Exam 70-236: *Configuring Microsoft Exchange Server 2007*

Objective	Location in Book
Installing and Configuring Microsoft Exchange Servers	
Prepare the infrastructure for Exchange installation.	Chapter 1, Lesson 1
Prepare the servers for Exchange installation.	Chapter 1, Lesson 2
Install Exchange.	Chapter 2, Lesson 1
Configure Exchange server roles.	Chapter 2, Lesson 2
Configuring Recipients and Public Folders	
Configure recipients.	Chapter 3, Lesson 1
Configure mail-enabled groups.	Chapter 3, Lesson 2
Configure resource mailboxes.	Chapter 3, Lesson 3
Configure public folders.	Chapter 4, Lesson 1
Move mailboxes.	Chapter 5, Lesson 1
Implement bulk management of mail-enabled objects	Chapter 5, Lesson 2
Configuring the Exchange Infrastructure	
Configure connectors.	Chapter 7, Lesson 1
Configure the antivirus and anti-spam system.	Chapter 6, Lesson 1
Configure transport rules and message compliance.	Chapter 6, Lesson 2
Configure policies.	Chapter 8, Lesson 1
Configure public folders.	Chapter 8, Lesson 2
Configure client connectivity.	Chapter 7, Lesson 2
Monitoring and Reporting	
Monitor mail queues.	Chapter 9, Lesson 1
Monitor system performance.	Chapter 9, Lesson 2
Perform message tracking.	Chapter 10, Lesson 1
Monitor client connectivity.	Chapter 10, Lesson 2
Create server reports.	Chapter 11, Lesson 1
Create usage reports.	Chapter 11, Lesson 2
Configuring Disaster Recovery	
Configure backups.	Chapter 12, Lesson 1
Recover messaging data.	Chapter 12, Lesson 2
Recover server roles.	Chapter 13, Lesson 1
Configure high availability.	Chapter 13, Lesson 2

Exam objectives   The exam objectives listed here are current as of this book's publication date. Exam objectives are subject to change at any time without prior notice and at Microsoft's sole discretion. Please visit the Microsoft Learning Web site for the most current listing of exam objectives: *http://www.microsoft.com/learning/mcp/.*

Microsoft®

Microsoft

MCTS Self-Paced Training Kit (Exam 70-236): Configuring Microsoft® Exchange Server 2007™

Ian McLean
Orin Thomas

PUBLISHED BY
Microsoft Press
A Division of Microsoft Corporation
One Microsoft Way
Redmond, Washington 98052-6399

Library of Congress Control Number: 2007934745

Printed and bound in the United States of America.

3 4 5 6 7 8 9   QWT   2 1 0 9

Distributed in Canada by H.B. Fenn and Company Ltd.

A CIP catalogue record for this book is available from the British Library.

Microsoft Press books are available through booksellers and distributors worldwide. For further information about international editions, contact your local Microsoft Corporation office or contact Microsoft Press International directly at fax (425) 936-7329. Visit our Web site at www.microsoft.com/mspress. Send comments to tkinput@microsoft.com.

Acquisitions Editor: Ken Jones
Developmental Editors: Jenny Moss Benson
Project Editor: Maureen Zimmerman
Editorial Production: S4Carlisle Publishing Services
Technical Reviewer: Bob Dean; Technical Review services provided by Content Master, a member of CM Group, Ltd.

Body Part No. X14-06985

This book is dedicated to my first grandchild,
Freya Isabella McLean, born September 5th, 2007.
Welcome to the world, Freya.

–Ian McLean

A deep and heartfelt thank you to the amazing team at Microsoft Press.
Your help, support, knowledge, and patience always
make authors come up looking far more
shiny than we are in real life!

–Orin Thomas

About the Authors

Ian McLean

Ian McLean, MCSE, MCITP, MCT, has 40 years' experience in industry, commerce, and education. He started his career as an electronics engineer before going into distance learning and then education as a university professor. Currently he runs his own consultancy company. Ian has written 20 books plus many papers and technical articles. He has been working with Microsoft Exchange Server since 1999.

Orin Thomas

Orin Thomas is a Windows Security MVP, an author, and a systems administrator. He has authored or co-authored more than a dozen books for Microsoft Press and is a contributing editor for Windows IT Pro magazine.

Contents at a Glance

Table of Contents

What do you think of this book? We want to hear from you!

Microsoft is interested in hearing your feedback so we can continually improve our books and learning resources for you. To participate in a brief online survey, please visit:

www.microsoft.com/learning/booksurvey/

What do you think of this book? We want to hear from you!

Microsoft is interested in hearing your feedback so we can continually improve our books and learning
resources for you. To participate in a brief online survey, please visit:

www.microsoft.com/learning/booksurvey/

Introduction

This training kit is designed for Exchange administrators who support Exchange Server 2007 in an enterprise environment and who plan to take the Microsoft Certified Technology Specialist (MCTS) exam 70-236. We assume that before you begin using this kit you have a solid foundation-level understanding of the Windows Server 2003 or Windows Server 2008 operating system and common Internet technologies.

By using this training kit, you will learn how to do the following:

- Install and manage Microsoft Exchange Server 2007.
- Manage messaging security by using Exchange Server 2007.
- Recover messaging servers and databases by using Exchange Server 2007.
- Monitor and troubleshoot Exchange Server 2007.

Hardware Requirements

We recommend that you use an isolated network that is not part of your production network to do the practice exercises in this book. The computer that you use to perform practices requires Internet connectivity. It is possible to perform all the practices in this training kit if you decide to use a single computer that is configured as a domain controller and has Exchange Server 2007 installed. Both the Windows Server and Exchange Server software need to be 64-bit editions. This means that the computer that you will perform your practices on requires a 64-bit processor. A 64-bit evaluation edition of Windows Server 2003 R2 can be obtained from the following address: *http://technet.microsoft.com/en-us/windowsserver/bb430831.aspx*. It is also possible to install Exchange Server 2007 SP1 on the 64-bit edition of Windows Server 2008 should the 64-bit evaluation edition of Windows Server 2003 R2 become unavailable at some point in the future.

You will find the practices closer to real life if you also have a client computer running either Microsoft Windows XP Professional or Windows Vista Business, Enterprise, or Ultimate on your network, but this is not essential. The client operating system does not need to be 64 bit. You can implement the client as a separate computer or as a virtual machine on the same computer. Your computer or computers should meet (at a minimum) the following hardware specification:

- Personal computer with a 1-GHz or faster 64-bit processor.
- 1.5 GB of RAM (2 GB if you plan to use virtual machine software).

- 60 GB of available hard disk space (100 GB if you plan to use virtual machine software).

- DVD-ROM drive.

- Keyboard and Microsoft mouse or compatible pointing device.

- The practices in Chapter 12, "Disaster Recovery," require a second hard disk, either internal or external. You can carry out the practices by using a high-capacity USB flash memory device (4 GB or greater), but the practices are closer to real life if you use a hard disk.

- Note that while the current edition of Microsoft Virtual PC and Virtual Server do not support 64-bit guest operating systems, third-party virtual machine host software such as VMware Server does. You must ensure that your processor's virtualization extensions are enabled when attempting to run 64-bit guest operating systems.

Software Requirements

The following software is required to complete the practice exercises:

- An evaluation or full edition of Windows Server 2003, Windows Server 2003 R2, or Windows Server 2008 64-bit Enterprise Edition.

- An evaluation or full edition of Windows Exchange Server 2007.

Using the CD and DVD

A companion CD and an evaluation software DVD set are included with this training kit. The companion CD contains the following:

- **Practice tests** You can reinforce your understanding of how to configure Exchange Server 2007 by using electronic practice tests you customize to meet your needs from the pool of Lesson Review questions in this book. Or you can practice for the 70-236 certification exam by using tests created from a pool of 300 realistic exam questions, which give you many practice exams to ensure that you are prepared.

- **An eBook** An electronic version (eBook) of this book is included for when you do not want to carry the printed book with you. The eBook is in Portable Document Format (PDF), and you can view it by using Adobe Acrobat or Adobe Reader.

An x64 evaluation edition of Exchange Server 2007 Enterprise Edition on two DVDs is supplied with this book. The book and the examination are written to the version of Exchange Server 2007 that is current at the time of publication.

The planned Exchange Server 2007 Service Pack 1 (SP1) release will contain a set of enhancements to the current version. The 70-236 exam might be updated in the future to include questions related to Exchange Server 2007 SPl.

NOTE **More on the changes in Service Pack 1**

To find out more about the changes made to Exchange Server 2007 with the release of Service Pack 1, consult the following TechNet article: *http://technet.microsoft.com/en-us/library/ bb676323.aspx*. When an evaluation version of Exchange Server 2007 SP1 is released, it will be available for free download on *http://www.microsoft.com*.

How to Install the Practice Tests

To install the practice test software from the companion CD to your hard disk, do the following:

1. Insert the companion CD into your CD drive and accept the license agreement. A CD menu appears.

   NOTE **If the CD menu does not appear**

   If the CD menu or the license agreement does not appear, AutoRun might be disabled on your computer. Refer to the Readme.txt file on the CD-ROM for alternate installation instructions.

   ---

2. Click Practice Tests and follow the instructions on the screen.

How to Use the Practice Tests

To start the practice test software, follow these steps:

1. Click Start/All Programs/Microsoft Press Training Kit Exam Prep. A window appears that shows all the Microsoft Press training kit exam prep suites installed on your computer.

2. Double-click the lesson review or practice test you want to use.

NOTE Lesson reviews vs. practice tests

Select the (70-236) Configuring Exchange Server 2007 *lesson review* to use the questions from the "Lesson Review" sections of this book. Select the (70-236) Configuring Exchange Server 2007 *practice test* to use a pool of 300 questions similar to those that appear on the 70-236 certification exam.

Lesson Review Options

When you start a lesson review, the Custom Mode dialog box appears so that you can configure your test. You can click OK to accept the defaults, or you can customize the number of questions you want, how the practice test software works, which exam objectives you want the questions to relate to, and whether you want your lesson review to be timed. If you are retaking a test, you can select whether you want to see all the questions again or only the questions you missed or did not answer.

After you click OK, your lesson review starts.

- To take the test, answer the questions and use the Next, Previous, and Go To buttons to move from question to question.

- After you answer an individual question, if you want to see which answers are correct—along with an explanation of each correct answer—click Explanation.

- If you prefer to wait until the end of the test to see how you did, answer all the questions and then click Score Test. You will see a summary of the exam objectives you chose and the percentage of questions you got right overall and per objective. You can print a copy of your test, review your answers, or retake the test.

Practice Test Options

When you start a practice test, you choose whether to take the test in Certification Mode, Study Mode, or Custom Mode:

- **Certification Mode**   Closely resembles the experience of taking a certification exam. The test has a set number of questions. It is timed, and you cannot pause and restart the timer.

- **Study Mode**   Creates an untimed test in which you can review the correct answers and the explanations after you answer each question.

- **Custom Mode**   Gives you full control over the test options so that you can customize them as you like.

In all modes, the user interface when you are taking the test is basically the same but with different options enabled or disabled depending on the mode. The main options are discussed in the previous section, "Lesson Review Options."

When you review your answer to an individual practice test question, a "References" section is provided that lists where in the training kit you can find the information that relates to that question and provides links to other sources of information. After you click Test Results to score your entire practice test, you can click the Learning Plan tab to see a list of references for every objective.

How to Uninstall the Practice Tests

To uninstall the practice test software for a training kit, use the Add Or Remove Programs option (Windows XP or Windows Server 2003) or the Program And Features option (Windows Vista or Windows Server 2008) in Windows Control Panel.

Microsoft Certified Professional Program

The Microsoft certifications provide the best method to prove your command of current Microsoft products and technologies. The exams and corresponding certifications are developed to validate your mastery of critical competencies as you design and develop or implement and support solutions with Microsoft products and technologies. Computer professionals who become Microsoft certified are recognized as experts and are sought after industry-wide. Certification brings a variety of benefits to the individual and to employers and organizations.

MORE INFO   All the Microsoft certifications

For a full list of Microsoft certifications, go to *http://www.microsoft.com/learning/mcp/default.asp*.

Technical Support

Every effort has been made to ensure the accuracy of this book and the contents of the companion CD. If you have comments, questions, or ideas regarding this book or the companion CD, please send them to Microsoft Press by using either of the following methods:

E-mail: tkinput@microsoft.com

Postal Mail:

Microsoft Press

Attn: MCTS Self-Paced Training Kit (Exam 70-236): Configuring Microsoft Exchange Server 2007 *Editor*

One Microsoft Way

Redmond, WA 98052-6399

For additional support information regarding this book and the CD-ROM (including answers to commonly asked questions about installation and use), visit the Microsoft Press Technical Support Web site at *http://www.microsoft.com/learning/support/ books*. To connect directly to the Microsoft Knowledge Base and enter a query, visit *http://support.microsoft.com/search*. For support information regarding Microsoft software, connect to *http://support.microsoft.com*.

Chapter 1

Preparing for Exchange Installation

An old adage says, measure twice, cut once. This adage applies to most tasks in network administration, but none more than the installation of Exchange Server 2007. Exchange Server 2007 is a complicated piece of software that has a significant influence not only on the operation of your network's infrastructure but also on the operation of your organization in general. If you do not prepare properly for the installation of Exchange Server 2007, you—and your organization—might be living with the consequences for a significant length of time. In this chapter, you will not actually install Exchange Server 2007 (which is covered in Chapter 2, "Installing Exchange Server and Configuring Roles"), but you will learn about the preparation that is required before the software can be deployed successfully. Exchange Server 2007 does not exist on the network in isolation. Before it can be utilized to its fullest extent, the network environment must be prepared properly. This chapter examines both the network infrastructure preparation and the server software preparation tasks that must be completed prior to the installation of Exchange Server 2007.

Exam objectives in this chapter:
- Prepare the infrastructure for Exchange installation.
- Prepare the servers for Exchange installation.

Lessons in this chapter:

Before You Begin

To complete the lessons in this chapter, you must have done the following:

- Have access to a computer running the 64-bit edition of Windows Server 2003 SP1 or R2 and access to the Exchange Server 2007 installation media.

No additional configuration is required for this chapter.

Real World

Orin Thomas

Installing any version of Exchange can be intimidating, though Exchange Server 2007 vastly simplifies the process. Exchange has always required an exhaustive amount of preparation prior to installation, and even when you have performed the task several times, a little voice at the back of your mind always asks you, "Have I forgotten something important?" The first Exchange environment I worked on had been installed by someone who had a "throw it in, run install, and figure it out later" approach to deployment. The deployment functioned only with the assistance of an elaborate series of workarounds. Those workarounds could have been avoided if the person who made the original deployment had spent some time with the documentation prior to attempting installation. Because of my experience having to manage a not-quite-right deployment, I was rather nervous when I first fully deployed Exchange in a production environment. I did not want future IT pros taking my name in vain the way I'd muttered in the server room about the guy who'd put together that original Exchange 5.5 box.

The best way to deal with these sorts of concerns is to perform multiple practice deployments. I do not mean running a pilot program at your organization, though you should do that as well. I mean using virtual machine software to repeatedly build up and tear down Exchange Server 2007 deployments until the process itself becomes second nature. Exchange Server 2007 is, if not the heart of an organization, the circulatory system that keeps everything moving. Virtual deployments give you a chance to learn from your mistakes and work out the kinks in any deployment plan long before any real e-mail gets put through the system.

Virtual machines also can be used as an excellent study tool. If it has enough RAM and hard disk space, a computer that meets the system requirements spelled out for this book is capable of running Exchange Server in a virtual machine rather than natively on the hardware. When you use this technique, you will be configuring a 64-bit edition of Windows Server 2003 to run within a virtual environment hosted on a 64-bit edition of Windows Server 2003. Just remember, though, that you can not run a 64-bit virtual machine on a 32-bit host operating system!

Lesson 1: Preparing the Infrastructure for Exchange Installation

Installing Exchange Server 2007 is not just a matter of placing the installation media in the nearest DVD-ROM drive and clicking through a wizard. The network infrastructure into which you will introduce Exchange needs to be prepared. Certain modifications and extensions need to be made to Active Directory before Exchange can be installed successfully. These modifications and extensions are significant. As you are likely to be aware from your study of Active Directory, rolling back changes can be difficult. You need to know what to do and how to do it. If you do not, at best you will have a failed Exchange installation that you will need to restart from the beginning. At worst, you will have messed up your network infrastructure and might have to pull it all apart and then put it back together. This lesson will also touch on Exchange Administrator roles and what steps need to be taken to prepare environments that have a previous Exchange deployment for the introduction of Exchange Server 2007.

After this lesson, you will be able to:

- Extend Active Directory schema.
- Prepare Active Directory in all domains where Exchange Server 2007 or mail-enabled objects will be deployed.
- Confirm Active Directory preparation, including permissions, groups, and schema.
- Understand the difference between and configure the four separate Exchange Administrator roles.
- Prepare an infrastructure utilizing a previous version of Exchange for migration to Exchange Server 2007.

Estimated lesson time: 40 minutes

Preparing Active Directory

Just as Active Directory forms the backbone of a Windows network, it also forms the backbone of an Exchange Server 2007 deployment. Although mailbox data, including e-mail and calendar appointments, is stored on Exchange Server 2007 computers, Active Directory stores almost all of Exchange Server 2007's configuration information.

Although, as discussed in Lesson 2, "Preparing the Servers for Exchange Installation," the server that will host the Exchange Server 2007 installation needs to have a 64-bit processor and a 64-bit edition of Windows Server 2003 or later installed, the network infrastructure servers, such as domain controllers and DNS servers in the environment, can have 32-bit processors and the 32-bit edition of Windows Server 2003 or later installed. Although as a matter of good practice all servers in your environment should be patched with the most recent updates, the installation of Exchange Server 2007 requires that the server that hosts the Schema Master role be patched with Service Pack 1 or higher if running Windows Server 2003 or be running Windows Server 2003 R2 or later. Exchange Server 2007 requires that there be a global catalog server deployed in each site in which Exchange is deployed. These global catalog servers also must be patched with Service Pack 1 or higher if running Windows Server 2003 or be running Windows Server 2003 R2 or later.

Setting Domain and Forest Functional Levels

To get the most out of Exchange Server 2007, it is necessary to set the functional levels of the host Windows Active Directory environment to the highest level possible. There are two different types of functional level in Windows Server 2003: the domain functional level and the forest functional level. The available domain functional levels are the following:

- **Windows 2000 mixed** This domain functional level supports Windows NT 4.0, Windows 2000, and Windows Server 2003 domain controllers.

- **Windows 2000 native** This domain functional level supports Windows 2000 and Windows Server 2003 domain controllers.

- **Windows Server 2003 interim** This domain functional level supports only Windows Server 2003 and Windows NT 4.0 domain controllers.

- **Windows Server 2003** This domain functional level supports only Windows Server 2003 domain controllers.

    Certain forest functional levels can be set only if all the domains in the forest are already set to a particular functional level. The available forest functional levels are the following:

- **Windows 2000** This forest functional level is available when domains in the forest are at any functional level.

- **Windows Server 2003 interim** This forest functional level is available only when the minimum level of all domains in the forest is Windows Server 2003 interim.

- **Windows Server 2003** This forest functional level can be set only if all domains in the forest are set to the Windows Server 2003 functional level.

Raising functional levels is a one-way operation. Once the functional level is raised, you cannot return it to a previous level. If you raise the domain functional level to Windows Server 2003 and then discover that you want to add an extra Windows 2000 domain controller, you will have to upgrade that computer to Windows Server 2003.

MORE INFO   **Functional levels**

To find out more about domain and forest functional levels, consult the following TechNet article: *http://technet2.microsoft.com/WindowsServer/en/library/4a589ca2-b572-48cd-94d2-7d5b0c817f411033.mspx?mfr=true*.

The primary limitation of raising the domain functional level is reducing the types of domain controllers that can be used in the domain. If a forgotten Windows NT4 or Windows 2000 domain controller exists in some far-flung office of your organization, raising the domain functional level could cause a problem. Prior to rolling out Exchange Server 2007, you will need to know what servers are located out in those remote offices and upgrade them if necessary. It makes no sense to have elaborate plans about rolling out Exchange Server 2007 when your existing infrastructure simply will not support it. All domains in the forest where you intend to install Exchange Server 2007 or host recipients must be set to the Windows 2000 Server domain functional level or higher. Raising domain and forest functional levels is covered by the practices at the end of this lesson.

NOTE   **Windows Server 2008 functional levels**

Windows Server 2008 domains support the Windows 2000 native, Windows Server 2003, and Windows Server 2008 domain functional levels and the Windows 2000, Windows Server 2003, and Windows Server 2008 forest functional levels. This means that if you are installing Exchange Server 2007 in a forest with Windows Server 2008 domain controllers, you will not need to modify the functional levels to support the new Exchange organization.

Extending the Active Directory Schema

Active Directory schema is a set of formal definitions for all object classes that can exist within an Active Directory forest. As Exchange Server 2007 uses new objects that have not been formally defined in the existing schema, it is necessary to add the new definitions that are relevant to Exchange-specific objects to the existing Active Directory schema. This process is called *schema extension* and is the first step in all new Exchange Server 2007 deployments.

Setting Legacy Permissions   If your environment has an existing Exchange 2000 or Exchange Server 2003 organization present, it is necessary to run an extra command prior to performing the normal schema and domain preparation. Running this extra command will update existing Exchange settings and permissions in preparation for the modifications made by deploying Exchange Server 2007. The user who executes this command must be a member of the Enterprise Admins group. This command needs to be run from the root directory of the Exchange Server 2007 installation media. The syntax of the command is the following:

```
Setup /PrepareLegacyExchangePermissions
```

Running the command as a member of the Enterprise Admins group will prepare all domains in the forest. It is possible to run this command against a single domain rather than all domains in the forest. If this is done, the user running the command must specify the fully qualified domain name of the domain, be a member of the Exchange Organization Administrators group, and be a member of the Domain Admins group in the domain to be prepared. For example, if Kim Akers wishes to prepare a child domain in the Tailspintoys.internal forest called child.tailspintoys.internal and she has the requisite group memberships, she would issue the following command:

```
Setup /PrepareLegacyExchangePermissions:child.tailspintoys.internal
```

If the entire forest is not prepared and preparation is performed on a domain-by-domain basis, it will be necessary to run this command in all domains where Exchange 2000 or Exchange Server 2003 has been deployed, prior to performing any other steps in the Exchange Server 2007 deployment process. If this command is not run in all domains where Exchange 2000 or Exchange Server 2003 has been deployed by executing it either on the forest level or on a domain-by-domain basis, it is possible that the deployment will fail.

NOTE   Running commands on 32-Bit computers

The version of setup.exe that comes with the Exchange Server 2007 installation media will run only on computers with a 64-bit operating system. In many environments, existing domain controllers will be running the 32-bit version of Windows Server 2003. This means that you can not run the setup.exe commands necessary to prepare the domain off the Exchange Server 2007 installation media, as it has been compiled for an alternate processor architecture. One way to deal with this problem is to obtain the 32-bit evaluation version of Exchange Server 2007 from Microsoft's Web site. You can use the 32-bit evaluation edition to prepare the forest and domains prior to installing the full 64-bit edition of Exchange Server 2007. You can obtain the 32-bit evaluation software by navigating to *http://www.microsoft.com/technet/prodtechnol/eval/exchange/default.mspx* and providing registration details. It is also possible to obtain the 64-bit Exchange Server 2007 evaluation from this location.

Preparing the Active Directory Schema from the Command Line   The Active Directory schema is extended by running the *Setup /PrepareSchema* command. This command must be run in the same site and domain as the computer that holds the schema master Flexible Single Master Operations (FSMO) role. Unless the Schema Master role has been moved, this server that hosts it will be located in the forest root domain on the first domain controller that was installed in the organization. You can locate the Schema Master using the technique detailed in Practice 2, "Extending the Active Directory Schema," at the end of this lesson. Prior to running the command, you must ensure that the .NET Framework version 2.0 and Windows PowerShell are installed. The Active Directory schema is prepared for Exchange Server 2007 by issuing the following command:

```
Setup /PrepareSchema
```

This command can be successfully executed only by a user account that is a member of both the Schema Admins and the Enterprise Admins group. If there are earlier versions of Exchange in your environment and the */PrepareLegacyExchangePermissions* command has not been executed, *Setup /PrepareSchema* will automatically execute this command against the forest prior to extending the schema.

MORE INFO   PowerShell version

Ensure that the version of PowerShell that you install is appropriate for your operating system. Separate versions of PowerShell are available for 32- and 64-bit editions of Windows as well as separate versions for Windows XP, Vista, Windows Server 2003, and Windows Server 2008. The different versions of PowerShell can be obtained by navigating to the following link: *http://www.microsoft.com/windowsserver2003/technologies/management/powershell/download.mspx*.

Quick Check

1. What are the minimum domain and forest functional levels required for the installation of Exchange Server 2007?
2. What components must be installed to run *Setup /PrepareSchema*?

Quick Check Answers

1. Windows 2000 native.
2. Windows .NET Framework version 2.0 and Windows PowerShell.

Domain Preparation

Each domain that will host an Exchange Server 2007 computer or that will host Exchange recipients needs to be prepared using the *Setup /PrepareAD* command. The first time this command is run, you also have to include the organization name. For example, after *Setup /PrepareSchema* is run on the schema master of the Tailspin-toys.internal forest, Active Directory can be prepared for the deployment of the new Tailspintoys Exchange Server 2007 organization by running the following command:

```
Setup /PrepareAD /OrganizationName:Tailspintoys
```

In the event that the organization already exists, it is not necessary to append the */OrganizationName* option.

Running this command will do the following:

- Configure global Exchange objects in Active Directory
- Create Exchange universal security groups in the root domain
- Set permissions on Exchange configuration objects
- Prepare the current domain

This command can be run only by a member of the Enterprise Administrators group. If there is an existing Exchange Server 2003 organization, the user running the command needs to be not only a member of the Enterprise Administrators group but also an Exchange full administrator.

Organization Name Limitations

The name that can be assigned to an Exchange organization has several limitations. An Exchange organization name cannot contain whitespaces at the beginning or the end, though it can contain whitespaces between characters. Usually, the Exchange organization reflects the name of the organization. In addition to the limitation on the use of whitespaces, Exchange organization names cannot contain any of the characters listed in Table 1-1.

Verifying Preparation

You can verify that the schema extension and domain preparation tasks have been completed correctly by viewing the output of the command-line utilities or by examining Active Directory Users and Computers in the forest root domain. If you examine Active Directory Users and Computers in the forest root domain, you will notice a new container called Microsoft Exchange Security Groups. Within that container are five new universal security groups with the following names:

- Exchange organization administrators
- Exchange recipient administrators
- Exchange servers
- Exchange view-only administrators
- ExchangeLegacyInterop

Table 1-1 Symbols That Cannot Be Used in the Name of an Exchange Organization

Symbol	Name	Symbol	Name	Symbol	Name
~	Tilde	&	Ampersand	[]	Brackets
!	Exclamation	*	Asterisk	|	Vertical bar
@	At sign	()	Parentheses	\	Backslash
#	Number sign	_	Underscore	:	Colon
$	Dollar sign	+	Plus sign	;	Semicolon
%	Percent sign	=	Equals sign	"	Quotation mark
^	Caret	{}	Braces	'	Apostrophe
<>	Angle brackets	,	Comma	.	Period
?	Question mark	/	Slash mark		

The new container and security groups are displayed in Figure 1-1. These groups are used to assign Exchange Server 2007 roles, which are covered later in this lesson.

MORE INFO   Preparing Active Directory and domains

For more information about preparing Active Directory and domains for the installation of Exchange Server 2007, consult the following article: *http://technet.microsoft.com/en-us/library/bb125224.aspx.*

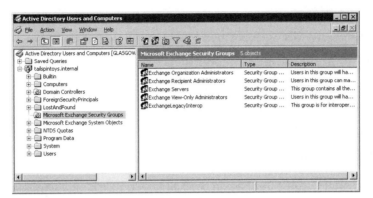

Figure 1-1   New Exchange objects

If you run the Exchange Server 2007 setup routine with a Windows account that has all the requisite permissions, the schema and domain preparation steps occur automatically. Given this, you might wonder why you would want to go manually through the command-line preparation steps. The answer is that going through the command-line preparation steps gives you a finer degree of control over the Exchange Server 2007 deployment process. Diagnosing problems in large, complex environments is more difficult if you try the "all at once" approach.

Local Server Role Requirements

Once you have prepared the schema and the domain, it is time to ensure that the location where you will place Exchange Server 2007 is suitably readied. A site is a set of IP subnets that are defined in Active Directory. Sites are configured using the Active Directory Sites And Services management console and are used to define distinct locations in an organization's network. For example, you work for a company that has its head office in Melbourne, Australia, and regional offices in the outback towns of Wagga Wagga, Cootamundra, and Wangaratta. Each office would use one or more separate IP subnets. Using the Active Directory Sites And Services console, the subnets used by each office would be collected into Active Directory sites. Sites help facilitate replication between domain controllers.

Each site at which you plan to install an Exchange Server 2007 computer needs a Windows Server 2003 SP1+ or R2 global catalog server. Global catalog servers can be installed only on computers that are already domain controllers. It is not necessary for the domain controllers or global catalog servers to be running a 64-bit version of Windows Server 2003. Although a global catalog server always existed at each site in Windows 2000 domains, the Windows Server 2003 universal group membership caching feature means that there is not always a global catalog server at each site.

To make an existing domain controller a global catalog server, you need to open Active Directory Sites And Services, locate the server that you wish to convert under the Servers node, expand that node, and edit the NTDS Settings. On the General tab, ensure that the Global Catalog option is selected, as shown in Figure 1-2.

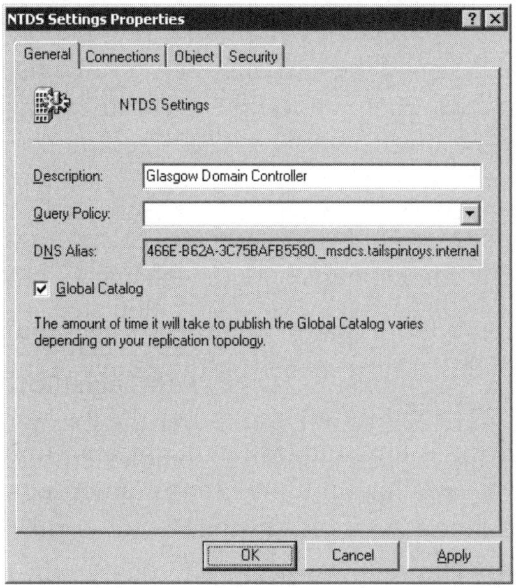

Figure 1-2   Setting a domain controller to be a global catalog server

Configuring Exchange Administrator Roles

Once the schema and domain preparation commands have been issued, several new groups will be added to a new organizational unit in the root domain of the forest. These groups are universal in scope, meaning that user accounts from any domain in the forest can be added to them. Adding a user account to one of these groups confers the group role on that account. These roles have the following properties:

- **Exchange Organization Administrator**   A user who is a member of this group has complete access to all Exchange properties and objects within the organization.

- **Exchange Recipient Administrator**   A user assigned the Exchange Recipient Administrator role can edit Exchange properties on Active Directory objects. This includes user accounts, contacts, groups, dynamic distribution lists, and public folders. Exchange recipient administrators can also edit client access mailbox settings and unified messaging mailbox settings.

- **Exchange View-Only Administrator**   A user assigned the Exchange View-Only Administrator role has read-only access to the Exchange organization tree and read-only access to those domain controllers that host Exchange recipient objects. This role is used primarily for auditing purposes.

- **Exchange Server Administrator**   This role is different from other assigned roles because its scope is limited to a particular computer or computers running Exchange Server 2007. A user assigned the Exchange Server Administrator role for a specific Exchange Server 2007 computer cannot perform Exchange Server Administrator tasks on any other Exchange Server 2007 computer within the organization.

In addition, new security groups apply to computers in the Exchange organization. Computer accounts that are added to these groups have the following properties:

- **Exchange Servers**   All computers with Exchange Server 2007 installed are members of this group. Members of this group can manage the Exchange information store, mail queues, and mail interchange.

- **Exchange2003Interop**   This group is for Exchange 2000 Server and Exchange Server 2003 bridgehead servers. It allows routing group connections between Exchange Server 2007 and earlier versions of Exchange.

- **Exchange Install Domain Servers**   This security group is located in the Microsoft Exchange System Objects container, which is visible only if the Advanced Features View option is enabled in Active Directory Users And Computers. This group contains all domain controllers with Exchange installed.

Link State and Coexistence with Previous Versions of Exchange

Prior to introducing Exchange Server 2007 to an existing Exchange environment, the existing Exchange environment must be prepared. This preparation involves either migrating data off existing servers and retiring them or ensuring that these servers have the most recent service packs and updates applied. Exchange Server 2007 can be introduced to the organization under the following conditions:

- No Exchange Server 5.5 server is present in the forest. If Exchange Server 5.5 is present and you wish to deploy Exchange Server 2007, it will be necessary to migrate users and data off these servers to Exchange 2000 or Exchange Server 2003 prior to attempting to deploy the new version of Exchange. It is not possible to directly upgrade from Exchange 5.5 to Exchange Server 2003, or Exchange Server 2007.

■ All Exchange Server 2003 servers in the forest have Exchange Server 2003 Service Pack (SP) 2 or higher applied.

■ All Exchange 2000 Servers in the forest have Exchange 2000 Server SP3 and the SP3 update rollup (KB870540) installed.

In the event that two or more routing groups exist in an Exchange Server 2003 deployment in which you wish to deploy Exchange Server 2007, it will be necessary to disable link state. Link state is used to route traffic in large Exchange Server 2003 deployments. Exchange Server 2007 does not propagate link state routing updates. If an organization is configured to use two or more routing groups and Exchange Server 2007 is introduced, routing loops will occur. To disable link state in an existing Exchange Server 2003 organization, it is necessary to edit the registry on all Exchange 2000 and Exchange Server 2003 computers in the organization. It is necessary to add the registry key *HKEY_LOCAL_MACHINE\System\CurrentControlSet\Services\ RESvc\Parameters\SuppressStateChanges* and to set its DWORD value to 1.

It is not possible to directly upgrade a computer running Exchange Server 2003 to Exchange Server 2007. It is possible to migrate all the mailboxes off an earlier version of Exchange to Exchange Server 2007, perform a complete server rebuild, install Exchange Server 2007, and then migrate the mailboxes back, but a direct migration is impossible.

Exam Tip   The Exchange Server exams have always had a reputation for requiring a solid background knowledge of network infrastructure and Active Directory principles. Other Microsoft products, such as Internet Security and Acceleration Server 2006, Windows Software Update Services, and Microsoft Operations Manager, can make tangential appearances in exam questions. You do not need to know all the technical details of these products, but you do need to have a basic understanding of how they interrelate with an Exchange Server deployment.

Practice: Preparing the Network Infrastructure for the Installation of Exchange Server 2007

In these practices, you will perform several exercises by which you will become familiar with preparing your network infrastructure for the installation of Exchange Server 2007. Prior to beginning these practice exercises, you should have configured a Windows Server 2003 64-bit edition computer in the following way:

■ Configure the computer with the name Glasgow.

■ Configure a static IP address and subnet mask that allow access to the Internet in your local network environment.

- Promote the computer to domain controller.

- Ensure that you configure the new domain so that it exists in a new forest.

- Configure the domain name to be Tailspintoys.internal

- Ensure that Database, Log, and Sysvol files are hosted in default locations.

- Configure the DNS service to be hosted locally.

- Ensure that permissions are configured to be compatible only with Windows 2000 or Windows Server 2003.

- Configure the Administrator account password and Active Directory restore mode password as P@ssw0rd.

- Download and install Windows Server 2003 SP2. This service pack can be applied to both Windows Server 2003 and Windows Server 2003 R2. Installing this service pack will also ensure that Microsoft Management Console (MMC) version 3.0 is present on your computer. Keep the SP2 file in a known location, as it will be necessary to reapply the service pack after adding additional components to Windows Server 2003.

- This computer can run on its own hardware or within a virtual machine, though if it is running in a virtual machine, you must ensure that the host operating system is also 64 bit.

BEST PRACTICES Slipstreaming

It is possible to slipstream the service pack into the installation files of the nonevaluation versions of Windows Server 2003. The process of slipstreaming updates the original installation files. When the installation files have been updated via slipstreaming, it is not necessary to reapply the service pack after components have been added to Windows. It is not possible to perform a slipstream update the installation files of an evaluation version of Windows Server 2003.

▶ **Practice 1: Configuring Domain and Forest Functional Levels**

In this practice, you will configure the domain and forest functional levels of your practice environment to Windows Server 2003 native. Setting this level will allow all features of Exchange Server 2007 to be implemented. To complete this practice, perform the following steps:

1. Log on to the computer using the default Administrator account.

2. Open Active Directory Users And Computers from the Administrative Tools menu. Right-click Tailspintoys.Internal and click Raise Domain Functional Level from the shortcut menu as shown in Figure 1-3.

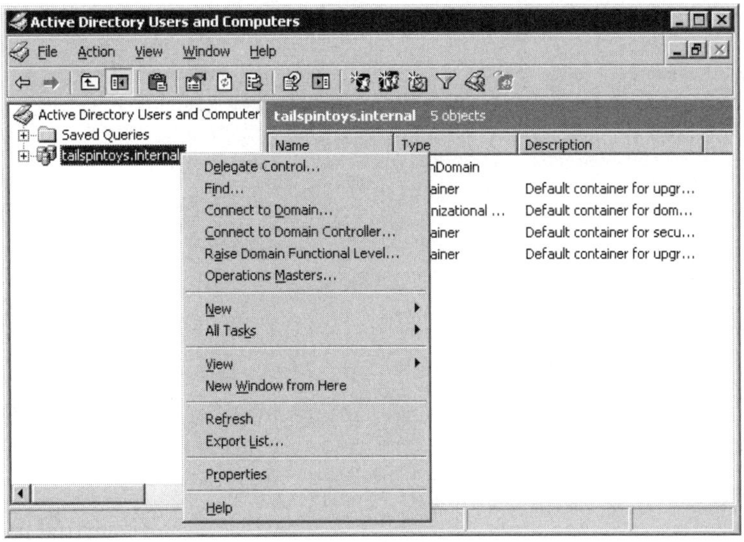

Figure 1-3 Raise domain functional level

3. Set the new domain functional level to Windows Server 2003 and click Raise.

4. In the Raise Domain Functional Level dialog box, click OK.

5. Click OK to dismiss the notification informing you that the domain functional level was raised successfully.

6. Close the Active Directory Users And Computers console.

7. Open Active Directory Domains And Trusts from the Administrative Tools menu.

8. Right-click Active Directory Domains And Trusts and then click Raise Forest Functional Level.

9. Verify that Windows Server 2003 is selected in the Select An Available Forest Functional Level dialog box as shown in Figure 1-4 and then click Raise.

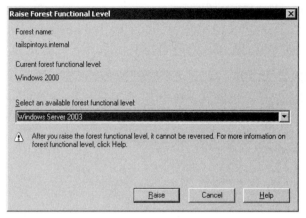

Figure 1-4   Raise forest functional level

10. At the warning dialog box, click OK.

11. Click OK to dismiss the message informing you that the functional level was raised successfully.

12. Close Active Directory Domains And Trusts.

▶ **Practice 2: Extending the Active Directory Schema**

The best place to extend the Active Directory schema is on the computer that holds the Schema Master role in the forest. In complicated Active Directory environments, you may need to locate the schema master. Although almost all the practices in this book involve a single computer that serves as domain controller, Exchange server, and holder of all FSMO roles, this practice will assume that you need to locate the schema master and then prepare it so that you can extend the schema. To complete this practice, perform the following steps:

1. While logged on as administrator, click Start and then click Run.

2. In the Run dialog box, type **regsvr32 schmmgmt.dll.**

3. Click OK to dismiss the dialog box informing you that the registration of this DLL file has succeeded.

4. In the Run dialog box, type **MMC** and then click OK.

5. Add the Active Directory Schema snap-in to the new console.

6. In the console, right-click Active Directory Schema and then click Operations Master. This will display the dialog box shown in Figure 1-5, which will inform you of which computer in the forest currently holds the Schema Master role.

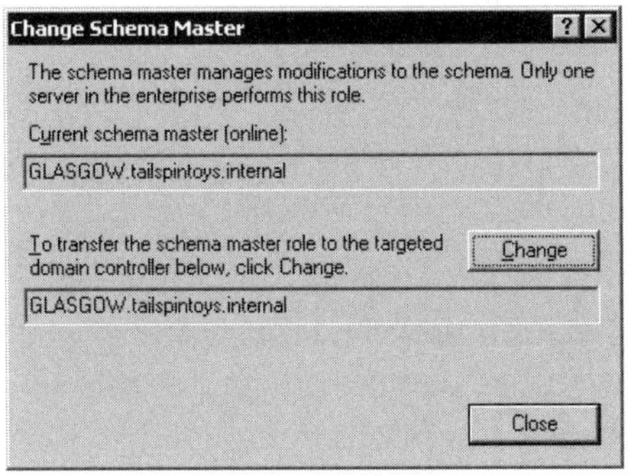

Figure 1-5 Locating the schema master

7. Close the console.

TIP **Find the schema master**

At this point in a production environment, you would log on to the schema master computer itself.

---

8. Open the Add/Remove Programs item in Control Panel and then click Add/Remove Windows Components.

9. Select the Microsoft .NET Framework 2.0 component and then click Next. This component will be available in the component list if you have installed Windows Server 2003 SP2 for x64.

10. Open Internet Explorer and navigate to *http://www.microsoft.com/powershell.* Locate and download the Windows PowerShell binary for Windows Server 2003 x64.

BEST PRACTICES **Do not surf from servers**

Best practice is not to browse the Internet directly from any server. In a production environment, you should use a desktop computer to obtain software that needs to be downloaded and then transfer the installation files across the network to the server.

---

11. Double-click the Windows PowerShell installation file that you have downloaded from Microsoft's Web site and install PowerShell by following the prompts.

12. When the PowerShell installation routine completes, place the Exchange Server 2007 installation media into the DVD-ROM drive. If the Exchange Server 2007 screen is displayed, click Close.

13. Click Start and open a command prompt from the Accessories menu.

14. In the command prompt environment, change to the DVD-ROM drive and issue the command *setup /prepareschema*.

15. During the schema preparation, the routine will check that the organization is at the appropriate functional levels and then extend the Active Directory schema.

16. At the end of the schema preparation process, you should get a message informing you that the setup operation has completed successfully. If you do not get this message, verify that you have successfully completed all steps in Practices 1 and 2.

▶ **Practice 3: Performing Domain Preparation**

Once the Active Directory schema has been prepared, you need to perform the domain preparation step. To complete this step, you need to use an account that is a member of the Enterprise Administrators group. For the purposes of this practice, the default Administrator account will suffice. To complete this practice, perform the following steps:

1. Ensure that the Exchange Server 2007 installation media is still present in the computer's DVD-ROM drive.

2. Open a command prompt and change to the DVD-ROM drive.

3. Enter the command **setup /PrepareAD /OrganizationName:Tailspintoys**

4. When the command completes execution, you will receive the message displayed in Figure 1-6.

Figure 1-6   Successful completion of Active Directory preparation

Lesson Summary

- *Setup /PrepareLegacyExchange Permissions* should be run if there is a preexisting Exchange 2000 or Exchange Server 2003 organization.

- *Setup /PrepareSchema* must be run in the same Active Directory site and domain as the computer that hosts the Schema Master role.

- *Setup /PrepareAD* must be run in all domains that will host Exchange servers or Exchange recipients.

- If an existing Exchange 2000 or Exchange Server 2003 organization contains more than two routing groups, link state must be disabled.

Lesson Review

You can use the following questions to test your knowledge of the information in Lesson 1, "Preparing the Infrastructure for Exchange Installation." The questions are also available on the companion CD if you prefer to review them in electronic form.

NOTE Answers

Answers to these questions and explanations of why each answer choice is correct or incorrect are located in the "Answers" section at the end of the book.

---

1. You are intending to introduce Exchange Server 2007 to an existing network consisting of Windows 2000 and Windows Server 2003 domain controllers and Exchange 5.5, Exchange 2000, and Exchange Server 2003 servers. Which of the following steps must you take prior to introducing Exchange Server 2007?

   A. Upgrade all Windows 2000 Server domain controllers to Windows Server 2003

   B. Upgrade all Exchange 2000 servers to Exchange Server 2003

   C. Upgrade all Exchange 5.5 servers to Exchange Server 2003

   D. Migrate all users and data from Exchange 5.5 to Exchange Server 2003

2. You are planning on installing a computer running Exchange Server 2007 at the Cootamundra branch office of Tailspintoys. The Tailspintoys forest has a single domain, and Exchange Server 2007 has already been deployed at the head office site. The Cootamundra office has a Windows Server 2003 R2 32-bit domain controller configured to use universal group membership caching, a Windows

Server 2003 SP1 32-bit file server, and 20 desktop computers running Windows Vista enterprise edition. Exchange will be installed on a new server running Windows Server 2003 R2 64 bit with SP2. Which of the following configuration changes should you make prior to deploying Exchange Server 2007?

A. Run *Setup /Prepareschema* on the Cootamundra domain controller

B. Run *Setup /PrepareAD* on the Cootamundra domain controller

C. Upgrade the Cootamundra domain controller to Windows Server 2003 R2 64-bit edition

D. Configure the Cootamundra domain controller as a global catalog server

E. Promote the Cootamundra file server to domain controller

3. Which of the following groups must your user account be a member of to run the command *Setup /PrepareSchema* in a forest that does not have an existing Exchange deployment? (Choose all that apply.)

A. Schema Admins

B. Enterprise Admins

C. Exchange Organization Administrators

D. Domain Admins

E. Account Operators

4. Which of the following commands should you execute first if you are going to introduce Exchange Server 2007 to an existing Exchange Server 2003 environment?

A. *Setup /PrepareSchema*

B. *Setup /PrepareAD*

C. *Setup /PrepareLegacyExchangePermissions*

D. *DCDIAG*

E. *NETDIAG*

5. Which of the following Exchange Server 2007 organization names are valid?

A. Tailspintoys-Corporation

B. Tailspintoys_Corporation

C. Tailspintoys:Corporation

D. TailspintoysCorporation!

E. Tailspintoys%Corporation

6. Under what conditions is it necessary to disable link state prior to installing Exchange Server 2007 in an organization that already has an Exchange Server 2003 deployment?

    A. If Outlook Web Access is available on any of the Exchange Server 2003 computers

    B. If multiple routing groups are in use

    C. If multiple administrative groups are in use

    D. If a front-end/back-end configuration is in use

Lesson 2: Preparing the Servers for Exchange Installation

Once the network infrastructure is prepared for the deployment of Exchange Server 2007, it is necessary to prepare the computer that will host Exchange Server 2007. As mentioned earlier, Exchange Server 2007 is an extremely sophisticated piece of software that requires planning and preparation to install. At the start of the installation process, covered in detail in Chapter 2, an application runs that checks that the appropriate components have been installed and settings have been applied. If these components are not installed, the installation routine will terminate, reminding you that you need to install component X or change setting Y. If you have not prepared properly for this, you will find yourself constantly restarting the installation process and returning to Microsoft's Web site yet again to download another required component. Rather than taking this stop-and-start approach to Exchange deployment, it is far simpler to download and install the relevant components in one go prior to launching Exchange installation. This lesson will examine all the components and extra software that need to be installed on the computer that will host Exchange Server 2007 before it is possible to successfully install the product.

> **After this lesson, you will be able to:**
> - Prepare a Windows Server 2003 computer for the installation of Exchange Server 2007.
> - Ensure that the server meets the minimum hardware requirements.
> - Ensure that the appropriate server components are installed.
> - Verify that DNS has been configured appropriately.
>
> **Estimated lesson time: 40 minutes**

Exchange 2007 Operating System and Hardware Requirements

The first step in determining whether a computer is capable of running Exchange Server 2007 is to determine whether it meets the minimum hardware requirements. Most organizations have a complex process when it comes to ordering new servers, and you do not want to go through filling out all those forms and then find that the server that you ordered either will not run Exchange Server 2007 well or cannot run it at all. The following list details the hardware requirements of the computer that will host Exchange Server 2007:

- x64 architecture–based processor that supports the Intel EM64T or AMD64 instruction set

- 2 GB of RAM plus 5 MB of RAM per mailbox

- 1.2 GB of disk space on the volume on which Exchange is installed plus 500 MB per unified messaging language pack that is to be installed

- 200 MB of free disk space on the system volume

Once you have verified that the computer you wish to install Exchange Server 2007 on has met the hardware requirements, you need to verify that the software environment computer meets the Exchange Server 2007 requirements.

BEST PRACTICES   **Fresh is best**

Although you can install Exchange Server 2007 on any computer that meets the minimum requirements, best practice is to install Exchange on a fresh install of Windows Server 2003 or Windows Server 2003 R2 rather than one that has been used for another task. A computer that has been explicitly prepared to run Exchange Server 2007 will provide better performance than a computer that was configured for another task and that has then had Exchange Server 2007 installed on it.

Prior to the installation of Exchange, the software environment should meet the following requirements:

- 64-bit edition of Windows Server 2003 or Windows Server 2003 R2. If you plan to use single-copy cluster or cluster continuous replication, the enterprise editions of Windows Server 2003 and Windows Server 2003 R2 are required.

- The following volumes must be formatted with the NTFS file system:
    1. System volume
    2. Volumes that store Exchange program files, storage group files, transaction log files, database files, and all other Exchange files

- Microsoft .NET Framework version 2.0.

- Microsoft Windows PowerShell. This can be downloaded from Microsoft's Web site. Consult Microsoft Knowledge Base Article 926139.

- MMC 3.0. This version of the MMC is included with Windows Server 2003 R2 but not with Windows Server 2003. This MMC is installed when you apply SP2 to Windows Server 2003.

- Update for Windows Server 2003 x64 edition KB904639.

- Update for Windows Server 2003 x64 edition KB918980.

- The Simple Mail Transfer Protocol (SMTP) and Network News Transfer Protocol (NNTP) service must not be installed.

NOTE   Does not work with Itanium

Exchange Server 2007 requires a processor that conforms to the x64 (also known as x86-64, AMD64, or EMT64T) architecture. The IA64 Itanium processor architecture, even though it is also 64 bit, uses a different instruction set to the x64 architecture. This means that Exchange Server 2007 will not run on the IA64 Itanium processor even though it is also 64 bit.

Although the different Exchange Server 2007 roles are discussed in Chapter 2, the following section will detail the prerequisite software environment that is necessary for particular Windows components to be installed. These components can be added to the server through the Add/Remove Programs item in Control Panel.

Windows Server 2008 Roles

In Windows, Server 2008 components are called *roles*. Roles are added through the Roles node of the new Server Manager console. Roles that can be added to Windows Server 2008 include Web server, DNS server, fax server, and file services. Windows Server 2008 also has a separate way of adding components called *features*. Features that can be added include Microsoft .NET Framework version 3.0 and PowerShell. Whereas the preparation for installing Exchange Server 2007 on Windows Server 2003 R2 still requires you to download files from Microsoft's Web site, it is possible to install Exchange Server 2007 on Windows Server 2008 by adding roles and features directly from the operating system installation media.

Do not worry if you do not understand what the different role types mean initially; you can refer back to this section once you've read about the tasks that each can be used to achieve in Chapter 2.

MORE INFO   System requirements

To find out more about the Exchange Server 2007 system requirements, navigate to the following link: *http://technet.microsoft.com/en-us/library/aa996719.aspx.*

Mailbox Server Role

If the computer on which you are going to install Exchange Server 2007 will be assigned the Mailbox server role, it will be necessary to install the following Internet Information Services (IIS) 6.0 components prior to installation:

- COM+ Access

- IIS
- World Wide Web Service

Client Access Server Role

If the computer on which you are going to install Exchange Server 2007 will be assigned the Client Access server role, it will be necessary to install the following components prior to installation:

- World Wide Web Service
- Remote procedure call (RPC) over HTTP Proxy
- ASP.NET version 2.0

Unified Messaging Server Role

If the computer on which you are going to install Exchange Server 2007 will be assigned the Unified Messaging server role, it will be necessary to install the following components prior to installation:

- Microsoft Windows Media Encoder
- Microsoft Windows Media Audio Voice Codec
- Microsoft Core XML Services (MSXML) 6.0

Hub Transport Server Role

The Hub Transport server role does not require any extra components to be installed other than those listed in the minimum specifications section.

Edge Transport Server Role

Edge Transport servers require that Active Directory Application Mode (ADAM) be installed. This software can be added using the Add/Remove Programs item on computers running Windows Server 2003 R2 or can be downloaded from Microsoft's Web site at *http://www.microsoft.com/adam*. ADAM is a directory service similar to Active Directory but runs as a user service rather than as a system service. ADAM can be installed on servers without requiring that they be promoted to domain controllers in an Active Directory domain. ADAM also has the advantage of being able to be installed on stand-alone servers that are not members of an Active Directory forest.

MORE INFO   **Application mode**

To find out more about Active Directory application mode, navigate to the following link: *http://www.microsoft.com/windowsserver2003/adam/ADAMfaq.mspx.*

Exchange Server 2007 on Domain Controllers

Even though the practices in this book have you install Exchange Server 2007 on a domain controller, this is done for the sake of expediency rather than as a recommended deployment option. Ideally, you should install Exchange Server 2007 only on a member server or as a stand-alone in the case of the edge transport. One limitation of installing Exchange Server 2007 is that you will not be able to use the *DCPROMO* command to add or remove the directory server role. You can not promote a member server that has Exchange installed to a domain controller, and you can not demote a domain controller that has Exchange installed to the status of member server.

Quick Check

1. Which components should you ensure are not installed on a Windows Server 2003 R2 computer prior to attempting the installation of Exchange Server 2007?

2. Which Exchange Server 2007 role does not require any special components to be installed above the minimum components required to install Exchange?

Quick Check Answers

1. SMTP and NNTP components.

2. Hub Transport server role.

Networking Configuration

A computer that is going to host Exchange Server 2007 needs to have a static IP address and the appropriate records created in DNS to support the exchange of mail. You can verify that a computer has a static IP address configured by opening a command prompt and issuing the *IPCONFIG /ALL* command. As shown in Figure 1-7, the DHCP Enabled line should read No. If this line does not read No, it will be necessary to edit the properties of the TCP/IP protocol for that adapter and to assign a static IP address.

```
Command Prompt                                                    _ □ X

C:\Documents and Settings\Administrator>ipconfig /all

Windows IP Configuration

        Host Name . . . . . . . . . . . . : GLASGOW
        Primary Dns Suffix  . . . . . . . : tailspintoys.internal
        Node Type . . . . . . . . . . . . : Unknown
        IP Routing Enabled. . . . . . . . : No
        WINS Proxy Enabled. . . . . . . . : No
        DNS Suffix Search List. . . . . . : tailspintoys.internal

Ethernet adapter Local Area Connection:

        Connection-specific DNS Suffix  . :
        Description . . . . . . . . . . . : Intel(R) PRO/1000 MT Network Connection
        Physical Address. . . . . . . . . : 00-0C-29-83-1C-6C
        DHCP Enabled. . . . . . . . . . . : No
        IP Address. . . . . . . . . . . . : 10.254.81.113
        Subnet Mask . . . . . . . . . . . : 255.255.255.0
        Default Gateway . . . . . . . . . : 10.254.81.1
        DNS Servers . . . . . . . . . . . : 127.0.0.1

C:\Documents and Settings\Administrator>_
```

Figure 1-7   Verifying static IP address configuration

For a mail server to send and receive mail, an MX record must exist within the DNS zone that it will answer mail for. For example, for the host glasgow.tailspintoys.internal to receive mail for the tailspintoys.internal DNS zone, an MX record must be configured in the tailspintoys.internal DNS zone that points to glasgow.tailspintoys.internal. You can determine which MX records exist for a DNS zone by using the *nslookup* command from the command prompt. The commands that you enter to determine the MX records for a DNS zone are the following:

```
nslookup -querytype=mx <dns.zone>
```

Each MX record can be assigned a priority, with the default priority being 10. The higher the assigned number, the lower its priority. For example, an MX record with a priority of 10 will be favored over an MX record with a priority of 30. Priorities are used in mail transport, with a connection attempted to the highest-priority mail server first and then connections attempted to lower-priority mail servers if that initial connection fails. The process of creating an MX record is demonstrated in Practice 3 at the end of this lesson.

Security Configuration Wizard

The Security Configuration Wizard (SCW) is a tool that can be used to reduce the attack surface of a computer running Windows Server 2003. The attack surface can be thought of as operational ports and services on a computer. The more services and ports that are open to the network, the greater the attack surface. The SCW works by limiting the number of operating services and open ports to only those that are required to carry out the server's function. The SCW is a component that can be installed by using the Add/Remove Programs item on computers running Windows Server 2003 with SP1 or Windows Server 2003 R2.

You have to have Exchange Server 2007 installed to access the Exchange Server 2007 Security Configuration Wizard templates as these are not available in the default installation of this application. Once you have installed the Security Configuration Wizard on a computer that hosts an Exchange Server 2007 role, you need to manually register the Exchange Server 2007 Security Configuration Wizard templates by issuing the following command:

```
scwcmd register /kbname:Ex2007KB /kbfile:"%programfiles%\Microsoft\Exchange
Server\scripts\Exchange2007.xml"
```

Practice 2 at the end of this lesson provides a walk-through of the SCW.

MORE INFO   Security Configuration Wizard

You can find out more about the Security Configuration Wizard with Exchange Server 2007 by navigating to the following link: *http://technet.microsoft.com/en-us/library/aa998208.aspx.*

The Exchange Best Practices Analyzer

The Exchange Best Practices Analyzer, shown in Figure 1-8, is a tool designed to assist in tuning an Exchange installation, diagnosing common misconfiguration issues with the intention of making Exchange function as efficiently as possible. Once the tool is run, a detailed report will be generated that lists a set of recommendations that can be made to the environment to achieve greater performance, scalability, and uptime. The Exchange Best Practices Analyzer is located in the Toolbox of the Exchange Management Console. This tool is presently available only after you have installed Exchange Server 2007. To perform the readiness check, install the tool without assigning any roles to the server.

NOTE   Use the included version

At the time of this writing, you need to use the Exchange Best Practices Analyzer included with Exchange Server 2007 rather than the one that is available from Microsoft's Web site, as there are difficulties installing the utility if Microsoft .NET Framework 2.0 rather than 1.1 is installed.

The Exchange Best Practices Analyzer can be configured to perform the following scans:

- **Health check** This check examines the Exchange environment for errors, warnings, and configuration settings that differ from the default.

- **Permission check** This check examines the Exchange administrative groups and the permissions assigned to Exchange servers and reports on critical issues and settings that deviate from the installation defaults.

- **Connectivity test** This check tests network connectivity. It is often used to verify that firewall configuration is not impeding Exchange.

- **Baseline** This scan reports on all settings that differ from a user-configured baseline.

- **Exchange 2007 readiness check** Used prior to an exchange deployment, this check will highlight issues in the network infrastructure that may cause deployment problems.

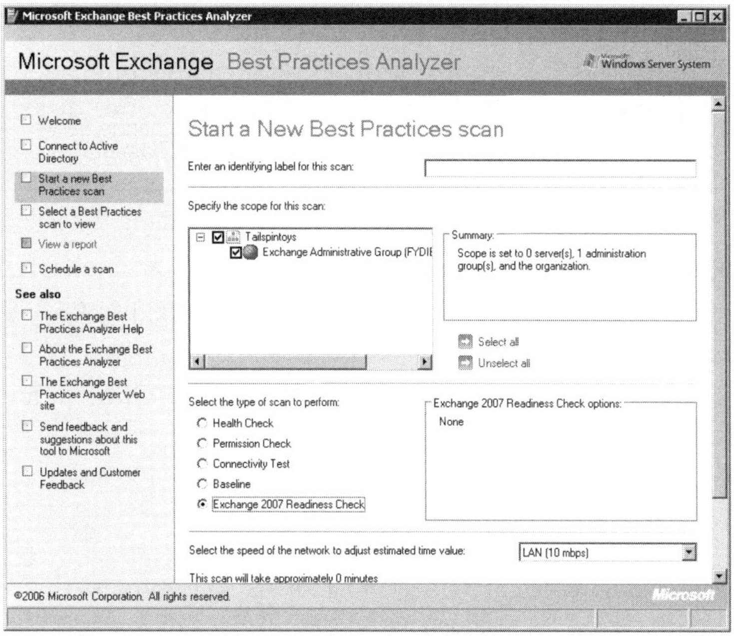

Figure 1-8   Exchange Best Practices Analyzer tool

Multiple Volumes

Although it is possible to install Exchange on the same volume as the Windows Server 2003 operating system, there are benefits of having multiple disks and multiple volumes. This involves performing a custom installation, the process for which will be covered in more detail in Chapter 2. Windows Server 2003 supports several levels of RAID (redundant array of independent disks) functionality that can be utilized to support an Exchange Server 2007 deployment. These are configured through the Disk Management node of the Computer Management console.

- RAID 0, also known as disk striping, improves disk read and write performance at the expense of redundancy. It achieves this by spreading data across two or more volumes. Data can be written and read from both disks at the same time, increasing performance. If one of the disks in a RAID 0 set fails, all data on the volume is lost. RAID 0 is supported through software on Windows Server 2003.

- RAID 1, also known as disk mirroring, provides redundancy. A RAID 1 volume involves a pair of disks with the data on the first disk mirrored on the second disk. In the event that one disk fails, the other disk can still be used without the loss of data. RAID 1 provides no performance benefit. RAID 1 is supported through software on Windows Server 2003.

- RAID 5, also known as disk striping with parity, provides redundancy and a performance improvement. RAID 5 requires a minimum of three disks. Data in a volume is spread across all disks in the RAID 5 array. Parity data, used in data recovery should a disk in the RAID array fail, is also spread across all disks. The data on a volume can be recovered if a disk fails by replacing the failed disk.

- Other types of RAID, including RAID 1+0 and RAID 0+1, are available, but these require the use of special hardware and cannot be implemented directly through the Windows Server 2003 operating system.

MORE INFO   **More on RAID**

You can find out more about RAID by navigating to the following Web site: *http://technet2.microsoft.com/windowsserver/en/library/cb871b6c-8ce7-4eb7-9aba-52b36e31d2a11033.mspx?mfr=true.*

In most situations, you would want to place mailbox data on volumes that are redundant. In the event that a disk failure occurs on the Exchange Server 2007 computer, data hosted on a redundant volume can be quickly recovered. The choice of which method of redundancy to use is determined by the costs involved. Small to medium-sized businesses are generally able to implement only RAID 1 on their mail servers, whereas large businesses can afford to buy the equipment necessary to implement RAID 1+0 or 0+1.

Exam Tip   It is likely that knowledge of which components are required for each role will be a topic presented on the exam. Use Microsoft PowerPoint or similar software to create a set of flash cards so that you can build an association in your mind between components and roles. You'd be surprised how you can adapt software that you already have available to improving your chances of passing a certification exam.

Practice: Preparing the Server for the Installation of Exchange Server 2007

In these practices, you will perform several exercises that will prepare your Windows Server 2003 x64 computer for the installation of Exchange Server 2007. You will also familiarize yourself with the SCW and the Exchange Best Practices Analyzer.

▶ **Practice 1: Installing Software Components**

In Chapter 2, you will install Exchange Server 2007 with all roles except the Edge Transport server role. In this practice, you will install all extra components that are not located on the Exchange Server 2007 installation media so that when you reach the practices in Chapter 2, the installation process will run without interruption. In Practice 2 of Lesson 1 in this chapter, you installed the Microsoft .NET Framework version 2 and Windows PowerShell on the schema master. If you are going to install Exchange Server 2007 on a computer other than the one functioning as schema master, you will need to perform steps 8 through 11 of Practice 1 on the computer that you will deploy Exchange on prior to beginning this practice. To complete this practice, log on to the computer on which you will be deploying Exchange Server 2007 using the Administrator account and perform the following steps:

1. Navigate to the following four links on Microsoft's Web site. Download these updates to the server's desktop:

   a. *http://go.microsoft.com/fwlink/?linkid=74465*

   b. *http://go.microsoft.com/fwlink/?LinkId=67406*

   c. *http://go.microsoft.com/fwlink/?LinkId=67407*

   d. *http://go.microsoft.com/fwlink/?LinkId=70796 (Ensure that you download the x64 version of this update.)*

IMPORTANT .NET hotfix

Even though you have already installed the Microsoft .NET Framework version 2.0 using the Add/Remove Programs item in an earlier practice, the Exchange Server 2007 installation requires that you install a hotfix for this software prior to deployment.

---

2. Install each of these updates. Ensure that you install the Windows Media Encoder before you install the update to the encoder.

3. Open the Add/Remove Programs item in Control Panel and select Add/Remove Windows Components.

4. Click Application Server and then click Details.

5. Select the Enable network COM+ Access item.

6. Select the Internet Information Services item and then click Details.

7. Verify that the NNTP and SMTP services are not enabled.

8. Select the World Wide Web Service item and then click OK twice.

9. Select the Networking Services item and then click Details.

10. Select the RPC Over HTTP Proxy item and then click OK.

11. Click Next to install these items. Click Finish when the items are installed.

BEST PRACTICES   Reapply SP2

After installing critical components, you should reboot the computer and reapply Windows Server 2003 SP2. This will update the newly installed components. A common mistake made by systems administrators is to forget to reapply service packs after modifying the components of a server. Reapplying service packs is not necessary if you have used the Slipstream technique on the installation files.

▶ **Practice 2: Installing and Running the SCW**

In this practice, you will explore the functionality of the SCW. In the best of worlds, this wizard should be run after all applications and services that the server will provide to the network are made active. If you apply the results of the SCW to a computer prior to installing necessary services, you may block something that you will need later. In this practice, you will go through the SCW process and then roll the computer back to its original configuration. Although this practice is long, it will give you a good overview of the SCW's capabilities. This practice is being performed prior to the full installation of Exchange Server 2007 so to ensure that important services are not accidentally disabled. To complete this practice, perform the following steps:

1. Select the Add/Remove Programs item from Control Panel.

2. Click on Add/Remove Windows Components, place a check next to the Security Configuration Wizard component, and then click Next to complete the installation. Open the SCW from the Administrative Tools menu.

3. On the Welcome page, click Next.

4. On the Configuration Action page of the wizard, select Create A New Security Policy and then click Next.

5. Verify that the current server name appears on the Select Server page and then click Next.

6. On the Processing Security Configuration Database page, click View Configuration Database. This will bring up the current configuration. Scroll down to the Domain Controller entry and expand it as shown in Figure 1-9.

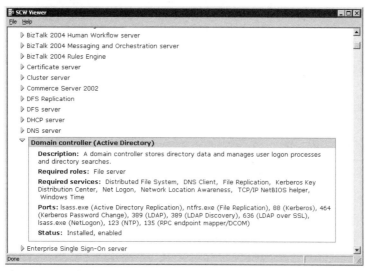

Figure 1-9   The SCW Viewer displays information about ports and services required for specific roles

7. Close the SCW Viewer and then click Next on the Processing Security Configuration Database page.

8. On the Select Server Roles page, examine which roles the SCW has detected and then click Next.

9. On the Select Client Features page, shown in Figure 1-10, examine the list of features that the SCW has detected and then click Next.

10. On the Select Administration And Other Options page, review the detected administration options and then click Next.

11. On the Select Additional Services page, review the additional services that the server requires and then click Next.

12. On the Handling Unspecified Services node, ensure that the Do Not Change The Startup Mode Of The Service option is selected and then click Next.

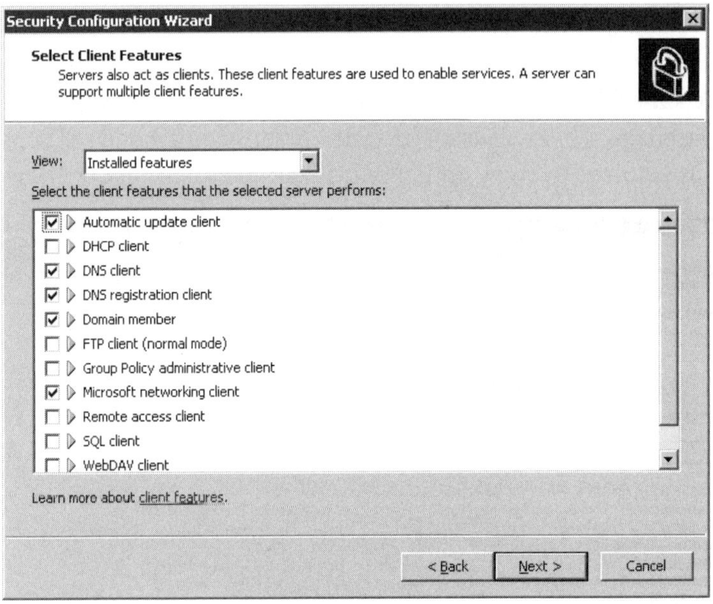

Figure 1-10 A list of installed features as detected by the SCW

13. On the Confirm Service Changes page, shown in Figure 1-11, review the list of services that have had their configuration changed and then click Next.

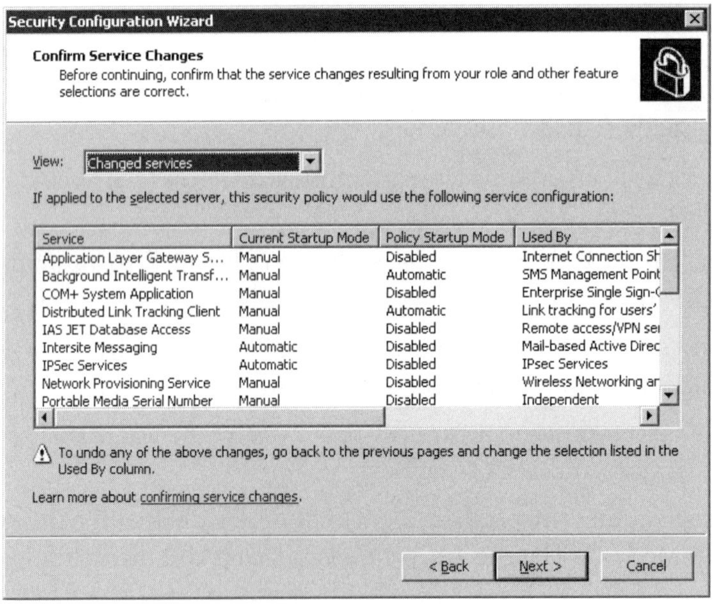

Figure 1-11 Services modified by the SCW

14. On the Network Security page, ensure that the Skip This Section option is not selected and then click Next.

15. On the Open Ports And Approve Applications page, review the ports that are being used by the computer and then click Next.

16. On the Confirm Port Configuration page, shown in Figure 1-12, check which ports have been left open and which ports have been closed and then click Next.

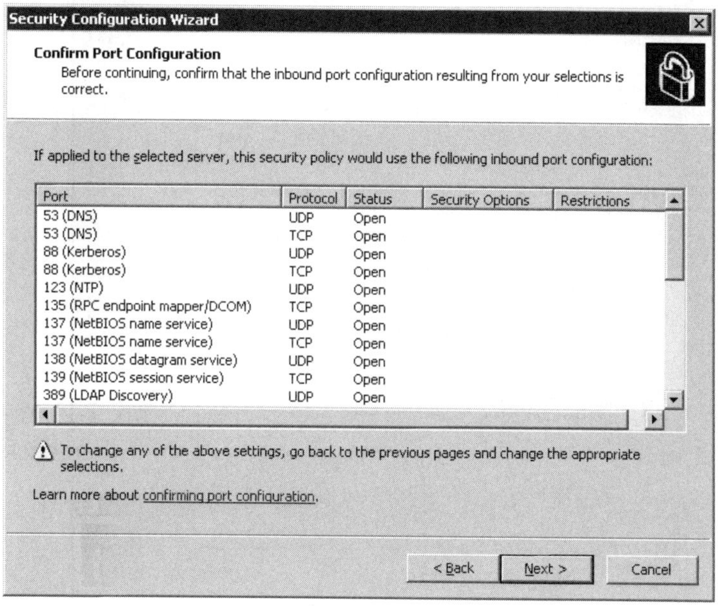

Figure 1-12   Confirming port configuration

17. On the Registry Settings page, verify that the Skip This Section option is not selected and then click Next.

18. On the Require SMB Security Signatures page, verify that both the All Computers That Connect To It Satisfy The Following Minimum Operating System Requirements and the It Has Surplus Processor Capacity That Can Be Used To Sign File And Print Traffic options are enabled. Click Next.

CAUTION   Using older editions of Windows with Exchange Server 2007

You should note that selecting these options does not mean that Windows NT 4.0, Windows 95, or Windows 98 computers will not be able to connect to the computer hosting Exchange Server 2007; it just means that each of these clients will require that the appropriate updates are installed.

---

19. On the Require LDAP Signing page, verify that the Windows 2000 Service Pack 3 Or Later option is not selected. This option should be enabled only if all clients are running Windows 2000 SP3 or later. Click Next.

20. On the Outbound Authentication Methods page, verify that only the Domain Accounts option, shown in Figure 1-13, is enabled and then click Next.

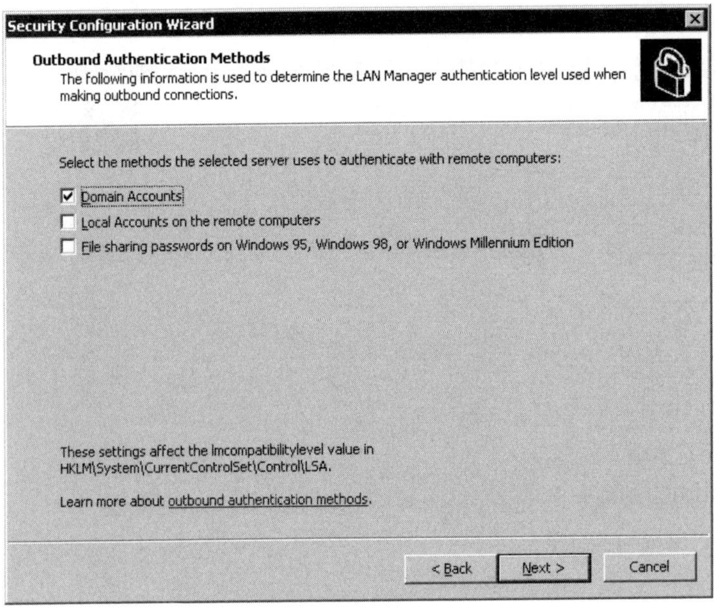

Figure 1-13   Confirming port configuration

21. On the Outbound Authentication Using Domain Accounts page, verify that the Windows NT 4.0 Service Pack 6a Or Later Operating System and the Clocks That Are Synchronized With The Selected Server's Clock options are selected and then click Next.

22. On the Inbound Authentication Methods page, verify that only the Computers That Have Not Been Configured To Use NTLMv2 Authentication and the Computers Using RAS Or VPN To Connect To RAS Server That Are Not Running Windows Server 2003 Service Pack 1 Or Later options are selected and click Next.

23. On the Registry Settings Summary page, review the settings and then click Next.

24. On the Audit Policy page, ensure that the Skip This Section option is not selected and then click Next.

25. On the System Audit Policy, select the Audit Successful And Unsuccessful Activities option and then click Next.

26. On the Audit Policy Summary page, review the settings and answer the questions below. Ensure that the Also Include The SCWAudit.inf Security Template option is not selected and then click Next.

27. On the Save Security Policy page, click Next.

28. Enter the security policy file name as **70-236-Chapter1.xml** and click Next.

29. Click OK to dismiss the reboot warning and then select the Apply Now option. Click Next. The security policy will now be applied to your computer. When the policy has been applied to your computer, click Next and then click Finish.

NOTE   If a reboot is required

You should not have to reboot your computer after applying the policy, but in the event that you do, once the computer has rebooted, log back on with administrator credentials.

---

30. Restart the SCW and then click Next.

31. On the Configure Action page, select the Rollback The Last Applied Security Policy option and then click Next.

32. On the Select Server page, ensure that the local computer is selected and then click Next.

33. On the Rollback Security Configuration page, click Next. After the rollback completes, click Next and then click Finish.

Quick Check

1. Which audit event type will not be audited if the settings outlined in step 26 are applied?

2. What caveat exists in applying the SCWAudit.inf security template using the SCW?

Quick Check Answers

1. The Privilege Used audit event type will not be audited.

2. The Audit Policy Summary page explains that the SCWAudit.inf SACLs cannot be used using the SCW rollback action.

▶ **Practice 3: Configuring an MX Record in DNS**

In this practice, you will perform the necessary steps to create an MX record for the future Exchange Server 2007 computer within the DNS system. To complete this practice, perform the following steps:

1. Open a command prompt and run the *IPCONFIG* command to determine the IP address of the computer that will host Exchange Server 2007. As mentioned earlier in the lesson, this IP address should be statically configured.

2. From the Administrative Tools menu, open the DNS console.

3. Expand the Forward Lookup Zones node, then the tailspintoys.internal node. Verify that the host record for Glasgow.tailspintoys.internal exists, as shown in Figure 1-14. This record should have been created when you installed the server operating system and Active Directory as described at the start of the practices in Lesson 1. If this record does not exist, it will be necessary for you to create it. Map the host name Glasgow.tailspintoys.internal to the IP address of the server and proceed to the next step.

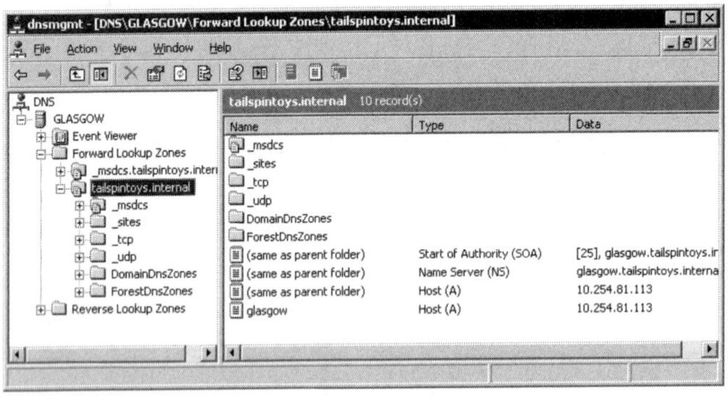

Figure 1-14   Confirming the existing host record

4. Right-click the tailspintoys.internal node and then click New Mail Exchanger. This will bring up the New Resource Record dialog box.

5. Click on Browse, navigate to the host record for glasgow.tailspintoys.internal, and then click OK.

6. Verify that the details match those in Figure 1-15 and then click OK.

7. Open a command prompt and issue the following command:

   ```
   nslookup -querytype=mx tailspintoys.internal
   ```

8. Verify that Glasgow.tailspintoys.internal is returned as the mail server for the tailspintoys.internal domain.

9. Type **Exit** to leave the command prompt.

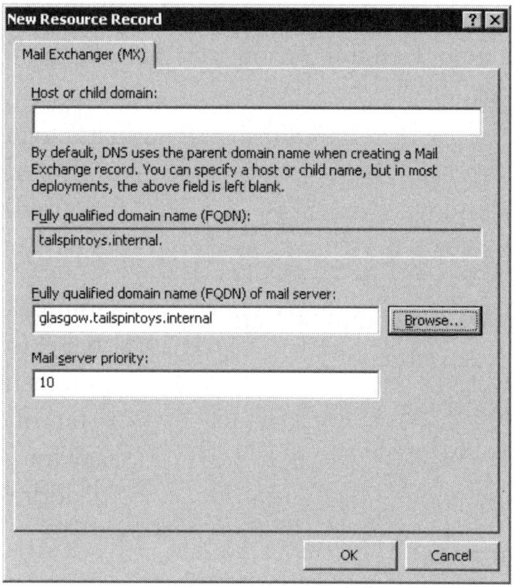

Figure 1-15   Creating an MX record

Lesson Summary

- Exchange Server 2007 must be installed on a computer running a 64-bit edition of the Windows Server 2003 operating system. The operating system needs to be patched to SP1 or R2.

- It is necessary to install several software components, some of which must be downloaded from Microsoft's Web site and some of which can be added using the Add/Remove Programs item prior to installing Exchange Server 2007.

- The SCW can be used to lock down a computer so that only those services that the computer provides to the network are enabled.

- The Exchange Best Practices Analyzer can examine your environment for problems that might cause the deployment of Exchange Server 2007 to fail.

- Exchange servers should be configured with static IP addresses. MX records on the DNS servers should be created and point to the host records of the computers that will host Exchange Server.

Lesson Review

You can use the following questions to test your knowledge of the information in Lesson 2. The questions are also available on the companion CD if you prefer to review them in electronic form.

NOTE Answers

Answers to these questions and explanations of why each answer choice is correct or incorrect are located in the "Answers" section at the end of the book.

---

1. Five Windows Server 2003 R2 computers are located at a remote site in your organization. The servers have the following roles:

   ❑ Server A: Domain controller and global catalog server

   ❑ Server B: File and print server

   ❑ Server C: SQL Server 2005 database server

   ❑ Server D: Exchange Server 2007 server

   ❑ Server E: Intranet Server

   Server A fails completely and needs to be replaced. It will be several days before you can install a replacement. Although users can currently log on over the WAN, you would like to temporarily promote one of the other servers at the site to act as a domain controller. Which of the following servers can you promote? (Choose all that apply.)

   A. Server A

   B. Server B

   C. Server C

   D. Server D

   E. Server E

2. Which of the following components need to be installed if an Exchange Server 2007 computer is to be assigned the Mailbox server role? (Choose all that apply.)

   A. COM+ Access

   B. IIS

   C. World Wide Web Service

   D. Windows PowerShell

   E. ASP.NET version 2.0

3. You are preparing a computer with Windows Server 2003 R2 x64 already installed for the installation of Exchange Server 2007. The Exchange Server will be assigned the Hub Transport server role. Which of the following components must you install prior to performing this deployment? (Choose all that apply.)

    A. Microsoft Core XML Services (MSXML) 6.0

    B. RPC over HTTP Proxy

    C. Microsoft .NET Framework version 2.0

    D. Microsoft Windows PowerShell

    E. MMC version 3.0

4. Which of the following checks should you perform using the Exchange Best Practices Analyzer prior to deploying Exchange Server 2007 in a new network environment?

    A. Health check

    B. Permissions check

    C. Connectivity test

    D. Baseline

    E. Exchange 2007 readiness check

5. Which of the following tools can you use to locate the mail servers in a DNS zone?

    A. Ping

    B. Telnet

    C. Pathping

    D. Tracert

    E. Nslookup

Chapter Review

To further practice and reinforce the skills you learned in this chapter, you can perform the following tasks:

- Review the chapter summary.
- Review the list of key terms introduced in this chapter.
- Complete the case scenarios. These scenarios set up real-world situations involving the topics of this chapter and ask you to create a solution.
- Complete the suggested practices.
- Take a practice test.

Chapter Summary

- Prior to installing Exchange Server 2007, it is necessary to extend the Active Directory schema and prepare each domain where Exchange objects will be hosted.
- When the root domain is prepared, security groups will be created that can be used to assign administrators varying levels of permissions. These include the Exchange organization administrators, Exchange recipient administrators, and the Exchange view-only administrators.
- If introducing Exchange 2007 into an existing environment, it is necessary to prepare legacy exchange permissions. It also may be necessary to disable link state.
- Exchange Server 2007 requires a 64-bit operating system and hardware. Several specific software components must be installed prior to performing the installation of Exchange.
- The Exchange Best Practices Analyzer can be used to locate problems that may cause an Exchange Server 2007 deployment to fail.

Key Terms

Do you know what these key terms mean? You can check your answers by looking up the terms in the glossary at the end of the book.

- Attack surface
- Link state

- MX recordRecord
- Schema
- Site

Case Scenarios

In the following case scenarios, you will apply what you've learned about preparing for the installation of Exchange Server 2007. You can find answers to these questions in the "Answers" section at the end of this book.

Case Scenario 1: Preparing the Active Directory Environment and Network Infrastructure at Tailspintoys for Exchange Deployment

You are planning to deploy Exchange Server 2007 at Tailspintoys. Tailspintoys has an existing Exchange Server 2003 deployment. As part of planning for the Exchange Server 2007 deployment, you must find the answer to several questions:

1. Under what conditions will it be necessary to disable link state on the Exchange Server 2003 servers?

2. To what group or groups must the user who runs *Setup /PrepareLegacyExchangePermissions* be a member if it is to be run for all domains in the forest?

3. At what location must *Setup /PrepareSchema* be run?

Case Scenario 2: Preparing a Windows Server 2003 Computer for Exchange Server Installation

A server that was going to be used for a now-canceled project has been forwarded to you in the hope that you can provision it to run Exchange Server 2007. You have access to the Windows Server 2003 R2 installation media in both 32-bit and 64-bit editions. The server itself has no operating system currently installed but has the following specifications:

- Intel Core 2 Duo Processor
- 4 GB of RAM
- Three, 1-terabyte SATA HDDs

1. Should you replace the processor with an AMD Opteron that has the same clock speed?

2. If assigned the Mailbox server role, approximately how many mailboxes could this server support?

3. What disk drive configuration could you use to ensure that no Exchange data is lost in the event that a hard disk drive fails?

Suggested Practices

To help you successfully master the exam objectives presented in this chapter, complete the following tasks.

Prepare the Infrastructure for Exchange Installation

Do all the practices in this section.

■ **Practice 1: Prepare Schema in the Exchange Server 2003 Environment** If you have access to the Exchange Server 2003 installation media, prepare a virtual environment, deploy Exchange Server 2003, and then prepare the schema for the deployment of Exchange Server 2007.

■ **Practice 2: Prepare Domain for Exchange Server 2007 Deployment** Create a child domain of your existing Tailspintoys.internal forest by adding a new domain controller.

■ Prepare this child domain for the deployment of Exchange Server 2007.

Prepare Servers for Exchange Installation

Do all the practices in this section.

Practice 1: MX Records Create two more host records in DNS.

■ Configure two MX records that point to these hosts.

Practice 2: Best Practices Analyzer Install the Microsoft Exchange Best Practices Analyzer from the Exchange Server 2007 installation media. Do not install any server roles.

■ Perform an Exchange 2007 readiness check on your environment.

Take a Practice Test

The practice tests on this book's companion CD offer many options. For example, you can test yourself on just one exam objective, or you can test yourself on all the 70-236 certification exam content. You can set up the test so that it closely simulates the experience of taking a certification exam, or you can set it up in study mode so that you can look at the correct answers and explanations after you answer each question.

MORE INFO   **Practice tests**

For details about all the practice test options available, see the "How to Use the Practice Tests" section in this book's Introduction.

Chapter 2

Installing Exchange Server and Configuring Server Roles

In the previous chapter, you prepared the Active Directory forest, individual domains, and server hardware and software for the installation of Exchange Server 2007. In this chapter, you will perform the Exchange Server 2007 installation itself. How you install Exchange Server 2007 depends on the number of Exchange servers that you need to deploy. If you are installing only a few Exchange servers, you are likely to personally run through the installation by running the Installation Wizard. If you are installing many Exchange servers, you are likely to use the scripted install process to simplify and automate deployment. In this chapter, you will also explore the most important decision that you will make in deploying each Exchange server: determining the particular roles the server will host. Once the roles have been installed, we will look at the steps that you will need to take to configure the roles for your environment, how to set up options such as clustering and load balancing, how to install Secure Sockets Layer (SSL) certificates to ensure security, and then how you can examine the installation records to verify that everything has gone according to plan.

Exam objectives in this chapter:
- Install Exchange.
- Configure Exchange server roles.

Lessons in this chapter:

Before You Begin

- Ensure that you have completed all practices in Lessons 1 and 2 of Chapter 1, "Preparing for Exchange Installation."

No additional configuration is required for this chapter.

Real World

Orin Thomas

Although unattended installations can be daunting, I have found that once you've got it working properly, you will find comfort in the fact that the process proceeds along a set path. I find that when I am repeatedly installing important software using wizards, I have a nagging feeling at the back of my mind that I've forgotten something. If you are tired and it is late on a Friday afternoon and you've been clicking through the same wizard multiple times for the last few hours, you tend to miss things. It might be a check box here or a setting there. You might miss something because you are interrupted in the middle of the process. You come back to the wizard after you've dealt with the interruption only to realize later that you've missed an important step after Exchange Server has been put into a production environment. Running an unattended installation bypasses this problem. Everything runs according to a script, and once it has started, you do not have to worry about zoning out and entering the wrong setting because you've already run through the Installation Wizard for the twenty-fifth successive time and you have 10 more to go before you clock off for the evening.

Lesson 1: Installing Exchange Server 2007

In this lesson, you will learn how to perform the installation of Exchange Server 2007 and ancillary components such as clustering, antivirus, and anti-spam. As part of the predeployment process, you will have determined which Exchange Server roles are appropriate for your organization and prepared the appropriate software environment for the installation of these roles. The lesson will then discuss the methods of installing Exchange Server 2007 and how to configure SSL and Network Load Balancing (NLB). The lesson will examine steps that should be taken prior to implementing clustering and adding antivirus and anti-spam protection to Exchange Server 2007.

After this lesson, you will be able to:

- Select the appropriate roles for an Exchange Server deployment given a set of organizational requirements.
- Perform a GUI-based, unattended, and command-line install of Exchange Server 2007.
- Install extra components, such as those that support clustering, load balancing, cryptography, antivirus, and spam-blocking functionality.

Estimated lesson time: 40 minutes

Choosing the Appropriate Role or Roles for the Server

The roles that you install on a computer running Exchange Server 2007 are determined by a set of needs. For example, if your organization is going to use only traditional e-mail and does not intend Exchange to meet voice-messaging or fax storage roles, you need not install the Unified Messaging server role. Part of the 70-236 exam involves being able to decide which roles to install on an Exchange Server 2007 computer given a specific set of organizational requirements. The first part of this lesson will provide you with the information that will help you make such a recommendation. In the second part of the lesson, we will examine the configuration of clustering, load balancing, and the steps that you should take to protect against spam and viruses. When determining which roles to deploy on a computer, remember that each Active Directory site in which clients will access Exchange resources requires at least one Mailbox server, a Hub Transport server, and a Client Access server.

MORE INFO   Typical Exchange Server 2007 setup

For more information on performing a typical Exchange Server 2007 setup, consult the following link: *http://technet.microsoft.com/en-us/library/bb123694.aspx.*

Edge Transport Role

Edge Tansport servers route messages between the Internet and your Exchange organization. Edge Transport servers are placed on an organization's perimeter network and are not members of the Active Directory environment. A perimeter network is a location between an outer firewall and an inner firewall. Other vendors sometimes refer to perimeter networks as screened subnets or demilitarized zones. Rather than traffic passing through a firewall directly to a protected internal network, perimeter networks are configured so that traffic can pass only from unprotected networks, such as the Internet, to the perimeter network or from the protected network to the perimeter network. Hosts located on the perimeter network are used to relay that traffic.

NOTE   To find out more about perimeter networks, access the following link: *http://technet2.microsoft.com/windowsserver/en/library/10e8360c-c0fe-4a52-87e8-cd8b42e446281033.mspx?mfr=true*

Edge Transport servers are often used as a blockade point for incoming and outgoing mail, ensuring that the mail is checked for viruses or unsolicited commercial e-mail, known colloquially as spam, prior to leaving the perimeter network. If problematic messages can be discarded on the perimeter of your organization's network, they will not clog up your internal mail infrastructure. If only 50 percent of the mail that is addressed to your organization is spam, dealing with it at the edge of your organization's network will halve the load on the rest of your mail infrastructure.

The main consideration with Edge Transport servers is that this role can be installed only if other roles are not present. Edge Transport servers should be placed only on perimeter networks. If your organization has no perimeter network, you should install the Hub Transport server role instead.

Hub Transport Role

The purpose of the Hub Transport role is to route traffic between Active Directory sites. If your organization has multiple Active Directory sites, any message you send to someone in a remote site will be routed to that site through your organization's Hub Transport servers. Exchange servers assigned the Hub Transport role are deployed on the protected network and are members of the Active Directory environment. At least one server assigned the Hub Transport role is required at each site for mail to be routed correctly. Servers with the Hub Transport role function in a manner similar to that of the bridgehead servers in earlier versions of Exchange.

In the event that you do not deploy an Edge Transport server, a server configured with the Hub Transport role can be used to receive and send mail traffic to the Internet. Many small and medium-sized organizations are likely to use the Hub Transport role to handle this traffic, especially if they have only a small number of computers running Exchange Server 2007. Like a server assigned the Edge Transport role, a server assigned the Hub Transport role can be configured to examine the traffic that it processes for viruses and spam. The Hub Transport role can coexist with the Client Access, Unified Messaging, and Mailbox server roles.

Client Access Role

The Client Access role provides a gateway between clients and their mailboxes. A client computer running Outlook or Exchange ActiveSync or connected using a Web browser to Outlook Web Access (OWA) connects to the Client Access server, which in turn connects to the appropriate Mailbox server. The Client Access server role is designed to optimize the performance of the Mailbox server by offloading the processing requirements. For example, rather than having the server hosting mailboxes be responsible for performing the necessary calculations to encrypt SSL traffic, this task is handled by the Client Access server. Of course, in many situations, the Client Access role will be hosted on the same computer as the Mailbox server role. The ability to separate these tasks onto a different computer allows administrators to optimize their Exchange organization.

If a single external URL of OWA or Exchange ActiveSync is required, Client Access servers must be configured for proxying. The Client Access server should be connected to the Mailbox servers it provides access to with a bandwidth of at least 100 Mbps. In enterprise environments, a gigabit connection is preferable. This means that you should have a Client Access server located in each site where there is a Mailbox server.

Mailbox Server Role

The Mailbox server role hosts mailboxes and public folders. Mailbox servers are where all the message data is stored, so they need to be provisioned with more disk space than any other role in your Exchange organization. There needs to be a computer hosting the Mailbox server role in each location where mail will be accessed. Besides storing message data, Mailbox servers also provide the scheduling services for Microsoft Office Outlook users.

Clustered Mailbox Roles

Clustered Mailbox servers provide high availability through the use of Windows Server 2003 and Windows Server 2008 clustering technology. You would choose this role over the standard Mailbox server role if you needed to ensure that mailboxes were always available. Of course, you want mailboxes to be available all the time anyway, but to ensure that they are, your organization will have to spend the money to host them on a cluster. Because of their reliance on clustering technology, you can install the Clustered Mailbox server roles only on computers running Windows Server 2003 enterprise edition or Windows Server 2008 enterprise edition. The standard editions of Windows Server software do not support the necessary form of clustering. Clustered Mailbox servers cannot share hardware with other server roles. If you select one of the Clustered Mailbox options during the installation process, as shown in Figure 2-1, you will not be able to install any other server roles.

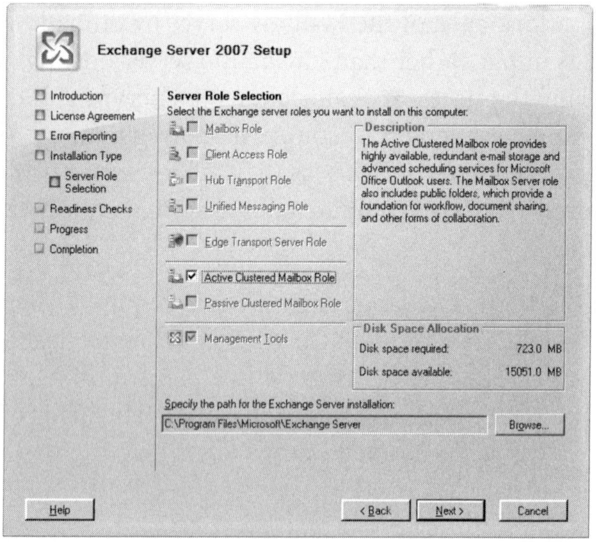

Figure 2-1   Installing the Active Clustered Mailbox role

There are two separate types of Clustered Mailbox role:

- **Active Clustered Mailbox role** This role provides highly available, redundant e-mail storage. Install this role on the active node of the cluster.

- **Passive Clustered Mailbox role** This role provides highly available, redundant e-mail storage. Install this role on the passive node of the cluster.

MORE INFO More on Mailbox servers

If you want to find out more about standard and Clustered Mailbox servers, consult the following link: *http://technet.microsoft.com/en-us/library/bb201699.aspx.*

Unified Messaging Server Role

Unified Messaging allows users to access their Exchange Server 2007 mailbox over an appropriately configured smart phone or telephone. You should deploy one Unified Messaging server in each site where you want to provide access to its services. When deployed, Unified Messaging provides the following features:

- Answering machine
- Fax reception
- Subscriber access
    - Access voice mail over telephone
    - Listen to, forward, and reply to e-mail messages over the telephone
    - Listen to calendar information over the telephone
    - Dial contacts stored within Exchange over the telephone
    - Respond to meeting requests over the telephone

Exam Tip The 70-236 exam objectives do not mention this role directly, but we thought it prudent to provide you with some information about the role's functionality in case the topic turns up in some capacity.

NOTE Unified Messaging

For more information on the capabilities of the Unified Messaging server role, consult the following link: *http://technet.microsoft.com/en-us/library/bb123911.aspx.*

Quick Check

1. What are the requirements that need to be met to install the Edge Transport role on a computer running Windows Server 2003 R2 64-bit edition?

2. Which server role can be used to manage the routing of e-mail into and out of an organization in the event that the Edge Transport server role is not deployed?

Quick Check Answers

1. The computer cannot be a member of the domain. Active Directory Application Mode (ADAM) must be installed. Server should be deployed on the perimeter network.

2. In the event that a server with the Edge Transport role is not deployed, a server with the Hub Transport role can manage the routing of e-mail into and out of the organization.

Preparing an Exchange Server 2007 Cluster

You can use clustering with Exchange Server 2007 only if you are also using Windows Server 2003 (or Windows Server 2008) enterprise edition. This is because Exchange Server 2007 relies on the Windows Cluster service, which is unavailable in the standard edition of Windows Server 2003. When you start Exchange Server 2007 setup on a node of an existing cluster, a version of Exchange that is compatible with clusters is installed. You cannot install Exchange Server 2007 on a server that is not a member of a cluster, join the server to a cluster, and then configure Exchange Server 2007 to work in a clustered configuration. If you want to shift from a standard Mailbox server role to a Clustered Mailbox server role, it will be necessary to remove Exchange entirely and reinstall the software before assigning the role. Chapter 13, "Recovering Server Roles and Configuring High Availability," covers Exchange Server 2007 clustering in more detail.

MORE INFO **More on High Availability**

To find out more about Exchange Server 2007 high-availability solutions, consult the following link: *http://technet.microsoft.com/en-us/library/bb124721.aspx.*

Load Balancing

When two or more servers are configured to load balance, they accept requests on the basis of their current workload. For example, if two servers are configured to load balance and the first server is under greater workload than the second server, client requests will be directed to the second server until such time as the workload is balanced more evenly between the computers in the load-balancing set. Load balancing is used primarily with the Client Access, Edge Transport, and Hub Transport server roles.

An advantage of load balancing is that it is not necessary to configure it prior to the installation of Exchange Server 2007. Another advantage is that you are able to add and remove nodes without a significant amount of effort. For example, if you have load-balanced Edge Transport servers that are straining under the weight of transmitting and receiving e-mail, it is relatively simple to add another Edge Transport server to the NLB cluster and have it automatically share the load with the existing servers. In the event that a server fails in an NLB cluster, the NLB service automatically reconfigures the way it distributes traffic until the failed server can be brought back online.

MORE INFO   NLB

To find out more about how to set up NLB, consult the following link: *http://go.microsoft.com/fwlink/ ?linkid=49315.*

Lesson 2 of Chapter 13 covers the configuration of network load balancing in Exchange Server 2007 in more detail. Round-robin DNS also provides a good way of load balancing Hub Transport roles within a particular site. The drawback of using round-robin DNS as a load balancing solution is that, unlike NLB, round-robin DNS cannot automatically detect the failure of one of the load-balanced hosts.

MORE INFO   Round-robin DNS

For more information about configuring round-robin DNS, consult the following link: *http:// technet2.microsoft.com/windowsserver/f/?en/library/e0f49958-f290-49fc-adb4-71ed8deefd621033.mspx.*

Installing Exchange Server 2007 Using the GUI

Exchange Server setup using the GUI can be completed using two options, as shown in Figure 2-2. Selecting the Typical Exchange Server Installation option with Hub Transport, Client Access, and Mailbox server roles. The Exchange Management tools will also be installed, as it is not possible to install any role without the management tools also being installed. It is possible to install the Edge Transport, Unified Messaging, or Clustered Mailbox server roles only if you select a custom install.

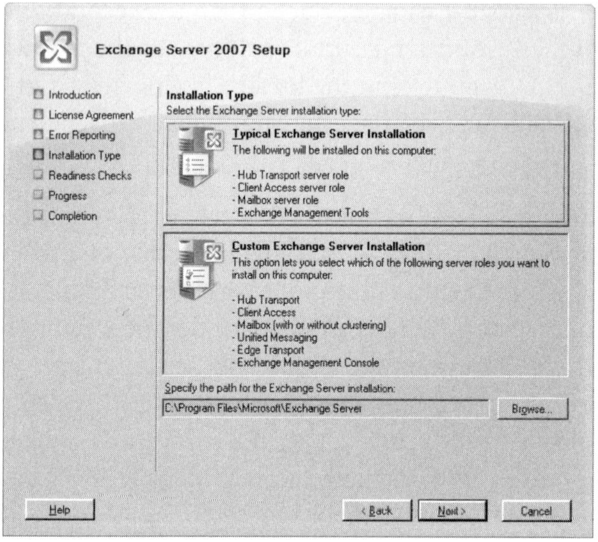

Figure 2-2 Selecting the installation type

Once you have selected the roles to be installed, either through the typical or the custom setup screen, the Exchange Server 2007 installation routine performs a series of readiness checks, shown in Figure 2-3, to determine that the environment is ready for installation. If the readiness checks are passed, the wizard proceeds to installation. If the readiness checks fail, you will be informed as to the reason for the failure, and the installation process will terminate. During the installation, the Exchange Server 2007 installation files will be copied to the server. This means that if you need to add or remove a role at a later date—assuming that you have installed a role that can coexist with other roles—you will not need to remember where you put the installation media.

When the installation process finishes, the Exchange Server 2007 Finalize Deployment checklist is displayed. The Finalize Deployment checklist reminds you to perform the following tasks:

- Enter the Exchange Server product key
- Run the Exchange Best Practices Analyzer
- Configure offline address book distribution for Outlook 2007 clients
- Configure offline address book distribution for Outlook 2003 and earlier clients
- Configure SSL for your Client Access server
- Configure Exchange ActiveSync
- Configure domains for which you will accept e-mail

- Subscribe the Edge Transport server
- Create a postmaster mailbox
- Configure Unified Messaging

The methods through which you can complete these tasks will be covered throughout the rest of this chapter.

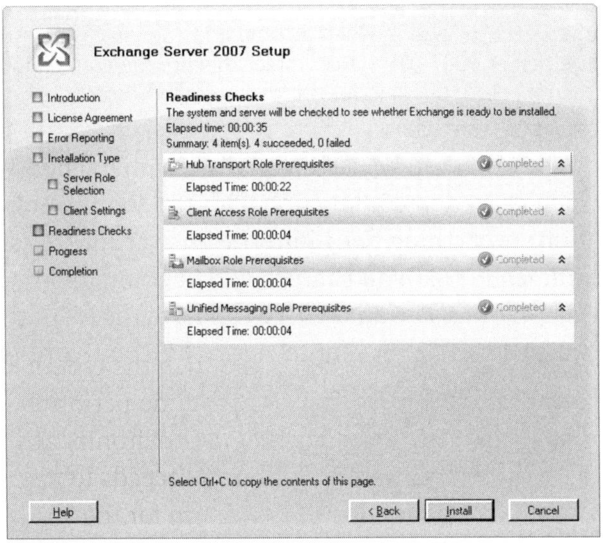

Figure 2-3   Readiness checks

Command-Line and Unattended Installations of Exchange Server 2007

You are unlikely to use the unattended installation features of Exchange Server 2007 if you need to configure only one or two Exchange servers. If you need to deploy 50 identically configured servers running Exchange Server 2007, the option to perform an unattended installation becomes far more attractive. The unattended installation feature allows you to perform large deployments of Exchange Server 2007 without having to constantly configure the same set of options through the GUI.

BEST PRACTICES   **Do it the easy way first**

You should be familiar with the requirements of a typical installation before you attempt to run your first unattended installation. Virtual machines are an excellent environment in which to test unattended installations to ensure that you've set everything up correctly. You do not want to run 50 unattended installations using the same script only to find that you've made a configuration error.

An unattended installation allows you to set all the Exchange server's configuration parameters at the start of the installation rather than having to provide them during the installation. Generally, this is done by configuring the options following a single setup command. Although you can use an answer file for part of the installation process, the answer file is used primarily for the installation of Clustered Mailbox roles.

BEST PRACTICES   Building a command

Although we talk about command-line installations, when a command contains as many options as the setup command for Exchange Server 2007 does, it is simpler to write the command to a batch file and execute the batch file than it is to type it all out on the command prompt.

Prior to examining all the options that can be used with the command line, we should examine the answer file, which is used in conjunction with the setup command. The first thing to realize is that not everything goes into the answer file. In fact, only a small set of the possible parameters that you can use with a command-line installation can be included in the answer file. The answer file can have the following parameters: CMSName, CMSIPAddress, CMSSharedStorage, CMSDataPath, NewCMS, RemoveCMS, RecoverCMS, UpgradeCMS, EnableLegacyOutlook, LegacyRoutingServer, ServerAdmin, ForeignForestFQDN, OrganizationName, DoNotStartTransport, UpdatesDir, EnableErrorReporting, NoSeltSignedCertificates, AdamLdapPort, and AdamSslPort.

A quick look at these parameters shows you that the majority of them have the CMS prefix. CMS is the acronym for Clustered Mailbox server. The answer file is used to ensure that nodes in a cluster have the same configuration. You use a single answer file for each node of the cluster. You generally do not use an answer file for a noncluster Exchange Server 2007 deployment.

The setup command has the following options:

```
Setup.com [/mode:<setup mode>] [/roles:<server roles to install>] [/OrganizationName:<name for
the new Exchange organization>] [/TargetDir:<target directory>] [/SourceDir:<source
directory>][/UpdatesDir:<directory from which to install updates>] [/DomainControler <FQDN of
domain controller>] [/AnswerFile <filename>] [/DoNotStartTransport]
[/EnableLegacyOutlook] [/LegacyRoutingServer] [/EnableErrorReporting]
[/NoSelfSignedCertificates] [/AdamLdapPort <port>] [/AdamSslPort <port>]
[/AddUmLanguagePack:<UM language pack name>] [/RemoveUmLanguagePack:<UM language pack name>]
[/NewProvisionedServer] [/RemoveProvisionedServer] [/ForeignForestFQDN] [/ServerAdmin <user
or group>] [/NewCms] [/RemoveCms] [/RecoverCms] [/CMSName:<name>] [/CMSIPAddress:<IP address>]
[/CMSSharedStorage] [/CMSDataPath:<CMS data path>] [/?]
```

Many of the options are self-explanatory, and you can use abbreviations rather than entering the full option. The most important ones include the following:

- **/mode or /m** You can set this to install, upgrade, uninstall, and recover Server.
- **/role, /roles, or /r** Specifies which roles to install. You can install the following:
  - ❑ **ClientAccess, CA, or C** Client Access role
  - ❑ **EdgeTransport, ET, or E** Edge Transport role
  - ❑ **HubTransport, HT, or H** Hub Transport role
  - ❑ **Mailbox, MB, or M** Mailbox role
  - ❑ **UnifiedMessaging, UM, or U** Unified Messaging role
  - ❑ **ManagementTools, MT, or T** Management tools (automatically installed if any other role is selected)
- **/OrganizationName or /on** Necessary only when setting up a new Exchange organization. If you have run *Setup /PrepAD*, then the */OrganizationName* switch is unnecessary.

MORE INFO   Command-line deployment

For more information about the command-line options not covered here, consult the following link: *http://technet.microsoft.com/en-us/library/aa997281.aspx.*

Installing an Edge Transport Server

Edge Transport servers should be stand-alone computers that are not members of the Active Directory forest. It follows that the user account used for the installation of the Exchange Server 2007 software does not need to be delegated any of the Exchange administrator roles. When installing the Edge Transport server role using the GUI, ensure that the Windows .NET Framework version 2.0, Windows PowerShell, ADAM with Service Pack 1, and Microsoft Management Console version 3.0 or higher are installed. You also need to ensure that the fully qualified domain name (FQDN) for the server that will host the Edge Transport role is set. You can set this information from the Computer Name tab of System Properties. Prior to installing the Edge Transport role, you should also ensure that the IP addresses assigned to the computer are registered in DNS and that MX records have been set appropriately.

MORE INFO   More on ADAM

To find out more about ADAM, consult the following link: *http://www.microsoft.com/ windowsserver2003/adam/default.mspx.*

You need to choose a custom Exchange Server installation on the Exchange Server 2007 Setup page to be able to select the Edge Transport server role on the Server Role Selection page. Once the role is installed, Exchange Management Console will launch and a list of postinstallation tasks be displayed. These tasks will be covered in more detail in Lesson 2 of this chapter.

Once the Edge Transport server role has been installed, it is possible to clone the configuration of the server so that you can install more Edge Transport servers to share the load. You run an Exchange Management Shell script to export the configuration from the original Edge Transport server to an XML file and then import that XML configuration file on the target server.

NOTE **Edge Transport server cloned configuration**

You can find out more about configuring Edge Transport servers using cloned configuration by navigating to the following link: *http://technet.microsoft.com/en-us/library/aa998622.aspx.*

> ### Quick Check
> 1. What do the majority of the possible parameters in the answer file relate to?
> 2. What command would you use from the command line to install the Edge Transport role on a stand-alone server?
>
> ### Quick Check Answers
> 1. Clustered Mailbox servers.
> 2. *Setup /mode:install /roles:EdgeTransport.*

Postinstallation Tasks

The quickest way to verify the configuration of a newly installed Exchange Server 2007 deployment is to open an Exchange Management Shell and issue the command *get-ExchangeServer | Format-List*. This command produces output in the format shown in Figure 2-4. By examining this output, you can determine which server roles have successfully installed as well as other important configuration information, including whether a valid license key has been input.

Figure 2-4 You can verify the configuration of an Exchange Server from Exchange Management Shell

Examining Logs for Problems

If you suspect that a deployment has not gone according to plan, you should examine the logs to tease out details of things that may have gone awry. You can search for information in two primary locations:

- Check the installation logs. The installation logs are located at C:\Program Files\Microsoft\Exchange Server\Logging\SetupLogs.

- Check the event logs. Events related to Exchange Server 2007 are written to the Application event log. Exchange events include warning, information, and critical errors.

In most cases, you can resolve the issue and then attempt to reinstall the role. You can do this either through Add/Remove Programs or using the *setup /mode:reinstall* option from the command line.

Applying Updates and Service Packs

In general, you should apply all available updates and service packs to Windows Server 2003 (or Windows Server 2008 in the event you are using it as the host operating system) prior to the installation of Exchange Server 2007. Once the installation process has been successfully completed, you should check whether new service packs or updates exist for Exchange Server 2007. Service packs provide updates and sometimes add new functionality. The best time to deploy updates and service packs is directly after installation. This way, you do not have to worry about taking management's mailboxes offline while you do maintenance, as you will not have deployed management mailboxes to the server yet.

Assigning Users Roles

Chapter 1 examined what each of the Exchange Server 2007 administrative roles is used for. Once Exchange is installed, it is possible to use the Exchange Management Console to apply these roles to particular users. To do this, open the Exchange Management Console, right-click the Organization Configuration node, and then click Add Exchange Administrator. This will start the Add Exchange Administrator Wizard. As shown in Figure 2-5, you browse to select a user or group and select the role and scope of the role. It is necessary to specify servers for a role only if the Exchange Server administrator role is assigned. If you are assigning the Exchange Server administrator role, you must ensure that the user or group you have assigned this role to is a member of the Local Administrators group on the server you have designated. If the user or group does not have membership of the Local Administrators group, they will be unable to perform some or all of their tasks.

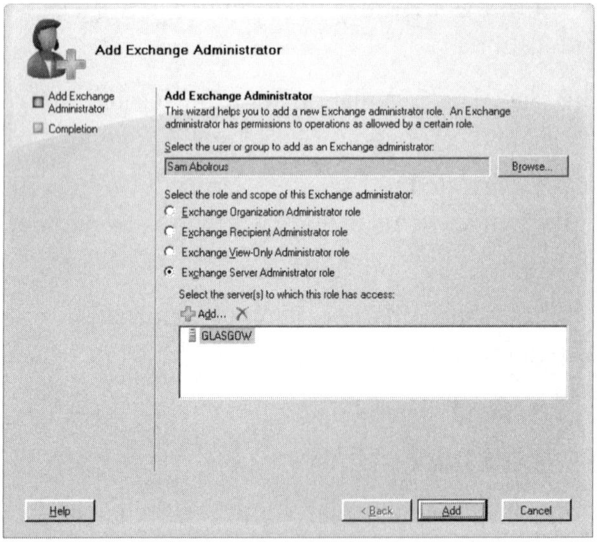

Figure 2-5   Adding an Exchange administrator

You can also assign roles to users and groups using Exchange Management Shell. The configuration setting shown in the previous figure can be achieved by entering the following command:

```
Add-ExchangeAdministrator -Identity 'tailspintoys.internal/Users/Sam Abolrous' -Role
'ServerAdmin' -Scope 'GLASGOW'
```

It is also possible to apply these roles to users by adding user accounts and groups to the appropriate security group in Active Directory Users and Computers, the method used in Chapter 1.

MORE INFO   Adding groups to administrator roles

For more information about adding users and groups to administrator roles within an Exchange organization, consult the following link: *http://technet.microsoft.com/en-us/library/aa998008.aspx*.

Exam Tip   Try to keep the purpose of each Exchange Server 2007 role clear in your mind, as there are likely to be questions exploring the differences between each role.

Enter the Product Key

In previous versions of Exchange, you entered a product key during the installation process. If you did not have the product key, you could not complete the installation. With Exchange Server 2007, the license key is entered during a 120-day period after the installation process has been completed. Until the product key is entered, Exchange Server 2007 runs in trial mode. This is functionally equivalent to the normal operational mode of Exchange Server 2007 except that the trial period lasts only 120 days.

As an administrator, this gives you a grace period to ensure that the server you install and activate is deployed in the location that best benefits your organization. It also gives you a chance to be certain that you have configured a server correctly. If you are rushed into product activation, you may activate a server only to find that you have to reinstall from scratch because of some configuration problem that you did not initially notice. You do not need to rush to enter the product key, but also make sure that you do not do it at the last moment.

When you are ready to enter the product key, open the Exchange Management Console, click Server Configuration, select the server that you wish to enter the product key for, and then click Enter Product Key in the Actions box. You then enter the product key in the dialog box shown in Figure 2-6. When you click Enter, the product ID will be generated, and Exchange Server 2007 will be licensed.

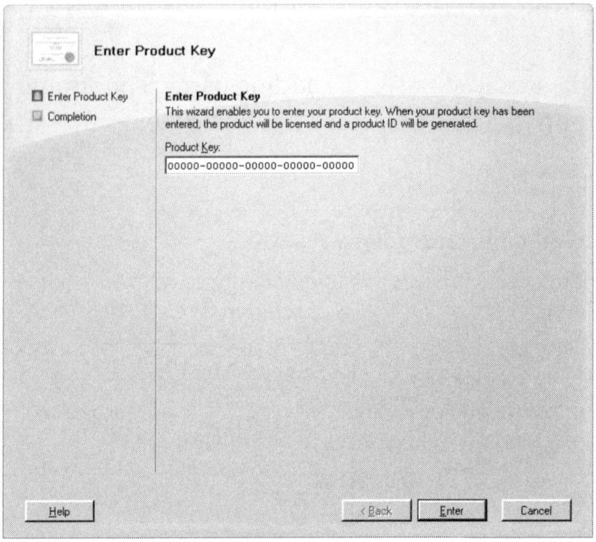

Figure 2-6   Entering the product key

Installing Antivirus and Anti-spam

E-mail communication is the lifeblood of many businesses. E-mail is also the conduit through which harmful material can enter and exit the organization in the form of viruses. Spam, also known as unsolicited commercial e-mail, is less harmful than viruses in terms of damaging computers and infrastructure. However, dealing with spam does take valuable time away from other tasks. An evaluation of Forefront Security for Exchange Server 2007 is included with the Exchange Server 2007 installation media. In this section, we will briefly look at setting up Forefront. Chapter 6, "Spam, Viruses, and Compliance," provides more detail on the application and how it can be used to protect your network environment.

During the setup of Forefront Security for Exchange Server, five separate antivirus scanning engines can be installed. You can either go with the random selection of engines performed by the Setup Wizard or choose four engines in addition to the Microsoft Antimalware engine, as shown in Figure 2-7. The engines that you can install as a part of Forefront Security include the following:

- AhnLab Antivirus Scan Engine
- CA InoculateIT

- CA Vet

- Authentium Command Antivirus

- Kaspersky Antivirus Technology

- Norman Virus Control

- Sophos Virus Detection

- VirusBuster Antivirus

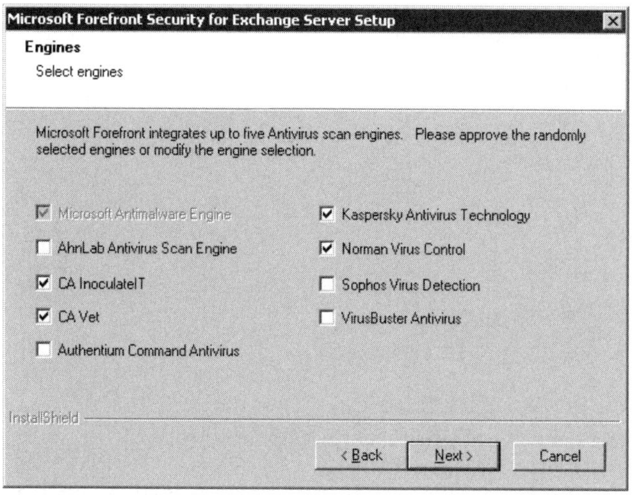

Figure 2-7   Antivirus engine selection

The antivirus engines will be updated on an hourly basis. You cannot configure a proxy server during installation through which the updates can be obtained, though you can use the Forefront Server Security Administrator tool to configure proxy information so that updates can occur. The installation of Forefront is covered by a practice exercise at the end of this lesson.

Securing Communication

SSL provides a way of encrypting traffic between a client and a server and also provides a method of verifying the server's identity. You most likely have used SSL before when performing activities like shopping online. When the Client Access server role is installed, a self-signed SSL certificate is generated and installed for the default Web site in Internet Information Services. You can view this certificate by clicking View Certificate on the Directory Security tab of the default Web site properties in Internet Information Services. The downside to this automatically generated certificate is that it is issued by an authority that will not be trusted by any clients, including, as Figure 2-8 demonstrates, the computer that issued the certificate.

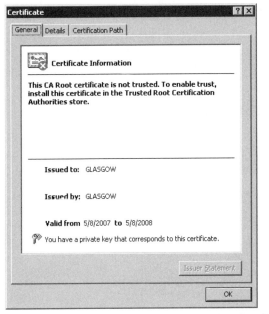

Figure 2-8   The SSL certificate generated by the Client Access server role

By default, client computers and devices trust only certain issuing authorities. You can view such a list of trusted authorities by clicking Certificates in the Content tab of Internet Properties or Internet Options (depending on which version of Windows you are using) in Control Panel. Although in a managed environment it is possible to configure clients to trust the self-generated certificate created with the installation of the Client Access role, it may be cheaper to obtain an SSL certificate from an issuing authority that is already a trusted publisher than to configure a new trusted publisher for all clients that will access Exchange Server 2007 using SSL. Trusted SSL certificates do cost money, but it also costs your organization money to have you spending many hours configuring clients to accept a new certificate-issuing authority as trustworthy. The money saved on not buying a certificate is lost on paying you to configure devices to trust another certification authority (CA).

To obtain an SSL certificate for a server, you have to provide identity details about the server, specifically the server's DNS name information. If you later decide to change the server's name, you will need to obtain a new SSL certificate that reflects this name change. You can generate a certificate request file by running the Web

Server Certificate Wizard. It is also possible to generate a certificate request from Exchange Management Shell by issuing the following command: *New-ExchangeCertificate –GenerateRequest –FriendlyName "SSL Access to Exchange 2007" –DomainName glasgow.tailspintoys.internal –path c:\sslrequest.txt.* The certificate request file is then forwarded to a trusted issuing authority that will issue the SSL certificate, generally for a certain fee. The process of requesting and installing an SSL certificate is covered in more detail by a practice exercise at the end of this lesson.

Practice: Exchange Server 2007 Installation and Setup

In these practices, you will perform several exercises that will familiarize you with installing Exchange Server 2007 and performing some postconfiguration steps. Practices 2 and 3 achieve the same goal by different routes, and you should perform only one of these practices before moving on to Practice 4.

NOTE   If you are using virtual machine software that allows for rollbacks or snapshots, it is possible to perform each installation practice, rolling back to the noninstalled configuration after each practice is completed.

▶ **Practice 1: Installing Exchange Server Using Graphical Tools**

In this practice, you will create user accounts that will be used in the installation and configuration of Exchange Server 2007 in later practices. To complete this practice, perform the following steps:

1. Log on to the computer that you prepared for the installation of Exchange Server 2007 in the practices at the end of Lesson 2 in Chapter 1.

2. Open Active Directory Users and Computers and create the following user accounts and add them to the security groups in the table:

Name	Account Name	Group
Kim Akers	Kim_Akers	Administrators, Domain Admins, Domain Users, Enterprise Admins, Exchange Organization Administrators
Sam Abolrous	Sam_Abolrous	Domain Users, Backup Operators
Terry Adams	Terry_Adams	Domain Users, Backup Operators

3. Set the password of all these accounts to *P@ssw0rd* and configure the password to never expire.

NOTE In a real-world environment, you would not configure a password to never expire, but this configuration setting simplifies things for the purposes of the practices in this training kit.

---

4. Log off.

▶ **Practice 2: Installing Exchange Server Using Graphical Tools**

In this practice, you will install Exchange Server 2007 using graphical tools. Even if you end up using primarily command-line and scripted installation to deploy Exchange, you will likely be using the graphical tools the first time you deploy Exchange. If you perform Practice 2, it is not necessary to perform Practice 3. To complete this practice, perform the following steps:

1. Log on with the Kim_Akers account.

2. Insert the Exchange Server 2007 installation media. If the Exchange Server 2007 splash screen does not appear, open a command prompt, change to the drive that contains the Exchange Server 2007 installation media, and type **setup**.

3. Verify that the first three steps under the Install category are grayed out, as shown in Figure 2-9. These steps are grayed out because you installed these components in an earlier lesson. Click Step 4: Install Microsoft Exchange.

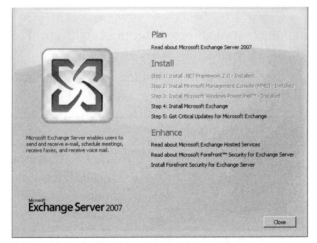

Figure 2-9   The Exchange Server splash screen

4. On the Introduction page, click Next.

5. On the License Agreement page, review the license terms. Once you have reviewed the terms, select I Accept The Terms In The License Agreement and then click Next.

6. On the Error Reporting page, click Next.

7. On the Installation Type page, click Custom Exchange Server Installation and then click Next.

8. On the Server Role Selection page, shown in Figure 2-10, select the Mailbox Role, Client Access Role, Hub Transport Role, and Unified Messaging Role options. Click Next.

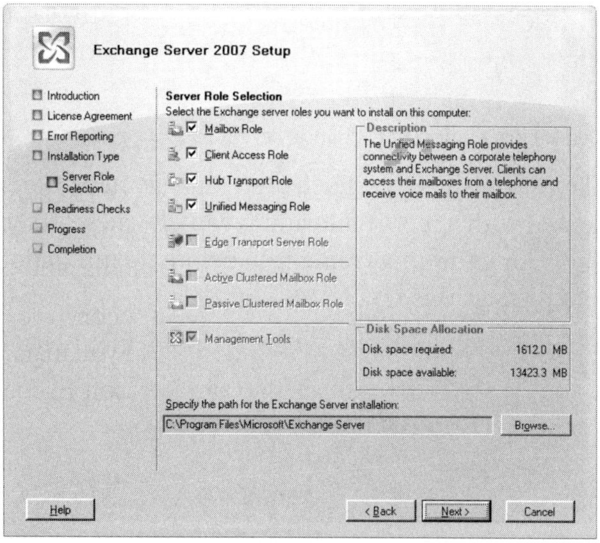

Figure 2-10 The Exchange Server splash screen

9. On the Client Settings page, review the information about Outlook 2003 and Entourage. Verify that No is selected and then click Next.

10. The Exchange Server 2007 setup process will now perform readiness checks. As you have already installed the required components, this should produce no errors. Once the readiness checks are complete, click Install.

11. The installation process will take between 20 and 50 minutes to complete, depending on the speed of the computer that you are installing it on. Exchange files will be copied to the server, and then the selected roles will be installed.

12. When all the roles have been installed, you will get a message informing you that Exchange has successfully installed with no errors, as shown in Figure 2-11. Ensure that the Finalize Installation Using The Exchange Management Console option is selected and then click Finish.

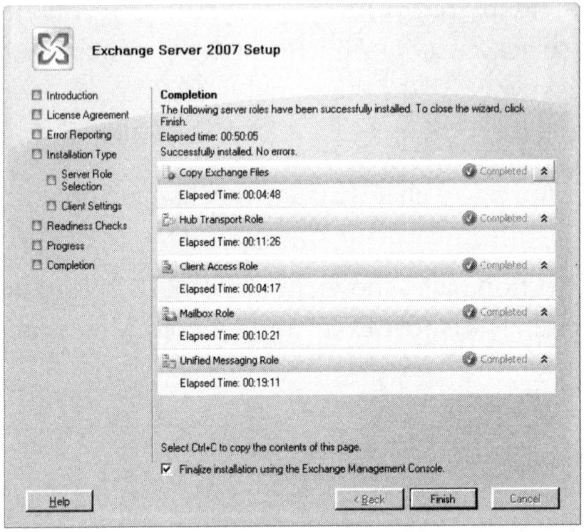

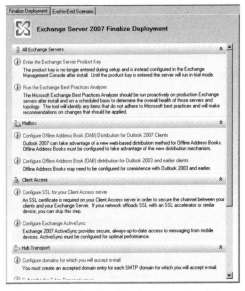

Figure 2-11   Successful installation of Exchange server roles

13. Once the installation finishes, the Exchange Management Console will open. You will be presented with a report informing you of which servers are currently unlicensed and how long they may remain so before their functionality is diminished. Click OK to dismiss this report.

14. You will then be presented with the Finalize Deployment checklist shown in Figure 2-12.

Figure 2-12   Finalize Deployment checklist

> ## Quick Check
> ■ According to the information on the Client Settings page of the Exchange Server 2007 Setup Wizard, what will happen if you inform the installation wizard that there are client computers running Outlook 2003 or Entourage in your organization?
>
> ### Quick Check Answer
> ■ A public folder database will be created during setup. For more information on why a public folder database is necessary for computers running Outlook 2003 or Entourage, see Chapter 4, "Configuring Public Folders."

▶ **Practice 3: Installing Exchange Server Using the Command Line**

When you have to deploy multiple Exchange multiple times, you will find it more efficient to use the command line rather than the graphical tools. In this practice, you will perform a command-line installation of Exchange Server 2003, adding exactly the same roles as were added in Practice 2. In essence, this practice achieves the same results as Practice 2 but does so using an alternate method. If you have performed Practice 2, it is not necessary to complete this practice. To complete this practice, perform the following steps:

1. Log on with the Kim_Akers account.

2. Insert the Exchange Server 2007 installation media. If the Exchange Server 2007 splash screen does not appear, open a command prompt and change to the drive that contains the Exchange Server 2007 installation media.

3. Enter the command:

    setup /mode:install
    /roles:HubTransport,ClientAccess,Mailbox,UnifiedMessaging

---

NOTE Exchange Management tools

The Exchange Management tools will be automatically installed when the other roles are installed.

▶ **Practice 4: Assigning Users Administrative Roles**

In this practice, you will assign two of the user accounts that you created in the first practice. To complete this practice, perform the following steps:

1. Log on to the computer on which you have installed Exchange Server 2007 with the Kim_Akers user account.

2. Open the Exchange Management Console.

3. Select the Organization Configuration node, right-click, and then click Add Exchange Administrator.

4. On the Add Exchange Administrator dialog box shown in Figure 2-13, click Browse and navigate to the Sam Abolrous account. Select the Exchange View-Only Administrator role and then click Add.

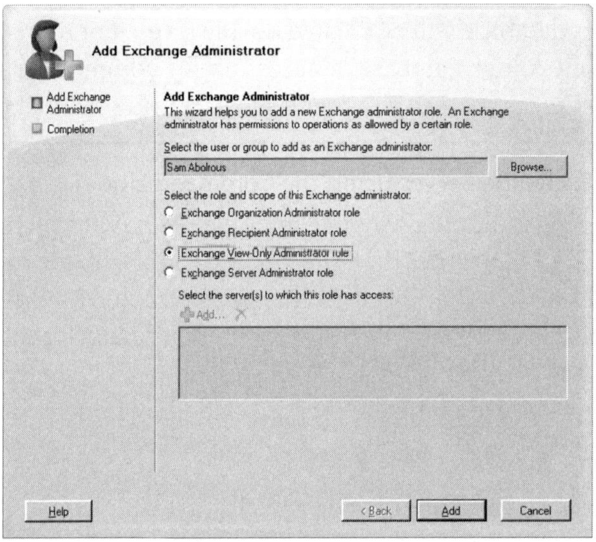

Figure 2-13 Configuring Exchange administrator roles

5. Click Finish to close the Completion dialog box.

6. Right-click the Organization Configuration node and then click Add Exchange Administrator.

7. Click Browse and navigate to the Terry Adams user account.

8. Select the Exchange Server Administrator role option and then click Add.

9. In the Select Exchange Server dialog box, shown in Figure 2-14, select GLAS-GOW and then click OK.

10. Click Add in the Add Exchange Administrator dialog box.

11. Review the warning and then click Finish.

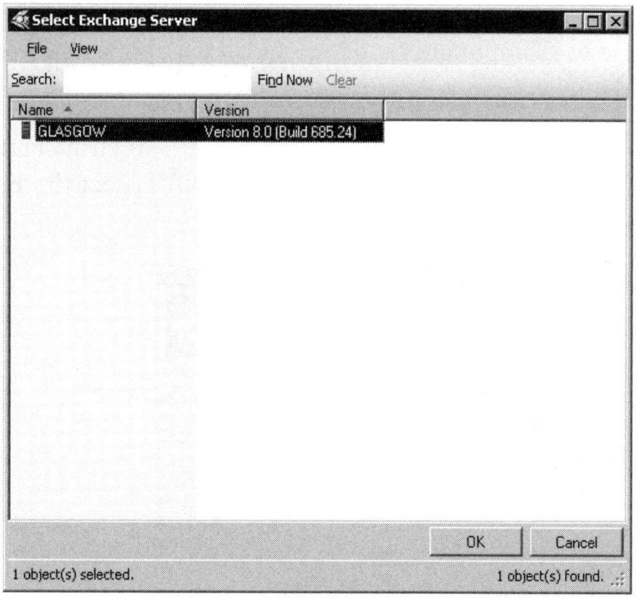

Figure 2-14   Configuring the Exchange Server Administrator role

---

Quick Check

1. What does the warning instruct you to do?

Quick Check Answer

1. The warning instructs you to add the Terry Adams user account to the Local Administrators group on the computer hosting Exchange Server 2007.

▶ **Practice 5: Installing an SSL Certificate on Exchange Server 2007**

In this practice, you will install an Enterprise Root Certificate Authority and configure it to generate SSL certificates. Although Exchange will automatically generate an SSL certificate and install it when you install the Client Access server role, clients attempting to access the server using SSL will not trust the issuing CA. By installing a CA and performing a request for an SSL certificate, this practice will simulate the steps you would take in requesting and installing an SSL certificate trusted by a third-party CA.

You will then install an SSL certificate on Exchange. To complete this practice, you will need access to the Windows Server 2003 installation media. Once you have verified that you have access to the installation media, perform the following steps:

1. Log on to the computer that hosts Exchange Server 2007 using the Kim_Akers account.

2. From Control Panel, open Add Or Remove Programs and then click Add/ Remove Windows Components.

3. Select Certificate Services. Click Yes to dismiss the warning that informs you that the computer name and domain membership cannot be changed. Click Next.

4. On the CA Type page of the Windows Components Wizard, select Enterprise Root CA, as shown in Figure 2-15, and then click Next.

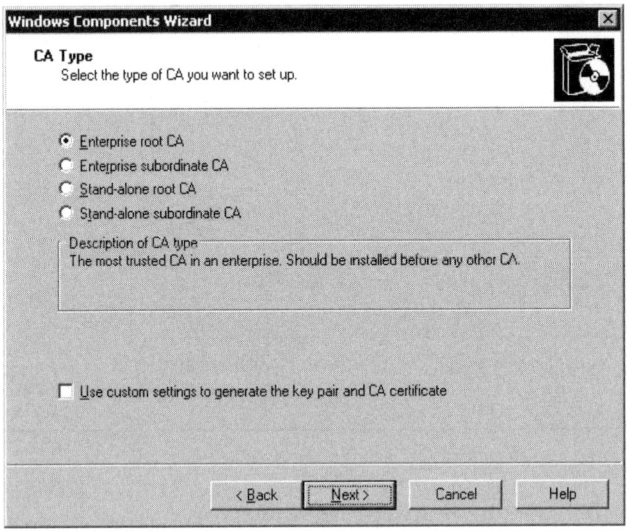

Figure 2-15   Installing an Enterprise Root CA

5. On the CA Identifying Information page, enter the common name for the CA as *Glasgow* and then click Next.

6. On the Certificate Database Settings page, review the default locations and then click Next.

7. In the warning dialog box that informs you that Internet Information Services needs to be temporarily stopped, click Yes. Certificate Services will now be installed. You will be prompted for the Windows Server 2003 installation media during the installation process.

8. You will be asked to enable Active Server Pages as a part of the Certificate Services installation process. Click Yes.

9. On the Completing The Windows Components Wizard page, click Finish.

10. Open Internet Information Services and expand the Server And Web Sites node.

11. Right-click Default Web Site and select Properties.

12. Click the Directory Security tab and then click the Server Certificate button. This will start the Web Server Certificate Wizard. Click Next.

13. On the Modify The Current Certificate Assignment page, select Remove The Current Certificate and then click Next twice. Click Finish.

14. Click the Server Certificate button again to restart the wizard and then click Next.

15. Select Create A New Certificate and click Next. Select Send The Request Immediately To An Online Certification Authority and then click Next.

16. Set the name for the certificate to OWA and then click Next.

17. Set the organization to Tailspin Toys and the organizational unit to Exchange and then click Next.

18. Leave the default common name and then click Next.

19. Set the state/province to Washington and the city/locality to Redmond and then click Next twice.

20. Leave the default SSL port and click Next.

21. Select GLASGOW.tailspintoys.internal\glasgow as the CA to process the request and click Next twice. Click Finish.

22. Click OK to close Default Website Properties.

23. In Internet Explorer, open the site *https://glasgow/certsrv*.

24. On the Security Warning About Trusted Sites List page, click Yes.

25. Click Download A CA Certificate, Certificate Chain, Or CRL.

26. Click Download CA Certificate and save it to the desktop.

27. Open the certificate and then install it using the Certificate Import Wizard.

▶ **Practice 6: Installing the Evaluation Version of Forefront**

WARNING   Optional practice

Warning: Installing Forefront Security for Exchange Server dramatically increases memory requirements. Do not perform this practice unless the computer you have installed Exchange Server 2007 on has more than 2 GB of memory.

An evaluation version of Forefront Security for Exchange Server is included with the Exchange Server 2007 installation media. Although you would normally perform message screening on an Edge Tansport server on a perimeter network, we will install this package on the computer assigned the Hub Transport server role.

NOTE Downloading Forefront Security for Exchange Server

Although included on the Exchange Server 2007 installation media, an evaluation version of Forefront Security for Exchange Server can be downloaded by accessing the following link: *http://www.microsoft.com/technet/prodtechnol/eval/fses/default.mspx.*

To complete this practice, perform the following steps:

1. Log on to the computer hosting Exchange Server 2007 using the Kim_Akers account.

2. Navigate to the Forefront directory on the Exchange Server 2007 installation media and double-click Setup.exe. This will start the Microsoft Forefront Security for Exchange Server Installation Wizard, as shown in Figure 2-16. Click Next to continue.

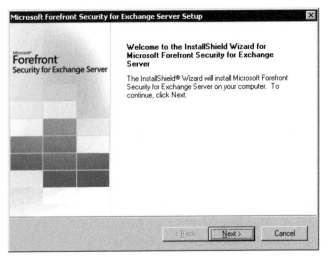

Figure 2-16 Starting installation of Forefront for Exchange Server

3. Review the license agreement and then click Yes.

4. On the Customer Information page, click Next.

5. On the Installation Location page, ensure that Local Installation is selected and then click Next.

6. On the Installation Type page, ensure that Full Installation is selected, as shown in Figure 2-17, and then click Next.

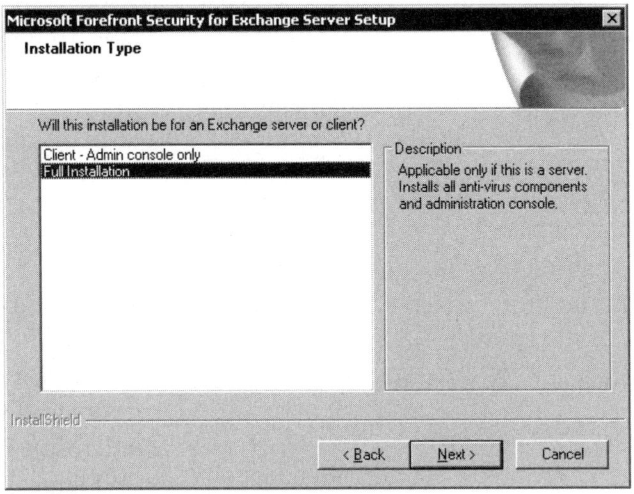

Figure 2-17   Forefront installation type

7. On the Quarantine Security Settings page, ensure that Secure Mode is selected and then click Next.

8. Review the five randomly selected antivirus scan engines and then click Next.

9. Review the information on the Engine Updates Required page and then click Next.

10. On the Choose Destination Location page, review the installation location and then click Next.

11. In the Select Program Folder, review the location the program icons will be installed to and then click Next.

12. On the Start Copying Files page, review the installation settings and then click Next. The installation process will now commence.

13. During the installation process, you will be asked if you would like setup to restart the Exchange Transport service. Click Next to have the service restarted.

BEST PRACTICES   Restarting Transport Service

In a production environment, you might choose to wait until an off-peak period to perform this operation. In general, you would add a component such as this during a period when having the server offline would cause minimal impact to your organization's operations.

---

14. After the service has been restarted, click Next and then click Finish. The readme file for Forefront Security for Exchange will open automatically. Review its contents and then close the file.

15. Restart the computer.

NOTE Restart optional

Restarting the computer is not strictly necessary but will refresh all services that Exchange Server 2007 relies on.

---

16. When the computer has restarted, log back on using the Kim_Akers user account. From the Programs menu, open Forefront Server Security Administrator. Click OK in the Connect To Server dialog box to open the local instance of this program. Click OK to dismiss the License Notice dialog box.

17. Click Scanner Updates under Settings.

18. Click Update Now in the right-hand-side pane of Forefront Server Security Administrator when Scanner Updates is selected, as shown in Figure 2-18.

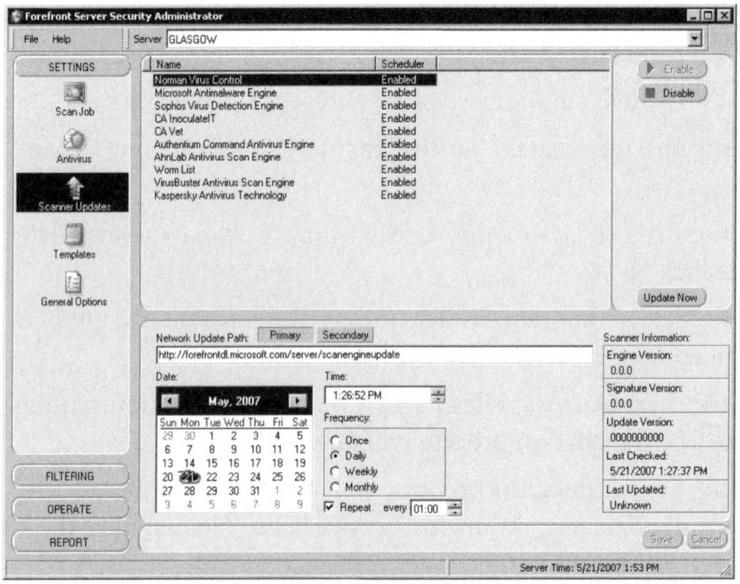

Figure 2-18 Updating virus definitions

Lesson Summary

- Mailbox servers host message data. Client Access servers allow access to Mailbox servers. Hub Transport servers route message data. Edge Transport servers route messages to and from the Internet, though this can also be done by Hub Transport servers. Unified Messaging servers store voice and fax data.

- The active Clustered Mailbox, passive Clustered Mailbox, and Edge Transport server roles cannot be installed with other roles.

- Computers assigned the Edge Transport server role are located on perimeter networks. They should not be members of an Active Directory environment.

- The standard way to set up Exchange Server 2007 is using a wizard that allows you to perform either a typical install, which installs the Client Access, Mailbox, and Hub Transport roles, or a custom install, where the combination of roles is selected by the administrator. The Unified Messaging, Edge Transport, and Clustered Mailbox roles can be installed graphically only by using a custom install.

- Command-line installation allows for a greater number of configuration options than the graphic installation. The majority of setup options must be passed directly from the command line. Answer files are used primarily to set up clusters.

- Communications with Client Access servers are encrypted using SSL. Installing the Client Access server role creates a default SSL certificate, though this will not be trusted by clients.

- Clustered roles require that the host server already be a node in a cluster. Clusters can be implemented on the enterprise editions of Windows Server 2003 and Windows Server 2008. You can implement active or passive mailbox clusters.

- Load balancing can be used to ensure that computers that host the Client Access, Hub Transport, and Edge Transport roles are not overwhelmed. This is done by adding servers hosting identical roles as nodes in an NLB cluster.

- An evaluation version of Forefront Security for Exchange Server is included with the Exchange Server 2007 installation media.

Lesson Review

You can use the following questions to test your knowledge of the information in Lesson 1, "Installing Exchange Server." The questions are also available on the companion CD if you prefer to review them in electronic form.

NOTE   Answers

Answers to these questions and explanations of why each answer choice is correct or incorrect are located in the "Answers" section at the end of the book.

---

1. You are preparing a new deployment of Exchange Server 2007 in a single-domain environment spread over five separate Active Directory sites. Users at all sites will need speedy access to mail. Branch office sites are connected by a virtual private network (VPN) tunnel to the head office site, where you have already deployed an Edge Transport server and a server with the Hub Transport, Client Access, and Mailbox server roles. A single computer running Exchange Server 2007 will be deployed at each site. Which of the following roles should be deployed on these computers? (Choose all that apply.)

    A. Edge Transport

    B. Hub Transport

    C. Client Access

    D. Mailbox server

    E. Unified Messaging server

2. In which of the following network locations should you deploy an Edge Transport server?

    A. Direct connection to the Internet

    B. Perimeter network

    C. Internal network

    D. Encrypted network

3. Which of the following digital certificate templates should you use when requesting and installing a digital certificate on a computer that will provide the OWA service to remote clients?

    A. Code signing

    B. SSL

    C. IPSec

    D. EFS

4. Your organization has a single computer with Exchange Server 2007 installed. This Exchange Server 2007 computer hosts the Hub Transport, Client Access, and Mailbox server roles. Users in your organization, who use primarily OWA, report slow connections to the server. You examine the performance of the server and find that although only 25 percent of the disk space on the server is consumed by mailbox databases, the processor usage statistics are consistently above 80 percent. To alleviate this problem, you will install a second computer running Exchange Server 2007. If you were to deploy only a single role on that computer, removing it from the existing server, which of the roles would you deploy to improve performance?

   A. Hub Transport

   B. Client Access

   C. Edge Transport

   D. Mailbox server

5. Which of the following Exchange Server 2007 setup commands will install the Client Access, Hub Transport, and Mailbox server roles on a computer in an existing Exchange 2007 organization?

   A. *setup /mode:install /roles:ClientAccess,Mailbox,EdgeTransport*

   B. *setup /mode:install /r:C,E,M,H*

   C. *setup /mode:upgrade /r:C,E,M,H*

   D. *setup /mode:install /r:C,M,H,U*

   E. *setup /mode:install /r::Mailbox,UnifiedMessaging,ClientAccess*

6. Each Exchange Server computer at your single site organization is assigned only one Exchange Server role. Your organization has five computers running Exchange Server 2007. You want to deal with messages containing spam or viruses before they reach user mailboxes. Which of the following computers running Exchange Server 2007 should you deploy Forefront Security for Exchange Server on? (Choose all that apply.)

   A. The computer assigned the Edge Transport server role

   B. The computer assigned the Hub Transport server role

   C. The computer assigned the Client Access server role

   D. The computer assigned the Mailbox server role

   E. The computer assigned the Unified Messaging server role

Lesson 2: Configuring Exchange Server Roles

Installing roles is not the end point of deploying Exchange 2007. Once roles are deployed, it is necessary to configure them. Configuring a role to best meet the needs of your organization is a critical part of the postinstallation process. Although when you install a role it is configured to suit the needs of most organizations, you will find that you can make a number of tweaks that best suit your organization. Although later chapters in this book look in more detail at specific configuration settings, this lesson provides an overview of the general postinstallation tasks an Exchange administrator would carry out on servers assigned these roles.

After this lesson, you will be able to:

■ Configure Exchange Server roles.

❑ Configure the Hub Transport server role.

❑ Configure the Edge Transport server role.

❑ Configure the Client Access server role.

- Configure Outlook Anywhere.

- Configure the server to enable client and mobile device connectivity.

- Configure OWA for changing passwords.

- Configure OWA for file sharing.

- Configure OWA for SharePoint.

❑ Configure the Mailbox server role.

- Create, modify, and delete databases and storage groups.

- Manage mailbox size limits.

❑ Add and remove roles.

❑ Remove the Exchange Server.

Estimated lesson time: 40 minutes

Configuring the Edge Transport Server Role

Once the Edge Transport server role is installed, you need to configure it to work with EdgeSync. EdgeSync links Active Directory with ADAM. Prior to establishing replication from Active Directory to ADAM, it is necessary to create an Edge subscription file. Each Edge Transport server requires a unique Edge subscription file. Three Edge Transport servers means three separate Edge subscription files.

To create an Edge subscription file, perform the following steps:

1. Verify that the Edge Transport server can resolve the FQDN of the Hub Transport server to an IP address using the nslookup command-line utility. Verify that the Hub Transport server can resolve the FQDN of the Edge Transport server to an IP address using the nslookup command-line utility.

2. Create the Edge subscription file on the Edge Transport server by issuing the following command from Exchange Management Shell: *New-EdgeSubscription –file "C:\EdgeSubExport.xml."*

NOTE **Loss of manual configuration settings**

When you configure an Edge Transport server to be managed by EdgeSync, you will lose configuration settings that may have already been made to the Edge Transport server manually, such as accepted domains, message classifications, remote domains, and send connectors. Once the subscription is configured, the Exchange Management Shell commands that allow you to make these configuration settings will be blocked on the Edge Transport server. All these settings will be configured through the organization-wide Hub Transport settings.

---

3. Copy the exported file to a Hub Transport server. This file needs to be imported within 1,440 minutes (24 hours) of creating the file; otherwise, you will need to re-create it.

4. On the Hub Transport server, open the Exchange Management Console and click on Hub Transport under Organization Configuration.

5. Click the Edge Subscriptions tab and then click New Edge Subscription in the Actions pane.

6. This will launch the New Edge Subscription Wizard, shown in Figure 2-19. Ensure that you have selected the site for which the Edge Transport server will become a member and then click Browse to locate the subscription file.

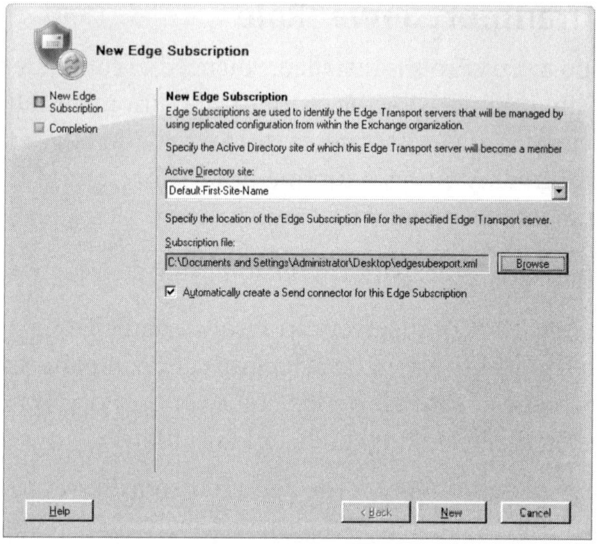

Figure 2-19 Enabling anti-spam updates

7. Click New to create the new subscription.

Once an Edge Transport server is subscribed, all Hub Transport servers located in the site to which the Edge Transport server is subscribed can contribute to the EdgeSync process. This does not apply to any new Hub Transport servers added to the site after the subscription has occurred. If you add more Hub Transport servers to the site, it will be necessary to remove and re-create the Edge subscription. In the event that the licensing status of the Edge Transport server changes, for example, if you created the subscription prior to activating the Edge Transport server, it will be necessary to perform the subscription process again.

MORE INFO **Subscribing the Edge Transport server**

For more information on subscribing the Edge Transport server to your Exchange organization, consult the following link: *http://technet.microsoft.com/en-us/library/bb125236.aspx*.

For successful synchronization between Active Directory and ADAM to occur, the firewall between the secure network and the perimeter network needs to have TCP/IP port 50636 open. Once the subscription has been set up, the Hub Transport server will periodically sync with the Edge Transport server, transmitting information about accepted domains, remote domains, and internal Simple Mail Transfer Protocol (SMTP) servers. To force synchronization, issue the *Start-EdgeSynchronization* command in the Exchange Management Shell.

Configuring the Hub Transport Server Role

Hub Transport servers are configured both at the server and at the organizational level. Server-level configuration includes external and internal DNS configuration, domain controller, and global catalog server configuration and message limit configurations. The domains for which your Exchange Server 2007 computers will accept e-mail are configured on an organizational level rather than a per server level. The New Accepted Domain Wizard allows you to configure Exchange Server 2007 to be authoritative for a domain. This configures your Exchange organization to accept e-mail sent to particular e-mail addresses, such as @tailspintoys.com or @wingtiptoys.com. If mail arrives at the server and is not addressed to a domain on the accepted domain list, it will bounce. The accepted domain list stops nefarious third parties from using your mail servers as relays to send spam and viruses.

You can configure an accepted domain through the wizard or from the Exchange Management Shell by issuing the command *new-AcceptedDomain –Name 'tailspintoys.com' –DomainType 'Authoritative,'* where you substitute tailspintoys.com for the domain name for which you wish your Exchange organization to accept mail.

You can also use the New Accepted Domain Wizard to configure an internal relay domain and an external relay domain. The internal relay domain option is used if you want e-mail relayed to another Active Directory forest within your organization. An external relay domain is used to relay traffic to an e-mail server outside the Exchange organization.

Any e-mail received by the Hub Transport server that is not addressed to an accepted domain will be dropped. As companies often change their names, it is important to ensure that messages addressed to previously registered domain names will still be received properly. For example, Tailspintoys.com was known several years ago as Wingtiptoys.com. Several customers might still send e-mail to wingtiptoys.com addresses. If Wingtiptoys.com is not on the list of accepted domains, this e-mail will be dropped by the server.

Configuring Remote Domains

Remote domains allow the configuration of formatting and messaging policies to specific remote domains. For example, if you know that a partner company requires specifically configured e-mail, you can set up a remote domain policy for all e-mail sent to that particular domain. Remote domain policies can be applied to a specific domain only or to all subdomains of that specific domain. Configuring mail for specific destinations is covered in more detail in Chapter 7, "Connectors and Connectivity."

Create a Postmaster Mailbox

The postmaster address is the address listed on nondelivery reports and other delivery status notifications. The postmaster at a particular mail domain is the person whom you contact if you want to follow up on an offensive or problematic e-mail. The standard postmaster alias allows anyone to send an e-mail for whatever reason to the person in charge of the e-mail servers at a particular organization.

Each Transport server will have a separate postmaster address. To view the currently assigned postmaster address, issue the following command in Exchange Management Shell:

```
Get-TransportServer | Format-List Name,ExternalPostMasterAddress
```

In the event that you want to redirect the postmaster address to another address, you can use the following Exchange Management Shell command:

```
Set-TransportServer -Identity 'ServerName' -ExternalPostMasterAddress
'newpostmaster@tailspintoys.com'
```

Alternatively, you could then assign the postmaster address as a secondary address on the user account that will be responsible for dealing with postmaster inquiries. In the event that person leaves your organization, you can move the postmaster address, as necessary. Ensuring that the postmaster address is watched is an important part of the responsibility of being a mail administrator. For example, if someone from within your organization has been sending spam, the postmaster e-mail address is the first place that some notification about it will exist. It is better to monitor this address than to find out that your mail domain has been placed on a blocking list because you were not aware that a rogue user was sending out unsolicited commercial e-mail.

Enabling Anti-spam Features on Transport Servers

Although Edge Transport servers have anti-spam features enabled by default, Hub Transport servers do not. To enable the Exchange Server 2007 anti-spam features on a computer with the Hub Transport server role installed, issue the following Exchange Management Shell command:

```
Set-TransportServer -Identity 'ServerName' -AntispamAgentsEnabled $true
```

You will then need to restart the Exchange Server Transport service and any open Exchange Management Consoles before the anti-spam features are enabled. You can verify that anti-spam features have been enabled, as the Enable Anti-Spam Updates item will now be available in the Actions pane when the Hub Transport server is selected under Server Configuration in the Exchange Management Console. The Anti-spam tab will also become available in the Actions pane when the Hub Transport option is selected under Organization Configuration in Exchange Management Console.

Clicking on Enable Anti-spam Updates in the Action pane allows you to configure how the anti-spam definitions and application will be updated, as shown in Figure 2-20. You can allow automatic updating of spam signatures as well as IP reputation updates. Configuring anti-spam settings is covered in more detail in Chapter 6.

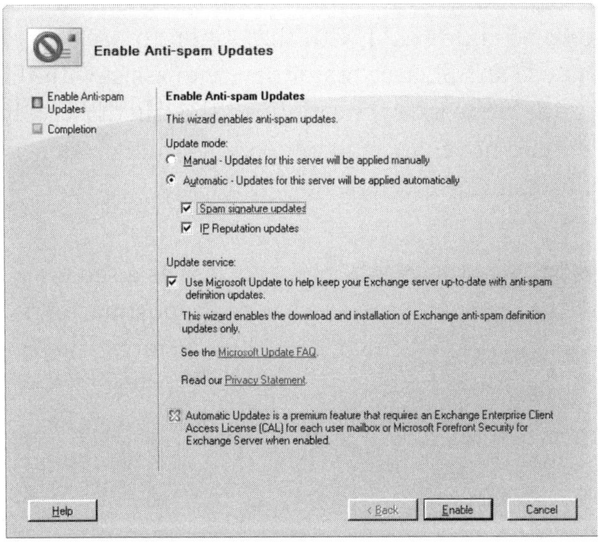

Figure 2-20   Enabling anti-spam updates

Configuring the Client Access Server Role

The Client Access role is the gateway between clients and their mailbox data. It is possible to use NLB to load balance the Client Access role in the event that client traffic is putting too much strain on resources. In most instances, you can install the client access server role, and your users will automatically be able to access e-mail. If you are using SSL, you should remember that clients will not trust the default SSL certificate generated during the installation of the Client Access server role. You have to either obtain an SSL certificate from a commercial and trusted source or find a way for your organization to manage and generate its own SSL certificate.

Configuring Outlook Anywhere

Outlook Anywhere allows clients using Microsoft Outlook 2007 and Outlook 2003 to access Exchange Server 2007 using the RPC over HTTP protocol. The primary benefit of using Outlook Anywhere is that it simplifies the configuration of remote access to Exchange. Access can be granted without having to use VPN connections, and rules allowing the quick setup of RPC over HTTP access to Exchange are built into Internet Security and Acceleration (ISA) Server, Microsoft's firewall and proxy product.

Outlook Anywhere can be enabled by clicking on Enable Outlook Anywhere on the Actions pane when the Client Access role is selected under the Server Configuration node. When configuring Outlook Anywhere, you need to specify the external host name, the authentication type, and whether you want to allow SSL offloading. The authentication options are Basic and NTLM with the option to use SSL offloading. SSL offloading allows you to use an SSL accelerator device to assist with the processing load involved in encrypting network connections to the Client Access server, as shown in Figure 2-21. You should not enable SSL offloading unless your server has an SSL accelerator device, as this can cause connection problems.

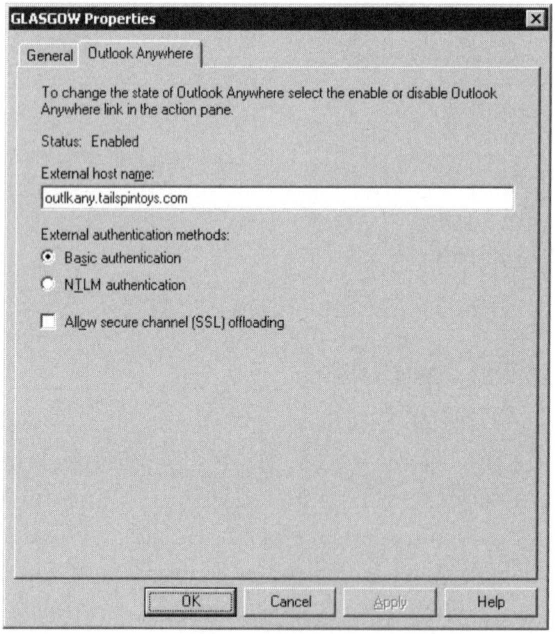

Figure 2-21   Outlook Anywhere properties

You can also enable Outlook Anywhere from the Exchange Management Shell by issuing the following command:

```
Enable-OutlookAnywhere -Server 'GLASGOW' -ExternalHostname 'externalhostname.
tailspintoys.com' -ExternalAuthenticationMethod 'Basic' -SSLOffloading $false
```

MORE INFO   **Enabling Outlook Anywhere**

To find out more about Outlook Anywhere, access the following link: *http://technet.microsoft.com/ en-us/library/bb123741.aspx.*

Configuring Client and Mobile Device Connectivity

Exchange ActiveSync is automatically enabled when the Client Access server role is installed on a computer running Exchange Server 2007. ActiveSync allows for the synchronization of data between mobile devices and Exchange Server 2007. Supported devices include Pocket PC 2002, Pocket PC 2003, and Windows Mobile 5.0. Windows Mobile 5.0 devices that have the Messaging Security and Feature Pack installed also support Direct Push, a technology that keeps a mobile device continuously synchronized with Exchange Server 2007.

The primary configuration that you have to make is on the clients themselves. Lesson 2 of Chapter 7 provides more information on configuring mobile device policies.

MORE INFO   **Managing ActiveSync**

For more information on managing ActiveSync, consult the following link: *http://tech- net.microsoft.com/en-us/library/bb124396.aspx.*

Configuring OWA

OWA can be used for more than just reading and responding to e-mail. Depending on how the Client Access role is configured, OWA clients can use their browser to access standard file shares or SharePoint sites. Access to Windows file shares and Windows SharePoint services can be enabled on the basis of whether a remote user is accessing OWA using a public or shared computer or is using a private computer. This way, you can disable access to Windows file shares or SharePoint when a user is connecting to OWA from an Internet café but allow access to Windows file shares and SharePoint when connecting to OWA from a company mobile computer using a café's WiFi connection. This demarcation relies on the user selecting the correct option when logging on to OWA, as shown in Figure 2-22.

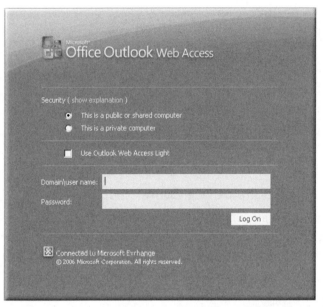

Figure 2-22   When logging on to OWA, the users specify whether they are using a public or a private computer

This access is granted by setting options within the OWA Web site's Properties dialog box. The Public Computer File Access tab allows you to configure the access granted to users accessing OWA from computers designated as public or shared. The Private Computer File Access tab allows you to configure the access granted to users accessing OWA from computers designated as private.

Once you have determined what type of access you want to grant users who are connecting remotely to OWA from public, shared, and private computers, you can configure the specific servers on your local network that they can access. You perform this task on the Remote File Servers tab of the OWA Web site properties, as shown in Figure 2-23.

The Remote File Servers tab has four items that can be configured:

- **Block list** A list of servers that OWA clients cannot access. Items on this list override items on the allow list.

- **Allow list** A list of servers that OWA clients can access.

- **Unknown servers** How servers not on either the block list or the allow list are to be treated. The default option is Block. This setting can also be configured to Allow.

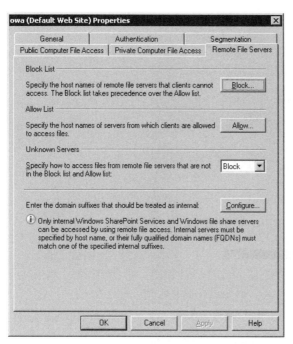

Figure 2-23   Remote File Servers tab

■ **Domain suffixes that should be treated as internal** OWA clients can access only servers that are recognized as internal. If a server that an OWA client attempts to access has a DNS suffix that is not on the list, it will be considered external and will not be accessible to the client.

By their nature, OWA clients are usually using computers that are not managed by your organization. You can not always be 100 percent certain that the person logging in using the publicly available computer in an airport in Volgograd, Russia, is actually your company's sales rep who is currently traveling in the area. It is not unheard of for nefarious third parties to place keylogging devices on public computers at airports or Internet cafés in an attempt to capture user names and passwords from the unwary. Although considering these threats might lead you to block off remote access to OWA entirely, some options that you can use to limit the damage are available. One configurable option allows you to block the ability to make password changes using OWA. In the event that a password is compromised, at least the person who has stolen the password will be unable to entirely hijack the compromised account by changing the password to something unknown to the user. To configure the option to block password changes for OWA users, edit the properties of the OWA Web site in Exchange

Management Console, click the Segmentation tab, and then disable the Change Password feature, as shown in Figure 2-24.

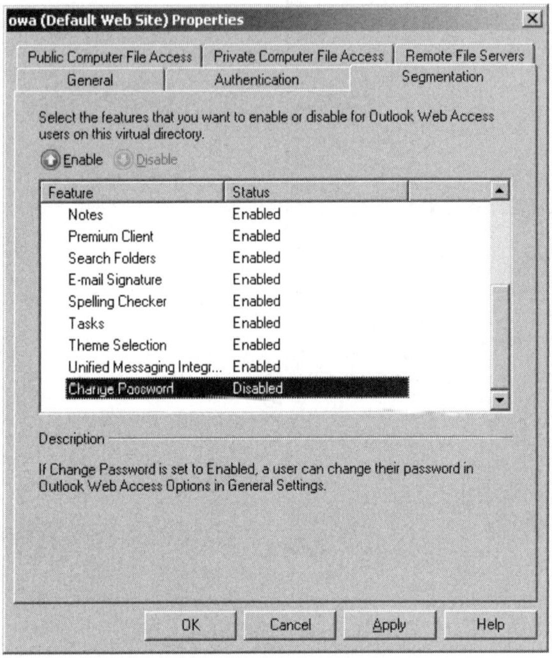

Figure 2-24   Blocking password change

MORE INFO   Managing OWA

For more information on managing OWA, navigate to the following link: *http://technet.microsoft.com/en-us/library/aa996373.aspx*.

POP3 and IMAP4

POP3 and IMAP4 are disabled by default on a computer configured with the Client Access role. As almost all e-mail clients use one of these protocols to retrieve e-mail, it is necessary to activate them prior to putting the Client Access role into a production environment. You can activate these services using two methods: using the Services console or using the NET START command from a command prompt. You should use the Services console, as this will also allow you to change the service startup type from manual to automatic. If you do not do this, you may reboot the server after applying updates and forget that neither the POP3 nor the IMAP4 service starts automatically. To enable each service, right-click on it within the Services console and select Properties. Change the start-up type to automatic and then click Start, as shown in Figure 2-25.

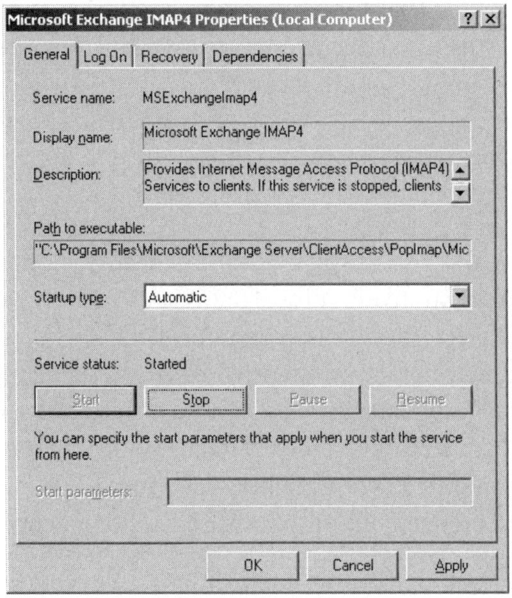

Figure 2-25   Setting the start-up type of the IMAP4 service

Quick Check

1. How does OWA determine whether a remote client is using a public or shared computer or a private computer?

2. Which SharePoint sites does a client connecting to OWA have access to by default?

Quick Check Answers

1. The remote client is queried when connected to OWA.

2. None. Sites must be added explicitly or by domain suffix.

Configuring the Mailbox Server Role

The immediate postinstallation tasks that you need to perform on a computer hosting the Mailbox server role are creating, modifying, and deleting databases and storage groups. Prior to performing those acts, you need to understand the differences between the two editions of Exchange Server 2007:

- The standard edition of Exchange Server 2007 supports five storage groups and five mailbox databases per server. The standard edition supports a maximum of five mailbox databases in a single storage group, one of which is reserved for recovery.

- The enterprise edition of Exchange Server 2007 supports up to 50 storage groups and a maximum of 50 databases per server, with a maximum of five mailbox databases per storage group.

Microsoft recommends that you allocate only one mailbox database per storage group, although it is possible to locate five mailbox databases in a single storage group. All databases within the same storage group share the same backup schedule. Having only a single database within a storage group provides greater flexibility in setting backup schedules on a per mailbox database basis. Storage groups are managed by separate server processes, and separating mailbox databases into their own separate storage group reduces transaction log complexity. Chapter 12, "Configuring Disaster Recovery," provides more information on backups and storage groups.

Storage groups can be created using the GUI by clicking New Storage Group in the Actions pane. You can also manage storage groups from Exchange Management Shell. The following Exchange Management Console command will create a storage group named Second Storage Group in the location C:\Program Files\Microsoft\Exchange Server\Mailbox\Second Storage Group:

```
new-StorageGroup –Server 'GLASGOW' –Name 'Second Storage Group' –LogFolderPath 'C:\Program
Files\Microsoft\Exchange Server\Mailbox\Second Storage Group' –SystemFolderPath 'C:\Program
Files\Microsoft\Exchange Server\Mailbox\Second Storage Group'
```

To create a new mailbox database, select the storage group that will host the database and then click New Mailbox Database. You can achieve the same thing using the Exchange Management Shell by issuing the following command:

```
new-mailboxdatabase -StorageGroup 'CN=Second Storage
Group,CN=InformationStore,CN=GLASGOW,CN=Servers,CN=Exchange Administrative Group
(FYDIBOHF23SPDLT),CN=Administrative Groups,CN=Tailspintoys,CN=Microsoft
Exchange,CN=Services,CN=Configuration,DC=tailspintoys,DC=internal' -Name 'Second Mailbox
Database' -EdbFilePath 'C:\Program Files\Microsoft\Exchange Server\Mailbox\Second Storage
Group\Second Mailbox Database.edb'
```

This command creates a mailbox database called Second Mailbox Database in the Second Storage Group of a server named *Glasgow*. You will create this database and storage group in the practices at the end of this lesson.

You can view the location mailbox database by viewing the Mailbox Database properties, as shown in Figure 2-26. From this dialog box, it is possible to view the last time the mailbox database was backed up and the location of the database mailbox copy if local continuous replication is enabled and to configure the mailbox maintenance schedule.

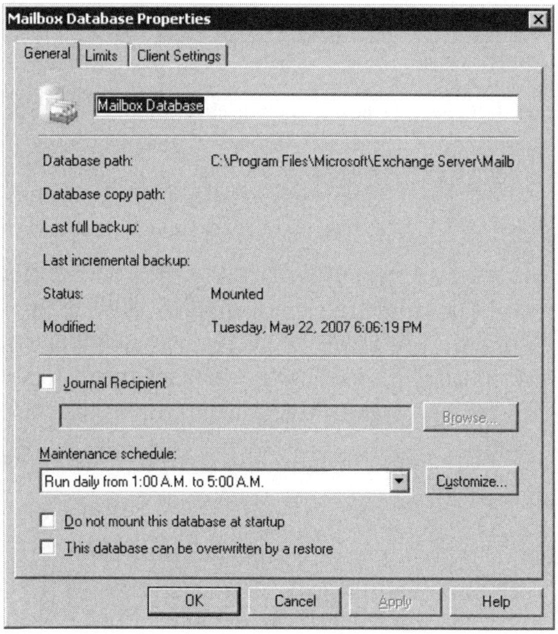

Figure 2-26 Mailbox database properties

During the period specified in the maintenance schedule, the following tasks are completed:

- Dumpster cleanup involves the removal of deleted messages that have passed the deleted item retention date.

- Public folder expiration involves messages posted to public folders expiring after a certain amount of time and being removed by the maintenance process.

- Deleted mailboxes are cleaned up.

- An online defragmentation of the mailbox is performed.

Managing Mailbox Size Limits

Although on a per gigabyte basis hard disk drive storage costs are always dropping, at some point you will most likely want to limit the amount of information that users can store in a mailbox. Although some users will be diligent about removing unnecessary material, the mailboxes of other users will continue to grow unless they reach some preconfigured limit. Some users never delete an attachment, even if it is completely outdated and has not been relevant for several years. If you do not impose mailbox limits, it is possible that a small number of mailboxes might account for the majority of the disk space on your mailbox servers.

BEST PRACTICES   The 80/20 rule

One common rule of thumb in many fields, including systems administration, is that 80 percent of resources will be consumed by 20 percent of the users. This applies to mailbox usage. You will find that without mailbox size limits, 20 percent (or less) of your users will end up taking 80 percent (or more) of the available disk space.

Besides the issue of a small number of users using a disproportionate amount of disk space, another practical reason for limiting the size of mailboxes involves backups. Data can be backed up and restored at only a finite rate. The larger the mailboxes, the longer the backup process is and the greater the amount of backup media that will be required. Larger mailboxes have a similar impact on restore operations. It takes longer to restore data from backups containing larger mailboxes than it does to restore data from backups containing smaller mailboxes.

You can manage mailbox size limits by editing the properties of the mailbox database and clicking the Limits tab. From this tab, it is possible to configure the following properties:

- **Issue Warning At (KB)** The threshold in kilobytes when a warning is automatically issued to the user about the amount of data stored in a mailbox.

- **Prohibit Send At (KB)** The threshold in kilobytes when the user is no longer able to send e-mail.

- **Prohibit Send And Receive At (KB)** The threshold in kilobytes when the user is no longer able to send and receive e-mail.

- **Warning Message Interval** The schedule by which warning messages will be sent to users who have mailboxes larger than the specified thresholds.

- **Keep Deleted Items For (Days)** How long deleted items are kept before being removed from the mailbox database.

- **Keep Deleted Mailboxes For (Days)** How long a deleted mailbox is kept in the database before being permanently deleted.

■ **Do Not Permanently Delete Items Until The Database Has Been Backed Up**
This option overrides the previous settings, keeping deleted items past their
expiration date until the database has been backed up.

Mailbox limits are configured in a practice at the end of this lesson.

Removing Exchange Server 2007

Three separate Exchange Server 2007 removal scenarios exist, each of which must be
treated differently. These include removing of one or more roles from an Exchange
Server while keeping the server operational, removing Exchange Server 2007 in its
entirety from a computer, and removing the Exchange Server 2007 organization from
an Active Directory forest. Also covered in this section are the steps that must be taken
to remove a final Exchange Server 2003 or Exchange 2000 from a mixed Exchange
environment.

Removing Roles

To remove roles that have been previously installed on a computer running Exchange
Server 2007, your user account must have been added to the Exchange organization
administrator role. To remove the roles, open Add Or Remove Programs, click
Microsoft Exchange Server 2007, and then click Change. This will bring up the
Exchange Server 2007 Setup Wizard in Exchange Maintenance Mode, as shown in
Figure 2-27. On the next page of the wizard, you select the roles that you wish to unin-
stall from the server. Readiness checks are performed, warning you of potential prob-
lems, and then the role removal is completed.

When removing the Mailbox server role, ensure that existing mailboxes have been
either moved, disabled, or deleted. You should also ensure that all public folders and
public folder replicas have been migrated to another Mailbox server. Similarly, if
removing a Client Access server, ensure that clients that are directly connecting to
OWA are redirected to an appropriate alternative.

Roles can be removed from an Exchange Server using setup from the command line.
The command *setup /mode:uninstall /roles:<roles to remove>* will remove the specified
roles from the computer running Exchange Server. If, in the future, you decide to reinstall the Mailbox server role on a computer that has had that role removed, it will be
necessary to manually remove the existing database and log files from the server.

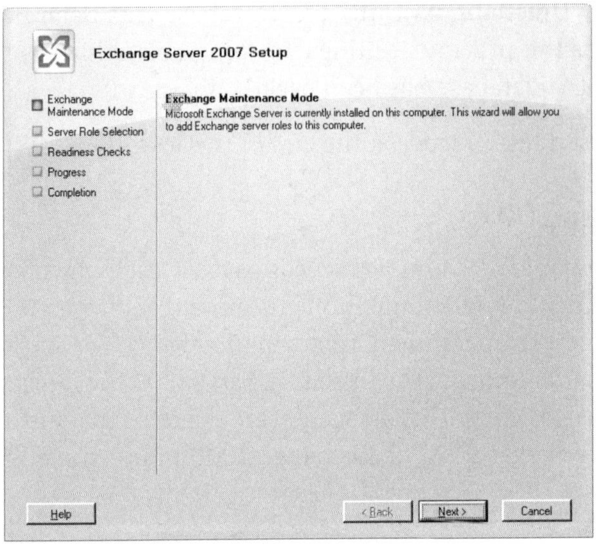

Figure 2-27   Removing roles using the GUI

Removing Exchange from a Server

In some cases you may want to remove not only an Exchange role but the entire program itself. It is important to perform a proper uninstall rather than just wiping the server and reinstalling the operating system, as a proper installation updates the rest of the Exchange organization about the status of the decommissioned server. Removing Exchange Server 2007 entirely includes removing all server roles, installation files, the Exchange Server object, and all the associated child objects from the Active Directory forest. For this reason, you can perform a complete removal of Exchange Server 2007 only by using an account that has been delegated the Exchange organization administrator role.

Prior to attempting to remove Exchange Server 2007 entirely, ensure that any mailboxes hosted on the computer have been deleted, disabled, or moved. Also verify that public folders and public folder replicas have been migrated to another server. Removal of Exchange Server 2007 is accomplished using the Add/Remove Programs item in Control Panel. It can also be achieved using the command *setup /mode:uninstall*. As with the removal and reinstallation of the Mailbox server role mentioned earlier, if you reinstall Exchange with the Mailbox server role on a computer that has hosted this role in the past, it is necessary to remove the existing database and log files from the server.

Removing an Exchange 2007 Organization

In the event that you want to completely remove an Exchange Server 2007 organization, you must first remove Exchange from all servers in the organization. Once Exchange is removed from all servers, the following data and settings will remain:

- Microsoft Exchange System Objects container in Active Directory
- Exchange Configuration container in Active Directory
- Active Directory schema modification
- User data, including database files, log files, public folder, and public folder replica data

Although it is relatively simple to remove the Active Directory containers and objects as well as the leftover user data, rolling back the schema modifications made by Active Directory setup is technically possible but very difficult to implement in a production environment. Unless you are well prepared, returning a large environment to the precise state it was in prior to the deployment of Exchange Server 2007 is next to impossible. This is another reason why you need to get deployment right from the start.

MORE INFO Schema rollback

To learn how Microsoft manages its Active Directory schema, including some techniques used for rolling back schema changes, consult the following link: *http://www.microsoft.com/technet/ itshowcase/content/adschemamgmt.mspx.*

Removing the Last Exchange 2000 or Exchange Server 2003 Server in a Coexistence Environment

Many organizations that implement Exchange Server 2007 are likely to have an existing Exchange Server infrastructure. As you roll out Exchange Server 2007 across your organization, you are likely to want to decommission the previous versions of Exchange. Before decommissioning legacy Exchange server computers, you need to ensure that people in your organization are not using services that only those editions of Exchange provide and that all relevant user data has been migrated to Exchange Server 2007.

Just as Exchange Server 2007 includes new features not available in previous editions, previous editions of Exchange Server have features that do not exist in Exchange Server 2007. If your organization still uses these services, you will need to migrate users to alternatives prior to removing the legacy Exchange servers that support them. The features that you have to be careful about are the following:

■ **Exchange Server 2003.** Novell GroupWise connector and NNTP Protocol

■ **Exchange 2000 Server.** Mobile Information Server, Instant Messaging Service, Exchange Chat Service, Exchange 2000 Conferencing Server, Key Management Service, cc: Mail connector, and MS Mail connector

You do not want to remove a prior version of Exchange server only to discover that it provides a critical service to some department in your organization of which you were unaware. Other steps that you need to take prior to decommissioning a legacy Exchange Server include the following:

■ Move all mailboxes to a computer running Exchange Server 2007.

■ Move all public folder replicas to a computer running Exchange Server 2007.

■ Move all offline address book generation processes to a computer running Exchange Server 2007.

■ Configure send connectors on a computer hosting the Exchange Server 2007 Hub or Edge Transport roles (depending on your Exchange architecture) to replace all existing outbound SMTP connectors.

■ Alter DNS MX records to ensure that they resolve to computers running Exchange Server 2007 with the Hub or Edge Transport roles installed. Ensure that no DNS MX records point to the computer hosting the legacy edition of Exchange.

■ Ensure that inbound protocol services, including ActiveSync, OWA, POP3, and IMAP4, point to a computer running Exchange 2007 with the Client Access role installed.

■ Remove routing group connectors connecting legacy Exchange routing groups to the Exchange 2007 routing group.

MORE INFO   **Removing and modifying Exchange Server 2007**

For more information on how to remove Microsoft Exchange Server 2007 server roles from a computer on which they are already installed, consult the following link: *http://technet.microsoft.com/en-us/library/aa998193.aspx*.

Exam Tip   When sitting the exam, take a moment to reread the question before you look at the answers. Many people taking multiple-choice exams glance at the answers before they have fully comprehended the question. When they reread the question, they have an incorrect answer in their mind, bending their interpretation of the question text. A helpful technique is to write the answer down on the scratch pad before glancing at the answers on the screen. That way, you will not be tempted to try to fit a wrong answer to the question setup.

Practice: Exchange Server Role Configuration

In these practices, you will perform several exercises that will familiarize you with the configuration of Exchange Server 2007 roles. Each of the practices in this section relates to the most common role configuration tasks that you will have to perform as an Exchange Server 2007 administrator. Before attempting these practices, ensure that you have performed all the practices in Lesson 1 of this chapter.

▶ **Practice 1: Configuring the Hub Transport Role**

In this practice, we will examine Hub Transport role configuration on both the server and the organizational level. We will be examining organizational policies in more detail in later chapters, and the coverage of organizational configuration is intended only to familiarize you with the configuration options that are available at both the server and the organizational level. To complete this practice, perform the following steps:

1. Log on to the Exchange Server 2007 computer using the Kim_Akers user account.

2. Open Exchange Management Console. Dismiss the unlicensed server warning and expand the Server Configuration node.

3. Click Hub Transport, then right-click the GLASGOW entry and select Properties. This will bring up the GLASGOW Properties dialog box, as shown in Figure 2-28.

4. Verify that the domain controller and global catalog servers being used by Exchange are set to GLASGOW.tailspintoys.internal. Click the External DNS Lookups tab.

5. On the External DNS Lookups tab, select the Use These DNS Servers option. In the field, enter the IP address 207.68.160.190 and then click Add.

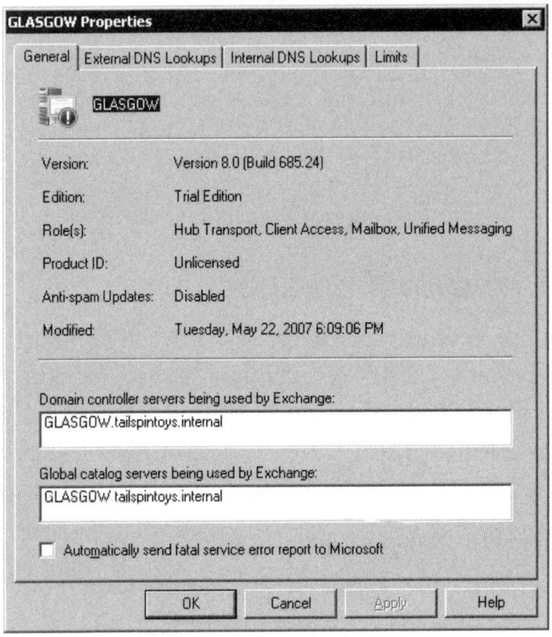

Figure 2-28   Hub Transport server general properties

6. Click the Limits tab. Change the settings so that the value for transient failure retry attempts is set to 10, that the maximum time since submission for message expiration is three days, and that senders will be notified if their message is delayed more than one hour, as shown in Figure 2-29. Click OK to close the Glasgow Properties dialog box.

7. Under Microsoft Exchange, expand the Organization Configuration node and then click the Hub Transport node.

8. Click the Accepted Domains tab and then click New Accepted Domains under Actions. This will start the New Accepted Domain Wizard.

9. On the New Accepted Domain page, enter **Tailspintoys.com** in the Name box and **tailspintoys.com** in Accepted Domain. Verify that the Authoritative Domain option is selected, as shown in Figure 2-30. Click New.

10. Flick Finish to close the wizard. The Exchange Server 2007 organization that you deployed in the first lesson of this chapter is now authoritative for both the tailspintoys.com and the tailspintoys.internal domain.

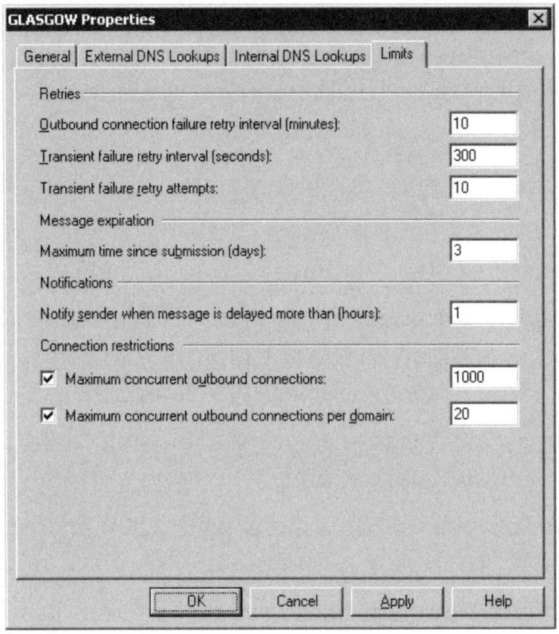

Figure 2-29   Hub Transport server limits

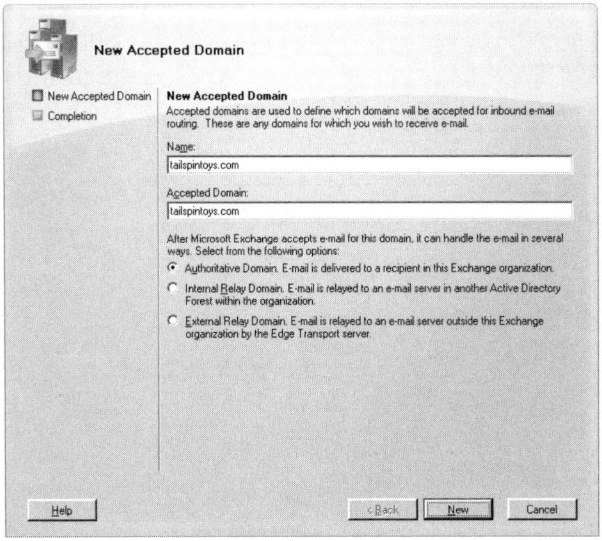

Figure 2-30   New accepted domain

► **Practice 2: Configuring Client Access Server Role**

In this practice, you will configure OWA so that remote users can change their password. You will also configure OWA so that remote users can access File Shares and SharePoint sites. To complete this practice, perform the following steps:

1. Log on to the Exchange Server 2007 computer using the Kim_Akers user account.

2. Open the DNS console from the Administrative Tools menu.

3. Create a new primary forward lookup zone called Tailspintoys.com. Create a new host record called outlkany in the tailspintoys.com zone. Assign the new host the IP address of the Exchange Server 2007 computer.

4. Open Exchange Management Console. Dismiss the unlicensed server warning and expand the Server Configuration node.

5. Click the Client Access node. In the Actions pane, click Enable Outlook Anywhere.

6. On the Enable Outlook Anywhere page, set the external host name to outlkany.tailspintoys.com and verify that basic authentication is set, as shown in Figure 2-31, and then click Enable.

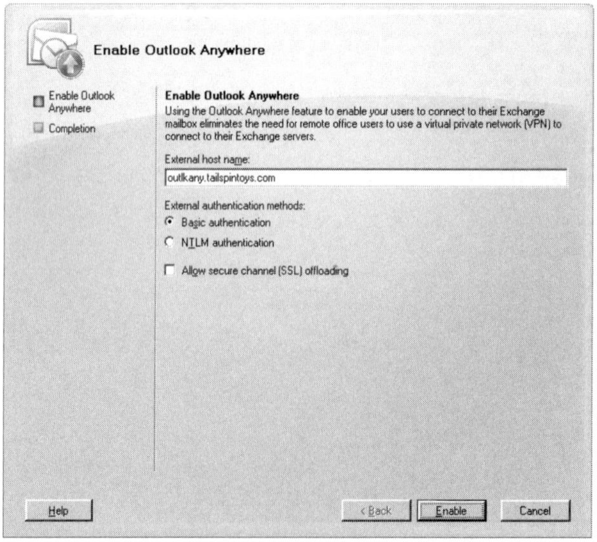

Figure 2-31   Enable Outlook Anywhere

7. When the Completion page is shown, click Finish.

8. Under the Outlook Web Access tab, right-click owa (Default Web Site) and then click Properties.

9. Click the Segmentation tab, as shown in Figure 2-32. Verify that the Change Password item is set to be enabled.

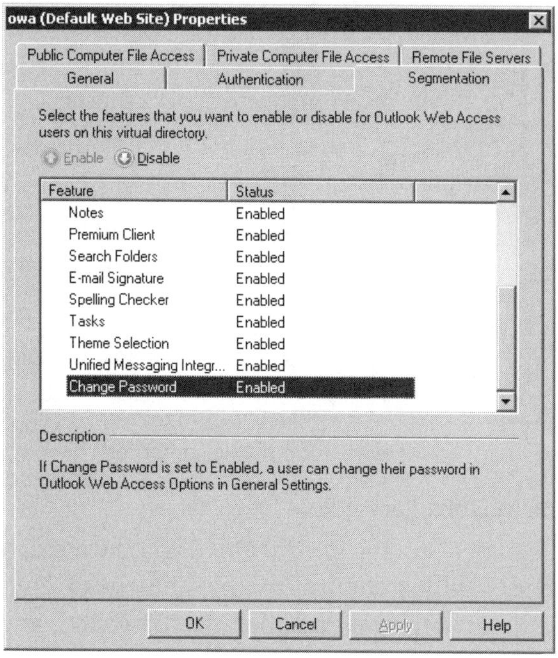

Figure 2-32   Allowing OWA users to change passwords

10. Click the Public Computer File Access tab and remove the checks next to the Windows File Shares and Windows SharePoint Services items, as shown in Figure 2-33. Click Apply.

11. Click the Remote File Servers tab and then click Allow.

12. In the Allow list, enter the hosts **sharepoint.tailspintoys.internal** and **fileserver. tailspintoys.internal** and click OK twice to close the dialog box.

13. From the Administrative Tools Program menu, open the Services console.

14. Right-click the Microsoft Exchange IMAP4 service and then click Properties.

15. On the General tab, change Startup Type to Automatic and then click Start. Click OK to close the Properties dialog box.

16. Repeat this process for the Microsoft Exchange POP3 service.

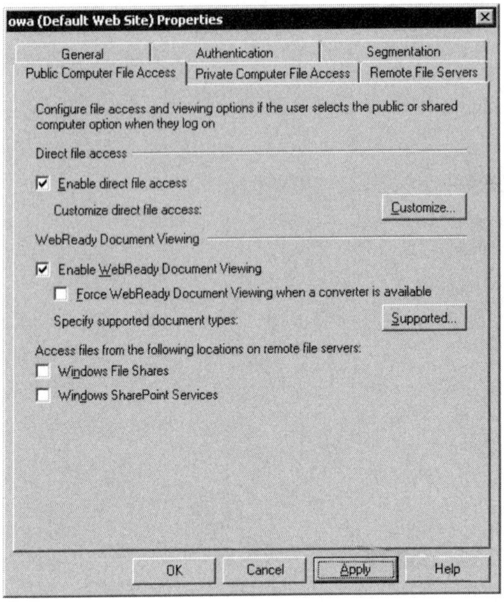

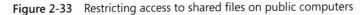

Figure 2-33   Restricting access to shared files on public computers

▶ **Practice 3: Configuring the Mailbox Server Role**

In this practice, you will create a storage group. Once you have created the storage group, you will create a new mailbox database within the group. You will then also configure the retention settings of the new mailbox database. To complete this practice, perform the following steps:

1. Log on to the Exchange Server 2007 computer using the Kim_Akers user account.

2. Open the Exchange Management Console. Dismiss the unlicensed server warning and expand the Server Configuration node.

3. Click the Mailbox item.

4. In the Actions pane, click New Storage Group. This will bring up the New Storage Group dialog box.

5. Enter the name **Second Storage Group** in the Storage group name text box and accept the default values for the Log Files And System Files path, as shown in Figure 2-34. Click New.

6. Click Finish to close the New Storage Group Wizard.

7. Verify the creation of the new storage group by examining the Database Management pane when the Mailbox node is selected under Server Configuration. Click Second Storage Group.

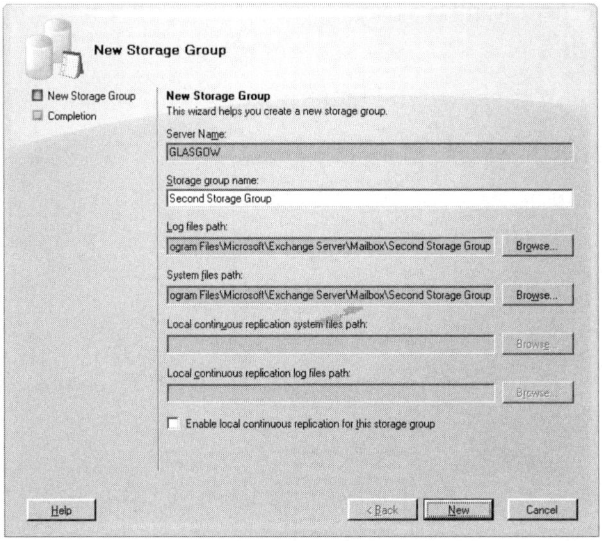

Figure 2-34   New Storage Group dialog box

8. With the Second Storage Group highlighted, in the Actions pane, click New Mailbox Database. This will bring up the New Mailbox Database page.

9. Enter **Second Mailbox Database** in the Mailbox database name text box, as shown in Figure 2-35, and then click New.

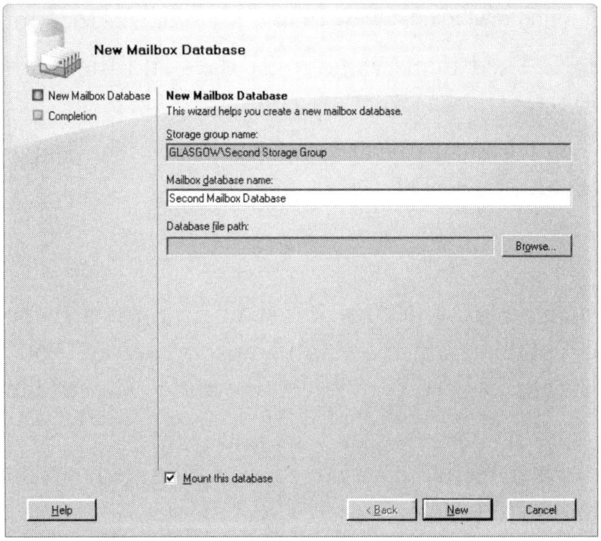

Figure 2-35   New Mailbox Database dialog box

10. The exchange mailbox will be created and then mounted, click Finish.

11. Right-click on Second Mailbox Database under the Second Storage group and then click Properties.

12. Click the Limits tab, as shown in Figure 2-36.

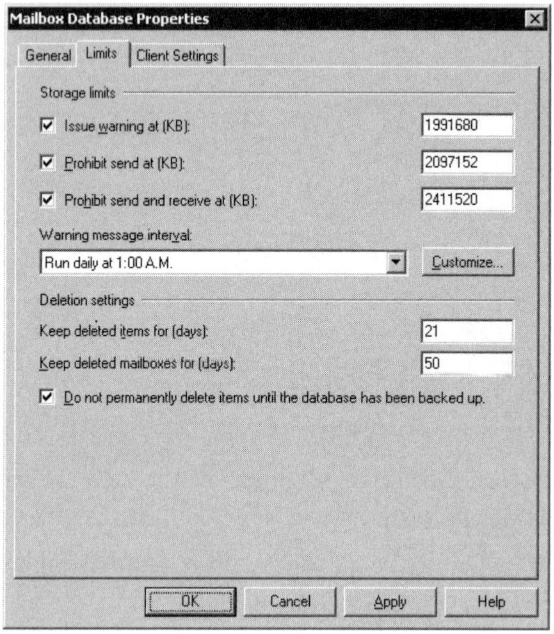

Figure 2-36   Configuring mailbox database limits

13. Change the Keep Deleted Items value to 21 days and the Keep Deleted Mailboxes value to 50 days.

14. Check the Do Not Permanently Delete Items Until The Database Has Been Backed Up option and then click OK.

Lesson Summary

- By default, Exchange Server 2007's anti-spam features are enabled on Edge Transport servers but not enabled on Hub Transport servers. You can enable this feature on Hub Transport servers by executing an Exchange Management Shell command.

- Edge Transport servers need to have EdgeSync configured to replicate data from Active Directory to ADAM.

- Outlook Anywhere replaces RPC over HTTP, allowing remote clients to access Exchange Server 2007 without connecting through a VPN.

- By default, mobile devices can access servers configured with the Client Access server role.

- OWA can be configured to differentiate access to File Shares and SharePoint servers based on whether a client is connecting using a public or shared computer or a private computer. You can allow or block password changes by accessing SharePoint properties.

- The standard edition of Exchange Server 2007 can host five mailbox databases and five storage groups. The enterprise edition of Exchange Server 2007 can host up to 50 mailbox databases and 50 storage groups.

Lesson Review

You can use the following questions to test your knowledge of the information in Lesson 2. The questions are also available on the companion CD if you prefer to review them in electronic form.

NOTE Answers

Answers to these questions and explanations of why each answer choice is correct or incorrect are located in the "Answers" section at the end of the book.

---

1. You have recently deployed Exchange Server 2007 for Coho Vineyard, a large local wine manufacturer. The deployment involves a single computer running Exchange Server 2007 with the Hub Transport, Mailbox, and Client Access roles deployed. You receive a complaint from the manager of the winery that several long-term clients have called to complain that their e-mails have bounced back. One clue to the problem is that the messages were sent to addresses using the cohowinery.com domain, an address used by the winery for many years. Messages addressed to people in the cohovineyard.com domain always arrive successfully at their destination. Which of the following configuration changes could you make to Exchange Server 2007 to ensure that e-mails from these long-term clients do not bounce?

   A. Configure cohowinery.com as an authoritative domain in accepted domains

   B. Configure cohovineyard.com as an authoritative domain in accepted domains

   C. Configure cohowinery.com as an internal relay domain in accepted domains

    D. Configure cohowinery.com as a remote domain

    E. Configure cohovineyard.com as a remote domain

2. Which of the following Exchange Server 2007 roles would you configure to ensure that users received a warning when their mailbox was becoming too large?

    A. Client Access

    B. Mailbox

    C. Hub Transport

    D. Edge Transport

3. You want to allow OWA clients in your organization the ability to access the SharePoint site hosted on server sharepoint.tailspintoys.internal. You do not want them to access the SharePoint site hosted on server secureshare.tailspin-toys.internal. Which of the following steps do you need to take to allow this to occur?

    A. Add the site sharepoint.tailspintoys.internal to the block list on the Remote File Servers tab of the OWA Web site properties

    B. Add the site sharepoint.tailspintoys.internal to the allow list on the Remote File Servers tab of the OWA Web site properties

    C. Add the site secureshare.tailspintoys.internal to the block list on the Remote File Servers tab of the OWA Web site properties

    D. Add the domain suffix tailspintoys.internal to the list of domain suffixes that should be treated as internal

    E. Add the site secure.tailspintoys.internal to the allow list on the Remote File Servers tab of the OWA Web site properties

4. You are planning the deployment of Exchange Server 2007 enterprise edition. This server will host the Mailbox server role. The server will host 16 mailbox databases. What is the minimum number of storage groups that will be necessary to host these mailbox databases?

    A. One

    B. Two

    C. Three

    D. Four

    E. Five

5. Your Exchange Server 2007 organization has a single site and a single server. The server's name is Canberra. This server hosts the Hub Transport, Mailbox, and Client Access server roles. You want to enable Exchange's anti-spam features on this server but cannot locate the Enable Anti-spam item in the Actions pane when the Hub Transport server is selected. Which of the following must you do prior to enabling the anti-spam features of Exchange Server 2007?

   A. Install the Edge Transport role

   B. Run the command *Set-TransportServer –Identity 'Canberra' –AntispamAgents Enabled $true* from the Exchange Management Shell

   C. Install Forefront Security for Exchange Server

   D. Reinstall the Hub Transport role

6. Several months ago, you removed the Mailbox server role from a computer running Exchange Server 2007. The computer retained the Client Access server role. Conditions at the location where the server is deployed have changed, and you need to reinstall the Mailbox server role. Which of the following steps must you take before reinstalling this role?

   A. Remove the Client Access server role

   B. Remove the Mailbox server role

   C. Remove the computer hosting Exchange from the domain and then rejoin the computer to the domain

   D. Manually remove the existing Mailbox database files and log files

   E. Reinstall the Client Access server role

Chapter Review

To further practice and reinforce the skills you learned in this chapter, you can perform the following tasks:

- Review the chapter summary.
- Review the list of key terms introduced in this chapter.
- Complete the case scenarios. These scenarios set up real-word situations involving the topics of this chapter and ask you to create a solution.
- Complete the suggested practices.
- Take a practice test.

Chapter Summary

- The roles that can be installed on an Exchange Server 2007 computer are the Edge Transport, Hub Transport, Mailbox, active Clustered Mailbox, passive Clustered Mailbox, and Client Access. You can install Exchange using a wizard or from the command line. The wizard provides more helpful hints if a prerequisite is missing.
- You can install the active Clustered Mailbox and passive Clustered Mailbox roles only on a server that is already part of a cluster. NLB is best suited for the Hub Transport, Edge Transport, and Client Access roles.
- Installation of the Client Access role generates a self-signed SSL certificate. As clients require special configuration to trust this certificate, installing an SSL certificate from a trusted CA is often more convenient.
- OWA can be configured to allow access to internal SharePoint servers and file shares. You can configure the security options to deny OWA users the ability to change their passwords.
- If Exchange Server 2007 is removed entirely from your organization, you have to manually remove the objects that it has created in Active Directory. Rolling back the schema to the condition it was in prior to the deployment of Exchange is possible, though it is a complex operation.

Key Terms

Do you know what these key terms mean? You can check your answers by looking up the terms in the glossary at the end of the book.

- Perimeter network
- Spam
- SSL (Secure Sockets Layer)
- Virus

Case Scenarios

In the following case scenarios, you will apply what you've learned about installing Exchange Server and configuring server roles. You can find answers to these questions in the "Answers" section at the end of this book.

Case Scenario 1: Wingtip Toys Exchange Server 2007 Deployment

Wingtip Toys, formerly known as Tailspin Toys, is considering a new Exchange Server 2007 deployment. Wingtip Toys has three separate sites. Two sites are connected to the third site by a dedicated Integrated Services Digital Network (ISDN) line. Incoming and outgoing traffic to the Internet pass through a Windows Server 2003 computer with ISA Server 2006 installed:

1. What is the minimum number of Edge Transport servers you need to deploy at Wingtip Toys?

2. How many Hub Transport servers should you deploy at Wingtip Toys?

3. How can you ensure that mail sent to tailspintoys.com addresses will not be rejected by Exchange Server?

Case Scenario 2: Contoso Postdeployment Role Configuration

Exchange Server 2007 was deployed several months ago at Contoso. Since then, there have been some teething problems that they have asked you to come in to resolve. The problems are as follows:

1. A member of the sales team was recently traveling through the South Pacific, accessing e-mail through OWA in Internet cafés. One of the computers was infected with a Trojan that logged keyboard data and forwarded it to hackers. The account password was changed, and the member of the sales team was locked out. How can you ensure that a user whose account is compromised can not be locked out from that account by a changed password?

2. Currently, OWA users are able to access the three SharePoint sites that are located on the Contoso internal network. You need to limit this to a single Share-Point site. How could you achieve this?

Suggested Practices

To help you successfully master the exam objectives presented in this chapter, complete the following tasks.

Install Exchange

Do all the practices in this section.

- **Practice 1: Edge Transport Server**   Install the Edge Transport server role on a stand-alone computer that is not a member of your domain, running Windows Server 2003.

- Correctly configure a subscription relationship with a Hub Transport server.

- Install the Forefront Security for Exchange Server 2007 evaluation on the Edge Transport server role.

- **Practice 2: Enable Anti-spam**   Enable the anti-spam features of Exchange using Exchange Management Shell.

- Enable automatic updating of Exchange's anti-spam features.

Configure Exchange Server Roles

Do all the practices in this section.

- **Practice 1: OWA Configuration**   Configure the Client Access server role so that OWA clients are able to use notes and e-mail signatures and to select OWA themes.

- Configure the Client Access server role so that OWA clients are able to access Windows SharePoint Services but not Windows file shares.

- **Practice 2: Mailbox Server Role Configuration**   Create an additional storage group and add a mailbox database.

- Change the settings on the new mailbox database so that deleted mailboxes are kept for 90 days.

- **Practice 3: Hub Transport Role Configuration**   Configure the computer to accept mail for the Contoso.com domain.

- Configure Fabrikam.com as an internal relay domain.

- Configure an Edge subscription for an Edge Transport server if there is one in your test environment.

Take a Practice Test

The practice tests on this book's companion CD offer many options. For example, you can test yourself on just one exam objective, or you can test yourself on all the 70-236 certification exam content. You can set up the test so that it closely simulates the experience of taking a certification exam, or you can set it up in study mode so that you can look at the correct answers and explanations after you answer each question.

MORE INFO   Practice tests

For details about all the practice test options available, see the "How to Use the Practice Tests" section in this book's Introduction.

Chapter 3

Configuring Recipients, Groups, and Mailboxes

As an Exchange organization administrator or Exchange recipient administrator, one of your many tasks will be to create recipients. This chapter looks at mailbox-enabled users, mail-enabled users, and contacts. It discusses the function of each recipient type and when you would use them. You will learn how to create each type, how to mailbox-enable or mail-enable a user account, how to configure recipient properties, and how to remove or disable a recipient.

Mail-enabled groups allow users to send a single e-mail message to the group. The message then goes to every group member. The chapter discusses universal distribution groups, dynamic distribution groups, and mail-enabled universal security groups and the functions of each. You will learn how to create, mail-enable, configure, disable, and remove each type of group.

You can create resource mailboxes for rooms and equipment. These enable users to book a resource by including its resource mailbox in a meeting request, to discover what resources are available, and to inspect resource usage schedules. You will learn how to create resource mailboxes and use custom resources to indicate the properties of a resource, for example, which rooms contain data projectors.

Exam objectives in this chapter:
- Configure recipients.
- Configure mail-enabled groups.
- Configure resource mailboxes.

Lessons in this chapter:

Before You Begin

To complete the lessons in this chapter, you must have done the following:

■ Installed Windows Exchange Server 2007 with the Mailbox, Client Access, Hub Transport, and Unified Messaging roles on a Windows domain controller in the Tailspintoys.internal domain as described in Chapter 2, "Installing Exchange Server and Configuring Roles."

Real World

Ian McLean

Sometimes (not very often) I manage to impress people who don't know me very well. I like to think this is because of long experience, although low cunning is probably a better description.

One of my party tricks (I go to very boring parties) is to carry out Exchange tasks very quickly and with minimum effort. I do this by using a command-line tool called Exchange Management Shell. Admittedly, I've been around computers for a very long time and have a lot of experience with command-line interfaces (CLIs), but, on the other hand, I am one of the world's slowest and least accurate typists and certainly would not call myself a command-line wizard.

Exchange Management Shell might look a bit complex at first sight, but it is actually quite easy to use. I make it even easier for myself by never typing the same thing twice. If I'm keying in an Exchange Management Shell command, I do so in a text editor and add the command to a text file. I then copy it from my text editor and paste it into the Exchange Management Shell console. Before saving the text file, I add a few comments and type in a few key words to help me find the command again. If I need to repeat the same task, I find the command, paste it into Exchange Management Shell, and change a few parameter values if required.

Using a CLI is usually much faster than working through the pages of a graphical user interface (GUI) such as Exchange Management Console, and some tasks, such as creating public folders, simply cannot be done with the GUI. In addition, you can put CLI commands into script files so that you can do the same task many times. If you wanted to create 100 mailbox-enabled users, for example, it would be very tedious to do this through the GUI. Chapter 4, "Configuring Public Folders" and Chapter 5, "Moving Mailboxes, and Implementing Bulk Management," discuss public folders and script files.

So my advice is to learn to use and love Exchange Management Shell. However, I do appreciate that CLIs can look scary if you're not used to them. Fortunately, Exchange Server 2007 provides a very neat way of introducing CLI commands to GUI users. If you use the Exchange Management Console GUI to carry out a task, the GUI's Completion page lists the Exchange Management Shell command that performs the same function. You can copy these commands and paste them into a text file and then experiment with changing parameter values and pasting the commands into the CLI. I think you will be surprised how easy this is compared to wading through GUI wizard pages filling in dialog boxes.

By the way, I'm not suggesting pasting commands generated by the GUI straight into the CLI. Some parameters, such as Password, will need a bit of work first. In addition, automatically generated commands are never as short or efficient as commands that you code and enter manually. I am instead recommending that you compare the examples given in this chapter with the commands automatically generated in the GUI and then edit and test the GUI-generated commands. In my experience, this is a good and very fast way of learning how to use a CLI.

In this chapter, I take a gentle approach, using the GUI in the practice sessions but encouraging you to paste the CLI commands into a text file and experiment with them. In the third lesson of this chapter, you get to use CLI commands in a practice for real. Chapter 4 is full of them. Happy coding!

Lesson 1: Configuring Recipients

> **After this lesson, you will be able to:**
> - Create and configure mailbox-enabled and mail-enabled user accounts.
> - Mailbox-enable and mail-enable existing user accounts.
> - Modify, disable, and remove mailbox-enabled and mail-enabled user accounts.
> - Create, modify, disable, and remove mail-enabled contacts.
>
> **Estimated lesson time: 50 minutes**

Creating and Configuring Mailbox-Enabled User Accounts

A mailbox-enabled user has an e-mail address and an Exchange mailbox in an organization. Most employees in an organization will be mailbox-enabled. The exceptions are likely to be external consultants or other staff who are working in your organization's premises on a temporary basis and are permanently based elsewhere.

> ### A Mailbox Contains More Than E-Mail
>
> An Exchange mailbox contains an Inbox to hold the e-mail that is sent to you and a sent items folder that holds the e-mail messages you have sent. The Outbox holds messages you are currently sending. You also have a deleted items folder to hold items you deleted from the Inbox or sent items folder. A drafts folder stores any messages that you were in the process of completing but have not yet sent. A mailbox holds e-mails and e-mail attachments.
>
> Mailboxes also hold calendar information. You can check your own calendar and add or remove appointments and check your colleagues' calendars (provided these have been made public) and find out their availability before you schedule an appointment. If scheduling has been enabled in resource mailboxes that represent bookable rooms or equipment, you can look at the calendars for such mailboxes and determine when resources are available. You can book resources by including resource mailboxes as required or optional attendees in a meeting request.
>
> A mailbox can also include a folder that stores suspected spam messages that have not been blocked by a spam filter. You have a folder in which you can store notes and a folder that contains files that will be deleted at the next scheduled system cleanup. Your mailbox contains your personal list of contacts and a list of tasks. It also contains any out-of-office messages you have composed. If journaling is enabled, your mailbox and other mailboxes in your organization will contain information that allows implementation of this feature.

Because of all the items that can be stored in a mailbox, the temptation for you and users you support is to use a personal mailbox as a convenient container to store personal files rather than backing them up or copying them to removable media. I confess to having e-mailed work in progress to myself so that I can continue to work on it at home, especially when I did not have a USB pen drive handy. However, excessive use of this facility clogs up mailbox stores. As an administrator, you need to enforce strict mailbox limits and retention policies—and be prepared to explain to a senior manager why a message and attachment she sent to a colleague three years ago is no longer in her sent items folder.

MORE INFO Journaling

For more information about journaling, access *http://technet.microsoft.com/en-us/library/aa998649.aspx*.

If an existing user in Active Directory does not have a mailbox, you can create one by using either the Exchange Management Console GUI or Exchange Management Shell CLI. These tools also enable you to create a mailbox-enabled user if no user account currently exists and to reconfigure an existing mailbox-enabled user's properties.

Using Exchange Management Console to Create a Mailbox-Enabled User

To create a mailbox-enabled user by using the Exchange Management Console GUI, you start Exchange Management Console from the Microsoft Exchange Server 2007 menu, accessed from All Programs in the Start menu; expand the Recipient Configuration node in the console tree; and click Mailbox. You then click New Mailbox in the Actions pane to start the New Mailbox Wizard, as shown in Figure 3-1.

You specify that you want to create a user mailbox for a new user and then fill in information about the user and the mailbox. Practice 1 of this lesson goes through these steps in detail. To provide information about the user, you complete the following boxes on the User Information page:

- **Organizational Unit** By default, the New Mailbox Wizard displays the Users container in Active Directory. You can change this setting by clicking Browse and then selecting the appropriate organizational unit (OU).
- **First Name** The first name of the user (optional).

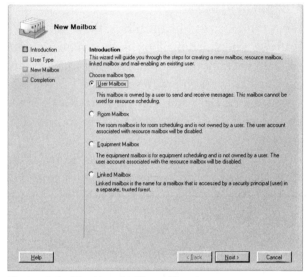

Figure 3-1   The New Mailbox Wizard

- **Initials**   The initials of the user (optional).

- **Last Name**   The last name of the user (optional).

- **Name**   If you enter information in the First Name, Initials, and Last Name fields, the Name field is populated with this information by default. You can modify the name in this field.

- **User Logon Name (User Principal Name)**   This is the name the user will use to log on to the domain. It consists of a user name and a suffix. Typically, the suffix is the domain name in which the user account resides, for example, don.hall@tailspintoys.internal.

- **User Logon Name (pre-Windows 2000)**   A user name that is compatible with versions of Microsoft Windows prior to the release of Windows 2000 Server. This field is, by default, populated on the basis of the information in the User Logon Name (User Principal Name) field.

- **Password**   The password that the user uses to log on to the domain.

- **Confirm Password**   You need to confirm the information you entered in the Password field.

- **User Must Change Password At Next Logon**   You select this check box to require the user to create a new password at first logon.

Figure 3-2 shows the User Information page.

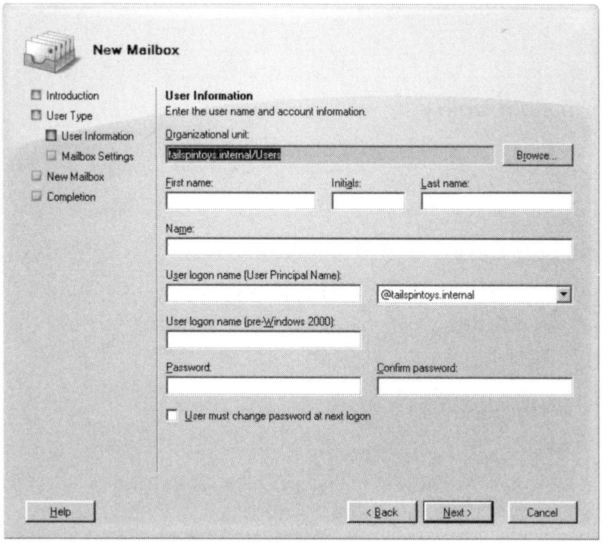

Figure 3-2   User Information page

NOTE   **Security account manager account name**

The user logon name (pre–Windows 2000) is also known as the security account manager account name (SAMAccountName). It is used for Windows Internet Naming Service (WINS) name resolution and must be unique within the domain.

You then provide information about the mailbox on the Mailbox Settings page. On this page, you complete the following fields:

- **Alias**   By default, this field contains the user's first and last name, with no space between the names. You can modify the alias in this field.

- **Server**   If you need to change the default server, select the server you want from the list in this field.

- **Storage Group**   If you need to change the default storage group, select the storage you want from the list in this field.

- **Mailbox Database**   If you need to change the default mailbox database, select the mailbox database you want from the list in this field.

- **Managed Folder Mailbox Policy**   If you have configured recipient policies, described in Chapter 8, "Policies and Public Folders," you can specify a mailbox policy in this field. You could, for example, use this option if you want to specify a policy that determines the retention period for the mailbox data. This field is optional.

MORE INFO   Managed folder mailbox policy

For more information about Managed folder mailbox policies and how to create them, access *http://technet.microsoft.com/en-us/aa996359.aspx*.

- **Exchange ActiveSync Mailbox Policy**   If you have previously configured Exchange ActiveSync mailbox policies, you can specify a policy by selecting the ActiveSync Mailbox Policy check box and clicking Browse to select the policy to be associated with this mailbox. This field is optional.

MORE INFO   Exchange ActiveSync

For more information about Exchange ActiveSync mailbox policies, search for "Overview of Exchange ActiveSync" in Microsoft Exchange Server 2007 Help or access *http://technet. microsoft.com/en-us/bb123484.aspx*.

Figure 3-9 in the practice session for this lesson shows the Mailbox Settings page.

The New Mailbox page presents you with the Configuration Summary. To make any configuration changes, click Back. To create the new mailbox, click New. On the Completion page, the summary states whether the mailbox was successfully created and displays the Exchange Management Shell command that was used to create the mailbox. Click Finish to close the wizard.

NOTE   Exchange Management Console acts as a command generator

When you use Exchange Management Console to generate an entity such as a mailbox in Exchange Server 2007, what actually happens is that Exchange Management Console generates a command (shown in the Completion page) that is then automatically passed to Exchange Management Shell. Exchange Management Shell implements the command to create the entity.

Using Exchange Management Shell to Create a Mailbox-Enabled Account

The Exchange Management Shell lets you perform tasks such as creating, removing, or disabling a mailbox-enabled user with a single command line. The following is an example of an Exchange Management Shell command:

```
New-mailbox -UserPrincipalName don.hall@tailspintoys.internal -database "First Storage
Group\Mailbox Database" -Name don.hall -OrganizationalUnit Users -DisplayName "Don Hall"
-ResetPasswordOnNextLogon $true
```

This command creates the user Don Hall in Active Directory. The mailbox don.hall@tailspintoys.internal is created in the Mailbox Database in the First Storage Group. The password must be reset at the next logon. Because the Password variable is not specified, Exchange Management Server prompts you to enter a password after you enter the command and assigns that password to the variable as a SecureString object (that is, it is encrypted). You cannot specify a password directly in the command (which would be bad security practice in any case, especially if you are saving the command in a text file).

You can, if you want to, specify a password before you create a mailbox-enabled user. You do this by using the $password variable. You first need to indicate how the value in the variable is specified (by entering it on the host machine) and that it is stored as a secure string. The command to do this is as follows:

```
$password = Read-Host "Enter password" –AsSecureString
```

When you enter this command, Exchange Management Shell prompts you for a password. When you have entered the password, you can create the mailbox-enabled user with the following command:

```
New-mailbox -UserPrincipalName don.hall@tailspintoys.internal -database "First Storage
Group\Mailbox Database" -Name don.hall -OrganizationalUnit Users –Password $password
-ResetPasswordOnNextLogon $true
```

NOTE **The password is not displayed on the New Mailbox Wizard's Completion page**

If you create a new mailbox-enabled user (or a new mail-enabled user) by using Exchange Management Console, the Exchange Management Shell command displayed on the New Mailbox Wizard's Completion page does not show the user's password in clear text (because a third party could read the information on the screen). Instead, the password value is given as "SystemSecuritySecureString."

MORE INFO **Storage Groups and Databases**

For more information about Exchange storage groups and databases, search for "Managing Storage Groups and Databases" in Exchange Server 2007 Help or access *http://technet.microsoft. com/en-us/library/aa998926.aspx.*

Using Exchange Management Console to Create a Mailbox for an Existing User

A user account can exist in Active Directory but not have an associated mailbox. For example, a domain administrator might have created the account by using Active Directory Users and Computers, or you might have previously disabled an existing mailbox-enabled user without removing the user's Active Directory account. To create a mailbox for an existing user, start the New Mailbox Wizard as before, specify User Mailbox, and then specify Existing User. Then click Browse and select the user. You do not need to supply user details, and the wizard takes you directly to the Mailbox Settings page described earlier in this lesson. You fill in the fields in this page and then complete the wizard as before.

Quick Check

- What two tools can you use to create a new mailbox-enabled user or to mailbox-enable an existing user?

Quick Check Answer

- Exchange Management Console and Exchange Management Shell.

Using Exchange Management Console to Disable or Remove a Mailbox-Enabled User

You can choose either to disable e-mail for a mailbox-enabled user or to remove the user completely. Removing a mailbox-enabled user removes that user from Active Directory. If you want the user to be able to log on to the domain but not to have a mailbox, disable the mailbox instead. You reenable a mailbox by re-creating it for an existing user. Typically, you might disable a mailbox-enabled user if the user is on extended leave but will eventually return to the organization. If you have removed a mailbox-enabled user account and want to re-create it, you need to perform a recovery operation or create a new mailbox-enabled user from scratch.

In either case, start the Exchange Management Console, expand the Recipient Configuration node in the console tree, and click Mailbox. In the Result pane (the middle pane), select the mailbox-enabled user and in the Actions pane, under the name of the user, click either Disable or Remove. Then click Yes to clear the Warning dialog box and either disable the mailbox or remove the user.

IMPORTANT Removing a Mailbox Removes the Mailbox-Enabled User

Take care when removing mailboxes. Remember that if you remove a mailbox, you also remove the associated user account, and the user can no longer log on to Active Directory. It is also worth remembering that if you delete the user, you can still recover the mailbox if required. Chapter 11, "Configuring Disaster Recovery," discusses mailbox recovery in depth. However, it is good practice to disable rather than remove mailboxes because someone always wants access to a mailbox just after you have removed it.

Using Exchange Management Shell to Remove, Disable, or Enable a Mailbox-Enabled User

You can also use Exchange Management Shell to disable or remove a mailbox. For example, the command *Remove-Mailbox -Identity don.hall@tailspintoys.internal* removes the user Don Hall and the mailbox don.hall@tailspintoys.internal. The command *Disable-Mailbox -Identity don.hall@tailspintoys.internal* disables e-mail but does not delete the user. When you enter either of these two commands, Exchange Management Shell prompts you to confirm that you want to carry out the operation. The default is Y for yes.

You can enable a disabled mailbox provided that you have not removed the mailbox-enabled user. The command requires that you supply the name of the Exchange database that contains the mailbox, for example, *Enable-Mailbox -Identity don.hall@ tailspintoys.internal –Database "Mailbox database"*.

MORE INFO Remove-Mailbox, Disable-Mailbox, and Enable-Mailbox

For more information about the *Remove-Mailbox, Disable-Mailbox, and Enable-Mailbox* cmdlets, access *http://technet.microsoft.com/en-us/aa995948.aspx*, *http://technet.microsoft.com/en-us/library/aa997210.aspx*, and *http://technet.microsoft.com/en-us/library/aa998251.aspx*, respectively.

Using Exchange Management Console to Configure Mailbox User Properties

You can use the Exchange Management Console to configure mailbox and mailbox user properties. For example, you might want to configure a mailbox to use Outlook Web Access (OWA), or you might want to enable or disable ActiveSync or specify storage quotas or message size restrictions for a mailbox user.

NOTE ActiveSync

ActiveSync lets you apply a common set of policy or security settings to a user or group of users. A link to enable you to obtain more information about Exchange ActiveSync policies was provided earlier in this lesson.

To configure user or mailbox properties, open the Exchange Management Console, expand Recipient Configuration, click Mailbox, and specify the mailbox-enabled user in the Result pane. Then click Properties in the Actions pane under the user's name. The Mailbox Settings tab of the Mailbox User Properties dialog box enables you to configure Messaging Records Management and Storage Quotas. You can configure a setting by double-clicking it. Figure 3-3 shows the Mailbox Settings tab.

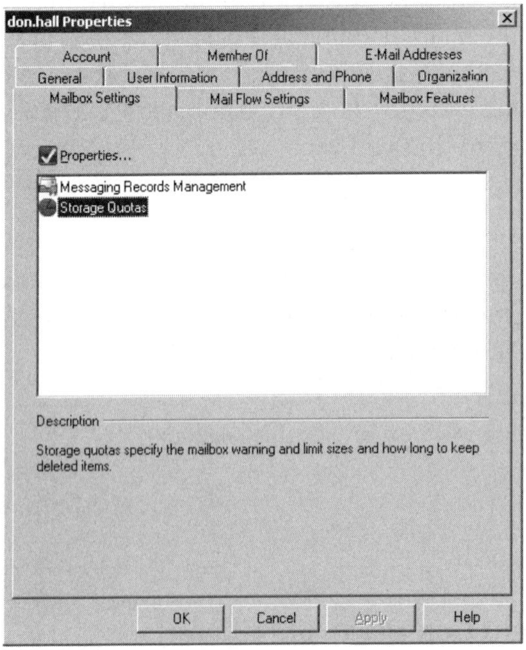

Figure 3-3   The Mailbox Settings tab of the Mailbox User Properties dialog box

The Mail Flow Settings tab of the Mailbox User Properties dialog box lets you configure Delivery Options, Message Size Restrictions, and Message Delivery Restrictions. Figure 3-4 shows the Mail Flow Settings tab.

The Mailbox Features tab of the Mailbox User Properties dialog box lets you enable or disable OWA, Exchange ActiveSync, Unified Messaging, and MAPI. You can disable or enable a feature by selecting it and clicking Disable or Enable. Figure 3-5 shows the Mailbox Features tab.

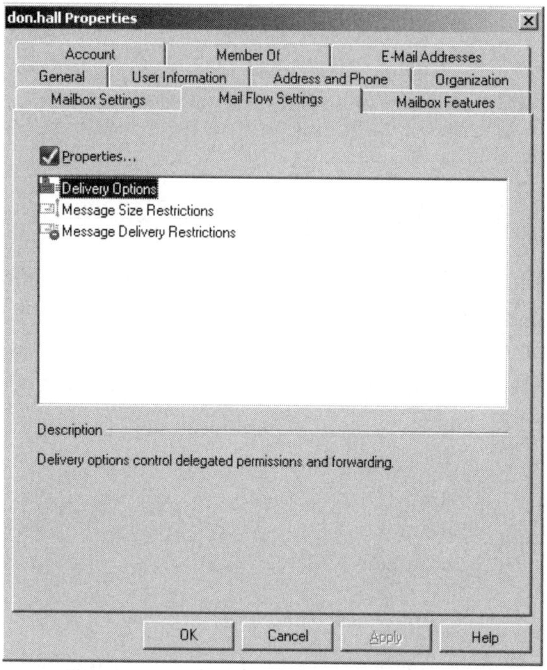

Figure 3-4   The Mail Flow Settings tab of the Mailbox User Properties dialog box

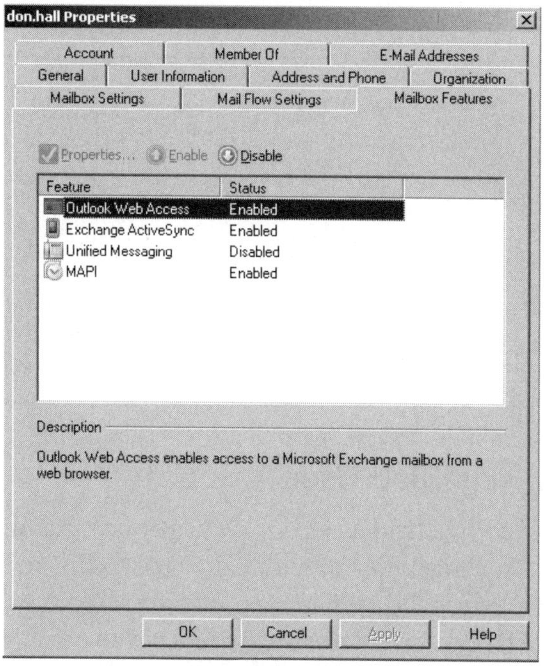

Figure 3-5   The Mailbox Features tab of the Mailbox User Properties dialog box

Exam Tip If you click Modify The Maximum Number Of Recipients To Display under Mailbox in the Actions pane, this lets you modify the maximum number of recipients displayed in the Recipient Configuration Result pane. It does not modify the selected mailbox. Be wary of answers in examination questions that suggest clicking Modify The Mailbox to configure mailbox features.

Using Exchange Management Shell to Configure Properties

You can also use Exchange Management Shell to configure mailbox properties. For example, the command *Set-CASMailbox -Identity don.hall@tailspintoys.internal -OWA Enabled $True* enables OWA for Don Hall. The command *Set-CASMailbox -Identity don.hall@tailspintoys.internal -OWAEnabled $False* disables OWA for the same user.

MORE INFO Set-CASMailbox

For more information about the *Set-CASMailbox* cmdlet, search for "Set-CASMailbox" in Exchange Server 2007 Help or access *http://technet.microsoft.com/en-us/bb125264.aspx*.

NOTE Get-Help

You can use Get-Help in Exchange Management Shell to get more information about any Exchange Management Shell cmdlet, for example, *Get-Help Set-CASMailbox*.

Quick Check
- What is the difference between removing and disabling a mailbox-enabled user?

Quick Check Answer
- Removing a user removes the user's mailbox and also removes the user's account from Active Directory so that the user can no longer log on to the domain. Disabling the user removes the user's mailbox but does not remove the user account in Active Directory.

Creating and Configuring Mail-Enabled User Accounts

A mail-enabled user has an e-mail address and user account in an organization but does not have an Exchange mailbox. All e-mail messages that are sent to the mail-enabled user are forwarded to a specified external e-mail address. Mail-enabled user accounts are created, for example, when external consultants are working in an organization but are not employed by that organization and do not have mailboxes allocated to them on that organization's Microsoft Exchange Server 2007 sever.

You can use both the Exchange Management Console GUI and the Exchange Management Shell to create a mail-enabled user, as described in the next two sections of this lesson.

Using Exchange Management Console to Create a Mail-Enabled Account

To use the Exchange Management Console GUI to create a new mail-enabled user, expand Recipient Configuration and click Mail Contact. Then select New Mail User in the Actions pane to start the New Mail User Wizard. Specify that you want to create a new user and supply the information needed to create that user. The First Name, Initials, Last Name, Name, User Logon Name (User Principal Name), User Logon Name (pre-Windows 2000), Password, Confirm Password, and User Must Change Password At Next Logon fields are the same as those described previously in this lesson for creating a mailbox-enabled user.

The Organizational Unit field performs the same function as the same field for a mailbox-enabled user, but the method of determining the default value in this field is different because a mailbox-enabled user has an account in the domain, whereas a mail-enabled user might have an account in another domain in the forest.

For mail-enabled users, the default value of the Organizational Unit field depends on the recipient scope set in the Recipient Configuration node. If the recipient scope is set to the forest, the default value is set to the Users container in the Active Directory domain that contains the computer on which the Exchange Management Console is running. If the recipient scope is set to a specific domain, the Users container in that domain is selected by default (which is the same default as for a mailbox-enabled user). If the recipient scope is set to a specific OU, that OU is selected by default. To change the default OU, click Browse and then select the OU you want.

MORE INFO   Recipient scope

For more information about recipient scope, consult the following link: *http://technet.microsoft.com/en-us/library/aa996861.aspx.*

When you have entered the required new user information, specify mail settings. On the Mail Settings page, complete the following fields:

- **Alias**   You specify the alias in this field. Typically, it is the same as the User Logon Name.

■ **External E-Mail Address**   You can specify the external e-mail address by using one of the following methods:

❑ To specify a Simple Mail Transfer Protocol (SMTP) e-mail address, click Edit, and then in E-Mail Address, type the external SMTP e-mail address of the user, for example, sean.alexander@contoso.com.

❑ To specify a custom e-mail address, click the arrow next to Edit, click Custom Address, and then in E-Mail Address, specify the e-mail address, for example, /pn=sean.alexander/PRMD=contoso/ADMD=attmail/C=us/, and the e-mail type, for example, X400.

NOTE   **All non-SMTP addresses are custom addresses**

In Exchange Server 2007, all non-SMTP e-mail addresses are considered to be custom addresses, and unique dialog boxes or property pages do not exist for X.400, GroupWise, or Lotus Notes e-mail address types. If you add a non-SMTP custom e-mail address, the appropriate dynamic-link library files need to be installed; otherwise, the following error will be logged in Event Viewer: "The e-mail address description object in the Microsoft Exchange directory for the 'SADF' address type on 'i386' machines is missing."

On the New Mail User page, you can review the configuration summary. As before, click Back to make changes or New to create the mail-enabled user. On the Completion page, the summary states whether the mail-enabled user was successfully created. The summary also displays the Exchange Management Shell command that was used to create the new mail-enabled user. Click Finish to complete the task.

Using Exchange Management Shell to Create a Mail-Enabled Account

You can use the Exchange Management Shell *New-MailUser* cmdlet to create a new mail-enabled user. The following is an Exchange Management Shell command that creates the mail-enabled user James R. Hamilton:

```
New-MailUser -Name "James R. Hamilton" -ExternalEmailAddress SMTP:james.hamilton@contoso.com
-UserPrincipalName jrhamilton@tailspintoys.internal -OrganizationalUnit Users -
ResetPasswordOnNextLogon $true
```

As with the command to create a new mailbox-enabled user earlier in this lesson, you will be prompted for a password, and this will be stored as a secure string. If you want to specify the password before you create the user, you can use the $password variable in exactly the same way as was described previously for a mailbox-enabled user.

Using Exchange Management Console to Mail-Enable User Accounts

To mail-enable an existing user account, start the New Mail User Wizard as before and then select Existing User and click Browse to select the user. When you click Next, the wizard takes you directly to the Mail Settings page, where you specify an alias (if necessary) and an external e-mail address. Complete the wizard in the same way as for a new mail-enabled user.

Using Exchange Management Console to Disable and Remove Mail-Enabled Users

To disable e-mail for a mail-enabled user, start the Exchange Management Console, expand Recipient Configuration in the console tree, and then click Mail Contact. In the Result pane, select the mail-enabled user account for which you want to disable mail and then click Disable under the name of the user in the Actions pane. Then click Yes to close the Warning dialog box. The procedure for deleting a mail-enabled user is almost identical to that for disabling e-mail except that you click Delete rather than Disable in the Result pane. Disabling e-mail does not remove the user from Active Directory; removing the user does.

Using Exchange Management Shell to Remove, Disable, or Enable a Mail-Enabled User

You can also use Exchange Management Shell to disable or remove a mail-enabled user. For example, the command *Remove-MailUser -Identity "James R. Hamilton"* removes the user James R. Hamilton. The command *Disable-MailUser -Identity "James R. Hamilton"* disables e-mail but does not delete the user. When you enter either of these two commands, Exchange Management Shell prompts you to confirm that you want to carry out the operation. The default is Y for yes.

You can enable a disabled mail-enabled user provided that you have not removed the user account. The command requires that you supply the user's external e-mail address, for example, *Enable-MailUser -Identity "James R. Hamilton" –ExternalEmailAddress james.hamilton@contoso.com.*

MORE INFO   **Remove-MailUser, Disable-MailUser, and Enable-MailUser**

For more information about the *Remove-MailUser, Disable-MailUser,* and *Enable-Mailuser* cmdlets, access *http://technet.microsoft.com/en-us/library/bb125260.aspx, http://technet.microsoft.com/en-us/library/aa998578.aspx,* and *http://technet.microsoft.com/en-us/library/aa996549.aspx,* respectively.

Using Exchange Management Console to Configure Mail-Enabled User Properties

To configure properties for a mail-enabled user, start the Exchange Management Console, expand Recipient Configuration, and click Mail Contact. You then select the mail-enabled user in the Result pane and in the Actions pane, under the user's name, click Properties. On the E-Mail Addresses tab of the Mail-Enabled User Properties dialog box, you can edit the user's e-mail addresses and specify new addresses. On the Mail Flow Settings tab, you can configure message size and message delivery restrictions. The E-Mail Addresses tab is shown in Figure 3-6.

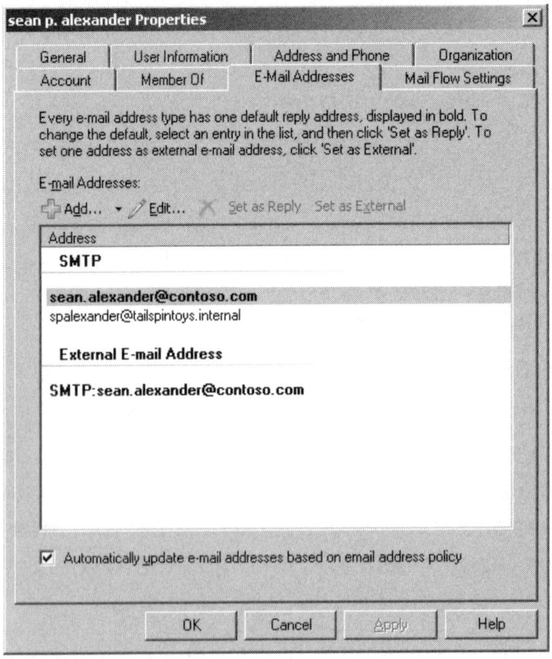

Figure 3-6   The E-Mail Addresses tab of the Mail-Enabled User Properties dialog box

Using Exchange Management Shell to Configure Mail-Enabled User Properties

You can use the Exchange Management Shell cmdlet *Set-MailUser* to configure e-mail properties for a mail-enabled user. Suppose, for example, that James R. Hamilton moved from Contoso, Ltd, to the A. Datum Corporation but still had a mail-enabled account at Tailspin Toys. You could change his external e-mail address by using the command *Set-MailUser "James R. Hamilton" –ExternalEmailAddress james.hamilton@ adatum.com.*

MORE INFO   Set-MailUser

For more information about the *Set-MailUser* cmdlet, access *http://technet.microsoft.com/en-us/library/aa995971.aspx*.

Configuring Mail-Enabled Contacts

A contact is a mail-enabled Active Directory directory service object (not a user account) that contains information about people or organizations that exist outside an Exchange organization. A contact does not have a mailbox on the Exchange Server 2007 server or an account in Active Directory and cannot log on to your organization's domain.

Users can specify a contact name in the To or Cc line in an e-mail message without needing to remember the contact's e-mail address. Users can also browse a list of contacts. Contacts can be placed in universal distribution groups, and they can be included in dynamic distribution groups, depending on their properties. Lesson 2 of this chapter discusses distribution groups.

You can use both the Exchange Management Console and the Exchange Management Shell to create, delete, and modify mail-enabled contacts in Exchange Server 2007.

Using Exchange Management Console to Create Mail-Enabled Contacts

To create a mail-enabled contact, open the Exchange Management Console, expand Recipient Configuration in the console tree, and then click Mail Contact. In the Action pane, click New Mail Contact to start the New Mail Contact Wizard, as shown in Figure 3-7.

On the Introduction page, select New Contact. On the Contact Information page, complete the required fields. The Organizational Unit, First Name, Initials, Last Name, and Name fields are the same as those defined earlier in this lesson for a mailbox-enabled user. Specify the Alias and External E-Mail Address fields in the same way as you did for a mail-enabled user.

On the New Mail Contact page, you can review the configuration summary, click Back to make changes, or click New to create the new mail contact. On the Completion page, the summary states whether the contact was successfully created. The summary also displays the Exchange Management Shell command that was used to create the new mail contact. As with other recipient objects, you can (if you want to) copy the page (including the Exchange Management Shell command) into a text editor, edit the command as necessary, and use the Exchange Management Shell to create additional mail-enabled contacts. Click Finish to complete the task.

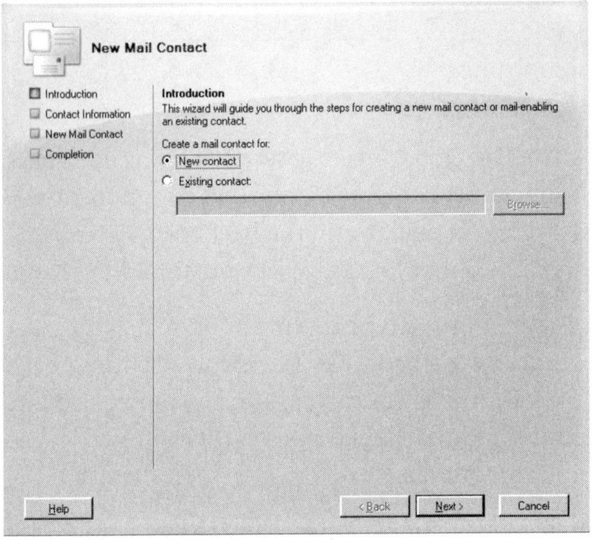

Figure 3-7 The New Mail Contact Wizard

Quick Check

■ All employees at Trey Research have a mailbox and a user account in the company's Active Directory domain. What type of users are they?

Quick Check Answer

■ Mailbox-enabled users.

Using Exchange Management Console to Mail-Enable an Existing Contact

Typically, you create contacts so that your users can send e-mail to them. However, if you have disabled e-mail for a contact without removing the contact, then that contact exists in Active Directory but is not mail-enabled. If you want to mail-enable such a contact, start the New Mail Contact Wizard as before and then select Existing Contact and click Browse to select the contact. When you click Next, the wizard takes you to the Contact Information page, where the information about the contact should be there by default, and you specify an external e-mail address. Complete the wizard in the same way as for a new mail-enabled contact.

Using Exchange Management Console to Remove or Disable a Mail-Enabled Contact

You remove or delete a mail-enabled contact in exactly the same way as a mail-enabled user. When you expand Recipient Configuration in the Exchange Management Console and click Mail Contact, both mail-enabled users and mail-enabled contacts are listed in the Result pane. Then select a mail-enabled contact and in the Actions pane, under the name of the mail contact, click either Disable or Remove. Then click Yes to clear the Warning dialog box.

Using Exchange Management Console to Modify Mail-Enabled Contact Properties

You modify the properties for a mail-enabled contact in the same way as for a mail-enabled user. As previously stated, when you expand Recipient Configuration in the Exchange Management Console and click Mail Contact, both mail-enabled users and mail-enabled contacts are listed in the Result pane. Then select a mail-enabled contact and in the Actions pane, under the name of the mail contact, click Properties. The Email-Addresses and Mail Flow settings tabs in a mail-enabled contact's Properties dialog box contain the same information as the same tabs in a mail-enabled user's Properties dialog box.

Using Exchange Management Shell to Configure Mail Contacts

You can use the Exchange Management Shell cmdlet *New-MailContact* to create a mail contact, for example, *New-MailContact -Name "Michael Allen" -ExternalEmailAddress m.allen@fabricam.com -OrganizationalUnit Users*. Mail contacts do not have user accounts in Active Directory, so you do not need to specify a password.

You can use Exchange Management Shell to remove, disable, or enable a mail contact. For example, *Remove-MailContact "Jeff Hay"* would remove that contact. If you wanted to restore the contact, you would need to either recover it or re-create it from scratch. *Disable-MailContact "Michael Allen"* would disable the mail contact Michael Allan, but you could reenable it if you want to. Both the remove and disable functions require that you confirm that you want to carry out the operation. The default is Y for yes.

If you have disabled but not removed a mail contact, you can enable it by using the *Enable-MailContact* cmdlet. You need to specify the contact's external e-mail add-ress, for example, *Enable-MailContact "Michael Allen" −ExternalEmailAddress m.allen@ fabricam.com*. You can also use Exchange Management Shell to configure a mail contact's properties, for example, *Set-MailContact "Michael Allen" −MaxReceiveSize 1000*.

MORE INFO   Configuring mail contacts

For more information about the Exchange Management Shell cmdlets that configure mail contacts, access *http://technet.microsoft.com/en-us/library/bb123561.aspx*, *http://technet.microsoft.com/en-us/ library/aa997465.aspx*, *http://technet.microsoft.com/en-us/library/aa996001.aspx*, and *http://technet. microsoft.com/en-us/library/aa995950.aspx*.

Practice: Configuring Recipient Accounts

In this practice session, you will create a mailbox-enabled user, a mail-enabled user, and a mail-enabled contact. The practices ask you to log on using the Kim_Akers domain administrator account. Domain administrators by default have the Exchange Organization Administrator role. You can also complete the practices if you are logged on with an account that has the Exchange Organization Administrator or Exchange Recipient Administrator role.

▶ **Practice 1: Creating a Mailbox-Enabled User**

In this practice, you will create the mailbox-enabled user Don Hall. You can extend the practice by copying the Exchange Management Shell command that the procedure generates and modifying it to create additional mailbox-enabled users:

1. Log on to the domain controller by using the Kim_Akers account.

2. Open the Exchange Management Console.

3. Expand the Recipient Configuration node in the console tree and click Mailbox.

4. Click New Mailbox in the Actions pane. The New Mailbox Wizard starts.

5. On the Introduction page (shown previously in Figure 3-1), select User Mailbox and then click Next.

6. On the User Type page, select New User and then click Next.

7. Fill in the elements on the User Information page as instructed in Table 3-1.

Table 3-1   User Information for Don Hall

Element	Instruction
Organizational Unit	Leave as default (tailspintoys.internal\Users)
First Name	don
Initials	Leave this blank
Last Name	hall

Table 3-1   User Information for Don Hall

Element	Instruction
Name	don.hall
User Logon Name (User Principal Name)	don.hall (@tailspintoys.internal should be specified by default)
User Logon Name (pre-Windows 2000)	Leave as default
Password	P@ssw0rd
Confirm Password	P@ssw0rd
User Must Change Password At Next Logon	Not selected

NOTE **Passwords**

For convenience, the same password is used in all the practices in this chapter, and the user is not required to change the password at logon. In a production environment, you might decide to use the same initial password (although this is not considered good security practice). You would, however, require users to change their passwords at next logon.

8. The User Information page should look similar to Figure 3-8. Click Next.

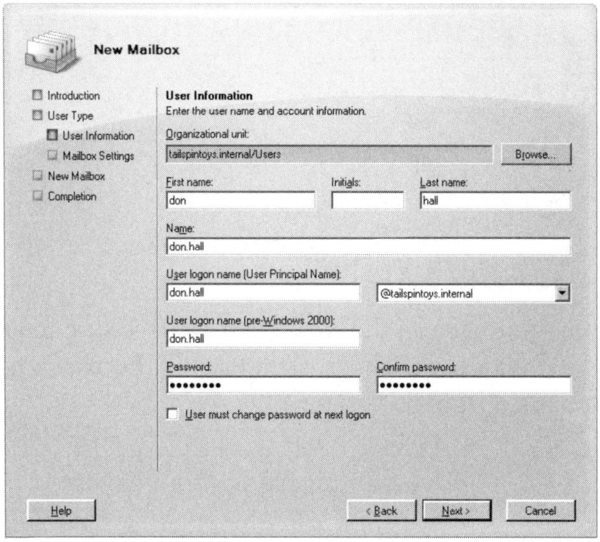

Figure 3-8   User information for Don Hall

9. Fill in the elements of the Mailbox Settings page as instructed in Table 3-2.

Table 3-2   Mailbox Settings for Don Hall

Element	Instruction
Alias	Check that this is don.hall
Server	Leave as default
Storage Group	Leave as default
Mailbox Database	Leave as default
Managed Folder Mailbox Policy	Do not configure
Exchange ActiveSync Mailbox Policy	Do not configure

10. The Mailbox Settings page should look like Figure 3-9. Click Next.

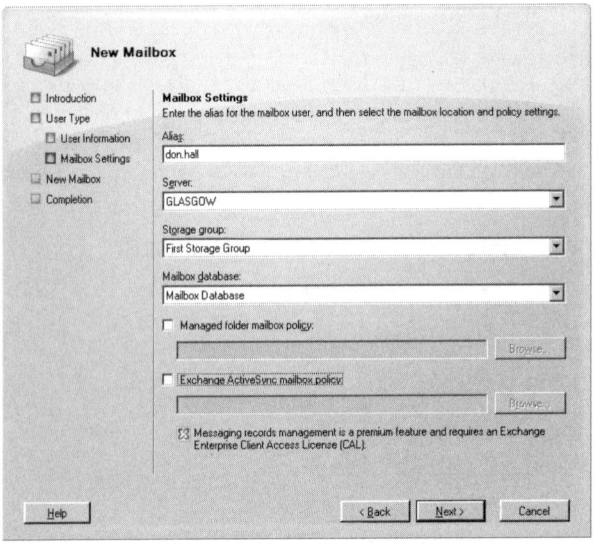

Figure 3-9   Mailbox Settings for Don Hall

11. The Configuration Summary on the New Mailbox page should look like Figure 3-10. If you need to make any changes, click Back. Otherwise, click New to create the mailbox-enabled user.

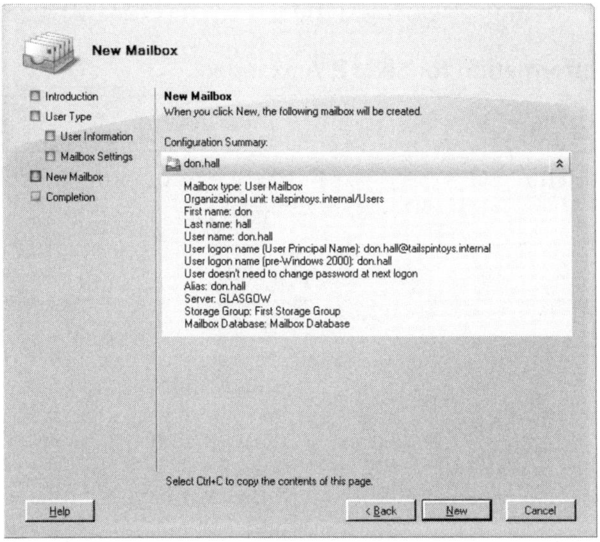

Figure 3-10 Configuration Summary for Don Hall

12. On the Completion page, press Ctrl+C to copy the page and paste it into a text editor. Copy the Exchange Management Shell command and paste it into a text file. If you want to expand the practice, you can modify this command and use it to create additional mailbox-enabled users.

13. Click Finish.

▶ **Practice 2: Creating a Mail-Enabled User**

In this practice, you will create the mail-enabled user Sean P. Alexander. As with the previous practice, you can extend this practice by copying the Exchange Management Shell command that the procedure generates and modifying it to create additional mail-enabled users:

1. If necessary, log on to the domain controller by using the Kim_Akers account.

2. Open the Exchange Management Console.

3. Expand the Recipient Configuration node in the console tree and click Mail Contact.

4. Select New Mail User in the Actions pane. The New Mail User Wizard starts.

5. In the Introduction page of the New Mail User Wizard, select New User. Click Next.

6. On the User Information Page, fill in the information as instructed in Table 3-3.

Table 3-3   User Information for Sean P. Alexander

Element	Instruction
Organizational Unit	Leave as default (tailspintoys.internal/Users)
First Name	sean
Initials	p
Last Name	alexander
Name	Check that this is sean p. alexander
User Logon Name (User Principal Name)	spalexander (@tailspintoys.internal should be specified automatically)
User Logon Name (pre-Windows 2000)	Leave as default
Password	P@ssw0rd
Confirm Password	P@ssw0rd
User Must Change Password At Next Logon	Not selected

7. The User Information page should look similar to Figure 3-11. Click Next.

8. On the Mail Settings page, fill in the information as instructed in Table 3-4. You need to click Edit to specify the external e-mail address.

Table 3-4   Mail Settings for Sean P. Alexander

Element	Instruction
Alias	spalexander
External E-Mail Address	sean.alexander@contoso.com

9. The Mail Settings page should look similar to Figure 3-12. Click Next.

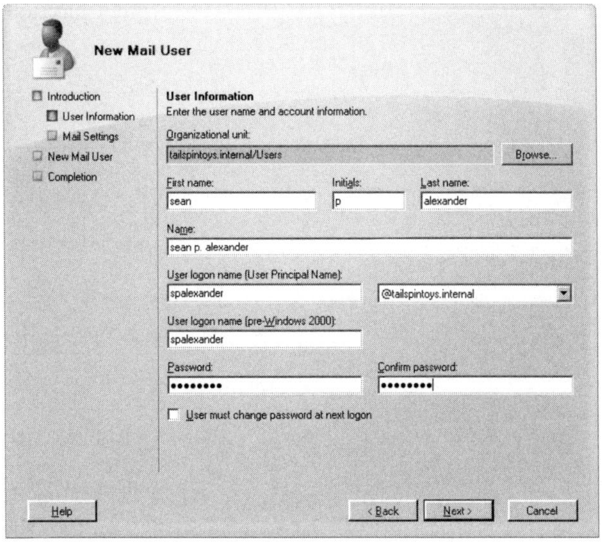

Figure 3-11 User Information page for Sean P. Alexander

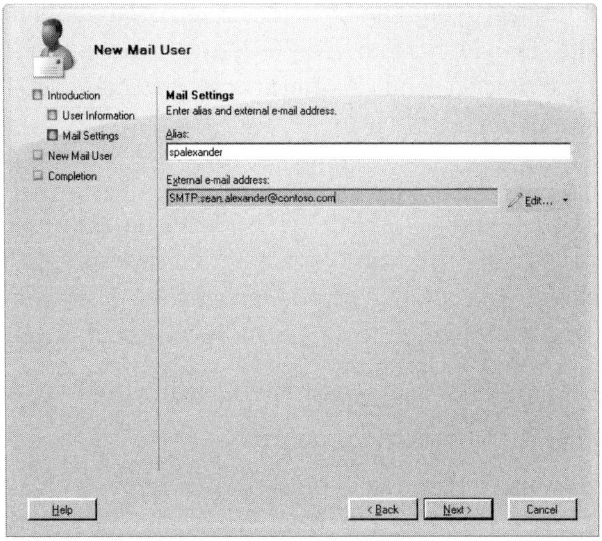

Figure 3-12 Mail Settings page for Sean P. Alexander

10. On the New Mail User page, review the Configuration Summary, which should look similar to Figure 3-13. If you need to make changes, click Back. Otherwise, click New.

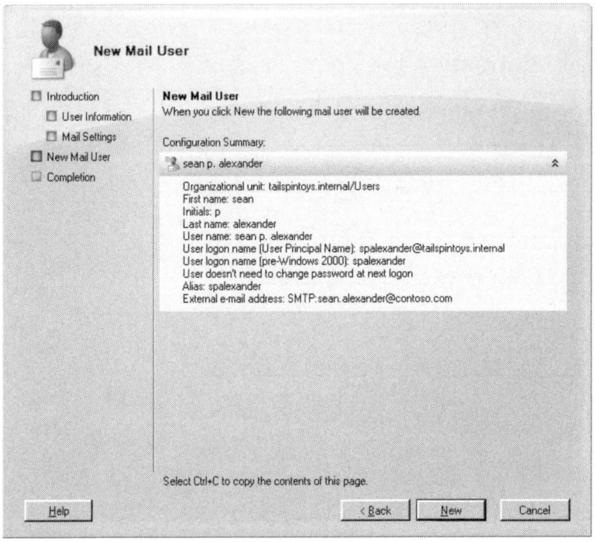

Figure 3-13   Configuration Summary page for Sean P. Alexander

11. On the Completion page, copy the Exchange Management Shell command that was used to create the new mail-enabled user and paste it into a text file. If you want to expand the practice, you can modify this command and use it to create additional mail-enabled users.

12. Click Finish.

▶ **Practice 3: Creating a Mail Contact**

In this practice, you will create the mail contact Simon Pearson. As before, you can extend the practice by copying the Exchange Management Shell command that the procedure generates and modifying it to create additional mail contacts:

1. If necessary, log on to the domain controller by using the Kim_Akers account.

2. Open the Exchange Management Console.

3. Expand the Recipient Configuration node in the console tree and click Mail Contact.

4. Select New Mail Contact in the Actions pane. The New Mail Contact Wizard starts.

5. In the Introduction page of the New Mail Contact Wizard, select New Contact.

6. Click Next.

7. On the Contact Information page, complete the fields as specified in Table 3-5.

Table 3-5 Contact Information for Simon Pearson

Element	Instruction
Organizational Unit	Leave as default (tailspintoys.internal/Users)
First Name	simon
Initials	Leave blank
Last Name	pearson
Name	Check that this is simon pearson
Alias	Check that this is simonpearson
External E-Mail Address	Click Edit; in E-Mail Address, enter **s.pearson@ adatum.com**

NOTE **Contacts Organizational Unit**

In the real world, you probably want to put contacts into a separate OU container rather than in the Users container. If you are a domain administrator as well as an Exchange administrator, you should create this OU before you create mail contacts. If you are not a domain administrator, you need to ask the person with these rights to do this for you.

8. The Contact Information page should look similar to Figure 3-14. Click Next.

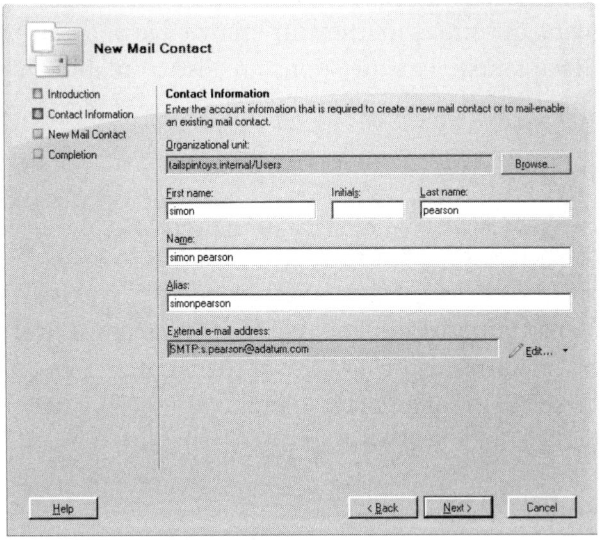

Figure 3-14 Contact Information page for Simon Pearson

9. On the New Mail Contact page, review the configuration summary. If you need to make changes, click Back. Otherwise, click New.

10. On the Completion page, copy the page and paste the Exchange Management Shell command into a text file. If you want to expand the practice, you can modify this command and use it to create additional mail contacts.

11. Click Finish.

Lesson Summary

- A mailbox-enabled user has a mailbox in the domain and a user account in Active Directory. The user can log in to Active Directory and access his or her mailbox.

- A mail-enabled user has a user account in Active Directory but does not have a mailbox in the domain. The user has an external e-mail address, and e-mail is forwarded to this address.

- A mail contact does not have a user account or a user name in Active Directory, and does not have a mailbox in the domain. The contact has an alias, and e-mail messages with this alias in the To or Cc line are sent to the contact's external e-mail address.

- You can use Exchange Management Console and Exchange Management Shell to create, configure, disable, or remove Exchange recipients.

Lesson Review

You can use the following questions to test your knowledge of the information in Lesson 1, "Configuring Recipients." The questions are also available on the companion CD if you prefer to review them in electronic form.

NOTE   Answers

Answers to these questions and explanations of why each answer choice is correct or incorrect are located in the "Answers" section at the end of the book.

---

1. You are the Exchange administrator at Lucerne Publishing. Lucerne's employees frequently send e-mail to David Hamilton at the Graphic Design Institute. They want to be able to select the alias david_hamilton in the To line rather than needing to enter David's e-mail address each time. How do you add David to your Exchange organization?

    A. As a mailbox-enabled user

    B. As a mail-enabled user

    C. As a mail contact

    D. As a mailbox-enabled user but with his mailbox disabled

2. You are the Exchange administrator at Coho Winery. Terry Adam is employed by Coho Vineyards but spends a lot of time working at Coho Winery. Terry has a mailbox at Coho Vineyards. You want Terry to be able to log on to the Coho Winery Active Directory domain and for incoming e-mail sent to him to be forwarded to his @cohovineyard.com address. How do you add Terry to your Exchange organization?

    A. As a mailbox-enabled user

    B. As a mail-enabled user

    C. As a mail contact

    D. As a mailbox-enabled user but with his mailbox disabled

3. Which of the following fields are mandatory when creating a mail contact? (Choose all that apply.)

    A. First Name

    B. Initials

    C. Last Name

    D. Alias

    E. External E-Mail Address

4. What does the following Exchange Management Shell command do?

```
New-MailUser -Name "Carol Philips" -ExternalEmailAddress SMTP:carol.philips@contoso.com
-UserPrincipalName cphilips@tailspintoys.internal -OrganizationalUnit Users
ResetPasswordOnNextLogon $true
```

    A. Creates a mailbox-enabled user Carol Philips and a mailbox cphilips@tailspintoys.internal

    B. Creates a mailbox-enabled user Carol Philips and a mailbox carol.philips@contoso.com

    C. Creates a mail-enabled user Carol Philips and specifies an external e-mail address carol.philips@contoso.com

    D. Creates a mail-enabled user Carol Philips and specifies an external e-mail address cphilips@tailspintoys.internal

5. You are creating a new mailbox-enabled user. Which of the following are fields on the Mailbox Settings page of the New Mailbox Wizard? (Choose all that apply.)

   A. Mailbox Database

   B. Organizational Unit

   C. Alias

   D. Server

   E. User Logon Name (User Principal Name)

   F. Storage Group

Lesson 2: Configuring Mail-Enabled Groups

Distribution groups are mail-enabled Active Directory directory service group objects that are created to expedite the mass sending of e-mail messages and other information within an Exchange organization. Security groups are Active Directory directory service group objects that are used mainly to set security permissions for the user accounts that are members of that group.

A typical distribution group in an organization could be, for example, Customer Support Personnel, whose members have no specific permissions but could each receive e-mail sent to the entire group. A typical security group could be Backup Operators, whose members require specific security permissions to carry out their job. Distribution groups are typically mail-enabled. Security groups can be mail-enabled, although many are not.

Exchange Server 2007 lets you create and configure mail-enabled universal distribution groups, mail-enabled universal security groups, and dynamic distribution groups.

After this lesson, you will be able to:

- Create a universal distribution group.
- Create a dynamic distribution group.
- Create a mail-enabled universal security group.
- Mail-enable a distribution group or a universal security group.
- Modify a mail-enabled group.

Estimated lesson time: 50 minutes

Creating Distribution Groups

When you create a universal distribution group, you add members to it manually, as opposed to a dynamic distribution group, where members are selected automatically depending on attributes you specify. You would use a universal distribution group in situations where group membership seldom changes, such as employees in a department. You would use a dynamic distribution group in situations where the group membership changes frequently but group members have at least one attribute in common, such as a group of consultants all of whom have external e-mail addresses.

Groups in Exchange Server 2007 and Active Directory

Distribution groups are used primarily for e-mail and replace mailing lists in earlier versions of Exchange. Typically, they are mail-enabled, but you can disable a distribution group if you do not want e-mail to be sent to it at present but you might want to reenable it sometime in the future. Universal distribution groups have a fixed membership, and you need to add or remove users manually. The membership of a dynamic distribution group is determined in Active Directory by applying conditions and filters each time an e-mail message is sent to the group. Dynamic distribution groups are most efficient if their membership is unlikely to exceed 25 recipients. For larger memberships, it is preferable to use universal distribution groups.

Security groups are used to assign permissions. As a result, all members of a security group need to have accounts in Active Directory. You cannot place mail contacts in a security group. Typically, security groups are not mail-enabled, but you can mail-enable universal security groups if you want to. Suppose, for example, that an organization with multiple domains in a forest already had a universal security group called Sales to grant members of sales departments throughout the forest access to interdomain sales resources. Rather than create an additional universal distribution group with exactly the same membership to allow a single e-mail to be sent to all group members, you could simply mail-enable the Sales universal security group.

If a universal distribution group exists and a domain administrator decides to use it to configure permissions, then the group can be converted to a universal security group (provided all its members have user accounts in the domain or in the forest). A security group cannot be converted to a distribution group. Security groups cannot be dynamic because they are used to configure security settings. Only administrators with the appropriate rights can add users to a security group; users cannot be added automatically.

IMPORTANT   **You can mail-enable only universal security groups**

The Exchange Management tools permit you to mail-enable only universal security groups. If you create a new mail-enabled security group, it is created as a universal security group.

Creating a Universal Distribution Group

A universal distribution group (sometimes known simply as a distribution group) is a group of recipients that you create to expedite the mass sending of e-mail messages and other information. For example, you could create a universal distribution group called Marketing if you wanted your users to be able to send a single e-mail that would then go to all members of the Marketing department (as opposed to sending a separate e-mail to each employee in Marketing).

Using Exchange Management Console to Create a Universal Distribution Group

You can create a universal distribution group by opening the Exchange Management Console, expanding Recipient Configuration in the console tree, and clicking Distribution Group. Then click New Distribution Group in the Actions pane to open the New Distribution Group Wizard, shown in Figure 3-15.

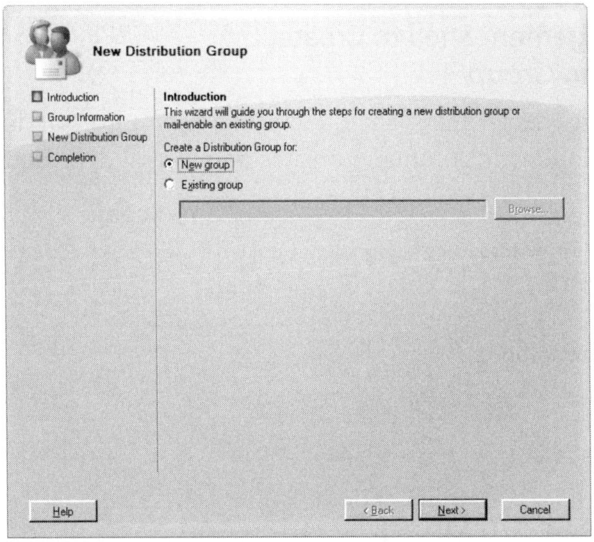

Figure 3-15   The New Distribution Group Wizard

Select New Group on the Introduction page and complete the following fields on the Group Information page:

- **Group Type**   Specify Distribution.

- **Organizational Unit**   By default, the New Distribution Group Wizard displays the Users container in the Active Directory directory service as the OU. If you want to change this, click Browse and then select an OU.

- **Name**   Specify the name of the group.

- **Name (pre-Windows 2000)**   This field is automatically populated based on the Name field.

- **Alias**   By default, the alias is the same as the group name. You can modify the alias if required.

On the New Distribution Group page, you can review the configuration summary. Click Back if you want to make any changes. Otherwise, click New to create the universal distribution group.

On the Completion page, the summary displays the Exchange Management Shell command that was used to create the distribution group. You can copy the page by pressing Ctrl+C and paste the information into a text editor. You can then copy the Exchange Management Shell command, paste it into a text file, and modify it to create additional universal distribution groups. Click Finish to close the wizard.

Using Exchange Management Shell to Create a Universal Distribution Group

You can also use Exchange Management Shell to create a new universal distribution group. For example, the following command creates a universal distribution group called Human Resources:

```
New-DistributionGroup -Name "Human Resources" -OrganizationalUnit Users -SAMAccountName "Human
Resources" -Type Distribution.
```

MORE INFO   New-DistributionGroup

For more information about the *New-DistributionGroup* cmdlet, access *http://technet.microsoft.com/en-us/library/aa998856.aspx*.

Creating a Dynamic Distribution Group

A dynamic distribution group does not have a fixed membership. It instead uses recipient filters and conditions to derive its membership at the time a message is sent. For example, a dynamic distribution group might specify a recipient filter, such as "users with external e-mail addresses," and a condition, such as "recipient works for Fabrikam, Inc." When someone sends a message to this dynamic distribution group, Exchange 2007 Server queries Active Directory for all recipients that match the filter and condition specified. For example, the query could return a list of all external recipients that work for a specified company, and Exchange would send the e-mail message to that list of recipients.

Using Exchange Management Console to Create a Dynamic Distribution Group

You can create a mail-enabled dynamic distribution group by opening the Exchange Management Console, expanding Recipient Configuration in the console tree, and clicking Distribution Group. Then select New Dynamic Distribution Group in the Actions pane to open the New Dynamic Distribution Group Wizard.

On the Introduction page, complete the Organizational Unit, Name, and Alias fields as described previously in this lesson for a universal distribution group. Then click Next to access the Filter Settings page.

On the Filter Settings page, you can click Browse and select the OU that contains the recipients that potentially can become group members, or you can accept the default. A dynamic distribution group can contain any recipients that are in the specified OU and any other OUs under it. You can then either select All Recipient Types or The Following Specific Type. If you choose the latter, you need to specify at least one recipient type. The recipient types are shown in Figure 3-18 in the practice session later in this lesson.

On the Conditions page, you can optionally define additional conditions to filter the recipients included in the dynamic distribution group. If, for example, you select Recipient Is In A Company, the wizard provides you with a hyperlink that lets you select one or more companies. This is a multistep procedure that you perform in the practice session later in this lesson. You can specify conditions such that only recipients that are in a specific state or province, who work in a specific department, who work for one or more specific companies, or who have specific values for custom attributes can become members of the dynamic distribution group.

When you have configured the filter settings you require, click Preview to view the recipients that will be contained in the dynamic distribution group. If you are satisfied that you have set up the conditions correctly, click Next to review the configuration summary. You can then click Back to amend the settings or New to create the dynamic distribution group.

The Completion page displays the Exchange Management Shell command that was used to create the dynamic distribution group. You can copy this page, paste it into a text editor, copy the Exchange Management Shell command, and amend it to create additional dynamic distribution groups or to specify a custom query for the dynamic distribution group. The filter and condition settings for dynamic distribution groups that have custom recipient filters can be managed only by using the Exchange Management Shell and are not available from within the Exchange Management Console GUI. Clicking Finish closes the wizard.

MORE INFO   Custom Queries

For more information about creating a dynamic distribution group with a custom query, search for "Use the Exchange Management Shell to create a new dynamic distribution group" in Exchange Server 2007 Help. For more information about recipient filters, search for "Creating Filters in Recipient Commands" in the help files or access *http://technet.microsoft.com/en-us/library/bb124268.aspx*.

Using Exchange Management Shell to Create New Dynamic Distribution Groups

You can also use Exchange Management Shell to create a new dynamic distribution group. The following command creates a dynamic distribution group called Contoso Consultants that contains mail-enabled users and contacts that have a Company attribute Contoso, Inc:

```
New-DynamicDistributionGroup -Name "Contoso Consultants" -IncludedRecipients "MailUsers,
MailContacts" -OrganizationalUnit Users -ConditionalCompany "Contoso, Inc"
-RecipientContainer Users
```

MORE INFO   New-DynamicDistributionGroup

For more information about the *New-DynamicDistributionGroup* cmdlet, access *http://technet. microsoft.com/en-us/library/bb125127.aspx*.

Disabling, Enabling, and Removing Distribution Groups

A newly created distribution group (universal or dynamic) is always mail-enabled. The function of such groups is to distribute e-mail messages to their members. However, you can choose to disable a universal distribution group if you do not want it to receive and distribute e-mail. Typically, you would disable a universal distribution group rather than remove it if you plan to enable it at a later date and do not want to re-create it from scratch. If, on the other hand, you do not intend to use the distribution group again, you can remove it.

Exam Tip   A dynamic distribution group is always mail-enabled. You can remove it, but you cannot disable it. It therefore follows that you cannot enable it because it is already enabled. Be wary of answers to examination questions that suggest disabling or enabling a dynamic distribution group.

Using Exchange Management Console to Mail-Enable Universal Distribution Groups

If a universal distribution group is not mail-enabled, you cannot send e-mail to the group, although you can still send e-mail to the group members individually. To mail-enable a universal distribution group, open Exchange Management Console, expand Recipient Configuration in the console tree, and click Distribution Group. Then click New Distribution Group in the Action pane to start the New Distribution Group Wizard.

On the Introduction page, click Existing Group, browse for the group you want to mail-enable, select it, click OK, and click Next. On the Group Information page, you can optionally change the Alias fields. By default, both the display name and the alias are the same as the group name. On the New Distribution Group page, click Back if you want to make any changes. Clicking New mail-enables the selected group. As with previously described Exchange Management Console procedures, the Completion page displays the Exchange Management Shell command that was used to mail-enable the distribution group. Click Finish to close the wizard.

Quick Check
- What type of group does not have a fixed membership?

Quick Check Answer
- A dynamic distribution group.

Using Exchange Management Console to Remove or Disable a Distribution Group

To remove a distribution group (universal or dynamic), start the Exchange Management Console as before, expand Recipient Configuration, and click Distribution Group. In the Result pane, select the distribution group that you want to remove, and in the Actions pane, under the name of the distribution group, click Remove. When you click Yes to clear the Warning dialog box, the group (but not the group members) is removed from Active Directory.

You can disable universal distribution groups, but you cannot disable dynamic distribution groups. Disabling stops e-mail from being sent to the group, although e-mail can still be sent to individual group members. The procedure for disabling a universal security group is the same as for removing it, except that you click Disable under the group name in the Actions pane. When you click Yes to clear the Warning dialog box, the group's mailbox is disabled.

Using Exchange Management Shell to Remove, Disable, or Enable a Distribution Group

You can also use Exchange Management Shell to remove, disable, or enable a universal distribution group and to remove a dynamic distribution group. However, if you are removing a distribution group, you require different cmdlets, depending on whether the group is a universal or a dynamic distribution group. For example, the command *Remove-DistributionGroup Sales* would remove a universal distribution group called Sales. The command *Remove-DynamicDistributionGroup "Contoso Consultants"* would remove a dynamic distribution group called Contoso Consultants.

The command *Disable-DistributionGroup Sales* would disable e-mail for the Sales universal distribution group. The command *Enable-DistributionGroup Sales* would enable the same group (assuming you had previously disabled it).

Modifying Distribution Group Properties

You can use either Exchange Management Console or Exchange Management Shell to configure the properties of a distribution group. For example, you can configure message size restrictions for both universal and dynamic distribution groups, or you can remove a member from or add a member to a universal distribution group. Note that you cannot remove members from or add members to a dynamic distribution group because membership is not fixed and a list of members is created whenever an e-mail message is sent to the group.

Using Exchange Management Console to Modify Distribution Group Properties

You can modify the properties of a distribution group by starting the Exchange Management Console, expanding Recipient Configuration, and clicking Distribution Group. In the Result pane, select the distribution group you want to modify, and in the Actions pane, click Properties under the group name. The Properties dialog box for a distribution group called Sales is shown in Figure 3-16. Don Hall's account has been added to the group.

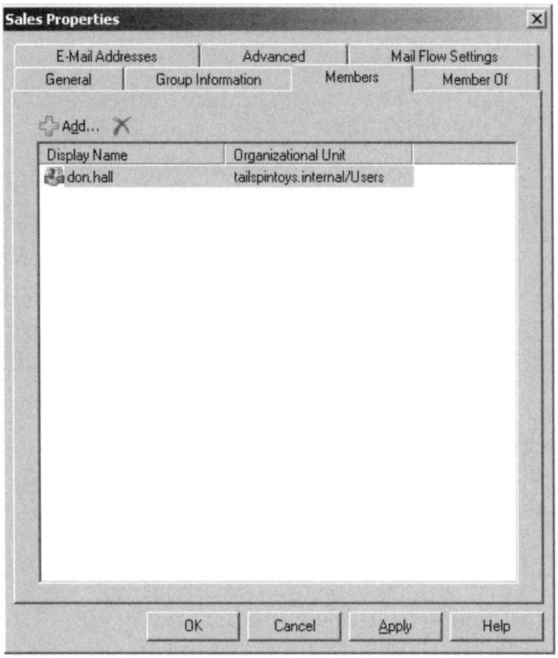

Figure 3-16   The Members tab of the Sales distribution group Properties dialog box

If you wanted, for example, to remove Don Hall from the Sales universal distribution group, you would select the Members tab, click don.hall, and then click the red cross. Clicking OK closes the Properties dialog box. You cannot delete members from a dynamic distribution group because group membership is derived dynamically from information held in Active Directory when an e-mail message is sent to the group.

Using Exchange Management Shell to Add Members to a Universal Distribution Group

Adding members to a distribution group is one of the tasks that you would normally do with a CLI rather than a GUI because it is repetitive and can be scripted. Chapter 5 discusses scripts in detail. For example, to add the user Don Hall to the universal distribution group Sales, use the command *Add-DistributionGroupMember Sales –Member "Don Hall"*.

Using Exchange Management Shell to List Group Members and to Remove a Member

To list the members of a universal distribution group, you would use the *Get-DistributionGroupMembers* cmdlet, for example, *Get-DistributionGroupMember Sales*.

To remove Don Hall from this distribution group, you would enter *Remove-Distribu-tionGroupMember Sales –Member "Don Hall"*.

Configuring Mail-Enabled Security Groups

Security groups are used to group users with similar functions and assign permissions to group members. Typically, a domain administrator, account operator, or local administrator creates a security group. Global and domain local security groups are scoped to the domain. Local security groups are scoped to the local PC, and universal security groups can contain members from, and be used to assign permissions to resources in, multiple domains in a forest.

MORE INFO   Security groups in Active Directory

For more information about managing Active Directory security groups, access *http://technet2.microsoft.com/WindowsServer/en/library/b3674c9b-fab9-4c1e-a8f6-7871264712711033.mspx?mfr=true* and follow the links.

As an Exchange organization administrator or Exchange recipient administrator, you can create and mail-enable universal security groups. However, you cannot add members to these groups or configure NTFS permissions granted to users through membership of these security groups unless you have the appropriate administrative rights to the domain or (in the case of a multiple-domain forest) to the forest.

Using Exchange Management Console to Create New Mail-Enabled Security Groups

To create a security group, open Exchange Management Console, expand Recipient Configuration, and click Distribution Group. Then click New Distribution Group in the Actions pane to open the New Distribution Group Wizard.

Real World

Ian McLean

It does appear counterintuitive that you use the New Distribution Group Wizard to create a security group or that you click Mail Contact in the console tree when creating or removing a mail-enabled user. However, when wizards in a GUI such as the Exchange Management Console use an identical route to get to a page where the actual action to be carried out is defined, it is more efficient to have a common routine to access that page than to have two different wizards. Unnecessary code leads to inefficiency, increased memory and disk usage, and the increased likelihood of coding errors.

Similarly, you use the Exchange Management Shell cmdlet *New-Distribution-Group* to create a new mail-enabled universal security group. The value in the Type parameter specifies whether the new group is a universal security group or a universal distribution group. This is done to minimize and optimize the code that implements the CLI.

Cynics will tell you that the occasional oddity in how a tool operates gives a Microsoft examiner some fine opportunities to ask tricky questions and makes answers more difficult to guess. Well, maybe it does, but this is not the purpose. Programmers are looking for efficiency and (you can believe me on this) have no interest in making life easy for examiners.

On the Introduction page of the New Distribution Group Wizard, specify New Group. On the Group Information page, specify the group type as Security, select an OU (or take the default), and type a group name. By default, the pre-Windows 2000 name and the alias are the same as the group name, although you can amend these if you want to.

As with previously described procedures, the New Distribution Group page displays the configuration summary, and you can click Back or New. The Completion page displays the Exchange Management Shell command. Click Finish to close the wizard.

Using Exchange Management Shell to Create New Mail-Enabled Security Groups

Creating a new mail-enabled universal security group by using Exchange Management Shell is very similar to creating a new universal distribution group, except that the Type parameter is set to Security. For example, the command *New-Distribution-Group -Name "Managers" -OrganizationalUnit Users -SAMAccountName Managers -Type Security* creates a security group called Managers.

Using Exchange Management Console to Enable, Modify, Disable, and Remove Security Groups

The procedures for mail-enabling a universal security group, modifying group properties, and disabling or removing the group are exactly the same as the procedures described earlier for a distribution group. The Select Group dialog box in the New

Distribution Group Wizard lists both security and distribution groups, and you select the appropriate group. You should take care when removing a security group because it might be used to assign permissions to resources in your organization.

Using Exchange Management Shell to Remove, Disable, or Enable Security Groups

The Exchange Management Shell commands that remove, disable, or enable a universal security group are exactly the same as the commands that implement the same operations on a universal distribution group. For example, the command *Disable-Distribution-Group Managers* would disable e-mail for the Managers universal security group. The command *Enable-DistributionGroup Managers* would enable the same group. The command *Remove-DistributionGroup Managers* would remove the security group.

You can use the Exchange Management Shell or the Exchange Management Console to add members to or remove members from a universal security group. However, an administrator with the appropriate rights in the domain and the forest would typically use Active Directory Users and Computers to perform this task. However, you can use the *Set-DistributionGroup* cmdlet to configure a security group's e-mail settings, for example, *Set-DistributionGroup MaxReceiveSize 1MB*.

Practice: Creating a Dynamic Distribution Group

In this practice session, you will specify that the mail-enabled user Sean P. Alexander is an employee of Contoso, Ltd. You then create a dynamic distribution group whose members have an external e-mail address and are employees of Contoso, Ltd. Before you can carry out the practices in this session, you need to have created a mail-enabled user account for Sean P. Alexander, as described in Practice 2 of the previous lesson.

▶ **Practice 1: Specifying That Sean P. Alexander Is an employee of Contoso, Ltd.**

In this practice, you will configure the properties of the mail-enabled user Sean P. Alexander to set his Company attribute to Contoso, Ltd. If you want to expand the practice, create additional mail-enabled users and configure the same Company attribute by using both Exchange Management Console and Exchange Management Shell. You can also create mail-enabled users with different Country attributes:

1. If necessary, log on to the domain controller by using the Kim_Akers account.

2. Open the Exchange Management Console.

3. Expand the Recipient Configuration node in the console tree and click Mail Contact.

4. In the Result pane, click sean p. alexander.

5. On the Actions pane under sean p. alexander, click Properties.

6. In the Properties dialog box, select the Organization tab.

7. Specify **Contoso, Ltd.** under Company, as shown in Figure 3-17, and click OK.

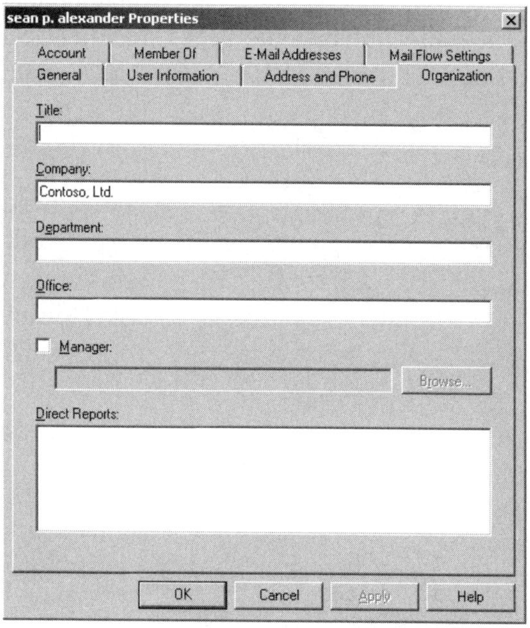

Figure 3-17 Specifying the Company attribute for Sean P. Alexander

▶ **Practice 2: Creating a Dynamic Distribution Group**

In this practice, you will create a dynamic distribution book whose members have external e-mail addresses and a Company attribute Contoso, Inc. You check that Sean P. Alexander is a member of this group. You need to complete Practice 1 before you attempt Practice 2. If you expanded the first practice as suggested, check that only the mail-enabled users with a Company attribute Contoso, Inc. are added to this group. If you want to expand this practice, you can use Exchange Management Shell to create additional dynamic distribution groups with different membership conditions:

1. If necessary, log on to the domain controller by using the Kim_Akers account.

2. Open the Exchange Management Console.

3. Expand the Recipient Configuration node in the console tree and click Distribution Group.

4. In the Actions pane, click New Dynamic Distribution Group.

5. In the Introduction page of the New Dynamic Distribution Group Wizard, specify Name as **Contoso Employees.** Check that the Alias is ContosoEmployees.

6. Click Next.

7. On the Filter Settings page, check that the recipient container is tailspintoys. internal/Users. Select The Following Specific Types and then select Users With External E-Mail Addresses, as shown in Figure 3-18.

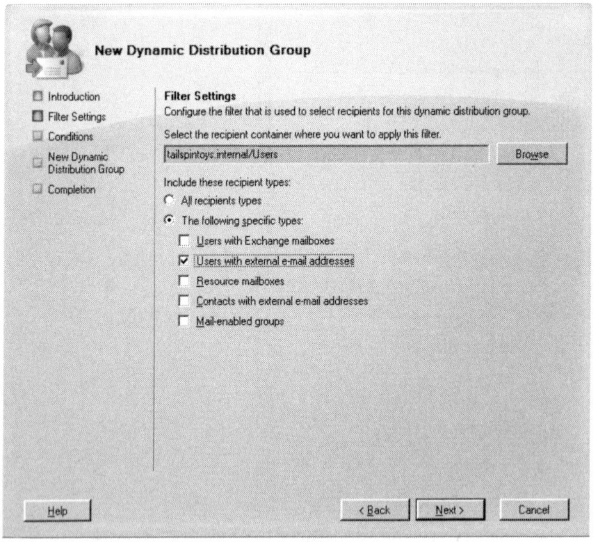

Figure 3-18   Specifying the filter settings

8. On the Conditions page in the Step 1 box, select Recipient Is In A Company. A hyperlink (specified) appears in the Step 2 box, as shown in Figure 3-19.

9. Click the hyperlink. In the Specify Company dialog box, type **Contoso, Ltd.** and then click Add. The dialog box should look similar to Figure 3-20.

10. Click OK to return to the New Distribution Group Wizard. Click Preview to check that sean p. alexander is a member of the dynamic distribution group, as shown in Figure 3-21. If this account does not appear, check that you have specified exactly the same information (Contoso, Ltd.), including punctuation, in both the New Distribution Group Wizard and the user's Properties dialog box.

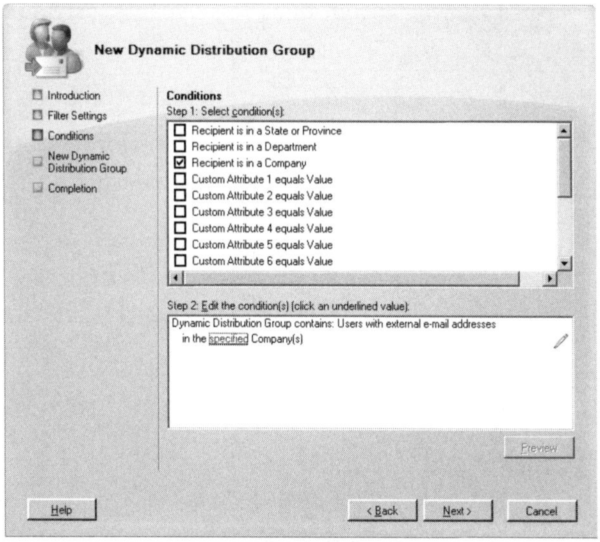

Figure 3-19   Specifying the Recipient Is In A Company condition

Figure 3-20   Specifying a company

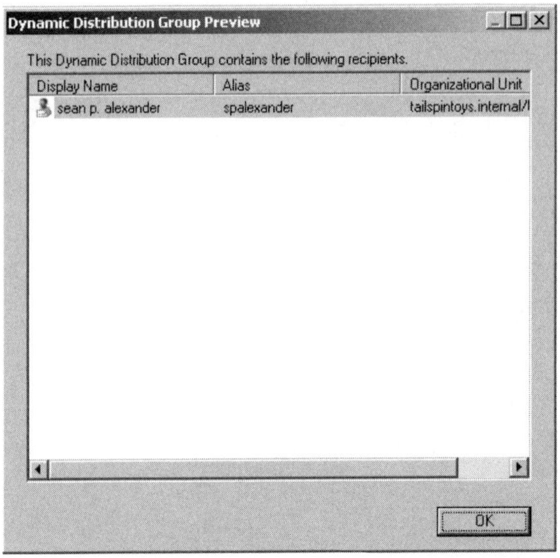

Figure 3-21   Dynamic distribution group membership

11. Click OK. Click Next. If you are happy with the information in the configuration summary, click New to create the dynamic distribution group.

12. Copy the page content and paste it into a text editor. Copy the Exchange Management Shell command and add it to a text file. If you want to extend this practice as suggested in the introduction, you can edit this command and use it to create additional groups by using Exchange Management Shell.

13. Click Finish to close the wizard.

Lesson Summary

- If you create a universal distribution group (sometimes known simply as a distribution group), then an e-mail message sent to the group will go to every group member.

- The membership of a dynamic distribution group is determined by filter settings and conditions. Group membership can change if the properties of group members alter or if new recipients are created that meet these filters and conditions. You cannot manually add members to or remove members from a dynamic distribution group. An e-mail message sent to the group will go to every current group member.

- The main function of a security group is to specify rights and permissions for group members. You can, however, mail-enable a universal security group or create a new mail-enabled universal security group. If you do so, an e-mail message sent to the group will go to every group member.

■ Distribution groups (universal or dynamic) cannot be used to grant rights and permissions.

Lesson Review

You can use the following questions to test your knowledge of the information in Lesson 2, "Configuring Mail-Enabled Groups." The questions are also available on the companion CD if you prefer to review them in electronic form.

NOTE Answers

Answers to these questions and explanations of why each answer choice is correct or incorrect are located in the "Answers" section at the end of the book.

---

1. You are an Exchange administrator at Contoso, Ltd. A group of consultants from Trey Research works closely with Contoso, and members of the group have mail-enabled accounts in Contoso's Active Directory domain. The group membership changes frequently, and you create and remove mail-enabled Trey Research users on a regular basis. You want to ensure that group e-mails sent to the Trey Research Consultants group go to all consultants who currently have mail-enabled accounts at Contoso. You also want to ensure that these e-mails are not sent to consultants who no longer have user accounts at Contoso because this results in nondelivery returns. How best can you achieve this?

    A. Create a mail-enabled universal security group

    B. Create a dynamic distribution group

    C. Create a universal distribution group

    D. Create a universal security group but disable its mailbox

2. You are an Exchange organization administrator at Trey Research. You have no administrative rights on the domain. Your boss has asked you to mail-enable the Sales universal security group so that a single e-mail sent to the group goes to all sales staff. Two new salespersons have recently joined the company, and your boss wants you to add them to the mail-enabled group. What do you tell her?

    A. You can mail-enable the group but cannot add the new members.

    B. As an Exchange organization administrator, you have control over all mail-enabled groups, and you can do as she asks.

     C. You cannot mail-enable a security group. Only a domain administrator can do that.

     D. Security groups cannot be mail-enabled. You need to create a universal distribution group.

3. Your company management has decided that e-mail should no longer be sent to a universal distribution group in your organization called Golfers. You know that a new chief executive officer will soon be joining the organization, and you also know he is a keen golfer. You suspect that it will not be long before you are asked to restore the group. What should you do?

     A. Do not remove or disable the group. Instead, remove all members from the group.

     B. Remove the group.

     C. Change the group type from universal distribution group to dynamic distribution group.

     D. Disable the group.

4. What does the following Exchange Management Shell command do?

```
New-DistributionGroup -Name "Manufacturing" -OrganizationalUnit Users -SAMAccountName
Manufacturing -Type Security
```

     A. Creates a mail-enabled local security group called Manufacturing

     B. Creates a mail-enabled universal security group called Manufacturing

     C. Creates a universal distribution group called Manufacturing

     D. Creates a dynamic distribution group called Manufacturing

Lesson 3: Configuring Resource Mailboxes

Resource mailboxes are mailboxes that represent conference rooms or shared equipment. Users can include these mailboxes in meeting requests. This provides a simple and efficient way to utilize resources in an organization.

When a user includes the resource mailbox as a required or optional attendee in a meeting request and if automatic booking is enabled, the mailbox automatically accepts or rejects the request, depending on whether the resource is available. If the meeting request is accepted, the resource is booked for the meeting. If automatic booking is not enabled, a user can still access the resource mailbox's calendar and book the resource manually.

NOTE   Auto Accept Agent

In Exchange Server 2003, you needed to download and install Microsoft Auto Accept Agent to enable users to include a resource mailbox as a required or optional attendee in a meeting request. This functionality is built into Exchange Server 2007, and Auto Accept Agent is no longer required.

A user can also look at the calendar for the resource and confirm that the resource is available and then include the resource mailbox as an attendee in a meeting request—automatic booking and the calendar function are not mutually exclusive. You can also set up custom resource properties for a resource mailbox so that a user can, for example, check whether a room has audiovisual facilities before including that room in a meeting request.

Microsoft Exchange Server 2007 provides two types of resource mailboxes: room and equipment. Room mailboxes are assigned to a meeting location, such as a conference room, auditorium, videoconferencing facility, or training room. Equipment mailboxes are assigned to a resource that is not location specific, such as a portable data projector, laptop computer, Webcam, or microphone headset.

> **After this lesson, you will be able to:**
> - Create, delete, and modify a resource mailbox.
>
> **Estimated lesson time: 30 minutes**

Creating Resource Mailboxes

You can create resource mailboxes by using Exchange Management Console or Exchange Management Shell. If you use the former method, the New Mailbox Wizard lets you create both room and equipment mailboxes.

NOTE Resource management

When you create a room or equipment mailbox in Exchange Server 2007, the mailbox does not need to be owned by a user (as was the case with previous versions of Exchange Server). There is a user account associated with a resource mailbox, but this is disabled automatically when the resource mailbox is created so that no one can log in as, for example, auditorium or data projector.

Using Exchange Management Console to Create Room Mailboxes

To create a room mailbox, start the Exchange Management Console, expand Recipient Configuration, and click Mailbox. Selecting New Mailbox in the Actions pane starts the New Mailbox Wizard.

On the wizard's Introduction page, select Room Mailbox. On the User Type page, select New User. On the Mailbox Information page, complete the Organizational Unit, First Name, Initials, Last Name, User Name, User Logon Name, User Logon Name (User Principal Name), User Logon Name (pre-Windows 2000), Password, and Confirm Password fields as appropriate. You are unlikely to select User Must Change Password At Next Logon because the user is a resource and never logs on.

On the Mailbox Settings page, specify the Alias, Sever, Storage Group, and Mailbox Database fields as appropriate. You can also choose to select the Managed Folder Mailbox Policy and the Exchange ActiveSync Mailbox Policy check boxes if you want to specify predefined policies. Complete the wizard as you did previously when creating a mailbox-enabled user. You will create a room mailbox in the practice session later in this lesson.

Using Exchange Management Console to Create Equipment Mailboxes

The procedure for creating an equipment mailbox is almost identical to that for creating a room mailbox (which, in turn, is almost identical to the procedure for creating a new mailbox-enabled user). The only procedural difference is the type of mailbox you select in the New Mailbox Wizard's Introduction page.

Using Exchange Management Shell to Create Resource Mailboxes

The Exchange Management Shell command to create a resource mailbox is almost identical to the command to create a new mailbox-enabled user, except that the -Room parameter is added for a room mailbox and the −Equipment parameter for an equipment mailbox. For example, the command *New-mailbox -UserPrincipalName MeetingRoom2@tailspintoys.internal -database "First Storage Group\Mailbox Database" -Name "Meeting Room 2" -OrganizationalUnit Users -DisplayName "Meeting Room 2" -ResetPasswordOnNextLogon $false −Room* creates a room mailbox called Meeting Room 1; the command *New-mailbox -UserPrincipalName Projector@tailspintoys.internal -database "First Storage Group\Mailbox Database" -Name Projector OrganizationalUnit Users -DisplayName Projector -ResetPasswordOnNextLogon $false −Equipment* creates an equipment mailbox called Projector.

Quick Check

- You want to create a mailbox that lets employees book one of your company's limited number of portable data projectors. What type of mailbox would you create?

Quick Check Answer

- An equipment mailbox.

Modifying Resource Mailboxes

You can use Exchange Management Console and Exchange Management Shell in combination to modify the properties of a resource mailbox. Exchange Management Console allows you to access the mailbox Properties dialog box. However, if a configuration change requires that you expand the resource schema or if you want to disable or enable automatic booking on a resource mailbox, you need to use Exchange Management Shell.

You can use Exchange Management Console to access a resource mailbox Properties dialog box in the same way as you access the Properties dialog box of a mailbox-enabled user. However, the Properties dialog box for a resource mailbox includes the Resource Information tab. On this tab, you can specify the Resource Capacity and add custom resource properties. You will do this in the practice session later in this lesson.

Custom resource properties help users select the most appropriate room or equipment by providing additional information about the resource. For example, you can create a custom property for room mailboxes called NetworkProjector. You can add this property to all rooms that have a network projector. This allows users to identify lecture or conference rooms that have network projectors available. However, before you do this, you need to expand the resource schema by using an Exchange Management Shell command. For example, to add a resource called NetworkProjector to the schema, you would use the following command:

```
Set-ResourceConfig -DomainController glasgow.tailspintoys.internal -ResourcePropertySchema
Room/NetworkProjector
```

NOTE   Room and equipment resources

Although a network projector is indisputably an item of equipment, it is treated as a room custom resource because it is used to identify the rooms that contain network projectors. You might use a different type of custom resource for equipment. For example, you could create a custom resource equipment property Wireless to identify wireless equipment by using the following Exchange Management Shell command: *Set-ResourceConfig -DomainController glasgow.tailspintoys.internal -ResourcePropertySchema Equipment/Wireless*.

MORE INFO   Configuring custom resource properties for a resource mailbox

For more information about configuring custom resource properties for a resource mailbox, access *http://technet.microsoft.com/en-us/library/bb201697.aspx*.

Enabling and Disabling Automatic Booking on a Resource Mailbox

Automatic booking enables users to book a resource automatically by including the resource mailbox as an attendee in a meeting request. If automatic booking is disabled, a user can still access the calendar for the resource and book the resource manually. You can use the Exchange Management Shell to enable automatic booking on a resource mailbox. For example, to enable automatic booking for a room mailbox called Auditorium, you would use the following command:

```
Set-MailboxCalendarSettings Auditorium -AutomateProcessing:AutoAccept
```

To disable automatic booking on the Auditorium resource mailbox, you would use the following Exchange Management Shell command:

```
Set-MailboxCalendarSettings Auditorium -AutomateProcessing:None
```

MORE INFO   Resource booking policies

Resource booking policies can be used to determine who can schedule a resource, when the resource can be scheduled, what meeting information is visible on the resource's calendar, and the response message that meeting organizers receive. For more information about resource booking policies, search for "How to Set Resource Booking Policies" in Exchange Server 2007 Help.

Setting Delegates on Resource Mailboxes

Users configured as delegates for resource mailboxes can control scheduling for the related resources. For example, if Don Hall is responsible for scheduling bookings for several meeting rooms at your company headquarters, you can configure each meeting room with a room mailbox and configure Don as a delegate for each of these room mailboxes. The following Exchange Management Shell command would configure Don Hall as a delegate for the room mailbox MeetingRoom2:

```
Set-MailboxCalendarSettings -Identity "MeetingRoom2" -ResourceDelegates "Don Hall"
```

MORE INFO   **Setting delegates**

For more information about setting delegates for resource mailboxes, search for "How to Set a Delegate on a Resource Mailbox" in Exchange Server Help or access *http://technet.microsoft.com/en-us/library/bb124973.aspx*.

IMPORTANT   **Do not set a delegate for a user mailbox**

Do not set a delegate on a user mailbox. This causes the user's mail to be forwarded to the assigned delegate and not to the user.

Removing and Disabling Resource Mailboxes

You remove or disable a resource mailbox in the same way that you remove or disable a mailbox-enabled user (in both Exchange Management Console and Exchange Management Shell). If you have disabled a resource mailbox and want to reenable it in exchange Management Console, you use the New Mailbox Wizard and select Existing User in the User Type page.

Practice: Creating and Configuring a Room Mailbox

In this practice session, you will create a room mailbox for a room called Auditorium. The room has a network projector, so you create a custom property called NetworkProjector and add it to the room mailbox properties.

▶ **Practice 1: Creating a Room Mailbox**

1. If necessary, log on to the domain controller by using the Kim_Akers account.

2. Open the Exchange Management Console.

3. Expand the Recipient Configuration node in the console tree and click Mailbox.

4. Click New Mailbox in the Actions pane. The New Mailbox Wizard starts.

5. On the Introduction page, select Room Mailbox and then click Next.

6. On the User Type page, select New User and then click Next.

7. Fill in the elements on the User Information page, as instructed in Table 3-6.

Table 3-6   User Information for the Auditorium Room Mailbox

Element	Instruction
Organizational Unit	Leave as default (tailspintoys.internal\Users)
First Name	Leave this blank
Initials	Leave this blank
Last Name	Leave this blank
Name	Auditorium
User Logon Name (User Principal Name)	Auditorium (@tailspintoys.internal should be specified by default)
User Logon Name (pre-Windows 2000)	Leave as default
Password	P@ssw0rd
Confirm Password	P@ssw0rd
User Must Change Password At Next Logon	Not selected

8. The User Information page should look similar to Figure 3-22. Click Next.

9. Fill in the elements of the Mailbox Settings page, as instructed in Table 3-7.

10. Click Next.

11. If you are happy with the configuration summary, click New.

12. As you did in previous practice sessions, copy the Exchange Management Shell command and paste it into a text file. If you want to expand the practice, you can modify this command and use it to create additional resource mailboxes. Click Finish to close the wizard.

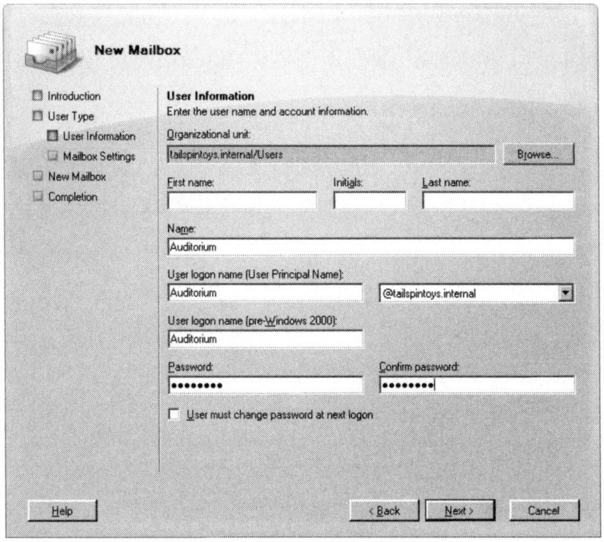

Figure 3-22   User Information page for the Auditorium room mailbox

Table 3-7   **Mailbox Settings for the Auditorium Room Mailbox**

Element	Instruction
Alias	Check that this is Auditorium
Server	Leave as default
Storage Group	Leave as default
Mailbox Database	Leave as default
Managed Folder Mailbox Policy	Do not configure
Exchange ActiveSync Mailbox Policy	Do not configure

▶ **Practice 2: Creating a Custom Property and Applying It to the Auditorium Room Mailbox**

1. If necessary, log on to the domain controller by using the Kim_Akers account.

2. Open Exchange Management Shell.

3. Enter the command: **Set-ResourceConfig -DomainController glasgow.tail-spintoys.internal -ResourcePropertySchema Room/NetworkProjector**

4. Open the Exchange Management Console.

5. Expand the Recipient Configuration node in the console tree and click Mailbox.

6. In the Result pane, click Auditorium.

7. In the Actions pane under Auditorium, click Properties.

8. In the Auditorium Properties dialog box, select the Resource Information tab.

9. There is only one Auditorium, so type 1 in the box under Resource Capacity.

10. Under Resource Custom Properties, click Add.

11. In the Select Resource Custom Property dialog box shown in Figure 3-23, ensure that NetworkProjector is selected, and Click OK.

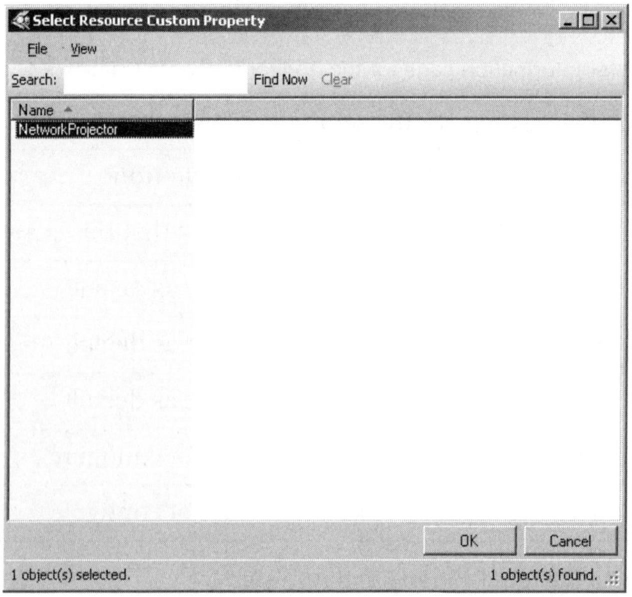

Figure 3-23   The Select Resource Custom Property dialog box

12. The Resource Information tab of the Auditorium Properties dialog box should look similar to Figure 3-24 Click OK.

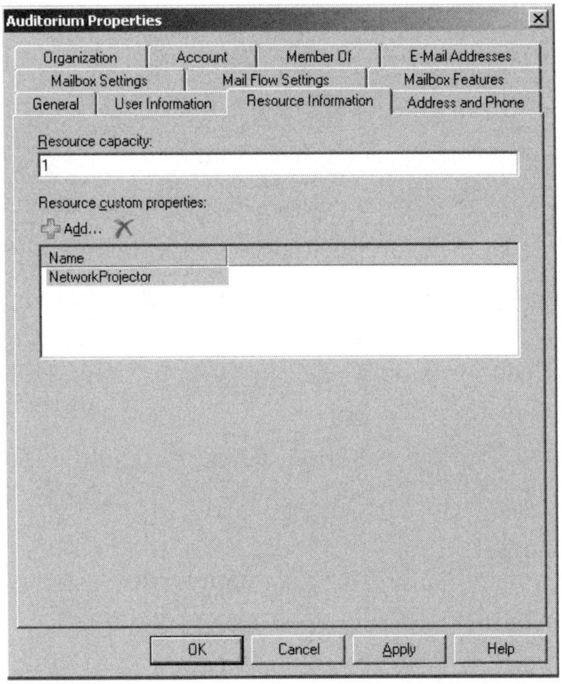

Figure 3-24   Adding the NetworkProjector resource custom property

Lesson Summary

■ You can create, remove, enable, and disable resource mailboxes that allow users to identify and reserve available rooms and equipment.

■ You can use Exchange Management Shell commands to enable and disable scheduling on a resource mailbox and to create custom properties.

Lesson Review

You can use the following questions to test your knowledge of the information in Lesson 3, "Configuring Resource Mailboxes." The questions are also available on the companion CD if you prefer to review them in electronic form.

NOTE   Answers

Answers to these questions and explanations of why each answer choice is correct or incorrect are located in the "Answers" section at the end of the book.

---

1. What does the following Exchange Management Shell command do?

   ```
   Set-MailboxCalendarSettings Auditorium -AutomateProcessing:None
   ```

   A. Enables scheduling of a resource mailbox called Auditorium

   B. Creates a custom property called Auditorium

   C. Disables scheduling of a resource mailbox called Auditorium

   D. Creates a custom property in the Auditorium room mailbox

2. You want your company's employees to be able to identify rooms that contain network projectors. Your company considers network projectors to be fixed resources, and they cannot be moved from room to room. How best can you achieve this aim?

   A. Create a room mailbox for each room. Create a custom resource called NetworkProjector and add it in each relevant room mailbox's Resource Information tab.

   B. Create an equipment mailbox for each network projector. Create a custom resource for each room and add the appropriate room custom resource in the Resource Information tab of each corresponding equipment mailbox.

   C. Create a dynamic distribution group called NetworkProjectors. Specify that network projector equipment resource mailboxes are members of this group.

   D. Create a mail-enabled security group called network projectors. Ask the domain administrator to add the users associated with every network projector equipment mailbox to that group.

Chapter Review

To further practice and reinforce the skills you learned in this chapter, you can perform the following tasks:

- Review the chapter summary.
- Review the list of key terms introduced in this chapter.
- Complete the case scenarios. These scenarios set up real-world situations involving the topics of this chapter and ask you to create a solution.
- Complete the suggested practices.
- Take a practice test.

Chapter Summary

- You can use Exchange Management Console or Exchange Management Shell to create, mail-enable, configure, disable, or delete mailbox-enabled users, mail-enabled users, mail contacts, universal distribution groups, dynamic distribution groups, mail-enabled universal security groups, room resource mailboxes, and equipment resource mailboxes.
- Mailbox-enabled users have mailboxes and user accounts in the domain. Mail-enabled users have user accounts but no mailboxes. Mail contacts do not have user accounts or mailboxes in the domain.
- Universal distribution groups have a fixed membership, and members need to be added and removed explicitly. Dynamic distribution groups do not have a fixed membership. Security groups can be used to grant permissions to group members. Universal security groups can be mail-enabled.
- You can use Exchange Management Shell to configure custom properties for resource mailboxes and to specify whether scheduling is enabled or disabled on a resource mailbox.

Key Terms

Do you know what these key terms mean? You can check your answers by looking up the terms in the glossary at the end of the book.

- Contact
- Custom attribute

- Dynamic distribution group
- Equipment mailbox
- Mailbox-enabled user
- Mail-enabled user
- Resource mailbox
- Room mailbox
- Security group
- Universal distribution group

Case Scenarios

In the following case scenarios, you will apply what you have learned about configuring recipients, groups, and mailboxes. You can find answers to these questions in the "Answers" section at the end of this book.

Case Scenario 1: Creating Recipients

You are an Exchange recipient administrator for Coho Winery. You create mailbox-enabled users, mail-enabled users, and contacts as appropriate. Answer the following questions:

1. Kim Abercrombie has recently joined the Human Resources Department. She has an account in Coho Winery's Active Directory and needs to be able to receive e-mail at k.abercrombie@cohowinery.com. What action do you take with regard to Kim's account?

2. Several Coho Winery employees send e-mails to Claus Hansen at Consolidated Messenger. His e-mail address is claus.hansen@consolidatedmessenger.com. Your colleagues find it tedious to type in this address every time. How can you make it easier to send e-mail to Claus?

3. Michelle Alexander works for Coho Vineyard but spends at least two days per week on the premises of Coho Winery. She needs access to some documents stored on Coho Winery's file server and as a result has had an account created for her in Active Directory. All mail, internal and external, sent to m.alexander@cohowinery.com should be redirected to Michelle's mailbox, michelle.alexander@cohovineyard.com. How do you make this happen?

Case Scenario 2: Creating Mail-Enabled Groups and Resource Mailboxes

You are a domain administrator at the Baldwin Museum of Science, and your responsibilities also include administering the museum's Exchange organization. Answer the following questions:

1. Only members of a universal security group called Researchers have access to files in a folder called Research Reports. The museum wants to set up a facility that enables members of the public to e-mail Research@baldwinmuseumof-science.com with queries related to the museum's research. How do you set this up?

2. A number of academics from the local university work in the museum on a project regularly. You have created user accounts for them in the museum's Active Directory and granted these accounts Read permission to a folder containing some of the museum's document files. However, the academics have external mailboxes at the university and do not have mailboxes at the museum. The membership of this group changes frequently. Sometimes, museum staff members need to send an e-mail to all academics currently on the project. What is the most efficient way in which you can provide this facility?

3. Only two rooms in the museum have audiovisual facilities. Members of staff need an efficient method of identifying these rooms and booking the facilities. Members of staff also sometimes need to book other rooms, for example, for meetings. How do you set up these facilities in an efficient manner?

Suggested Practices

To help you successfully master the exam objectives presented in this chapter, complete the following tasks.

Add and Configure Recipients

Do all the practices in this section.

■ **Practice 1: Use Exchange Management Shell**   In this chapter, all the practices that create recipients used Exchange Management Console. Use Exchange Management Shell to perform similar operations. You can either edit the Exchange

Management Shell commands that you pasted into a text file or create commands from scratch using the examples given in this chapter.

■ **Practice 2: Configure Recipient Properties**   Exchange Management Console lets you access the Properties dialog box for users and contacts. Experiment with configuring these properties. Find out which reconfigurations require you to have domain administrator privileges.

Create and Configure Groups and Resource Mailboxes

Do Practice 1 and Practice 2 in this section. Practice 3 is optional.

■ **Practice 1: Use Exchange Management Shell**   Use Exchange Management Shell commands to create additional distribution and security groups.

■ **Practice 2: Create Resource Mailboxes**   Create and configure room and equipment mailboxes. Become familiar with the Exchange Management Shell commands that enable and disable resource mailbox scheduling and create custom attributes.

■ **Practice 3: (optional) Log in at a Client, Send E-Mail to Users and Groups, and Set Up a Meeting**   You can carry out this practice if you join a PC running an Exchange client (for example, Microsoft Outlook 2007) to the domain or if you create a virtual machine, install a client operating system, install Outlook, and join the machine to the domain. Log on to the domain at the client PC as a mailbox-enabled user you have created (for example, don.hall) and send e-mail to other users or groups. Check that other mailbox-enabled users you have created and added to distribution groups get these messages. Set up a meeting and include the Auditorium room mailbox as an attendee. Check that mailbox's calendar and confirm that you have booked it for the meeting (if not, enable automatic booking and try again). Log on to the domain as another mailbox-enabled user and try to book the same resource for the same time. Check that you are told the resource has already been booked.

Take a Practice Test

The practice tests on this book's companion CD offer many options. For example, you can test yourself on just one exam objective, or you can test yourself on all the 70-236 certification exam content. You can set up the test so that it closely simulates the experience of taking a certification exam, or you can set it up in study mode so that you can look at the correct answers and explanations after you answer each question.

MORE INFO   **Practice tests**

For details about all the practice test options available, see the "How to Use the Practice Tests" section in this book's Introduction.

Chapter 4
Configuring Public Folders

A public folder is a place where the public folder owner can post information and store documents and where everyone in the organization (or users selected by the public folder owner) can read the folder contents and, if they have the appropriate permissions, post replies to them. As an administrator, you might also need to create public folders and public folder hierarchies where your organization can store company information. This chapter looks at how you create, modify, and delete public folders.

NOTE Mailbox server role

The Mailbox server role needs to be installed on your Exchange Server 2007 server if you want to install a public folder database. If you want more than one public folder database, you need more than one mailbox server.

Exam objectives in this chapter:
- Configure public folders.

Lessons in this chapter:

Before You Begin

To complete the lesson in this chapter, you must have done the following:

- Installed Windows Exchange Server 2007 with the Mailbox, Client Access, Hub Transport, and Unified Messaging roles on a Windows domain controller in the Tailspintoys.internal domain. To do this, you need to have completed all the practices in Lessons 1 and 2 of Chapter 1, "Preparing for Exchange Installation," and Lesson 1 of Chapter 2, "Installing Exchange Server and Configuring Roles."

Real World

Ian McLean

I have always been rather fond of public folders.

They provide an apparently simple and easily understood method of storing information that others can access. If you want to find out more about your conditions of employment, you access your organization's Human Resources public folder. Even relatively unsophisticated users can create and post information to personal public folders and share that information with colleagues. We dinosaurs are comfortable with public folders.

Of course, much more sophisticated methods of collaboration now exist. Public folders do not support versioning and other collaboration facilities. Collaboration underpins the entire Microsoft Office 2007 suite. Tools such as SharePoint Designer, SharePoint Server, and Groove 2007 provide a rich collaboration environment. Really Simple Syndication feeds are replacing traditional newsgroups, and we all have our own blogs.

Nevertheless, it came as a bit of a shock when I installed my first beta version of Exchange Server 2007 and found that I could not create public folders because no public folder database to put them in existed. A public folder database (or public folder store) has been a default Exchange feature since I first started looking at Exchange way back in the last millennium. I was relieved to find it was an easy matter to create and mount such a database. It seems that the concept of public folders had not been abandoned after all.

Maybe public folders will not in the future be used for as many purposes as they have been in the past, but they are alive and well and feature heavily in the objectives of the 70-236 examination. Unlike the dinosaurs, they are not an endangered species.

MORE INFO   **Collaboration tools in Microsoft Office 2007**

For more information about the collaboration tools provided by the Microsoft Office 2007 suite, access *http://office.microsoft.com/en-gb/products/FX100487641033.aspx.*

Lesson 1: Configuring Public Folders

You and the users you support can use public folders for shared communication, including shared e-mail messages, discussions through message posts, contact lists, group calendars, and archiving distribution list posts. You can also use public folders for shared content management. They can be used to store content such as document files and for sharing content, provided you do not require versioning and provisioning. Public folders can provide a repository if you require offline or replicated information storage. You can also configure public folders to enable multiple users to access and add information to threaded discussions, although SharePoint Server is possibly becoming the preferred tool for this purpose.

You should, however, try to discourage users from archiving personal data in public folders. Personal folder (.pst) files were designed for this purpose, and using public folders has resource implications for public folder servers and undermines the goal of mailbox limits. Bear in mind that public folders are not designed for document sharing and collaboration. They do not provide versioning or other document management features, such as automatic content change notifications that are provided by products such as Microsoft Groove 2007.

MORE INFO   **Best practices for public folders**

For an excellent series of articles about public folder best practices, access *http:// www.microsoft.com/technet/prodtechnol/exchange/2003/pubfoldersbp.mspx* and click the Best Practices For Microsoft Exchange Server Public Folders download link. These articles were written before Exchange Server 2007 and Microsoft Outlook 2007 were released, but they are not particularly technology specific and contain a lot of good advice.

> **After this lesson, you will be able to:**
> - Create, modify, and delete public folders.
>
> **Estimated lesson time: 50 minutes**

Using Public Folders

Public folders implement shared access and provide an easy, effective way for users to collect, organize, and share information with other people in their organization. Public folders can be used to share files. They can store data, such as calendars and contacts, that is shared by two or more people. Public folders are organized in public folder hierarchies and stored in dedicated public folder databases (databases that can store only public folders). They can be replicated between Exchange servers.

Public Folders May Not Be Necessary in Exchange Server 2007

Unlike in previous versions of Exchange, public folders can be an optional feature in Exchange Server 2007. Provided that all client computers in your organization are running Microsoft Office Outlook 2007, Exchange no longer depends on public folders for features such as offline address book (OAB) and free/busy information downloads. In Exchange 2007, these features are serviced by the Autodiscover and Availability services; the System Attendant service, which communicates with Active Directory to retrieve and cache directory information; and the Exchange File Distribution service, which distributes files to Client Access servers and Unified Messaging servers.

When you install the Mailbox server role on the first Exchange Server 2007 server in a pure Exchange 2007 organization (that is, an organization where all Exchange servers run Exchange Server 2007), the setup procedure asks you whether you have any client computers in your organization running Outlook 2003 and earlier or Microsoft Entourage. If the answer is yes, a public folder database is created. If the answer is no, a public folder database (previously called the public folder store) is not created. In the latter case, if you decide to use public folders, which provide a convenient method of sharing information that your users are accustomed to using, you need to create and mount a public folder database.

If client computers in your organization run Outlook 2003 and earlier or Microsoft Entourage, they require a public folder database to connect to Exchange Server 2007. In a mixed Exchange organization, to ensure backward compatibility to pre–Exchange 2007 versions, a public folder database is created by default. This public folder database will support earlier Schedule+ free/busy functionality.

Exchange 2007 is the first version of Exchange that provides the option to not use public folders. However, until all client computers in your organization are running Outlook 2007, you should continue using public folders. This is why the Exchange 2007 Server Setup Wizard asks you whether Outlook 2003 or Entourage clients exist in your organization.

MORE INFO The Autodiscover service

The Autodiscover service must be deployed and configured correctly for Outlook 2007 clients to automatically connect to Microsoft Exchange features, such as the OAB, the Availability service, and Unified Messaging. For more information about the Autodiscover service, access *http://technet. microsoft.com/en-us/library/b03c0f21-cbc2-4be8-ad03-73a7dac16ffc.aspx*.

MORE INFO The Availability service

The Availability service is a Web service that is deployed on the Client Access server role. Outlook 2007 clients discover the Availability service via the Autodiscover service. The Outlook 2007 and Outlook Web Access Scheduling Assistants use the Availability service to retrieve live and published free/busy information, view attendee working hours, and show meeting time suggestions. For more information about the Availability service, access *http://technet.microsoft.com/en-us/library/ bb232134.aspx* and *http://msexchangeteam.com/archive/2006/10/23/429296.aspx*.

NOTE Other mail clients

The Exchange 2007 Server Setup Wizard asks only about Microsoft clients (Outlook and Entourage). It does not ask about third-party clients, such as Thunderbird or Eudora, or about the Windows mail client in Vista. If you specify that no Outlook clients previous to Outlook 2007 exist and that no Entourage clients exist, a public folder database will not be created.

Accessing Public Folders with Outlook Web Access (OWA)

Although users cannot directly access public folders by using OWA in the same way that they use the tool to access e-mail messages, OWA supports public folder access by using the virtual directory /public. In order to allow this functionality, the Exchange Server 2007 organization must meet the following requirements:

- The home public folder server for the mailbox database must be a server that is running Microsoft Exchange Server 2003 or Microsoft Exchange 2000 Server. You can set the home public server by using the *Set-MailboxDatabase* cmdlet and the publicfolderdatabase parameter.

- You must use a dedicated server for the Client Access server role. If the server that hosts the Client Access server role also hosts the Mailbox server role, public folder access may not be reliable through that server when users are accessing OWA through the Internet.

Public folders do not appear in the default OWA user interface. To reach public folders through an Exchange Server 2007 server that has the Client Access server role installed, you use the /public virtual directory. For example, if you log on to OWA by using the URL *http://tailspintoys.com/owa*, you would reach your organization's public folders through the URL *http://tailspintoys.com/public*.

By default, the /public virtual directory is not configured to use Secure Sockets Layer (SSL). If you want the /public virtual directory to require SSL, you must obtain the relevant certificate and configure the directory to do this. If SSL is used, the URL in the previous example would become *https://tailspintoys.com/public*.

MORE INFO   Using OWA to access public folders

For more information about using OWA to access public folders, search for "How to Allow Users to Access Public Folders from Outlook Web Access" in Exchange Server 2007 Help or access *http:// technet.microsoft.com/en-us/library/bb430795.aspx*.

NOTE   OWA and Exchange Server 2007

Because the home public folder server for the mailbox database must be a server that is running Microsoft Exchange Server 2003 or Microsoft Exchange 2000 Server, you cannot currently access public folders by using OWA in a pure Exchange Server 2007 organization, Currently, the beta version of Exchange Server 2007 Service Pack 1, issued for evaluation purposes, implements this functionality, but it is at present unsupported in a production environment. This situation might have changed by the time you read this book.

Public Folder Hierarchy

Unlike Exchange Server 2003, which also supported General Purpose public folder hierarchy, Exchange Server 2007 supports only the default Messaging Application Programming Interface (MAPI) Top Level Hierarchy (TLH). The MAPI TLH is divided into the public folders and system folders subtrees. You cannot create General Purpose public folders in Exchange Server 2007.

MORE INFO   General Purpose public folders

If you want to find out more about General Purpose public folders that were used in previous versions of Exchange, you can access *http://www.msexchange.org/tutorials/General-Purpose-Public-Folder-Trees-Exchange2003.html*. However, it is unlikely that General Purpose public folders will be tested in the 70-236 examination.

Public Folder Subtree

The public folder subtree contains public folders that users can access directly by using client applications such as Outlook. The public folder subtree is also known as the Interpersonal Message (IPM) Subtree. You should be careful when designing a public folder hierarchy, as public folders inherit settings from parent folders, and a complex hierarchical structure can be difficult to understand and administer.

In general, a deep hierarchy—where you have children of top-level folders each with its own children and with children of the children—is better than a wide hierarchy where a large number of high-level folders and few child folders are created. This has advantages for both replication and assigning permissions. Chapter 8, "Policies and Public Folders," discusses public folder permissions and replication. Figures 4-1 and 4-2 show examples of wide and deep public folder hierarchies.

Figure 4-1   Wide public folder hierarchy

System Folder Subtree

The system folder subtree contains folders that users cannot access directly by using conventional methods. The information in these folders is accessed by applications and is accessible only if users open the appropriate application. Client applications such as Outlook use these folders to store information such as free/busy data, OABs, and organizational forms. Other system folders contain configuration information that is used by custom applications or by Exchange itself. The system folder subtree is also known as the Non_IPM_Subtree. Examples of system folders include the following:

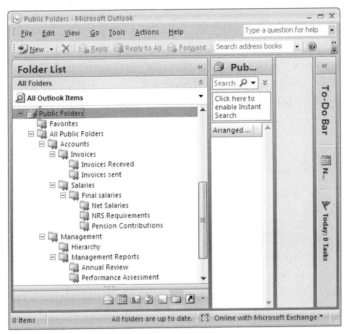

Figure 4-2 Deep public folder hierarchy

- **EForms Registry and Events Root folders** By default, one content replica of each of these folders resides in the default public folder database on the first Exchange 2007 server that is installed in the first administrative group. This is the location where organizational forms are stored for earlier Outlook clients (pre–Outlook 2007).

- **Site folders** In most respects, these folders function in the same manner as other public folders except that the OAB folder and the free/busy folder automatically contain a subfolder for each administrative group (or site) in an Exchange organization's topology. By default, a content replica of a specific administrative group folder resides on the first server that is installed in the administrative group. These folders are used to store free/busy information and OAB data for earlier (pre–Outlook 2007) Outlook clients. Such clients do not understand the new features in Exchange 2007 that manage free/busy information and OAB data.

- **OWAScratchPad folders**   Each public folder database has an OWAScratchPad folder, which is used to temporarily store attachments that are being accessed by using OWA. Do not modify this folder. OWA running on Exchange 2007 Client Access servers does not use these folders to store attachment data, and you cannot access Exchange 2007 public folders by using OWA. Nevertheless, this folder is created during a pure installation of Exchange 2007.

- **StoreEvents folders**   Each public folder database has a StoreEvents folder that holds registration information for custom Exchange store events. Do not modify these folders.

- **Other folders**   To support internal Exchange store operations, a tree may contain several other system folders. Do not modify these folders.

Figure 4-3 shows a list of system folders in the Non_IPM_Subtree.

Figure 4-3   System folders

NOTE   The Documents and Settings\Administrator folder

Even when the name of the Administrator account has been changed in line with good security practice, Exchange Management Shell uses the Documents and Settings\Administrator folder. This is a system folder, and its name does not change when you rename the Administrator account in Active Directory. If, however, you create a new account with administrative privileges and log in by using this account, the Exchange Management Shell prompt will then change, for example, to Documents and Settings\Kim_Akers. This makes no difference to the procedures and practices described in this and other chapters.

Mail-Enabled Public Folders

A mail-enabled folder is a public folder that has an e-mail address. Depending on how the folder is configured, it may appear in the global address list. Each mail-enabled folder has an object in Active Directory that stores its e-mail address, address list name, and other mail-related attributes. E-mail sent to a mail-enabled public folder is directed to the public folder database instead of to a mailbox in the mailbox database.

If you mail-enable a public folder, users can send e-mail messages to and, if the folder is configured appropriately, receive e-mail messages from it in addition to being able to post messages to the folder. If you are developing custom applications, you can use this feature to move messages or documents into or out of public folders.

Why Use Public Folders?

Public folders are typically used by an organization to store information that is frequently accessed by a large number of readers but seldom changes, although this is not invariably the case. The Human Resources Department might, for example, store conditions of service documents or blank absence request forms in a public folder. Documentation on how to use a business application could be stored in a Technical Support public folder.

It is true that such information can be stored on shared folders within an organization, with the Distributed File System (DFS) configured so that users do not need to know what server the folder is stored on. Like public folder replicas, DFS replicas can be configured so that information is available even if a server goes offline. (Public folder replication is discussed in Chapter 8.)

However, users are often more comfortable using Microsoft Outlook, which they use all the time for reading and sending e-mail, than they are with My Network Places or with typing Universal Naming Convention paths into the Run box. In addition, My Network Places is often disabled in enterprise environments.

When it comes to creating personal public folders through Outlook, the procedure (if permitted) could not be simpler. The user does not need to know where the public folder is created and by default can post to it while other users can read the posts. Users are typically less comfortable sharing folders and configuring permissions.

Public folders allow users to post messages and to post messages with attachments. Users can send e-mail to public folders that can be forwarded to the public folder owner. E-mail–enabled public folders can acknowledge such messages.

Public folders are in general more easily accessed remotely than are shared folders. In particular, if your Exchange organization is such that public folders can be accessed through OWA, remote access is very easy indeed. The facility to access public folders remotely through OWA is a persuasive argument for their use.

Public folders are possibly not the best mechanism for collaboration. Tools such as SharePoint Client, SharePoint Server, Microsoft Groove, and Web-based Distributed Authoring and Versioning offer a rich collaborative environment. However, when it comes to a simple, easily understood, and familiar method of distributing information, public folders have a great deal to offer.

Using the Exchange Management Shell to Manage Public Folders

The Exchange Management Shell is the primary tool in Microsoft Exchange Server 2007 for managing public folders (although you can also perform a limited number of public folder database management tasks by using Exchange Management Console). Chapter 3, "Configuring Recipients, Groups, and Mailboxes," introduced this tool and encouraged you to use Exchange Management Shell commands to create recipients, groups, and resource mailboxes. This chapter, however, requires extensive use of Exchange Management Shell commands, so we need to look at the tool in more detail.

NOTE Roles and permissions

To create and configure public folders by using Exchange Management Shell commands, you need to be a domain administrator or be added to the Exchange Organization Administrator role. A user that has been added to the Exchange View-Only Administrator role can obtain information about public folders or public folder servers but cannot use any of the configuration commands.

Using Cmdlets

Cmdlets are verb–noun combinations (For example, *Get-PublicFolder*) that define what Exchange Management Shell commands do. An Exchange Management Shell command typically consists of a cmdlet followed by parameters and parameter values. You can use the following cmdlets to perform common public folder management tasks:

- **New-PublicFolder**   Creates a new public folder with a specified name, for example, *New-PublicFolder -Name Accounts*. Before you can create a public folder on an Exchange Server 2007 server, the server needs to have a public folder database. In a pure Exchange Server 2007 installation in which you have specified during the install process that no Outlook 2003 or Microsoft Entourage clients exist, no public folder database is created by default. Creating a public folder database is one of the tasks for which you can use Exchange Management Console. You create a public folder database and public folders in the practice session later in this lesson.

- **Remove-PublicFolder**   Removes a specified public folder, for example, *Remove-PublicFolder −Identity \ Accounts*.

- **Set-PublicFolder**   Sets public folder attributes, for example, *Set-PublicFolder − Identity \ Accounts -ReplicationSchedule "Saturday.3:00 AM-Monday.3:00 AM"*.

NOTE   **The Identity parameter**

You can omit the Identity parameter in Exchange Management Shell commands. For example, "-Identity \Accounts" would become "\Accounts." Also note that the public folder Identity parameter must always contain the hierarchy that identifies the public folder. In this example, Accounts is a top-level folder under the root public folder (\) and is identified as \Accounts. If the Salaries public folder were a subfolder (or child) of Accounts, its Identity parameter would be \Accounts\Salaries.

- **Update-PublicFolder**   Starts public folder content synchronization, for example, *Update-PublicFolder \Accounts -Server Glasgow*.

NOTE   **Spaces in parameter values**

If a parameter value contains one or more spaces, you need to put quotation marks around it, for example, *Update-PublicFolder \ Accounts -Server "Server A."*

- **Get-PublicFolder**   Lists a public folder or a set of public folders and shows the parent path. For example, *Get-PublicFolder -Identity \ Accounts −Recurse* lists the top-level public folder Accounts and the public hierarchy underneath that public folder. Commands that use the *Get-PublicFolder* cmdlet can include either the Recurse or the GetChildren parameter but not both. Recurse and GetChildren are parameters of the type System.Management.Automation.SwitchParameter and return information about public folder hierarchies. The Recurse parameter specifies that the command must return the specified public folder and all its children. The GetChildren parameter returns only the children of the folder specified by the Identity parameter. If you use the command with neither the Recurse nor the GetChildren parameter, it lists only the public folder specified and its path. Figure 4-4 shows the output from the command *Get-PublicFolder \Management -Recurse*. You create the Management Public folder and its child Management Reports in the practice session later in this lesson.

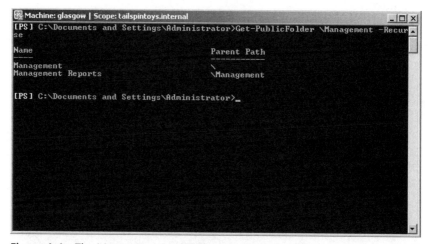

Figure 4-4   The Management public folder and its hierarchy

- **Get-PublicFolderStatistics**   Returns statistical information about public folder servers or public folders, such as last log-on time and folder size, for example, *Get-PublicFolderStatistics -Server Glasgow*. Figure 4-5 shows the public folder statistics for the Exchange Server 2007 server Glasgow. The public folders have just been created and as yet have no content.

NOTE   **Mail-related public folder information**

You can use the *Get-PublicFolder* and *Set-PublicFolder* cmdlets to get and set public folder information that is not mail related to e-mail. If, however, you want to get or set mail-related information, you need to use the *Get-MailPublicFolder* and *Set-MailPublicFolder* cmdlets, described in the next section of this lesson.

Using Cmdlets to Configure Mail-Enabled Public Folders

You can mail-enable a public folder and give it an e-mail address. This enables users to send e-mail messages to and sometimes to receive e-mail messages from the public folder in addition to being able to post messages. A message posted in a public folder appears in the folder, and any user who can view the folder can read the message. An e-mail message posted to a public folder can be forwarded to the folder owner. Anyone who knows a public folder's e-mail address can (unless specifically blocked) send an e-mail message to the public folder, while only users with appropriate permissions can post to it. A mail-enabled folder has an object in the Active Directory directory service that stores its e-mail address, address book name, and other mail-related attributes.

```
Machine: glasgow | Scope: tailspintoys.internal                          _ | □ | X |
[PS] C:\Documents and Settings\Administrator>Get-PublicFolderStatistics -Server
Glasgow

Name                                         ItemCount            LastAccessTime
----                                         ---------            --------------
Default                                      0                    4/23/2007 8:01:23 PM
EX:/o=Tailspintoys/ou=Exchange Administr     0                    4/24/2007 6:27:26 PM
ative Group (FYDIBOHF23SPDLT)
EX:/o=Tailspintoys/ou=Exchange Administr     0                    4/23/2007 8:01:23 PM
ative Group (FYDIBOHF23SPDLT)
exchangeV1                                   401                  4/23/2007 8:01:23 PM
globalevents                                 0                    4/23/2007 8:01:23 PM
internal                                     0                    4/23/2007 8:01:23 PM
Management Reports                           0                    4/24/2007 7:08:05 PM
Management                                   0                    4/24/2007 7:08:05 PM
microsoft                                    0                    4/23/2007 8:01:23 PM
OWAScratchPad{90C42429-357F-4C68-B68B-52     0                    4/23/2007 8:01:23 PM
218CA05C83}
schema-root                                  0                    4/23/2007 8:01:23 PM
StoreEvents{90C42429-357F-4C68-B68B-5221     0                    4/23/2007 8:01:23 PM
8CA05C83}
/o=Tailspintoys/cn=addrlists/cn=oabs/cn=     0                    4/23/2007 8:01:23 PM
Default Offline Address Book

[PS] C:\Documents and Settings\Administrator>_
```

Figure 4-5   Statistics for the Glasgow server

Exchange Management Shell provides a set of cmdlets that you use specifically to mail-enable public folders and to perform operations on mail-enabled public folders. You need to create a public folder before you can mail-enable it.

Exam Tip   Because you can create, for example, a mailbox-enabled user or a mail-enabled universal distribution group with a single operation, it is easy to forget that you need to create a public folder and then to mail-enable it. Beware of answers to examination questions that specify that a single command creates and mail-enables a public folder.

You can enable, disable, and configure mail-enabled public folders and obtain information about them by using the following cmdlets:

■ **Enable-MailPublicFolder**   Mail-enables an existing public folder, for example, *Enable-MailPublicFolder \ Accounts*. You mail-enable a public folder in the practice session later in this lesson.

- **Disable-MailPublicFolder** Mail-disables a public folder, for example, *Disable-MailPublicFolder \ Accounts*. The public folder is not removed, but users can no longer send e-mail to it. You disable a public folder in the practice session later in this lesson.

- **Set-MailPublicFolder** Configures the mail-related settings of mail-enabled public folders, for example, *Set-MailPublicFolder \ Accounts -PrimarySmtpAddress AccountInfo@tailspintoys.internal −MaxReceiveSize 1000*. Figure 4-6 shows this command being used to configure a mail-enabled public folder called Accounts.

Figure 4-6   Configuring a mail-enabled public folder

NOTE Configuring a primary e-mail address

By default, the primary e-mail address for a public folder is set through e-mail address policy. If you want to use the PrimarySmtpAddress parameter to change this, you must first set the EmailAddressPolicyEnabled parameter to False, for example, *Set-MailPublicFolder \Accounts −EmailAddressPolicyEnabled $False*.

- **Get-MailPublicFolder** Returns mail-related information about mail-enabled public folders, for example, *Get-MailPublicFolder \Accounts*. Used without an Identity parameter, the cmdlet returns information about all public folders.

- **Get-MailboxFolderStatistics** Returns statistical information about the mail-enabled public folders in a specified mailbox, such as the number and size of items in the folder and the folder name, for example, *Get-MailboxFolderStatistics -Identity tailspintoys\Kim_Akers*. Figure 4-7 shows some of the output from this command.

Figure 4-7   Statistical information about public folders in the Kim_Akers mailbox

---

Quick Check

- You want to get information about the top-level public folder Human Resources and all public folders in its hierarchy. What command do you use?

Quick Check Answer

- *Get-PublicFolder "\Human Resources" –Recurse (or Get-PublicFolder –Identity "\Human Resources" –Recurse).*

Using Cmdlets to Configure Public Folder Databases

You can use Exchange Management Shell to create, configure, remove, and get information about public folder databases. Creating a public folder database is one of the few operations that you can also carry out by using Exchange Management Console. You do this in the practice session later in this lesson.

NOTE   Using Exchange Management Console

You can perform public folder database management tasks in Exchange Management Console. Database management tasks, such as creating or removing a database, are the only public folder tasks that can be performed in Exchange Management Console. All other public folder management tasks are performed in Exchange Management Shell.

You need to be a domain administrator or a local administrator on the Exchange Server 2003 server or be added to at least the Exchange Server Administrator role to create configure or remove public folder databases. You can view public folder database settings if you are added to the Exchange View-Only Administrator role. The following cmdlets perform public folder database tasks:

- **New-PublicFolderDatabase**   Creates a public folder database in a specified storage group, for example, *New-PublicFolderDatabase -Name "First Glasgow Database" -StorageGroup "First Storage Group"*. Note that an Exchange Server 2007 mailbox server can contain only one public folder database.

MORE INFO   Storage groups and databases

For more information about Exchange storage groups and databases, search for "Managing Storage Groups and Databases" in Exchange Server 2007 Help or access *http:// technet.microsoft.com/en-us/library/aa998926.aspx*.

- **Mount-Database**   Mounts a database, for example, *Mount-Database "First Glasgow Database"*. You need to mount a public folder database after you have created it. You can also cause a public database to mount at start-up by using the *Set-PublicFolderDatabase* cmdlet (described next).

- **Set-PublicFolderDatabase**   Sets the attributes of a public folder database, for example, *Set-PublicFolderDatabase -Identity "Glasgow\First Glasgow Database" – MountAtStartup $True*.

- **Remove-PublicFolderDatabase**   Removes a public folder database if all the prerequisites have been met. For example, all the public folders in the database need to be removed or moved to another database. You need to be added to at least the Exchange Organization Administrator role in order to remove a database. The following is an example of an Exchange Management Shell command to remove a public folder database: *Remove-PublicFolderDatabase "Glasgow\First Storage Group\First Glasgow Database"*.

MORE INFO   Removing a public folder database

For more information about the prerequisites for removing a public folder database and the procedure for removing a database by using the Exchange Management Console, search for "How to Remove a Public Folder Database" in Exchange Server 2003 Help or access *http:// technet.microsoft.com/en-us/library/aa998329.aspx*.

- **Get-PublicFolderDatabase**   Returns public folder database settings, for example, *Get-PublicFolderDatabase -Identity "First Glasgow Database"*. You can use this command if you are added to at least the Exchange View-Only Administrator role. Figure 4-8 shows the output from this command.

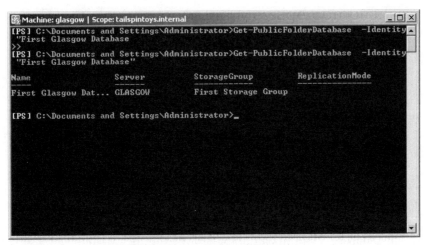

Figure 4-8 Get-PublicFolderDatabase command output

MORE INFO **Public folder referrals, permissions, and replication**

Lesson 2, "Configuring Public Folders," of Chapter 8 discusses public folder referrals, permissions, and replication. If you want more information in the meantime, you can find a list of cmdlets to configure public folder permissions and replication at *http://technet.microsoft.com/en-us/library/bb232202.aspx*. You will also find a good general discussion of Exchange Server 2007 permissions at *http://technet.microsoft.com/en-us/library/aa996881.aspx*.

Creating Public Folders

This section explains how to use the Exchange Management Shell to create new public folders. When you create a new public folder, the only required attribute is the folder name. After the folder has been created, you can use the *Set-PublicFolder* cmdlet to configure other folder properties.

> ### Real World
>
> *Ian McLean*
>
> Creating public folders cannot be a problem—after all, anyone can do it.
>
> Users can create their own public folders by using a client program such as Microsoft Outlook 2007. To create a personal public folder in Outlook, all a user needs to do is right-click Public Folder in the Navigation pane and then click New Folder. However, users do not need to create public folders in bulk. They do

> not need to create organization-wide public folders and configure who can and cannot write to them. They typically do not create public folder hierarchies. They do not set permissions or configure replication. They are not concerned with creating and mounting a public folder database. To the ordinary user, public folders are not a problem, nor should they be.
>
> This is because as an administrator, you have set up high-level folders in which users can create their own public folders and have configured public folder settings to make using them easy for the ordinary user. It's what administrators do.

Before you can create a public folder, you need a public folder database to put it in. If you have a pure Exchange Server 2007 organization and have specified during installation that your organization has no pre–Outlook 2007 or Microsoft Entourage clients, then no public folder database will have been created during that installation. (If you do specify that you have clients other than Outlook 2007, a public folder database will be created.) In the former case, you can use either Exchange Management Shell or Exchange Management Console to create a public folder database.

NOTE   Public folder inheritance

By default, a public folder inherits the settings of its parent folder.

To create a new public database, you need to be a domain administrator or a local administrator on the Exchange Server 2007 server or be added to the Exchange Organization Administrator role. You can create a public folder database with an Exchange Management Shell command that uses the *New-PublicFolderDatabase* cmdlet, or you can use Exchange Management Console. The practice session later in this lesson uses Exchange Management Console to create a public folder database.

To create a public folder database, open Exchange Management Console, expand Server Configuration in the console tree, and then click Mailbox. In the Result pane (the middle pane), click the server on which you want to create the new public folder database. In the Work pane, click the storage group in which you want to create the new public folder database, and in the Actions pane, click New Public Folder Database. This starts the New Public Folder Database Wizard.

In the Public Folder Database Name box, type the name of the new public folder database. If you want to specify the location of the public folder database files, click

Browse and enter the name and location of the new Exchange database file (file type .edb) for the public folder.

You need to mount a database before you can use it, so typically you would select the Mount This Database check box. This mounts the database at the completion of the wizard. To create the database, click New. The Completion page appears, indicating whether the public folder database was created successfully. This page also displays the Exchange Management Shell command that was used to create the public folder database.

When you have created a public folder database, you then use Exchange Management Shell to create a new public folder. To create a new public folder in the root of the public folder tree on a mailbox server that has a public folder database, enter the Exchange Management Shell command *New-PublicFolder -Name <name of public folder>*. You do this in the practice session later in this lesson.

To create a new public folder you need to be a domain administrator or a local administrator on the Exchange Server 2007 server or be added to at least the Exchange Server Administrator role. The Exchange Management Shell command to create a new public folder has the syntax *New-PublicFolder -Name <String> [-DomainController <Fqdn>] [-Path <PublicFolderIdParameter>] [-Server <ServerIdParameter>]*.

- The Name parameter is required. It specifies the name for the public folder, for example, AccountsPublicFolder.

- The DomainController parameter is optional. It specifies the domain controller that will write the configuration change to Active Directory. Use the fully qualified domain name of the domain controller, for example, Glasgow.tailspin-toys.internal.

- The Path parameter is optional if you are creating top-level folders. It specifies the location of the folder in the folder hierarchy. If, for example, you had a public folder hierarchy and you wanted to create a public folder called Wills as a child of a public folder called Legal, you would specify the path as \Legal. If you do not specify a value for the Path parameter, the public folder will be created as a child of the root folder.

- The Server parameter is optional. It specifies the server on which to create the public folder, for example, Glasgow. If you do not specify a server, Exchange Management Shell checks that the local server is an Exchange Server 2007 mailbox server and that it has a public folder database. If both conditions are met, the public folder is created locally. If it is not, Exchange finds the closest Exchange

2007 mailbox server that has a public folder database on which to create the public folder.

Removing Public Folders

To remove a public folder, you use an Exchange Management Shell command with the syntax *Remove-PublicFolder -Identity <PublicFolderIdParameter> [-DomainController <Fqdn>] [-Recurse <SwitchParameter>] [-Server <ServerIdParameter>]*.

The Identity parameter is required, although the parameter label "-Identity" can be omitted. This can be the mailbox name, for example, AccountInfo@tailspintoys.internal, or you can specify the public folder identity, for example, \Accounts.

You remove a public folder in the practice session later in this lesson. You can test this command without making any modifications by using the WhatIf parameter, for example, *Remove-PublicFolder -Identity <public folder identity> -WhatIf*.

To remove a named public folder and all of its subfolders (that is, to run the command recursively), you use the Recurse parameter, for example, *Remove PublicFolder -Identity <public folder identity> -Recurse*.

Modifying Public Folder Properties

You can use *Set-PublicFolder* Exchange Management Shell cmdlet to configure public folder properties that are not mail related. You cannot, however, use this cmdlet to mail-enable or mail-disable a public folder. Table 4-1 gives examples of the use of this cmdlet.

Table 4-1   Using the Set-PublicFolder Cmdlet

Command	What It Does
Set-PublicFolder \Accounts -UseDatabaseQuotaDefaults: $False	Specifies that the Accounts public folder can use storage size limits other than the values that are set on the public folder database.
Set-PublicFolder \Accounts -StorageQuota 10MB	Specifies that over-storage-quota warnings should be sent when the size of the Accounts public folder exceeds 10 MB. Note that the -StorageQuota parameter cannot be used when the −UseDatabaseQuotaDefaults parameter is set to $True.

Table 4-1   Using the Set-PublicFolder Cmdlet

Command	What It Does
Set-PublicFolder \Accounts -ReplicationSchedule Always	Specifies that the Accounts public folder always uses the default replication schedule of the public folder database.
Set-PublicFolder \Accounts -Use-DatabaseReplicationSchedule: $False	Specifies that the Accounts public folder does not use the default replication schedule of the public folder database.
Set-PublicFolder \Accounts -ReplicationSchedule "Sunday.12:00 AM-Monday.12:00 AM"	Specifies that the Accounts public folder replicates only on Sundays.

NOTE   Public folder replication schedule format

The public folder replication schedule uses the "Weekday.Hour:Minute [AM/PM] - Weekday.Hour: Minute [AM/PM]" format.

MORE INFO   Set-PublicFolder

For more information about the *Set-PublicFolder* cmdlet and the full syntax of *Set-PublicFolder* commands, search for "Set-PublicFolder" in Exchange Server 2007 Help or access *http:// technet.microsoft.com/en-us/library/bb124772.aspx*.

MORE INFO   Quota messages

For more information about quota messages, search for "Understanding Quota Messages" in Exchange Server 2007 Help or access *http://technet.microsoft.com/en-us/library/bb232173.aspx*.

Exam Tip   It is unlikely that you will be expected to remember all the parameters that can be used with the *Set-PublicFolder* cmdlet. However, you should know or be able to work out what the more commonly used parameters do, such as those listed in Table 4-1. Fortunately, the parameter names (for example, UseDataReplicationShedule) are fairly descriptive.

Setting Public Folder Database Limits

You can configure settings for individual public folders, but if you want to configure settings for all public folders, you can use commands based on the *Set-PublicFolder-Database* cmdlet to specify settings that apply to all public folders unless overridden by individual public folder settings. Typically, you would use commands based on this cmdlet to set public folder quotas and limits. Table 4-2 lists parameters that you can use with the *Set-PublicFolderDatabase cmdlet.*

Table 4-2   Limits That Can Be Set on a Public Folder Database

Parameter	Description
IssueWarningQuota	This parameter specifies the public folder size at which a warning is issued to public folder owners stating that the folder is almost full.
ItemRetentionPeriod	This parameter specifies the length of time that items are retained in a folder before they are deleted during store maintenance.
MaxItemSize	This parameter specifies the maximum size of an item that can be posted to or received by a public folder.
ProhibitPostQuota	This parameter specifies the size of a public folder at which users are notified that the public folder is full. Users cannot post to a folder that is larger than the ProhibitPost-Quota parameter value.

MORE INFO   Public folder database parameters

For more information about the parameters, search for "Set-PublicFolderDatabase" in Exchange Server 2007 Help or access *http://technet.microsoft.com/en-us/library/aa997225.aspx.*

MORE INFO   Moving public folders

You can move public folders between public folder databases on different Exchange Server 2007 mailbox servers. For more information, search for "How to Move Public Folder Content from One Public Folder Database to Another Public Folder Database" in Exchange 2007 Help or access *http://technet.microsoft.com/en-us/library/bb331970.aspx.*

Mail-Enabling and Disabling Public Folders

Earlier in this lesson, we saw that the command *Enable-MailPublicFolder \Accounts* mail-enable the Accounts public folder. If you want to mail-enable a public folder on a remote server in your Exchange organization, you can specify that server, for example, *Enable-MailPublicFolder \Accounts -Server Edinburgh*. If you want to mail-enable a public folder but hide the folder in address lists, you can set the HideFromAddress-ListsEnabled parameter, for example, *Enable-MailPublicFolder \Accounts -HiddenFrom AddressListsEnabled $True*.

MORE INFO   **Enable-MailPublicFolder**

For more information about the *Enable-MailPublicFolder* cmdlet, search for "Enable-MailPublic-Folder" in Exchange Server 2007 Help or access *http://technet.microsoft.com/en-us/library/aa998824.aspx*.

The command *Disable-MailPublicFolder \Accounts* disables the Accounts public folder (assuming it was mail-enabled). As with mail-enabling a public folder, you can specify a remote server by using the Server parameter.

Quick Check

- How would you specify that the Human Resources public folder on the server Edinburgh always uses the default replication schedule of the public folder database?

Quick Check Answer

- Use the command *Set-PublicFolder "\Human Resources" –Server Edinburgh – ReplicationSchedule Always*.

Configuring Public Folder E-Mail Properties

As described earlier in this lesson, you use the *Enable-MailPublicFolder* cmdlet to mail-enable a public folder and the *Disable-MailPublicFolder* cmdlet to mail-disable a public folder. To configure mail-related settings of mail-enabled public folders, you use the *Set-MailPublicFolder* cmdlet.

You could, for example, use *Set-MailPublicFolder \Accounts -EmailAddresses Finance@ toyspintoys.internal* to set a proxy address for the Accounts public folder or *Set-Mail-PublicFolder \Accounts -PrimarySmtpAddress CashInfo@tailspintoys.internal* to specify the primary e-mail address of the folder. By default, the primary e-mail address for a public folder is set through e-mail address policy. If you want to use the EmailAddresses or PrimarySmtpAddress parameter to change either address, you must first set the EmailAddressPolicyEnabled parameter to False, for example, *Set-MailPublicFolder \Accounts –EmailAddressPolicyEnabled $False*.

NOTE   EmailAddresses and PrimarySmtpAddress

If you set proxy addresses by using the EmailAddresses parameter, the first of these addresses becomes the primary e-mail address. Therefore, you cannot use the EmailAddresses and PrimarySmtpAddress parameters in the same command.

MORE INFO   Set-MailPublicFolder

For more information about the *Set-MailPublicFolder* cmdlet and the full syntax of *Set-MailPublicFolder* commands, search for "Set-MailPublicFolder" in Exchange Server 2007 Help or access *http://technet.microsoft.com/en-us/library/bb123707.aspx*.

Obtaining Public Folder Information

Commands that enable you to obtain information about public folders use the Get-*PublicFolder* cmdlet. However, these commands return only information that is not related to e-mail settings. If you want to get mail-related information about mail-enabled public folders, you need to use the use the *Get-MailPublicFolder* cmdlet.

The root public folder (\) exists by default above each top-level public folder. It forms part of an Identity parameter value, for example, \Accounts. If you want to obtain information about the root public folder, you can use the command *Get-PublicFolder with no parameters, or Get-PublicFolder –Identity "\"*. To get a list of the names of the root public folder and all the public folders below it in the hierarchy, you can use the command *Get-PublicFolder -Recurse | Format-List Name*. Note the optional use of the pipe (|) operator in this command. This transfers the output of the *Get-PublicFolder –Recurse* command into the *Format-List Name* command, which lists the public folder names. Figure 4-9 shows the output of a *Get-PublicFolder –Recurse* command piped into *Format-List Name*.

To get information about a specific public folder, you can use the *Get-Public Folder* cmdlet, followed by the identity of the folder (for example, \Accounts). Optionally, you can pipe the output into Format-List Name. If you want information about the public folder and its children, you specify the Recurse parameter. If you want information only about the children of the public folder you have specified, you replace the

Recurse parameter with the GetChildren parameter. You cannot have both Recurse and GetChildren in the command.

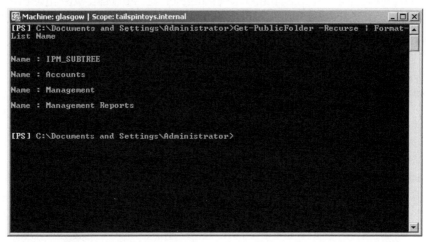

Figure 4-9   Public folder name list

By default, the maximum number of public folders about which information is returned is 10,000. You can change this default number by using the ResultSize parameter. The ResultSize parameter must be used in combination with either the Recurse or the GetChildren parameter.

Thus, in the somewhat unlikely event that the hierarchy below the Accounts public folder contains more than 10,000 public folders, you would use the command *Get-PublicFolder \Accounts −Recurse -ResultSize Unlimited | Format-List Name* to list the folder names. More practically, you might want to get a list of the names of the public folders in the hierarchy under the top-level public folder Manufacturing but limit the list size to 100. In this case, you would use the command *Get-PublicFolder \Manufacturing -GetChildren -ResultSize 100 | Format-List Name.*

By default, *Get-PublicFolder* commands do not display system folders (even if you list the root folder and all child folders). To view the system folders, you must specify the system folder root \NON_IPM_SUBTREE, for example, *Get-PublicFolder -Identity \NON_IPM_SUBTREE -Recurse | Format-List Name.* Figure 4-3 earlier in this lesson showed a list of public folders generated by a Get-PublicFolder command.

MORE INFO   **Get-PublicFolder**

For more information about the *Get-PublicFolder* cmdlet, search for "Get-PublicFolder" in Exchange Server 2007 Help or access *http://technet.microsoft.com/en-us/library/aa997615.aspx.*

To obtain mail-related public folder information about a mail-enabled public folder, you use the *Get-MailPublicFolder* cmdlet followed by the folder's identity, for example, *Get-MailPublicFolder \Accounts*. If you want to get information about all public folders in a public folder store, you can use the cmdlet without specifying the Identity parameter. For example, if you wanted a list of the names of all mail-enabled public folders on the Exchange Server 2007 server Glasgow, you could enter **Get-MailPublicFolder | Format-List Name** on that server or **Get-MailPublicFolder –Server Glasgow | Format-List Name** from any Exchange Server 2007 server in the organization.

If you want a different display of results, you can use the SortBy parameter to sort results by specifying a criterion, for example, alias. You cannot use the Recurse or GetChildren parameters with the *Get-MailPublicFolder* cmdlet, but you can use the Filter parameter to specify attributes used to construct a query that retrieves a set of mail-enabled public folders, for example, *Get-MailPublicFolder –Filter { (Name -eq "Management") –or (Name –eq "Accounts") } –SortBy Alias*. Figure 4-10 shows the result of this query.

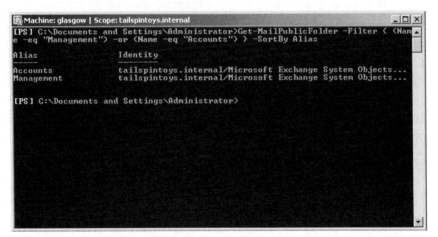

Figure 4-10   Query using Filter and SortBy parameters

Exam Tip   The *Get-PublicFolder* cmdlet can use the Recurse and GetChildren parameters. The *Get-MailPublicFolder* cmdlet cannot. You can reject any answer that uses either of these parameters with the *GetMailPublicFolder* cmdlet.

To retrieve information about the folders in a specified mailbox, for example, the number and size of items in the folder, the folder name, and its identity, you can use the *Get-MailboxFolderStatistics* cmdlet. Figure 4-7 earlier in this lesson shows sample output from a command that uses this cmdlet.

MORE INFO Get-MailPublicFolder and Get-MailboxFolderStatistics

For more information about these cmdlets and the syntax of commands that use them, search for "Get-MailPublicFolder" and "Get-MailboxFolderStatistics" in Exchange Server 2007 Help or access *http://technet.microsoft.com/en-us/library/bb124772.aspx* and *http://technet.microsoft.com/en-us/library/aa996762.aspx*.

Practice: Creating and Configuring Public Folders

In this practice session, you use Exchange Management Console to create and mount a public folder database. You then create a top-level public folder Management. Under that folder, you create a child public folder Management Reports. You mail-enable both public folders and specify primary Simple Mail Transfer Protocol addresses. You then get information about these public folders. Finally, you first disable and then delete the Management Reports folder.

▶ **Practice 1: Creating and Mounting a Public Folder Database**

In this practice, you use Exchange Management Console to create and mount a public folder database. If you prefer to use Exchange Management Shell to perform the same tasks, the commands to do this are given in this lesson. If you have configured a test network with a single Exchange Server 2007 server and specified that you have no Microsoft Outlook 2003 or Microsoft Entourage clients on your network, then no public folder database will have been created during installation. In this case, you need to create and mount the database before you can create public folders.

If a public folder database already exists in your Exchange organization, then you can create public folders, and you cannot create an additional public folder database. In this case, you should not carry out this practice. To create and mount a public server database, carry out the following procedure:

1. If necessary, log on by using the Kim_Akers account.
2. Open Exchange Management Console, expand Server Configuration in the console tree, and click Mailbox.
3. In the Result pane (middle pane), click Glasgow.
4. Under Database Management (the Work pane), click First Storage Group.
5. In the Actions pane, click New Public Folder Database. The New Public Folder Database Wizard starts, as shown in Figure 4-11.

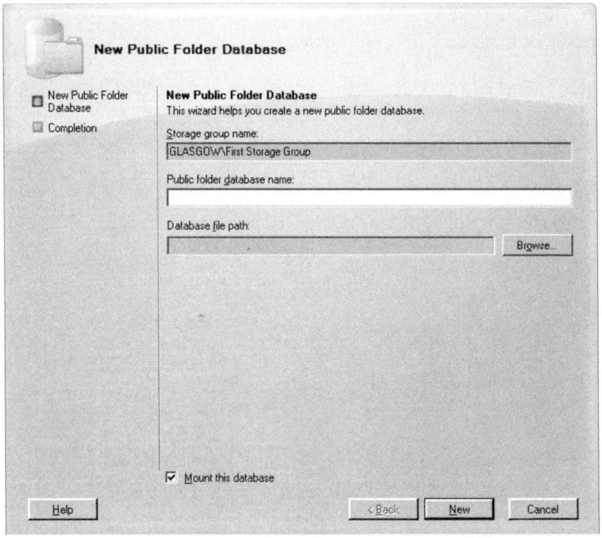

Figure 4-11   The New Public Folder Database Wizard

6. In the Public Folder Database Name box, type **First Glasgow Database**.

7. Ensure that the Mount This Database check box is selected. Do not change the Database File Path default. The New Folder Database page should look similar to Figure 4-12.

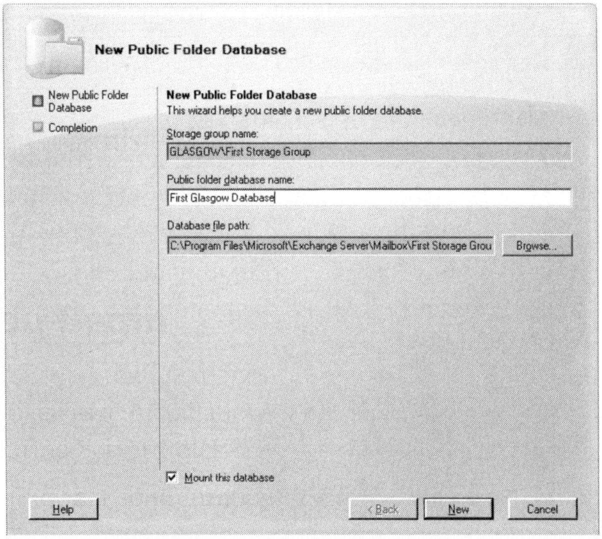

Figure 4-12   Specifying a new public folder database

8. Click New.

9. The Completion page appears, indicating that the public folder database was created successfully. This page also displays the Exchange Management Shell command that was used to create the public folder database.

10. Click Finish to close the wizard.

11. Exchange Management Console should list the new public folder database, as shown in Figure 4-13. Close Exchange Management Console.

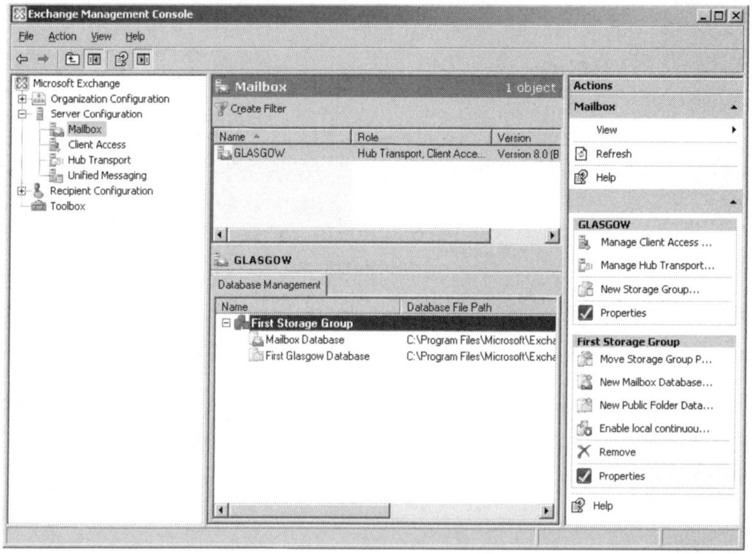

Figure 4-13 New public folder database created

▶ **Practice 2: Creating and Mail-Enabling Public Folders**

In this practice, you create the Management and Management Reports databases. If no public folder database exists by default in your Exchange organization, you need to complete Practice 1 before starting this practice. If you want to expand this practice, log on with the Kim_Akers account to a PC in the domain that is running Microsoft Outlook 2007 and post files and send e-mails to the public folders you have created. To create and mail-enable public folders, carry out the following procedure:

1. If necessary, log on by using the Kim_Akers account.

2. Open Exchange Management Shell.

3. Enter the command **New-PublicFolder -Name Management.** The Exchange Management Shell console should look similar to Figure 4-14.

Figure 4-14   Creating a top-level public folder

4. Enter the command **New-PublicFolder -Name "Management Reports" −Path \Management**. The Exchange Management Shell console should look similar to Figure 4-15.

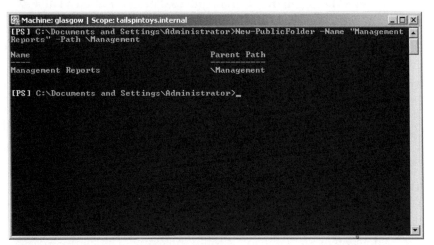

Figure 4-15   Creating a child public folder

5. You now mail-enable the public folders. Enter the command **Enable-MailPublicFolder \Management**.

6. Enter the command **Enable-MailPublicFolder "\Management\Management Reports"**. The Exchange Management Shell console should look similar to Figure 4-16.

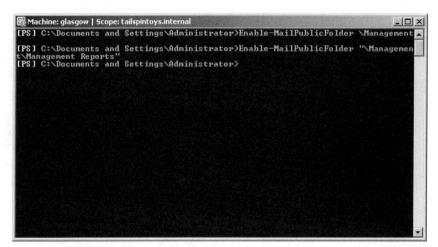

Figure 4-16 Mail-enabling public folders

7. You do not want to use the public folder database default settings for the primary e-mail addresses of the Management public folder. Enter **Set-MailPublic-Folder \Management –EmailAddressPolicyEnabled $False**.

8. You can now specify a primary e-mail address for the Management public folder. Enter **Set-MailPublicFolder \Management -PrimarySmtpAddress Manage@tailspintoys.internal**.

9. You need to disable the public folder database default settings for each public folder for which you want to specify a primary e-mail address. To do this for the Management Reports public folder, enter **Set-MailPublicFolder "\Management\Management Reports" –EmailAddressPolicyEnabled $False**.

10. You can now specify a primary e-mail address for the Management Reports public folder. Enter **Set-MailPublicFolder "\Management\Management Reports" -PrimarySmtpAddress ManageReport@tailspintoys.internal**. The Exchange Management Shell console should look similar to Figure 4-17.

11. Use the technique described in this practice to create, mail-enable, and configure a public folder called Accounts. This step is not essential, but if you do not create this folder, the Exchange Management Shell output in the next practice will look slightly different to the figure in that practice.

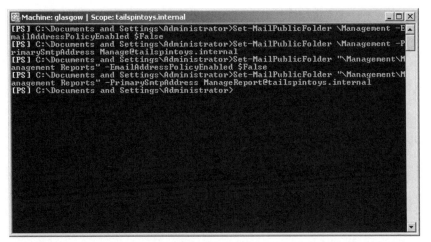

Figure 4-17   Setting primary e-mail addresses

▶ **Practice 3: Getting Information about Public Folders**

In this practice, you obtain mail-related information about the Accounts and Management public folders and a list of all mail-enabled public folders in the public folder store:

1. If necessary, log on by using the Kim_Akers account.

2. Open Exchange Management Shell.

3. To list all public folders, enter the command **Get-PublicFolder −Recurse | Format-List Name**. Figure 4-9 earlier in this lesson shows the output from this command.

4. To get mail-related information about the Accounts and Management mail-enabled public folders in the public folder database, enter the command **Get-MailPublicFolder −Filter { (Name −eq "Management") −or (Name −eq "Accounts") } −SortBy Alias**.

5. To list all mail-enabled public folders in the public folder database, enter the command **Get-MailPublicFolder | Format-List Name**. The Exchange Management Shell console should look similar to Figure 4-18.

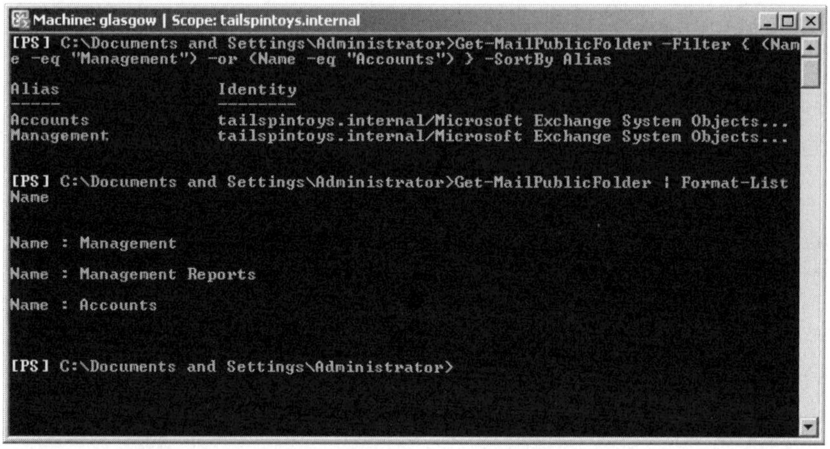

Figure 4-18   Mail-related information

▶ **Practice 4: Disabling and Removing a Public Folder**

In this practice, you first disable and then remove the Management Reports public folder. You do not need to disable a public folder before you remove it, but the procedure lets you practice doing both. If you want to extend the practice, attempt to post and send e-mail to the public folder after you have disabled it but before you remove it. You should be able to do the former (logged on as Kim_Akers) but not the latter. When you have removed the public folder, you should not be able to post to it. To disable and then remove a public folder, carry out the following procedure:

1. If necessary, log on by using the Kim_Akers account.

2. Open Exchange Management Shell.

3. To disable the Management Reports Public folder enter the command **Disable-MailPublicFolder "\Management\Management Reports"**. When prompted, enter Y for Yes.

4. To remove the Management Reports Public folder, enter the command **Remove-PublicFolder "\Management\Management Reports"**. When prompted, enter Y for Yes. The Exchange Management Shell console should look similar to Figure 4-19.

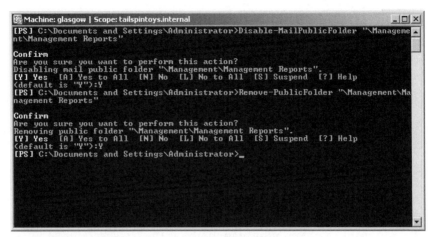

Figure 4-19   Disabling and removing a public folder

Lesson Summary

- Exchange Management Shell is the primary tool that you use to manage public folders. A limited number of public folder database tasks can also be carried out by using Exchange Management Console.

- You cannot create public folders unless a public folder database exists and is mounted.

- An Exchange Management Shell command consists of a cmdlet followed by parameters and parameter values.

- Public folders are not mail-enabled by default. You need separate sets of commands to manage the mail-related configuration of public folders and the general public folder parameters.

- System folders are in a different subtree from public folders. They are used by the system and typically you do not configure them.

Lesson Review

You can use the following questions to test your knowledge of the information in Lesson 1, "Configuring Public Folders." The questions are also available on the companion CD if you prefer to review them in electronic form.

1. You want to obtain information about the root public folder and the public folder hierarchy below it. What command should you use?

    A. *Get-PublicFolder*

    B. *Get-PublicFolder –Identity "\"*

    C. *Get-PublicFolder –Recurse*

    D. *Get-PublicFolder -GetChildren*

2. You want to obtain information about the top-level public folder Contoso and public folders in its hierarchy. However, you know that many public folders exist under Contoso and you want to limit the results to 50 folders, including the Contoso public folder itself. What command should you use?

    A. *Get-PublicFolder Contoso –Recurse –ResultSize 50*

    B. *Get-PublicFolder \Contoso –Recurse –ResultSize Unlimited*

    C. *Get-PublicFolder \NON_IPM_SUBTREE\Contoso –Recurse –ResultSize 50*

    D. *Get-PublicFolder \Contoso –Recurse –ResultSize 50*

3. What does the following command do?

    ```
    New-PublicFolder -Name "Meeting Minutes" -Path "\Contoso\Management"
    ```

    A. Creates a new public folder Meeting Minutes as a child of Management, which in turn is a child of Contoso. The public folder is not mail-enabled.

    B. Creates a new mail-enabled public folder Meeting Minutes as a child of Management, which in turn is a child of Contoso.

    C. Creates a new public folder Meeting Minutes as a child of the top-level public folder Management. The public folder is not mail-enabled.

    D. Creates a new mail-enabled public folder Meeting Minutes as a child of the top-level public folder Contoso.

4. What does the following command do?

```
Set-PublicFolder "\Human Resources" -ReplicationSchedule "Saturday.12:00 AM
-Monday.12:00 AM"
```

   A. Specifies that the Human Resources public folder replicates only on Saturday and Sunday.

   B. Specifies that the Human Resources public folder replicates only on Saturday, Sunday, and Monday.

   C. Specifies that the Human Resources public folder replicates only on Sunday.

   D. Specifies that the Human Resources public folder always uses the default replication schedule of the public folder database.

5. You are unable to create public folders because there is no public folder database. You open Exchange Management Console and start the New Database Wizard. You specify the name of the database as MyDatabase and click New on the Configuration page and Finish on the Completion page to create the database and close the wizard. You still cannot create public folders. Why not?

   A. You cannot use MyDatabase as a database name. The name needs to be "First <servername> Database" where <servername> is the name of the Exchange Server 2007 server on which you are creating the database.

   B. You have not mounted the database.

   C. You cannot create a public folder database by using Exchange Management Console. You need to use Exchange Management Shell.

   D. You need to restart the Exchange Server 2007 server to create the database.

6. You want to get mail-related information about the mail-enabled public folders Management and Management Reports. Management is a top-level folder, and Management Reports is a child of Management. You want to use a single command to do this. What command do you use?

   A. *Get-MailPublicFolder "Management" -Recurse*

   B. *Get-MailPublicFolder −Filter { (Name -eq "Management") −or (Name −eq "Management Reports") }*

   C. *Get-PublicFolder "Management" -Recurse*

   D. *Get-PublicFolder "Management" -GetChildren*

Chapter Review

To further practice and reinforce the skills you learned in this chapter, you can perform the following tasks:

- Review the chapter summary.
- Review the list of key terms introduced in this chapter.
- Complete the case scenarios. These scenarios set up real-world situations involving the topics of this chapter and ask you to create a solution.
- Complete the suggested practices.
- Take a practice test.

Chapter Summary

- You typically use Exchange Management Shell commands to create and manage public folders. You can also use Exchange Management Console to create and mount public folder databases.
- You can mail-enable a public folder so users can send e-mail messages to it as well as posts. Public folders are not mail-enabled by default.
- A pure Exchange Server 2007 organization that does not have Microsoft Outlook 2003 or earlier or Microsoft Entourage clients will have no public folder database by default. If you want to use public folders in such an organization, you need to create and mount a public folder database.

Key Terms

Do you know what these key terms mean? You can check your answers by looking up the terms in the glossary at the end of the book.

- Mounting a database
- Public folder
- Public folder database
- Public folder hierarchy
- Public folder replication
- Root public folder
- Storage quota
- System folder
- Top-level public folder

Case Scenarios

In the following case scenarios, you will apply what you've learned about configuring public folders. You can find answers to these questions in the "Answers" section at the end of this book.

Case Scenario 1: Creating and Mounting a Public Folder Database

You have been added to the Exchange Organization Administrator role at Trey Research. You have completed a clean install of Exchange Server 2007 enterprise edition and created the required recipients. You have not installed any service packs. Trey Research uses only Microsoft Outlook 2007 clients internally, although some workers use Outlook Web Access from home. Management has decided that the company needs a public folder hierarchy because its employees are accustomed to using public folders and are comfortable with them. Answer the following questions:

1. Don Hall, the marketing manager, has tried to create a personal public folder but cannot do so. What do you need to do before he can?

2. Your boss is concerned that you plan to install and mount only one public folder database. She understands that public folders and system folders are in two different hierarchies and believes you need two separate databases. How do you reassure her?

3. Don Hall has created a personal public folder by using Microsoft Outlook 2007 while in the office. He tries to access it from home using OWA but is unable to do so. He reports this as an error and asks you to enable the public folder database for access to OWA. What do you tell him?

Case Scenario 2: Creating, Configuring, and Mail-Enabling Public Folders

You are a member of the Exchange Server 2007 administration team at Contoso, Ltd. It is part of your job to create public folders as required for general company use and to configure the properties of existing public folders. Sometimes you are required to mail-enable public folders. Answer the following questions:

1. You have been asked to create a public folder called Payment Receipts, which is a child of Invoices, which in turn is a child of Finance. What command do you use to do this?

2. You have been asked to set the storage quota of the Payment Receipts public folder so that warnings are sent if a quota of 10 MB is exceeded. This is not the database default. What two commands do you need to enter?

3. You need to mail-enable the Payment Receipts public folder and give it a primary e-mail address, Receipts@Contoso.com. This is not the public folder database default. You need three commands to do this. What are they?

Suggested Practices

To help you successfully master the exam objectives presented in this chapter, complete the following tasks.

Configure Public Folders

Do Practice 1 and Practice 2 in this section. Practice 3 is optional.

■ **Practice 1: Use the Set-PublicFolder Commands**   Investigate the many parameters in the commands based on the *Set-PublicFolder* cmdlet. Practice using them, read the help files to determine what they do, and find out what values are acceptable for each parameter.

■ **Practice 2: Create and Mount a Public Folder Database**   In the practice session, you used Exchange Management Console to create and mount a public folder database. Use Exchange Management Shell commands to prepare the database so it can be removed, to remove it, to create another public folder database, to mount it, and to re-create the public folders you deleted.

■ **Practice 3: Use Public Folders**   Log in as Kim_Akers on a client PC running Microsoft Outlook 2007. Test the effect of various parameter settings on public folders by posting to them and sending e-mail messages to them. Log on to the Exchange Server 2007 server and reconfigure the public folders. From the client PC, test the effect of the changes you made.

Configure Public Folder E-Mail Settings

Do both of the practices in this session.

■ **Practice 1: Use the Get-MailPublicFolder Commands**   Investigate the commands based on the *Get-MailPublicFolder* and *Get-PublicFolderStatistics* cmdlets.

Practice using them, read the help files to determine what they do, and find out what values are acceptable for each parameter.

■ **Practice 2: Use the Set-MailPublicFolder Commands**   Investigate the commands based on the *Set-MailPublicFolder* cmdlet. Practice using them, read the help files to determine what they do, and find out what values are acceptable for each parameter. Determine the effect of overriding public folder database defaults for individual folders and find out what settings can be configured at the individual public folder level.

Take a Practice Test

The practice tests on this book's companion CD offer many options. For example, you can test yourself on just one exam objective, or you can test yourself on all the 70-236 certification exam content. You can set up the test so that it closely simulates the experience of taking a certification exam, or you can set it up in study mode so that you can look at the correct answers and explanations after you answer each question.

MORE INFO   **Practice Tests**

For details about all the practice test options available, see the "How to Use the Practice Tests" section in this book's Introduction.

Chapter 5

Moving Mailboxes and Implementing Bulk Management

As an Exchange administrator, moving mailboxes is likely to be one of your responsibilities. It is a straightforward task to move a single mailbox, but you also need to know how to schedule mailbox moves, implement bulk moves, and verify the policies that apply to mailboxes. This chapter covers all these topics.

Managing e-mail in bulk is an important part of an administrator's job, particularly in a large organization with a lot of recipients. This chapter discusses bulk management and bulk management tools such as comma-separated value (CSV) files, PowerShell scripts, and the Exchange Management Console graphical user interface (GUI). It also discusses scheduling bulk management operations.

Exam objectives in this chapter:
- Move mailboxes.
- Implement bulk management of mail-enabled objects.

Lessons in this chapter:

Before You Begin

To complete the lessons in this chapter, you must have done the following:

- Installed Windows Exchange Server 2007 with the Mailbox, Client Access, Hub Transport, and Unified Messaging roles on a Windows domain controller in the Tailspintoys.internal domain. To do this, you need to have completed all the practices in Lessons 1 and 2 of Chapter 1, "Preparing for Exchange Installation," and Lesson 1 of Chapter 2, "Installing Exchange Server and Configuring Roles."

Real World

Ian McLean

For success, a lot of things need to be correct. For failure, only one thing needs to go wrong.

This becomes most apparent when you are performing one operation that depends on another that in turn depends on a third. For example, you might want to create a mailbox template to enable you to create mailboxes with parameter settings you specify for the template. You might then want to set a variable that specifies that template. You might want to store a list of mailbox names and other parameters, such as primary e-mail addresses in a CSV file. Finally, you might want to extract the information from the CSV file and feed it into a *New-Mailbox* command that uses this information to create multiple mailboxes based on the template you created.

If you make a mistake in the template, the procedure will not work as anticipated. If you do not set up your template variable correctly, the procedure will not work at all. If you make a mistake in your CSV file, the process might fail, or, even worse, you might end up with a mailbox called Users. Finally, if you enter the *New-Mailbox* command incorrectly, the only result of your efforts is likely to be some brightly colored error messages in your Exchange Management Shell console. (Do you not just love that shade of red?)

So why try? Because if you are creating, modifying, and configuring large numbers of mailboxes (or other Exchange objects), you need to use bulk management techniques. Carrying out such operations one mailbox at a time is frustrating, time consuming, and boring.

When you first try out the procedures described in this chapter, you will probably get something wrong. I certainly did. After I had used the same technique a hundred times, however, I usually got everything right the first time. My typing accuracy had not improved, and I would probably lost a few more brain cells to the aging process, so the only other explanation was that I started to get good at it. Also, I found that I could automate a lot of procedures by using scripts, so I was not typing in the same code time and time again.

You might find the same.

Lesson 1: Moving Mailboxes

You can move mailboxes between mailbox databases, servers, domains, Active Directory directory service sites, and forests. You can also move mailboxes between different versions of Exchange Server. You can use the Move Mailbox Wizard, which you access from Exchange Management Console, to move mailboxes, or you can use Exchange Management Shell commands based on the *Move-Mailbox* cmdlet. You cannot use the Move Mailbox Wizard to move mailboxes across forests. To move a mailbox from one forest to another, you must use Exchange Management Shell.

This lesson discusses the various scenarios in which you might want to move mailboxes, how to schedule mailbox moves, and how to move mailboxes in bulk. It also covers mailbox policies and how you would go about verifying them. However, before you can move multiple mailboxes, you need multiple mailboxes to move. This chapter therefore also describes how you use Exchange Management Shell to create multiple mailbox-enabled users.

After this lesson, you will be able to:

- Implement scheduled and bulk mailbox moves.
- Verify mailbox policies.

Estimated lesson time: 55 minutes

Investigating Scenarios That Require Mailbox Moves

You might need to move mailboxes for a variety of reasons. The following are typical scenarios where mailbox moves might be required:

- **Moving to databases with different settings** You might want to move mailboxes to mailbox databases that provide different default settings. For example, Don Hall has just been promoted to a managerial position, and managers have larger mailbox size limits. You can move Don's mailbox to a database that has a larger mailbox quota setting.

- **A user changes location** You can move mailboxes to a server in a different Active Directory site. For example, Sean Alexander has moved from your company's New York office to its manufacturing plant in Seattle. You need to move Sean's mailbox from an Exchange Sever 2007 server in the New York Active Directory site to a similar server in the Seattle site.

- **Load balancing**   You can move mailboxes between servers to balance server load. Typically, you would select a criterion that determines which mailboxes to use. For example, you might choose to move mailboxes with a size greater than a specified limit.

- **You have moved a mailbox database**   If you have moved a database file to a new location, you can use the Exchange Management Shell *Move-Mailbox* cmdlet to change the configuration information in Active Directory so that all the mailboxes point to the new database location. You can perform this type of database move only within a single forest, and you cannot use Exchange Management Console to carry out this operation.

- **Problem investigation**   If you need to investigate issues that have arisen with one or more mailboxes, you can move the mailboxes to a different sever. This enables you to troubleshoot without interfering with the normal operation of mailboxes that do not have any problems and to investigate the situation where all mailboxes on several servers have the same problem. For example, if a number of mailboxes have corrupted messages, you might want to move all of them to one server.

- **Merging mailboxes**   Typically, you would merge the contents of one mailbox into another mailbox by using the Exchange Management Shell *Move-Mailbox* cmdlet with the AllowMerge parameter when you are moving mailboxes between forests and want to minimize disruption to user service.

MORE INFO   Merging mailboxes

For more information about merging mailboxes, search for "How to Merge Mailboxes" in Exchange Server 2007 Help or access *http://technet.microsoft.com/en-us/library/bb201751.aspx*.

- **An organizational change**   If, for example, your organization has acquired or merged with another or has divested an asset that is not vital to its core business, you might have two separate Exchange forests operating in a cross-forest scenario, and you might need to move mailboxes into a single forest. You do this by using the Exchange Management Shell *Move-Mailbox* cmdlet. This is one situation where you can use the AllowMerge parameter to minimize user disruption.

- **Administrative considerations**   Typically, an Exchange recipient administrator or Exchange organization administrator administers mailboxes while the domain administrator team administers Active Directory accounts. Your organization might want to separate these functions further by moving mailboxes from the current Active Directory forest into a resource forest. In this scenario, mailboxes reside in one forest and their associated user accounts in a separate forest.

Resource Forests

In the resource forest scenario, user mailboxes exist in a different forest from user accounts. Typically, this is done when an organization wants to outsource the administration of e-mail and retain the administration of Windows user accounts. This is usually invisible to users who can still access their mailboxes and receive and send e-mail messages in the normal way. If you move mailboxes but not user accounts to another forest, user accounts are created in the second forest but are disabled. These disabled user accounts need to exist to enable the mailboxes to exist in the forest but do not have the properties and permissions of the user accounts in the original forest. If you want to move user accounts between forests, you need to use the appropriate tool, for example, Active Directory Migration Tool version 3 (ADMT v3).

Sometimes an organization that has previously outsourced e-mail administration decides that it now wants to administer e-mail internally. In this case, you might need to move mailboxes back from a resource forest to their original forest so that e-mail and user accounts can be managed from within the same forest.

Moving Mailboxes between Versions of Exchange

When you upgrade an existing Microsoft Exchange Server 2003 or Exchange 2000 Server organization to Exchange Server 2007, you need to move mailboxes from the existing Exchange servers to an Exchange Server 2007 server that has the Mailbox server role installed. You can perform these moves within a single forest or across forests.

It is rather less likely that you will need to move Exchange Server 2007 mailboxes to an Exchange Server 2003 or Exchange 2000 Server organization, but you can do this if required. You cannot move Exchange Server 2007 mailboxes to a pure Exchange 2000 Server organization in another forest. To move Exchange Server 2007 mailboxes to an Exchange 2000 Server organization in another forest, you need to have at least one Exchange Server 2003 server in both forests.

You can use the Exchange Management *Move-Mailbox* cmdlet or the Exchange Management Console Move Mailbox Wizard in Exchange Server 2007 to move Exchange Server 2003 and Exchange 2000 Server mailboxes. You can use the same tools to move Exchange Server 2007 mailboxes to an Exchange 2003 server and to an Exchange 2000 server within the same forest.

You cannot move mailboxes directly from Microsoft Exchange Server version 5.5 to Exchange Server 2007. To move mailboxes from Exchange Server 5.5 to Exchange Server 2007, you must first move the mailboxes to either an Exchange Server 2003 server or a server running Exchange 2000 Server and then move the mailboxes to Exchange Server 2007.

Previous versions of Exchange Server do not support resource mailboxes (discussed in Chapter 3, "Configuring Recipients, Groups, and Mailboxes") but instead use shared mailboxes to represent resources. A shared mailbox is a mailbox with multiple users. Exchange Server 2007 supports both resource mailboxes and, for backward compatibility, shared mailboxes.

If you move a shared mailbox from an Exchange Server 2003 or Exchange 2000 Server organization to an Exchange Server 2007 organization, the *Move-Mailbox* cmdlet creates the mailbox as a shared Exchange Server 2007 mailbox. After you move the mailbox to Exchange Server 2007, you can convert it to a resource mailbox. If you need to move a resource mailbox from Exchange Server 2007 to an Exchange Server 2003 or Exchange 2000 Server organization, you should first convert it to a shared mailbox.

MORE INFO   Moving mailboxes

For more information about moving mailboxes between different versions of Exchange, search Exchange 2007 Help for "Moving Mailboxes" or access *http://technet.microsoft.com/en-us/library/bb124797.aspx.*

MORE INFO   Mailbox conversion

For more information about mailbox conversion, search for "How to Convert a Mailbox" in Exchange Server 2007 Help or access *http://technet.microsoft.com/en-us/library/bb201749.aspx.*

IMPORTANT Delays using Outlook Web Access

After you move a mailbox, a user may experience a delay of several minutes when accessing the moved mailbox by using Outlook Web Access (OWA). OWA requests a message table from Exchange Server 2007, and building the message table can take some time, especially if the user's mailbox contains a lot of data. This is normal operation, but you might have to explain the delay to users you support or choose a time for the move when few users are likely to be accessing mailboxes. Scheduling mailbox moves is discussed later in this lesson.

Creating Multiple Mailbox-Enabled Users

Later in this lesson, you will learn how to implement bulk mailbox moves. Before you do this, however, you need to create some mailboxes to move. You can use Exchange Management Shell to create multiple mailbox-enabled users by using an existing recipient as a template. Using a recipient template allows you to configure settings for a recipient that are not available in a *New-Mailbox* cmdlet. For example, you can modify a mailbox template to set the expansion server attribute, but you cannot specify this attribute as a parameter in a command based on the *New-Mailbox* cmdlet.

This technique also allows you to configure the mailbox you copy to create the template with nondefault settings. For example, you could use a command based on the *Set-Mailbox* cmdlet to alter the issue warning quota or the maximum message size from the database defaults. When you use this mailbox as a template, the same settings are used for the additional mailboxes you create. When you use a template to create a new mailbox, all properties are copied to the new mailbox, except the mandatory properties for the corresponding *New-Mailbox* cmdlet and the properties that must be unique in the organization.

NOTE Creating recipients by using templates

You cannot use the Exchange Management Console to create recipients by using templates.

To create a new mailbox by using a mailbox template, you start the Exchange Management Shell and select or create a mailbox that you want to use as a template. You can use an ordinary mailbox (For example, the don.hall@tailspintoys.internal mailbox you created in Chapter 3), but it is preferable to create a new mailbox specifically for use as a template. You could, for example, specify the mailbox name such as _Template. You can then configure any mailbox properties that you want to apply to the mailboxes you will be creating. If, for example, you wanted to apply a nondefault ActiveSync mailbox policy to all mailboxes created by using a specific template, you could specify a value for the ActiveSyncMailboxPolicy parameter in the command to create the mailbox.

NOTE **Template mailbox names**

It is traditional to start template names with an underscore (_) character. This distinguishes them from ordinary mailboxes and has the additional advantage that the template names appear together at the start of any alphabetically ordered list of mailbox names.

You can then create a single mailbox-enabled user, Stephan Adolphi, with the following commands:

```
$Template = Get-Mailbox _Template
New-Mailbox -Name "Stephan Adolphi" -UserPrincipalName stephan.adolphi@tailspintoys.internal
-Database "First Storage Group\Mailbox Database" -OrganizationalUnit Users -TemplateInstance
$Template
```

You then enter the password for the new user when prompted. Figure 5-1 shows the result of these commands.

Figure 5-1 Creating a template and creating a single user by using the template

It is, however, more efficient to use a text editor or spreadsheet to create a CSV file that has a list of mailboxes you want to create. For example, you could create a file called CreateUsers.csv containing the name, log-on name, organizational unit, and initial password for each user. In the example given, the file has been saved to the root of the C:\ drive, but you would probably put it in another location. You create this file in the practice session later in this lesson.

To create multiple mailboxes by using a CSV file and a mailbox template, you use the following commands:

```
$Template = Get-Mailbox "_Template"
Import-CSV "C:\CreateUsers.csv" | ForEach-Object -process {$Temp = ConvertTo-SecureString
$_.Password -asPlainText -force;New-Mailbox -Name $_.Name -UserPrincipalName $_.UPN
-OrganizationalUnit $_.OU -Database "First Storage Group\Mailbox Database" -Password $Temp
-TemplateInstance $Template}
```

The *Import-CSV* command reads the contents of the CreateUsers.csv file. The content of the CSV file is then piped into the *ForEach-Object* command, which executes a script block to create the new mailboxes for each line item listed in the CSV file. The variables Name, UPN, OU, and Password are extracted from the CSV file for each user mailbox. The *ConvertTo-SecureString* command converts the plain-text password in the CSV file to a secure string and stores it in the temporary variable $Temp. The *New-Mailbox* command creates the new mailbox and uses the $Temp variable to create the password for the new user.

IMPORTANT   Security considerations

Although the password for each user is converted to a secure string when the mailboxes are created, passwords are stored in clear text in the CSV file. Therefore, if you are using this technique, it is highly advisable to force users to change password at the next logon. You should also store the CSV file in an encrypted folder and not in the root of the C:\ drive.

MORE INFO   Using scripts in Exchange Management Shell

For more information about using scripts in the Exchange Management Shell, refer to Lesson 2 in this chapter, "Implementing Bulk Management of Mail-Enabled Objects"; search for "Scripting with the Exchange Management Shell" in Exchange Server 2007 Help; or access *http://technet. microsoft.com/en-us/library/bb123798.aspx*.

You can also use a list of variables in a CSV file to create a new universal distribution groups, new mail-enabled universal security groups, new mail contacts, and new mail-enabled users.

Quick Check

- What Exchange Management Shell command sets the Template variable used by the TemplateInstance parameter to the value "_ManagerTemplate"?

Quick Check Answer

- $Template = Get-Mailbox "_ManagerTemplate."

Moving Mailboxes and Scheduling Mailbox Moves

You can move a mailbox within a single forest, move a mailbox across forests, move several mailboxes simultaneously, and schedule when mailbox moves occur. You can use Exchange Management Shell for all these operations. You can also use Exchange Management Console, but this tool will not move mailboxes between forests. To move mailboxes, you must be delegated at least the Exchange Recipient Administrator role and the Exchange Server Administrator role for both source and target servers. You also need to be a local administrator on both servers. If you are moving mailboxes between mailbox databases on the same server, you need to be delegated the same roles and group membership, but the server-specific requirements are for only the one server.

If you are running Exchange Server 2007 on a computer that also functions as a domain controller and you want to move a mailbox to a database on this server, you must be delegated the Exchange Server Administrator role, but you do not need to be delegated the Exchange Recipient Administrator role.

Moving Mailboxes and Scheduling Moves within a Single Forest by Using Exchange Management Console

If you move a mailbox within a forest, items in the transport dumpster on a server with the Hub Transport role, which is used for cluster continuous replication, will not be moved. However, items in the Deleted Items folder will be moved.

MORE INFO **The transport dumpster**

For more information about the transport dumpster, search for "How to Configure the Transport Dumpster" in Exchange Server 2007 Help or access *http://technet.microsoft.com/en-us/library/ 4f2d92fd-ab33-4601-bdc2-cc208a36e5cb.aspx.*

If you elect to use the Move Mailbox Wizard in the Exchange Management Console to move a mailbox, you can open only one instance of the wizard within the tool. You can then move several mailboxes but only if the destination server, storage group, and mailbox database and the rules for handling corrupted messages are the same. You can also use the Move Mailbox Wizard to schedule the move, but again all the mailboxes would move at the same time. However, you can open multiple instances of Exchange Management Console and start the Move Mailbox Wizard in each. You can then select different mailboxes and specify a different destination, a corrupted message rule, and a schedule for each instance.

To use the Exchange Management Console to move a mailbox, start the console, expand Recipient Configuration in the console tree, and click Mailbox. In the Result pane, click the mailbox or mailboxes that you want to move and in the Actions pane click Move Mailbox. This starts the Move Mailbox Wizard, as shown in Figure 5-2.

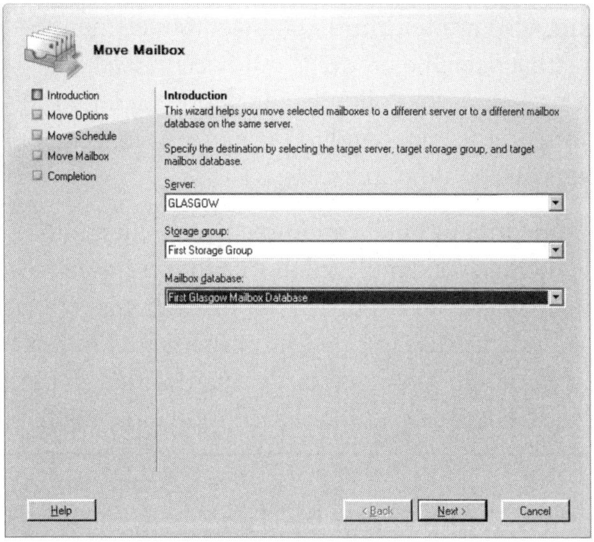

Figure 5-2   The Move Mailbox Wizard

On the wizard's Introduction page, select the server, storage group, and mailbox database to where you want to move the mailbox. On the Move Options page, you can select an option for handling corrupted messages in a mailbox, and on the Move Schedule page you can specify when the move should occur. On the Move Mailbox page, you can review the summary to confirm the mailbox moves and then click Move. On the Completion page, click Finish to close the wizard.

You use the Exchange Management Console to move mailboxes in the practice session later in this lesson.

How Exchange Management Console Schedules a Move

When you use the Move Mailbox Wizard and schedule a mailbox move to occur at a later time, the wizard remains open until the scheduled time for the move, and the Completion page does not appear until the mailboxes have been moved. If you want to move other mailboxes in the interim, you need to open another instance of Exchange Management Console.

To understand this behavior, you need to bear in mind how Exchange Management Console works. It is basically a code generator that generates Exchange Management Shell commands. The commands are passed to Exchange Management Shell, which implements the required operation, in this case a mailbox move. There is no cmdlet or parameter in Exchange Management Shell that directly specifies the time that a mailbox move should occur. Exchange Management Console therefore uses the scheduling facilities provided by the server's operating system (OS) to send the command to Exchange Management Shell at the time you specify the move should occur.

In addition, Exchange Management Shell can implement bulk mailbox moves on the basis of specified criteria, for example, all the mailboxes in a mailbox database, but when you specify mailboxes to be moved in Exchange Management Console, you select them individually from a list on the screen rather than by specifying a criterion. Exchange Management Console then generates an Exchange Management Shell command to move each individual mailbox.

Moving Mailboxes within a Single Forest by Using Exchange Management Shell

To use the Exchange Management Shell to move a mailbox to a destination in the same forest, you use commands based on the *Move-Mailbox* cmdlet. For example, to move Don Hall's mailbox to the First Glasgow Mailbox Database in the First Storage Group on the same server, you would use the following command:

```
Move-Mailbox "Don Hall" -TargetDatabase "First Storage Group\First Glasgow Mailbox Database"
```

Figure 5-3 shows the result of this command. Note that for this command to work, the First Glasgow Mailbox Database must already exist in the First Storage Group. You create this database in the practice session later in this lesson.

If you want to specify the number of corrupt messages—that is, messages that cannot display properly in client software, such as Microsoft Outlook 2007—that can be skipped before the move fails, you can set the BadItemLimit parameter. If you wanted to move Don Hall's mailbox as before but limit the number of corrupt messages to five and abort the move if more than five corrupt messages are encountered, you would use the following command:

```
Move-Mailbox "Don Hall" -TargetDatabase "First Storage Group\First Glasgow Mailbox Database"
-BadItemLimit 5
```

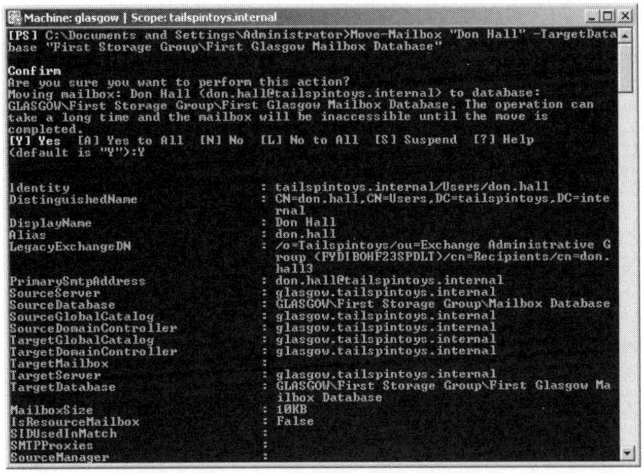

Figure 5-3   Moving a mailbox by using Exchange Management Shell

---

NOTE   **Moving mailboxes to Exchange 2000 Server or Exchange Server 2003 servers in the same forest**

If you attempt to move a mailbox from a Microsoft Exchange Server 2007 server to an Exchange 2000 Server or Exchange Server 2003 server and the mailbox has rules that occupy more than 32 KB of storage space, the move will fail. To avoid this, you can use the IgnoreRuleLimitErrors parameter. For example,

```
Move-Mailbox "Don Hall" -TargetDatabase "First Storage Group\First Glasgow Mailbox Database"
-IgnoreRuleLimitErrors
```

If you are moving an entire database to a new location, you can move the database file and then use the *Move-Mailbox* command to change the configuration information in the Active Directory directory service so that all the mailboxes point to the new location of the database. To do this, you use the ConfigurationOnly parameter. For example,

```
Move-Mailbox "Don Hall" -ConfigurationOnly -TargetDatabase "First Storage Group\Mailbox
Database" -Server Edinburgh
```

If the size limit on the source mailbox exceeds the size limit of the target database, the move fails by default. If you want to use the mailbox size limit of the source mailbox instead of the size limit of the target database, you can specify the PreserveMailbox-SizeLimit parameter. This sets the mailbox size limit for the source mailbox on the target mailbox. If a size limit for an individual source mailbox is not set, the size limit for the source database will be applied to the target mailbox. If, for example, you want to move Don Hall's mailbox and preserve the source mailbox size limit, you would use the following command:

```
Move-Mailbox "Don Hall" -TargetDatabase "First Storage Group\First Glasgow Mailbox Database"
-PreserveMailboxSizeLimit
```

When moving mailboxes between forests, the *Move-Mailbox* command does not delete the source mailbox by default. If you want to delete the source mailbox after it is moved to the target location, use the SourceMailboxCleanupOptions parameter. For example,

```
Move-Mailbox "Don Hall" -TargetDatabase "First Storage Group\First Glasgow Mailbox Database"
-SourceMailboxCleanupOptions DeleteSourceMailbox
```

Figure 5-4 shows the result of this command.

Figure 5-4   Moving a mailbox and deleting the source mailbox

To specify the time-out limit for moving a mailbox, you use the RetryTimeout parameter. If a mailbox move takes longer than the specified time, the mailbox is not moved from its source location. If you are performing a bulk move, mailboxes that have already moved will remain at the target location. Using Exchange Management Shell to move mailboxes in bulk is discussed later in this lesson. You can also specify the interval for displaying mailbox status information by using the RetryInterval parameter. For example,

```
Move-Mailbox "Don Hall" -TargetDatabase "First Storage Group\First Glasgow Mailbox Database"
-RetryTimeout 1:00:00 -RetryInterval 5:00
```

You can filter the messages that are moved to the target mailbox by using any of the following filter parameters:

- AttachmentFilenames
- ExcludeFolders
- IncludeFolders
- ContentKeywords
- SubjectKeywords
- AllContentKeywords
- Locale
- StartDate
- EndDate

For example, the following command moves Don Hall's mailbox to the Second Mailbox Database in the First Storage Group. It moves attachments with a .doc file type (Microsoft Word files). It does not move e-mail that is in the Personal or OldProjects folder in Don's Inbox. It moves all messages (other than those in the excluded folders) that have "Important" in their subject field and "merger" in the message content.

```
Move-Mailbox "Don Hall" -TargetDatabase "First Storage Group\First Glasgow Mailbox Database"
-AttachmentFilenames *.doc -ExcludeFolders \Inbox\Personal,\Inbox\OldProjects
-ContentKeywords merger -SubjectKeywords Important
```

Moving Mailboxes across Forests

You use Exchange Management Shell to move mailboxes across forests. You cannot perform this task by using Exchange Management Console. To move a mailbox from one forest to another, you must be delegated the Exchange Recipient Administrator role for both the source Exchange organization and the target Exchange organization and the Exchange Server Administrator role for both the source and the target server. You also need to be a member of the Local Administrators group on both the source and the target server.

When you move a mailbox across a forest, the mailbox-enabled user's Active Directory account does not move. However, if the user account does not already exist in the target forest, this procedure creates a disabled user account in the target forest. As a result, the source forest will contain an enabled user account, and the target forest will contain a disabled user account and the mailbox for that user account. This is known as a "resource forest scenario." As stated previously in this lesson, the use of a resource scenario is invisible to users who access their mailboxes in the normal fashion.

If you want to move both the user account and the corresponding mailbox to the target forest, you must use an appropriate Active Directory tool to move the user account, for example, ADMT v3. You can run this tool before or after you move the mailboxes. You can also use ADMT v3 to move contacts and distribution groups from one forest to another.

MORE INFO Active Directory Migration Tool

If you want to learn more about ADMT v3, you can download a guide at *http://www.microsoft.com/downloads/details.aspx?familyid=D99EF770-3BBB-4B9E-A8BC-01E9F7EF7342&displaylang=en*. To download the tool itself, access *http://www.microsoft.com/downloads/details.aspx?FamilyId=6F86937B-533A-466D-A8E8-AFF85AD3D212&displaylang=en*.

If you move a mailbox across forests, items in the transport dumpster will not be moved unless you are merging mailboxes by using the AllowMerge parameter. Items in the Deleted Items folder will be moved. You can move mailboxes from an Exchange Server 2003 forest to an Exchange Server 2007 forest (and vice versa). However, if you are moving mailboxes between an Exchange 2000 Server forest and an Exchange Server 2007 forest, you need to have at least one Windows Server 2003 domain controller in each forest.

Quick Check

1. When you move a mailbox from its source forest to a target forest, what happens to the corresponding user's Active Directory account?

2. What is the purpose of the ADMT v3 tool?

Quick Check Answers

1. The user's Active Directory account in the source forest is not moved or disabled. A disabled Active Directory account is created for the user in the target directory.

2. You can use the ADMT v3 tool to move a user's Active Directory account between forests.

You can use Exchange Management Shell on an Exchange Server 2007 server in the destination forest to move a mailbox from the source forest. In this case, you should be logged on with an account in the target forest that has the appropriate rights and Exchange Administrator roles. However, you need to provide account credentials for the source forest. To do specify an account in the source forest, you enter the following command:

```
$c = Get-Credential
```

You are prompted for credentials. You need to have an account in the source forest that has permissions to move mailboxes in that forest. You can then enter the following command to move the mailbox:

```
Move-Mailbox "Don Hall" -TargetDatabase "First Storage Group\Mailbox Database"
-SourceForestGlobalCatalog glasgow.tailspintoys.internal -DomainController
brisbane.fabrikam.com -NTAccountOU "CN=Users,DC=fabrikam,DC=com" -SourceForestCredential $c
```

This command, run in the target forest, moves Don Hall's mailbox from the source forest tailspintoys.internal to the target forest fabricam.com. The GlobalCatalog and SourceForestGlobalCatalog parameters specifiy the global catalogs in which to perform search operations in the target and source forests. Glasgow.tailspintoys.internal is a domain controller with the global catalog server role in the source forest. The GlobalCatalog parameter specifies a global catalog server in the target forest. However, this parameter is optional. If you do not specify a target forest global catalog, the forest for the local computer on which you are running the *Move-Mailbox* command is used identifies a global catalog server. If you omit the GlobalCatalog parameter, you must specify a SourceForestGlobalCatalog parameter. You cannot omit both.

The DomainController parameter is used to identify a specific domain controller in the target forest for the mailbox move, in this case Brisbane.fabricam.com. This domain controller is used during the migration for Active Directory write operations. If you do not specify a target forest domain controller, the local forest on which you are running the *Move-Mailbox* command identifies a domain controller to use.

Quick Check

- You are running commands on an Exchange Server 2007 server in a target forest to move mailboxes from a source forest. You enter the command *$c = Get-Credential* and are prompted for credentials. What account credentials do you provide?

Quick Check Answer
- You enter the credentials of an account in the source forest that has permissions to move mailboxes in that forest.

The NTAccountOU parameter is used to specify the organizational unit in the target forest where the disabled user account for the mailbox is created. However, if you do not want to interrupt user access to a mailbox, you can instead specify the Allow-Merge parameter. This parameter specifies that you want to merge the mailbox with a mailbox that already exists in the target forest. You need to create the relevant mailbox or mailboxes in the target forest before you can use the *Move-Mailbox* cmdlet with the AllowMerge parameter. The resulting command moves the source mailbox and merges it with the target mailbox. You cannot use both the NTAccountOU and the AllowMerge parameter in the same command.

The following parameters were described earlier in this lesson when we looked at moving mailboxes within a single forest, and the lesson gave examples of their use. They perform the same functions as described when you are moving mailboxes across forests:

- RetryTimeout
- RetryInterval
- IgnorePolicyMatch
- AttachmentFilenames
- ExcludeFolders
- IncludeFolders
- ContentKeywords
- SubjectKeywords

By default, the *Move-Mailbox* command does not delete the source mailbox or the source user account. If you are moving a user's mailbox to a new forest and if you have already moved the user account to the new forest by using, for example, the ADMT and if you want to delete both the source mailbox and the source user account after the mailbox is moved, you can use the DeleteSourceNTAccount option of the Source-MailboxCleanupOptions parameter. For example,

```
Move-Mailbox "Don Hall" -TargetDatabase "First Storage Group\Mailbox Database"
-SourceForestGlobalCatalog glasgow.tailspintoys.internal -DomainController
```

```
brisbane.fabrikam.com -NTAccountOU "CN=Users,DC=fabrikam,DC=com" -SourceForestCredential $c
-SourceMailboxCleanupOptions DeleteSourceNTAccount
```

IMPORTANT   Deleting source user accounts

Moving a user account to another forest by using a tool such as ADMT v3 typically disables the user account in the source forest. You cannot use the DeleteSourceNTAccount setting of the SourceMailboxCleanupOptions parameter unless the user account you are deleting is disabled.

Implementing Bulk Moves

If you use the Move Mailbox Wizard in Exchange Management Console, you can select the mailboxes you want to move in the Result pane before you start the wizard. This procedure moves mailboxes that are listed for a particular database and storage group. If you want to move, say, 10 mailboxes from one storage group to another, this is a good way to do so.

However, if you want to move a large number of mailboxes (say, more than a hundred) or mailboxes from several databases or storage groups or if you want to move mailboxes based on predefined parameter values, you can use Exchange Management Shell. To do this, you use a command based on the *Get-Mailbox* cmdlet. Such commands return a list of mailboxes determined by the values of the command parameters and by default display this list on the screen. However, you can pipe the output of a command into a command based on the *Move-Mailbox* cmdlet, which then moves all the mailboxes on the list to a specified destination. You used the pipe function in Chapter 4, "Configuring Public Folders," when you piped command output into the *Format-List* cmdlet.

For example, the following command moves all the mailboxes in the database "First Glasgow Mailbox Database" into the database "Mailbox Database" in the same storage group:

```
Get-Mailbox -Database "First Storage Group\First Glasgow Mailbox Database" | Move-Mailbox
-TargetDatabase "First Storage Group\Mailbox Database"
```

By default, you are prompted to confirm the move for each mailbox. However, you can enter **A** for "Yes to All." You can also specify a filter condition that determines what mailboxes you move. For example,

```
Get-Mailbox -Filter { (Name -eq "Don Hall") -or (Name -eq "Stephan Adolphi ") -or (Name -eq
"Kim Akers") } | Move-Mailbox -TargetDatabase "First Storage Group\Mailbox Database"
```

Figure 5-5 shows the result of this operation.

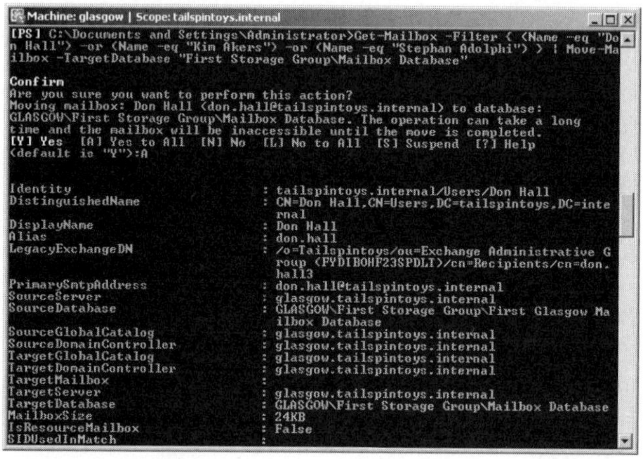

Figure 5-5   Moving multiple mailboxes by using Exchange Management Shell

Sometimes, if you are lucky, the names of the mailboxes you want to move have a common initial character string. In this case, you can use an ambiguous name resolution search by using the Anr parameter. Suppose, for example, you wanted to move the Jim Corbin, Jimmy Bischoff, Jim Daly, Jim Glynn, and Jim Hance mailboxes. You could then use the following command:

```
Get-Mailbox –Anr Jim | Move-Mailbox -TargetDatabase "First Storage Group\Mailbox Database"
```

You would, however, need to check carefully that no other mailbox names start with the character string "Jim."

Depending on the *Move-Mailbox* command in the second part of this multiple command, you can move mailboxes in bulk within a forest or between forests. You can specify parameter values as described previously. For example, you can delete the source mailboxes after the mailboxes are moved by using the DeleteSourceMailbox option of the SourceMailboxCleanupOptions parameter.

NOTE   Deleting source mailboxes

By default, moving a mailbox across forests does not delete the source mailbox. This gives a fallback situation should a mailbox move, particularly a bulk mailbox move, fail. The original mailboxes are still in the source forest, and you can try the move again. In general, it is a good idea to check that mailboxes have been moved successfully before deleting the source mailboxes. However, once you have checked that the cross-forest move has occurred without errors, you should delete the source mailboxes. The SourceMailboxCleanupOptions parameter lets you delete a source mailbox as part of a mailbox move, but you should use this with care. It is not necessary to specifiy the SourceMailboxCleanupOptions parameter when moving mailboxes within a single forest.

You can also use PowerShell scripts to implement mailbox moves and CSV files to specify the mailboxes to move. These techniques are described in Lesson 2 of this chapter.

Quick Check

- You want to move a mailbox from one forest to another. You want to delete the mailbox in the source forest. What parameter do you use, and what value do you set it to?

Quick Check Answer

- You use the SourceMailboxCleanupOptions parameter and set it to Delete-SourceMailbox.

Scheduling Mailbox Moves

We saw earlier in this chapter that you can schedule when a mailbox move takes place if you use Exchange Management Console and specify a start time in the Move Mailbox Wizard. However, this does not create an Exchange Management Shell command to implement scheduling. Instead, the wizard uses the scheduling function provided by the server software to delay issuing the command to move the mailbox until the appropriate time. The Exchange Management Shell command to move the mailbox is then generated.

Because Exchange Management Shell does not have a native scheduling facility, you can schedule Exchange Management Shell commands only if they are in an executable file, for example, a script file or a batch file. You can then use the scheduler provided by the OS to schedule when that file will run. Lesson 2 of this chapter discusses executable files.

Setting and Verifying Applicable Policies

Mailbox policies are, by default, determined by mailbox database policies, and default settings can be changed for individual mailboxes. Some policy settings are specified when the mailbox is created, but policy changes are typically applied to an individual mailbox by using the *Set-Mailbox* cmdlet. You can also change the mailbox database defaults by using the *Set-MailboxDatabase* commands. You can verify policy settings by using the *Get-MailboxDatabase* and *Get-Mailbox* commands.

When you move mailboxes, you can determine whether they retain their original policy settings or inherit the settings of the mailbox database to which you move them. For example, earlier in this lesson we discussed specifying the PreserveMailboxSize-Limit parameter in a *Move-Mailbox* command so that the move does not fail if you are moving a mailbox that is larger than the size limit specified in the target database.

Setting and Verifying Policies at the Database Level

When you use the *New-MailboxDatabase* cmdlet to create a mailbox database, you can optionally specify a path for the database (.edb) file and the associated address book for the new mailbox database. Neither of these settings can be changed at the mailbox level. However, you can use the *Set-MailboxDatabase* cmdlet to configure a number of database-level settings that are applied to mailboxes in the database by default, as listed in Table 5-1.

Table 5-1 Policy Settings Configurable at the Database Level

Policy Parameter	Description
DeletedItemRetention	Specifies the length of time to keep deleted items. Values are entered in the format dd.hh:mm:ss, where d = days, h = hours, m = minutes, and s = seconds. For example, to specify a 12-hour interval, enter **12:00:00**. By default, deleted items are retained for 14 days.
IssueWarningQuota	Specifies the mailbox size at which a warning message is sent to the user. The default value is 1.9 GB.
ProhibitSendQuota	Specifies the mailbox size at which users can no longer send messages.
ProhibitSendReceiveQuota	Specifies the mailbox size at which users can no longer send or receive messages.

You can also use the *Set-MailboxDatabase* cmdlet to configure backup, restore, and maintenance schedule settings, but these cannot be reconfigured at the mailbox level.

The *Get-MailboxDatabase* cmdlet does not return the settings of a mailbox database that are related to mailboxes (such as the issue warning and prohibit send quotas). If you want to verify these settings, you need to do so for an individual mailbox.

Setting and Verifying Policies at the Mailbox Level

When you use the *New-Mailbox* cmdlet to create a mailbox you can optionally specify policy parameter settings. When you have created the mailbox, you can use the *Set-Mailbox* cmdlet to configure further settings. The parameters you can configure when creating a mailbox are listed in Table 5-2.

Table 5-2   Policy Settings Configurable When Creating a Mailbox

Policy Parameter	Description
ActiveSyncMailboxPolicy	Specifies the ActiveSync mailbox policy that is enabled for the mailbox.
ManagedFolderMailboxPolicy	Specifies the managed folder mailbox policy that is enabled for the mailbox.
ManagedFolderMailboxPolicy Allowed	If you specify this parameter, Exchange Server 2007 server does not warn you that messaging records management features are not supported for e-mail clients using versions of Microsoft Outlook earlier than Outlook 2007.

MORE INFO   **ActiveSync mailbox policies and managed folder mailbox policies**

For more information about these policies, search for "Client Features in Exchange ActiveSync" and "How to Create a Managed Folder Mailbox Policy" in Exchange Server 2007 Server Help or access *http://technet.microsoft.com/en-us/library/aa996303.aspx* and *http://technet.microsoft.com/en-us/library/aa996359.aspx*.

The parameters you can configure on an existing mailbox by using the *Set-Mailbox* cmdlet are listed in Table 5-3. Because a very large number of these parameters exists, only those related to quotas, message retention, send and receive policies, and e-mail address format are listed in the table. Settings related to, for example, out-of-office settings and spam are discussed in Chapter 6, "Configuring Exchange Infrastructure."

Table 5-3 Policy Settings Configurable on an Existing Mailbox

Policy Parameter	Description
AcceptMessagesOnly-From	Specifies the recipients from whom messages will be accepted.
AcceptMessagesOnly-FromDLMembers	Specifies the distribution list members from whom messages will be accepted.
DeliverToMailboxAndForward	Specifies whether messages sent to the mailbox will be forwarded to another address.
EmailAddressPolicyEnabled	Specifies whether the e-mail address policy for the mailbox is enabled.
ForwardingAddress	Specifies a forwarding address. If DeliverToMailboxAndForward is set to $True, messages that are sent to the mailbox will be forwarded to the address specified.
GrantSendOnBehalfTo	Specifies the distinguished names of other mailboxes that can send messages on behalf of the mailbox.
HiddenFromAddressListsEnabled	Specifies whether the mailbox is hidden from other address lists.
IssueWarningQuota	Specifies the mailbox size at which a warning message is sent to the user.
ManagedFolderMailbox-Policy	Specifies a managed folder mailbox policy.
ManagedFolderMailbox-PolicyAllowed	Bypasses the warning that messaging records management (MRM) features are not supported for e-mail clients running versions of Outlook earlier than Outlook 2007.
MaxBlockedSenders	Specifies the maximum number of senders that can be included in the blocked senders list.
MaxReceiveSize	Specifies the maximum size of messages that the mailbox can receive.

Table 5-3 Policy Settings Configurable on an Existing Mailbox

Policy Parameter	Description
MaxSafeSenders	Specifies the maximum number of senders that can be included in the safe senders list.
MaxSendSize	Specifies the maximum size of messages that the mailbox can send.
ProhibitSendQuota	Specifies the mailbox size at which the user can no longer send messages.
ProhibitSendReceive-Quota	Specifies the mailbox size at which the user can no longer send or receive messages.
RecipientLimits	Specifies the maximum number of recipients per message to which the mailbox can send.
RejectMessagesFrom	Specifies the recipients from whom messages will be rejected.
RejectMessagesFrom-DLMembers	Specifies distribution lists. Messages from any member of these distribution lists will be rejected.
RequireSenderAuthentica-tionEnabled	Specifies whether senders must be authenticated.
ResourceCapacity	Specifies the capacity of a resource mailbox.
RetainDeletedItemsFor	Specifies the length of time to keep deleted items.
RetainDeletedItemsUntil-Backup	Specifies whether to retain deleted items until the next backup.
RulesQuota	Specifies the size limit for enabled rules for the mailbox.
UseDatabaseQuotaDe-faults	Specifies that the mailbox uses the quota attributes specified for the mailbox database.
UseDatabaseRetentionDe-faults	Specifies that the mailbox uses the MailboxRetention attribute specified for the mailbox database.

You can use the *Get-Mailbox* cmdlet to view mailbox objects and attributes and populate property pages. The cmdlet can also supply mailbox information or a list of mailboxes to other tasks. For example its output can be piped into a command that uses the *Move-Mailbox* cmdlet to move the listed mailboxes. You can use the *Get-Mailbox-Statistics* cmdlet to obtain information about a mailbox, for example, the size of the mailbox, the number of messages it contains, and the last time it was accessed. The *Get-Mailbox* cmdlet was discussed earlier in this lesson.

Retaining Polices When Moving Mailboxes

When you move mailboxes, by default they inherit the settings of the target mailbox database. Sometimes, however, this is not what you want. You might have created a template by specifying a number of the parameters listed in Table 5-3 and want these settings to be retained. A mailbox you want to move might be larger than the maximum size limit of the target database, in which case the move will fail.

The *Move-Mailbox* cmdlet supports a number of parameters that allow you to change the default behavior when you are moving mailboxes. These were discussed earlier in this lesson but are listed in Table 5-4 for convenience.

Table 5-4   Parameters That Specify Recipient Policy Configuration When Moving Mailboxes

Parameter	Description
IgnorePolicyMatch	Specifies whether to match recipient policies.
IgnoreRuleLimitErrors	Used when moving a mailbox to an Exchange Server 2003 or Exchange 2000 Server organization to circumvent the Microsoft Outlook 32-KB rules limit.
PreserveMailboxSizeLimit	Specifies whether to apply the size limit options of the source mailbox to the target mailbox.

The IgnoreRuleLimitErrors and PreserveMailboxSizeLimit parameters were discussed earlier in this lesson. However, arguably the most useful of these parameters is IgnorePolicyMatch. This enables you to retain all the recipient policies configured on a mailbox when the mailbox is moved. For example,

```
Move-Mailbox "Don Hall" -TargetDatabase "First Storage Group\Mailbox Database"
-IgnorePolicyMatch
```

Practice: Creating and Moving Mailboxes in Bulk

In this practice session, you first create a number of mailbox-enabled users whose details are held in a CSV file. You then create and mount a new mailbox database and use Exchange Management Shell to move the mailboxes you created to the new database. Finally, you use Exchange Management Shell to move them back into the original database.

▶ **Practice 1: Creating Bulk Users**

In this practice, you create a mailbox template and a CSV file that holds the data for five mailbox-enabled users. You then use Exchange Management Shell to create these users. As the practice is written, you create the CSV file by using a text editor, for example, Microsoft Notepad. If you prefer, you can enter user data into a spreadsheet such as Microsoft Excel and save this data as a CSV file. Many organizations have a list of employees held in a spreadsheet file.

1. If necessary, log on by using the Kim_Akers account.

2. Open Exchange Management Shell.

3. Use a text editor to create a file similar to that shown in Figure 5-6. Save this in the root of the C:\ drive as CreateUser.csv. If you choose to save the file in an alternative folder or with another name, take a note of these details and amend the practice accordingly. The file must have a .csv file type.

Figure 5-6 CSV file used to create users

4. You now create a mailbox template. Enter the following command in Exchange Management Shell:

```
New-Mailbox –Name _Template -UserPrincipalName _Template@tailspintoys.external
–Database "First Storage Group\Mailbox Database" -OrganizationalUnit Users
–ResetPasswordOnNextLogon $True
```

5. When prompted for a password, enter **P@ssw0rd.** The creation of a mailbox template was shown in Figure 5-1 earlier in this lesson.

6. You now set the variable $Template so that it identifies the _Template mailbox. Enter the following command:

```
$Template = Get-Mailbox _Template
```

7. You now set the $Temp variable so that it contains a secure string generated from the password P@ssw0rd. Because of how you have specified the template, the user will be asked to change password at first logon. Enter the following command:

```
$Temp = ConvertTo-SecureString P@ssw0rd -asPlainText -Force
```

8. You now create the mail-enabled users. Enter the following command:

```
Import-CSV "C:\CreateUsers.csv" | ForEach-Object -Process {New-Mailbox -Name $_.Name
-UserPrincipalName $_.UPN -OrganizationalUnit $_.OU -Database "First Storage
Group\Mailbox Database" -Password $Temp -TemplateInstance $Template}
```

Figure 5-7 shows the new mailbox-enabled users.

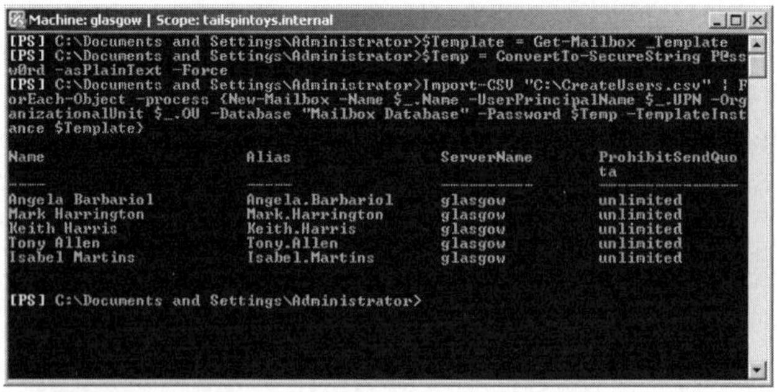

Figure 5-7   Mailbox-enabled users created by bulk command

MORE INFO   **Shell variable**

Variables starting with $_ are Exchange Management Shell variables that contain a pipeline object. Thus, the variable $_.Name contains a string imported from the CSV file and piped to the Name parameter in the *New-Mailbox* command. For more information about shell variables, search for "Shell Variables" in Exchange Server 2007 Help or access *http://technet.microsoft.com/en-us/library/a601c3d9-534d-4155-9a8e-73ef2c2229f2.aspx.*

▶ **Practice 2: Moving Users into a New Database**

In this practice, you create and mount a new mailbox database and use Exchange Management Console to move the mailboxes you have created into it. The practice assumes that the First Glasgow Mailbox Database does not already exist.

1. If necessary, log on by using the Kim_Akers account.

2. Open Exchange Management Shell.

3. Enter the following commands:

   ```
   New-MailboxDatabase "First Glasgow Mailbox Database" –StorageGroup "First Storage Group"
   Mount-Database "First Glasgow Mailbox Database"
   ```

4. Open Exchange Management Console.

5. Expand Recipient Configuration and click Mailbox.

6. Select the mailboxes to move, as shown in Figure 5-8.

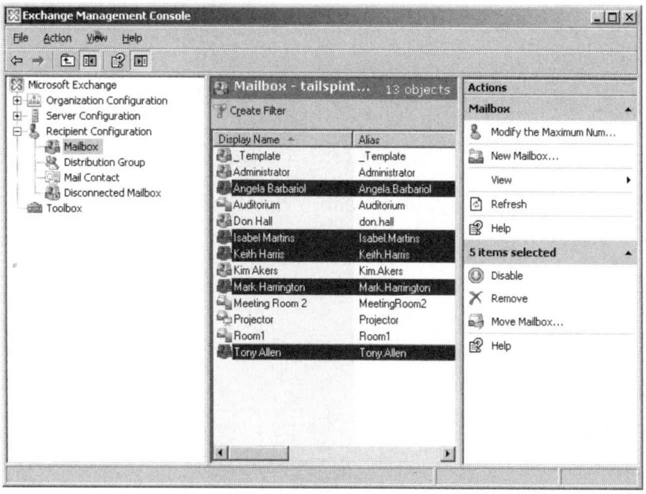

Figure 5-8 Selecting mailboxes

7. In the Actions pane, click Move Mailbox. The Move Mailbox Wizard starts.

8. Specify First Glasgow Mailbox Database, as shown in Figure 5-9. Click Next.

NOTE **New Mailbox Wizard does not display new database**

If the New Mailbox Wizard does not display the new database First Glasgow Mailbox Database, expand Server Configuration, right-click Mailbox, and click Refresh.

---

9. On the Move Options page, specify that up to five corrupted messages can be skipped, as shown in Figure 5-10. Click Next.

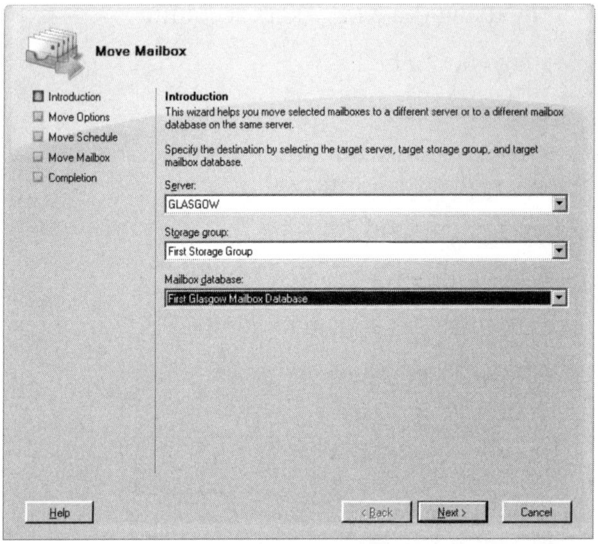

Figure 5-9 Specifying the destination mailbox database

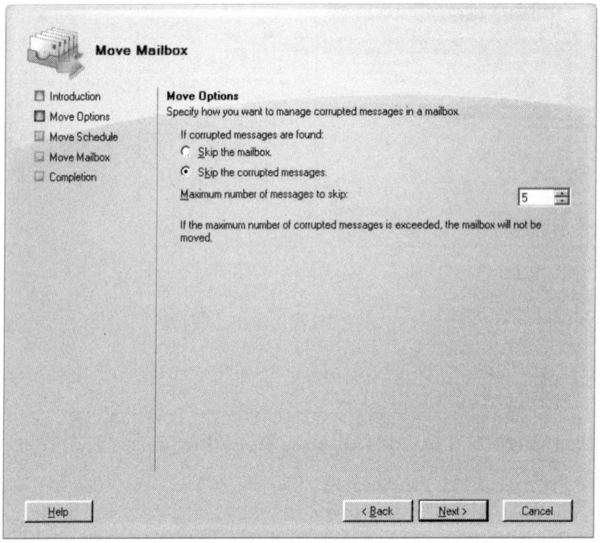

Figure 5-10 Specifying move options

10. On the Move Schedule page, specify that the mailboxes should be moved immediately, as shown in Figure 5-11. Click Next.

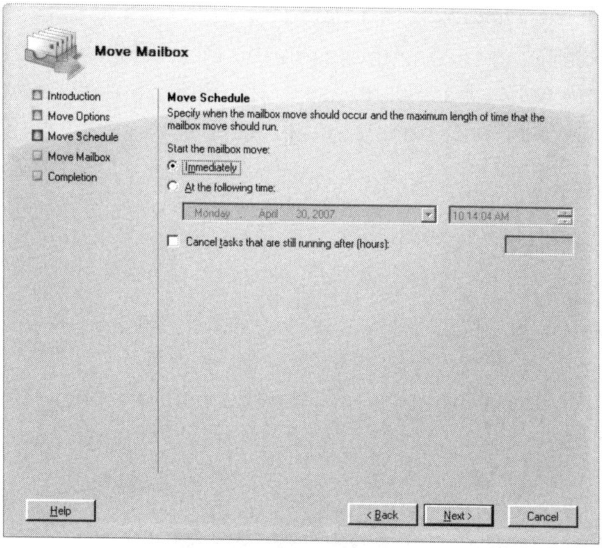

Figure 5-11   Specifying move options

11. On the Move Mailbox page, shown in Figure 5-12, check that all the mailboxes to be moved are listed. Click Move.

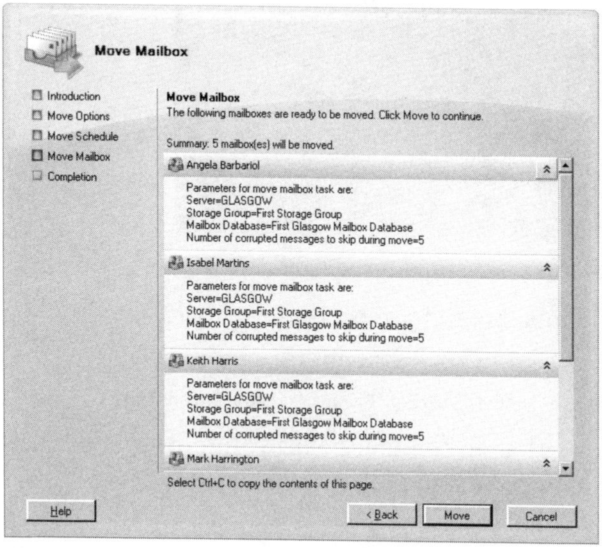

Figure 5-12   List of mailboxes to be moved

12. When the multiple move is complete, click Finish to close the wizard.

▶ **Practice 3: Moving All the Mailboxes in a Database**

In this practice, you move all the mailboxes in the First Glasgow Mailbox Database database into the Mailbox Database database in the First Storage Group. You need to have completed Practice 2 before you attempt Practice 3.

1. If necessary, log on by using the Kim_Akers account.

2. Open Exchange Management Shell.

3. Enter the following command:

```
Get-Mailbox –Database "First Glasgow Mailbox Database" | Move-Mailbox –TargetDatabase
"First Storage Group\Mailbox Database"
```

Confirm the action when prompted. When the mailboxes have been moved into the Mailbox Database database, your Exchange Management Shell console should look similar to Figure 5-13.

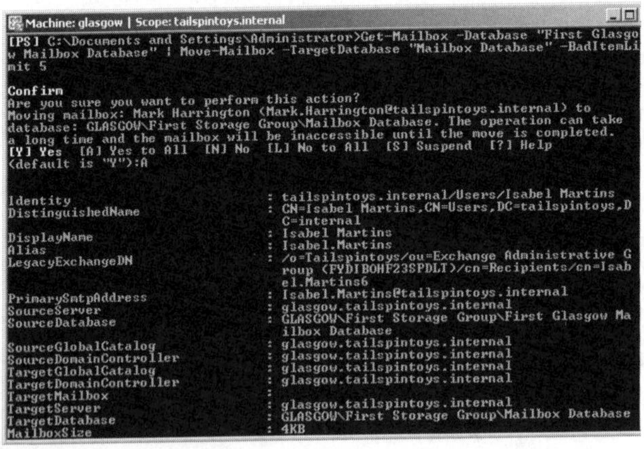

Figure 5-13 Bulk mailboxes move using Exchange Management Shell

4. To check that the mailboxes have been moved back into the Mailbox Database database, enter the following command:

```
Get-Mailbox –Database "First Storage Group\Mailbox Database"
```

Figure 5-14 shows that all the mailboxes you moved in the previous practice have now been moved back to their original location.

NOTE Specifying the storage group

If you have not created any additional storage groups, you could use the command *Get-Mailbox –Database "Mailbox Database"* in step 4 of Practice 3. However, you might have created additional storage groups and placed a mailbox database called Mailbox Database in each.

```
Machine: glasgow | Scope: tailspintoys.internal                        _ □ ×
[PS] C:\Documents and Settings\Administrator>Get-Mailbox -Database "First Storag
e Group\Mailbox Database"

Name                       Alias                   ServerName      ProhibitSendQuo
                                                                   ta
----                       -----                   ----------      ----------------
Administrator              Administrator           glasgow         unlimited
Auditorium                 Auditorium              glasgow         unlimited
Don Hall                   don.hall                glasgow         2GB
Room1                      Room1                   glasgow         unlimited
Meeting Room 2             MeetingRoom2            glasgow         unlimited
Projector                  Projector               glasgow         unlimited
Kim Akers                  Kim.Akers               glasgow         unlimited
_Template                  _Template               glasgow         unlimited
Angela Barbariol           Angela.Barbariol        glasgow         unlimited
Mark Harrington            Mark.Harrington         glasgow         unlimited
Keith Harris               Keith.Harris            glasgow         unlimited
Tony Allen                 Tony.Allen              glasgow         unlimited
Isabel Martins             Isabel.Martins          glasgow         unlimited


[PS] C:\Documents and Settings\Administrator>_
```

Figure 5-14   Listing the mailboxes in the Mailbox Database database

Lesson Summary

- You can move mailboxes within a forest by using either Exchange Management Console or Exchange Management Shell. If you want to move mailboxes across forests, you need to use Exchange Management Shell.

- You can implement bulk moves directly in Exchange Management Console. One technique for implementing bulk moves in Exchange Management Shell is to select mailboxes by using a *Get-Mailbox* command and then pipe the output of this command into a *Move-Mailbox* command.

- You can use the information in CSV files for bulk operations, such as creating multiple mailboxes.

Lesson Review

You can use the following questions to test your knowledge of the information in Lesson 1, "Moving Mailboxes." The questions are also available on the companion CD if you prefer to review them in electronic form.

NOTE Answers

Answers to these questions and explanations of why each answer choice is correct or incorrect are located in the "Answers" section at the end of the book.

1. You are using Exchange Management Console to move selected mailboxes to another database. You select the mailboxes and step through the pages of the wizard. On the Move Schedule page, you specify that the mailboxes should be moved at 11:30 PM that day, and you click Next. On the Move Mailbox page, you click Move. What then happens?

   A. You click Finish, and a single command to move the mailboxes is sent to Exchange Management Shell. Exchange Management Shell uses the scheduling facilities of the OS to delay the execution of the command until the appropriate time.

   B. You click Finish, and multiple commands to move each mailbox individually are sent to Exchange Management Shell. Exchange Management Shell uses the scheduling facilities of the OS to delay the execution of the commands until the appropriate time.

   C. You cannot close the Move Mailbox Wizard because the wizard remains on the the Move Mailbox page until the scheduled time is reached. At 11:30 PM, a single command is sent to Exchange Management Shell to implement all the mailbox moves. After the mailboxes have been moved, you can click Finish to close the wizard.

   D. You cannot close the Move Mailbox Wizard because the wizard remains on the the Move Mailbox page until the scheduled time is reached. At 11:30 PM, multiple commands are sent to Exchange Management Shell, each of which implements a mailbox move. After the mailboxes have been moved, you can click Finish to close the wizard.

2. You enter the command *Move-Mailbox "Don Hall" -TargetDatabase "First Storage Group\First Glasgow Mailbox Database" -BadItemLimit 5*. Don Hall's mailbox contains six corrupted messages. What is the result of the command?

   A. Don Hall's mailbox is moved with all corrupted messages removed.

   B. Don Hall's mailbox is not moved.

   C. Don Hall's mailbox is moved with five corrupted messages removed. The sixth corrupted message is moved with the mailbox.

   D. Don Hall's mailbox is moved along with the first five corrupted messages. The sixth corrupted message is not moved.

3. Kim Akers's mailbox is in the database Mailbox Database in the storage group First Storage Group. Five of the messages contained in the mailbox are corrupted. What does the following command do?

```
Move-Mailbox "Kim Akers" -TargetDatabase "First Storage Group\First Glasgow Mailbox
Database" -SourceMailboxCleanupOptions DeleteSourceMailbox
```

A. Moves Kim Akers's mailbox to the database First Glasgow Mailbox Database in the storage group First Storage Group and deletes Kim Akers's mailbox in the database Mailbox Database in the storage group First Storage Group. All messages are moved, including the corrupted messages.

B. Moves Kim Akers's mailbox to the database First Glasgow Mailbox Database in the storage group First Storage Group but does not delete Kim Akers's mailbox in the database Mailbox Database in the storage group First Storage Group. All messages are moved, including the corrupted messages.

C. Moves Kim Akers's mailbox to the database First Glasgow Mailbox Database in the storage group First Storage Group and deletes Kim Akers's mailbox in the database Mailbox Database in the storage group First Storage Group. All messages are moved except the corrupted messages.

D. Does not move Kim Akers's mailbox.

4. Kim Akers is the Exchange organization administrator at Coho Winery. Don Hall is the Exchange organization administrator at Coho Vineyard. There is a requirement to move a group of mailboxes from the Coho Winery forest to the Coho Vineyard forest. In preparation, the *c = Get-Credential* command is used to obtain the credentials required by the *Move-Mailbox* command. Who enters the command, and what credentials are supplied?

A. Don Hall enters the command and provides Kim Akers's credentials.

B. Don Hall enters the command and provides his own credentials.

C. Kim Akers enters the command and provides Don Hall's credentials.

D. Kim Akers enters the command and provides her own credentials.

5. Which of the following settings are configurable when you create a mailbox? Choose all that apply.

A. IssueWarningQuota

B. ActiveSyncMailboxPolicy

C. ManagedFolderMailboxPolicy

D. MaxReceiveSize

E. ManagedFolderMailboxPolicyAllowed

F. RejectMessagesFrom

Lesson 2: Implementing Bulk Management of Mail-Enabled Objects

Configuring the settings for a mailbox and moving a single mailbox are relatively straightforward operations. Things start getting complex when you need to deal with large numbers of mailboxes and other Exchange objects, such as public folders. In the previous lesson, you saw how to use CSV files to create a number of users with a single command and how you could select mailboxes by using the *Get-Mailbox* cmdlet and then move the selected mailboxes by piping the output from a *Get-Mailbox* command into a *Move-Mailbox* command. In this lesson, you expand and combine these techniques.

You also saw that the Exchange Management Console GUI could be used to select multiple mailboxes, move them in bulk, and schedule the move. This lesson investigates how the GUI can be used to filter the mailboxes to be moved.

If you want to perform the same task a large number of times or automate a task so that it performs without errors, you would typically generate a script file. Exchange Management Shell is based on Microsoft PowerShell, and this lesson investigates the use of PowerShell scripts to implement bulk management of Exchange objects and how to specify batch files that run PowerShell scripts from the Command Console and whose operation can be scheduled.

After this lesson, you will be able to:

- ■ Configure bulk management by using PowerShell scripts or the GUI.
- ■ Schedule bulk management.

Estimated lesson time: 50 minutes

Configuring Bulk Management

In the previous lesson, you saw that you could move all the mailboxes in a mailbox database by using a command based on the *Get-Mailbox* cmdlet and piping the result into a command based on the *Move-Mailbox* cmdlet. However, if you wanted to move specific mailboxes rather than all mailboxes, you needed to use the Filter parameter. If you want to move a lot of mailboxes but not all of them, this can be a rather tedious and error-prone method.

Typically, it is easier and more efficient to use a CSV file that holds the identities of the mailboxes you want to move. Such a file can be very simple and contain only identities or can be more complex and contain other information, such as configuration settings if you want to configure mailboxes rather than move them. Figure 5-15 shows the simple CSV file IdentifyUsers.csv, which contains mailbox identities. This file can be generated by editing the CSV file that you used to create mailbox-enabled users in the first instance.

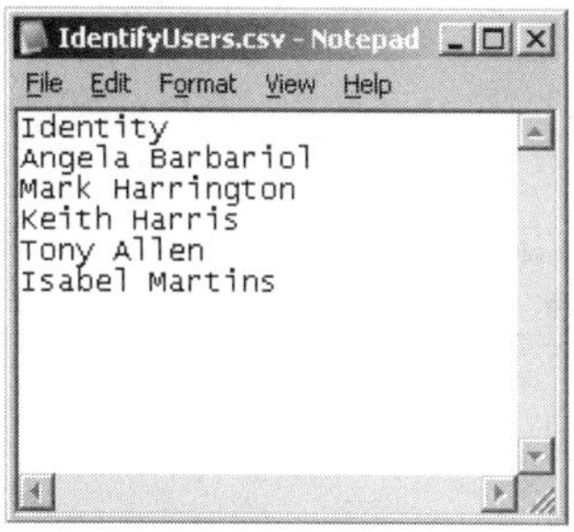

Figure 5-15   Mailbox identities in a CSV file

Assuming that this file is saved to the root of the C:\ drive (you can change the path specification if you store it elsewhere), you can list the mailboxes by using the following command:

```
Import-CSV "C:\IdentifyUsers.csv" | ForEach-Object –Process {Get-Mailbox –Identity
$_.Identity}
```

Figure 5-16 shows the output from this command.

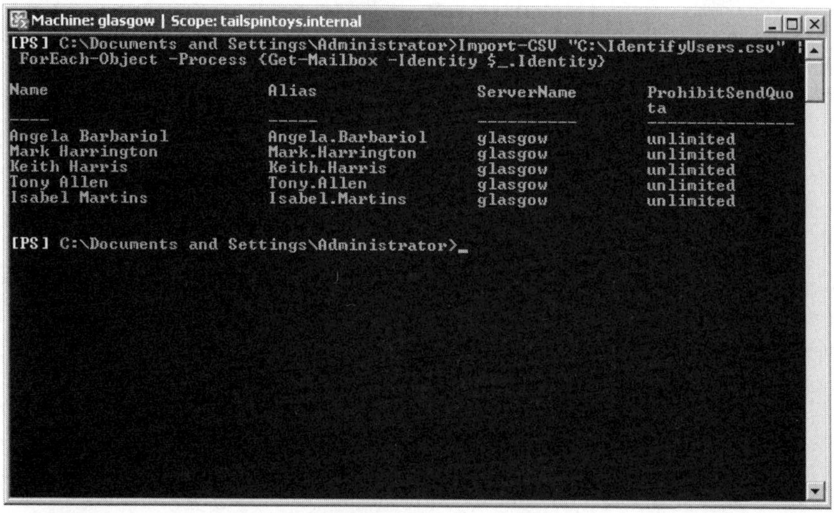

Figure 5-16   Listing mailboxes identified by a CSV file

If you want to move these users from the default mailbox database (First Storage Group\Mailbox Database) to the database First Glasgow Mailbox Database in the same storage group, you could pipe the output of the previous command into an appropriate command based on the *Move-Mailbox* cmdlet as follows:

```
Import-CSV "C:\IdentifyUsers.csv" | ForEach-Object -Process {Get-Mailbox -Identity
$_.Identity} | Move-Mailbox -TargetDatabase "First Storage Group\First Glasgow Mailbox
Database"
```

The output from this command is shown in Figure 5-17.

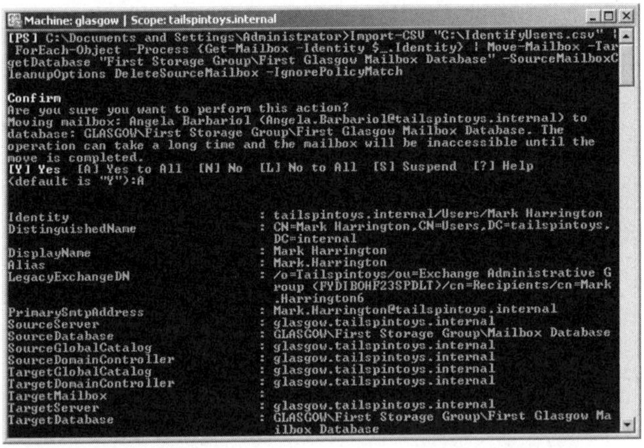

Figure 5-17   Moving mailboxes identified by a CSV file

Real World

Ian McLean

Never try to solve a big problem when you can solve several small problems instead.

Bulk management can look very complex. For example, you might feed the information in a CSV file into a command that identifies mailboxes and pipe the output into another command that does something with them. Think about it all at once, and your brain might give up the uneven struggle and switch to a state of confusion (or, in my case, blind panic).

But a CSV file is a simple thing. It consists of a line of variables, separated by commas, a line of values for these variables, another line of values for these variables, and so on. You can use a text editor to generate the file directly, or you can type the lines into spreadsheet rows with one cell for each variable and value and save this as a CSV file. There are no special symbols and no special formatting. About the only thing you need to remember is not to put spaces after the commas or at the end of lines.

The commands based on the *Get-Mailbox* cmdlet are not particularly complex. You can specify a lot of parameters, but each parameter has its own defined function, there is not a high degree of interdependency, and you typically do not need to worry about the order in which you define them. The same can be said of commands based on the *New-Mailbox* and *Set-Mailbox* cmdlets. You've used the commands before—you're simply using them with parameter values extracted from a CSV file. Remember that if you're piping the output from such commands into another command, you can first run the command without the pipe and check that the output is what you expected.

Finally, the command that actually does something with the output of another command piped into it is also relatively straightforward. You've used, for example, the *Move-Mailbox* cmdlet before in the previous lesson. It has a number of parameters, but most of them are reasonably self-explanatory.

So the large, complex problem is broken down into three small problems. In the previous example, you get the CSV file correct, ensure that the command based on the *Get-Mailbox* cmdlet gives the output you expect, and then feed that output into the command based on the *Move-Mailbox* cmdlet. You've done all three before.

Bulk management really is much easier than it looks.

Quick Check

- What does the following command do?

```
Import-CSV "C:\UserList.csv" | ForEach-Object –Process {Get-Mailbox –Identity
$_.Identity} | Move-Mailbox –TargetDatabase "Second Storage Group\Mailbox Database"
```

Quick Check Answer

- Moves the mailboxes listed in the C:\UserList.csv file to the database Mailbox Database in the storage group Second Storage Group.

You can also configure mailbox settings in bulk by using the *Set-Mailbox* cmdlet with a CSV file. For example, you can use the simple IdentifyUsers.csv file to set a maximum receive size limit (the maximum size of any single message that the mailbox can receive) of 2 MB for the mailboxes identified by the file. The command to do this is as follows:

```
Import-CSV "C:\IdentifyUsers.csv" | ForEach-Object -Process {Set-Mailbox -Identity $_.Identity
-MaxReceiveSize 2MB}
```

However, you can add a little more sophistication to a CSV file, although very few CSV files can be described as complex. For example, you might want to set a different set of quotas for each mailbox. In this case, you could use a CSV file similar to the Set-Quotas.csv file shown in Figure 5-18.

Figure 5-18   CSV file specifying quota settings

WARNING   Do not put blank lines or unnecessary spaces in CSV files

It is easy to accidentally put a space after a comma in a CSV file, and you need to take care not to do this. In addition, you also need to check that there are no space characters at the end of lines or extra blank lines at the end of the file.

Assuming that the CSV file is saved in the root of the C:\ drive, you can set mailbox quotas with the following command:

```
Import-CSV "C:\SetQuotas.csv" | ForEach-Object -Process {Set-Mailbox -Identity $_.Identity
-ProhibitSendReceiveQuota $_.Receive -ProhibitSendQuota $_.Send -IssueWarningQuota
$_.Warning}
```

You can also use CSV files to specify mailboxes to disable or remove. In both cases, you need to confirm the operation for each mailbox. The commands to disable and delete the mailboxes specified in the IdentityUsers.csv file are, respectively, the following:

```
Import-CSV "C:\IdentifyUsers.csv" | ForEach-Object -Process {Disable-Mailbox -Identity
$_.Identity}
Import-CSV "C:\IdentifyUsers.csv" | ForEach-Object -Process {Remove-Mailbox -Identity
$_.Identity}
```

NOTE Removing mailboxes

If you have disabled a mailbox, the user is no longer identified as a mailbox user. You cannot, therefore, use *Remove-Mailbox* to remove a disabled mailbox.

Sometimes you want to work with user attributes, for example, Department. In some organizations, you can identify a user's department from the OU parameter in that user's mailbox, such as when all the accountants' user accounts are in the accounting OU. However, in Active Directory structures where OUs are not created for each department, you might need to use the user's Department attribute instead. You can specify attributes in commands based on the *Get-User* and *Set-User* cmdlets.

You might, for example, want to set the Department attribute for a list of existing users by using a CSV file similar to the UserDepatment.csv file shown in Figure 5-19.

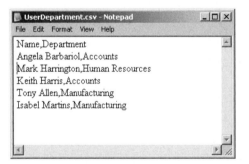

Figure 5-19 CSV file specifying departments

Assuming that the file is saved in the root of the C: drive, you can use the following command to set the Department attribute for each of the listed users:

```
Import-CSV "C:\UserDepartment.csv" | ForEach-Object -Process {Set-User -Identity $_.Name
-Department $_.Department}
```

If you then wanted to move the mailboxes of the users in the Manufacturing department to the database First Glasgow Mailbox Database in the storage group First Storage Group, you can use the following command:

```
Get-User -Filter { Department -eq "Manufacturing" } | Move-Mailbox -TargetDatabase "First
Storage Group\First Glasgow Mailbox Database"
```

MORE INFO   **Using the Exchange Management Shell for bulk recipient management**

For further examples of the use of Exchange Management Shell commands and CSV files and an excellent article about this technique, access *http://technet.microsoft.com/en-us/library/bb310752.aspx.*

Creating Bulk Management Tasks by Using the GUI

In the previous lesson, you used the Exchange Management Console to move mailboxes in bulk. In the practice session, you moved five mailboxes. In the production environment, however, you might need to move hundreds and possibly thousands of mailboxes, and you need a filtering mechanism to help you select the mailboxes to move.

When you open Exchange Management Console and expand Recipient Configuration, you can perform a first level of filtering by selecting Mailbox, Distribution Group, Mail Contact, or Disconnected Mailbox. If you want to move, disable, or remove mailboxes in bulk, you would select Mailbox. To set up a filter, you click Create Filter above the list of mailboxes. In the left-hand pull-down menu, you can set a filter parameter, as shown in Figure 5-20.

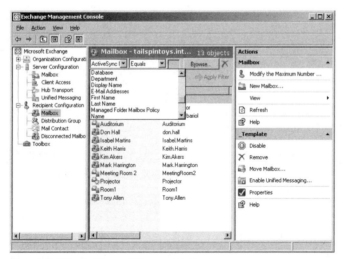

Figure 5-20   Setting a filter parameter

You can choose from a number of different parameters, including e-mail addresses and custom attributes. If, for example, you want to move all the mailboxes in a particular department, you can choose Department. You can then select a filter condition, as shown in Figure 5-21. If you want to select all the mailboxes in a department, you specify Equals, but you could also specify that you want to select all the mailboxes except those in a particular department or all mailboxes whose name contains or does not contain a specified letter.

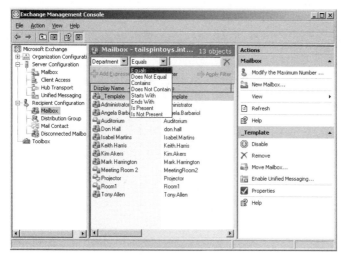

Figure 5-21   Setting a filter condition

On the third filter condition box, you can set a parameter value, either by typing it in or by selecting Browse. The Browse facility is available only for certain parameters. In the case of the Department parameter, you type the name of the department. Figure 5-22 shows the filter configured for Department Equals Manufacturing.

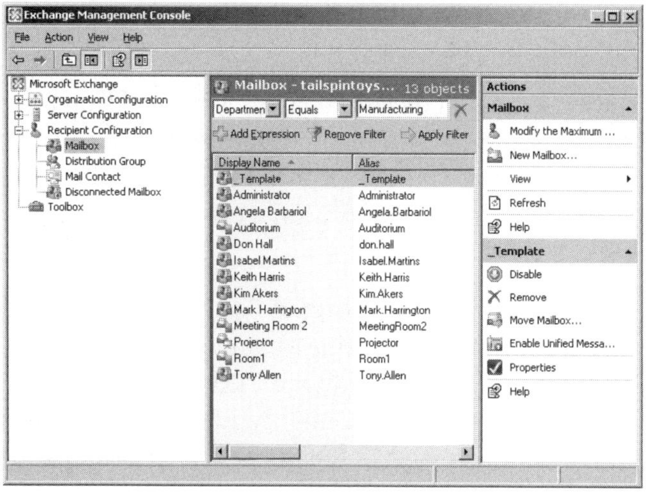

Figure 5-22   Setting a filter value

You then click Apply Filter to obtain a filtered list of mailboxes, as shown in Figure 5-23. You can select all these mailboxes and move, disable, or delete them. If you choose to move the mailboxes, the Move Mailbox Wizard allows you to schedule the move as described in Lesson 1. You also have the option of filtering the list further by clicking Add Filter Condition or of removing the filter.

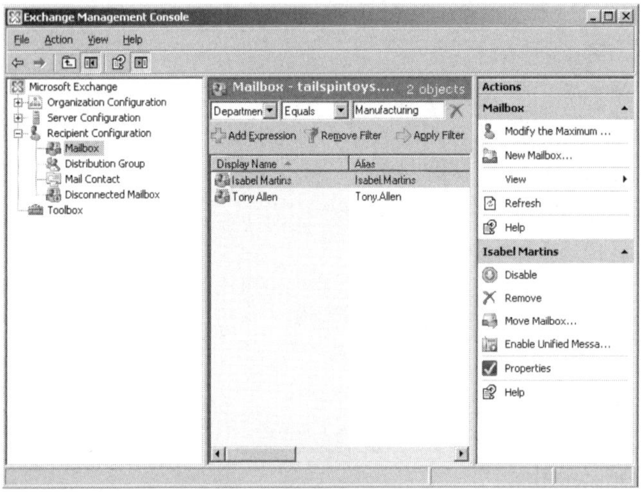

Figure 5-23   Applying the filter

Using PowerShell Scripts for Bulk Management

Typically, you can carry out most bulk management tasks by using CSV files and by piping the output from one Exchange Management Shell command into another. However, if you need to do a task frequently and, in particular, if the task is complex, you might find it advantageous to create a script file.

You might previously have used batch files that have a .bat extension and run from the Command Console. Such files contain the commands that otherwise you would type into the console to carry out the required operation. PowerShell script files are similar, except they run in Exchange Management Shell and have a .ps1 extension.

Exchange Management Shell cmdlets are a subset of PowerShell cmdlets and follow the same verb–noun construct. Instead of entering a command directly into Exchange Management Shell, you can type it into a text editor and save it with a .ps1 extension. Exchange Server 2007 provides a set of preconfigured PowerShell scripts that are stored in the C:\Program Files\Microsoft\Exchange Server\Scripts subdirectory.

Figure 5-24 shows a list of the files in this subdirectory. Script files that you store in the C:\Program Files\Microsoft\Exchange Server\Scripts subdirectory can be run directly from Exchange Management Shell without specifying a path.

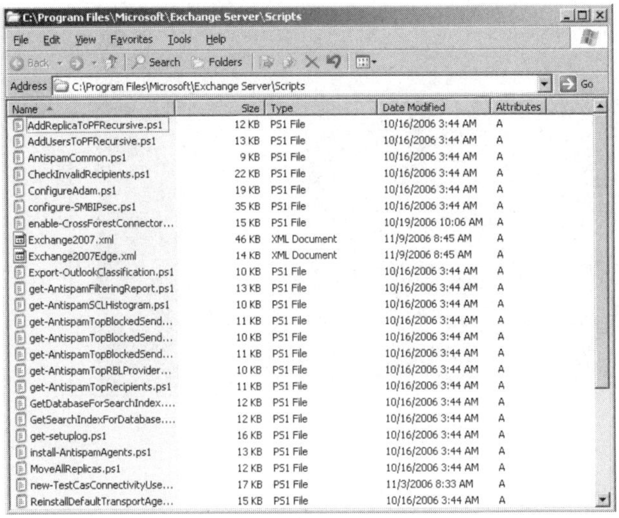

Figure 5-24 The PSHome subdirectory

NOTE The PSHome subdirectory

By default, the PowerShell variable $PSHome points to the Windows PowerShell directory (C:\WINDOWS\system32\WindowsPowerShell\v1.0). While it is possible to point the PowerShell variable $PSHome to the location of the C:\Program Files\Microsoft\Exchange Server\Scripts subfolder, this is seldom necessary because the C:\Program Files\Microsoft\Exchange Server\Scripts subfolder is included in the system search path. To display the search path, use the $env:path command.

You run a PowerShell script file by typing its name into Exchange Management Shell, typically followed by the parameters you want to specify. Some script files require parameters in order to run, while with others the parameters are optional. If you wanted to identify all invalid recipients in your Exchange organization, for example, mailboxes that have more than one primary SMTP address, you can enter *CheckInvalidRecipients.ps1*. If, on the other hand, you wanted to list any invalid recipients in a specific OU, you can enter the OU as a parameter, for example, *CheckInvalidRecipients.ps1 -OrganizationalUnit Users*. If you add the FixErrors parameter, PowerShell will attempt to repair any errors it encounters. In this case, the command is *CheckInvalidRecipients.ps1 -OrganizationalUnit Users -FixErrors*. Figure 5-25 shows these commands in Exchange Management Shell. The outputs are not particularly interesting because you are unlikely to have errors in your test environment at this stage. You might get different results in a production environment, particularly after a large migration from another organization.

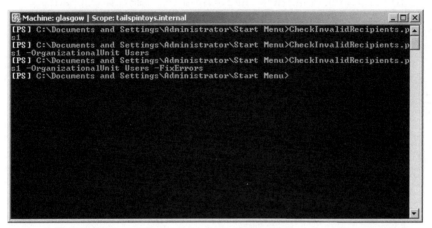

Figure 5-25   Using the CheckInvalidRecipients.ps1 file

Creating PowerShell Scripts to Manage Recipients

PowerShell provides a very powerful and fully featured scripting language that gives programmers direct access to the entire .NET common language run time plus the ability to script existing COM (ActiveX) and Windows Management Instrumentation objects. However, this book and the 70-236 examination are not about complex programming functions and routines. You can generate simple PowerShell scripts as easily as you type commands into Exchange Management Shell. If you carry out tasks repeatedly, even this fairly basic use of PowerShell can save you a lot of time and effort. But remember that there is a lot more to PowerShell than is described in this brief section.

MORE INFO   **Sample PowerShell scripts**

Many examples of PowerShell scripts exist on the Internet, and more are being posted on blogs every day. However, to get information about the scripts that Microsoft has identified as the best of their kind, access *http://www.microsoft.com/technet/scriptcenter/scripts/msh/default.mspx?mfr=true.*

To create a simple PowerShell script, type the following into a text editor:

```
Move-Mailbox "Don Hall" -TargetDatabase "First Storage Group\First Glasgow Mailbox Database"
```

Save the file in the C:\Program Files\ Microsoft\ Exchange Server\Scripts subdirectory as MoveDon.ps1. Open Exchange Management Shell and enter **MoveDon.ps1**.

You should get an Exchange Management Shell screen similar to Figure 5-26. If you want to move Don, enter **Y**; otherwise, enter **N**. It may not have done much, but you have just created and run a PowerShell script.

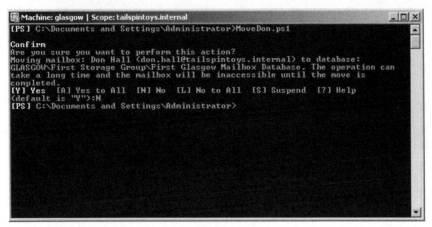

Figure 5-26   Running a simple PowerShell script

You can now write a PowerShell script that uses a parameter that is specified as part of the command line, for example, the Identity parameter used to identify a mailbox. Amend the MoveDon.ps1 file so that it contains the following:

```
Param(
[string] $Identity
)
Move-Mailbox -Identity $Identity -TargetDatabase "First Storage Group\First Glasgow Mailbox
Database"
```

Save the file in the C:\Program Files\ Microsoft\ Exchange Server\Scripts subdirectory as MoveAnyone.ps1. In Exchange Management Shell, enter **MoveAnyone.ps1 −Identity "Tony Allen"** (if you have not created the mailbox-enabled user Tony Allen in the previous lesson, then specify a user that you have created). Figure 5-27 shows the result of this entry. Note that you need to specify the parameter before you include it in the command.

To manage recipients (or other Exchange entities) in bulk, you need to be able to define more than one of them. This can be done using a CSV file. For example, you could create a PowerShell script file containing the command:

```
Import-CSV "C:\IdentifyUsers.csv" | ForEach-Object -Process {Get-Mailbox -Identity
$_.Identity} | Move-Mailbox -TargetDatabase "First Storage Group\First Glasgow Mailbox
Database"
```

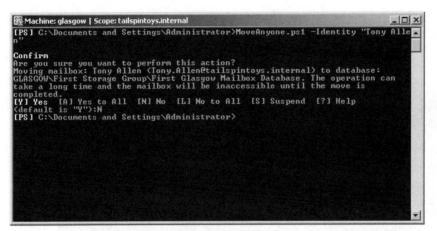

Figure 5-27   Specifying a PowerShell parameter

This, however, would be inflexible. You might want to specify other CSV files, possibly in locations other than the root of the C:\ drive. To do this, you create a PowerShell script that takes the parameter Source. This file contains the following code:

```
Param(
[string] $Source
)
Import-CSV $Source | ForEach-Object –Process {Get-Mailbox –Identity $_.Identity} | Move-
Mailbox –TargetDatabase "First Storage Group\First Glasgow Mailbox Database"
```

You save this script as MoveMultiple.ps1 and then specify the CSV file you want to use and the path to it. For example, in Exchange Management Shell, you enter the following:

```
MoveMultiple.ps1 –Source C:\IdentifyUsers.csv
```

Figure 5-28 shows the result of this operation. You can expand the technique so that you can specify the target database as a parameter as well as the CSV file. This is a suggested practice.

NOTE   **PowerShell scripts and CSV files**

It is possible to write a PowerShell script or to use other scripting tools to extract information from Active Directory and place it in a CSV file. However, writing this level of script is beyond the scope of the 70-236 examination.

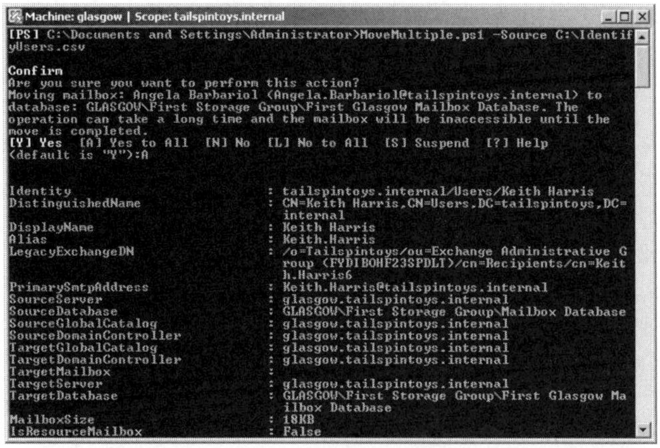

Figure 5-28 Moving multiple user mailboxes specified by a CSV file

---

Quick Check

■ You want to create a PowerShell script that lets you specify the name and location of a CSV file containing mailbox identities and configures a quota warning limit of 4 GB for these mailboxes. What should you enter into the text file that you save as the PowerShell script?

Quick Check Answer

■ You should create a PowerShell script containing the following code:

```
Param(
[string] $Source
)
Import-CSV $Source | ForEach-Object -Process {Get-Mailbox -Identity $_.Identity} |
Set-Mailbox -IssueWarningQuota 4GB
```

Using PowerShell Scripts to Manage Public Folders

You can use the scripts supplied with Exchange Server 2007 to manage both recipients and public folders. For example, to move all the public folders on an Exchange Server 2007 server called Glasgow to an Exchange Server 2007 server called Melbourne, you would use the following command:

```
MoveAllReplicas.ps1 -Server Glasgow -NewServer Melbourne
```

If you wanted to move the public folder Marketing and all the folders within the Marketing hierarchy from the Exchange Server 2007 server Glasgow to the Exchange Server 2007 server Melbourne, you can run the following command:

```
ReplaceReplicaOnPFRecursive.ps1 -TopPublicFolder "\Marketing" -ServerToAdd Melbourne
-ServerToRemove Glasgow
```

MORE INFO   **Managing public folders by using PowerShell scripts**

For more information about managing public folders by using PowerShell scripts, search Exchange Server 2007 Help for "How to Move Public Folder Content from One Public Folder Database to Another Public Folder Database" and "Scripts for Managing Public Folders in the Exchange Management Shell" or access *http://technet.microsoft.com/en-us/library/bb331970.aspx* and *http:// technet.microsoft.com/en-us/library/aa997966.aspx*.

Scheduling Bulk Management

If you move mailboxes singly or in bulk by using Exchange Management Console, the Move Schedule page of the Move Mailbox Wizard, shown in Figure 5-11 earlier in this chapter, lets you schedule the move by delaying when the *Move-Mailbox* command or commands are sent to Exchange Management Shell. However, this is the only event that you can schedule within Exchange Management Console.

Most bulk management operations are implemented in Exchange Management Shell, which has no built-in scheduling facilities. You cannot directly schedule Exchange Management Shell commands based, for example, on the *Move-Mailbox, Get-Mailbox, Set-Mailbox, Get-User,* or *Set-User* cmdlets directly within Exchange Management Shell.

If you need to schedule a bulk management operation, your first step is to put it in a PowerShell script, as described earlier in this lesson. However, PowerShell scripts need to run in Exchange Management Shell, and Exchange Management Shell has no scheduling facilities.

You can schedule commands that run from the Command Console. PowerShell commands cannot run directly from the Command Console, but the command to start PowerShell, *PowerShell.exe*, can. Exchange Management Shell is a PowerShell snap-in implemented in the file ExShell.psc1, which is typically located in the C:\Program Files\Microsoft\Exchange Server\Bin subdirectory. You can use the parameter PSConsoleFile to specify a snap-in for PowerShell.exe. Therefore, the code to identify a command stored in a PowerShell script file and run it from the Command Console is the following:

```
PowerShell.exe -PSConsoleFile "C:\Program Files\Microsoft\Exchange Server\Bin\ExShell.psc1"
<specify the command>
```

This command does not work immediately because we need to identify the Power-Shell script that holds the command. The parameter that does this is Command. The Command parameter takes the following format:

```
-Command ". '<Path to the PowerShell script>'"
```

Note the space after the full stop and the use of single and double quotation marks. Unfortunately, the Command Console does not know the path to the PSHome sub-directory, so if you want to run files in that directory, you need to specify the path. If you choose to use another subdirectory to store your PowerShell scripts, you specify the path to that subdirectory instead. Thus, the command to run the MoveDon.ps1 PowerShell script from the Command Console is the following:

```
PowerShell.exe -PSConsoleFile "C:\Program Files\Microsoft\Exchange Server\Bin\ExShell.psc1"
-Command ". 'C:\Program Files\Microsoft\Exchange Server\Scripts\MoveDon.ps1'"
```

As advised in the "Real World" sidebar earlier in this lesson, this is not as complicated as it looks if you take the process a step at a time. Figure 5-29 shows this command running from the Command Console.

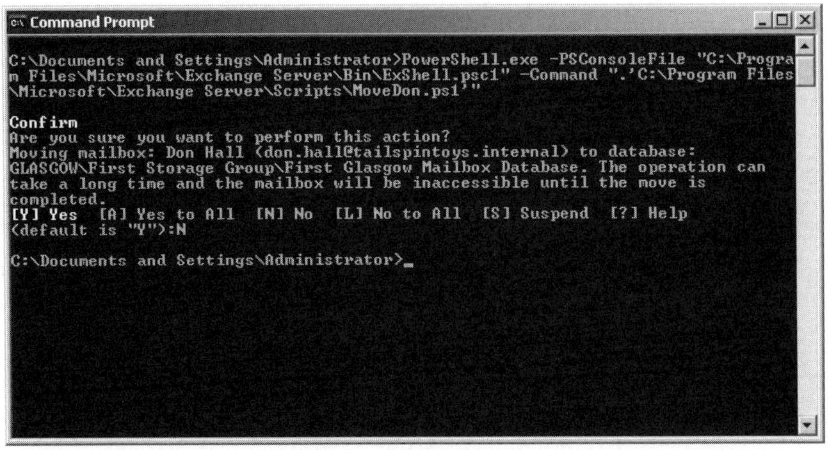

Figure 5-29   Running a PowerShell script from the Command Console

Typing in a command like the one shown in Figure 5-29 every time you wanted to use a command would be tedious in the extreme. You would therefore type it into a text editor instead and save it as a batch file in a convenient location, for example, as the file MoveDon.bat in a folder you have created with the path C:\Batch files. Figure 5-30 shows the batch file running from the Command Console (cmd.exe).

Figure 5-30   Running a batch file from the Command Console

Quick Check

- What PowerShell parameter specifies a file that loads a PowerShell snap-in (for example, Exchange Management Shell)?

Quick Check Answer
- PSConsoleFile.

When you create a batch file that runs a PowerShell script from the Command Console, you have the facility to schedule when the batch file runs. Note that the very simple MoveDon.ps1 file was used to illustrate the procedure. In practice, you would run a more complex file that implements bulk management and does not require manual confirmation.

To schedule a batch file, you access the Scheduled Tasks applet in Control Panel and click Add Selected Task to open the Scheduled Task Wizard. You browse for the batch file and specify when it should be run. You can run batch files regularly or once only. You then specify a time for the batch file to be run. You also need to specify a user account (typically your own) under which the file runs and enter and confirm a password. You create a PowerShell script, put it in a batch file, and schedule its operation in the practice session later in this lesson.

Practice: Using and Scheduling a PowerShell Script to Create Mailbox-Enabled Users

In this practice session, you create a CSV file that specifies mailbox-enabled users, create and test a PowerShell script that uses Exchange Management Shell commands to create the users, create a batch file that runs the PowerShell script, and schedule the batch file. Before you attempt this practice session, you need to have created the template mailbox –Template. You did this in Practice 1 of Lesson 1. If you have not created this mailbox, you can specify any mailbox you have created as a template.

▶ **Practice 1: Creating a CSV File**

In this practice, you use Microsoft Excel to create a CSV file. Although using a text editor is arguably more straightforward, many organizations store the information used to create or manage mailboxes in spreadsheet files. If you do not have Microsoft Excel installed on your computer, almost any spreadsheet can be used to create CSV files. If you prefer, you can create the CSV file by using a text editor and then complete the practice.

1. If necessary, log on by using the Kim_Akers account.

2. Open Microsoft Excel. If you do not have Microsoft Excel installed on your computer, open the spreadsheet or text editor that you want to use to create CSV files.

3. Enter the information shown in Figure 5-31.

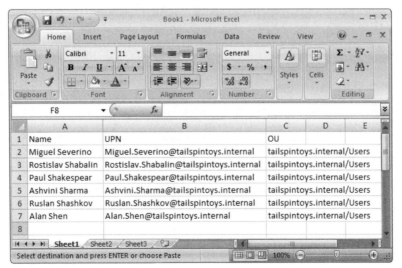

Figure 5-31   New user information entered in Excel

4. Save the file in CSV format as NewUsers.csv in the root of the C:\ drive, as shown in Figure 5-32.

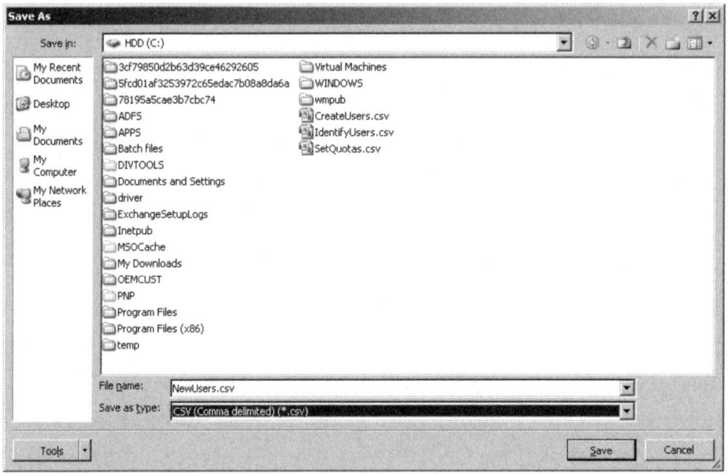

Figure 5-32   Saving a spreadsheet file in CSV format

5. Click OK to save only the active sheet, and then click Yes to retain the CSV format.

▶ **Practice 2: Creating a PowerShell Script**

In this practice, you create a PowerShell Script that creates the new users. You specify the CSV file and mailbox template to use as the script parameters. You need to have completed Practice 1 before you attempt Practice 2.

1. If necessary, log on by using the Kim_Akers account.

2. Type the following into a text editor:

```
Param(
[string] $MailboxTemplate,
[string] $CSVFile
)
$Temp = ConvertTo-SecureString P@ssw0rd -asPlainText –Force
$Template = Get-Mailbox "$MailboxTemplate"
Import-CSV $CSVFile | ForEach-Object -Process {New-Mailbox -Name $_.Name
-UserPrincipalName $_.UPN -OrganizationalUnit $_.OU -Database "First Storage
Group\Mailbox Database" -Password $Temp -TemplateInstance $Template}
```

3. Save the file in the C:\Program Files\Microsoft\ Exchange Server\Scripts subdi-rectory as CreateNewUser.ps1, as shown in Figure 5-33.

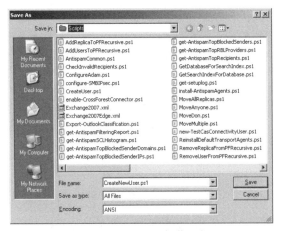

Figure 5-33 Saving a PowerShell script

4. Open Exchange Management Shell.

5. Run the following command:

```
CreateNewUser.ps1 –MailboxTemplate "_Template" –CSVFile "C:\NewUsers.csv"
```

Your screen should look similar to Figure 5-34.

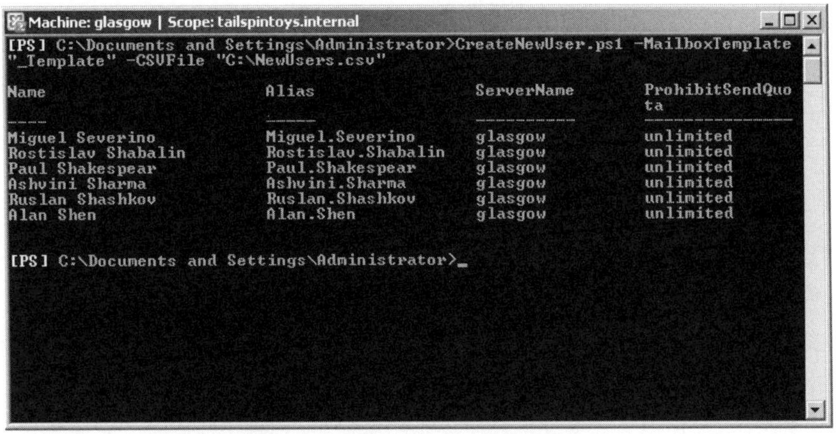

Figure 5-34 Creating new users with a PowerShell script

NOTE CSV file cannot be opened

If you get an error message saying that the C:\NewUsers.csv file cannot be opened, open the file with a text editor such as Notepad and ensure that there are no blank lines under the text. Save the file in the root of the C:\ drive—you might need to delete the original file before you can do so—and then run the command in step 5 of Practice 2 again.

▶ **Practice 3: Scheduling Mailbox Creation**

In this practice, you use the procedures you tested in the last two practices to create additional mailbox-enabled users, but you schedule the task so that it does not happen immediately. You need to have completed Practice 2 before you attempt this practice. This practice assumes that the $ExScripts variable points to the subdirectory C:\Program Files\Microsoft\Exchange Server\Scripts. If the $ExScripts variable does not points to the subdirectory C:\Program Files\Microsoft\Exchange Server\Scripts, amend the practice accordingly.

1. If necessary, log on by using the Kim_Akers account.

2. Create the CSV file shown in Figure 5-35 and save it as C:\MoreUsers.csv.

Figure 5-35   CSV file to create more mailbox-enabled users

3. Type the following into a text editor as a single line:

```
PowerShell.exe -PSConsoleFile "C:\Program Files\Microsoft\Exchange
Server\Bin\ExShell.psc1" -Command ". 'C:\Program Files\Microsoft\Exchange
Server\Scripts\CreateNewUser.ps1' -MailboxTemplate "_Template" -CSVFile
"C:\MoreUsers.csv"
```

4. Save the file in the C:\Batch files folder as MoreUsers.bat.

5. In Control Panel, click Scheduled Tasks. Select Add Scheduled Task.

6. On the Introduction page of the Scheduled Task Wizard, click Next.

7. On the Program Selection page, shown in Figure 5-36, click Browse.

8. Browse to C:\Batch files and click MoreUsers.bat. Click Open.

9. Leave the task name as the default (MoreUsers) and specify that it will run One Time Only, as shown in Figure 5-37. Click Next.

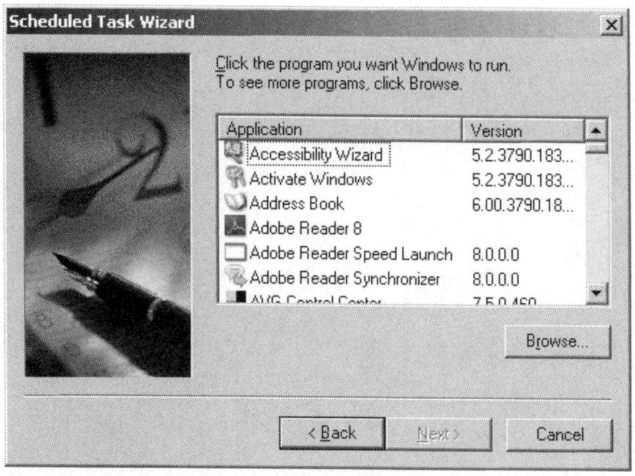

Figure 5-36   Program selection

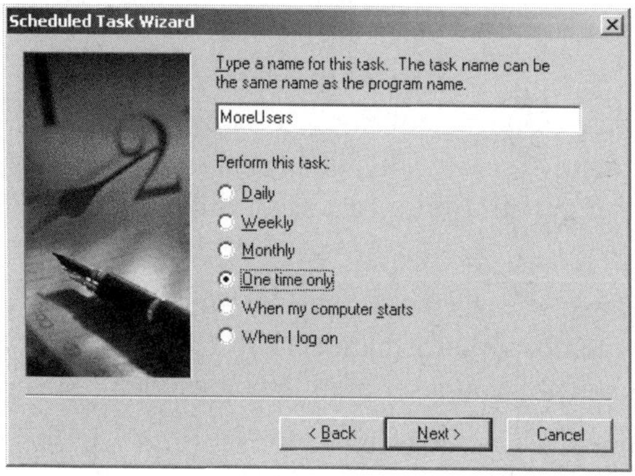

Figure 5-37   Specifying how often a task will run

10. Choose a start time. In a production environment, you might specify midnight or possibly on a Saturday. For the purposes of this practice, specify a time a couple of minutes into the future. Click Next.

11. Enter and confirm the password for the Kim_Akers account. Click Next. Click Finish. The scheduled bulk management task runs, and the new users are created, as shown in Figure 5-38.

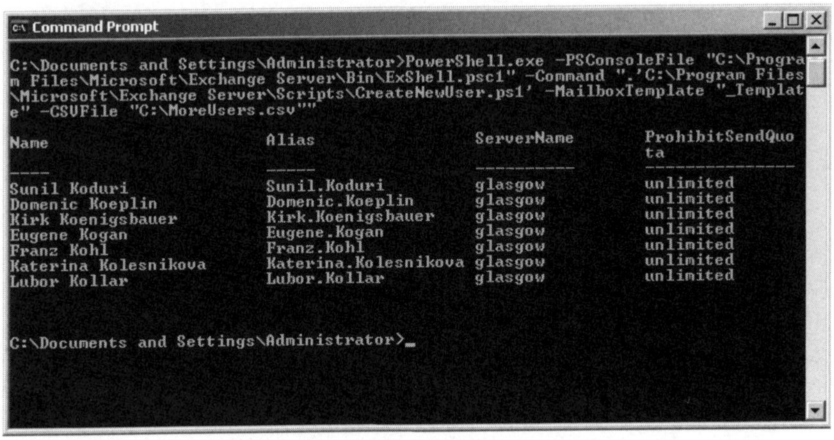

Figure 5-38 The scheduled bulk management task runs

Lesson Summary

- You can use Exchange Management Shell commands and CSV files to implement bulk management. Typically, this involves using one command to obtain information and piping its output into a second command that performs the required operation.

- You can save Exchange Management Shell commands in PowerShell scripts. PowerShell scripts can obtain information from CSV files, and you can define script parameters when you run a script in Exchange Management Shell.

- You can use one or more filters to select mailboxes (and other recipient objects) in Exchange Management Console. You can select a number of mailboxes and remove, disable, or move them. Only mailbox moves can be scheduled in Exchange Management Console.

- To schedule a bulk management task, you need to write a PowerShell script that performs the task and create code in Command Console that opens PowerShell, loads the Exchange Management Shell PowerShell snap-in, and then runs the PowerShell script. You can save this code in a batch file and use the Scheduled Tasks applet in Control Panel to schedule the batch file.

Lesson Review

You can use the following questions to test your knowledge of the information in Lesson 2 of this chapter. The questions are also available on the companion CD if you prefer to review them in electronic form.

NOTE Answers

Answers to these questions and explanations of why each answer choice is correct or incorrect are located in the "Answers" section at the end of the book.

1. What does the following command do?

    ```
    Get-User -Filter { Department -eq "Accounts" } | Move-Mailbox -TargetDatabase "Second
    Storage Group\Mailbox Database"
    ```

    A. Moves all the mailboxes of users with a Department attribute "Accounts" from the database Mailbox Database in the storage group Second Storage Group to the database Mailbox Database in the storage group First Storage Group.

    B. Moves all the mailboxes of users with a Department attribute "Accounts" to the database Mailbox Database in the storage group Second Storage Group.

    C. Moves all the mailboxes of users with accounts in the Accounts OU from the database Mailbox Database in the storage group Second Storage Group to the database Mailbox Database in the storage group First Storage Group.

    D. Moves all the mailboxes of users with accounts in the Accounts OU to the database Mailbox Database in the storage group Second Storage Group.

2. What is the error or errors in the CSV file shown in Figure 5-39?

    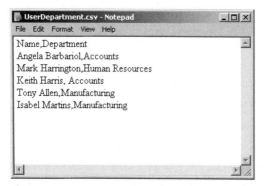

    Figure 5-39   CSV file with error or errors

    A. There should be no spaces in the user names. For example "Angela Barbariol" should be "AngelaBarbariol."

    B. You need quotation marks round the items that have spaces in them. For example, the user names and "Human Resources."

    C. There should be a space after each comma.

    D. There should not be a space after the comma in the fourth line.

3. What file implements Exchange Management Shell as a PowerShell snap-in?

    A. ExShell.psc1

    B. PowerShell.exe

    C. PSConsoleFile

    D. ExShell.Mcf1

4. You are writing a PowerShell script that takes the identity of a mailbox as a parameter, moves the mailbox to the database First Glasgow Mailbox Database in the storage group First Storage Group, and removes the mailbox from its original location. What should be the contents of the PowerShell script file?

```
A.  Param(
    [string] $Identity
    )
    Move-Mailbox -Identity $Identity -TargetDatabase "First Storage Group\First
    Glasgow Mailbox Database" -SourceMailboxCleanupOptions DeleteSourceMailbox
```

```
B.  Move-Mailbox -Identity $Identity -TargetDatabase "First Storage Group\ First
    Glasgow Mailbox Database"
    Param(
    [string] $Identity
    )
```

```
C.  Move-Mailbox -Identity $Identity -TargetDatabase "First Storage Group\ First
    Glasgow Mailbox Database" -SourceMailboxCleanupOptions DeleteSourceMailbox
```

```
D.  Param(
    [string] $Mailbox
    )
    Move-Mailbox -Identity $Identity -TargetDatabase "First Storage Group\ First
    Glasgow Mailbox Database"
```

5. You want to set storage quotas and define the replication schedule for all the mailboxes in the database First Glasgow Mailbox Database in the storage group First Storage Group. You want to schedule this operation so that it runs at midnight. What procedure do you use?

    A. In Exchange Management Console, filter by Database and select all the mailboxes in the database First Glasgow Mailbox Database in the storage group First Storage Group. Click Properties and specify storage quotas and replication schedule. On the Schedule page of the Set Properties Wizard, schedule the change to occur at midnight.

    B. Use a command based on the *Set-Mailbox* cmdlet in Exchange Management Shell. Schedule the command in Exchange Management Shell.

C. Write a PowerShell script that implements the configuration changes. Schedule the script file in Exchange Management Shell.

D. Write a PowerShell script that implements the configuration changes. Write a batch file that opens PowerShell from the Command Console, starts the Exchange Management Shell snap-in, and runs the PowerShell script. In Control Panel, click Scheduled Tasks. Select Add Scheduled Task and specify the batch file. Schedule the batch file to run once at midnight.

Chapter Review

To further practice and reinforce the skills you learned in this chapter, you can perform the following tasks:

- Review the chapter summary.
- Review the list of key terms introduced in this chapter.
- Complete the case scenarios. These scenarios set up real-world situations involving the topics of this chapter and ask you to create a solution.
- Complete the suggested practices.
- Take a practice test.

Chapter Summary

- You can manage mailboxes by using either Exchange Management Console or Exchange Management Shell. Exchange Management Shell commands give you more options and also allow you to move mailboxes across forests.
- You can remove, disable, or move mailboxes in bulk in Exchange Management Console, but you can schedule only mailbox moves. Exchange Management Shell uses CSV files and the pipe function to implement bulk management. You can create PowerShell scripts to automate Exchange Management Shell operations.
- You can use one or more filters to select mailboxes (and other recipient objects) in Exchange Management Console.
- To schedule a bulk management task that uses Exchange Management Shell commands, you need to generate code in the Command Console that enables PowerShell and Exchange Management Shell to run from that console. You can use the Scheduled Tasks applet in Control Panel to schedule a batch file that holds this code.

Key Terms

Do you know what these key terms mean? You can check your answers by looking up the terms in the glossary at the end of the book.

- Bulk management
- Cluster continuous replication (CCR)
- Comma-separated value (CSV) file

- Mailbox database
- Recipient template
- Resource forest
- Storage group

Case Scenarios

In the following case scenarios, you will apply what you've learned about configuring public folders, moving mailboxes, and implementing bulk management. You can find answers to these questions in the "Answers" section at the end of this book.

Case Scenario 1: Configuring and Moving Mailboxes

You are an Exchange organization administrator for The Adatum Corporation. Two of your tasks are to configure mailbox settings and to move mailboxes both individually and in bulk within the Adatum.com forest. Answer the following questions:

1. You want to move all the mailboxes in the database Mailbox Database in the storage group First Storage Group to the database Adatum Employees Mailbox Database in the storage group Second Storage Group. You plan to apply different quotas to the mailboxes after you have moved them to the target database. What command should you use?

2. You want to set the quota warning limit for all mailboxes in the database Adatum Employees Mailbox Database in the storage group Second Storage Group to 4 GB. Currently, this quota is at its default value (1.9 GB) for all mailboxes in the database. What command do you use?

3. You want to move Kim Akers's mailbox to the database Adatum Employees Mailbox Database in the storage group Second Storage Group. You want to increase mailbox quotas after you have moved the mailbox to the target database. You want the moved mailbox to retain its current recipient policies. What command do you use?

Case Scenario 2: Implementing Bulk Management

You are a member of the Exchange Administration team at Contoso Ltd. The company is expanding rapidly, and you frequently need to generate mailboxes for new members of staff. You need to configure mailboxes to meet changing company requirements and move mailboxes between mailbox databases. Some operations need to be done at night, when employees are less likely to be accessing their mailboxes. Answer the following questions:

1. The Human Resources Department sends you an e-mail with an attached spreadsheet file that lists the new employees that will be joining the company on the following Monday and the departments in which they will work. You need to create mailbox-enabled accounts for these users. What do you do with the spreadsheet file?

2. You want to create a PowerShell script that moves mailboxes in bulk to a mailbox database called Second Contoso Mailbox Database in the storage group First Storage Group. The moved mailboxes will be assigned increased mailbox quotas. You have been given a text file that contains the identities of the mailboxes that need to be moved. What do you do to the text file, and what code should you include in the script file?

3. You have written a PowerShell script named ConfigureQuotas.ps1 that configures warning quotas for all the mailboxes in the database Second Contoso Mailbox Database. The script file does not require any command-line parameters. You need to schedule the file to run during the night. You know that if you create a batch file, you can schedule when the batch file runs. The $ExScripts variable that points to C:\Program Files\Microsoft\Exchange Server\Scripts. What code should the batch file contain?

Suggested Practices

To help you successfully master the exam objectives presented in this chapter, complete the following tasks.

Moving Mailboxes

Do the first two practices in this section. The third practice is optional.

■ **Practice 1: Investigate the Relevant Exchange Management Shell Commands**   Study the help file information about the Exchange Management Shell *Move-Mailbox, Get-Mailbox, Set-Mailbox, Set-MailboxDatabase, Get-User,* and *Set-User* cmdlets and their associated parameters. Experiment with the available commands.

■ **Practice 2: Experiment with the Pipe Function**   Experiment with piping the output of commands that obtain information (for example, commands based on the *Get-Mailbox* and *Get-User* cmdlets) into commands that perform operations (for example, commands based on the *Move-Mailbox* cmdlet).

- **Practice 3: Move Mailboxes between Forests**   If your test network is large enough to create two forests each with an Exchange organization, experiment with moving mailboxes from one forest to another.

Bulk Management

Do the first two practices in this section. The third practice is optional.

- **Practice 1: Expand the PowerShell Script for Moving Mailboxes**   In Lesson 2, you created a PowerShell script that let you specify a CSV file that contained a list of mailbox identities and moved the corresponding mailboxes. Expand this technique so that you can also specify the target mailbox database as a parameter.

- **Practice 2: Run PowerShell Scripts from the Command Console**   Practice creating batch files that run PowerShell scripts from the Command Console and scheduling these batch files. This process looks difficult at first sight but becomes easy with practice.

- **Practice 3: Learn the PowerShell Scripting Language**   Many PowerShell scripts of varying complexity can be found in the Internet. Download scripts and try to understand them. Take care, however, that you test any script you download thoroughly before you use it in the production environment. Find out more about the features of .NET Framework. Read the text files you find in the C:\WINDOWS\system32\WindowsPowerShell\v1.0 subdirectory of your Exchange Server 2007 server. They provide a lot of good information about writing PowerShell scripts.

Take a Practice Test

The practice tests on this book's companion CD offer many options. For example, you can test yourself on just one exam objective, or you can test yourself on all the 70-236 certification exam content. You can set up the test so that it closely simulates the experience of taking a certification exam, or you can set it up in study mode so that you can look at the correct answers and explanations after you answer each question.

MORE INFO   **Practice tests**

For details about all the practice test options available, see the "How to Use the Practice Tests" section in this book's Introduction.

Chapter 6

Spam, Viruses, and Compliance

Not only do members of your organization spend valuable time deleting spam, but spam can also disrupt people's attention, drawing their minds from their work. Spam also has the effect of clogging up your organization's connection to the Internet and of consuming disk space on your mailbox database servers. Every megabyte that is used to store undeleted spam is a megabyte that is not being used to store e-mail that people actually want to read. Viruses are even worse than spam, as they are a direct attack on your organization. A successful virus infection can take hours to disinfect or, worse, be used to compromise company security by forwarding sensitive communication to nefarious third parties. The architecture of Exchange Server 2007 allows you to deal preemptively with these dual threats out on the perimeter of your network rather than in the more vulnerable core. You can configure an edge transport server to block viruses and spam from passing across your organization's firewall so that users are unaware of its existence.

Compliance is another issue that is becoming increasingly important to mail administrators. Compliance is about ensuring that important business communication is stored according to policies that meet appropriate legislative requirements. These requirements are different, depending on the jurisdiction your organization falls under. Compliance is one of those unusual areas where systems administration practice is as much dictated by technical realities as it is by your organization's lawyers. Implementing compliance policies involves taking legal guidelines and applying them using the Exchange Server 2007 administration tools.

Exam objectives in this chapter:
- Configure the antivirus and anti-spam system.
- Configure transport rules and message compliance.

Lessons in this chapter:

Before You Begin

To complete the lessons in this chapter, you must have done the following:

■ Ensure that you have completed all the end-of-lesson practice exercises in Chapter 1, "Preparing for Exchange Installation," Chapter 2, "Installing Exchange Server and Configuring Server Roles," and Chapter 3, "Configuring Recipients, Groups and Mailboxes."

No additional configuration is required for this chapter.

Real World

Orin Thomas

In the past, I have provided support to small and medium-sized businesses running earlier versions of Exchange and other mail servers. One problem anyone supporting small and medium-sized businesses has is that it is often necessary to deal with a mail server incorrectly configured by someone else. In many cases, I found two specific problems. The first is that the mail server had not been locked down and had been used as a mail relay for spam. The second was having to figure out which block list providers had put the mail server in the list of untrustworthy mail servers. Although blocking an open relay was a bit cumbersome with some older mail servers, the problem does not exist with Exchange Server 2007. Exchange Server 2007 will not relay mail by default, and you will not have to worry about it turning up on block lists unless users from within the organization are intentionally spamming. As for removing the server from a block list provider, often it was a matter of asking the administrators at organizations where local users were unable to send messages, which providers they were using, and proceeding from there. If the users at your organization have problems getting their e-mail received by only a particular organization, it is likely that some sort of block is in place that you will need to resolve.

Lesson 1: Configuring the Antivirus and Anti-Spam System

In this lesson, you will learn about the configuration changes you can make to Exchange Server 2007 to reduce the volume of spam and virus traffic reaching your organization's mailboxes. The lesson examines what you can do to reduce spam and viruses using Exchange Server 2007's functionality and the improvements that installing Forefront Security for Exchange Server can make.

After this lesson, you will be able to:

- Configure the antivirus and anti-spam system (e.g., configure deny lists, block lists, allow lists, and specific exceptions).

Estimated lesson time: 40 minutes

The best place to deal with spam and viruses is on a perimeter network. Although in the best situation your organization would not ever receive spam or viruses through e-mail, cleaning the flow of traffic before it reaches the internal network is a superior strategy to letting the mail filters and antivirus software of desktop computers deal with it. The key component in fighting spam and viruses in an Exchange Server 2007 organization is the edge transport server. This server is the first port of call for any mail received from external sources, so it makes sense that you would use it to discard communication that is harmful to your organization's health.

It is, of course, possible to configure a server assigned the Hub Transport server role to deal with spam and viruses, but not all the available anti-spam and antivirus transport agents function on the Hub Transport server role. By default, user mailboxes in an organization that uses an edge transport server will receive fewer virus and spam messages than user mailboxes in an organization that does not use an edge transport server. This is something to keep in mind when arguing with your manager about the need for this extra Exchange Server 2007 installation.

Configuring Exchange Server 2007 Anti-Spam Features

Exchange Server 2007 has a series of transport agents that incoming messages must pass through before they are forwarded to user's mailboxes. Each of these transport agents concentrates on a different aspect of the incoming message. For example, one transport agent deals with the IP address of the Simple Mail Transfer Protocol (SMTP) server that the message originates from, another examines the sender's address, and another analyzes the incoming message and rates the likelihood that the message is actually spam.

You can view the transport agents in the order of their priority by entering the following Exchange Management Shell command:

```
Get-TransportAgent
```

The output of this command, when run on an edge transport server, is displayed in Figure 6-1.

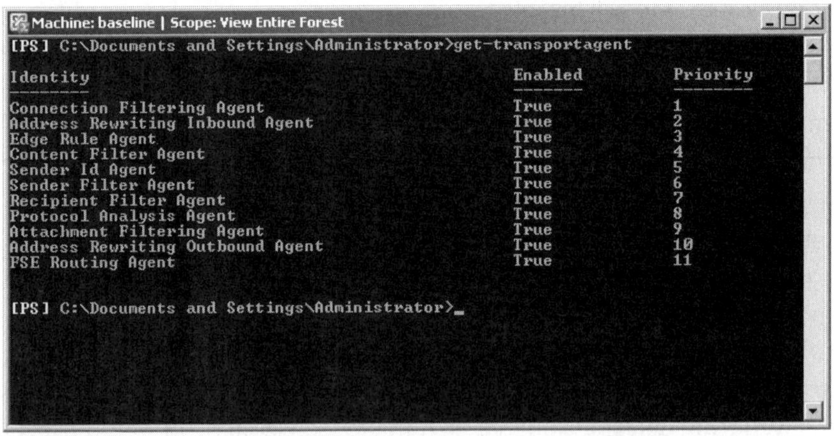

Figure 6-1   Active transport agents in the order of their priority.

Connection Filtering

When an incoming message arrives on an edge transport server and connection filtering is enabled, the IP address of the SMTP server that sent the message is compared against IP allow and block lists. If the forwarding SMTP server's IP address is on the allow list, the message is forwarded into the Exchange organization. If the SMTP server's IP address is on the block list, the message is dropped. If the SMTP server's IP address is not on either list, the message will pass through other anti-spam agents on the configured server.

Unlike addresses on the allow list, you can configure addresses on the block list to expire, as shown in Figure 6-2. Most SMTP servers that send spam are doing so because a third party has compromised them. Implementing a limited-duration block gives the administrator the time to patch the server so that it is not used by spammers.

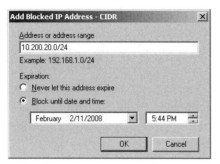

Figure 6-2 Setting a blocked address to expire

IP block and allow lists can be configured in two ways. The simplest is for e-mail administrators within your organization to add entries to each as the need arises. A more complex method involve subscribing to block and allow list providers. Block lists are also sometimes known as real-time block lists, as the block list is queried each time mail arrives at your organization from a new IP address. Block lists have the advantage of allowing a third-party organization to keep your list of spam-sending IP addresses up to date. IP block list providers generate their list on the basis of spam reports and the spam that they have received themselves from SMTP servers located on the Internet. Finally, messages that are received from SMTP servers on the blocked addresses list will always be discarded as spam, unless the SMTP servers also appear on the allowed addresses list. To receive e-mail from an SMTP server on a block list is to remove it from the block list or grant an exception by adding the SMTP server to the IP allow list. In some cases, this may require the administrator of the blocked SMTP server interceding with the real-time block list provider.

MORE INFO **More on connection filtering**

For more information on connection filtering, consult the following TechNet article: *http://technet.microsoft.com/en-us/library/bb124320.aspx.*

Filtering Content

Content filtering uses algorithms to assess the contents of message to provide a rating on how likely that message is to be spam. How the message is treated depends on the threshold values that you set. You can configure Exchange to drop any message that has even minimal spamlike characteristics, or, alternatively, you can configure Exchange to reject only those messages that are very likely to be spam.

Content filtering does not work only by looking for specific words within messages; it also looks for patterns within messages. The algorithms that search through messages are updated on a regular basis, as spammers are always doing their best to get around detection software so that they can deliver their important message to you. It is possible to disable these anti-spam updates. Do so by selecting the edge transport server under Server Configuration in Exchange Management Console and click Disable Anti-spam Updates in the Actions pane. This method will also work in the event that you have enabled anti-spam functionality on a hub transport server.

The Custom Words tab of the Content Filtering Properties dialog box, shown in Figure 6-3, allows you to enter words or phrases that, if encountered, will automatically mean that a message will or will not be blocked. If you are running a business that makes a very specific product (e.g., hovercraft, as shown in the figure), it is reasonable to assume that any incoming communication that mentions that product is something that someone within your organization would want to read. It is possible to use the Exceptions tab to enter recipient addresses that you wish to exempt from the content-filtering process.

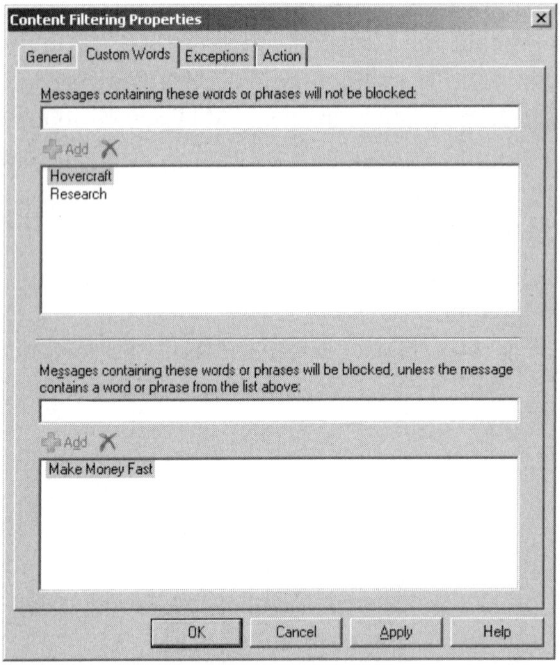

Figure 6-3   Overriding the anti-spam settings to allow certain messages in

After analyzing the content of a message, the content filter will assign a spam confidence level (SCL) rating to the message. How those messages are treated depends on the configuration of the Action tab of Content Filtering Properties, shown in Figure 6-4. In the figure, any messages that have an SCL rating of 5 or 6 will be forwarded to the quarantine mailbox. Any messages that have an SCL rating of 7 or 8 will be rejected. Any messages with an SCL rating of 9 will be automatically deleted. The difference between rejection and deletion is that senders will be informed that their message has been rejected. In the case of deletion, they will receive no response at all.

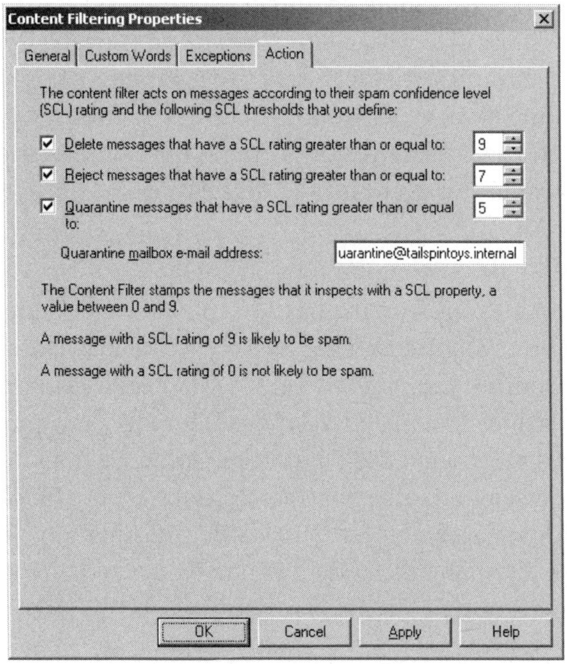

Figure 6-4   Configuring actions based on SCL ratings

If you are going to use message quarantine, you will need to configure a quarantine mailbox. This is a specially created mailbox to which all messages that are scored between your threshold will be forwarded. Microsoft recommends that you place the quarantine mailbox in a separate mailbox database in its own storage group. It is also very important, if you are going to use quarantine, that someone actually check the quarantine mailbox on a regular basis to see if it is full of legitimate e-mail or full of spam. By assessing the contents of the quarantine mailbox, you can make a determination about adjusting the SCL sliders.

MORE INFO **More on content filtering**

For more information on configuring content filtering for Exchange Server 2007, consult the following TechNet article: *http://technet.microsoft.com/en-us/library/bb123737.aspx.*

Filtering Recipients

Recipient filtering allows you to block messages on the basis of who they are sent to. This technology is most often used to block messages sent to recipients that are not listed in the global address list (GAL). Some spammers send messages to common names at a particular address, hoping to get a hit. If this setting is enabled, messages will be forwarded from an edge transport server to an internal hub transport server only if the recipient is listed in the GAL. GAL information is stored within Active Directory Application Mode. If this setting is not enabled, the hub transport server must generate a non-delivery report for every invalid address.

Sender Filtering and Sender ID

Sender filtering is used to drop messages on the basis of the message sender's e-mail address. Sender filtering can be configured on the basis of a specific sender address or a sender's domain. For example, you can filter the sender address kim_akers@ tailspintoys.com specifically or filter all e-mail that comes from the @tailspintoys.com mail domain. Sender filtering is most often used to block incoming e-mail from e-mail domains that provide free addresses. It is also possible to configure the blocked senders list to automatically block messages that have no sender information. To do this, ensure that the Block Messages From Blank Senders option is checked on the Blocked Senders tab of Sender Filtering Properties.

As shown in Figure 6-5, there are two actions that you can configure for messages that have a sender that appears on the blocked sender's list:

- **Reject message** When this setting is configured, the message is deleted. Microsoft recommends this option be used.
- **Stamp message with blocked sender and continue processing** When this setting is selected, the message's metadata is modified to indicate that the message has come from a blocked sender.

MORE INFO **Understanding sender filtering**

For more on sender filtering, consult the following TechNet link: *http://technet.microsoft.com/en-us/ library/bb124354.aspx.*

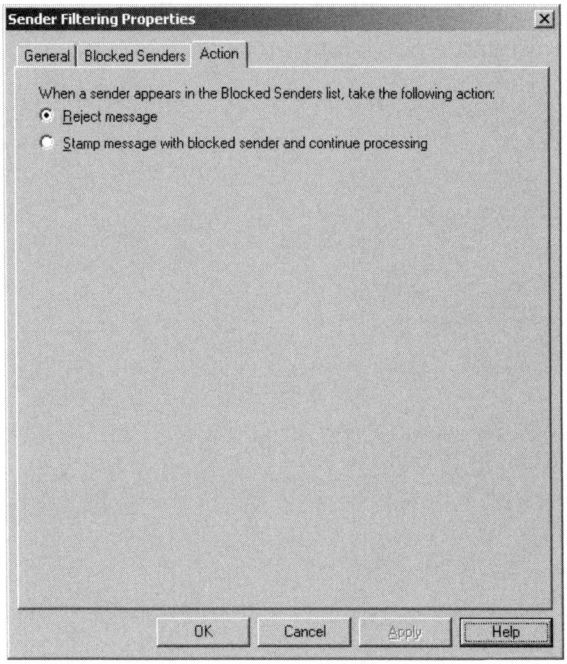

Figure 6-5   Sender filtering action

Quick Check

1. Which filtering technology would you use to block incoming messages going to internal distribution lists?

2. Which filtering technology should you use to permanently block messages from a specific sender?

Quick Check Answers

1. Recipient filtering.

2. Sender filtering.

Sender Reputation

Sender reputation is used to add SMTP servers to the IP block list for a limited duration based on the characteristics of the sending host (open proxy) and the messages received from that host. If enough messages are transmitted from an SMTP server at a particular IP that are recognized as spam, it has a corresponding impact on the sender reputation level (SRL) metric. The higher the SRL metric, the more likely it is that the SMTP server is being used by spammers. As shown in Figure 6-6, you can configure an

SMTP server's IP address to be automatically blocked for a certain number of hours once a certain threshold value has been reached.

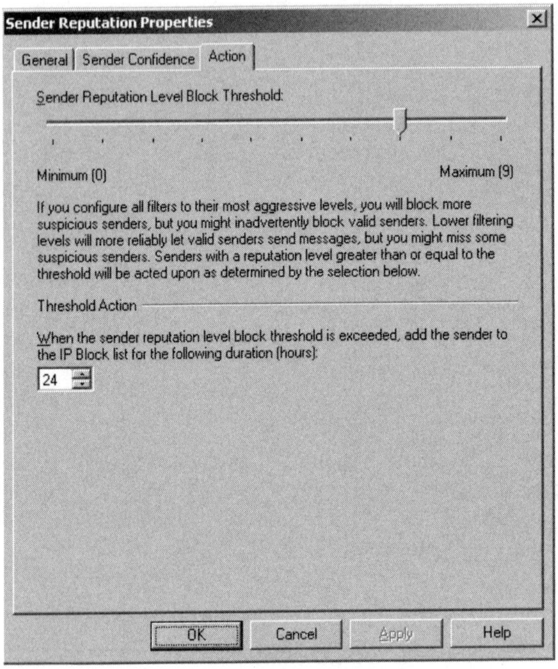

Figure 6-6 Sender reputation properties

MORE INFO **More on sender reputation**

For more information on configuring sender reputation, navigate to the following page on TechNet: *http://technet.microsoft.com/en-us/library/aa998344.aspx*.

Configuring Attachment Filtering

Attachment filtering is a method of antivirus protection where e-mail attachments are dropped on the basis of file name, file extension, or Multipurpose Internet Mail Extension (MIME) type. Attachment filtering can be implemented only on edge transport servers and is not available on hub transport servers. Attachment filtering is also unusual in that it can be configured only by using Exchange Management Shell on the actual edge transport server and cannot be configured from the Exchange Management Console. If your organization has multiple edge transport servers, you need to be aware that attachment filters can be configured only on a per-server basis. For complete coverage, it will be necessary to add the same attachment filter manually to all edge transport servers rather than adding it to only one.

Attachment filtering is a broad-brush strategy. Rather than have an antivirus program analyze an attachment and see if it matches the characteristics of known viruses, attachment filtering drops everything of the specified type regardless of whether the file is actually harmful. Attachment filters are enabled by default on edge transport servers and the following extensions are automatically filtered: .xnk, .wsh, .wsf, .wsc, .vbs, .vbe, .vb, .url, .shs, .shb, .sct, .scr, .scf, .reg, .prg, .prf, .pif, pcd, .ops, .mst, .msp, .msi, .psc2, .psc1, .ps2mxl, .ps2, .ps11xml, .ps11, .ps1mxl, .ps1, .msc, .mdz, .mdw, .mdt, .mde, .mdb, .mda, .lnk, .ksh, .jse, .js, .isp, .ins, .inf, .hta, .hlp, .fxp, .exe, .csh, .crt, .cpl, .com, .cmd, .chm, .bat, .bas, .asx, .app, .adp, and .ade.

TIP **Do not memorize the list!**

This list is provided for your information, and it is unlikely that you will actually have to remember all these file types for the exam. Just make a note that files like .com, .bat, and .vbs are filtered, while file types such as .doc, .jpg, and .zip are not.

Attachment filters can be created for MIME types or for particular file names. To create a new attachment filter that filters on the basis of MIME content type, use the following syntax:

```
Add-AttachmentFilterEntry -Name <MIMEContentType> -Type ContentType
```

For example, entering the command *Add-AttachmentFilterEntry -Name image/BMP -Type ContentType* would filter all bitmap image types. Alternatively, if you want to create an attachment filter that works on the basis of file names, you would use the following syntax:

```
Add-AttachmentFilterEntry -Name <FileName> -Type FileName
```

For example, if you wanted to filter all scripts with the .pl extension, you would type the following into Exchange Management Shell: **Add-AttachmentFilterEntry -Name *.pl -Type FileName**. Alternatively, if you want to filter a specific file, such as virus.exe, specify the entire file name and do not use the wildcard option.

If you are unsure as to which attachments are filtered by edge transport servers, you can get a list by issuing the following command:

```
Get-AttachmentFilterEntry
```

This will list all existing filters on the edge transport server. The default settings make this list quite long, and it is likely that most of the attachments that you would want to filter, such as .exe, .com, and .bat files, are already included. The file types that you will have to be careful about are the common documents, such as .doc and .xls, as well as archives, such as .zip. Blocking these file types will decrease the likelihood of a virus infection but most likely will not be appreciated by people who need to share documents with others outside the organization.

All messages that match an attachment filter entry on an edge transport server are dealt with in the same way. The three options are the following:

- **Reject**   When reject is selected, the message and attachment are not delivered to the recipient, and a non-delivery report (NDR) failure message is sent to the sender. It is possible to configure a specific NDR response using the RejectResponse option of the command used to configure attachment filter behavior.

- **Strip**   The attachment is stripped, and the message is forwarded to the recipient with an included message informing the recipient of the action taken. This is the default setting.

- **SilentDelete**   When SilentDelete is configured, the message is deleted without the sender or the recipient being informed.

As there will always be cases where a banned file type needs to be transmitted by e-mail, you will need to come up with a policy by which these files can be received. What you do not want to happen is all your employees deciding to use free Web mail as a way of getting around these restrictions, which just provides a back door for viruses to get into your organization.

One solution is to configure a list of connectors that are exempt from attachment filtering. You might configure this option if your organization has a trusted partner organization. To configure the attachment filter action, issue the following command:

```
Set-AttachmentFilterListConfig -Action -Reject -RejectResponse "Your attachment has been
deleted by the tailspintoys.com mailserver. Please resend your message without the
attachment."
```

MORE INFO   More on attachment filtering

For more information on how to configure attachment filtering, navigate to the following address: *http://technet.microsoft.com/en-us/library/aa997139.aspx.*

Exam Tip   A good way to remember whether a particular attachment is going to be filtered is to ask yourself whether the attachment is executable. Applications and scripts are generally considered harmful, whereas Word documents and PowerPoint presentations are not.

Forefront Security for Exchange Server

Forefront Security for Exchange Server, which was introduced in Chapter 2, "Installing Exchange Server and Configuring Server Roles," is an antivirus service that works specifically with Exchange Server 2007. Forefront Security for Exchange Server uses multiple antivirus scan engines from different vendors, provides distributed protection on all Exchange Server roles, provides detailed notification for administrators on the viruses that have been found, and provides filtering by file size as well as name and extension.

Rather than just using a single antivirus scanning engine, Forefront uses licensed engines from multiple vendors. Using multiple engines increases the likelihood that incoming viruses will be detected. Although antivirus vendors are always improving their detection databases, it is possible that one vendor may be aware of a virus or a virus variant that another does not yet know about.

Forefront scans using two separate methods:

- Forefront scans messages on edge and hub transport servers using the Forefront AV agent.
- Forefront scans messages stored within mailbox stores using the Forefront VSAPI.dll, which is loaded by the Exchange store.

Another benefit of Forefront is that it keeps track of which messages have been scanned. This means that a message that has already been scanned when it first arrives from the Internet at the organization's edge transport server will not be rescanned when it reaches a hub transport server or is placed in the user mailbox store. The reason that Forefront is able to scan both the mailbox stores and the transport servers is that not every harmful virus that enters an organization will come from the outside. It is also important to remember that messages posted to public folders might also contain viruses. The scan-once capability of Forefront can be disabled, although this does introduce a performance cost, as the message will be scanned each time it moves to a new server role within your organization. It is also possible to configure Forefront to rescan mailbox content when virus signatures are updated. In this way, messages that might be infected by viruses that were not detected by initial scans because the virus was so new that it had not been cataloged can be detected when updated signatures become available.

The most common Forefront scan-once scenarios are the following:

- **Scan inbound mail**   In this scenario, messages are scanned only when they pass through the edge transport server. This is sometimes combined with scheduled scans of mailbox servers rather than a message scan as each new message arrives in the mailbox server.

- **Scan outbound mail**   In this scenario, messages are scanned only when they are passed to hub transport servers. Messages that transit the edge transport server are not scanned by any of the Forefront agents.

- **Scan internal mail**   In this scenario, mail is scanned at hub transport servers but not at the origin and destination mailbox servers.

By default, messages located in mailbox stores are scanned when they are first accessed only if they have not already been scanned by a hub or edge transport server. It is possible to configure messages located in mailbox stores to be rescanned if virus definitions have been updated since the last scan. This is achieved by setting the Scan On Scanner Update option under General Options in Settings. When the Scan On Scanner Update setting is enabled, not only messages in Mailbox stores but also messages stored in Public Folders will be rescanned using the new definitions. Microsoft recommends that you enable Scan On Scanner Update only in the event of a serious threat, as it incurs a significant impact performance.

Some of the other important scanning options that can be configured for Forefront include the following:

- **Delete corrupted compressed files**   Any compressed file that appears corrupted will be automatically quarantined. It is possible to configure this setting so that corrupted compressed files are automatically deleted.

- **Delete corrupted unencoded files**   Any unencoded file that exhibits corruption is deleted by default.

- **Delete encrypted compressed files**   Encrypted files cannot be scanned by Forefront. Forefront reports encrypted compressed files as an EncryptedCompressedFile virus. Because these files may be innocuous, it is often better to quarantine them rather than delete them.

- **Optimize for performance by not scanning messages that were already virus scanned—transport**   This setting is enabled by default. If one transport server has scanned the message, the message is marked so that other transport servers that forward the message on to its destination within the organization will not scan the message.

- **Perform reverse DNS lookups**   When enabled, Forefront uses reverse DNS to get the domain name for inbound and outbound mail traffic. The default setting is disabled. In the disabled configuration, message headers are used for inbound and outbound mail traffic.

- **Purge message if message body deleted—transport**   Some viruses are carried in the body of the message rather than as a separate attachment. When Forefront removes the virus, it places deletion text in its place and then forwards the message to the recipient. If you do not want the sanitized message forwarded to the recipient, you can enable this option.

- **Enable Forefront scan**   The options are Disable All, Enable Store Scanning, Enable Transport Scanning, and Enable All. These scanning options were discussed earlier in this lesson.

These options can be configured using the Settings/General Options box of Forefront Server Security Administrator, as shown in Figure 6-7.

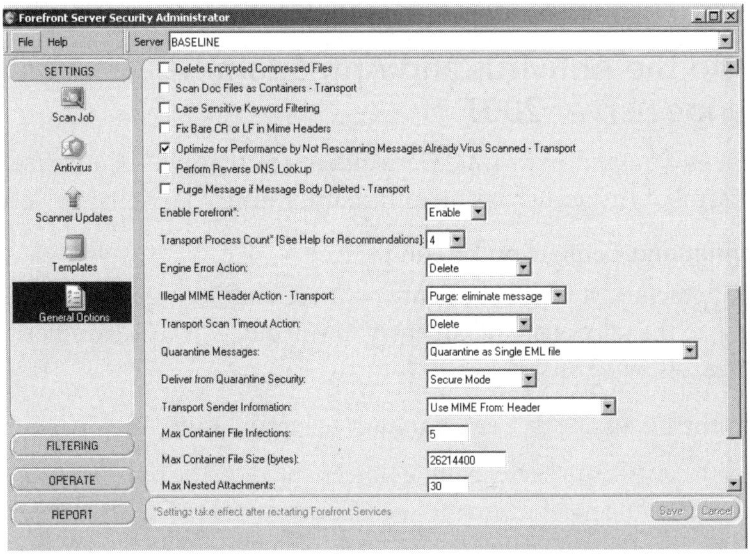

Figure 6-7   Configuring general options for Forefront Security for Exchange Server 2007

Forefront can be configured so that infected files are either deleted or placed in quarantine. In most cases, infected files should be automatically deleted, but there may be certain situations where you want to quarantine a file for later examination. For example, a file infected with a virus also contains important information that must be recovered.

Forefront can be configured to filter on the basis of the following message properties:

- Key word
- File
- Allowed senders
- Filter lists

These filters function in the same way as the anti-spam filters that are available in a default edge transport server deployment of Exchange Server 2007 covered earlier in this lesson. These options can be configured by opening the Filtering box of Forefront Server Security Administrator.

MORE INFO Forefront Security for Exchange Server 2007 user guide

The user guide for Forefront Security for Exchange Server 2007 can be downloaded from the following Web site: *http://www.microsoft.com/technet/forefront/serversecurity/exchange/userguide/default.mspx?mfr=true.*

Practice: Setting Up the Antivirus and Anti-Spam Features of Exchange Server 2007

In these practices, you will perform several exercises that will familiarize you with configuring several of the antivirus and anti-spam features of Exchange Server 2007.

▶ **Practice 1: Configuring Connection Filtering**

In the following practice, you will configure connection filtering. This will be done by adding an entry to the allow list and an entry to the block list. To complete this practice, perform the following steps:

1. Log on to the Exchange Server Computer using the Kim_Akers account.

2. Verify that the anti-spam server settings are enabled on the hub transport server by issuing the Exchange Management Shell Command: *Set-TransportServer –Identity 'ServerName' –AntiSpamAgentsEnabled $true.* You should see a message in yellow informing you that no settings have been modified. If you do not get this message, it will be necessary to restart the Microsoft Exchange Transport service and Exchange Management Console.

3. In Exchange Management Console, click on the Hub Transport node under Organization Configuration and then click on the Anti-spam tab, as shown in Figure 6-8.

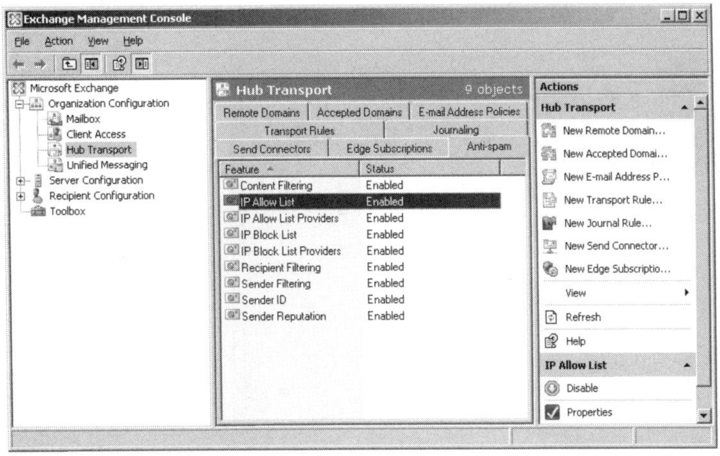

Figure 6-8   The Anti-spam section of the hub transport configuration at the organization level

4. Double-click IP Allow List. This will open the IP Allow List Properties dialog box. Click on the Allowed Addresses tab.

5. On the Allowed Addresses tab, click Add.

6. In the Add Allowed IP Address–CIDR, enter the network **10.100.10.0/24** and then click OK.

7. Verify that the list of allowed addresses matches that shown in Figure 6-9 and then click OK.

8. Double-click the IP Block List entry. This will open the IP Block List Properties item. Click the Blocked Addresses tab and then click Add.

9. Enter the address range **10.200.20.0/24** and set the Block Until Date value to January 1, 2012. Click OK twice to close the dialog box.

▶ **Practice 2: Configuring Sender Filtering**

In this practice, you will configure sender filtering to block incoming e-mail from specific domains. To complete this practice, perform the following steps:

1. Log on to the computer hosting Exchange Server 2007 using the Kim_Akers account.

2. Open Exchange Management Console and under Organization Configuration click Hub Transport and then click on the Anti-spam tab.

3. Double-click the Sender Filtering item to open Sender Filtering Properties.

4. Click the Blocked Senders tab and then click Add.

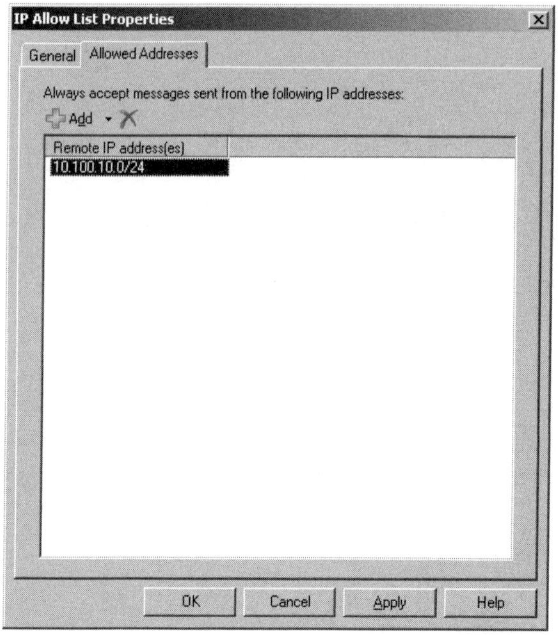

Figure 6-9   The Allowed Addresses tab of the IP Allow List Properties

5. Ensure that the Individual e-mail address option is selected and enter the address **Thomas_Axen@cpandl.com.** Click OK.

6. Click Add and then select the Domain option. Enter the domain **treyresearch.net** and click OK.

7. Verify that the Blocked Senders list is the same as the list shown in Figure 6-10 and then click OK.

▶ **Practice 3: Configuring Content Filtering**

In this practice, you will configure content filtering on a hub transport server that has anti-spam functionality installed to accept any messages that contain the word "Hovercraft," discard any messages that contain the phrase "Make Money Fast," and disable content filtering for any messages addressed to Kim Akers. You will also configure the SCL sliders to reject messages that appear to contain spam. To complete this practice, perform the following steps:

1. Log on to the computer hosting Exchange Server 2007 using the Kim_Akers account.

2. Open Exchange Management Console and under Organization Configuration click Hub Transport and then click on the Anti-spam tab.

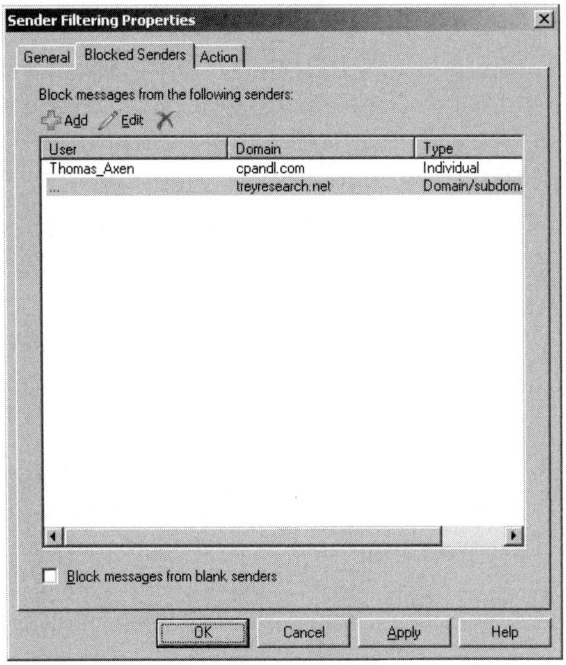

Figure 6-10 List of blocked senders and domains

3. Double-click on Content Filtering to open the Content Filtering Properties dialog box.

4. Click the Custom Words tab. In the Messages Containing These Words Or Phrases Will Not Be Blocked text box, type **Hovercraft** and then click Add.

5. In the Messages Containing These Words Or Phrases Will Be Blocked, Unless The Message Contains A Word Or Phrase From The List Above text box, type **Make Money Fast** and then click Add.

6. Click the Exceptions tab. In the Do Not Filter Content In Messages Addressed To The Following Recipients text box, type **Kim_Akers@tailspintoys.internal** and then click Add.

7. Click the Action tab. Ensure that the Reject Messages That Have A SCL Rating Greater Than Or Equal To option is selected and change the value to 5.

8. Ensure that the Delete Messages That Have A SCL Rating Greater Than Or Equal To option is selected and set the value to 7.

9. Click OK to close the Content Filtering Properties dialog box.

Lesson Summary

- Messages that are received from SMTP servers on the allowed addresses list will always be accepted and not discarded as spam. Messages that are received from SMTP servers on the blocked addresses list will be discarded as spam, unless they also appear on the allowed addresses list.

- Sender filtering is used to filter messages on the basis of the properties of the sender's address. Sender filtering can be configured on the basis of a specific e-mail address or an entire e-mail address domain.

- Attachment filtering enables you to have an edge transport server drop attachments on the basis of MIME type, file name, or file extension. The three settings are Reject, Strip, and SilentDelete.

- Forefront Security for Exchange (FSE) is an additional antivirus product that can be installed in an Exchange Server organization. FSE uses multiple antivirus engines to protect an Exchange organization. By default, FSE will scan a message only once. Where the message is scanned depends on FSE configuration. It is possible to have stored messages scanned each time the antivirus definitions are updated.

- Content filtering assigns an SCL score to a message on the basis of an analysis of the message contents. It is possible to configure content filtering to delete, reject, or quarantine a message on the basis of its SCL score. Content filtering can also be configured to automatically allow or block messages, depending on whether the message contains specific words.

Lesson Review

You can use the following questions to test your knowledge of the information in Lesson 1, "Configuring the Antivirus and Anti-Spam System" The questions are also available on the companion CD if you prefer to review them in electronic form.

NOTE Answers

Answers to these questions and explanations of why each answer choice is correct or incorrect are located in the "Answers" section at the end of the book.

---

1. You have configured attachment filtering on your organization's edge transport servers. Because some senders are transmitting files that are not harmful, you want to allow them to be informed that the message containing the attachment

has been rejected by your organization. Which of the following configuration settings should you make?

   A. Configure the attachment filtering behavior action to Strip

   B. Configure the attachment filtering behavior action to SilentDelete

   C. Configure the attachment filtering behavior action to Reject

   D. Configure a ConnectorException

2. You are the sole mail administrator for Contoso. Contoso uses an edge transport server to filter out spam and viruses from incoming message traffic. Last month, you printed out a list of addresses on the IP block list that you configured. Yesterday, you noticed a spam message in your Inbox from an IP address that is on your printed block list. You are the only person that configures the anti-spam settings for your organization. Which of the following steps can you take to ensure that the IP address of the spam-forwarding SMTP server remains blocked?

   A. Re-create the block list address entry. Set the address entry to never expire.

   B. Remove the IP address of the SMTP server from the allow list.

   C. Add the IP address of the SMTP server to the allow list.

   D. Remove the IP address of the SMTP server from the block list.

3. A former employee is sending e-mails to people in your organization attempting to recruit them to a new start-up company that he has created. E-mails are transmitted from an Internet service provider's SMTP server that is also used by several of your organization's clients. Management has asked you to block all e-mails sent from the new company's e-mail domain. Which of the following technologies should you implement?

   A. Attachment filtering

   B. Connection filtering

   C. Sender filtering

   D. Recipient filtering

4. Which of the following Forefront Security for Exchange Server 2007 settings should you enable to ensure that messages stored on mailbox servers are rechecked for viruses when antivirus definitions are updated?

   A. Optimize for Performance by Not Rescanning Messages Already Virus Scanned–Transport

   B. Perform Reverse DNS Lookups

    C. Scan On Scanner Update

    D. Quarantine Messages

5. You have installed Forefront Security for Exchange Server on servers in your Exchange organization. You want to ensure that messages are examined by anti-virus agents when transmitted through hub transport servers but do not want messages located on mailbox servers to be scanned. Which of the following Enable Forefront Security for Exchange Scan options should you select in Forefront Server Security Administrator?

    A. Disable All

    B. Enable Store Scanning

    C. Enable Transport Scanning

    D. Enable All

6. You work for Tailspin Toys, which sells toy hovercrafts. You want to make certain that any message that contains the word "Hovercraft" in its header or body is not rejected as spam by your organization's Exchange Server 2007 edge transport server. Which of the following can you do to ensure that this does not happen?

    A. Disable anti-spam updates on the edge transport server

    B. Configure the word "Hovercraft" as a nonblocked word on the Custom Words tab of Content Filtering Properties

    C. Configure the word "Hovercraft" as a blocked word on the Custom Words tab of Content Filtering Properties

    D. Configure the address hovercraft@tailspintoys.com on the Exceptions tab of the Content Filtering Properties

Lesson 2: Configuring Transport and Message Compliance

Almost all organizations must abide by certain rules with respect to the retention of business-related communication. Although these rules vary from jurisdiction to jurisdiction, it is possible to use features built in to Exchange Server 2007 to ensure that your organization remains compliant. Where message filtering is used primarily to sort out spam from legitimate messages entering the organization through the edge transport server, transport rules are used primarily to manage communication within the organization and communication from the organization to the rest of the world. Transport rules can be used to filter internal communication, performing actions on the basis of message properties, such as sender, receiver, message content, and classification.

After this lesson, you will be able to:
- Configure message compliance.
- Configure transport rules.

Estimated lesson time: 40 minutes

Configuring Message Compliance

Configuring message compliance is about configuring Exchange to meet compliance requirements in a particular jurisdiction rather than a specific set of global requirements. For example, in some countries it may be necessary for corporations to retain business-related communication for a period of several years, whereas in other countries it may be necessary for archives to be kept for only a matter of months. The key to configuring message compliance is being able to interpret regulations and conform to their principles by applying Exchange Server 2007 administrative techniques.

Configuring Messaging Records Management

As shown in Figure 6-11, managed folders are the default folders located in all users' mailboxes in Microsoft Office Outlook 2007. It is also possible to create custom managed folders. To create a new managed custom folder, click on the New Managed Custom Folder item in the Actions pane when the Mailbox node is selected under the Organization Configuration node in Exchange Management Console. A managed folder mailbox policy is a collection of managed folders. For example, a custom managed folder named Hovercraft_Specs and another called Hovercraft_Design could be linked to a managed folder mailbox policy called Hovercraft_Development. When the

Hovercraft_Development policy is applied to a user's mailbox, the managed folders that it contains are also applied to that user's mailbox in a single step.

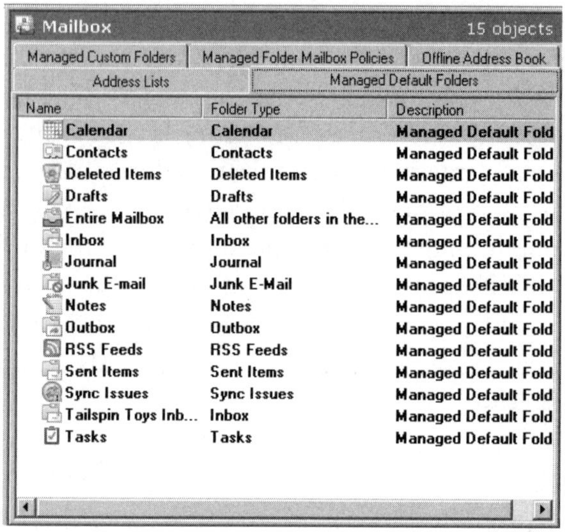

Figure 6-11   The list of default managed folders

Managed content settings, shown in Figure 6-12, determine how long items are retained before being deleted. A retention period is specified in days. The managed content settings also specify when the retention period starts and the action to take at the end of the retention period. The possible actions that can be taken at the end of the retention period are to move the item to the deleted items folder, move to a managed custom folder, delete and allow recovery, permanently delete, or mark as past retention limit. To set the Managed Content settings, right-click one of the managed default or custom folders and select New Managed Content Settings.

NOTE   Written policies are important

It is not just important to have policies on computers for the management of data retention. Written policies must also exist. If e-mail records are subpoenaed, it has to be clear how long e-mail is stored at your organization. If an organization's written retention policy is substantially different from what is implemented in practice, the organization could face additional problems in court. Ensure that your implementation follows the written policy as closely as possible. You do not want to be accused of allowing the deletion of important e-mail that should have been stored according to your company's policies.

In the event that a user is on vacation, you might wish to place a mailbox on retention hold. This disables messaging records management. To do this, edit the properties of the user's mailbox under the Mailbox node of Recipient Configuration in Exchange Management Console. On the Mailbox Settings tab, select Messaging Records Management and then click the Properties button. In the Messaging Records Management dialog box, shown in Figure 6-13, check the Enable Retention Hold For Items In This Mailbox option and specify a start and end date.

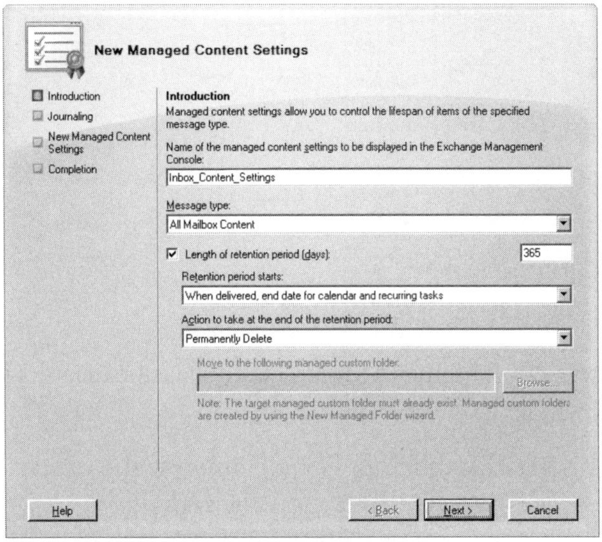

Figure 6-12 Managed Content Settings

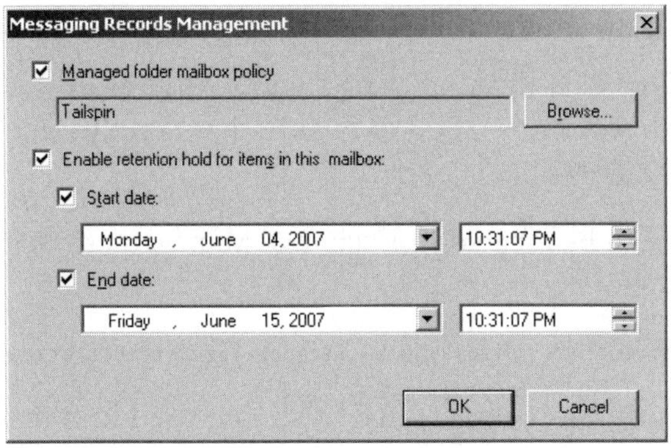

Figure 6-13 Configuring a retention hold

MORE INFO **More on managing messaging records**

For more information on managing messaging records with Exchange Server 2007, consult the following TechNet link: *http://technet.microsoft.com/en-us/library/bb123507.aspx*.

Configuring Message Classifications

Message classifications allow messages to be flagged for special handling. Special handling could mean that the message can be read only by certain users or might not be able to be sent to recipients outside the organization. Users who create a message using Outlook 2007 or Outlook Web Access have the option of assigning a classification to that message, as shown in Figure 6-14.

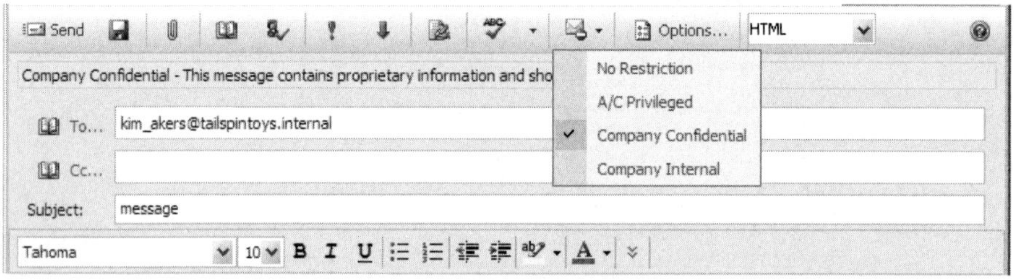

Figure 6-14 The four built-in message classifications

By default, Exchange Server 2007 includes three default classifications. These classifications include the following:

- **A/C privileged** This classification applies a banner to the header informing readers that the message is subject to attorney–client privilege.

- **Company confidential** This classification utilizes Microsoft Windows Rights Management Services for Windows Server 2003 to ensure that only users with appropriate permissions are able to access the message contents.

- **Company internal** This classification works with Windows Rights Management Services for Windows Server 2003 to ensure that the message cannot be transmitted to external recipients.

New message classifications can be created in Exchange Management Shell by using the following command:

```
New-MessageClassification –Name <string> -DisplayName <String> -SenderDescription <String>
```

Once the message classification has been created, it can be used in transport rules. Prior to being able to use message classification, it is necessary to update end-user computers with the message classification XML file that can be created by executing Export-OutlookClassification.ps1 script file located in the Exchange Server 2007 scripts directory.

MORE INFO **More on message classification**

To learn more about message classification, consult the following TechNet link: *http://technet. microsoft.com/en-us/library/bb124705.aspx*

Rights Management Services Exchange Agents

The section on configuring message classifications discussed the use of Windows Rights Management Services to restrict the distribution of messages. By default, the Rights Management Services agent is not enabled. To enable this functionality in Exchange Server 2007, it is necessary to perform the following steps:

1. Install Windows Rights Management Services Client with Service Pack 2 (SP2) on a server within your organization. This is an involved process and also requires the installation of an SQL Server 2005 instance to host logging and configuration information.

2. Download and install the Rights Management Services Client with SP2 on each hub transport server.

3. Register the Rightsmanagementwrapper.dll in Exchange Management Shell.

4. Enable the Rights Management Services Prelicensing Agent using the Exchange Management Service command:

   ```
   Enable-TransportAgent "AD RMS Prelicensing Agent"
   ```

5. Restart the Microsoft Exchange Transport Service.

MORE INFO **Rights Management Services Client with SP2**

The Rights Management Services Client with SP2 can be downloaded from Microsoft's Web site at the following address: *http://www.microsoft.com/downloads/details.aspx?familyid=02DA5107-2919-414B-A5A3-3102C7447838&displaylang=en.*

During the transport process, a license is acquired from the Rights Management Services server that allows the e-mail to be delivered to the user. If the user has not been granted permission to read the message, the attempt to deliver the message to the user's mailbox will fail. Users with appropriate rights are able to open mail protected by Rights Management Services even if they are not connected to the Rights Management Services server, for example, if they have a mobile computer and try to read e-mail on a business trip.

MORE INFO   Rights Management Services

For more information of Rights Management Services, consult the following Web site: *http://www.microsoft.com/windowsserver2003/technologies/rightsmgmt/default.mspx.*

Journaling

Journaling is the process where records are kept of all e-mail messages that pass through Hub Transport servers. Messaging journals can be thought of as log files, but are used to keep track of messaging so that companies can be in compliance with their legal and regulatory obligations. Journaling can be thought of as a mixture of message archiving and logging. Instead of storing data offline, journaling records who sent a particular message to a particular recipient at a particular time. Journaled messages are wrapped in journaling envelopes that contain detailed information about the sender, recipient, subject and other important data. Journaled messages are stored in Journal mailboxes. In some third-party solutions, journaling data is stored directly in a database. Exchange Server 2007 supports two types of journaling:

- **Standard Journaling.** Standard journaling is also called per-mailbox database journaling because it journals all messages sent to and from users that have their mailboxes stored in a particular mailbox database. Standard journaling is available in both versions of Exchange Server 2007.

- **Premium Journaling.** Also known as per-recipient journaling, this form of journaling provides more flexibility as it allows journaling of messages from or to individuals or groups of users. Premium journaling allows an administrator to journal messages sent within the organization or message traffic that is sent to or arrives from outside the organization. It is also possible to apply journaling to all messages. Premium journaling is only available with the Enterprise version of Exchange Server 2007.

Journal records are usually sent to an SMTP address, which is specified in a journal rule. The Journaled mailbox needs to be treated differently to standard mailboxes. They often need to be tamper proof as there is the possibility that the contents of such a mailbox might be used as evidence in legal proceedings. Depending on what data is Journaled and the period it needs to be retained for, it is often necessary to devote an entire mailbox database to a single Journaled mailbox.

Journal rules require that the Journaling agent be enabled. This can be achieved on a Hub Transport agent by using the command:

```
Enable-TransportAgent -Identity "Journaling agent"
```

To enable per-mailbox journaling on a particular mailbox database, you can edit the properties of the mailbox database through Exchange Management Console and specify a journal recipient mailbox SMTP address. To achieve the same goal through Exchange Management Shell, issue the command:

```
Set-MailboxDatabase <Mailbox Database Name> -JournalRecipient <journal@mailbox.address>
```

Premium journal rules can be created from Exchange Management Console by opening the journaling tab under Organization Configuration\Hub Transport and selecting the New Journal Rule item from the Actions pane. Alternatively, new journal rules can be created using Exchange Management shell by issuing the command:

```
New-JournalRule -Name <RuleName> -Recipient <Monitored SMTP Address> -JournalEmailAddress
journal@mailbox.address - Scope <Internal | External | Global> -Enabled <$True | $False>
```

Although journaling rules can be created in this manner using the standard version of Exchange Server 2007, the rules can only be activated if an Exchange Server 2007 Enterprise Client Access License (CAL) is present.

MORE INFO   Overview of Journaling

To get a more complete overview of journaling, including how the feature can be used to comply with relevant legislation, consult the following link: *http://technet.microsoft.com/en-us/library/aa998649.aspx*

> ## Quick Check
> 1. Which message classification should you assign to a message that should not be sent to people outside your organization?
> 2. What technology do you need to implement before you can successfully apply the company-confidential message classification?
>
> ### Quick Check Answers
> 1. You should assign the company-internal classification to messages that should not be sent to people outside your organization.
> 2. It is necessary to implement the Windows Rights Management Service in your organization prior to being able to successfully use the company-confidential message classification.

Configuring Transport Rules

Transport rules allow organizational message policies to be applied to e-mail that passes through hub and edge transport servers in an organization. Transport rules agents are used to enforce compliance policies. For example, it is possible to use transport rules to do the following:

- Prevent inappropriate content from entering or exiting the organization's messaging infrastructure
- Ensure that confidential information is filtered
- Track and archive messages on the basis of sender or recipient
- Redirect messages for inspection prior to delivery
- Apply legal disclaimers to messages

Transport rules can be managed using the Transport Rules tab, which is available when the Hub Transport node is selected under Organization Configuration in Exchange Management Console. It is also possible to manage transport rules using Exchange Management Shell. Because transport rules work at the organizational level, a transport rule that you create is applied via the Active Directory directory service to all other Hub Transport servers in the Exchange 2007 organization.

Transport rules are made up of conditions, exceptions, and actions. It is possible that a message may meet the conditions of multiple transport rules. In such a circumstance, the rules are applied in the order of priority listed under the Transport Rules section in Exchange Management Console. In the following sections, each of the available conditions, exceptions, and actions that make up Exchange Server 2007 transport rules are covered in more detail.

Conditions

Transport rule conditions, shown in Figure 6-15, determine which messages the transport rule will apply to. Transport rules without any conditions are applied to all messages, unless those messages meet a configured exception. It is possible for a rule to have multiple conditions. When a transport rule has multiple conditions, each one of those conditions must be met before the rule will be applied.

The following conditions can apply to a transport rule:

- From people (specify user account)
- From members of a distribution list (specify distribution list)

- From users inside or outside the organization (specify one or the other)
- Sent to people (specify user accounts)
- Sent to a member of a distribution list (specify distribution list)
- Sent to users inside or outside the organization (specify one or the other)
- When any of the recipients in the To field are people (specify user account)
- When any of the recipients in the To field are members of a distribution list (specify distribution list)
- When any of the recipients in the Cc field are people (specify user account)
- When any of the recipients in the Cc field are members of a distribution list (specify distribution list)
- When any of the recipients in the To or Cc field are people (specify user account)
- When any of the recipients in the To or Cc field are members of a distribution list (specify distribution list)
- Marked with classification (Select from existing classifications)
- When the Subject field contains specific words
- When the Subject field or the body of the message contains specific words
- When the From address contains specific words
- When the Subject field contains specific text patterns
- When the Subject field or the body of the message contains specific text patterns
- When the From address contains specific text patterns
- With an SCL rating that is greater than or equal to limit
- When the size of any attachment is greater than or equal to limit
- Marked with importance

In most situations, a transport rule with a single condition will be adequate. It is only in very specific circumstances that you will need to apply more than one condition to get the appropriate match.

Exceptions

Exceptions, some of which are shown in Figure 6-16, are used to used to exempt messages that match a transport rule's conditions from the actions of a transport rule. For example, you might want a transport rule to apply to all messages in your organization except for those sent by a particular person. In this instance, it is easier to have no conditions, which means the rule applies to all messages, and then to configure an exception for that one user than it would be to create a condition that applied to everyone but that one user. A transport rule can have multiple exceptions. Unlike conditions where every specified condition must be met for a rule to apply, only one exception condition must be met for the message to be exempted from the rule.

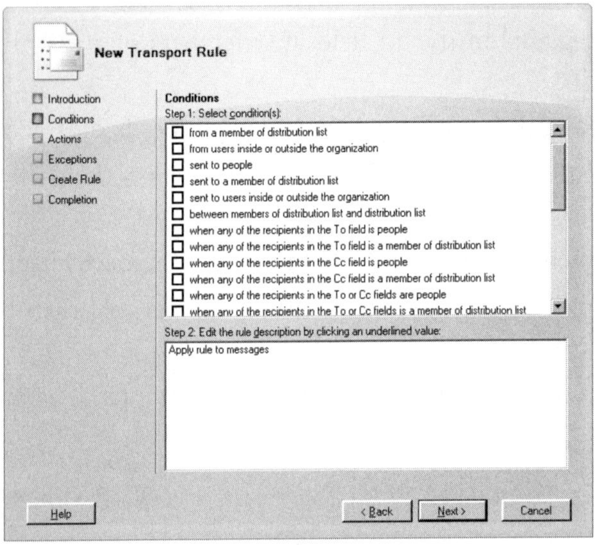

Figure 6-15   Some transport rule conditions

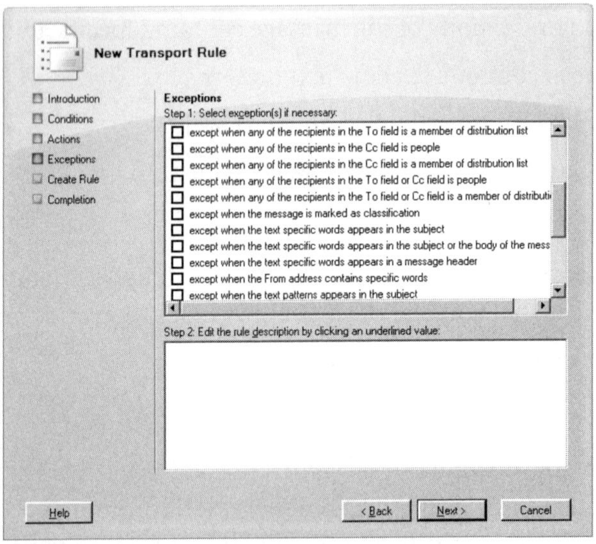

Figure 6-16   Some transport rule exceptions

The following exceptions can apply to a transport rule:

- Except When The Message Is From People (select users)
- Except When The Message Is From Member Of Distribution List (select list)
- Except When The Message Is From Users Inside Or Outside The Organization (select one)
- Except When The Message Is Sent to People (select users)
- Except When The Message Is Sent To Member Of Distribution List (select list)
- Except When The Message Is Sent To Users Inside Or Outside The Organization (select one)
- Except When Any Of The Recipients In The To Field Is People (select users)
- Except When Any Of The Recipients In The To Field Is A Member Of Distribution List (select list)
- Except When Any Of The Recipients In The Cc Field Is People (select users)
- Except When Any Of The Recipients In The Cc Field Is A Member Of Distribution List (select list)
- Except When Any Of The Recipients In The To Field Or Cc Field Is People (select users)
- Except When Any Of The Recipients In The To Field Or Cc Field Is A Member Of Distribution List (select list)
- Except When The Message Is Marked As Classification (select classification)
- Except When The Text Specific Words Appears In The Subject (enter text)
- Except When The Text Specific Words Appears In The Subject Or The Body Of The Message (enter text)
- Except When The Text Specific Words Appear In A Message Header (enter text)
- Except When The From Address Contains Text Patterns (enter text pattern)
- Except When The Text Pattern Appears In Any Attachment File Name (enter text pattern)
- Except With A Spam Confidence Level (SCL) That Is Greater Than Or Equal To Limit (set limit)
- Except When The Size Of Any Attachment Is Greater Than Or Equal To Limit (set limit)
- Except When The Message Is Marked As Importance (set importance)

When creating a transport rule using the wizard you configure exceptions after you configure actions. When considering the logic of a transport rule, it is best to define the set of messages that the actions should apply to first. When debugging transport rules, try to figure out why the conditions and exceptions might have missed a particular message before attempting to discover if the action was not applied.

Actions

Actions, some of which are shown in Figure 6-17, are applied to messages that meet transport rule conditions and do not meet any exceptions. Multiple actions can be applied to messages, although you should be careful when using multiple actions to ensure that they do not conflict with each other to produce an undesired result. When debugging transport rules, you should include the Log An Event action, as this will allow you to determine whether the rule was invoked by the conditions. Events are written to the local hub transport server's application log.

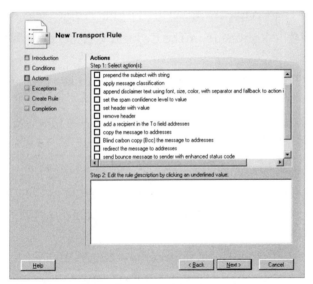

Figure 6-17   Some transport rule actions

The available actions that can be configured as part of a transport rule are the following:

- Log An Event With Message (specify message)
- Prepend The Subject With String (specify string)
- Apply Message Classification (select classification)

- Append Disclaimer Text Using Font, Size, Color, With Separator And Fallback Action If Unable To Apply (enter disclaimer text, select font, select font size, select fallback action)
- Set The Spam Confidence Level To Value (set value)
- Set Header With Value (set value)
- Remove Header (specify header to remove)
- Add A Recipient In The To Field Addresses (specify recipient)
- Copy The Message To Addresses (specify addresses)
- Blind Carbon Copy (BCC) The Message To Addresses (specify addresses)
- Redirect The Message To Addresses (specify addresses)
- Send Bounce Message To Sender With Enhanced Status Code (specify bounce message and status code)
- Silently Drop The Message

With the substantial number of conditions, exceptions, and actions available, transport rules can be customized to meet any organization's needs. The practices at the end of this lesson provide a detailed description of how to configure transport rules using some of these conditions.

Message Screening

Some organizations, especially those that are working on projects that are yet to be publicly announced or those that deal with confidential data, will want to ensure that employees are unable to forward sensitive information outside the organization. Exchange Server 2007 can be used to block the transmission of sensitive information within or outside the organization using a process known as message screening.

When configuring the conditions for message screening, as shown in Figure 6-18, use the conditions that search for particular text or text patterns contained in messages. Text patterns can be entered as regular expressions, which are a way of searching a block of text for particular strings of text.

MORE INFO   **Regular Expressions in Transport Rules**

For more information of using Regular Expressions in Transport Rules, consult the following link: *http://technet.microsoft.com/en-us/library/aa997187.aspx.*

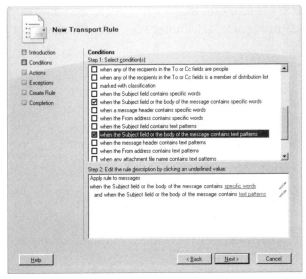

Figure 6-18 Screening messages based on content

When implementing message screening, you would configure one of the following actions:

- **Copy the message to addresses** When this option is selected, the recipient is aware that a third party also has been sent a copy of the message, though the sender will not be aware of this

- **Blind carbon copy the message to addresses** When this option is selected, the recipient still gets the message but will be unaware that a third party has also been sent a copy of the message. This is a good option if it is necessary to monitor communication but not interrupt it.

- **Redirect the message to addresses** When this option is selected, the recipient never receives the message but a specially configured third party might. For example, if you suspect that an employee is forwarding sensitive information, you can set up a condition that searches for specific key words in the employee's mail and redirects matching e-mail to the Human Resources Department for use in disciplinary proceedings.

As with any form of surveillance, ensure that you implement these types of rules in line with company policy. Part of the job of being an e-mail administrator is ensuring that you enforce company policy while respecting the rights of the people that you work with.

Legal Notice Disclaimers

A legal disclaimer is an addition that can be included on all e-mail messages sent by an organization. Generally, legal disclaimers provide legal information about the nature of the communication, reminding readers that the information is confidential and should not be forwarded. The precise text is usually written by an organization's lawyers and will vary depending on the organization's legal responsibilities. Exchange Server 2007 includes the ability to add legal disclaimers to e-mail messages processed by computers hosting the Hub Transport server role.

Legal disclaimers can be applied through transport rules. In conjunction with transport rules, it is possible to configure separate disclaimers for different countries or regions, different languages, and different regulatory environments. Disclaimer text is inserted into e-mail messages using the same format as the original message, so plain-text messages have plain-text disclaimers, and HTML-formatted messages have HTML-formatted disclaimers.

Legal disclaimers can be customized in the following ways:

- Each disclaimer can have unique text. This text can be formatted using different fonts, font sizes, and colors. Disclaimers can be configured to use the Arial, Courier New, or Veranda fonts.

- Disclaimers can be placed in different locations within the message body. For example, it is possible to place a disclaimer at the beginning of a message or to place a disclaimer at the end of a message.

- In the event that a disclaimer cannot be directly inserted into a message, for example, when the message is encrypted, you can configure Exchange to wrap the encrypted message with an attached disclaimer. Alternatively, you can configure the hub transport server to reject the message if a disclaimer cannot be added or allow the message to be transmitted without the disclaimer.

In Practice 3 at the end of this lesson, you will go through the process of configuring a legal disclaimer that is applied to all messages.

MORE INFO   **More on disclaimers**

For more information on configuring legal disclaimers to work with Exchange Server 2007, consult the following TechNet link: *http://technet.microsoft.com/en-us/library/bb124352.aspx*.

Practice: Setting Up Transport and Message Compliance

In these practices, you will perform several exercises that will familiarize you with setting up transport and message compliance.

▶ **Practice 1: Configuring a Transport Rule That Screens Messages**

In this practice, you will configure a transport rule to drop any messages containing the word "Kangaroo" sent to people outside the organization by user David Hamilton. To complete this practice, perform the following steps:

1. Log on to the computer hosting Exchange Server 2007 using the Kim_Akers account.

2. Open Exchange Management Console and click Mailbox under Recipient Configuration.

3. Click New Mailbox in the Actions pane. Ensure that User Mailbox is selected and then click Next.

4. Ensure that New User is selected and then click Next.

5. Create a user with the user log-on name David Hamilton and the password P@ssw0rd. Configure properties as shown in Figure 6-19 and click Next.

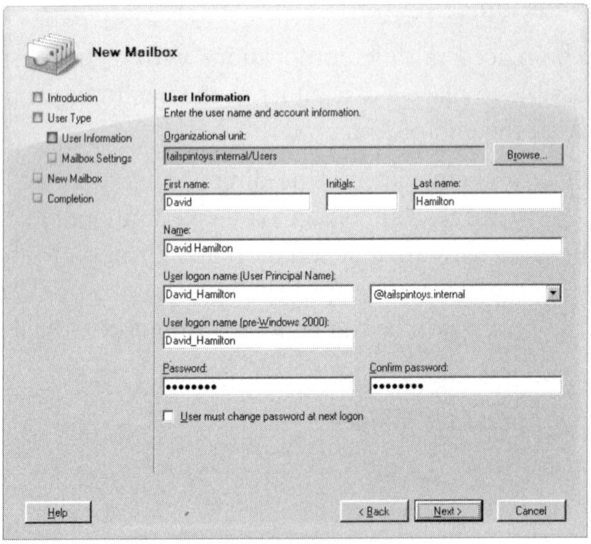

Figure 6-19 New Mailbox dialog box

6. Click Next and then click New to create the user and associated mailbox. When the mailbox is created, click Finish.

7. Open the Hub Transport node under Organization Configuration.

8. Click the Transport Rules tab and then click the New Transport Rule item in the Action pane. This will open the New Transport Rule wizard.

9. On the Introduction page, enter the rule name **David_Hamilton** and click Next.

10. Check the From People, Sent To Users Inside Or Outside The Organization and When The Subject Field Or The Body Of The Message Contains Specific Words items.

11. Click on the word "People" that is underlined and in blue and then click Add. Select David Hamilton and then click OK twice.

12. Click the word "Inside" that is underlined and in blue. Change the scope to Outside and click OK.

13. Click the specific words that are underlined and in blue. In the Specify Words dialog box, enter **Kangaroo**, click Add, and then click OK.

14. Verify that the New Transport dialog box appears similar to Figure 6-20 and then click Next.

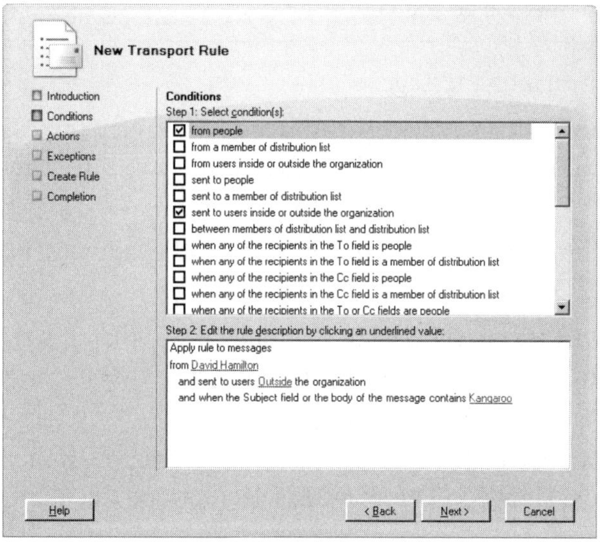

Figure 6-20   New rule for David Hamilton

15. On the Actions page, check the Silently Drop The Message option and click Next twice. Click New to create the transport rule and click Finish when the rule is created.

▶ **Practice 2: Configuring a Legal Disclaimer**

In this practice, you will configure a legal disclaimer that will be attached to all messages. The disclaimer text will be appended to all messages and will ask recipients to delete the message if they have received it in error. To complete this practice, perform the following steps:

1. Log on to the computer hosting Exchange Server 2007 using the Kim_Akers account.

2. Open Exchange Management Console and then open the Hub Transport node under Organization Configuration.

3. Click the Transport Rules tab and then click the New Transport Rule tab in the Action pane. This will open the New Transport Rule wizard.

4. In the Name field, enter **Legal Disclaimer** and click Next.

5. Ensure that no conditions are selected and click Next.

NOTE **No conditions**

When no conditions are selected, the transport rule applies to all e-mail messages. In this case, the legal disclaimer will be added to all messages.

---

6. Click Yes to the warning message.

7. On the Select Actions page, select the Append Disclaimer Text Using Font, Size, Color, With Separator And Fallback To Action If Unable To Apply, as shown in Figure 6-21.

8. Click the underlined words "Disclaimer Text" in the rule description. This will open the Specify Disclaimer Text dialog box.

9. Enter the following text in the Specify Disclaimer Text dialog box: **This is a legal disclaimer written by our organization's lawyers. This message is subject to unspecified terms and conditions.** Click OK.

10. Click the underlined word "Wrap" in the rule description. In the Select Fallback Action dialog box, shown in Figure 6-22, select Ignore. Click OK.

11. Click Next.

12. Ensure that no exceptions are selected and click Next.

13. On the Create Rule page, shown in Figure 6-23, click New and then click Finish.

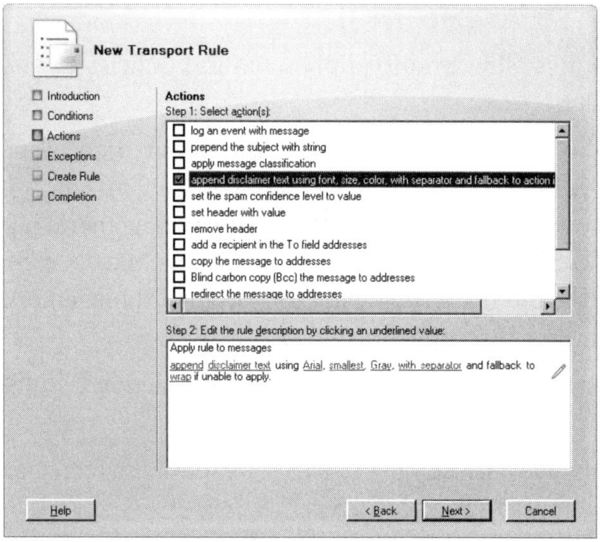

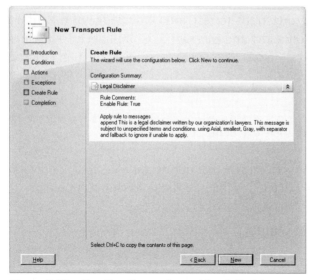

Figure 6-21 Configuring a legal disclaimer

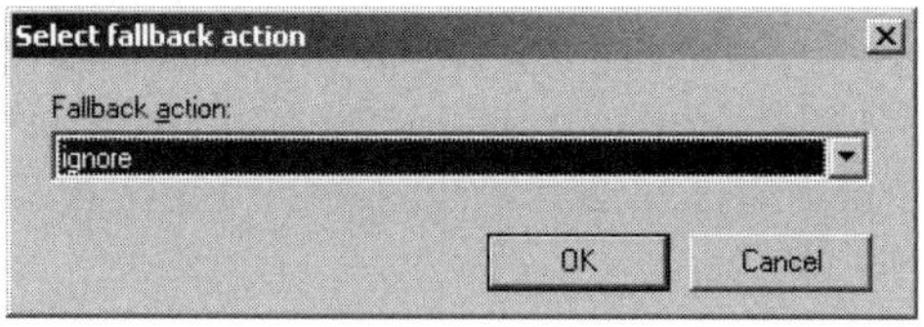

Figure 6-22 Configuring a fallback action

Figure 6-23 Creating the configured legal disclaimer

Lesson Summary

- Managed content settings allow you to apply retention policies to default managed and custom folders.

- To use Windows Rights Management to restrict the distribution of messages, it is necessary to have Windows Rights Management with SP2 installed on a server in the organization. You must then register the Rightsmanagemenwrapper.dll in Exchange Management Shell. You must then install Rights Management Services Client with SP2 and enable the Active Directory Rights Management Services Prelicensing Agent on each hub transport server.

- Transport rules consist of conditions, exceptions, and actions. Rules without conditions configured apply to all messages.

- Message screening involves scanning messages for particular text and taking appropriate action when that text is found.

- Legal disclaimers are added using transport rules on hub transport servers. They are often used to spell out the legal terms of communication originating from within the organization. Different disclaimers can be applied to messages on the basis of configured conditions. Disclaimers can be inserted at the front or at the end of messages and can be configured to conform to the message's original format.

Lesson Review

You can use the following questions to test your knowledge of the information in Lesson 2, "Configuring Transport and Messaging Compliance." The questions are also available on the companion CD if you prefer to review them in electronic form.

NOTE Answers

Answers to these questions and explanations of why each answer choice is correct or incorrect are located in the "Answers" section at the end of the book.

---

1. Your organization wants to ensure that important messages are reviewed before they are automatically deleted. Which of the following technologies would you implement to achieve this goal?

    A. Managed content settings

    B. Transport rule

    C. Retention hold

    D. Managed folder mailbox policy

2. Which of the following components must you install and enable on each hub transport server to ensure that messages can be opened only by people who have been assigned the appropriate permissions? Choose all that apply.

    A. Internet Information Services (IIS)

    B. Windows Rights Management Services Client with SP2

    C. Windows Rights Management Services server with SP2

    D. Active Directory Rights Management Services Prelicensing Agent

    E. IPSec

3. When applied to a message, which of the following default Exchange Server 2007 message classifications can only be read by users with appropriate permissions?

    A. A/C privilege

    B. Company confidential

    C. Company internal

    D. No restriction

4. At present, a transport rule has no conditions and is applied to all messages in your organization. What is the simplest way of ensuring that the same rule applies to all messages except those sent by the chief executive officer, Sam Abolrous?

    A. Create a new transport rule that has Sam Abolrous's account as a condition

    B. Edit the existing transport rule and configure Sam Abolrous's account as a condition

    C. Edit the existing transport rule and configure Sam Abolrous's account as an exception

    D. Create a new transport rule and configure Sam Abolrous's account as an exception

5. A senior manager at your company is under suspicion of forwarding sensitive information to a competitor. The chief executive officer (CEO) wants to be provided with a copy of all messages that the senior manager sends but does not want the senior manager to be aware that he is under surveillance. Which of the following actions would you configure when setting up a transport rule to screen the senior manager's messages?

    A. Blind carbon copy (Bcc) the message to addresses

    B. Add a recipient in the To field addresses

    C. Redirect the message To addresses

    D. Silently drop the message

6. You want to ensure that all messages transmitted by users in your organization have a legal disclaimer attached. Which of the following methods can you use to configure disclaimers?

    A. Configure accepted domains on hub transport servers

    B. Configure e-mail address policies on hub transport servers

    C. Configure content filtering rules on edge transport servers

    D. Configure transport rules on hub transport servers

Chapter Review

To further practice and reinforce the skills you learned in this chapter, you can perform the following tasks:

- Review the chapter summary.
- Review the list of key terms introduced in this chapter.
- Complete the case scenarios. These scenarios set up real-world situations involving the topics of this chapter and ask you to create a solution.
- Complete the suggested practices.
- Take a practice test.

Chapter Summary

- Exchange Server 2007 has built-in anti-spam functionality. Anti-spam functionality is enabled by default on edge transport servers and must be manually enabled.
- Attachment filtering, a functionality available only on edge transport servers, can be used to block attachments on the basis of file name, extension, or MIME type.
- Forefront Security for Exchange Server is an add-on solution from Microsoft that can be used to protect the Exchange infrastructure from viruses. Forefront includes commercial antivirus engines from several vendors. Forefront can be configured to scan messages once, marking them as scanned as they transit the Exchange infrastructure, or they can be configured to rescan stored messages each time new antivirus definitions become available.
- Managed folders are folders that have policies applied to them pertaining to retention of data. It is possible to configure policies for the default Outlook folders as well as to create new folders to which you apply policies.
- Windows Rights Management Services can be used in conjunction with Exchange Server 2007 to limit the dissemination of information so that it is accessible only to authorized users.
- Message classifications can be assigned by Outlook 2007 and Outlook Web Access users. Message classifications can be used to restrict access, to provide confidentiality warnings, and as the basis for transport rules.

- Message screening allows you to automate the examination of the content of messages through the use of transport rules. It is possible to use message screening to delete or reroute messages that contain specified content.

- It is possible to configure transport rules to automatically attach legal disclaimers to messages. Disclaimers can be placed at the beginning or the end of the message.

Key Terms

Do you know what these key terms mean? You can check your answers by looking up the terms in the glossary at the end of the book.

- Block list
- Compliance
- Retention
- Sender reputation level
- Spam confidence level

Case Scenarios

In the following case scenarios, you will apply what you've learned about spam, viruses, and compliance. You can find answers to these questions in the "Answers" section at the end of this book.

Case Scenario 1: Exchange Server 2007 as an Anti-Spam Solution for Coho Vineyard

The existing messaging infrastructure at Coho Vineyard has been swamped by spam. You have been asked by management at Coho Vineyard to explain how replacing the existing messaging infrastructure at Coho Vineyard with a messaging infrastructure based on Exchange Server 2007 could alleviate their problems. Management has three specific questions that they would like you to answer:

1. What technology exists to automatically block SMTP servers that repeatedly send spam to the organization?

2. How can they ensure that the IP address of their most valuable customers' SMTP servers are never blocked, even if their customers send them messages of a commercial nature?

3. How can they ensure that messages from the Internet containing words of an explicit nature are always blocked?

Case Scenario 2: Configuring Message and Transport Compliance for a Law Firm

You are helping a law firm implement Exchange Server 2007. The law firm has several compliance issues that they would like you to help them resolve. The issues are as follows:

1. Lawyers at the firm need some way to prominently mark certain communication as covered by attorney–client privilege. Which Exchange Server 2007 technology could you implement to achieve this?

2. The law firm handles matters for a prominent celebrity. The law firm is concerned that some employees might forward confidential information about the celebrity to the tabloids. They want you to stop any message that mentions the celebrity stopped from being sent outside the information and to be sent to the director instead. How can you achieve this?

3. What steps can you take to ensure that all messages that are sent by organizational staff to clients on the Internet are labeled with information about the terms and conditions under which communication with the law firm can be disseminated?

Suggested Practices

To help you successfully master the exam objectives presented in this chapter, complete the following tasks. Several of these tasks require an Edge Transport server. A suggested practice involving installing the Edge Transport server role was included in Chapter 2, "Installing Exchange Server and Configuring Server Roles."

Configure the Antivirus and Anti-spam System

Do all the practices in this section.

- **Practice 1: Configure Attachment Filtering on an Edge Transport Server** Configure an edge transport server to drop all script attachments that use the .dog extension.

- Configure an edge transport server to drop all attachments named newvirus.exe.

- **Practice 2: Configure Forefront Security for Exchange Server 2007 on an Edge Transport Server** Install and configure the Forefront evaluation on an edge transport server connected to your Exchange organization.

- Configure Forefront to delete encrypted compressed files and perform reverse DNS lookups.

- **Practice 3: Configure Forefront Security for Exchange Server 2007 on a Mailbox Server**   Configure the Forefront evaluation you installed during an optional practice in Chapter 2 to rescan messages stored on mailbox servers when antivirus definitions are updated.

- Configure the Forefront evaluation to update daily at 3:00 AM.

Transport Rules and Message Compliance

Do all the practices in this section.

- **Practice 1: Create Managed Folders**   Create a managed folder.

- Configure the managed folder that you created to retain messages for 180 days.

- **Practice 2: Message Classification**   Create a new message classification called Non Disclosure Agreement.

- Configure a transport rule that ensures that no messages marked with the classification Non Disclosure Agreement can be sent to addresses outside the organization.

- **Practice 3: Message Screening**   Configure any outgoing e-mails that include the word "Wombat" to be redirected to Kim Akers.

- Configure any e-mails that contain the word "Secret" to be blind carbon copied to Kim Akers.

Take a Practice Test

The practice tests on this book's companion CD offer many options. For example, you can test yourself on just one exam objective, or you can test yourself on all the 70-236 certification exam content. You can set up the test so that it closely simulates the experience of taking a certification exam, or you can set it up in study mode so that you can look at the correct answers and explanations after you answer each question.

MORE INFO   Practice tests

For details about all the practice test options available, see the "How to Use the Practice Tests" section in this book's Introduction.

Chapter 7

Connectors and Connectivity

Connectors are a collection of configuration settings that describe how Edge and Hub Transport servers communicate with each other, the Internet, servers running other messaging systems, and servers running previous versions of Exchange. The first lesson in this chapter examines connectors in detail, including how to add, modify, and remove them so that message traffic in and out of your organization flows as efficiently as possible.

The second part of the chapter looks at how Exchange Server 2007 can be configured to interact with mobile devices. Compatible mobile phones can be configured to work as clients of Exchange Server 2007, allowing users to keep up-to-date copies of the calendars and messages in their pockets rather than being able to access them only through a desktop or laptop computer. The second lesson also examines how to configure and support other services, such as Availability and Autodiscover, that assist client access to Exchange Server 2007.

Exam objectives in this chapter:
- Configure connectors.
- Configure client connectivity.

Lessons in this chapter:

Before You Begin

- Ensure that you have completed all practices in Chapter 1, "Preparing for Exchange Installation," and Chapter 2, "Installing Exchange Server and Configuring Server Roles."

No additional configuration is required for this chapter.

Real World

Orin Thomas

In some industries, the competition for customers is brutal. A salesperson's contact list can be one of his or her most valuable possessions. Increasingly important information is kept not in locked briefcases but in personal digital assistants and smart phones. Although conferences may sound relatively benign, there are industries where competitors would not think twice about pickpocketing a mobile device to get access to important information. At one company I worked for, the sales team was forbidden from taking their mobile devices to conferences because a phone containing customer information had once been lifted during a conference social event. The remote wipe technology available in Exchange Server 2007 allows mobile devices containing sensitive information to be sanitized in the event that they are misplaced or stolen. You should make the users of mobile devices in your organization aware of this technology. In the event that they have just lost the device, you can always replace the information. In the event that the device has in fact been stolen, remote wipe can be a way of ensuring that important customers are not snatched away by competitors.

Lesson 1: Configuring Connectors

Connectors allow administrators to customize how Edge and Hub Transport servers send and receive messages. During role deployment, basic connector functionality is implemented. All that is necessary to get message traffic flowing is ensuring that the Edge Transport server is properly subscribed to the rest of the Exchange organization. In this lesson, you will learn how to create custom connectors to deal with unusual message traffic that might not be appropriate for the default connectors installed with the Edge and Hub Transport server roles.

> **After this lesson, you will be able to:**
> - Understand the difference between Send and Receive connectors.
> - Create, modify, and remove connectors from Edge and Hub Transport servers.
>
> **Estimated lesson time: 40 minutes**

Receive Connectors

Receive connectors determine how incoming Simple Mail Transfer Protocol (SMTP) traffic is dealt with by an Edge or Hub Transport server. A Receive connector listens for incoming connections that match a specific configuration. Receive connectors are defined on a per-server basis and cannot be copied to other servers. Receive connector configuration is stored within Active Directory for Hub Transport servers and within Active Directory Application Mode for Edge Transport servers.

When you deploy the Edge Transport server role, the following Receive connectors are automatically created:

- Receive connector for incoming messages from the Internet
- Receive connector for incoming messages from the organization's Hub Transport servers

Although these connectors are automatically created, incoming and outgoing mail can be processed only once the Edge Transport server has undergone the Edge subscription process or has been configured manually. When the Hub Transport server role is deployed, the following connectors are created:

- **Client** This connector allows clients, such as Outlook Express, to send messages.
- **Default** This connector allows Exchange users, Exchange servers, and legacy Exchange servers to connect to this server.

You specify two parameters when you create a new Receive connector. These parameters are the Usage Type and the Permission Group. Usage Types determine the default security settings for the connector. As shown in Figure 7-1, the possible usage types are Custom, Internet, Internal, Client, and Partner. If no usage type is specified, the default usage type will be set to Custom.

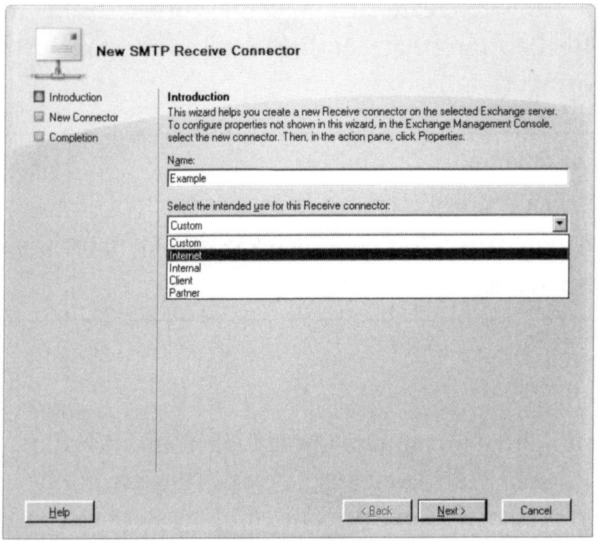

Figure 7-1 New Receive connector

The properties of each Receive connector usage types are as follows:

- The Client usage type has ExchangeUsers as the default permission group. This usage type uses Transport Layer Security (TLS), Basic Authentication plus TLS, and Integrated Microsoft Windows Authentication as default authentication mechanisms. This authentication type is used by internal clients to transmit messages. This usage type is not available on an Edge Transport server, as all client traffic must be routed through Hub Transport servers.

- The Custom usage type does not have a default permission group or a default authentication mechanism. The Custom usage type is used when configuring a connector to receive messages from Hub Transport servers in another forest. You would also configure a Custom connector on an Edge Transport server to allow it to receive e-mail from an external relay domain.

- The Internal usage type has ExchangeServers and ExchangeLegacyServers as the default permission groups. This authentication type uses Exchange Server authentication as the default authentication mechanism. When implemented on an Edge Transport server, the ExchangeLegacyServers permission group is not available. The Internal usage type is often created to receive e-mail from a legacy Exchange bridgehead server.

- The Internet usage type as the AnonymousUsers and Partner as its default permission groups. The Internet usage type generally does not use any authentication mechanism, as SMTP servers on the Internet need to be able to deliver mail to the organization through this connector and it is not possible to set up authentication for every SMTP server on the Internet.

- The Partner usage group uses the Partner default permission group. The default authentication type is mutual TLS authentication.

As stated earlier, connectors use both usage types and permission groups. Permission groups specify which users or computers can utilize the connector. The available Receive connector permission groups are detailed in Table 7-1.

Table 7-1   Receive Connector Permission Groups

Permission Group	Security Principles
Anonymous users	Anonymous users
Exchange users	Authenticated users
Exchange servers	Hub Transport, Edge Transport, and externally secured servers
Legacy Exchange Servers	Exchange legacy interoperability
Partner	Partner Server account

You can edit an existing Receive connector's properties by right-clicking the Receive connector, located in the Exchange Management Console under the Server Configuration\Hub Transport node (or under the Edge Transport node if you are working on an Edge Transport server), and selecting properties. The General tab, shown in Figure 7-2, allows you to configure the protocol logging level and the name that the connector will provide to incoming connection attempts. If multiple fully qualified domain names (FQDNs) are assigned to the transport server that the Receive connector is on, you should ensure that the appropriate one is listed on this tab of the connector's properties dialog box.

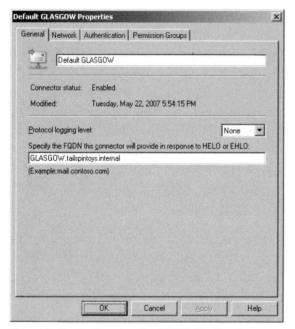

Figure 7-2 Configuring the FQDN of a Receive connector

The Network tab of a Receive connector's properties dialog box is shown in Figure 7-3. There are two sections in this dialog box: the Local IP address section and the Remote IP address section. The Local IP address section determines which server IP address the connector will listen on. For example, if your Hub Transport server has multiple network cards, you can configure the connector to listen only for traffic on an IP address assigned to one of these cards rather than both of them. The default setting is to listen for traffic on port 25 on all interfaces. The Remote IP address section is used to specify which remote servers can forward mail to the local server. By default, the Receive connector will accept mail from all IP addresses. In some situations, you may wish to limit the settings in this dialog box to a specific range of IP addresses, such as those in use within your organization, though you should keep in mind that there are more effective tools for fighting spam and viruses, such as transport rules, which were covered in Chapter 6, "Spam, Viruses, and Compliance." Unless there is a great reason to do otherwise, you should configure Receive connectors to receive all incoming messages and then let other aspects of Exchange, such as transport rules, deal with filtering messages on the basis of source address or content.

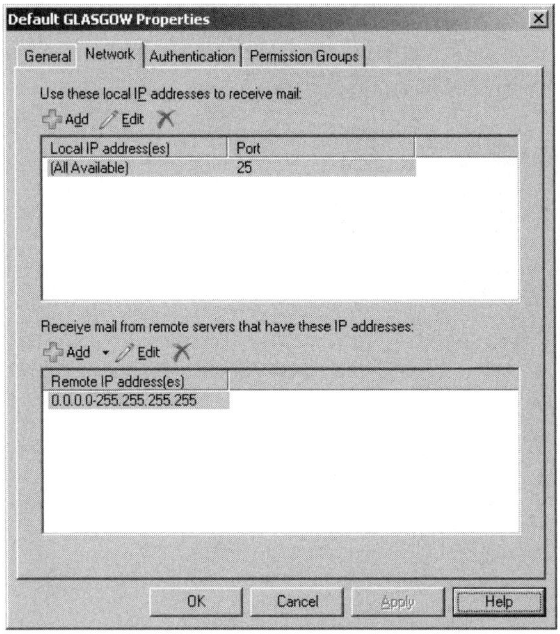

Figure 7-3   Receive connector network settings

The Authentication tab, shown in Figure 7-4, allows you different authentication options. The available authentication options are the following:

- TLS requires the installation of a TLS certificate and is generally used between trusted organizations.

- Basic authentication uses unencrypted user names and passwords.

- Exchange Server authentication is used to authenticate with smart hosts and uses TLS direct trust or Kerberos through TLS.

- Integrated Windows authentication uses NTLM or Kerberos authentication.

- The Externally Secured option is used in the event that the network is secured (such as a direct line) or Internet Protocol security (IPSec) has been implemented.

The Permission Groups tab, shown in Figure 7-5, allows you to specify which network users or computers are able to utilize this Receive connector. The permission groups that are available were listed earlier in this lesson in Table 7-1. In general, if your connector will receive traffic from outside the organization, you will select Anonymous Users or the Partners permission group. For communication within the organization, you will generally select the Exchange Users, Exchange Server, or Legacy Exchange

Servers permission group. The permission groups that are assigned determine exactly which SMTP functionality (submitting messages and bypassing spam filters) is available for the connector based on authentication.

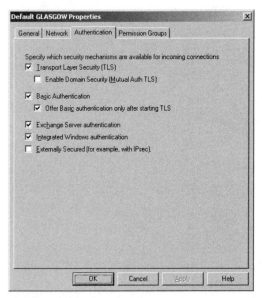

Figure 7-4 Receive connector authentication settings

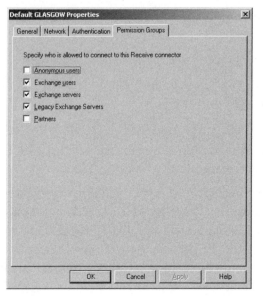

Figure 7-5 Receive connector permission groups

Quick Check

1. Which connector usage type cannot be implemented on an Edge Transport server?

2. What connector usage type would you implement to receive mail from an external relay domain, and what type of transport server would you create it on?

Quick Check Answers

1. The Client usage type cannot be implemented on an Edge Transport server.

2. You would use the Custom usage type on an Edge Transport server.

Send Connectors

Send connectors determine how messages are forwarded from a Hub or Edge Transport server to another mail server, either within the organization or located on the Internet. Send connectors are not explicitly created when the Hub or Edge Transport role is installed on a computer, though invisible Send connectors are created on the basis of the Active Directory site topology so that mail can flow within the Exchange organization. As mentioned earlier, message flow to and from hosts on the Internet requires that an Edge Transport server be subscribed to Hub Transport servers by the Edge subscription process or that special manual configuration be performed. If you want to configure a Hub Transport server to receive and transmit messages to the Internet (for example, when an organization does not use an Edge Transport server), connectors must be manually configured to allow message transmission.

When you create a Send connector for a Hub Transport server, the connector can be used by any Hub Transport server within your organization. This is because the connector configuration data is stored within Active Directory. For example, if you configure a Send connector to forward messages to an external domain, any Hub Transport server in your organization will use the information within that connector to route messages destined for that domain. During the connector creation process, covered later in this lesson, you can select which Hub Transport servers you wish to associate the connector with. It is possible to associate any number of Hub Transport servers in your organization with a connector as long as you do not also associate an Edge Transport server with the connector. It is not possible to associate the same Send connector with both Edge and Hub Transport servers; one or the other type of transport server must be chosen.

Send connectors can be configured for the following intended usages:

- **Internal** This type is used to send messages to other servers in your Exchange organization. It is rare that you need to configure this type of Send connector, as they are automatically created when Hub Transport servers are deployed.

- **Internet** This type of connector sends mail directly to the Internet and will use Domain Name System (DNS) mail exchanger (MX) records to route e-mail.

- **Partner** This type of connector is used to forward messages to partner domains. Partner connectors allow connections only to SMTP servers that authenticate using TLS certificates.

- **Custom** This type allows an administrator to configure a mix of settings.

When configuring a custom Send connector, you specify the address space that the Send connector applies to, the smart host (if any) that messages addressed to or are forwarded to, how DNS resolution occurs, and which transport servers within the organization the Send connector will be applied to. A smart host is a special host that forwards mail to a specific destination. They are most often used when you want to route mail using a more direct route than passing it across the Internet. You will configure a Send connector during the practice exercises at the end of this lesson.

MORE INFO **More on Send connectors**

For more information on Send connectors, consult the following TechNet article: *http://technet.microsoft.com/en-us/library/aa998662.aspx*.

Foreign Connectors

Foreign connectors are a special type of connector that can be installed only on a Hub Transport server. Foreign connectors use drop directories to transmit messages to a local messaging server that uses a transport mechanism other than SMTP. The foreign gateway server is configured to obtain messages from the drop directory and forward them from there. An example of this type of server is a third-party fax server where Exchange deposits messages that are to be forwarded via fax into a special drop directory and the third-party fax software takes over from there. You can find out more about foreign connectors by navigating to the following link: *http://technet.microsoft.com/en-us/library/aa996779.aspx*.

Using Telnet to Test SMTP Communication

Telnet was once the Internet's primary remote access protocol. It was used for decades on the Internet to connect to servers on local and remote networks. Telnet transmits data in an unencrypted way, which means that Telnet traffic can be monitored. This has led to a decline in its use as a remote access protocol. Because Telnet works in a very basic way, it can still be used to test networking functionality. You can use Telnet to simulate some of the commands used to interact with a mail server. This allows you to verify that SMTP is functioning. The Telnet utility is included with all versions of Windows.

Normally, Telnet will connect to TCP port 23, but by specifying an alternate port when opening a connection, it is possible to initiate a network connection to another port. SMTP uses TCP port 25, so to connect to the SMTP service on mail server mail.tailspintoys.internal, you would issue the following command from the command prompt: *telnet mail.tailspintoys.internal 25*. When the connection is established, you will see a message in the command line identifying the mail server name and the time at which your connection was initiated, similar to the following:

```
220 GLASGOW.tailspintoys.internal Microsoft ESMTP MAIL Service ready at Fri, 29 Jun 2007
20:17:24 +1000
```

Once the connection has been established, you can begin to interact with the SMTP server by typing commands in directly. It is important to note that you cannot use the backspace key when connected to an SMTP server through a Telnet session, even though Telnet might make it appear that you can. In the event that you enter an incorrect character, you will need to press Enter and retype the command from the beginning. Practice 3 at the end of this chapter covers how to connect to an SMTP server using Telnet.

MORE INFO **Testing SMTP with Telnet**

For a more detailed look at how you can test SMTP functionality using the Telnet utility, consult the following TechNet article: *http://technet.microsoft.com/en-us/library/bb123686.aspx*.

Exam Tip The main thing to keep clear in your head is the difference between connector types and their scope. Receive connectors are configured locally for each computer, and Send connectors can be configured organization-wide for some or all computers.

Practice: Connector Configuration

In these practices, you will perform several exercises that will familiarize you with configuring connectors on Exchange Server 2007.

▶ **Practice 1: Create a Receive Connector**

In this practice, you will create a Receive connector to allow local traffic using a non-standard SMTP port. To complete this practice, perform the following steps:

1. Log on to the Exchange Server 2007 computer using the Kim_Akers user account.

2. In the Exchange Management Console, select the Hub Transport node under Server Configuration.

3. In the Actions pane, click the New Receive Connector item. This will launch the New SMTP Receive Connector Wizard.

4. In the Name option, enter the **Special Tailspin Receive Connector.** Ensure that the Intended Use is set to Custom and click Next.

5. On the Local Network Settings page, select the (All Available) entry and click Edit.

6. On the Edit Receive Connector Binding page, shown in Figure 7-6, change the port value to 24 and click OK. This will close the Edit Receive Connector Bindings page and return you to the Local Network Settings page.

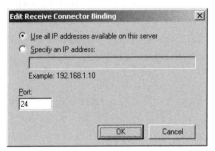

Figure 7-6 Setting the connector to listen on TCP/IP port 24

7. On the Local Network Settings page, in the Specify The FQDN This Connector Will Provide In Response To HELO Or EHLO, enter **glasgow.tailspintoys.internal** and click Next.

8. On the Remote Network Settings page, click Edit.

9. In the Start Address text option, enter **10.0.0.0**, and in the End Address text option, enter **10.255.255.255**, as shown in Figure 7-7. Click OK.

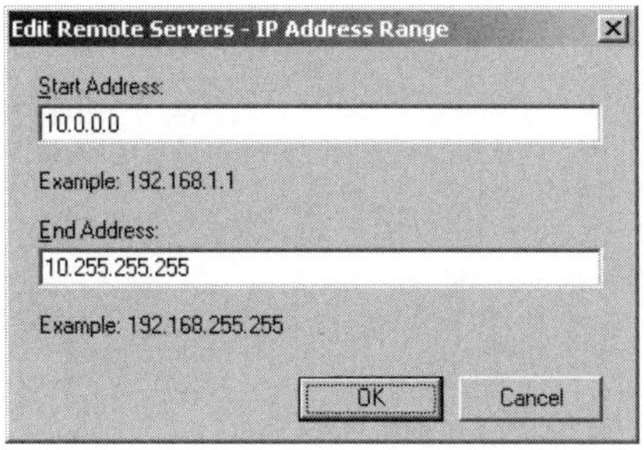

Figure 7-7   Configuring remote server addresses

10. Click Next and then click New. When you see the Completion page, click Finish.

11. Right-click the new connector and select Properties.

12. Click on the Permission Groups tab and select the Anonymous users permission group. Click OK.

▶ **Practice 2: Create a Send Connector**

In this practice, you will create a Send connector for the domain Contoso.com. You will then modify the properties of that Send connector, adding an additional address space. To complete this practice, perform the following steps:

1. Log on to the Exchange Server 2007 computer using the Kim_Akers user account.

2. Open the Exchange Management Console and under Organization Configuration, select the Hub Transport node.

3. In the Actions pane, click New Send Connector Item. This will start the New SMTP Send Connector Wizard.

4. In the Name text box, enter **Contoso Connector**. Ensure that the Intended Use For This Send Connector drop-down is set to Custom and click Next.

5. On the Address Space page, click Add. In the Domain text box, enter **Contoso. com** and check the Include All Subdomains option, as shown in Figure 7-8. Click OK.

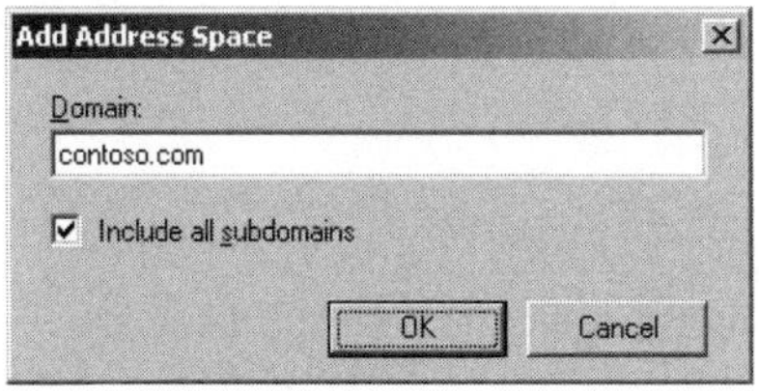

Figure 7-8   Configuring a Send connector's address space

6. Click Next.

7. On the Network Settings page, select the Route Mail Through The Following Smart Hosts option and click Add.

8. In the Add Smart Host dialog box, enter the FQDN **smarthost.tailspintoys. internal**, as shown in Figure 7-9. Click OK.

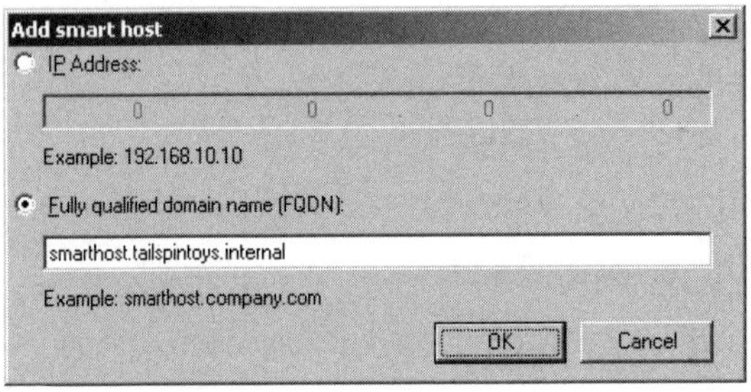

Figure 7-9   Configuring a smart host

9. Click Next.

10. On the Configure Smart Host Authentication Settings page, ensure that the None option is selected and click Next.

11. On the Source Server page, ensure that the server Glasgow is selected, as shown in Figure 7-10, and then click Next.

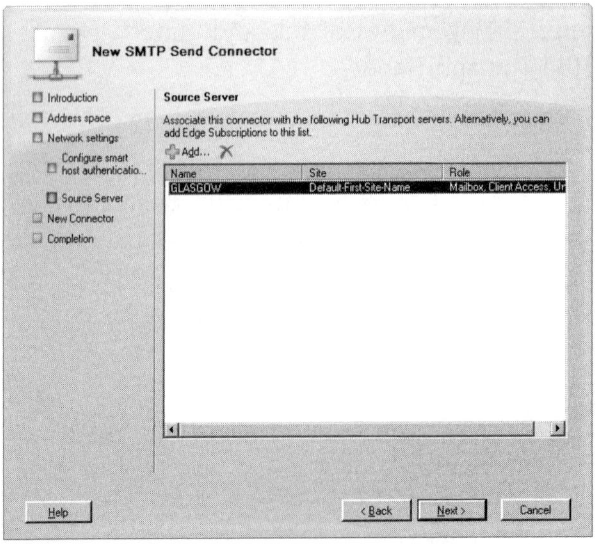

Figure 7-10   Applying the connector to a specific Hub Transport server

12. On the New Connector page, click New. Once the connector is created, click Finish.

▶ **Practice 3: Using Telnet to Test the SMTP Service**

In this practice, you will use Telnet to test whether the SMTP service on the Hub Transport server Glasgow is functional. The Telnet utility offers a quick method by which you can determine whether the SMTP server is functional and whether it is accepting messages.

NOTE   4-GB free disk space

Prior to starting this practice, verify that you have at least 4 GB of free disk space on the Exchange Server; otherwise, you may encounter an error.

To complete this practice, perform the following steps:

1. Log on to the Exchange Server 2007 computer using the Kim_Akers user account.

2. Open a command prompt and type **Telnet** and press Enter.

3. Type the command **set localecho** and press Enter.

4. Type the command **open glasgow.tailspintoys.internal 25** and press Enter. This will open a Telnet session to port 25 of the server glasgow.tailspintoys. internal, which should be the local computer.

5. Verify that the response from the server appears similar to the following:

   ```
   220 GLASGOW.tailspintoys.internal Microsoft ESMTP MAIL Service ready at Fri, 29 Jun 2007
   21:34:10 +1000
   ```

6. Type the command **EHLO tailspintoys.internal** and then press Enter. The ELHO command identifies the transmitting domain to the mail server.

7. Type **MAIL FROM:kim_akers@tailspintoys.internal** and then press Enter.

NOTE   Connection to host lost

Because we are connecting to a Hub Transport server that does not accept unauthenticated mail, the connection is dropped. If you tried the same commands on an Edge Transport server, which is designed to receive unauthenticated e-mail from the Internet, the connection would be sustained, and you could continue.

---

8. Type **quit**. This will exit Telnet.

Lesson Summary

- Until an Edge Transport server is subscribed to the Exchange organization, mail flow to and from the Internet will not occur. When you subscribe an Edge Transport Server, a Receive connector for incoming messages from the Internet and a Receive connector for incoming messages from the organization's Hub Transport servers are created.

- Receive connectors can be configured to listen for messages on nonstandard ports. It is also possible to configure a Receive connector to listen on a specific IP address or to a specific network range.

- Receive connectors are configured on a per-server basis.

- If an organization does not have an Edge Transport server, connectors can be configured to allow it to send and receive messages from the Internet.

- Send connectors can be applied to any or all Hub Transport servers in an organization. Alternatively, they can be applied to any or all Edge Transport servers in an organization. It is impossible to apply a Send connector to both Hub and Edge Transport servers at the same time.

- The Telnet application can be used to verify that an SMTP Receive connector is functional. This is done by opening a direct connection to the SMTP server's port and determining whether the server is responding to SMTP commands in a normal way.

Lesson Review

You can use the following questions to test your knowledge of the information in Lesson 1, "Configuring Connectors." The questions are also available on the companion CD if you prefer to review them in electronic form.

NOTE Answers

Answers to these questions and explanations of why each answer choice is correct or incorrect are located in the "Answers" section at the end of the book.

---

1. You have just added a second Edge Transport server to your perimeter network and configured DNS round-robin to support it. The new server does not appear to be transporting mail in the same manner that the existing Edge Transport server does. Which of the following steps should you take to resolve this problem?

    A. Configure a Send connector.

    B. Configure a Receive connector.

    C. Re-create the Edge subscription for the existing Edge Transport server.

    D. Create an Edge subscription for the new Edge Transport server.

2. Which of the following Receive connector usage types uses Exchange Server authentication as its default authentication mechanism?

    A. Client

    B. Internal

    C. Internet

    D. Partner

3. Which authentication type would be used by a Hub Transport server to receive traffic from an Exchange 2000 bridgehead server?

    A. Internet

    B. Client

    C. Internal

    D. Partner

4. Your organization has four Hub Transport servers and one Edge Transport server. The Edge Transport server is subscribed to your organization through the Edge subscription process. You want to create a Send connector that can be used by all of the Hub Transport servers. How many times must the Send connector be configured?

    A. One

    B. Two

    C. Three

    D. Four

    E. Five

5. Which type of connector would you create to forward all e-mail addressed to a specific e-mail domain for a company that your organization is not partnered with that is located in a foreign country through a smart host?

    A. Internal send

    B. Internal receive

    C. Internet send

    D. Internet receive

6. Which of the following commands would you enter from within the built-in Windows Telnet application to connect to the SMTP service on host mail. contoso.com?

   A. *open mail.tailspintoys.internal 25*

   B. *open mail.contoso.com 23*

   C. *open mail.contoso.com 25*

   D. *smtp mail.contoso.com 23*

   E. *smtp mail.contoso.com 25*

Lesson 2: Configuring Client Connectivity

In this lesson, you will learn how to set policies to manage mobile devices that many modern workers use to keep up with office communication. You will also learn how to configure services that help clients interact with your Exchange Server 2007 infrastructure. These services can allow for Outlook 2007 to be automatically configured with a minimal amount of user input. The lesson also examines how to configure protocols such as Post Office Protocol version 3 (POP3) and Internet Message Access Protocol version 4 (IMAP4), which allow client software to retrieve mail from mailbox servers through Client Access servers.

After this lesson, you will be able to:

- Configure mobile device policies.
- Configure the Availability service.
- Configure Autodiscover.
- Configure Client Access protocols.

Estimated lesson time: 40 minutes

Configuring Mobile Device Policies

Exchange ActiveSync mailbox policies, also known as mobile device policies, govern how mobile devices interact with Exchange Server 2007. By default, Exchange Active-Sync is enabled for all mailbox-enabled users. Exchange ActiveSync mailbox policies allow you to do the following:

- Ensure that mobile device users use passwords.
- Ensure a minimum password length and complexity.
- Configure user data in a device to be wiped after a number of successive incorrect passwords are entered.
- Allow users to recover device passwords using Outlook Web Access (OWA).
- Ensure that all user data stored on the device is encrypted.
- Limit the size of attachments that can be downloaded to the device.
- Allow or restrict access to Windows file or SharePoint servers. Unlike OWA settings that allow you to grant access to specific servers, this is a blanket ban or allow on all servers.

■ Determine whether nonprovisionable devices are allowed to sync with the mailbox. A nonprovisionable device is one that may be unable to enforce all of the Exchange ActiveSync mailbox policies, for example, a device that does not support remote wipe. In environments where security is important, you should not allow nonprovisionable devices to sync with a user mailbox.

Exchange ActiveSync mailbox policies are created by clicking on the New Exchange ActiveSync Mailbox Policy item in the Actions pane when the Client Access node of Organization Configuration is selected in Exchange Management Console. You create the policy by editing the policy properties page, shown in Figure 7-11, and then clicking New. You will create an Exchange ActiveSync mailbox policy in one of the practice exercises at the end of this lesson.

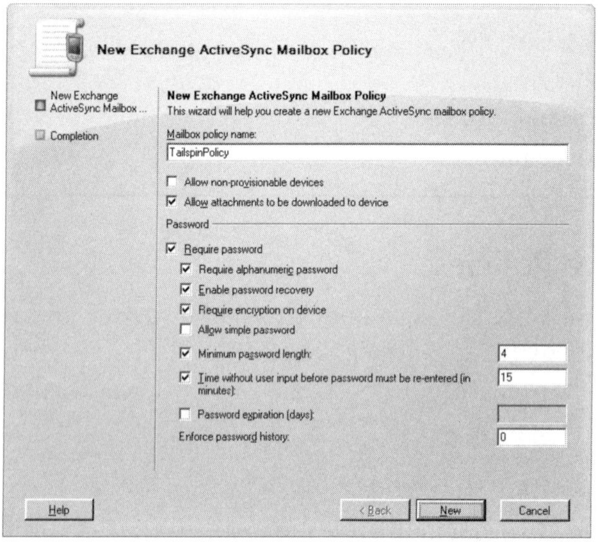

Figure 7-11 Creating a new Exchange ActiveSync mailbox policy

Once a policy is created, it is necessary to assign that policy to the user mailboxes. Policies are applied to users, and users are linked with specific devices. To apply a policy to a user, open the user's mailbox properties under the Recipient Configuration\Mailbox node of Exchange Management Console and click the Mailbox Features tab. Click Exchange ActiveSync and then click Properties. This will open the Exchange Active-Sync Properties dialog box, shown in Figure 7-12. On the dialog box, select the checkbox Apply an Exchange ActiveSync mailbox policy, then click Browse, select a policy to apply to the user, and then click OK.

Figure 7-12   Applying a policy to a user's mailbox

By default, any supported device can sync with Exchange if the correct configuration settings and password is entered. In organizations where security is a high priority, it is possible to restrict synchronization to a specific Windows mobile device. This is done by using the following Exchange Management Shell command:

```
Set-CASMailbox -Identity: "EmailAlias" -ActiveSyncAllowedDeviceIDs:
"<DeviceID_1>","<DeviceID_2>"
```

It is possible to allow a user's mailbox to be associated with multiple devices. Unfortunately, you must perform synchronization to determine the device ID, as it cannot be extracted by other means. Once you have performed synchronization, you can extract the device ID from the user mailbox by issuing the following Exchange Management Shell command:

```
Get-ActiveSyncDeviceStatistics -Mailbox:"Alias"
```

In secure environments, you might disable Exchange ActiveSync for a particular user's mailbox until you have an opportunity to extract the device ID. As you will have to help them through the synchronization process the first time, you can allow any device to connect to their mailbox. Once the first connection has occurred, you can extract the device ID and restrict the Exchange ActiveSync process for that user's mailbox to that single specific device. If the user attempts to sync another device with their mailbox, he or she will be unsuccessful.

To disable Exchange ActiveSync for a specific user mailbox, edit the user's mailbox properties by locating the mailbox under the Recipient Configuration\Mailbox node in Exchange Management Console. Navigate to the Mailbox Features tab, select the Exchange ActiveSync item, and click Disable, as shown in Figure 7-13.

MORE INFO   Configuring Windows mobile devices to sync with Exchange Server 2007

This lesson examines how to get Exchange Server 2007 to work with mobile devices. To learn how to configure a Windows mobile device to sync with Exchange, consult the following link: *http://technet.microsoft.com/en-us/library/bb123704.aspx.*

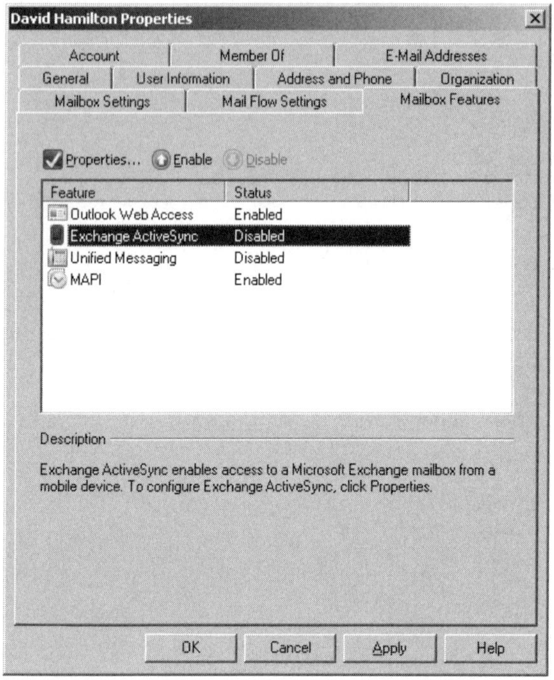

Figure 7-13   Disabling Exchange ActiveSync

Configuring Password Recovery

People forget passwords all the time. If people remembered their passwords all the time, there would be a lot of Help desk staff looking for a new job. As it is possible to configure a mobile device policy to wipe the device if a user enters a specific number of incorrect passwords, a forgotten password can go from being a minor nuisance to a significant problem. No one wants to tell the chief executive officer that her device has been reset to its factory defaults because she entered an incorrect password three times during a conference in Helsinki! In the event that a person realizes that he or she has forgotten a password and has not yet had the device wiped, he or she can call you for a recovery password.

To recover a user password, open the Recipient Configuration\Mailbox node in Exchange Management Console, select the user's mailbox, and then click Manage Mobile Device from the Actions pane. Note that the Manage Mobile Device action is ony available for mailboxes with an established device partnership. You can also learn the device's recovery password by issuing the following Exchange Management Shell command:

```
Get-ActiveSyncDeviceStatistics -Mailbox:"alias" -ShowRecoveryPassword:$true
```

Forgetful users can then enter the recovery password and access their device. Once they have access to their mobile device, they should set a new device password immediately. You should also remind users of mobile devices that their device password is not the same as their log-on password. Each exists independently of the other.

BEST PRACTICES   **Verify identity before resetting passwords**

A common hacker trick is to ring a Help desk and ask for a user's password to be reset. In the event that someone rings you from off-site asking for his or her mobile device password to be reset, you need to verify his or her identity. It could be someone who has stolen the mobile device and is hoping that you will give him or her the necessary information to gain access to the device. Always verify someone's identity before resetting a password. Ensure that there is a procedure in place for verifying the identity of someone who cannot come to your office to prove his or her identity directly.

Configuring Direct Push

Direct Push allows mobile users to get messages as soon as they arrive in a mailbox rather than waiting for users to initiate synchronization from their mobile device. A traditional drawback of mobile devices has been that users do not become aware of important messages sitting in their Inbox until they perform synchronization. If users forget to sync, they may find that a message they needed to respond to urgently is now half a day old. In today's highly competitive corporate environment, contracts can be lost if a quick response to a message is not forthcoming.

Direct Push is enabled by default in Exchange Server 2007 but works only with compatible devices. All Windows Mobile 6 devices and later support Direct Push. It is also possible to use Direct Push with a Windows Mobile 5.0 if the Messaging and Security Feature Pack has been installed.

Direct Push works by issuing an extended Secure HTTP (HTTPS) request (called a ping) to the Exchange server. Exchange monitors the user's mailbox and sends a response to the HTTPS request if there are any changes, such as new messages, contacts, or calendar items. When the device receives the update informing it of the changes, the device initiates synchronization. When synchronization is complete, a new extended HTTPS request is issued. These extended requests last for 15 minutes. Direct Push requires the mobile phone carrier to support long-standing HTTPS requests. It is also necessary for the organization's firewall to support these requests. In the event that a 15-minute request is not supported, the device will attempt shorter requests until the maximum request time (known as a heartbeat) is reached.

This process occurs automatically, and it is not necessary for an administrator to configure a specific heartbeat period on the Exchange server.

To configure firewalls to support Direct Push, make the following changes:

- Ensure that any internal firewalls between organization sites have TCP port 135 (remote procedure call [RPC] locator service) open. It is not necessary to open this port on the external firewall.

- Ensure that TCP port 443 (Secure Sockets Layer [SSL]) is open between the Internet and Exchange Server computers hosting the Client Access server role.

To improve performance, set the time-out value on the firewall to 30 minutes. This will not make any difference if the mobile phone carrier does not support such a lengthy time-out but will ensure that if the phone carrier's settings change, your Direct Push configuration will take advantage of it.

MORE INFO More on Direct Push

For more information on the implementation of Direct Push on Exchange Server 2007, consult the following TechNet link: *http://technet.microsoft.com/en-us/library/aa997252.aspx*.

Configuring Remote Wipe

Remote wipe allows you to remove all data from a device, returning it to the factory default settings. When you perform a remote wipe, the mobile applications installed on the device remain, but all the user data is gone. For most organizations, it is the user data that is important. It is possible to contact the service provider and block the device from connecting to a cellular network, but the main concerns of most organizations will be having data, such as client contact information, fall into the hands of competitors.

To perform a remote wipe, select the user's mailbox under the Recipient Configuration\Mailbox node, and then click Manage Mobile Device from the Actions pane. As mentioned, the Manage Mobile Device action is ony available for mailboxes with an established device partnership. Select the mobile device that you wish to remotely wipe and then click Clear in the Actions option. Alternatively, issue the following Exchange Management Shell command:

```
Clear-ActiveSyncDevice -Identity Device_ID
```

You can ascertain the device ID using the method outlined earlier in this lesson. It is possible to determine the device ID of any device that has gone through the Active-Sync process. Any device that has not gone through ActiveSync cannot be remote wiped because it has not interacted with your organization.

> **Quick Check**
>
> 1. How can you ensure that only devices with remote wipe functionality are able to perform ActiveSync with Exchange Server 2007 mailboxes?
> 2. Which firewall port on an organization's external firewall must be open to support Direct Push?
>
> **Quick Check Answers**
> 1. Configure an Exchange ActiveSync mailbox policy so that nonprovisionable devices are unable to sync.
> 2. TCP port 443.

Configuring Autodiscover

Autodiscover is a service new to Exchange Server 2007. This service is designed to support client computers running Microsoft Office Outlook 2007 and later. This service can also be used to configure supported Windows mobile devices. The Autodiscover service can automatically configure a user's profile on the basis of e-mail address or domain account. It is necessary for Autodiscover to be deployed and configured before Outlook 2007 clients will be able to automatically access the offline address book (OAB), the Availability service, and Exchange Server 2007's unified messaging features. The features that the Autodiscover service can configure include the following:

- The location of the user's mailbox server. In the event that the mailbox is moved, the Autodiscover service can automatically update Outlook 2007's information.
- Appropriate Client Access server settings for internal connectivity.
- Appropriate Outlook Anywhere server settings for external connectivity.
- Information for unified messaging and OAB functionality.

Autodiscover works through a virtual directory created under the default Web site on a Client Access server. When the Client Access server role is installed, an object is created in Active Directory called the service connection point (SCP). The SCP object stores an authoritative list of Autodiscover service URLs for the Exchange organization.

When Outlook Anywhere is deployed, it is necessary to configure external access to Exchange Server 2007 services for Autodiscover. To do this means providing URL information for the Availability service, Exchange Web Services, the OAB, and unified messaging if it is deployed. The following list provides the Exchange Management

Shell commands that an Exchange server administrator for the appropriate Client Access server must run. These commands need to be run on each Client Access server in the organization.

- To inform Autodiscover of the external host name for Outlook Anywhere, issue the command *Enable-OutlookAnywhere -Server ClientAccessServerName -External-Hostname "mail.domain.name" -ExternalAuthenticationMethod "Basic" -SSLOffloading:$False*.

- To inform Autodiscover of the external URL for the OAB, issue the command *Set-OABVirtualDirectory -identity "ClientAccessServer\OAB (Default Web Site)" -externalurl https://mail.domain.name/OAB -RequireSSL:$true*.

- To inform Autodiscover of the external URL for unified messaging, issue the command *Set-UMVirtualDirectory -identity "ClientAccessServer\UnifiedMessaging (Default Web Site)" -externalurl https://mail.domain.com/UnifiedMessaging/Service.asmx -BasicAuthentication:$True*.

If members of your organization are using Outlook Anywhere with Outlook 2007 and you wish to provide them with the automatic configuration options provided by Autodiscover, you must ensure that the SSL certificate on the Client Access server includes a subject alternative name for autodiscover.domain.name in addition to its common name. For example, if you were configuring the Exchange infrastructure at a company that had the domain name Tailspintoys.com and wanted to provide the Autodiscover service for Outlook 2007 clients connecting from an external location using Outlook Anywhere, you would need to ensure that the SSL certificates installed on your Client Access servers had the subject alternative name Autodiscover.tailspintoys.com in addition to whatever common name (such as cas.tailspintoys.com) has been assigned to the certificate.

MORE INFO **More on configuring Autodiscover for Internet access**

For more information on how to configure the Autodiscover service for Internet access, consult the following link: *http://technet.microsoft.com/en-us/library/aa995928.aspx*.

Autodiscover is supported for Windows Mobile 5.0 devices that have the Messaging and Security Feature Pack. Autodiscover is also supported for all devices that use Windows Mobile 6.0 and later. Autodiscover will be able to successfully provision a device only if the device's owner is subject to a mobile device policy. The device can then be provisioned by supplying the owner's user name and password.

MORE INFO   Configuring Autodiscover for ActiveSync

To learn more about configuring Autodiscover for Windows mobile devices, consult the following TechNet link: *http://technet.microsoft.com/en-us/library/aa996339.aspx*.

Although the closest server should be automatically contacted, sometimes it is necessary to configure the Autodiscover service to use site affinity. Site affinity defines a preferred Active Directory site that a client connects to for a particular Autodiscover service. To configure site affinity for the Autodiscover service, run the following command:

```
Set-ClientAccessServer -Identity "ServerName" -AutodiscoverServiceInternalURI "https://
internalsitename/autodiscover/autodiscover.xml" AutodiscoverSiteScope "SiteName"
```

Configuring the Availability Service

The Availability service works with the Autodiscover feature to allow Outlook 2007 clients to stay completely up to date with free/busy information. The Availability service works only with Outlook 2007, and other clients will need to perform a manual update to get the latest free/busy data. The Availability service is also a part of the Exchange 2007 API and is likely to be used by third-party developers to further Outlook and Exchange functionality. The Availability service is dependent on the Autodiscover service and cannot be configured to work separately.

If a user is having problems with the Availability or Autodiscover service, it is possible to perform diagnostics of these services on a per-user, per-Client Access server, and per-Active Directory site basis by using the Exchange Management Shell's *Test-OutlookWebServices* cmdlet. Use these tools in the event that a user or group of users is not receiving free/busy updates in Outlook 2007.

In the event that a single user is having troubles with the availability service, you can log on using an account that has the Exchange Server Administrator role and local administrator privileges on the Client Access server and issue the following Exchange Management Service command:

```
Test-OutlookWebServices -Identity: username@domain.name
```

If the problem appears to affect more than one user, you should search the event logs on the Client Access server for events containing the event source "MSExchange Availability." It is also possible to tease more information about a specific Client Access server out using the following Exchange Management Shell command:

```
Test-OutlookWebServices -ClientAccessServer ClientAccessServerName
```

Finally, should you need to resolve Availability service issues when there are multiple Client Access servers within a site, you should use the following Exchange Management Shell command:

```
Test-OutlookWebServices -Identity User1@Site1.Contoso.com -TargetAddress
User2@Site2.tailspintoys.com
```

MORE INFO   Deploying Autodiscover in your environment

For more information about deploying the Autodiscover service within your environment and how to resolve issues such as colocating Autodiscover on a server that is also used as a Web server, consult the following link: *http://technet.microsoft.com/en-us/library/aa997633.aspx*.

Configuring and Managing IMAP4 and POP3

Besides HTTP, IMAP4 and POP3 are the most commonly used mail access protocols on the Internet. POP3 is the most basic, allowing mail to be retrieved from the server. It is possible to keep messages on the server after they are retrieved, though client settings need to be managed to ensure that the space consumed by stored messages does not grow to the point where a user's mailbox becomes full. Most POP3 clients, such as Outlook Express or Windows Mail, allow for the deletion of messages through POP3 after a certain amount of time has elapsed. POP3 uses TCP and User Datagram Protocol (UDP) on port 110. If used in conjunction with SSL, POP3 uses TCP and UDP protocols on port 995. SSL connections will use the existing Client Access server SSL certificate, the configuration of which was discussed in Chapter 2.

IMAP4 differs from POP3 in that it allows continuous connection to a mailbox on the incoming mail server. IMAP4 also allows multiple e-mail clients to be connected to the same mailbox simultaneously. IMAP4 clients can create mail folders on the incoming mail server and move messages between these mail folders. By default, IMAP4 uses port 143 for normal traffic and port 993 for IMAP4 over SSL.

By default, the IMAP4 and POP3 services are not enabled on Client Access servers. These services need to be enabled by an administrator by opening the services console on the Client Access server and setting the service start-up type to Automatic. You configured the start-up type of the POP3 and IMAP4 services in Practice 2 of Lesson 2 in Chapter 2. In addition to the service start-up type, you can configure the service recover options, as shown in Figure 7-14. These options allow you to have the service automatically restart or run a program in the event that the service fails for some reason. This option can be configured through the Recovery tab of the service properties, available through the Services console.

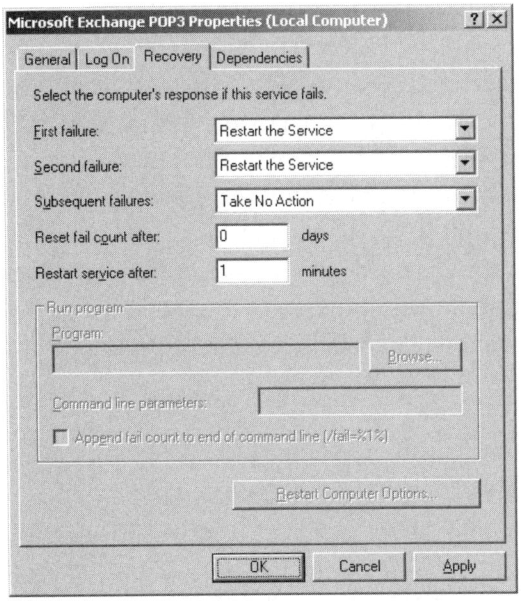

Figure 7-14   Configuring the POP3 service to automatically recover

Advanced POP3 Configuration   It is possible to configure calendaring options when POP3 is being used as the e-mail protocol for users. When configured using this option, calendar configuration information is transmitted through the POP3 protocol to the client. This configuration is done through the *Set-PopSettings* Exchange Management Shell cmdlet. This command must be run on the Client Access server. You can configure the following options:

- To have POP3 clients use the iCalendar standard, issue the command *Set-PopSettings –Identity ClientAccessServer –CalenderItemRetrievalOption 0*.

- To have POP3 users access calendar data from an internal server, issue the command *Set-PopSettings –Identity ClientAccessServer –CalenderItemRetrival-Option 1 – IntranetURL "CalendarServer"*.

- To have POP3 users access calendar data hosted on a server published via an external URL, issue the command *Set-PopSettings -CalenderItemRetrievalOption 2 -InternetURL https://external.calendar.url*.

■ To have POP3 users access calendar data through OWA, issue the command *Set -PopSettings −CalenderItemRetrievalOption 3 − OwaServerUrl "https://outlookwe-baccess.domain.name"*.

By default, a Client Access server with the POP3 service enabled will accept a maximum of 2,000 simultaneous connections. You can configure connection settings for the POP3 service by using the *Set-PopSettings* cmdlet. Settings that you can configure using this command are the maximum number of connections from a single IP address (the default is 20, the maximum is 1,000) and the maximum number of connections from a single user (the default is 10, the maximum is 1,000). Once you have altered the connection settings limits, it is necessary to manually restart the POP3 service. To change the maximum number of simultaneous connections the POP3 server will accept, issue the following Exchange Management Shell command:

```
Set-PopSettings -Identity ClientAccessServerName -MaxConnections Value
```

If external clients who are connecting through a virtual private network (VPN) to your Exchange Server organization are experiencing problems with their connection to the POP3 service timing out, you can alter the time-out settings with the command *Set-PopSettings −Identity ClientAccessServerName −PreAuthenticatedConnectionTimeout Timevalue*. To configure alternate IP address and port settings for the POP3 service, use the command *Set-PopSettings −UnencryptedOrTLSBindings IPaddress:Port*. To configure an alternate IP address and port settings for Exchange Server 2007 users who are accessing POP3 using SSL, issue the command *Set-PopSettings −SSLBindings: IPaddress:Port*. It is important to remember when configuring these alternate IP address settings that the server itself must be configured to use this IP address.

Although you may wish to enable POP3 generally, you may wish to disable it for specific users. To disable POP3, issue the Exchange Management Shell command *Set-CASMailbox −Identity user@domain.name −POP3Enabled $false*. To reenable POP3 access for a specific user, use the command *Set-CASMailbox −Identity user@domain.name −POP3Enabled $true*.

NOTE Per-user protocol settings

In the event that you want to configure certain users to use POP3 or IMAP4 protocol settings to other users, you can specify individual settings using the *Set-PopSettings* or *Set-ImapSettings* command. To find out more about configuring POP3 or IMAP4 settings on an individual user basis, consult the following link on TechNet: *http://technet.microsoft.com/en-us/library/bb124540.aspx*.

Advanced IMAP4 Configuration   Many of the commands used to configure advanced IMAP4 settings have similar syntax to the commands used to configure the POP3 service. The IMAP4 commands are almost identical to the POP3 configuration commands, and in the exam you should be careful to ensure that the appropriate protocol is configured using the appropriate command:

- To have IMAP4 clients use the iCalendar standard, issue the command *Set-ImapSettings −Identity ClientAccessServer −CalenderItemRetrievalOption 0*.

- To have IMAP4 users access calendar data from an internal server, issue the command *Set-ImapSettings −Identity ClientAccessServer −CalenderItemRetrivalOption 1 −IntranetURL "CalendarServer"*.

- To have IMAP4 users access calendar data hosted on a server published via an external URL, issue the command *Set-ImapSettings -CalenderItemRetrievalOption 2 InternetURL https://external.calendar.url*.

- To have IMAP4 users access calendar data through OWA, issue the command *Set-ImapSettings −CalenderItemRetrievalOption 3 − OwaServerUrl "https://outlook-webaccess.domain.name"*.

As most organizations will enable only IMAP4 or POP3, equal coverage will be given to the IMAP4 configuration commands even though many of them are similar to POP3.

Like the POP3 service, the IMAP4 service has a default maximum of 2,000 simultaneous connections. You can configure connection settings for the IMAP4 service by using the *Set-ImapSettings* cmdlet. Settings that you can configure using this command are the maximum number of connections from a single IP address (the default is 20, the maximum is 1,000) and the maximum number of connections from a single user (the default is 10, the maximum is 1,000). As with the POP3 service, once you have altered the connection settings limits, it is necessary to manually restart the IMAP4 service. To change the maximum number of simultaneous connections the IMAP4 server will accept, issue the following Exchange Management Shell command:

```
Set-ImapSettings -Identity ClientAccessServerName -MaxConnections Value
```

If IMAP4 clients connecting through a VPN to your Exchange Server organization are experiencing time-outs, you can alter the time-out settings with the command *Set-ImapSettings −Identity ClientAccessServerName −PreAuthenticatedConnectionTimeout Timevalue*. As with other commands mentioned in this section, this command uses very similar syntax to the command used to configure the POP3 service. To configure alternate IP address and port settings for the IMAP4 service, use the command *Set-ImapSettings –UnencryptedOrTLSBindings IPaddress:Port*. To configure an alternate IP address and port settings for Exchange Server 2007 users who are accessing IMAP4 using SSL, issue the command *Set-ImapSettings –SSLBindings: IPaddress:Port*. As mentioned earlier, when configuring these alternate IP address settings, the server itself must be configured to use this IP address.

Although you may wish to enable IMAP4 generally, you may wish to disable it for specific users. To disable IMAP4, issue the Exchange Management Shell command *Set-CASMailbox –Identity user@domain.name –IMAP4Enabled $false*. To reenable IMAP4 access for a specific user, use the command *Set-CASMailbox –Identity user@domain.name –IMAP4Enabled $true*.

In the event that your organization has Exchange Server 2007 Client Access servers interfacing with Exchange Server 2003 mailbox servers, it is necessary to disable SSL encryption and enable Basic authentication on the Exchange 2003 server. This can be achieved for IMAP4 using the command *Set-ImapSettings –ProxyTargetPort 143* and for POP3 using the command *Set-PopSettings –ProxyTargetPort 110*. Note that disabling SSL will mean that authentication information is transmitted between the Client Access server and the Exchange Server 2003 Mailbox server in an insecure format. Although this traffic is going to be transmitted across the internal network, in security-conscious environments you can secure this traffic using IPSec.

Exam Tip   Try to keep clear in your mind the purpose of the Autodiscover, Outlook Anywhere, and Availability services. Enabling and configuring Outlook Anywhere was covered in Chapter 2.

Practice: Managing Client Connectivity

In these practices, you will perform several exercises that will familiarize you with configuring mobile device policies and setting up client access settings.

▶ **Practice 1: Creating, Modifying, and Assigning an ActiveSync Mailbox Policy**

Exchange ActiveSync mailbox policies are used to manage how Windows mobile devices interact with Exchange Server 2007. In this practice, you will create a new Exchange ActiveSync mailbox policy and configure it to wipe all data and return the device to default settings after the password is incorrectly entered five times in succession. To complete this practice, perform the following steps:

1. Log on to the computer running Exchange Server 2007 and start the Exchange Management Console.

2. Click Client Access under the Organization Configuration node.

3. Click the New Exchange ActiveSync Policy item in the Actions pane. This will bring up the New Exchange ActiveSync Mailbox Policy Wizard.

4. In the Mailbox Policy Name text box, enter **Tailspin Policy**.

5. Ensure that the following policy items are selected:

   ❑ Allow Attachments To Be Downloaded To Device

   ❑ Require Password

   ❑ Require Alphanumeric Password

   ❑ Enable Password Recovery

   ❑ Require Encryption On Device

   ❑ Minimum Password Length

   ❑ Time Without User Input Before Password Must Be Re-Entered (in Minutes)

6. Click New to create the policy. After the wizard verifies that it has completed successfully, click Finish.

7. In the list of policies in the Client Access pane, select Tailspin Policy and then click Properties in the Actions pane.

8. On the Tailspin Policy Properties dialog box, click the Password tab. Change the number of failed attempts allowed to 5, as shown in Figure 7-15.

9. Click OK to close the password properties dialog box.

▶ Practice 2: **Configuring the POP3 Service**

In this practice, you will configure several settings for the Exchange Server 2007 POP3 service. Specifically, you will verify that the POP3 service is running, increase the maximum number of POP3 connections, and disable POP3 access for specific user accounts. To complete this practice, perform the following steps:

1. Log on to the Exchange Server 2007 computer using the Kim_Akers user account.

2. Open an Exchange Management Shell prompt and verify that the POP3 service is running by issuing the command *net start MSExchangePOP3* and pressing Enter. If the POP3 service is running, you will be informed that it has started. If the POP3 service is not running, it will start.

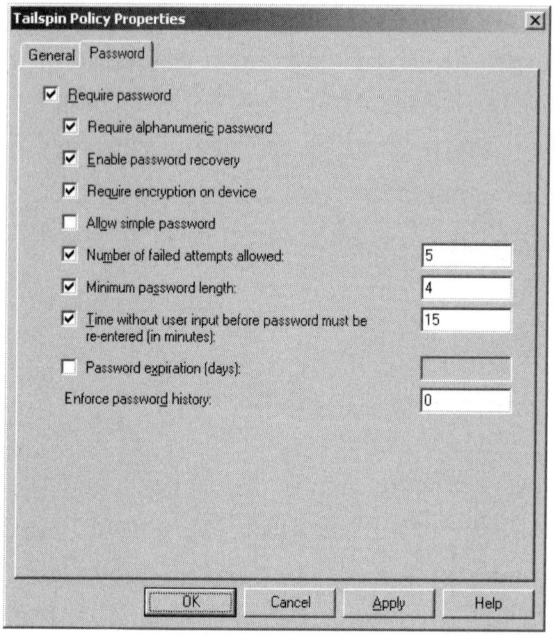

Figure 7-15   ActiveSync policy settings

NOTE   Remember Chapter 2

You configured the POP3 service in the practice exercises in Chapter 2. If you did not perform this practice, you can use Exchange Management Shell to automatically start the POP3 service, by issuing the command *Set-Service msExchangePOP3 –startuptype automatic.*

---

3. To increase the number of simultaneous connections that the POP3 service will accept, issue the command *Set-PopSettings -Identity Glasgow -MaxConnections 5000* and press Enter.

4. To disable POP3 access for Kim Akers's user account, issue the command *Set-CASMailbox -Identity kim_akers@tailspintoys.internal –POPEnabled $false.*

5. To reenable POP3 access for Kim Akers's user account, issue the command *Set-CASMailbox -Identity kim_akers@tailspintoys.internal –POPEnabled $true.*

Lesson Summary

■ Exchange ActiveSync mailbox policies are used to manage Windows mobile devices that synchronize with an organization's Exchange infrastructure.

- It is possible to determine a Windows mobile device ID only after synchronization has occurred. This is achieved by querying the device user's mailbox using Exchange Management Shell. It is possible to limit a user's ability to sync devices to specific device ID.

- Direct Push uses an extended HTTPS request to keep a connection to a Client Access server. If there is a change in the mailbox, such as a contact list being updated, a new appointment, or new messages, the request is responded to, and the device initiates synchronization. Once synchronization is complete, a new HTTPS request is issued.

- Remote wipe allows an administrator to remove all user data from a device, restoring it to its factory defaults. Remote wipe is used to ensure that sensitive data is not accessible to third parties in the event that the device is lost or stolen.

- The IMAP4 and POP3 services are not enabled by default on Client Access servers. It is possible to restrict individual users from using either protocol. It is also possible to use Exchange Management Shell commands to alter the ports and IP addresses that the protocols listen on and to adjust connection limits and time-out settings.

Lesson Review

You can use the following questions to test your knowledge of the information in Lesson 2, "Configuring Client Connectivity." The questions are also available on the companion CD if you prefer to review them in electronic form.

NOTE Answers

Answers to these questions and explanations of why each answer choice is correct or incorrect are located in the "Answers" section at the end of the book.

---

1. You have created an Exchange ActiveSync mailbox policy for the Research and Development Department at Wingtip Toys. You want to ensure that all user data on any mobile device used by members of the Research and Development Department will be automatically wiped in the event that an incorrect password is entered three times in succession. Which of the following policy properties should you configure?

    A. Time Without User Input Before Password Must Be Re-Entered

    B. Password Expiration

    C. Enable Password Recovery

    D. Require Encryption On Device

    E. Number Of Failed Attempts Allowed

2. David is at a conference in Queensland and has just called you in a panic because he has forgotten the password to his mobile device. He knows that the mobile device policy at your organization will wipe all personal data from his device if he enters an incorrect password five times. He has entered his password incorrectly four times and needs your help. You verify David's identity. What step should you take next?

    A. Reset his user account password in Active Directory Users and Computers

    B. Disable ActiveSync on David's mailbox

    C. Recover the device password using Exchange Management Shell

    D. Perform a remote wipe on the device

3. Which of the following must you configure to ensure that users connecting from home through their Internet service provider using Outlook 2007 and Outlook Anywhere are able to access Autodiscover features?

    A. Ensure that the IPSec certificate is configured with an appropriate subject alternative name

    B. Ensure that the SSL certificate is configured with an appropriate subject alternative name

    C. Ensure that the Encrypting File System (EFS) certificate is configured with an appropriate subject alternative name

    D. Ensure that the Client certificate is configured with an appropriate subject alternative name

4. Which of the following protocols or services should you configure to ensure that Outlook 2007 clients within your organization remain up to date on free/busy calendaring information?

    A. Outlook Anywhere

    B. IMAP4

    C. Availability service

    D. POP3

5. Which of the following commands disables IMAP4 access for Kim Akers's user account?

   A. *CASMailbox -Identity kim_akers@tailspintoys.internal −POPEnabled $true*

   B. *CASMailbox -Identity kim_akers@tailspintoys.internal −POPEnabled $false*

   C. *CASMailbox -Identity kim_akers@tailspintoys.internal −IMAPEnabled $true*

   D. *CASMailbox -Identity kim_akers@tailspintoys.internal −IMAPEnabled $false*

Chapter Review

To further practice and reinforce the skills you learned in this chapter, you can perform the following tasks:

- Review the chapter summary.
- Review the list of key terms introduced in this chapter.
- Complete the case scenarios. These scenarios set up real-world situations involving the topics of this chapter and ask you to create a solution.
- Complete the suggested practices.
- Take a practice test.

Chapter Summary

- Send connectors are used to forward traffic to particular domains from Edge or Hub Transport servers. They are often used to route messages in a specific manner rather than being forwarded through the Internet in a normal manner. Send connectors can be deployed to all Hub or Edge Transport servers in an organization but cannot be deployed to both Hub and Edge Transport servers at the same time.

- A Receive connector listens for specific SMTP traffic. A Receive connector can listen on a nonstandard port for message traffic and can also require the sending SMTP server to authenticate. Receive connectors are specific to the Hub or Edge Transport server that they are created on.

- Exchange ActiveSync mailbox policies are applied to users and through those users to mobile devices. To fully utilize Exchange ActiveSync mailbox policies, a device must have Windows Mobile 5.0 with the Messaging and Security Feature Pack installed or Windows Mobile 6.0 and later. These policies determine settings such as whether the device must store all data in an encrypted format, password policies, and whether the device can access Windows file or SharePoint servers.

- Direct Push allows mobile devices to remain completely up to date on messaging, contact list, and calendaring data. It works by using a series of lengthy HTTPS requests that are responded to by the Exchange server in the event that a user's mailbox is updated.

- Remote wipe allows an administrator to remove all user data from a remote device and restore it to its factory default settings. This functionality is most useful in the event that a device containing sensitive data is lost or has been stolen, as it can ensure that sensitive data cannot be retrieved by third parties.

- The Availability service provides Outlook 2007 clients with up-to-date free/busy information about calendar objects within the organization.

- The Autodiscover service allows for Outlook 2007 and compatible Windows mobile devices to be automatically configured on the basis of an e-mail address and password.

- The IMAP4 and POP3 protocols are not automatically enabled on a Client Access server. It is possible to disable a user's access to either protocol using Exchange Management Shell.

Key Terms

Do you know what these key terms mean? You can check your answers by looking up the terms in the glossary at the end of the book.

- ActiveSync
- Autodiscover
- Availability service
- Outlook Anywhere
- Receive connector
- Send connector

Case Scenarios

In the following case scenarios, you will apply what you have learned about connectors and connectivity. You can find answers to these questions in the "Answers" section at the end of this book.

Case Scenario 1: Contoso Connector Configuration

Contoso and Fabrikam have come to an agreement to collaborate on the design of a new hovercraft. You are assisting them in adapting their Exchange Server infrastructure to meet this challenge. In the course of the deployment, you need to deal with the following questions and issues:

1. Which type of connector should you configure for Contoso to accept messages from Fabrikam?

2. Messages to Fabrikam from Contoso should be forwarded through a smart host. Which type of connector should you configure to aid this?

3. How can you ensure that only the Fabrikam servers can use this particular connector?

Case Scenario 2: Coho Vineyard Mobile Devices

Coho Vineyard wants to integrate the Sales Department and the management team's mobile devices with the newly deployed Exchange Server 2007 infrastructure. They have asked you to assist them with the deployment of these devices. In the course of the deployment, you need to deal with the following questions and issues:

1. What requirements should the mobile phones purchased for Coho Vineyard meet?

2. Which service should you configure to ensure that the phones are automatically set up with a minimum of user information?

3. What steps can you take to protect data stored on mobile devices?

Suggested Practices

To help you successfully master the exam objectives presented in this chapter, complete the following tasks.

Adding, Removing, and Modifying Connectors

Do all the practices in this section.

- **Practice 1: Adding Connectors** Create a Receive connector that listens for traffic from IP address range 192.168.0.0 /24 on port 24.

- Create a Send connector for the Cohovineyard.com domain and all its subdomains. Configure the Send connector to route all SMTP traffic to these domains through a smart host at IP address 192.168.10.1.

■ **Practice 2: Modifying Connectors** Modify the permissions on the Receive connector you created so that it can be used by anonymous users.

Configuring Client Connectivity

Do all the practices in this section.

■ **Practice 1: Configuring Mobile Device Policies** Create a new Exchange ActiveSync mailbox policy and apply it to a new user account that you create using your own name.

■ Configure the Exchange ActiveSync mailbox policy so that it cannot be used to access Windows file or SharePoint servers.

■ **Practice 2: Configuring Client Access Protocols** Configure the IMAP4 service to accept up to 6,000 simultaneous connections.

■ Disable POP3 access for the user account that you create that has your own name.

Take a Practice Test

The practice tests on this book's companion CD offer many options. For example, you can test yourself on just one exam objective, or you can test yourself on all the 70-236 certification exam content. You can set up the test so that it closely simulates the experience of taking a certification exam, or you can set it up in study mode so that you can look at the correct answers and explanations after you answer each question.

MORE INFO **Practice tests**

For details about all the practice test options available, see the "How to Use the Practice Tests" section in this book's Introduction.

Chapter 8
Policies and Public Folders

Polices are used to ensure that a particular aspect of Exchange configuration conforms to a specific set of standards. Policies can be used to ensure that all Simple Mail Transfer Protocol (SMTP) addresses share a standard format. Policies can also be used to ensure that all mobile devices require a password to be reentered after they have not been used for a certain amount of time. Multiple policies can be applied so that the configuration settings that apply to one group are quite different to those applied to another. This chapter examines how you can apply certain types of policies using Exchange Server 2007 to meet the requirements of all parts of your organization.

As you learned in Chapter 4, "Configuring Public Folders," the traditional functionality serviced by Exchange public folders is now better addressed through products such as Windows SharePoint Services, which is included as an add-on component with Windows Server 2003 R2 and Windows Server 2008. Although many organizations have already made the transition to the new technology, there are still several important public folder management tools that you need to be aware of to successfully pass the 70-236 exam. These are covered in the second part of the chapter.

Exam objectives in this chapter:
- Configure policies.
- Configure public folders.

Lessons in this chapter:

Before You Begin

To complete the lessons in this chapter, you must have done the following:

- Installed Exchange Server 2007 with the Mailbox, Client Access, Hub Transport, and Unified Messaging roles on a Windows domain controller in the Tailspin-toys.internal domain. To do this, you need to have completed all the Practices in Lessons 1 and 2 of Chapter 1, "Preparing for Exchange Installation," and Lesson 1 of Chapter 2, "Installing Exchange Server and Configuring Roles."

- To complete the practice exercises in Lesson 2, you need to have completed all the practice exercises in Chapter 4.

No additional configuration is required for this chapter.

Real World

Orin Thomas

Without policies, chaos reigns. A hotshot on the sales team at one organization I worked for (that shall remain nameless) purchased a new sports car with a highly memorable personalized license plate. Needless to say, this guy wanted an e-mail address that matched the license plate, as he reasoned clients would only have to remember the car to remember what his e-mail address was. The best way to defeat these contortions of logic is to have a firm e-mail address policy that spells out the exact format of organizational e-mail addresses. Exchange makes this easy, automatically assigning e-mail addresses to recipients by applying a policy that puts together aspects of their user account properties such as first initial followed by surname.

Lesson 1: Configuring Policies

In this lesson, you will learn how to manage e-mail address policies, which are used to provide a consistent format for an organization's SMTP addresses. You will also learn how to create and manage offline address books (OABs), which can be helpful when people in your organization do not need access to all recipient data, just a certain portion of it. This lesson will examine mobile device policies in more detail than the brief coverage than they received in Chapter 7, "Connectors and Connectivity." The final part of the lesson will teach you how to diagnose and resolve problems that may arise with Exchange Search.

After this lesson, you will be able to:

- Create and manage e-mail address policies.
- Configure OAB settings.
- Manage mobile device policies.
- Manage content indexing.

Estimated lesson time: 40 minutes

E-Mail Address Policies

E-mail address policies are used to ensure that an organization's external SMTP addresses all use a consistent format. A consistent e-mail address policy allows an organization to maintain a professional Internet presence. Consistent e-mail address policies also make it easier for people outside the organization to guess the address of people within the organization if they are aware of someone else within the organization's address. For example, if you know that Kim Akers works for Tailspin Toys and that Kim's e-mail address is k.akers@tailspintoys.com, you can infer that David Hamilton, who works for the same organization, will have the e-mail address d.hamilton@tailspintoys.com.

When considering an e-mail address policy for your organization, you should take the following points into account:

- Do any people in your organization share the same surname and same first initial of their given name? If you chose a policy of the first initial of the given name followed by the surname, there may be confusion between John and Jeff Smith. A good e-mail address policy allows you to easily tell which person the message is addressed to.

- Do any people in your organization share the same given and surnames? In the event that they do, consider how you would differentiate these recipients.

- Would an e mail address policy unintentionally lead to a user having an inappropriate SMTP address? You would be surprised what words might appear when you adopt certain policies.

As with most tasks in Exchange Server 2007, there are two ways to create an e-mail address policy. The first is to use the New E-mail Address Policy Wizard, and the second is to use the Exchange Management Shell cmdlet *New-EmailAddressPolicy*. If you are using the wizard to create an e-mail address policy, you are provided with several basic options for an address format. These options are shown in Figure 8-1.

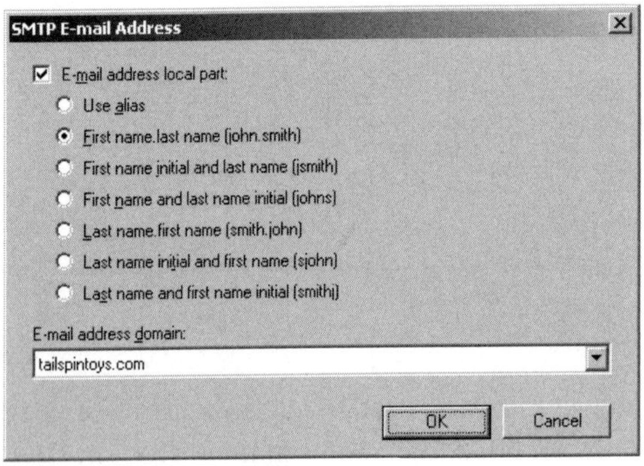

Figure 8-1 The default e-mail address formatting options

These default options meet the needs of most organizations. You will learn how to use the wizard to create an e-mail address policy at the end of this lesson. Creating an e-mail address policies using Exchange Management Shell allows for a greater degree of customization. When you create an e-mail address policy using this method, you specify the policy as a set of variables. Each of the variables represent some aspect of a user's account properties. The variables that you can use and the account properties that they represent are listed here:

- %g: Given name
- %i: Middle initial
- %s: Surname
- %d: Display name
- %m: Exchange alias

When using variables to construct an e-mail address policy, remember that if the variable is used by itself, the entire contents of the variable is used. For example, if you use %s, the entire surname will be used. If you want to use only part of the variable, such as the first letter of the given name, you need to insert a number into the variable. For example, %1g will provide the first letter of the given name, and %3g will provide the first three letters of the given name. Although it is not necessary, you can also separate variables using other characters, such as ".", "-", and "_". For example, Kim Akers would have the e-mail address ak.ki@tailspintoys.com if you executed the following command:

```
new-EmailAddressPolicy -Name 'PolicyName' -IncludedRecipients 'AllRecipients'
-EnabledEmailAddressTemplates 'SMTP:%2s.%2g@tailspintoys.com',
```

Kim would have the e-mail address ake_kim@tailspintoys.com if you executed the following command:

```
new-EmailAddressPolicy -Name 'PolicyName' -IncludedRecipients 'AllRecipients'
-EnabledEmailAddressTemplates 'SMTP:%3s_%3g@tailspintoys.com',
```

Before creating and enforcing a new e-mail address policy, check how the SMTP addresses of a small group of people would look if the policy were applied. You may find that the policy that you were originally going to use does not measure up when applied to the user accounts of actual people within the organization.

E-mail address policies do not have to apply to everyone in the organization. It is possible to apply policies to specific groups using filtering. The IncludedRecipients parameter can be filtered to apply the policy to a specific group of recipients, such as those who belong to a particular department or who are located in a particular state. In the practice at the end of this lesson, you will configure an e-mail address policy for a department within the Tailspin Toys organization so that the members of that department can use an entirely different e-mail address suffix to the rest of the organization.

NOTE Suffixes and accepted domains

An alternate suffix cannot be used in an e-mail address policy unless it has previously been configured as an accepted domain for the Exchange organization.

It is possible that multiple policies might apply to one user. The list of e-mail address policies under the E-Mail Address Policies tab shows that each is assigned a numerical priority. The policy that applies to a recipient who has the highest priority will be used as that recipient's default reply-to address. For example, if policy alpha applies to users from a particular state and policy beta applies to users from a particular department and if policy alpha is assigned priority 2 and policy beta priority 3, users from that particular state who are in that particular department will have their e-mail address set by policy alpha.

Finally, when you alter an e-mail address policy and people's SMTP addresses are altered, it does not mean that they can no longer receive messages from a previously configured SMTP address. As you can see from Figure 8-2, messages addressed to previously used SMTP addresses will still be delivered; it is just that the SMTP address configured by the e-mail address policy will be the default reply-to address.

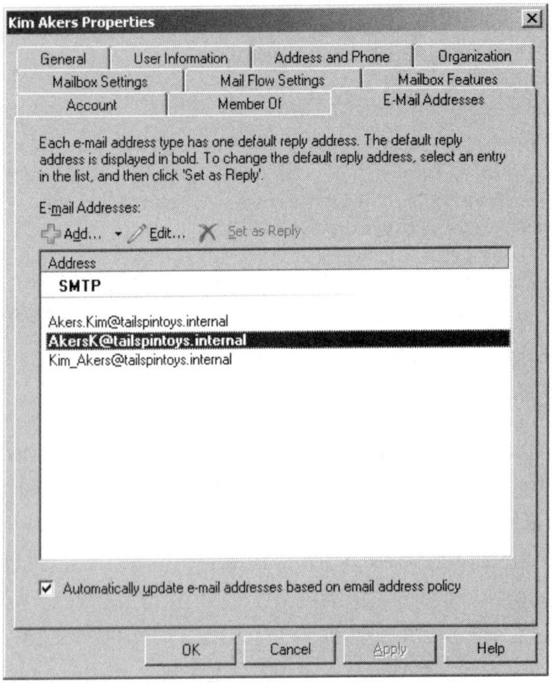

Figure 8-2 Messages can still be delivered to previously used SMTP addresses

---

Exam Tip The main thing to remember for the exam in respect to e-mail address policies and Exchange Management Shell is that %g is for given name and %s is for surname.

It is also possible to configure addresses to be rewritten as they pass through an Edge Transport server by configuring the Address Rewriting agent. Address rewriting differs from e-mail address policies, as the SMTP address is modified as the message passes through the Edge Transport server for an external destination. Address rewriting is most often used when third-party organizations are providing e-mail support and services under your organization's umbrella but are not a part of your Exchange infrastructure. Address rewriting can also be used to route inbound messages to internal recipients, allowing replies to sender addresses that were rewritten on outbound messages to reach the appropriate internal destination.

MORE INFO   **Understanding address rewriting**

To learn more about how address rewriting differs from e-mail address policies and the types of situations in which it can be useful, consult the following TechNet link: *http://technet.microsoft.com/ en-us/library/aa996806.aspx*.

Address Lists

Address lists are a method of organizing recipients. Address lists can be used to organize recipients on the basis of user account properties, such as department, company, or location. Clients are able to examine address lists to find recipients to which they wish to send messages. For example, a large organization has branches in many states. A separate address list has been created for each state. A client looking for the address details of a person she knows works in a particular state can just consult that state's address list rather than searching through all the addresses in the organization.

The following default address lists are created during the setup of Exchange:

- **Default Global Address List** Contains all mail-enabled users, contacts, and groups
- **Default Offline Address Book** Although strictly speaking not an address list, the OAB contains all items in the default global address list for offline use
- **All Contacts** A list of all mail-enabled contacts
- **All Users** All mailbox-enabled and e-mail-enabled accounts in the organization
- **All Groups** A list of all mail-enabled groups
- **All Rooms** All resource mailboxes for rooms
- **Public Folders** All e-mail-enabled public folders

Address lists can be managed in Exchange Management Console by opening the Mailbox node under Organization Configuration and selecting the Address Lists tab, as shown in Figure 8-3.

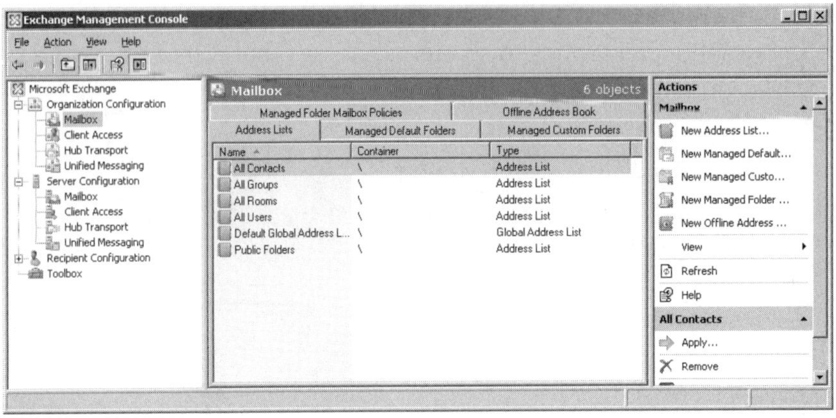

Figure 8-3   Default address lists

To create an address list that shows only a subset of all recipient objects within the Exchange organization, perform the following steps:

1. Navigate to the Mailbox node under Organization Configuration and click New Address List in the Actions pane.

2. On the Introduction page of the New Address List Wizard, shown in Figure 8-4, enter a name for the address list. Select a container location and specify the recipient types that should be included in the address list. The options are the following:

   ❑ Users with Exchange mailboxes

   ❑ Users with external e-mail addresses

   ❑ Resource mailboxes

   ❑ Contacts with external e-mail addresses

   ❑ Mail-enabled groups

3. The next step in creating an address list is to specify which conditions apply to the list. As with other Exchange objects of this type, you can filter by state or province, department, company, or a preconfigured custom attribute.

4. Once these tasks have been completed, you can choose to create the address list immediately or at some point in the future.

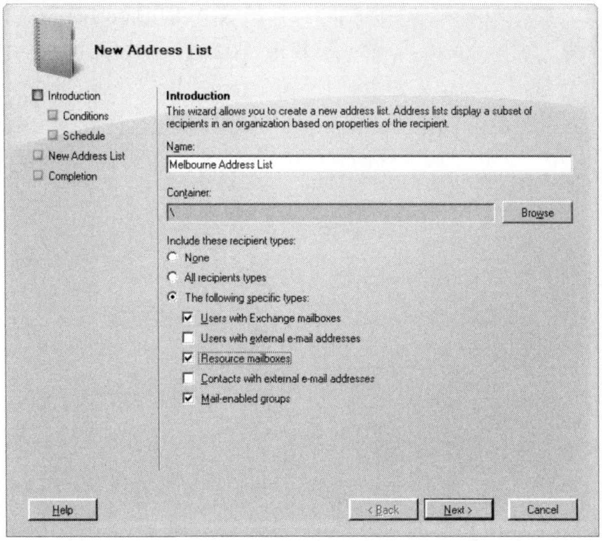

Figure 8-4 Creating a new address list

Address lists are regularly updated. If you want to force the update of an address list, right-click the address list and then click Apply. To create an address list using Exchange Management Shell, you use the *New-AddressList* cmdlet. For example, to create a new address list that lists all mail-enabled users in the state of Victoria, issue the following command:

```
New-AddressList -Name "Victoria Mailbox Users" -Container "\" -IncludedRecipients
"MailboxUsers" -ConditionalStateOrProvince "Victoria"
```

To modify an existing address list, use the *Set-AddressList* cmdlet; to update an address list, use the *Update-AddressList* cmdlet; and to remove an address list, use the *Remove-AddressList* cmdlet.

MORE INFO **Managing address lists**

To find out more about how you can managed address lists using Exchange Management Shell, consult the following link: *http://technet.microsoft.com/en-us/library/bb124700.aspx.*

Address Books

Like the global address list, the default OAB includes every recipient address in the organization. Just as you might want to look through an address list that contained only a specific portion of the entire list, a custom OAB allows the user of a mobile computer to accomplish the same goal. OABs are created with reference to an existing address list. For example, in Figure 8-5, an OAB is created on the basis of the Melbourne address list. New OABs can be created by starting the New Offline Address Book Wizard, located in the Actions pane when the Mailbox node is selected under Organization configuration in Exchange Management Console.

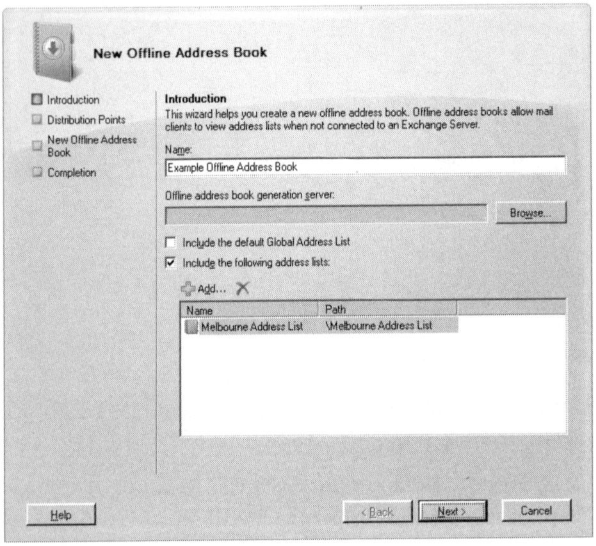

Figure 8-5 Creating a new OAB

During the process of creating a new OAB, you must select a specific server to be responsible for the generation of the OAB. This server can be any mailbox server located in your organization. It is also necessary to specify the OAB's distribution point. As you can see in Figure 8-6, the OAB can be distributed from a Web-based distribution point, usually the OAB virtual directory of a Client Access server, through a public folder distribution point, or through both. Public folder distribution points are generally used only with versions of Microsoft Outlook prior to Outlook 2007.

As the case with address lists, OABs need to be periodically rebuilt. The default setting is for OABs to be rebuilt at 5:00 AM (for example, the default OAB is rebuilt at 5:00 AM). You can modify this schedule by editing the properties of an OAB and selecting or creating a new update schedule, as shown in Figure 8-7. This can be particularly useful if there are multiple OABs hosted on the same mailbox server. Staggering the updates places less load on the server than having them all rebuild at once.

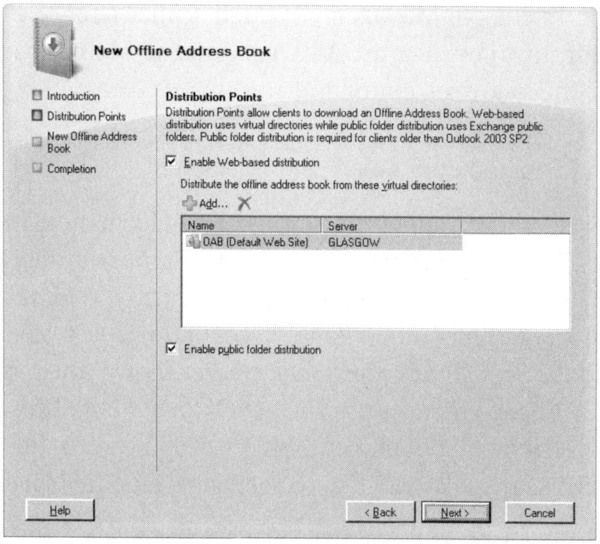

Figure 8-6   Setting OAB distribution points

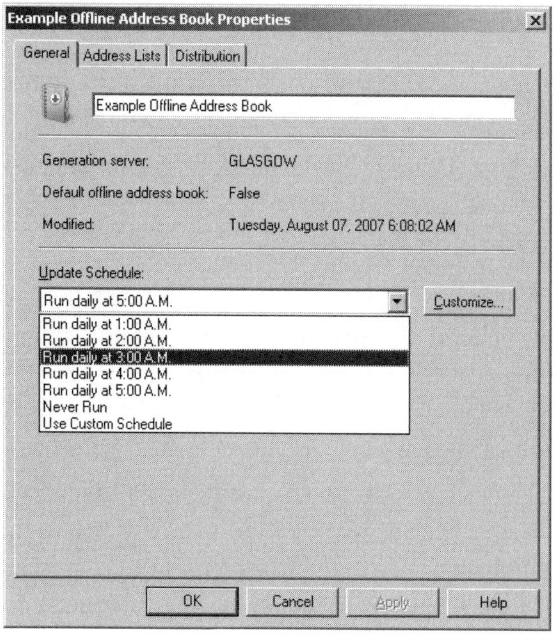

Figure 8-7   OAB update schedule

To create a new OAB using Exchange Management Shell, utilize the *New-OfflineAddressBook* cmdlet. For example, to create an OAB based on the Melbourne Mailbox Users address list, execute the following command:

```
New-OfflineAddressBook -Name MelbOAB -Server Glasgow -AddressLists "Melbourne Address List"
-VirtualDirectories "GLASGOW\OAB (Default Web Site)"
```

The *Get-OfflineAddressBook* cmdlet will allow you to view OAB information. In the event that you need to move an OAB, for example, if you are decommissioning a mailbox server or want to distribute the load more equitably, you can use the *Move-OfflineAddressBook* cmdlet. The *Update-OfflineAddressBook* cmdlet allows you to initiate an update of OAB content, and the *Set-OfflineAddressBook* cmdlet allows you to modify the properties of an existing OAB. You can also use the *Set-OfflineAddressBook* cmdlet to change which OAB is used as the default OAB. For example, if you want to have the MelbOAB to be the default OAB, use the following Exchange Management Shell command:

```
Set-OfflineAddressBook -Identity MelbOAB -IsDefault $True
```

Quick Check

1. How can you ensure that all SMTP addresses for employees at your company share a consistent format?

2. What happens to messages addressed to a previous SMTP address when organization's SMTP address format is altered?

Quick Check Answers

1. Configure an e-mail address policy.

2. These messages are still delivered to the intended recipient.

Out-of-Office Policies

An out-of-office message is one that is configured to be automatically sent when a message arrives at the mailbox of a user who is on vacation or is otherwise indisposed. The mailbox owner or an administrator must activate an out-of-office message. Out-of-office messages can be very useful within an organization, but in some situations you might not want out-of-office messages distributed outside your organization. Exchange Server 2007 allows you to block out-of-office messages on the basis of specific users; alternatively, you can block out-of-office messages on the basis of remote domains. Remote domains can apply to a specifically configured remote domain, or if you edit the properties of the default remote domain, as shown in Figure 8-8, all external traffic that is not covered by a specifically configured remote domain.

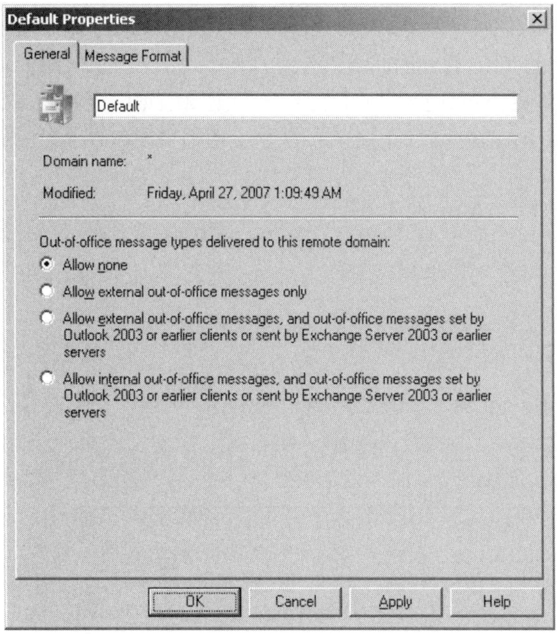

Figure 8-8   Configuring the out-of-office settings of the Default remote domain

The out-of-office policy settings that can be configured on a remote domain level are the following:

■ **Allow none** No out-of-office messages will be delivered to the remote domain.

■ **Allow external out-of-office messages only** Only out-of-office messages configured as external by an Outlook 2007 client or Outlook Web Access (OWA), where the client mailbox is located on an Exchange 2007 mailbox server are delivered to the remote domain.

■ **Allow external out-of-office messages, and out-of-office messages set by Outlook 2003 or earlier clients or sent by Exchange Server 2003 or earlier servers** This setting allows messages configured as external by Outlook 2007 and OWA clients, where the client mailbox is located on an Exchange 2007 mailbox server to be delivered to the remote domain. Where this setting differs from the previous setting is that out-of-office messages from Outlook 2003 or earlier clients, even if stored on Exchange 2003, will also be delivered to the remote domain.

■ **Allow internal out-of-office messages, and out-of-office messages set by Outlook 2003 or earlier clients or sent by Exchange Server 2003 or earlier servers** This setting is similar to the above setting, except that out-of-office messages marked by Outlook 2007 and OWA clients using Exchange 2007 mailbox servers will be delivered to the remote domain. This setting is most often used with partner organizations where it makes sense that out-of-office messages marked for internal distribution should be forwarded only to specific groups outside the organization.

To configure out-of-office settings for a remote domain using Exchange Management Shell, use the following command syntax:

```
Set-RemoteDomain -Identity RemoteDomainName -AllowedOOFType <External |
InternalLegacy | ExternalLegacy | None>
```

Out-of-office settings can also be set at the mailbox level using the *Set-Mailbox* cmdlet with the ExternalOofOptions parameter. Unlike configuring these settings at the remote domain level, the settings that can be applied to user's mailboxes are to allow out-of-office messages only to internal recipients or to allow out-of-office messages to all recipients. The syntax of the Exchange Management Shell command is the following:

```
Set-Mailbox -Identity "User Name" -ExternalOofOptions <External | InternalOnly>
```

Managing Mobile Device Policies

Lesson 2 of Chapter 7 examined the basics of Exchange ActiveSync mailbox policies, including how you can configure these policies using Exchange Management Console. Exchange ActiveSync mailbox policies are used to manage mobile devices in a way similar to how group policy objects (GPOs) in Active Directory are used to manage users and computers. Unlike GPOs, which can be applied to both user accounts and computer accounts, Exchange ActiveSync mailbox policies can be applied only to users. These policies are also applied only during the synchronization process rather than at regular intervals, like GPOs in an Active Directory environment.

The most effective use of Exchange ActiveSync mailbox policies requires devices running Windows Mobile 6.0. The Windows Mobile 6.0 operating system is designed to work directly with Exchange ActiveSync mailbox policies, and you can be certain that any policy setting that you configure will be enforced on a device. Windows Mobile 5.0 devices will enforce some but not all Exchange ActiveSync mailbox policy settings. Installation of the Messaging and Security Feature Pack on a Windows Mobile 5.0

device should make the device compliant with all Exchange ActiveSync mailbox policy settings, but some vendors' devices may not be fully compliant, and you should test these devices prior to deployment. Devices that are unable to enforce all Exchange ActiveSync mailbox policy settings are termed *nonprovisionable devices*. These devices also cannot be configured automatically through the Autodiscover service. When editing an Exchange ActiveSync mailbox policy, you can choose whether you want devices that are not fully compliant to be subject to the policy by enabling the Allow Non-Provisionable Devices option. If this option is not enabled, mobile devices that are not fully compliant will be unable to sync with Exchange. In a practice exercise at the end of this chapter, you will configure a policy setting that accomplishes this using Exchange Management Console. To allow devices running versions of Windows Mobile prior to version 6.0 to sync using Exchange Management Shell, issue the following command:

```
Set-ActiveSyncMailboxPolicy -Identity PolicyName -AllowNonProvisionableDevices $true
```

An important consideration for any organization deploying mobile devices is the cost of transmitting data. Although the Direct Push feature, covered in Chapter 7, does require a near constant connection, it does not have a large cost in terms of the amount of data actually transferred across the cellular phone provider's network. Although the ActiveSync process uses significantly more data than Direct Push, it is e-mail attachments that are the worst offenders when it comes to using up monthly data allowances. Unlike broadband providers, most mobile phone carriers have very spartan free data allowances. For this reason, administrators may wish to stop attachments being downloaded to mobile devices during the ActiveSync process or limit the attachments that can be downloaded to a specific size. To disable the downloading of attachments using Exchange Management Shell, issue the following command:

```
Set-ActiveSyncMailboxPolicy -Identity PolicyName -AttachmentsEnabled $false
```

To limit the size of attachments that can be downloaded to 250 KB, use the following Exchange Management Shell command:

```
Set-ActiveSyncMailboxPolicy -Identity PolicyName -AttachmentsEnabled $true
-MaxAttachmentSize 250KB
```

As is the case with OWA, modern mobile devices allow users to navigate to network shares and SharePoint sites. In some cases, you might want to restrict access so that files on these sites cannot directly be accessed by users with mobile devices. Unlike OWA, where it is possible to restrict access to a particular set of servers, Exchange ActiveSync mailbox policies work on a broader basis, either providing or restricting access to all Windows File Shares and/or SharePoint sites. It is important for administrators to remember that blocking access to one type of file share will not automatically block access to any other type of file share. To restrict access to Windows Files Shares and SharePoint sites using Exchange Management Shell, use the following command:

```
Set-ActiveSyncMailboxPolicy -Identity PolicyName -UNCAccessEnabled $false
-WSSAccessEnabled $false
```

Mobile device password policies are significantly different from standard Windows password policies. Administrators should also remember that mobile device passwords are separate from Active Directory log-on passwords. Password settings will be enforced only if the Require Password option is enabled. The possible password settings are the following:

- **Require Alphanumeric Password** Although this sounds as though only letters and numbers should be used, the policy requires that passwords include characters other than those in the alphabet. This includes symbols as well as numbers. The Exchange Management Shell parameter for this setting when using the *Set-ActiveSyncMailboxPolicy* cmdlet is AlphaNumericDevicePasswordRequired.

- **Enable Password Recovery** Enabling this option allows for a device recovery password to be stored on the server. The procedure for retrieving this password was covered in Chapter 7. The Exchange Management Shell parameter for this setting when using the *Set-ActiveSyncMailboxPolicy* cmdlet is PasswordRecovery-Enabled.

- **Require Encryption on Device** Enabling this option forces all data on the device to be stored in encrypted format. The Exchange Management Shell parameter for this setting when using the *Set-ActiveSyncMailboxPolicy* cmdlet is Device-EncryptionEnabled.

- **Allow Simple Password** This allows passwords such as AB12. You can have this setting enabled with the Require Alphanumeric Password setting. The Exchange Management Shell parameter for this setting when using the *Set-ActiveSyncMailboxPolicy* cmdlet is AllowSimpleDevicePassword.

- **Number of Failed Attempts Allowed** When a number of incorrect passwords exceeding this number is entered in succession, the device will automatically be wiped. The Exchange Management Shell parameter for this setting when using the *Set-ActiveSyncMailboxPolicy* cmdlet is MaxDevicePasswordFailedAttempts.

- **Minimum Password Length** A straightforward policy with a default value of 4. The Exchange Management Shell parameter for this setting when using the *Set-ActiveSyncMailboxPolicy* cmdlet is MinDevicePasswordLength.

- **Time without User Input Before Password Must Be Re-Entered** This option locks the device automatically after the specified interval has elapsed. The Exchange Management Shell parameter for this setting when using the *Set-ActiveSyncMailboxPolicy* cmdlet is MaxInactivityTimeDeviceLock.

- **Password Expiration (Days)** The number of days before the current mobile device password expires. The Exchange Management Shell parameter for this setting when using the *Set-ActiveSyncMailboxPolicy* cmdlet is DevicePasswordExpiration.

- **Enforce Password History** The number of previous passwords that are remembered by the device. It is used to ensure that device owners, when asked to change their password, are unable to select a recently used password. The Exchange Management Shell parameter for this setting when using the *Set-ActiveSyncMailboxPolicy* cmdlet is DevicePasswordHistory.

Exam Tip   Do not fret about remembering the exact names of each parameter for the *Set-Active-SyncMailboxPolicy* cmdlet. Each parameter name is intuitive.

Content Indexing

Messages contain important information. Most people get a large number of messages each day, equating to a larger number each week and so on. Unless an organization has a set of strict data retention and quota polices, it is not unknown for people to store years' worth of messages. Finding one piece of data in a message you received a long time ago can be a challenge. Content indexing allows Exchange Server to index mailbox data on the server so that a search request from a client can be quickly answered. Searching against the index is a superior method to having the mailbox server trawl through every message in the mailbox each time a client initiates a search. Content indexing works automatically on Exchange Server 2007, and there is not much scope for changing the indexing options other than turning indexes on or off. In this section of the lesson, you will learn several techniques that will help you diagnose why a search may not be working and the steps that you can take to resolve the problem.

In the event that something is awry with the indexing of mailbox content, the first step to take is to verify that the Microsoft Exchange Search Indexer service is working. This can be done by opening the Services control panel from the Administrative Tools menu and opening the service's properties by double-clicking it in the list of services. When examining the service properties, shown in Figure 8-9, verify that the service status is set to Started and that the start-up type is set to Automatic. If the service has stopped unexpectedly, you can configure it to automatically recover by clicking on the Recovery tab and ensuring that the computer's response after each failure is to automatically restart the service. Alternatively, it is possible to configure the service manager to run a program, such as an application that sends your cell phone a Short Messaging Service (SMS) informing you of the failure, anytime that this service fails. If the service is failing regularly, you will need to dig deeper to resolve the problem, as configuring an automatic restart is a temporary measure, not a long-term solution.

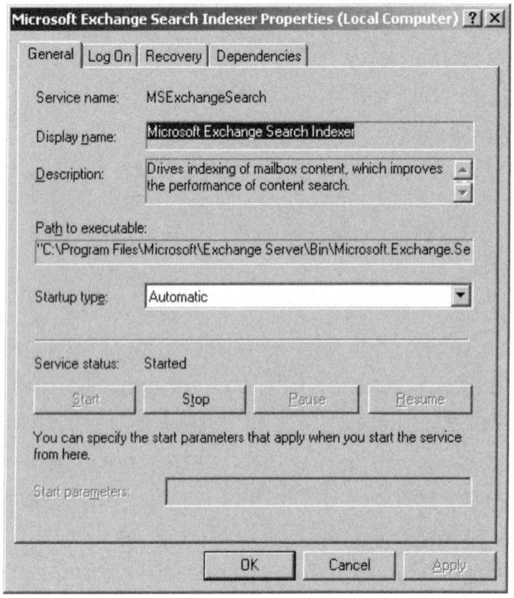

Figure 8-9 Properties of the Microsoft Exchange Search Indexer service

Once you have verified that the Microsoft Exchange Search Indexer service is running, you need to verify that indexing is enabled on each mailbox database. This can be accomplished using the following Exchange Management Shell cmdlet:

```
Get-MailboxDatabase | ft Name,IndexEnabled
```

The output of this command is shown in Figure 8-10.

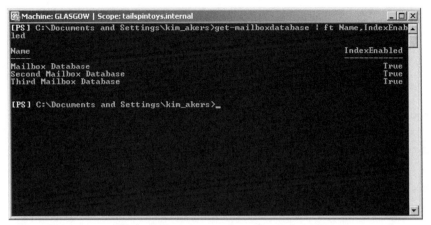

Figure 8-10   Verifying that full text is enabled on mailbox databases

To enable full text indexing on a mailbox database, use the following Exchange Management Shell command:

```
Set-MailboxDatabase -Identity <MailboxDatabaseName> -IndexEnabled $True
```

Exchange System Performance Monitor can be used to determine whether an Exchange database is being crawled by Exchange Search. The Full Crawl Mode Status counter of the MSexchange Search Indices Performance object will have a value of 1 during a crawl and 0 once a crawl is complete.

The final step to take in troubleshooting problems with Exchange Search is to use the *Test-ExchangeSearch* cmdlet. *Test-ExchangeSearch* works by creating a new message and attachment that only the Microsoft Exchange search function can find. The command waits for the created message to be indexed and then attempts to search for that message. *Test-ExchangeSearch* can be run against a specific mailbox or, if no mailbox is specified, is run against the System Attendant mailbox, as shown in Figure 8-11. The user account used to run the *Test-ExchangeSearch* cmdlet must be a member of at least the Exchange Recipient Administrator role and be a member of the Exchange Server Administrator role for the mailbox server as well as being a member of the mailbox server's Local Administrators group.

MORE INFO   **Exchange search management scripts**

To learn more about managing exchange search, including several scripts that are included in the \Exchange Server\Scripts directory, navigate to the following page: *http://technet.microsoft.com/en-us/library/aa998289.aspx.*

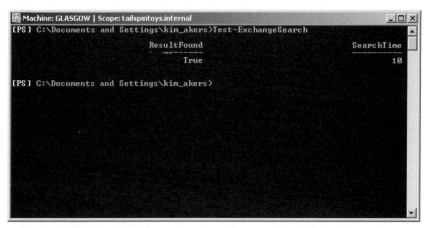

Figure 8-11   Output of the *Test-ExchangeSearch* command

Practice: Setting Policies

In these practices, you will perform several exercises that will familiarize you with the configuration of Exchange e-mail address and out-of-office policies. You will also learn how to use diagnostic tools to verify that content indexing is enabled on computers assigned the Mailbox server role.

▶ **Practice 1: Creating E-Mail Address Policies**

In this practice, you will use Exchange Management Console to create an e-mail address policy that applies to a specific department within your organization. This policy will allow members of this department to use a special reply-to address that has a different suffix from other regular mail users within the organization. To complete this practice, perform the following steps:

1. Log on to the computer that you installed Exchange Server 2007 on with the Kim Akers user account.

2. Open Exchange Management Console.

3. Select the Hub Transport node under the Organization Configuration node.

4. Click New Accepted Domain under the Actions pane.

5. In the Name text box, enter **Wingtip Toys**. In the Accepted domain text box, enter **wingtiptoys.com.** Ensure that the Authoritative Domain option is selected. Verify that the settings match those in Figure 8-12 and then click New. When the Accepted Domain Wizard has completed, click Finish.

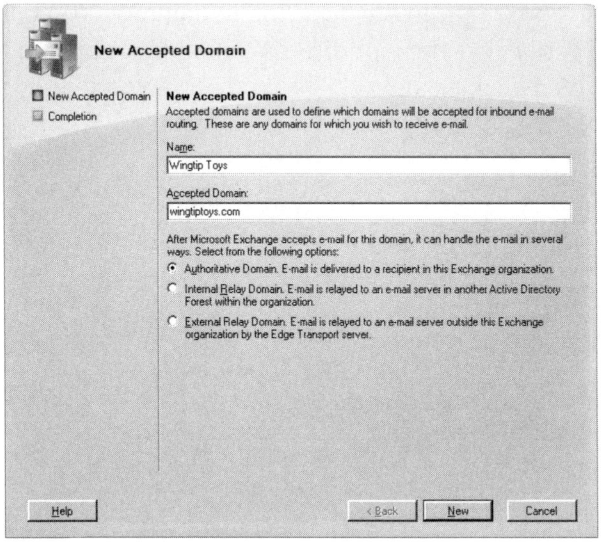

Figure 8-12   New Accepted Domain

6. Click on New E-mail Address Policy under the Actions pane. This will launch the New E-Mail Address Policy Wizard. In the Name text box, type **WINGTIPTOYS** and ensure that All recipient types is selected, as shown in Figure 8-13. Click Next.

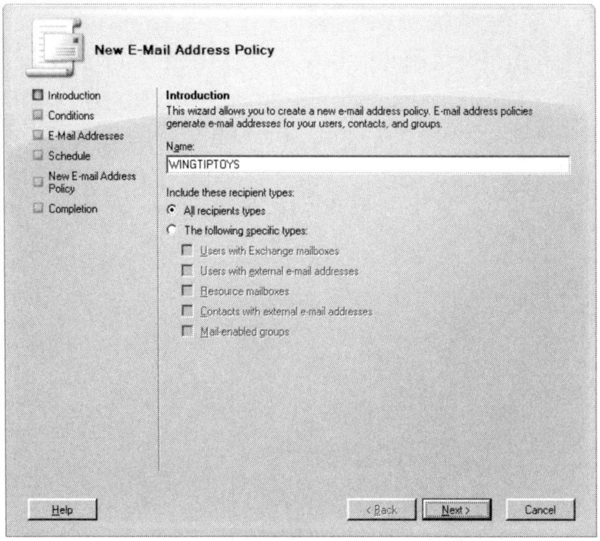

Figure 8-13   New E-Mail Address Policy Wizard

7. On the Conditions page, check Recipient is in a Department. In the Step 2 box, click the word *specified*, which is underlined in blue. This will open the Specify

Department dialog box. Type in the department name **WINGTIPTOYS** and click Add. Click OK. Verify that the Conditions dialog box appears the same as in Figure 8-14 and then click Next.

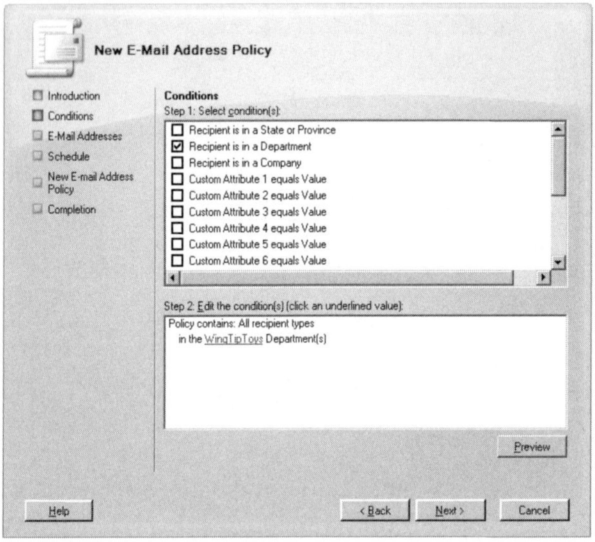

Figure 8-14   New E-Mail Address Policy Conditions

8.   On the E-Mail Addresses page, click Add.

9.   On the SMTP E-Mail Address dialog box, select the First name.last name option. In the E-Mail address domain drop-down, select wingtiptoys.com. Verify that the settings match those in Figure 8-15 and then click OK. Click Next.

Figure 8-15   New E-Mail Address Policy Address Format

10.   On the schedule page, ensure that the Immediately option is selected and click Next.

11. On the New Email Address policy page, verify that the settings match those in Figure 8-16 and then click New. Once the policy has been created and applied, click Finish.

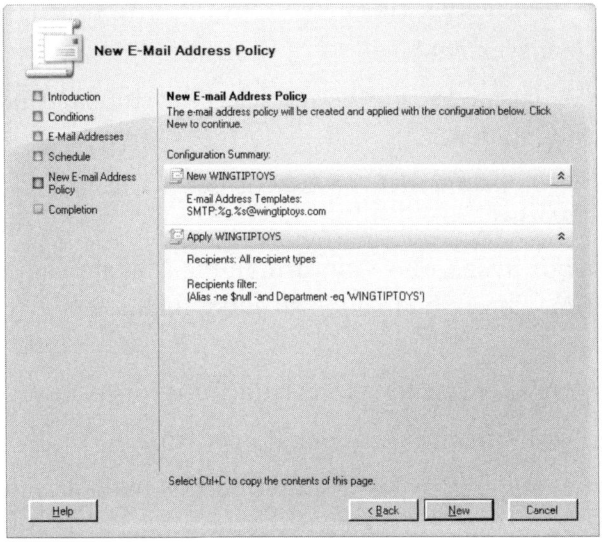

Figure 8-16   Finalizing the new policy

▶ **Practice 2: Configuring Out-of-Office Settings**

An out-of-office message is an automatic response that informs senders that recipients are unlikely to respond to messages because they are on holiday or are otherwise indisposed for a temporary period of time. Exchange Server 2007 allows you to limit the distribution of these messages, allowing them to be blocked from specific remote domains for ensuring that they do not get sent to external recipients. In this exercise, you will configure the out-of-office message settings for an individual user's mailbox and then configure the out-of-office message settings for an entire remote domain. To complete this practice, perform the following steps:

1. Log on to the computer that you installed Exchange Server 2007 on with the Kim Akers user account.

2. Open Exchange Management Shell.

3. To configure Kim Akers's mailbox so that out-of-office messages are only transmitted to internal recipients, enter the command **Set-Mailbox –Identity "Kim_Akers" –ExternalOofOptions InternalOnly**.

4. To verify the out-of-office settings of all users on a mailbox server and to verify that Kim Akers's settings have been applied correctly, enter the command **Get-Mailbox | Format-Table –Property Alias, ExternalOofOptions.** This will output a list of the settings applied to all mailboxes on the server.

5. Close Exchange Management Shell.

6. Open Exchange Management Console and select the Hub Transport node under Organization Configuration.

7. Click New Remote Domain under the Actions pane. This will bring up the New Remote Domain Wizard.

8. In the Name text box, type **Coho Vineyard**. In the Domain name text box, type **cohovineyard.com.** Check the Include all subdomains option. Click New and then click Finish.

9. Click on the Remote Domains tab in the Hub Transport pane.

10. Right-click Coho Vineyard and then click Properties.

11. Under Out-of-office message types delivered to this remote domain, select the Allow none option, as shown in Figure 8-17. Click OK.

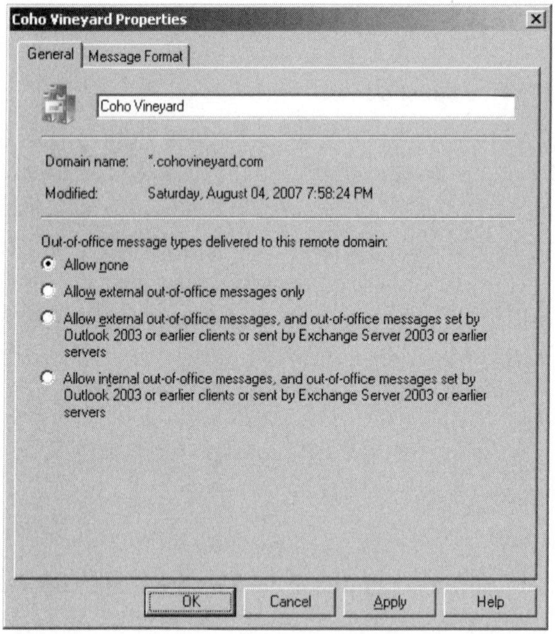

Figure 8-17   Configuring out-of-office options for a remote domain

▶ **Practice 3: Managing Content Indexing**

Being able to perform a search query does not prove that content indexing actually works. If an error has occurred with the indexing service, the indexed content could be weeks out of date. In this practice, you will run a diagnostic test against a mailbox server to verify that content indexing is functioning properly. To complete this practice, perform the following steps:

1. Log on to the computer that you installed Exchange Server 2007 on with the Kim Akers user account.

2. From the Administrative Tools menu, open the Services console. Scroll down and verify that the Microsoft Exchange Search Indexer service is started.

3. View the properties of the Microsoft Exchange Search Indexer service by double-clicking it from the list in the Services console. Verify that the service start-up type is set to Automatic. Click OK to close the service properties.

4. To verify that Full Text Search is enabled on each mailbox database on the server, enter the command **Get-MailboxDatabase | ft –Property Name,IndexEnabled.**

5. To test that Kim Akers's mailbox is indexing newly arrived content, enter the command **Test-ExchangeSearch –Identity "Kim_Akers".**

6. Verify that the output matches that displayed in Figure 8-18.

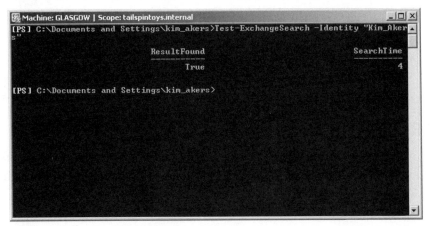

Figure 8-18   Output of *Test-ExchangeSearch*

Lesson Summary

- E-mail address policies ensure that SMTP addresses are configured in a consistent manner. Policies utilize user account properties, such as first name, middle name, last name, and display name. It is possible to specify a preexisting accepted domain only as an address suffix. The SMTP address dictated by the policy will be the recipient's default reply-to address.

- Address lists allow you to create small specific lists of addresses based on recipient properties. Custom OABs are based on existing address lists. Address lists are regenerated on a periodic basis, though it is possible to force them to be updated. OABs are generated on a specific mailbox server. The time at which the OAB is regenerated can be customized.

- Out-of-office options are used to determine whether a user's out-of-office message is transmitted beyond the boundaries of the organization. Out-of-office options can be configured on a per-remote-domain level, including the default remote domain, or on an individual mailbox level.

- Mobile device policies are applied to users. These policies are known as Exchange ActiveSync mailbox policies. You can configure these policies to allow only devices that are fully compliant to perform synchronization with Exchange. You can block or allow access to Windows File Servers and/or SharePoint servers within your organization. You can also configure device password policies and recoverability settings.

- Several tools, such as the *Test-ExchangeSearch* cmdlet, can be used to verify that new and existing content is being properly indexed by Exchange Search. It is also possible to disable Exchange Search on a per-mailbox-database basis.

Lesson Review

You can use the following questions to test your knowledge of the information in Lesson 1, "Configuring Policies." The questions are also available on the companion CD if you prefer to review them in electronic form.

NOTE   Answers

Answers to these questions and explanations of why each answer choice is correct or incorrect are located in the "Answers" section at the end of the book.

---

1. Your assistant will be tasked with regularly checking that search is enabled and messages are being indexed on your organization's mailbox servers. This check will be performed by utilizing the *Test-ExchangeSearch* cmdlet. Which of the following roles must your assistant's user account be added to achieve this goal without granting unnecessary rights or privileges? (Choose all that apply.)

   A. Exchange Organization Administrator

   B. Exchange Server Administrator on all mailbox servers

   C. Exchange Recipient Administrator

   D. Exchange View Only Administrator

   E. Membership of Local Administrators group on all mailbox servers

2. Which of the following commands will restrict Kim Akers from sending out-of-office messages to recipients outside your organization?

   A. *Set-Mailbox "Kim Akers" −ExternalOofOptions External*

   B. *Set-Mailbox "Kim Akers" −ExternalOofOptions InternalOnly*

   C. *Set-RemoteDomain "Kim Akers" −AllowedOOFType External*

   D. *Set-RemoteDomain "Kim Akers" −AllowedOOFType None*

3. What will happen if you execute the Exchange Management Shell command *Set-OfflineAddressBook -Identity NewOAB -IsDefault $true* using an account with the appropriate permissions?

   A. Updates the contents of the default OAB

   B. Changes the default OAB

   C. Moves the default OAB

   D. Reindexes the default OAB

4. Which of the following SMTP addresses would Kim Akers have if the Exchange Management Shell command *new-EmailAddressPolicy -Name 'NewPol' -Included-Recipients 'AllRecipients' -EnabledEmailAddressTemplates 'SMTP:%s%1g@ cohovineyard.com'* was issued by a person with a user account that had the requisite privileges?

   A. kim.akers@cohovineyard.com

   B. k.akers@cohovineyard.com

   C. akers.kim@cohovineyard.com

   D. akersk@cohovineyard.com

5. Which of the following Exchange Management Shell commands would you use to stop users of Windows Mobile 6.0 who are subject to the ContosoMobo Exchange ActiveSync policy from accessing Windows File Shares with these devices but continue to allow them to access your organization's SharePoint sites with the same devices?

   A. `Set-ActiveSyncMailboxPolicy –Identity ContosoMobo –UNCAccessEnabled $false –WSSAccessEnabled $true`

   B. `Set-ActiveSyncMailboxPolicy –Identity ContosoMobo –UNCAccessEnabled $true –WSSAccessEnabled $true`

   C. `Set-ActiveSyncMailboxPolicy –Identity ContosoMobo –UNCAccessEnabled $true –WSSAccessEnabled $false`

   D. `Set-ActiveSyncMailboxPolicy –Identity ContosoMobo –UNCAccessEnabled $false –WSSAccessEnabled $false`

6. Your organization has a mixture of mobile devices, all of which run the Windows Mobile operating system. Although the same Exchange ActiveSync mailbox policy applies to all the user accounts of people who have these devices, roughly 25 percent of these people are unable to synchronize their devices. Which of the following policy changes could you make to resolve this problem?

   A. Configure the policy so that nonprovisionable devices can sync.

   B. Configure the policy so that nonprovisionable devices cannot sync.

   C. Configure the policy so that all devices require a password.

   D. Configure the policy so that devices do not require a password.

Lesson 2: Configuring Public Folders

In Chapter 4, you learned how to create, delete, and modify the basic settings of Exchange Server 2007 public folders. During the course of this lesson, you will learn how to configure advanced public folder replication settings, including limiting the replication of a public folder to a specific set of mailbox servers and configuring a replication period that is separate from that of the host public folder database. You will also learn how to configure both client and administrator public folder permissions. At the end of the lesson, you will learn how to configure advanced mail settings for public folders. As mentioned in Chapter 4, almost all public folder configuration tasks involve using Exchange Management Shell. This is especially true in this lesson, as an Exchange Server 2007 public folder administrator has little recourse to graphic user interface (GUI) administration tools.

After this lesson, you will be able to:
- Configure public folder replication.
- Configure public folder permissions.
- Mail-enable folder access.

Estimated lesson time: 30 minutes

Public Folder Replication

Public folder replication settings are inherited from the settings configured at the public folder database level. The key to configuring public folder replication settings that are different from those of the parent public folder database is to set the UseDatabaseReplicationSchedule parameter to $False when using the *Set-PublicFolder* or *New-PublicFolder* cmdlet. At the public folder level, you can configure replication to occur throughout the day or during specified periods. You can configure replication schedule settings for public folders by using the ReplicationSchedule parameter with the *Set-PublicFolder* or *New-PublicFolder* cmdlet. The replication schedule must be specified in one of the following the formats:

- Weekday.Hour:Minute [AM/PM]-Weekday.Hour:Minute [AM/PM]
- Weekday.Hour:Minute-Weekday.Hour:Minute.

When using the second format, you must use a 24-hour clock, though both can be mixed. You can also use the full weekday name or an abbreviation. For example, if you want replication to occur between 2:15 in the morning on Sunday and 10:00 in the evening on Monday you can use the following with the ReplicationSchedule parameter:

- Sunday.2:15 AM-Monday.10:00 PM
- Sun.02:15-Mon.22:00
- Sun.2:15 AM-Monday.22:00

The Exchange Management Shell command used to apply this replication schedule to the \HR-Folder public folder is the following:

```
Set-PublicFolder \HR-Folder -ReplicationSchedule "Sun.2:15-Mon.22:00"
```

You can also set the ReplicationSchedule parameter to Always if you want a particular public folder to continuously replicate. This can be useful if you have one folder that contains important information that needs to be quickly and regularly replicated across your organization but where you have configured the public folder database to perform replication only after hours. To force replication of a single public folder, issue the following command:

```
Update-PublicFolder -Identity PublicFolderName
```

In the event that you want to force synchronization of the public folder hierarchy on a mailbox database server, issue the following command:

```
Update-PublicFolderHierarchy
```

It is also possible to suspend and resume public folder replication across the entire Exchange organization. To do this, the user account must be a member of the Exchange Organization Administrator role. The commands that can be used are *Suspend-PublicFolderReplication* and *Resume-PublicFolderReplication*.

The Replicas parameter allows you to control which mailbox servers a public folder replicates to. The specified servers must exist within Active Directory. You can also use this command to change the existing replica set for a public folder, adding and removing mailbox servers as necessary. To configure the public folder named \HR-Folder to replicate only to the mailbox servers HR-MBX2 and HR-MBX3, run the following command on the server that hosts the original \HR-Folder public folder:

```
Set-PublicFolder -Replicas "HR-MBX2,HR-MBX3"
```

> **Quick Check**
>
> 1. What step should you take when attempting to differentiate the replication settings of a public folder compared to its parent public folder database?
>
> 2. How can you ensure that a public folder is replicated to specific mailbox servers in your organization?
>
> **Quick Check Answers**
>
> 1. Be sure to include the parameter that disables database defaults.
>
> 2. Specify the mailbox servers that you want the public folder replicated to. If you do not specify a set of mailbox servers, the public folder will be replicated to all mailbox servers that host a public folder database.

Public Folder Permissions

Public folders can be assigned two types of permissions: administrator permissions and client permissions. The easiest way to differentiate these two types in your mind is to think of administrator permissions applying to the public folder itself and client permissions applying to the content.

Public folder administrator permissions are assigned to Active Directory Users and Groups using the *Add-PublicFolderAdministrativePermission* cmdlet. Permissions are assigned using roles. The roles that can be assigned and what a user assigned a role can accomplish are as follows:

- **ModifyPublicFolderACL** Users assigned this role have the right to modify client access permissions for the specified folder.

- **ModifyPublicFolderAdminACL** Users assigned this role have the right to modify administrator permissions for the specified public folder.

- **ModifyPublicFolderDeletedItemRetention** Users assigned this role have the right to modify the Public Folder Deleted Item Retention attributes.

- **ModifyPublicFolderExpiry** Users assigned this role have the right to modify the Public Folder Expiration attributes.

- **ModifyPublicFolderQuotas** Users assigned this role have the right to modify the Public Folder Quota attributes.

- **ModifyPublicFolderReplicaList** Users assigned this role have the right to modify the replica list attribute for the specified public folder.

- **AdministerInformationStore** Users assigned this role have the right to modify all other public folder properties that are not defined previously.

- **ViewInformationStore** Users assigned this role have the right to view public folder properties.

- **AllExtendedRights** Users assigned this role have the right to modify all public folder properties.

Unlike administrator permissions, client permissions are assigned to mailbox-enabled user accounts and mail-enabled security groups. You cannot assign client permissions to an Active Directory user account or group unless that user account or group is mail-enabled. Like administrator permissions, client permissions are assigned using roles. The available roles that can be assigned using the *Add-PublicFolderClientPermission* cmdlet are the following:

- **Contributor** Can create items but cannot view folder contents.

- **Reviewer** Read-only access.

- **Nonediting Author** Can create and read items in the folder.

- **Author** Can create and read items in the folder. Can modify and delete items that they created.

- **Publishing Author** Same as Author but can also create subfolders.

- **Editor** Users assigned this role are able to create, read, modify, and delete all items in a folder.

- **Publishing Editor** Users assigned this role are able to create, read, modify, and delete all items in a folder. Users granted this role can create subfolders.

- **Owner** Users assigned this role are able to create, read, modify, and delete all items in a folder. Users granted this role can create subfolders. Users granted this role can change permissions on folders.

The practice exercise at the end of this lesson involves configuring both administrator and client permissions on public folders using the *Add-PublicFolderClientPermission* and *Add-PublicFolderAministrativePermission* cmdlets.

Mail-Enabled Public Folder Settings

Mail-enabling a public folder allows users to send messages directly to public folders rather than posting them in a traditional manner. To mail-enable the public folder named \HR-Folder, execute the following Exchange Management Shell command:

```
Enable-MailPublicFolder -Identity "\HR-Folder"
```

Once the public folder is mail-enabled, you can manage the mail-specific settings for the public folder using the *Set-MailPublic Folder* command. For example, to limit the people that can send messages to the \HR-Folder public folder to members of the HR-list@tailspintoys.internal distribution list, execute the following command:

```
Set-MailPublicFolder -Identity "\HR-Folder" -AcceptMessagesOnlyFromDLMembers
HR-list@tailspintoys.internal
```

MORE INFO   **More on configuring mail-enabled public folders**

To learn what other settings you can apply to mail-enabled public folders, including how to config-ure contacts, aliases, and forwarding addresses, consult the following link: *http://technet. microsoft.com/en-us/library/bb123707.aspx.*

Practice: Public Folder Management

In these practices, you will perform several exercises that will familiarize you with managing public folders. To perform these practices, you must have completed the practice exercises in Chapter 4 that created the Management public folder.

▶ **Practice 1: Configuring Public Folder Permissions**

In this practice, you will examine and then modify the client and administrator permissions applied to the Management public folder that was created during the practice exercises in Chapter 4. To complete this practice, perform the following steps:

1. Log on to the computer running Exchange Server 2007 using the Kim_Akers user account.

2. Open Exchange Management Shell.

3. Enter the command **New-DistributionGroup -Name Managers -Type Distri-bution -SamAccountName Managers -OrganizationalUnit Users**. This distri-bution group will be assigned client permissions later in this practice.

4. Enter the command **Get-PublicFolderClientPermission "\Management" | Format-Table -Property User, AccessRights** and verify that the output is simi-lar to that displayed in Figure 8-19.

5. To add the Publishing Editor role to members of the managers@tailspin-toys.internal distribution group, enter the command **Add-PublicFolderClient-Permission -Identity "\Management" -AccessRights PublishingEditor -User managers@tailspintoys.internal**.

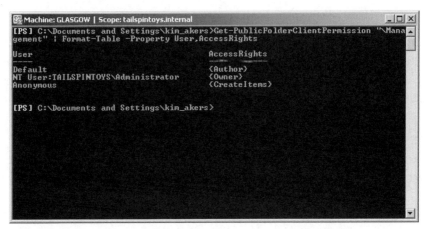

Figure 8-19   Client permissions for the Management public folder

6. Verify that the appropriate permission was added by reentering the command **Get-PublicFolderClientPermission "\Management" | Format-Table –Property User, AccessRights.**

7. To view existing administrator permissions on the Management public folder, enter the command **Get-PublicFolderAdministrativePermission "\Management" | Format-Table –Property User, AccessRights.**

8. To grant members of the Backup Operators group the ability to modify public folder quotas, enter the command **Add-PublicFolderAdministrativePermission –Identity "\Management" –AccessRights ModifyPublicFolderQuotas –User "Tailspintoys\Backup Operators".**

9. Verify that the appropriate permission has been applied by reentering the command **Get-PublicFolderAdministrativePermission "\Management" | Format-Table –Property User, AccessRights** and comparing it to Figure 8-20.

10. To configure the Management public folder so that it can receive only messages from members of the Managers distribution list, enter the command **Set-MailPublicFolder –Identity "\Management" –AcceptMessagesOnlyFromDLMembers managers@tailspintoys.internal.**

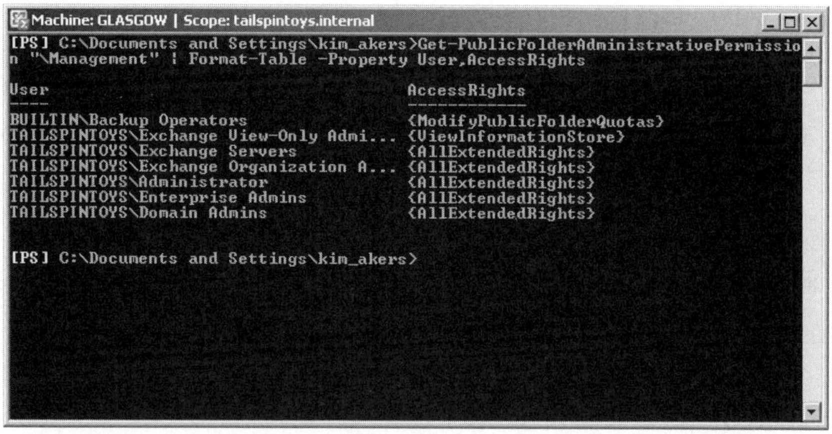

Figure 8-20   Administrator permissions for the Management public folder

▶ **Practice 2: Configuring Public Folder Database Replication and Retention Settings**

In this practice you will configure the replication period and deleted item retention settings of the Public Folder Database created during the practice exercises in Chapter 4. To complete this practice, perform the following steps:

1. Log on to the computer running Exchange Server 2007 using the Kim_Akers user account.

2. Open Exchange Management Shell.

3. To ensure that deleted items will not be removed until the public folder database has been backed up, issue the command **Set-PublicFolderDatabase –Identity "First Glasgow Database" –RetainDeletedItemsUntilBackup $True.**

4. To set the public folder database replication period to 30 minutes, issue the command **Set-PublicFolderDatabase –Identity "First Glasgow Database" –ReplicationPeriod 30.**

Lesson Summary

■ Replication can be configured at the public folder database level and at the public folder level. The default setting is for replication to occur automatically every 30 minutes and to replicate only messages under 300 KB.

■ It is possible to configure a particular folder or set of folders to replicate only to a specific group of mailbox servers. By default, only the public folder hierarchy is replicated to all other mailbox servers in an organization that host a public folder database.

- Replication can be configured to occur during certain periods or all the time. Many organizations configure replication to occur after hours so that replication traffic does not impede bandwidth usage.

- Quotas and deleted items settings can be configured at the public folder database level and at the public folder level. Settings configured at the public folder level override those configured at the public folder database level.

Lesson Review

You can use the following questions to test your knowledge of the information in Lesson 2, "Configuring Public Folders." The questions are also available on the companion CD if you prefer to review them in electronic form.

NOTE   Answers

Answers to these questions and explanations of why each answer choice is correct or incorrect are located in the "Answers" section at the end of the book.

---

1. Which of the following Exchange Management Shell cmdlets is used to configure the mail-related settings of mail-enabled public folders?

    A. *Set-MailPublicFolder*

    B. *Enable-MailPublicFolder*

    C. *Add-PublicFolderClientPermission*

    D. *Set-PublicFolderDatabase*

2. What will executing the command *Set-MailPublicFolder –Identity Research –AcceptMessagesOnlyFromDLMembers scientists@baldwinmuseumofscience.com* accomplish?

    A. Forward all messages posted to the public folder Research to the scientists@baldwinmuseumofscience.com distribution list.

    B. Forward all messages posted to the scientists@baldwinmuseumofscience.com distribution list to the Research public folder.

    C. Configure the distribution list scientists@baldwinmuseumofscience.com distribution list to accept only messages from the Research public folder.

    D. Configure the Research public folder to accept messages only from members of the scientisits@baldwinmuseumofscience.com distribution list.

3. Which of the following Exchange Management Shell cmdlets would form the basis of a command used to create public folder replicas?

   A. *Set-PublicFolderDatabase*

   B. *Set-MailPublicFolder*

   C. *Set-PublicFolder*

   D. *Update-PublicFolder*

4. Your organization has several mailbox servers that host public folders. A manager has complained that the contents of the HR public folder is often several hours out of date. Which of the following Exchange Management Shell cmdlets can you use as a part of a command that alters the replication schedule so that replicas of the HR public folder are updated on a more regular basis? (Choose all that apply.)

   A. *Set-PublicFolderDatabase*

   B. *Update-PublicFolder*

   C. *Set-PublicFolder*

   D. *Set-MailPublicFolder*

   E. *New-PublicFolder*

5. You need to determine which users have the right to modify the public folder replica list for the HR folder, hosted on several mailbox servers within your organization. Which of the following cmdlets would you use to accomplish this?

   A. *Add-PublicFolderAdministrativePermission*

   B. *Get-PublicFolderClientPermission*

   C. *Get-PublicFolderAdministrativePermission*

   D. *Add-PublicFolderClientPermission*

Chapter Review

To further practice and reinforce the skills you learned in this chapter, you can perform the following tasks:

- Review the chapter summary.
- Review the list of key terms introduced in this chapter.
- Complete the case scenarios. These scenarios set up real-world situations involving the topics of this chapter and ask you to create a solution.
- Complete the suggested practices.
- Take a practice test.

Chapter Summary

- You can use policies to configure recipient e-mail address formatting.
- Address lists are collections of recipient addresses that share common attributes, such as location or department.
- Mobile devices are managed by Exchange ActiveSync mailbox policies.
- Public folders can have separate replication settings to their host public folder databases. You can use public folder replication settings to limit which mailbox servers a public folder will be replicated to.
- Public folder administrator permissions can be used to determine which users can manage public folder settings, such as quotas and replication schedule. These permissions are applied to Active Directory Users and Groups. Public folder client permissions are applied to recipients and determine which users can access and manage public folder content.

Key Terms

Do you know what these key terms mean? You can check your answers by looking up the terms in the glossary at the end of the book.

- Address list
- E-mail address policy
- Exchange ActiveSync mailbox policy
- Offline address book
- Out-of-office message

Case Scenarios

In the following case scenarios, you will apply what you have learned about managing policies and public folders. You can find answers to these questions in the "Answers" section at the end of this book.

Case Scenario 1: Address Lists at Coho Vineyard

Coho Vineyard is a collection of wineries spread across Australia. Because there are so many wineries spread across the Barossa, Margaret River, Hunter Valley, Yarra Valley, and Mornington Peninsula areas, members of the Coho Vineyard organization often spend a lot of time tracking down a particular person's e-mail address. You have been asked to help improve this state of affairs. The most urgent issues are as follows:

1. Wine growers in the Barossa Valley region would like to be able to quickly view the contact details of other growers in the same region. What steps could you take to help them accomplish this?

2. All the wine growers have had their distributors added as mail-enabled contacts. All distributors have their Department attribute set to the value Distributor. There are other mail-enabled contacts in the organization. What method could you use to create a list that only includes distributors?

3. What steps need to be taken so that people in the organization can view a list of room mailboxes?

Case Scenario 2: Public Folder Management at Fabrikam

Fabrikam is a company that manages the information technology (IT) infrastructure of an Australian Outback school district connected by low-speed WAN links. Teacher materials are posted to public folders and then replicated out across the network. Both students, teachers, and support staff have mailbox-enabled accounts in the Exchange organization.

1. What steps can be taken to ensure that only teachers and support staff can post content to the public folders?

2. What steps can be taken to ensure that only support staff are able to modify public folder replication settings?

3. What steps can be taken to ensure that all public folders replicate over WAN links between the hours of 9:00 PM and 3:00 AM each weeknight?

Suggested Practices

To help you successfully master the exam objectives presented in this chapter, complete the following tasks.

Configuring Exchange Server 2007 Policies

Do all the practices in this section.

- **Practice 1: E-Mail Address Policies**

    - Create an e-mail address policy using Exchange Management Console that uses the givenname.surname@cohovineyard.com format within the Tailspin Toys organization for all users who have the Department attribute set to Winery.

    - Create an e-mail address policy using the appropriate Exchange Management Shell cmdlets that uses the firstinitial_surname@contoso.com format within the Tailspin Toys organization for all users who have the State or Province attribute set to Victoria.

- **Practice 2: Managing Address Lists**

    - Create an address list for all resource mailboxes located in the Accounting Department using Exchange Management Console.

    - Create an address list for all mail-enabled groups using the appropriate Exchange Management Shell cmdlets.

- **Practice 3: Mobile Device Policies**

    - Create an Exchange ActiveSync mailbox policy that allows access to internal SharePoint sites but not internal Windows File Shares.

    - Create an Exchange ActiveSync mailbox policy that requires devices to have an alphanumeric password with a minimum length of eight characters and that expires every 21 days.

Managing Exchange Server 2007 Public Folders

Do all the practices in this section.

- **Practice 1: Public Folder Replication**

    - Create a new public folder named Replicant. Configure the public folder replication settings to that the Replicant public folder replicates only between the hours of 8:30 PM and 11:30 PM Monday to Friday.

❑ Use the appropriate Exchange Management Shell cmdlets to suspend and then resume replication on the public folder named Replicant.

■ **Practice 2: Public Folder Permissions**

❑ Create a new public folder named Design. Mail-enable this public folder. Create a new distribution list named Designers. Configure the Design public folder to accept only messages from recipients on the Designers distribution list.

❑ Create a new security group named DesignAdmins. Configure the Design public folder so that members of the DesignAdmins group are able to configure the quota settings of the public folder.

Take a Practice Test

The practice tests on this book's companion CD offer many options. For example, you can test yourself on just one exam objective, or you can test yourself on all the 70-236 certification exam content. You can set up the test so that it closely simulates the experience of taking a certification exam, or you can set it up in study mode so that you can look at the correct answers and explanations after you answer each question.

MORE INFO   Practice tests

For details about all the practice test options available, see the "How to Use the Practice Tests" section in this book's Introduction.

Chapter 9
Monitoring

Users expect delivery and receipt of e-mail to be instantaneous. They are accustomed to sending messages to the other side of the world through an indeterminate number of networks in considerably less time than the blink of an eye. They will not be impressed if they do not immediately receive messages from a colleague in the same building.

As an administrator, you will be blamed for any internal mail delay and probably also when an anticipated message from an external source does not arrive at the expected time. As always, you will be ignored when everything is going well and reviled when things go wrong. It is therefore your job to ensure that things go right almost all the time. To do this, you need to monitor the operation of your servers and the flow of your e-mail and take action when you see a problem—long before your users see it. This chapter discusses monitoring and managing message queues and monitoring the performance of server hardware, services, and the operation of your network.

Exam objectives in this chapter:
- Monitor mail queues.
- Monitor system performance.

Lessons in this chapter:

Before You Begin

To complete the lessons in this chapter, you must have done the following:

- Installed Windows Exchange Server 2007 with the Mailbox, Client Access, Hub Transport, and Unified Messaging roles on a Windows domain controller in the Tailspintoys.internal domain. To do this, you need to have completed all the practices in Lessons 1 and 2 of Chapter 1, "Preparing for Exchange Installation," and Lesson 1 of Chapter 2, "Installing Exchange Server and Configuring Roles." Preferably, your test network should include a client machine running either Microsoft Outlook 2007 or Microsoft Outlook 2003.

- Created mailbox-enabled users Don Hall and Keith Harris as described in Chapter 3, "Configuring Recipients, Groups, and Mailboxes." If you have not created these users but have created other mailbox-enabled users, you can use their accounts instead.

You require Internet access to complete the practice session in Lesson 2.

Real World

Ian McLean

Once—and it was not that long ago—if I wanted to send a document to a colleague, I would photocopy it and put it in my out-tray. Eventually, it would be collected and placed in my colleague's in-tray. Now I attach a file to an e-mail message and send it.

This is to be applauded. It is more environmentally friendly (provided you can persuade users not to print out all their e-mail messages and attachments), faster, and more efficient. However, problems can sometimes arise with users who have not experienced the old method. They simply cannot understand the difference between their Outbox and Sent Items folders.

I was recently accosted by one such user. "I have sent a message, but it has not gone through," he told me. "I know it has been sent because it is in my Outbox." I explained that messages in the Outbox were queued for sending and that if they had been sent, they would be in his Sent Items folder. "OK," he said, "how do you move e-mails from Outbox to Sent Items?"

At this point, the message disappeared from Outbox. "I have lost the e-mail," my user complained, "now I will need to send it again." I showed him that it was now in Sent Items. "How did you do that?" he asked. You did not even touch the machine."

I did my best to explain. It was not easy.

Lesson 1: Monitoring Mail Queues

This lesson looks at monitoring the queues that hold e-mail messages and ensuring that messages are queued for the minimum amount of time. It discusses how you would filter a queue to find a specific message or messages (possibly a message that is blocking a queue) and how you would force a retry if messages in a queue were not being delivered. It looks at how you would set queue thresholds to determine the maximum number of messages in a queue and the maximum time that a message remains in a queue, how you would monitor thresholds, and the action you would take if a threshold were exceeded.

After this lesson, you will be able to:

- Find specific messages in queues and delete queued messages.
- Force retry messages in a queue.
- Set and monitor queue thresholds.
- Respond to exceeded queue thresholds.

Estimated lesson time: 50 minutes

Managing and Monitoring Queues

A queue is a temporary location that holds messages that are waiting to enter the next stage of processing. Each queue represents a set of messages that a transport server processes in a specific order.

You can use Exchange Management Shell and the Queue Viewer graphical user interface (GUI) to view the status and contents of queues and detailed message properties. You can also use these tools to manage queues or the messages in the queues.

In order to view queues on a computer that has the Hub Transport role installed (a Hub Transport server), your account needs to be added to the Exchange View Administrator role. In order to manage queues on a Hub Transport server, your account needs to be added to the Exchange Organization Administrator role. To perform the procedures described in this lesson on a computer that has the Edge Transport role installed (an Edge Transport server), you must log on by using an account that is a member of the Local Administrators group on that computer.

Messages to and from the Internet are queued at the computer that has the Edge Transport server role installed. Messages in transport within an Exchange 2007 organization are queued at the computer that has the Hub Transport server role installed.

Queue Viewer can connect to all Exchange 2007 servers with the Hub Transport or Edge Transport server role installed.

NOTE **Extensible Storage Engine database**

Exchange 2007 Server uses an Extensible Storage Engine (ESE) database for queue storage. ESE, formerly known as JET, defines a low-level application programming interface to the underlying database structures in Exchange. For more information about how to manage the queuing database, search for "Managing the Queue Database" in Exchange Server 2007 Help or access *http://technet.microsoft.com/en-us/library/aa996006.aspx*.

NOTE **Queue Viewer focus**

Queue Viewer can be installed on any Exchange Server 2007 server and also on client computers that act as management consoles. However, the tool can connect only to servers that have either the Edge Transport or the Hub Transport role installed. Typically, the tool is installed directly on these servers, but this is not always the case. When Queue Viewer connects to a server, the server is said to be the "focus" of the tool.

When monitoring and managing queues, you need to develop a queue baseline so that you can identify normal and abnormal behavior in your organization. You also need to set thresholds that warn you when abnormal behavior occurs. Typically, however, Queue Viewer is used on demand as the result of a support call reporting slow e-mail delivery or a delivery failure.

Determining Queue Types

How a message is routed determines the type of queue in which it is stored. The following types of queues are used in Exchange Server 2007:

- **Submission Queue** A submission queue is a persistent queue that the categorizer uses to store messages that need to be resolved, routed, and processed by transport agents. All messages that are received by a transport server are held in the submission queue before processing. Messages are submitted through Simple Mail Transfer Protocol (SMTP)-receive, the Pickup directory, or the store driver. The categorizer retrieves messages from this queue and determines the location of the recipient and the route to that location. After categorization, the message is moved to a delivery queue or to the unreachable queue. Only one submission queue exists on each Exchange Server 2007 transport server. Messages that are in the submission queue cannot be in other queues at the same time.

NOTE The categorizer

The categorizer is an Exchange transport component that processes all inbound messages and determines what to do with them on the basis of information about their intended recipients. In Exchange 2007, a server with the Edge Transport role uses the categorizer to route messages to their appropriate destinations. A server with the Hub Transport role uses the categorizer to expand distribution lists and to identify alternative recipients and forwarding addresses. After the categorizer retrieves full information about recipients, it uses that information to apply policies, route the message, and perform content conversion.

- **Mailbox Delivery Queue**   A mailbox delivery queue holds messages that are delivered to a mailbox server by using encrypted Exchange remote procedure call (RPC). Mailbox delivery queues exist only on servers with the Hub Transport role. A mailbox delivery queue holds messages that are being delivered to mailbox recipients whose mailbox data is stored on a mailbox server located in the same site as the Hub Transport server. Several mailbox delivery queues can exist on a server with the Hub Transport role. The next hop for a mailbox delivery queue is defined by the distinguished name of the mailbox store.

- **Remote Delivery Queue**   A remote delivery queue holds messages that are being delivered to a remote server by using SMTP. Remote delivery queues can exist on servers with both the Hub Transport and the Edge Transport role, and more than one remote delivery queue can exist on each server. A remote delivery queue contains messages that are being routed to recipients that have the same delivery destination. On a server with the Edge Transport role, these destinations are external SMTP domains or SMTP connectors. On a server with the Hub Transport role, the destinations are outside the Active Directory site in which server with the Hub Transport role is located. A server with the Hub Transport role can also route internet e-mail. Remote delivery queues are created dynamically as required and are automatically deleted from the server when they no longer hold messages and when their (configurable) expiration time has passed. By default, a remote delivery queue is deleted three minutes after the last message has left the queue. The next hop for a remote delivery queue is an SMTP domain name, a smart host name or IP address, or an Active Directory site name.

- **Poison Message Queue**   The poison message queue is a special queue that is used to isolate messages that are potentially harmful to Exchange Server 2007. This queue is typically empty. If no poison messages exist, the queue does not appear in queue-viewing interfaces such as Queue Viewer. The poison message queue is always in a ready state. By default, all messages in this queue are suspended. You can delete the messages if you judge that they are harmful to the system. If an event that causes a message to enter the poison message queue is unrelated to the message, message delivery can be resumed. If delivery is resumed, the message enters the submission queue.

MORE INFO   **Determining whether a message is a poison message**

A poison message is a message that has exceeded the maximum number of delivery attempts to an application. For more information about poison message identification and how these messages are handled, access *http://msdn2.microsoft.com/en-us/library/ ms789028.aspx*.

- **Unreachable Queue**   The unreachable queue contains messages that cannot be routed to their destinations. A transport server can have only one unreachable queue. Typically, an unreachable destination can be created when configuration changes modify the delivery routing path. All messages that have unreachable recipients reside in the unreachable queue.

When a message is received, a transport mail item is created and saved to the database, and a unique identifier is assigned to the item. If a message or transport mail item is being sent to more than one recipient, the item can have more than one destination. Each destination represents a separate routing solution for the transport mail item, and each routing solution causes a routed mail item to be created.

The routed mail item refers to the transport mail item. If a transport mail item has more than one routing solution, more than one routed mail item references the same transport mail item. A single message addressed to recipients in two different domains appears as two distinct messages in the delivery queues, even if there is only one transport mail item in the database.

Quick Check
- Which message queue is used to isolate messages that are potentially harmful to Exchange Server 2007?

Quick Check Answer
- The poison message queue.

Managing and Monitoring Queues with Queue Viewer

The Queue Viewer GUI is an Exchange Management Console snap-in that is installed with the Exchange Server 2007 Hub Transport server or the Edge Transport server role. You access Queue Viewer by starting Exchange Management Console and clicking Toolbox. You use this GUI to view information about queues on a transport server and the messages that are present in those queues and to manage queues and mail items. You can use Queue Viewer to troubleshoot mail flow and identify spam. (Chapter 6, "Spam, Viruses, and Compliance," discussed configuring and enabling anti-spam features.) Queue Viewer is shown in Figure 9-1.

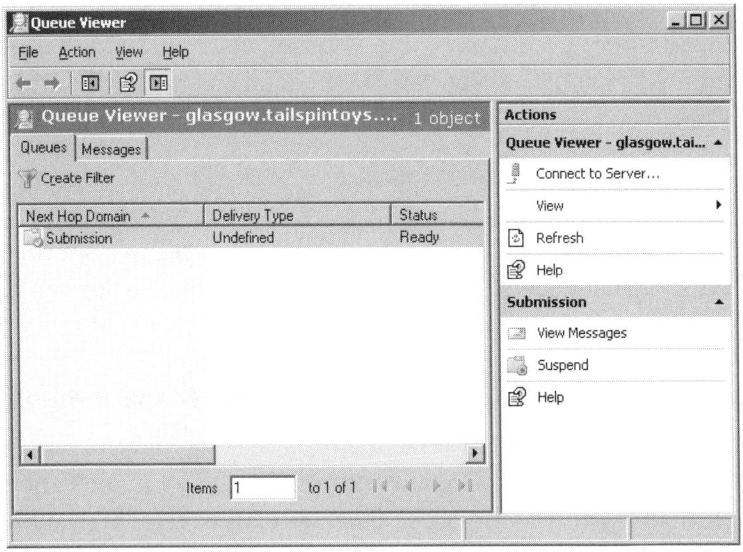

Figure 9-1   Queue Viewer

Before you use Queue Viewer to monitor and manage queues, you need to connect to a transport server. By default, Queue Viewer operates on the queuing database on the server on which the GUI runs. You can, however, also connect to a remote server and view the queues and messages on the remote server.

MORE INFO   Connecting Queue Viewer to a remote server

For more information about viewing queues on a remote server, search for "How to Connect to a Server by Using the Queue Viewer" in Exchange Server 2007 Help or access *http://technet. microsoft.com/en-us/library/aa998669.aspx*.

You can configure the options for the Queue Viewer to control the interval at which the list of queues and messages is refreshed and the number of items that are displayed on each page.

MORE INFO   Queue Viewer options

For more information about configuring Queue Viewer options, search Exchange Server 2007 Help for "How to Set Queue Viewer Options" or access *http://technet.microsoft.com/en-us/library/ aa995934.aspx.*

You can create a filter to display the specific set of queues or messages that you want to monitor and view the property information for these queues and messages. This can help you troubleshoot potential mail flow problems, such as messages that are queued for extended periods of time, peaks in queued messages, and spikes in queued messages.

In particular, you should look for large volumes of queued messages to one recipient or e-mail address. This can be a symptom of a spam attack or a denial-of-service (DoS) attack. On the other hand, a large volume of queued messages to a specific server or domain could indicate that a server is down, a service is stopped, a domain is unreachable, or a network disruption is preventing the system from establishing a connection.

Monitoring and Managing Queues with Exchange Management Shell

Queue Viewer is an Exchange Management Console snap-in, and the Exchange Management Console GUI is in turn a code generator that feeds commands into Exchange Management Shell. You can therefore use Exchange Management Shell to directly monitor and modify message queues and to identify spam. You can create PowerShell scripts that enable you to automate and schedule Exchange Management Shell operations. Chapter 5, "Moving Mailboxes and Implementing Bulk Management," describes how to use and schedule PowerShell scripts.

MORE INFO   The Exchange Server 2007 transport process

Exchange Management Shell monitoring and management tasks access data by connecting to the transport worker process RPCs. For more information about the Exchange Server 2007 transport process, search for "Transport Architecture" in Exchange Server 2007 Help or access *http:// technet.microsoft.com/en-us/library/aa996349.aspx.*

By default, Exchange Management Shell focuses on the local server. You can also connect to a remote server and view the queues and messages on that server by specifying the remote server name as part of the queue identity or by using the Server parameter with a filter, as described later in this lesson.

Using Exchange Management Shell Cmdlets

Exchange Management Shell cmdlets that perform specific operations on queues and messages are used throughout this lesson. Table 9-1 lists and summarizes the cmdlets you can use to monitor and manage queues and queued messages.

Figure 9-2 shows the *Get-Message* cmdlet used in a command that displays all messages currently queued on the server Glasgow.tailspintoys.internal.

Table 9-1   Cmdlets That Operate on Queues and Messages

Cmdlet	Usage
Export-Message	Saves a copy of a message in a specified file path.
Get-Message	Displays details of messages that are currently queued for delivery. You can use the *Get-Message* cmdlet to retrieve a set of messages and then pipe the results to one of the cmdlets that modify queues and messages.
Get-Queue	Lets you view the configuration details of the queues that are present on transport servers. You can use the *Get-Queue* cmdlet to retrieve a set of messages and then pipe the results to one of the cmdlets that modify queues and messages.
Remove-Message	Deletes a message from a queue. You can specify whether a non-delivery report (NDR) is sent.
Resume-Message	Resumes delivery of a previously suspended message. You can use the *Resume-Message* cmdlet to resubmit messages that are in the poison message queue to the submission queue so that the categorizer can reprocess them.
Resume-Queue	Resumes deliveries of messages from a previously suspended queue.
Retry-Queue	Forces a connection attempt for a queue that currently has a status of retry. This connection attempt overrides the next scheduled retry. You can also use the *Retry-Queue* cmdlet together with the Resubmit parameter to send messages that are in delivery queues or in the unreachable queue back to the submission queue so that the categorizer can reprocess them.

Table 9-1 Cmdlets That Operate on Queues and Messages

Cmdlet	Usage
Suspend-Message	Suspends delivery of a message that is located in a queue on an Exchange Server 2007 transport server.
Suspend-Queue	Suspends outgoing messages in a queue on an Exchange Server 2007 transport server.

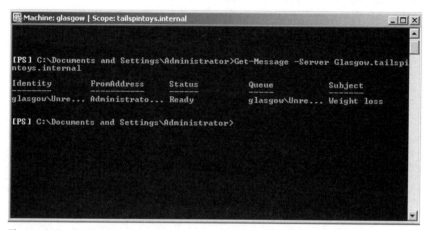

Figure 9-2 Retrieving messages by using Exchange Management Shell

---

NOTE Generating queues

In your internal test network, you will find it difficult to generate queues because the conditions of high volume and limited bandwidth that typically cause queuing do not exist. In a busy production network, this is not the case, and dealing with queues is likely to be an important part of your job.

Deleting Messages from Queues

You can use Queue Viewer or Exchange Management Shell to remove one or more messages from a queue on a computer that has the Hub Transport or the Edge Transport server role installed. To perform this operation, your account needs to be added to the Exchange Organization Administrator role. A message sent to multiple recipients might be located in more than one queue. To remove a message from more than one queue in a single operation, you need to use a filter. You can specify whether to send an NDR when you remove messages from a queue.

IMPORTANT Messages in the submission queue

You cannot remove a message from the submission queue.

Before you delete a message in a queue, you need to verify that you are connected to an Exchange Server 2007 transport server. By default, Queue Viewer and Exchange Management Shell operate on the local server.

Using Queue Viewer to Remove a Message

You open Queue Viewer by opening Exchange Management Console, clicking Tool-box in the console tree, selecting Queue Viewer in the Result pane, and clicking Open Tool in the Actions pane. If you are logged on to the Hub Transport server that holds the queue you want to access, you can use Queue Viewer immediately to view the queue and delete messages as required. Otherwise, you click Connect To Server in the Action pane, click Browse to view a list of available transport servers, and select a server from the list. Links to more information about connecting Queue Viewer to a server were given earlier in this lesson.

To view messages in Queue Viewer, select the Messages tab. This displays a list of all messages on the server to which you are connected. To view the messages in a single queue, click the Queues tab and double-click the queue name or right-click the queue and click View Messages. Figure 9-3 shows the messages (currently only one message) in the Unreachable Domain queue. The messages in a specified queue appear on the tab for that queue.

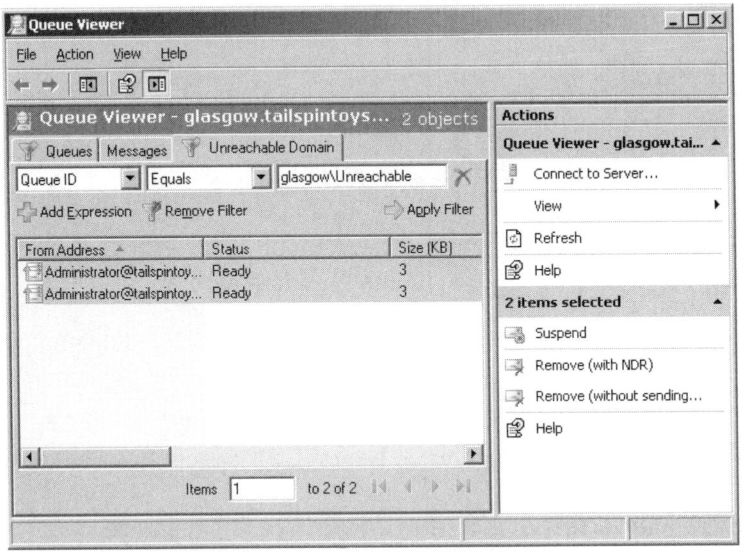

Figure 9-3 Viewing messages by using Queue Viewer

To remove a message, select it from the list, right-click on it, and then select Remove Messages (with NDR) or Remove Messages (without NDR). Click OK to remove the message. If you want to, you can select several messages and remove them with a single operation.

To remove all messages from a particular queue, click the Queues tab, select a queue, right-click the queue, and select Remove Messages (with NDR) or Remove Messages (without NDR). Click Yes to clear the confirmation dialog box and delete the queue.

Deleting Filtered Messages

If you have applied a filter, Queue Viewer might not display all the messages that a queue contains. If you then choose to delete all the messages on the Messages tab, a prompt appears informing you that this action will affect the items displayed. To expand the scope of the action to include all messages (filtered and unfiltered), you select the Expand The Scope Of This Action To Include All Items In This Filter check box, shown in Figure 9-4, before you click OK. Using filters to identify and select messages is discussed later in this lesson.

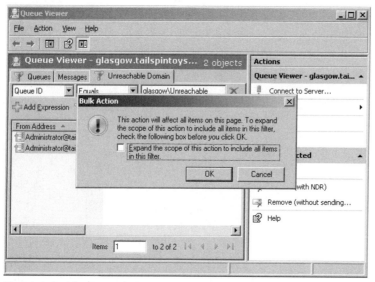

Figure 9-4 The Expand The Scope Of This Action To Include All Items In This Filter check box

Using Exchange Management Shell to Remove a Message

Like Queue Viewer, Exchange Management Shell operates by default on the server on which it is running. You can use the Server parameter to specify a remote server. The

Remove-Message cmdlet also lets you specify an Identity parameter that can optionally identify a message queue and server in addition to the message itself. The cmdlet also supports the WithNDR parameter, which specifies whether an NDR is sent to the sender. The default value is True.

If you specify an Identity parameter that matches only a single message, the message will be removed. However, an e-mail message can (and frequently is) sent to multiple recipients and can be held in several queues. In this case, the identity could match more than one message, and the command could fail. If you want to remove a message from more than one queue in a single operation, you can use the Filter parameter. You can filter messages by, for example, size, subject, status, spam confidence level (SCL), date received, and source address. You can use the *–and* logical operator to specify multiple filter criteria. Finding specific messages is discussed later in this lesson.

You can use an Identity parameter or a Filter parameter with Remove-Message. These two parameter sets are mutually exclusive, and you cannot use both of them in the same command. For example, to use the Filter parameter to identify and remove all messages from don.hall@tailspintoys.internal from all queues on the default server without sending an NDR, you would enter the following command:

```
Remove-Message –Filter {FromAddress –eq "don.hall@tailspintoys.internal"} –WithNDR $False
```

You can also use a command based on the *Get-Message* cmdlet and pipe its output into a command based on the *Remove-Message* cmdlet. However, the *Get-Message* cmdlet uses the same filter conditions as the *Remove-Message* cmdlet, and the value of this procedure is, at best, debatable.

MORE INFO   Remove-Message cmdlet

For more information about the *Remove-Message* cmdlet, including syntax and filter conditions, search Exchange Server 2007 Help for "Remove-Message" or access *http://technet.microsoft.com /en-us/library/aa996371.aspx*.

Finding Specific Messages in a Queue

You can use filters to locate and manage messages in queues by using either Queue Viewer or Exchange Management Shell. The list of messages changes when messages enter and leave the server. You can adjust your search by specifying search criteria to locate messages that might be causing a mail flow problem or are suspected spam. You can then perform operations that modify the status of those messages.

Quick Check

- What does the following command do?

  ```
  Remove-Message -Filter {FromAddress -eq "kim.akers@tailspintoys.internal"} -WithNDR
  $False
  ```

Quick Check Answer

- Removes all the messages from the e-mail address kim.akers@tailspintoys.internal in all message queues on the server and does not send an NDR.

When an e-mail message is sent to multiple recipients, the message might be located in multiple queues. When you filter by message properties, you can locate messages across all queues. You might filter a submission queue for messages that have the same subject criteria (for example, "lose weight" when you suspect that a high level of spam is being sent to your organization). Alternatively, you might create a filter that identifies all the messages from a specific domain. If you detect spam, you can remove all the offending messages without sending an NDR.

Using Filter Parameters and Message Properties

The filter parameters and the message properties on which they filter are the same in Queue Viewer and Exchange Management Shell. For example, setting the From Address filter condition in Queue Viewer to don.hall@tailspintoys.internal finds the same messages as the parameter *−Filter {FromAddress −eq "don.hall@tailspintoys.internal"}* in an Exchange Management Shell command based on the *Get-Message* or the *Remove-Message* cmdlet. In general the Exchange Management Shell conditions omit spaces in the middle of their names; for example, Date Received becomes Date-Received. The filter parameters and properties used by both tools are as follows:

- **Date Received**   Specifies the time when the message was received by the server that holds the queue in which the message is located.

- **Expiration Time**   Specifies the time when an undelivered message will expire and be deleted from the queue.

- **From Address**   Specifies the SMTP address of the message sender.

- **Identity**   An integer that represents a particular message. The queuing database assigns a message identity when the message is received for processing. You can include an optional server and queue identity. This value can be expressed as follows:

❑ Server\QueueId\MessageId

❑ Server\Poison\MessageId

❑ MessageId

❑ Server*\MessageId

■ **Internet Message ID** The value of the Message-ID message header field that is located in the message header. The value of this property is expressed as a global unique identifier (GUID) followed by the SMTP address of the sending server (for example, E77F966F4DC24E48A257656E52DBA546486CD7D1AE@glas-gow.tailspintoys.internal).

MORE INFO GUIDs

For more information about GUIDs, access *http://msdn2.microsoft.com/en-us/library/system.guid.aspx*. However, the 70-236 examination will not test you on GUID structure or how a GUID is generated.

■ **Last Error** The last error that was recorded for a message.

■ **Message Source Name** The name of the component that submitted the message to the queue.

■ **Queue ID** The identity of the queue that holds the message. This takes the form Server\destination, where destination is a remote domain, mailbox server, persistent queue name, or the queuing database identifier. The database identifier is an integer and can be determined by viewing the message properties.

■ **Retry Count** The number of times that delivery of a message to a destination was tried.

■ **SCL** The SCL of the message. A valid SCL entry is an integer from 0 through 9. An empty SCL property value indicates that the message has not been processed by the Content Filter agent.

■ **Size (KB)** The size of the message. In Exchange Management Shell (KB) is omitted.

■ **Source IP** The IP address of the external server that submitted the message.

■ **Status** The current message status. A message can have one of the following status values:

❑ Active—If the message is in a delivery queue, it is being delivered to its destination. If the message is in the submission queue, it is being processed by the categorizer.

❑ Suspended—The message was suspended by the administrator.

❑ PendingRemove—The message was deleted by the administrator but was already in delivery. The message will be deleted if the delivery ends in an error that causes the message to reenter the queue. Otherwise, delivery will continue.

❑ PendingSuspend—The message was suspended by the administrator but was already in delivery. The message will be suspended if a delivery error causes it to reenter the queue. Otherwise, delivery will continue.

❑ Ready—The message is waiting in the queue and is ready to be processed.

❑ Retry—The last connection attempt for the queue in which this message is located failed. The message is waiting for the next queue retry.

■ **Subject**   The subject of the message.

Using Filter Operators

Queue Viewer and Exchange Management Shell use the same comparison operators when filtering, although the representation in Exchange Management Shell is different from the representation in the pull-down menu in Queue Viewer. Table 9-2 lists the comparison operators.

Table 9-2 Filter Operators

Comparison Operator	Exchange Management Shell Representation	Function
Equals	-eq	The results must exactly match the property value that is supplied in the expression.
Does Not Equal	-ne	The results must not match the property value that is supplied in the expression.
Greater Than	-gt	The value of the specified property is greater than the value that is supplied in the expression.

Table 9-2 **Filter Operators**

Comparison Operator	Exchange Management Shell Representation	Function
Greater Than or Equals	-ge	The value of the specified property is greater than or equal to the value that is supplied in the expression.
Less Than	-lt	The value of the specified property is less than the value that is supplied in the expression.
Less Than or Equals	-le	This operator is used with properties where the value is expressed as an integer. The filter results include only messages where the value of the specified property is less than or equal to the value that is supplied in the expression.
Contains	-like	The filter results include only messages where the value of the specified property contains the text string that is supplied in the expression. You can include the * wildcard character in a -like statement that is applied to a text string field.

Using Queue Viewer to Filter Messages

Queue Viewer displays and filters messages on the Exchange Server 2007 transport server to which it is connected—by default, the server on which it is running. Earlier in this lesson, you saw how to connect Queue Viewer to another server when you wanted to view queues on that server.

To filter messages in Queue Viewer, open the tool from Toolbox in Exchange Management Console and click the Messages tab. A list of all messages in all queues on the server to which you are connected is displayed. If you want to limit the view to a single queue, you can click the Queues tab and double-click the queue name. You can right-click any message in the Messages tab and select Properties. This lists the properties of the message, including its identity and its GUID.

To filter messages in Queue Viewer, click Create Filter and select a message property from the Message Property drop-down list. Then select a comparison operator from the Comparison Operator drop-down list. If the property has fixed values, you can select a value from the Value drop-down list; otherwise, you can type in a value. If the property requires a date/time expression, edit the current date/time value or click the drop-down list to select a date from the calendar interface. Figure 9-5 shows a filter set to display messages with an SCL greater than or equal to 5. In Figure 9-5, no messages meet that criterion. You might get a different result depending on how you have configured your spam detection settings.

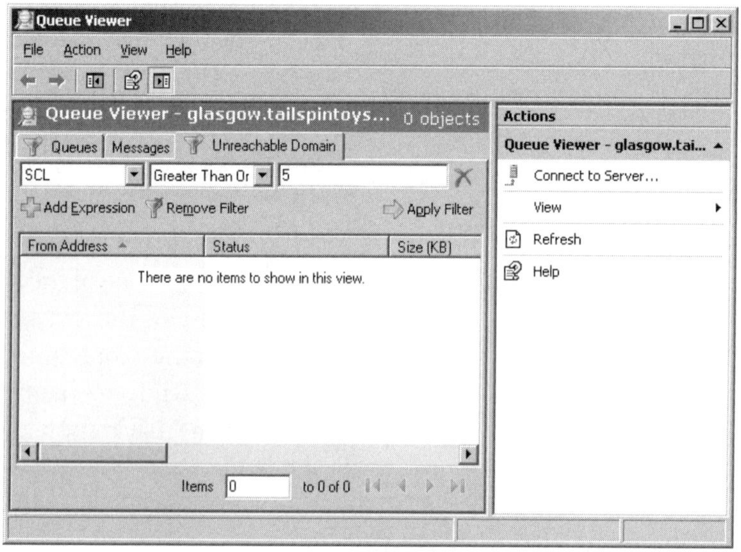

Figure 9-5 Filtering messages in Queue Viewer

If you want to add additional filter conditions, you can click Add Expression to specify additional filter criteria. Only messages that meet the criteria of all configured filters are displayed. You apply the filter condition or conditions you have specified by clicking Apply Filter.

Using Exchange Management Shell to Filter Messages

You can use the *Get-Message* cmdlet in Exchange Management Shell to list messages and to apply filter conditions to select messages. If you want to delete the messages you select, you can use the *Remove-Message* cmdlet, which supports the same filter criteria as the *Get-Message* cmdlet.

For example, if you wanted to list all messages with an SCL greater than or equal to 6, you would enter the following command:

```
Get-Message –Filter {SCL –ge 6}
```

To delete all messages with an SCL greater than or equal to 6, you would enter the following command:

```
Remove-Message –Filter {SCL –ge 6} –WithNDR $False
```

You can use wildcards. For example, to select all messages from addresses in the adatum.com domain, you could enter the following:

```
Get-Message –Filter {FromAddress –like "*@adatum.com"}
```

Wildcards are especially useful when you are filtering on the basis of the subject line. For example, to list all messages that have "lose weight" in the subject line, you could enter the following:

```
Get-Message –Filter {Subject –like "*lose weight*"}
```

Figure 9-6 shows the result of this command.

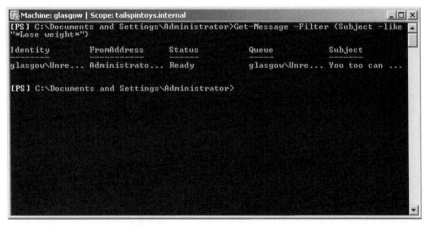

Figure 9-6   Filtering by subject

Similarly, if you wanted to remove all messages that have "lose weight" in the subject line, you could enter the following:

```
Remove-Message –Filter {Subject –like "*lose weight*"}
```

You can select messages by using parameters other than Filter, such as the following:

```
Get-Message -Identity glasgow\Unreachable\8
```

Figure 9-7 shows the result of this command.

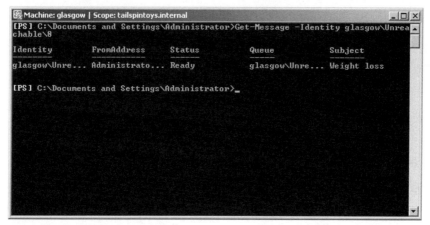

Figure 9-7   Filtering by identity

Finally, you can pipe the output of commands based on the *Get-Message* cmdlet into other commands. Typically, you would not pipe this output into the *Remove-Message* cmdlet, which has its own selection parameters (as has the *Suspend-Message* cmdlet), but you could, for example, pipe it into a command based on the *Export-Message* cmdlet. You need to suspend a message before you can export it, so you would need the following two commands:

```
Suspend-Message -Identity glasgow\Unreachable\8
Get-Message -Identity glasgow\Unreachable\8 | Export-Message -Path "C:\Email_Messages"
```

Figure 9-8 shows the result of these commands. The message is saved in the file glasgow_Unreachable_8.eml in the folder C:\Email_Messages.

MORE INFO   Get-Message

For more information about the *Get-Message* cmdlet and the syntax of associated commands, search Exchange 2007 Help for "Get-Message" or access *http://technet.microsoft.com/en-us/library/bb124738.aspx*.

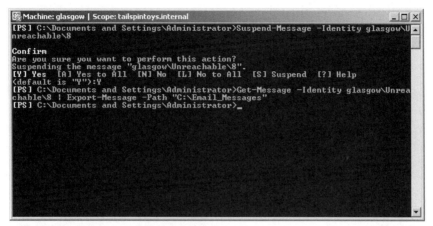

Figure 9-8   Filtering by identity

Forcing Retry Messages in a Queue

When an Exchange Server 2007 transport server—that is, a computer that has the Exchange Server 2007 Hub Transport server role or Edge Transport server role installed—cannot connect to the next hop, the delivery queue is put in a status of retry, and the server will attempt to connect to the next hop and send the queued messages on a scheduled basis. When you use Queue Viewer or Exchange Management Shell to retry a delivery queue, you force an immediate connection attempt and override the next scheduled retry time. If the connection is not successful, the retry interval timer is reset. The delivery queue must be in a status of retry for this action to have any effect.

Before you retry a queue, you need to ensure you are connected to the Exchange Server 2007 transport server that holds the queue. By default, Queue Viewer and Exchange Management Shell operate on the server where they run. You looked at how to connect Queue Viewer to a remote server and at the Server parameter in Exchange Management Shell commands earlier in this lesson.

Using Queue Viewer to Retry a Queue

To retry a queue in Queue Viewer, open the tool and select the Queues tab. You will see a list of all queues on the server to which Queue Viewer is connected. You can then select one or more queues that have a status of retry and select Retry Queue.

If you have a large number of queues on the server, you can list all the queues that have a status of retry by clicking Create Filter, selecting Status from the queue property drop-down list, selecting Equals from the comparison operator drop-down list and selecting Retry from the value drop-down list. When you then click Apply Filter, all queues that currently have a retry status are displayed.

Using Exchange Management Shell to Retry a Queue

You can use commands based on the Exchange Management Shell *Retry-Queue* cmdlet to retry a queue. You must use either an Identity or a Filter parameter to identify the queue or queues you want to retry. The Identity parameter and Filter parameter sets are mutually exclusive, and you cannot specify both.

The Filter parameter can specify values for one or more of the following criteria:

- DeliveryType
- Identity
- LastError
- LastRetryTime
- MessageCount
- NextHopConnector
- NextHopDomain
- NextRetryTime
- Status

You can specify multiple criteria by using the *-and* logical operator. Property values that are not expressed as an integer must be enclosed in quotation marks. For example, you can retry all the queues on the default server that have a status of retry by entering the following command:

```
Retry-Queue -Filter {status -eq "Retry"}
```

You can retry a queue addressed to the adatum.com domain that has a status of retry by entering the following command:

```
Retry-Queue -Filter {NextHopDomain -eq "adatum.com" -and Status -eq "Retry"}
```

You can retry a queue on the remote server Melbourne that is addressed to the adatum.com domain and that has a status of retry by entering the following command:

```
Retry-Queue –Server Melbourne -Filter {NextHopDomain -eq "adatum.com" -and Status -eq "Retry"}
```

You can also specify a remote server as part of the Identity parameter. For example, you can enter the following command to retry a queue on the remote server Edinburgh addressed to the contoso.com domain:

```
Retry-Queue -Identity "Edinburgh\contoso.com"
```

You can include the Resubmit parameter. The following command specifies whether the queue contents are resubmitted to the categorizer before a connection is established:

```
Retry-Queue -Server Melbourne -Filter {NextHopDomain -eq "adatum.com" -and Status -eq "Retry"}
-Resubmit $True
```

MORE INFO The Retry-Queue Cmdlet

For more information about the syntax of commands based on the *Retry-Queue* cmdlet and the parameters you can specify in these commands, search Exchange Server 2007 Help for "Retry-Queue" or access *http://technet.microsoft.com/en-us/library/bb124081.aspx*.

Monitoring Queue Thresholds

A threshold is a value for an operational parameter above or below which you need to be notified so that you can take the appropriate action. Typically, no definitive values exist for these thresholds. The values you specify depend on values you encounter when you monitor Exchange Server 2007 server operation during periods of low, average, and high activity.

You need to create a series of baselines that help you determine normal operational parameter value ranges and determine thresholds that should trigger warnings and actions. Baselines also help you judge whether the load on your servers is increasing or the performance of these servers is diminishing over time.

Exchange Server 2007 provides the Exchange Server Performance Monitor tool to enable you to monitor Exchange activity, establish baselines, set thresholds, and determine the action to be taken when a threshold level exceeds or falls below its specified value. You access this tool by opening Exchange Management Console, clicking Toolbox in the console tree, selecting Exchange Server Performance Monitor in the Result pane, and clicking Open Tool in the Actions pane. You can choose whether to monitor the counters on the Exchange Server 2007 server on which the tool is running or to connect to a remote Exchange Server 2007 server.

NOTE Exchange Server Performance Monitor

Lesson 2 of this chapter describes the use of data gathering tools such as Event Viewer to monitor system performance. The discussion in this lesson covers monitoring message traffic and queue thresholds.

You might already be familiar with the Microsoft Windows Performance tools, System Monitor, and Performance Logs and Alerts. Exchange Server Performance Monitor provides the same functionality as these tools but adds Exchange Server objects, each with its own set of counters. Figure 9-9 shows Exchange specific performance objects in Exchange Server Performance Monitor.

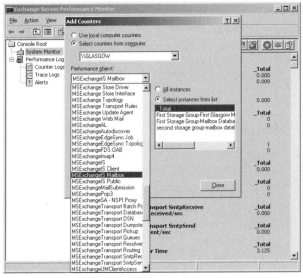

Figure 9-9 Exchange performance objects

You can use the counters provided by the Microsoft Exchange Information Store Mailbox (MSExchangeIS Mailbox) Performance Object to monitor message receipt, message delivery, and the length of delivery and incoming message queues. You can add and monitor the following counters either for all instances or for each mailbox database on the server:

- Messages Delivered/Sec
- Messages Sent/Sec
- Messages Queued For Submission
- Receive Queue Size

Figure 9-10 shows the Report view of the tool with these four counters added.

You can use the tool to create performance logs and record the values of the counters you are monitoring during quiet, normal, or busy times. You should repeat this exercise on a regular basis to determine increases in server load or degradation of server performance over time.

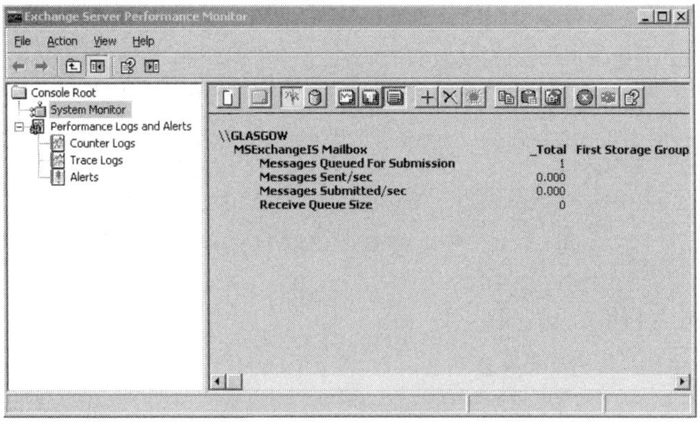

Figure 9-10   Monitored counters in report view

Interpreting Results and Responding to Exceeded Thresholds

It is not possible to give absolute values for thresholds. The number of messages queued for submission that triggers an alert in one organization might be perfectly normal and acceptable in another. This depends on many factors, for example, normal levels of message traffic, server resources, or business requirements. You can make this type of judgment only by baselining and determining typical counter values. For example, if you have captured a baseline that tells you that the typical value in a particular queue counter during a busy period is 100, you might decide to set an alert threshold of 200 for that counter. Setting threshold alerts is discussed in the next section of this lesson.

In addition, you frequently need the information from two or more counters to make a judgment. For example, if the value in the Receive Queue Size counter is high but the value in the Messages Delivered/sec is also high, your server is probably experiencing a traffic spike and is operating normally. If, on the other hand, the value in the Receive Queue Size counter is high but the value in the Messages Delivered/sec is low or zero, something is blocking message delivery, and you have a problem.

If Exchange Server Performance Monitor triggers an alert because a queue threshold has been exceeded, you can use Queue Viewer to obtain further information. For example, excessive queue lengths can indicate spam or DoS attacks, particularly if many of the messages are from the same source or have the same recipient. In this case, you delete the messages without sending NDRs, and it is probably a good idea to look at your e-mail security settings.

It is possible that a corrupt message or a message with a very large attachment is blocking a queue and that deleting that message (typically with an NDR) will solve the problem. It is also possible that a resource on your Exchange Server 2007 server is under stress. Lesson 2 of this chapter discusses how you monitor system performance.

Lesson 2 also discusses the Best Practice Analyzer tool and the Exchange Troubleshooting Assistant tools. While these are general tools for analyzing the health of your Exchange organization, the analyses they provide can assist when you detect queue problems resulting in exceeded thresholds.

Quick Check

- Which Exchange Performance Object provides the Messages Queued For Submission and Receipt Queue counters?

Quick Check Answer

- The MSExchangeIS Mailbox Performance Object.

Setting Queue Thresholds

You can use the Performance Logs and Alerts tool in Exchange Server Performance Monitor to alert you if the number of messages queued for submission reaches 100. As previously stated, the actual value you set for this alert depends on a number of factors, and the figure of 100 is for the purpose of demonstration only.

To set an alert, you expand Performance Logs And Alerts in the Exchange Server Performance Monitor Console Root, right-click Alerts, and select New Alert Settings. You give the alert a name, for example, Submission Queue, and click OK. You then click Add on the General tab. In the Add Counters dialog box, you select the MSExchangeIS Mailbox Performance Object, select All Instances, and then select the Messages Queued For Submission counter. Clicking Add adds this counter. You then specify Over in the Alert When The Value Is box and 100 in the Limit box. You need to set a limit for each instance of the counter, and you can optionally set different limits for each instance. You can also specify how often you want the counter to be scanned. Figure 9-11 shows these settings. If you want to, you can specify a user account under which the alert should run (by default, it runs under the logged-on account) and supply a password.

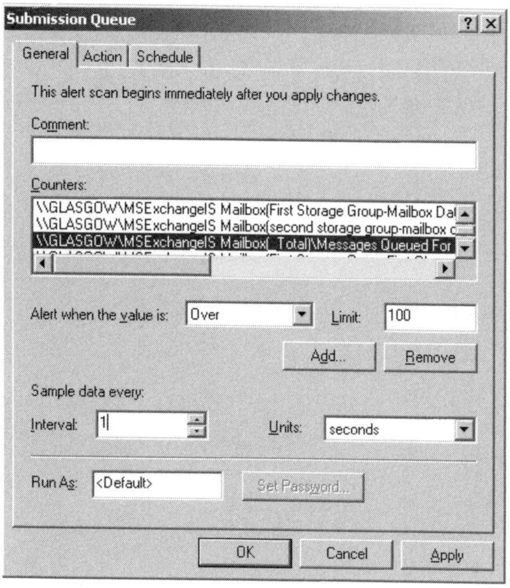

Figure 9-11 Specifying an alert

NOTE **The Over option**

In the Alerts tool, the Over option actually means "greater than or equal to." Therefore, if you specify a value of 100, the alert will trigger on a value of 100 (not 101).

You then select the Action tab and are presented with a choice of alert actions, as shown in Figure 9-12. By default, a triggered alert logs an entry in the Application log. You can also send a network message to an administrator's client computer, start a performance data log to record the values in other specified counters, or start a program—for example, to send an alert to a pager.

You can set an alert to start a performance data log in Exchange Server Performance Monitor and record values in additional counters, for example, Messages Delivered/ Sec. Alternatively, you can use System Monitor in the same tool to look at these counters immediately in real time. If you determine that you have a problem and the alert was not triggered by a traffic spike, you need to take corrective action. You can identify whether the problem is in a single storage group or in all storage groups by looking at instances of the counters.

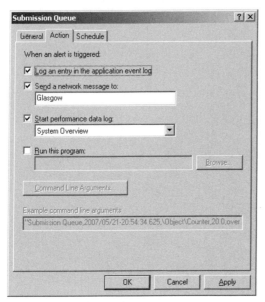

Figure 9-12   Alert actions

Microsoft Operations Manager

Microsoft Operations Manager (MOM) 2005 Service Pack 1 (SP1) provides an alternative and powerful method of monitoring Microsoft Exchange Server 2007 servers. MOM can use either Microsoft SQL Server 2005 or Microsoft SQL Server 2000 as its report server database. The tool is typically used in the enterprise environment to generate alerts when operational failures and performance problems occur and generate reports of operational health over time so that you can estimate future demands based on usage patterns and other performance data. MOM indicators represent the state of health of servers and server roles.

The Exchange 2007 Management Pack for MOM 2005 SP1 contains rules to monitor a comprehensive array of Exchange Server 2007 server health indicators and create alerts when problems are detected or when predefined thresholds are exceeded. Each rule starts with the word "Collect" to indicate that it is collecting data. Rules that collect data for reports end with "Report Collection." All performance data collection rules are related to a threshold rule or a report or provide data to another MOM rule.

The Exchange Server 2007 Management Pack monitors the following:

- Exchange services
- Databases
- Free disk space
- Microsoft Outlook 2007 connectivity
- Microsoft Outlook 2007 performance
- Mail flow between servers
- Exchange performance
- Exchange configuration
- Backups

Figure 9-13 shows the MOM console with the Exchange Server 2007 Management Pack imported.

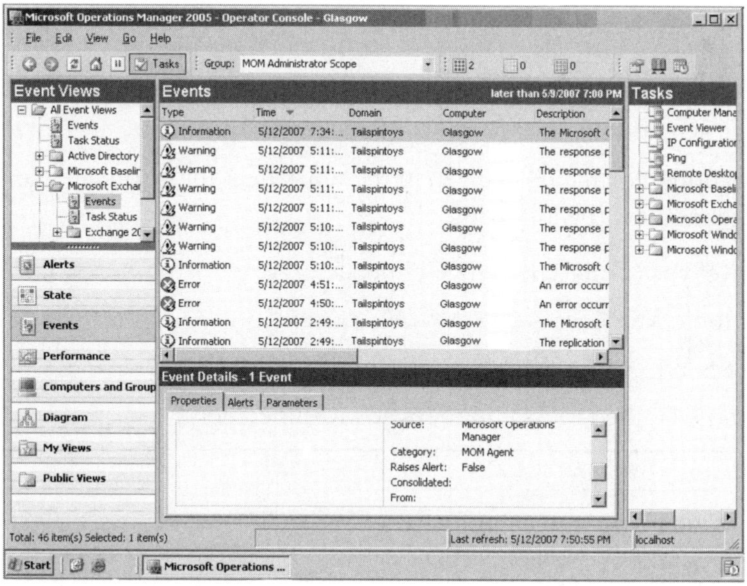

Figure 9-13   The MOM console

In order to use MOM, you need to install it and then import the Exchange Management Pack. Note that the workgroup version of MOM 2005 can monitor only up to 10 servers and does not support reporting. However, the full version requires

SQL Server 2000 or later, so if you want to look at MOM, you might decide to download the workgroup version to an Exchange server that has the Edge Transport role installed. You can find information about planning your monitoring strategy and about MOM 2005 installation at *http://www.microsoft. com/mom/ techinfo/planning/default.mspx*. You can download the installation file for the trial software from *http://www.microsoft.com/technet/mom/2005/downloads/ default.mspx*. You can download the ExchangeServer2007ManagementPack.akm file and Exchange2007Reports.xml files from *http://go.microsoft.com/fwlink/ ?linkid=78482*.

No configuration is required if you want to monitor the following:

- MAPI logons (Test-MAPIConnectivity)
- Mailflow (Test-Mailflow)
- Search (Test-ExchangeSearch)
- Services (Test-ServiceHealth)
- Configuration (Test-SystemHealth)
- Local Unified Messaging connectivity (Test-UMConnectivity)
- Edge synchronization (Test-EdgeSynchronization)

Configuration information is given in the tool's help files. You need to configure the tool to monitor the following:

- ActiveSync (Test-ActiveSyncConnectivity)
- Outlook Web Access (Test-OWAConnectivity)
- Web Services (Test-WebServicesConnectivity)
- Remote Unified Messaging (Test-UMConnectivity)

MORE INFO Using MOM to monitor Exchange Server 2007

For more information about using MOM to monitor Exchange Server 2007, search Exchange Server 2007 Help for "Monitoring Exchange 2007 with Microsoft Operations Manager 2005 SP1" or access *http://technet.microsoft.com/en-us/library/bb201735.aspx*. Follow all the links under this topic on the left pane of the console.

Exam Tip   MOM is not specifically mentioned in the objectives of the 70-236 examination, and it is most unlikely to be tested in depth. However, one objective is "Monitor Mail Queues," and MOM is a tool you can use for this purpose, so it could appear as one of the alternative answers in a question on this topic.

Practice: Locating and Monitoring E-Mail Messages

In this practice session, you log on to the domain as Don Hall and send a number of e-mail messages. These messages are to addresses in unreachable domains, and they are therefore queued. You locate queued messages in Queue Viewer and determine their properties. You then use Exchange Management Shell to locate, remove, suspend, and export messages.

IMPORTANT   **Disable spam filtering before attempting this practice session**

One of the purposes of searching for messages in queues is to identify potential spam or other malware. Although the built-in spam filter in a Hub Transport or Edge Transport server plus the anti-spam features of Microsoft Forefront provide very good protection, no system can be perfect. In addition, you might need to demonstrate the presence of spam in order to justify anti-spam configuration to management. The message subjects in this practice session have therefore been deliberately chosen to look like spam. However, if you configured spam filtering in Microsoft Forefront as described in Chapter 6, the practices might not work as written. Before attempting this practice session, disable spam filtering as described in Chapter 6. If the built-in spam filter on your Hub Transport server (Glasgow) has been enabled, you can disable it by entering the command *Set-TransportServer –Identity "Glasgow" –AntispamAgentsEnabled $False*. You need to restart the Microsoft Exchange Transport service when you enable or disable the built-in anti-spam features on a Hub Transport server.

▶ **Practice 1: Creating Message Queues**

This practice asks you to log on to the domain by using the Don.Hall account. You can do this at a client computer joined to the domain. If you do not have such a computer on your test network, you can carry out the practice by permitting the Don Hall and Keith Harris accounts to log on at the domain controller. It is not considered good security practice to permit ordinary users to log on locally on domain controllers, so the best procedure is to add the Don.Hall and Keith.Harris accounts to, for example, the Account Operators, Backup Operators, Print Operators, or Server Operators Domain Local security group. If you do not know how to do this, refer to your Server operating system help files:

1. Log on to the domain by using the Don.Hall account.

2. Send the e-mail messages detailed in Table 9-3. You can include whatever text you like (or no text at all) in the body of the e-mail. You can choose to send the messages by using Microsoft Outlook, Outlook Express, or Outlook Web Access (OWA).

Table 9-3   Don Hall's E-Mail Messages

Recipients	Subject
Michael.Patten@litwareinc.internal Laurent.Penisson@adatum.internal John.Peoples@contoso.internal	Lose weight now
Michael.Patten@litwareinc.internal Simon.Pearson@litwareinc.internal Flemming.Pedersen@litwareinc.internal	Confirm your bank account details
David.Pelton@adatum.internal Laurent.Penisson@adatum.internal Lori.Penor@adatum.internal Lionel.Penuchot@contoso.internal John.Peoples@contoso.internal Michel.Pereira@contoso.internal	Cheap prescription drugs

3. Find a file on the computer that is at least 10 KB in size.

4. Send an e-mail message to Simon.Pearson@litwareinc.internal with the subject "Here it is" and the file you selected attached.

5. Log on to the domain by using the Keith.Harris account.

6. Send the e-mail messages detailed in Table 9-4. You can include whatever text you like (or no text at all) in the body of the e-mail.

Table 9-4   Keith Harris's E-Mail Messages

Recipients	Subject
Michael.Patten@litwareinc.internal Simon.Pearson@litwareinc.internal Flemming.Pedersen@litwareinc.internal	Achieve your ideal weight

Table 9-4   Keith Harris's E-Mail Messages

Recipients	Subject
Michael.Patten@litwareinc.internal Laurent.Penisson@adatum.internal John.Peoples@contoso.internal	A criminal organization might know your bank account details
Lionel.Penuchot@contoso.internal John.Peoples@contoso.internal Michel.Pereira@contoso.internal	The cheapest drugs on the Internet

▶ **Practice 2: Using Queue Viewer to Monitor Queues and Messages**

In this practice, you view the queues you have created and the messages in these queues. You view message properties and filter messages by source address and size. You can expand the practice by filtering on additional criteria, both singly and in combination. You need to complete Practice 1 before attempting Practice 2:

1. Log on to the Exchange server in your domain by using the Kim_Akers account.

2. Start Queue Viewer as described earlier in this lesson.

3. On the Queues tab, right-click Unreachable Domain and click View Messages, as shown in Figure 9-14.

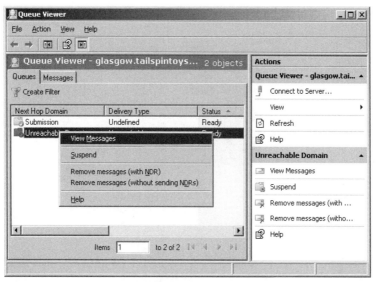

Figure 9-14   Selecting the Unreachable Domain queue

4. The messages in the Unreachable Domain queue are listed in the Unreachable Domain tab, as shown in Figure 9-15.

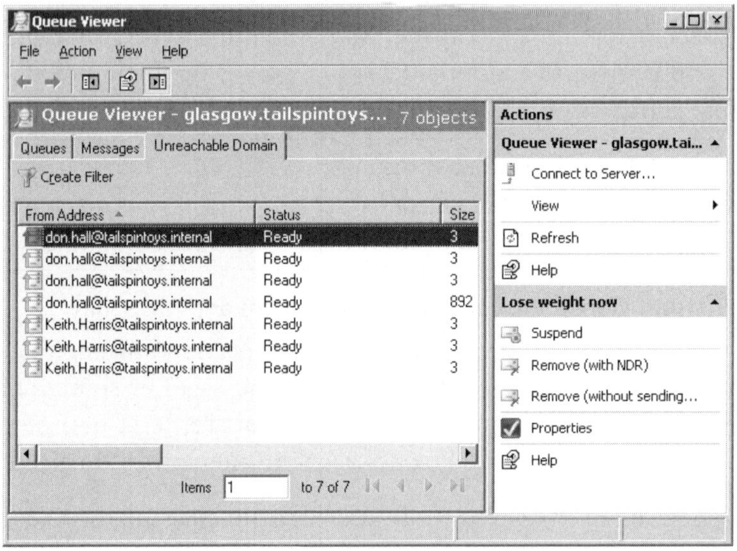

Figure 9-15   Messages in the Unreachable Domain queue

5. Click Create Filter. Set up a filter to display messages from address don.hall@ tailspintoys.internal. Click Apply Filter. E-mail messages from Don Hall are listed, as shown in Figure 9-16.

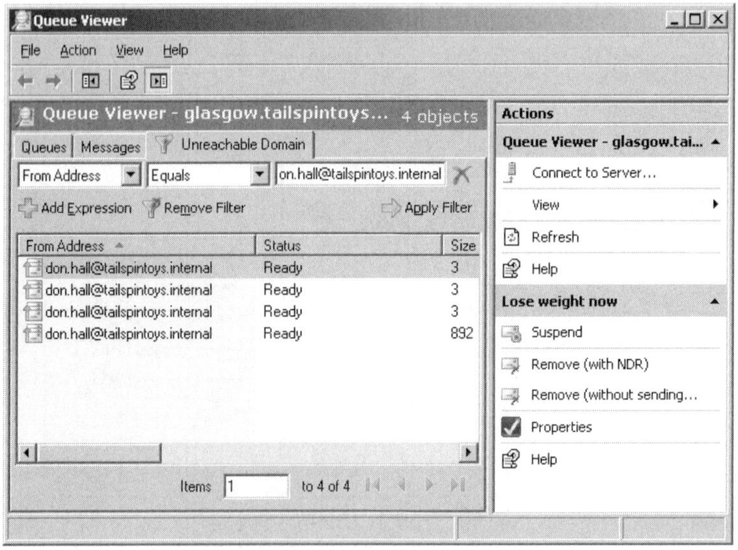

Figure 9-16   Messages from don.hall@tailspintoys.internal

6. Click Add Expression.

7. Set up a filter to display messages with a message size greater than 10 KB. Click Apply Filter. The message from Don Hall that was sent with an attachment is listed, as shown in Figure 9-17.

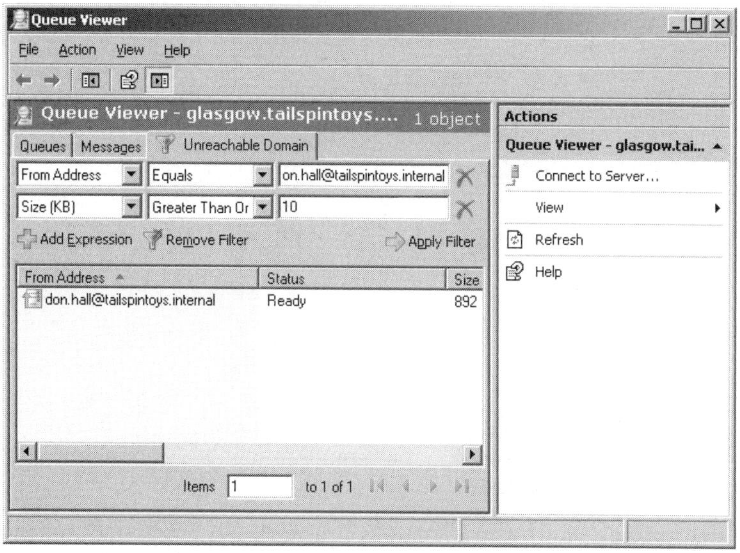

Figure 9-17   Large message from don.hall@tailspintoys.internal

8. Click Remove Filter.

9. Right-click the first message on the list and click Properties. The Properties box for the message is shown in Figure 9-18. Take a note of the message identity. You use this in Practice 3.

10. Close the Properties box. Close Queue Viewer.

▶ **Practice 3: Using Exchange Management Console to Monitor Queues and Messages**

In this practice, you use Exchange Management Shell to filter messages by message identity and subject. You remove a message from a specific sender whose subject contains a specified text string. You suspend messages whose subject contains another text string and export these messages to a folder. As with the previous practice, you can expand this practice by filtering on additional criteria, both singly and in combination. You need to complete Practice 2 before attempting Practice 3:

1. If necessary, log on to the Exchange server in your domain by using the Kim_Akers account.

2. Open Exchange Management Shell.

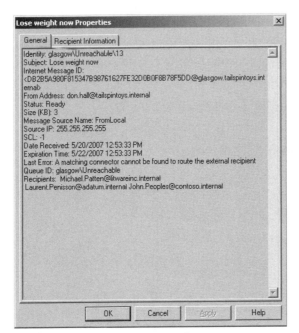

Figure 9-18   Message properties

3. List the message with the Identity parameter equal to the message identity that you noted in Practice 2. In Figure 9-19, this value is "glasgow\Unreachable\13." You will probably record and use a different value when you carry out the practices.

Figure 9-19   Filtering by message identity

4. You now list all the messages that have the string "drugs" in the subject line. Enter the following command:

```
Get-Message -Filter {Subject -like "*drugs*"}
```

Your screen should look similar to Figure 9-20.

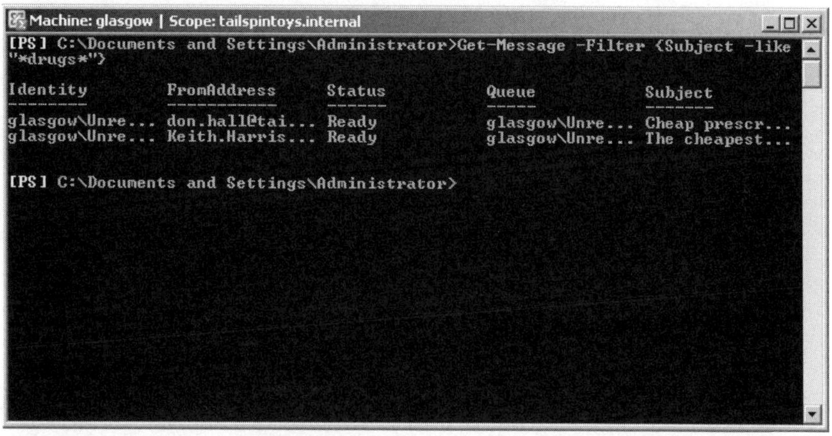

Figure 9-20   Filtering by subject contents

5. You now remove a message from don.hall@tailspintoys.internal whose subject contains the string "drugs" without sending an NDR. If several messages existed that met both of these criteria, they would all be removed. Enter the following command:

```
Remove-Message -Filter {Subject -like "*drugs*" -and FromAddress -like
"don.hall@tailspintoys.internal"} -WithNDR $False
```

Enter **Y** to confirm message removal. Your screen should look similar to Figure 9-21.

6. You now suspend all messages whose subject contains the string "bank account." Enter the following command:

```
Suspend-Message -Filter {Subject -like "*bank account*"}
```

7. Enter **Y** (or **A**) to confirm the operation. Having suspended the messages, you export them to the folder C:\Email_Messages. Note that this folder must already exist for this procedure to work. Enter the following command:

```
Get-Message -Filter {Subject -like "*bank account*"} | Export-Message -Path
"C:\Email_Messages"
```

Figure 9-21   Removing a message based on filter criteria

Your screen should look similar to Figure 9-22.

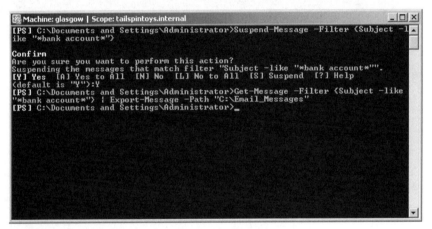

Figure 9-22   Suspending and exporting messages

8. Check that the messages have been exported to the specified folder, as shown in Figure 9-23.

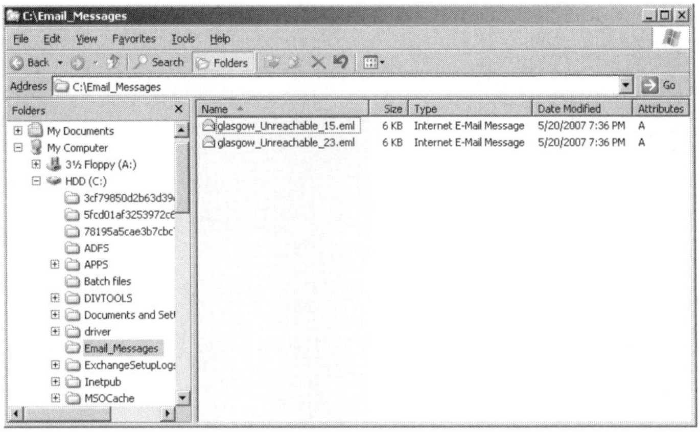

Figure 9-23　Exported messages

Lesson Summary

- You can use Queue Viewer and Exchange Management Shell to monitor and manage queues and the messages in these queues.

- You can filter messages by using either tool so that only the messages that meet specified filter criteria are listed.

- You can use either tool to remove, suspend, resume, or export queued messages and to force a queue retry.

- You can use Exchange Server Performance Monitor to look at the rates at which messages are received or sent and the lengths of queues. You can examine the counters that provide this information in log files or in real time. You can set an alert if a counter value exceeds or falls below a specific value.

Lesson Review

You can use the following questions to test your knowledge of the information in Lesson 1, "Monitoring Mail Queues." The questions are also available on the companion CD if you prefer to review them in electronic form.

NOTE　Answers

Answers to these questions and explanations of why each answer choice is correct or incorrect are located in the "Answers" section at the end of the book.

1. On which Exchange Server 2007 transport roles does Queue Viewer focus? (Choose all that apply.)

   A. Hub Transport role

   B. Client Access role

   C. Mailbox role

   D. Edge Transport role

   E. Unified Messaging role

2. Which queue holds all messages that are received by a transport server before processing?

   A. Unreachable queue

   B. Remote delivery queue

   C. Mailbox delivery queue

   D. Submission queue

3. You suspect that a queued message from don.hall@contoso.com might be corrupt. You enter the following command in Exchange Management Shell:

   ```
   Remove-Message -Filter {FromAddress -eq "don.hall@contoso.com" -and Identity -eq 100}
   ```

   What happens to the message?

   A. It is suspended and exported to the poison message queue.

   B. It is removed, and an NDR is sent to don.hall@contoso.com.

   C. It is removed, and an NDR is not sent to don.hall@contoso.com.

   D. It is transferred to the unreachable queue.

4. You want to list messages that are likely to be spam. You enter the following command:

   ```
   Get-Message -Filter {SCL -ge 6}
   ```

   What messages are not listed?

   A. Messages with an SCL of 6

   B. Messages with an SCL of 6 or greater

   C. Messages with an SCL less than 6

   D. Messages with an SCL greater than 6

5. You want to trigger an alert when the number of messages in the mailbox store's receive queue on an Exchange Server 2007 server reaches a defined value. What counter do you select when configuring the alert? (The question uses the notation <performance object>:<counter name>.)

   A. MSExchangeIS:Messages Queued For Submission

   B. MSExchangeIS:Receive Queue Size

   C. MSExchangeIS Mailbox:Messages Queued For Submission

   D. MSExchangeIS Mailbox:Receive Queue Size

Lesson 2: Monitoring System Performance

This lesson discusses how to use tools such as Event Viewer, Performance Logs and Alerts (Perfmon.exe), Network Monitor (Netmon.exe), and PowerShell scripts to detect system performance degradation. If a server has one or more subsystems—for example, memory, disk storage, network, and processor—that are underperforming, this might alter the responsiveness of the server, whose performance might fall below acceptable levels. In Exchange Server 2007, server performance degradation has the symptoms of rising mail queues and poor client response. Tools provided by Exchange Troubleshooting Assistant monitor the usage data for resources associated with these symptoms, return analysis reports, and suggest solutions when a problem is detected.

In this lesson, you learn how to use the tools provided to monitor the performance of server subsystems and how to monitor services and applications. The lesson also discusses how to use HTTP Monitoring Service (HTTPMon) to monitor Web sites and, in particular, OWA servers.

After this lesson, you will be able to:

- Monitor hardware.
- Use the Microsoft tools provided to monitor services.
- Monitor network activities.
- Set and monitor performance thresholds.
- Respond to exceeded performance thresholds.

Estimated lesson time: 55 minutes

Real World

Ian McLean

Monitoring your server hardware and the performance of your system is not especially difficult.

You have got lots of tools to do it with. What you monitor and when you monitor it depends on your equipment and business requirements, but many examples of good monitoring practice exist and can be found on the Internet. You can automate many monitoring tasks so that they happen in the background while you are busy doing something else.

What is difficult is finding the time to inspect, analyze, and document the results. You need to do this on a regular basis to build up a history of the stress on your server resources. If an alert occurs and you have identified a problem that you need to resolve, you'll find the time to deal with the situation. But if you need to check and record that the values returned in some significant counters, while still acceptable, indicate that traffic and resource pressure is building up in your system over time, you might decide to leave the task until later.

After all, if you skip the occasional check on your performance counters, who is to know? In the meantime, 40 new employees start work on the following Monday and need mailbox accounts, and your chief executive officer has opened Microsoft Word and is complaining that he cannot see his e-mail messages (again).

You need to find the time to check your monitor results. If you do not, your organization's network will continue to work fine—until one day it falls over completely. A good administrator solves problems before they occur and certainly before users notice them. When management is budgeting for equipment refresh, it will not allocate money for upgrades to the equipment you are responsible for unless you have the figures to justify this expenditure.

Spend some of your valuable time monitoring your system, recording the results, and documenting your reports. In the long run, it is your lifeline.

MORE INFO   **Best monitoring practice**

An Internet search for "monitoring best practice" or "best practice in monitoring" will give you access to a lot of advice and further information. However, a good place to start is *http://technet2.microsoft.com/windowsserver/en/library/b3d458a8-7d62-4f2a-80bb-c16e75994b1d1033.mspx?mfr=true*.

Monitoring Hardware

If you suspect a hardware failure of a system component, you can typically access a troubleshooter associated with the Server help files that assists you in diagnosing and repairing the problem. For example, if you had printing problems, you would access the Printing Troubleshooter, shown in Figure 9-24.

Sometimes the problem is caused by a corrupt or out-of-date driver or by an unsuitable driver being downloaded. In this case, you can access a device from Device Driver on the Hardware tab of the System tool in Control Panel, check whether the device is working properly, and, if necessary, update or roll back the driver. If you choose to update the diver, ensure that you have an Internet connection because new versions of device drivers are often available on the Microsoft Update Web site. Figure 9-25 shows the Driver tab of the Properties dialog box for an Ethernet controller.

Figure 9-24   Printing Troubleshooter

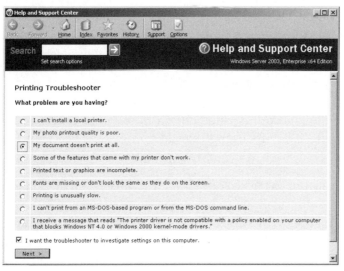

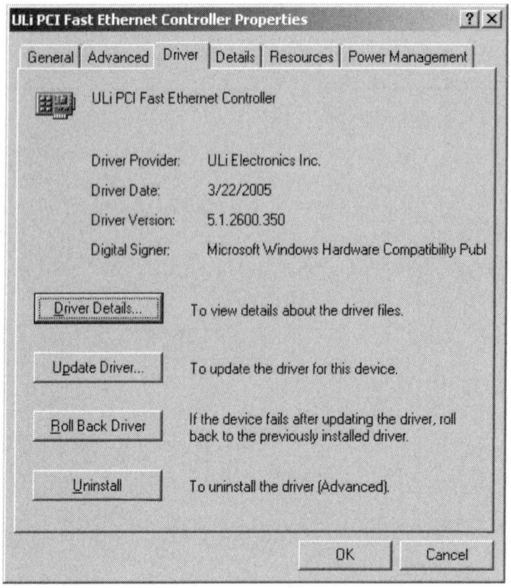

Figure 9-25   Options for working with drivers

However, hardware failures are rare, although they can happen. Typically, performance problems are caused by stressed resources. Your processor, for example, has not failed but is frequently running at over 99 percent usage for extended periods of time, and server performance is consequently very poor. Microsoft provides the Performance tools, System Monitor, and Performance Logs and Alerts, to check stress on resources, create performance baselines, and alert you if a counter associated with a resource exceeds or falls below a predefined threshold value. You can access the Exchange Server Performance Monitor from Exchange Management Console or Performance from the Administrative Tools menu. Essentially, both procedures access the same set of tools.

NOTE Task Manager

If you want an instant view of server performance without needing to specify counters, you can access the Performance and Networking tabs on Windows Task Manager. This tool is not as versatile as the Performance tools and does not provide a large number of counters to let you drill down to a specific issue, but it provides a quick and easy method of getting a snapshot of system performance.

Lesson 1 discussed the use of Performance tools to monitor counters specific to Exchange. However, in many instances, they are used to monitor the server subsystems: memory, disk storage, network, and processor.

Setting Performance Thresholds

System Monitor, shown in Figure 9-26, lets you monitor performance counters in real time. You could, for example, check the value of memory counters such as Pages/Sec; processor counters such as % Processor Time; disk counters such as Disk Bytes/Sec; and network counters such as Bytes Total/Sec in graph, histogram, or report view.

However, real-time checks are of limited long-term value, and you would typically add the counters you want to monitor to logs, which you would use to record values during quiet, busy, and normal periods to generate baselines. You would then repeat the process regularly to determine whether the load on the server and server subsystems is changing over time. You would also recalculate your baselines if there were any significant changes to your systems, such as the installation of a new disk array or the addition of a second processor. Typically, you view logs in System Monitor report view.

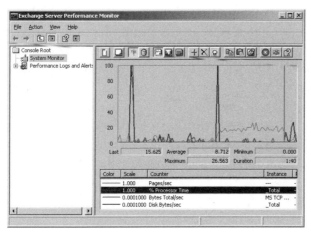

Figure 9-26 System Monitor graph view

Guidelines exist for some of the more frequently used counters. For example, Pages/Sec should not exceed 20 and should not have an average value greater than 5 (except on SQL Servers), and % Processor Time should not exceed 85 percent for extended periods of time (although it can and frequently does reach 100 percent for short periods). However, most of the thresholds you specify are determined by the specific load on your systems and the business requirements of your organization. As in setting thresholds for Exchange counters, described in Lesson 1, thresholds for your system counters are determined by your baseline statistics.

Quick Check
- What are the four main subsystems that determine server performance?

Quick Check Answer
- Memory, processor, disk, and network.

Monitoring Performance Thresholds

As described in Lesson 1, you monitor thresholds by setting alerts. Figure 9-27 shows an alert setting on the Pages/Sec counter.

Responding to Exceeded Performance Thresholds

An exceeded performance threshold might be caused by a sudden spike in demand. Spikes are often encountered in server operation and do not necessarily indicate a problem, so your first task when an alert occurs is to determine whether a problem exists. By default, a performance alert is logged in the Application log, which you can monitor in Event Viewer. You can, however, specify that an alert starts a performance log. For example, an unusually high Pages/Sec reading could start a log that records subsequent values of that counter in addition to other memory- and disk-related counters.

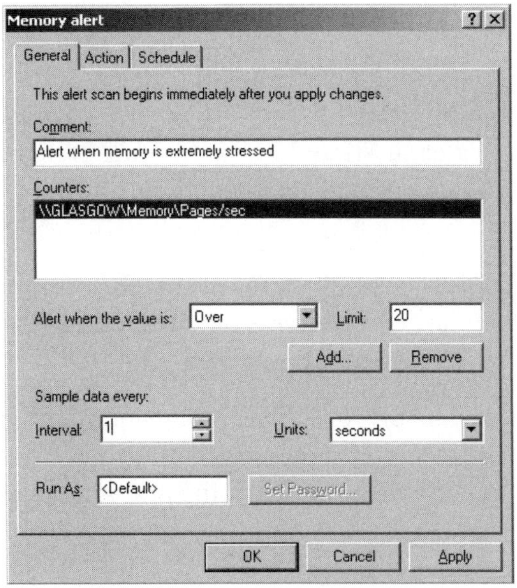

Figure 9-27   Alerting on Pages/Sec

Sometimes an alert indicates a potentially serious condition that you need to urgently investigate. For example, if the network counter Bytes/Sec is returning a very low or zero value on a busy server on a busy network, you need to know about this immediately. An alert can send an administrative message and start a program that could, for example, activate a pager. Figure 9-12 earlier in this chapter shows the choice of alert actions.

An alert can indicate equipment failure (for example, a faulty network card or hard disk), but it can also indicate stress on resources that are working but not coping with increased traffic. In an ideal world, you should detect this situation by regularly analyzing your baseline logs and detecting that the load on resources is increasing over time. However, in practice, an alert might be your first indication of overstressed resources.

In this case, you need to consider implementing resource upgrades. If your Hub Transport server cannot cope with your e-mail throughput and an alert on queue length notifies you of the problem, the solution is probably to install a second Hub Transport server to achieve load balancing. If a Client Access server shows excessive processor use, then you should consider either a faster processor or an additional processor. If your hard disks are becoming full, you need more disks or possibly a Storage Area Network solution. Your servers might need faster network controllers, or you might need to upgrade your local area network.

Monitoring with Event Viewer, HTTPMon, and PowerShell

Event Viewer is possibly the most widely used tool for monitoring system, services, and application events. Almost all the other tools mentioned in this chapter write to event logs, which you then monitor by using Event Viewer.

Monitoring Web sites and Web servers is an important activity, and in particular Microsoft recommends that you monitor OWA servers on a regular basis. The Windows Server Resource Kit provides HTTPMon for this purpose.

You can read specified logs directly by using PowerShell commands and place these commands in PowerShell scripts. Scripted commands can be scheduled to run regularly at a specified time of day. Chapter 5 discussed creating and scheduling PowerShell scripts in depth.

Using Event Viewer

You can access Event Viewer from the Administrative Tools menu. The tool displays event logs, which are files that record significant events on a server—for example, when a user logs on to the server or when an application encounters an error. You can use the information in event logs when troubleshooting problems with the Server OS, drivers, and application programs. The events recorded fall into the following categories:

- Error
- Warning
- Information

The security log contains two additional event categories that are used for auditing purposes: Audit Success and Audit Failure.

Figure 9-28 shows details of an error event. This is a failure in performance counter data collection for a particular service, which would be unfortunate if you were relying on these particular performance counters to diagnose a fault. The main point that this illustrates is, however, that event logs contain information about counters related to services in addition to system, application, and other types of information.

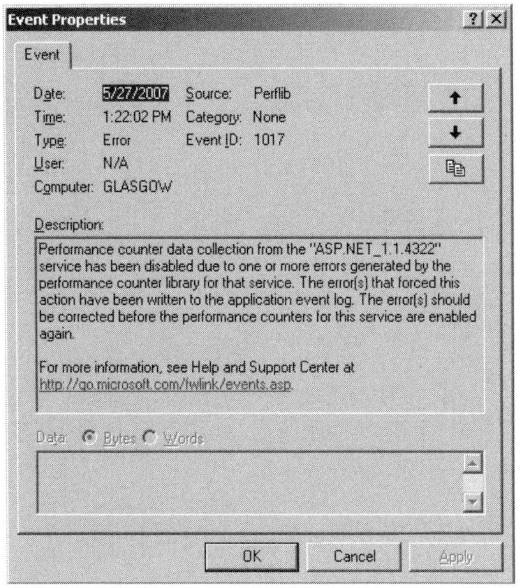

Figure 9-28 An error event

Event Viewer tracks information in various logs. Figure 9-29 shows the logs that are present on the Exchange Server 2007 server Glasgow in the test network used to write this book. The server is a domain controller that runs the File Replication Service and the Domain Name System. It also has Microsoft Office 2007 installed. This would be an unusual setup on a production network.

Windows logs include the following:

- **Application**   Stores program events. Events are classified as error, warning, or information, depending on the severity of the event. An error is a significant problem, such as loss of data. A warning is an event that is not necessarily significant but might indicate a possible future problem. An information event describes the successful operation of a program, driver, or service. The critical error classification is not used in the application log.

- **Security**   Stores security-related audit events that can be successful or failed. For example, the security log will record an audit success if a user trying to log on to the computer was successful.

■ **System**   Stores system events that are logged by Windows Server and Windows Server system services. System events are classified as error, warning, or information.

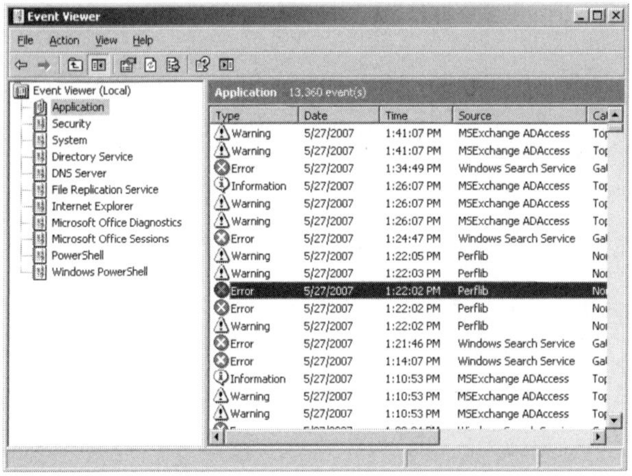

Figure 9-29   Windows logs on the Glasgow server

NOTE   **Critical classification**

Currently, Windows Server 2008 is released in beta. When the production version is released, it is possible that the system log might also include system events classed as critical.

■ **Directory Service**   Stores events related to the Active Directory directory service. Events are classified as error, warning, or information. This log is found only on domain controllers.

■ **DNS Server**   Stores events related to the Domain Name System (DNS). Events are classified as error, warning, or information. This log appears only on DNS servers. The DNS service is typically but not exclusively implemented on domain controllers. It is unusual in a production environment to implement the DNS service on an Exchange Server 2007 server.

■ **File Replication Service**   Stores events related to the File Replication Service, which is a multimaster replication service that is used to replicate files and folders between servers. Events are classified as error, warning, or information.

■ **Internet Explorer**   Stores Web browser events. Events are classified as error, warning, or information.

■ **Microsoft Office Diagnostics and Microsoft Office Sessions** Stores events related to Microsoft Office. These logs are not related to Exchange Server 2007 or the 70-236 examination.

■ **PowerShell** Stores events related to PowerShell. Events are classified as error, warning, or information.

■ **Windows PowerShell** The Windows PowerShell event log records details of Windows PowerShell operations, such as starting and stopping the program "engine," starting and stopping the Windows PowerShell providers, and details about Windows PowerShell commands.

Filtering Event Viewer Logs

You can filter a log by clicking Filter in the View menu or by right-clicking a log and selecting Properties in order to access the Filter tab in the log's Properties dialog box. You can filter by level, time logged, event source, category, event identity (ID), user, or computer. You are unlikely to specify all these criteria, but this facility enables you to refine your search to where you think a problem might be occurring rather than searching through a very large number of events. Figure 9-30 shows a filter specification.

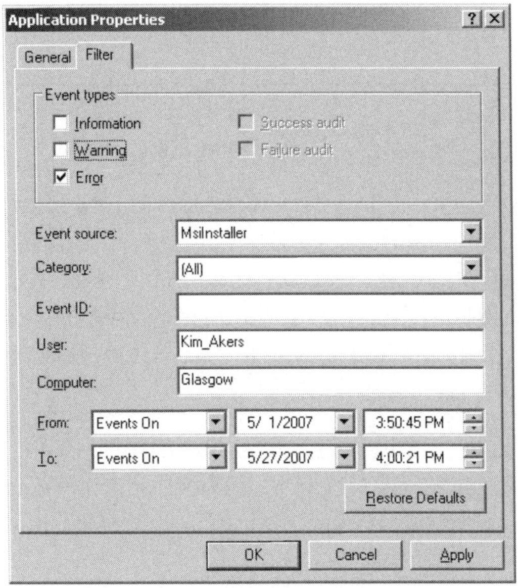

Figure 9-30   Event Viewer filter specification

Applying this filter to the application log results in the event list shown in Figure 9-31.

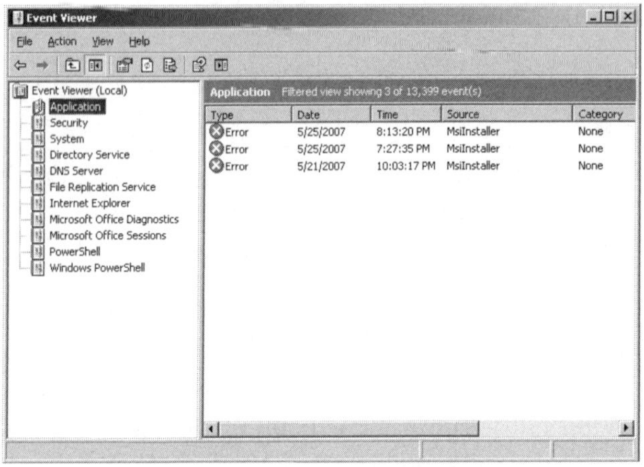

Figure 9-31   Filter applied to application log

Quick Check

- What log holds audit events that can be successful or failed?

Quick Check Answer
- The security log.

Monitoring Outlook Web Access Servers with HTTPMon

You can use the HTTP Monitoring Service to monitor Web sites and applications and, in particular, to identify and troubleshoot issues with OWA servers. You need to monitor OWA servers on a regular basis. Microsoft recommends that, on the basis of your organization's requirements, you should consider monitoring OWA servers weekly. You can increase or decrease the frequency of monitoring based on trend analysis of your OWA servers.

HTTPMon is a resource kit tool. It provides reports about the availability and response time of Web sites and applications and can also check several Web sites and applications simultaneously and export the results to a log file in CSV format or to the Windows Server event log.

You install HTTPMon from the resource kit by running setup.exe in the \apps\http-mon folder of the Microsoft Windows Server 2000 resource kit. (Currently, the tool is not available in the Windows Server 2003 and Windows server 2008 resource kits.)

After you install HTTPMon, you need to run HTTPMon Configuration Manager to configure global settings for your organization and add the OWA servers you want to monitor. You can use the Services tool on the Administration Tools menu to start HTTP Monitoring Service. After your tests start running, you can review the CSV files and analyze this data to detect problems with your OWA servers, and you can review the events logged by HTTPMon in Event Viewer.

HTTPMon consists of three components:

- **Real-time Sampling Service** Monitors OWA servers (and other Web servers) in real time

- **SQL Reporting Server** Gathers data from monitored servers and loads it into an SQL Server database

- **Client Monitor** Displays the results from the SQL Reporting Server database as a set of Web pages

To view the results of HTTP Monitoring Service, you can monitor Event Viewer manually or use, for example, Windows Management Instrumentation (WMI) to automate this process. You can import the CSV file output to Microsoft Excel, Access, or SQL Server for more analysis. You can also use SQL Server data and Client Monitor to track your servers and the reporting features of SQL Server to carry out additional data analysis.

Monitoring Events with PowerShell

PowerShell provides an additional method of monitoring event logs and looking for specific events. The advantage of this method is you can pipe the output of your PowerShell commands into other commands that perform additional functions or redirect the output into, for example, CSV files that can be analyzed by other software packages.

You can use a PowerShell command to list all instances of an event in a specified log. For example, to find all events with event ID 7026 in the system log you would enter the following command into either the PowerShell console or Exchange Management Shell:

```
Get-Eventlog System | where {$_.EventID -eq 7026}
```

Figure 9-32 shows the result of this command entered in Exchange Management Shell.

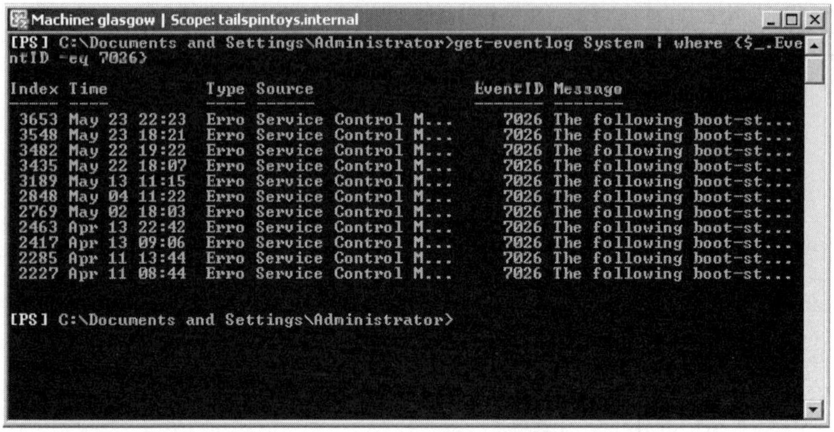

Figure 9-32 Listing events with a PowerShell command

This is an inflexible procedure, and you do not want to type in the full command every time you list events. To overcome these limitations, you can generate a Power-Shell script and specify Log and EventID as parameters. You do this by typing the following into a text editor and saving it with a file name GetEvent.ps1 in the ExScripts subdirectory (typically, C:\Program Files\Microsoft\Exchange Server\Scripts):

```
Param (
[string] $Log,
[string] $ID
)
Get-Eventlog $Log | where {$_.EventID -eq $ID}
```

You can then, for example, get a list of all events in the application log with EventID 1022 by entering the following command:

```
GetEvent.ps1 -Log "Application" -ID "1022"
```

Figure 9-33 shows the result of this command entered in Exchange Management Shell.

You can expand this technique by using the powerful features in the PowerShell scripting language. For example, because event logs can store a very large number of events, you might want to search logs incrementally, reporting only new hits that occurred since the last time you ran the script. You might want to identify several event IDs listed in, for example, a CSV file. If events corresponding to one or more of these IDs do not exist, you want the script to continue to list events that do exist rather than to stop with an error.

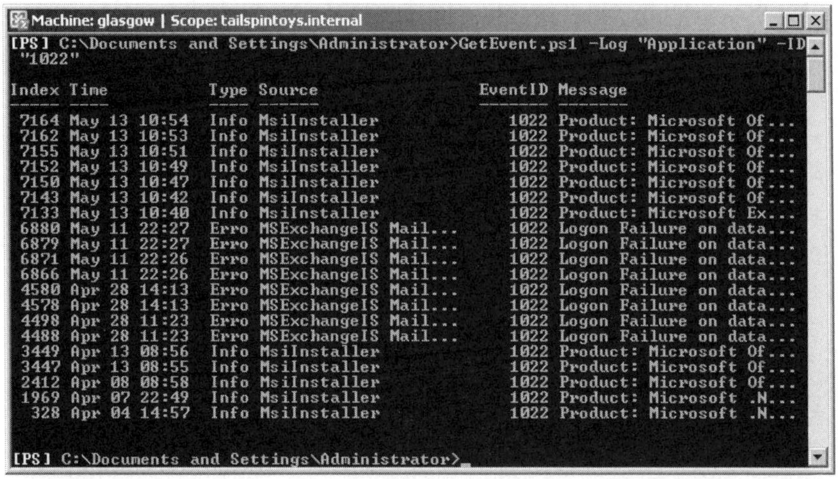

Figure 9-33 Using a PowerShell script

MORE INFO Scripting with PowerShell

For more information about PowerShell scripting and sample scripts including scripts for managing event logs, access *http://www.microsoft.com/technet/scriptcenter/scripts/msh/default.mspx?mfr=true.*

Exam Tip It is unlikely that the 70-236 examination will require you to create even very basic PowerShell scripts under examination conditions. The examination will not test you on scripts as complex as those described in the above link.

You might also want to schedule when the script runs. As described in Chapter 5, you can do this by creating a batch file that can run from the Command Console and then scheduling the batch file. A batch file that runs the GetEvent.ps1 script specifying the application log and EventID 1022 would contain the following code:

```
PowerShell.exe -PSConsoleFile "C:\Program Files\Microsoft\Exchange Server\Bin\ExShell.psc1"
-Command ". 'C:\Program Files\Microsoft\Exchange Server\Scripts\GetEvent.ps1' -Log
"Application" -ID "1022""
```

Quick Check

- What PowerShell cmdlet returns events in a specified event log?

Quick Check Answer

- *Get-Eventlog.*

Monitoring Network Activities by Using Network Monitor

Network Monitor (Netmon) is a protocol analyzer that you can use to analyze network traffic. By default, it is not installed during the installation of your operating system. You can install it by using the Windows Components Wizard available through the Add Or Remove Programs tool in Control Panel. Figure 9-34 shows the tools available when you select the Management And Monitoring Tools check box and click Details. If you select Network Monitor Tools, this results in the installation of both Network Monitor and Network Monitor Driver.

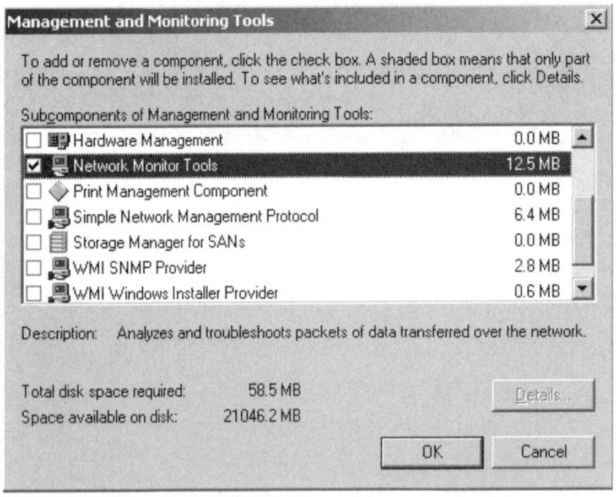

Figure 9-34 Management and monitoring tools

You can use Network Monitor to perform the following tasks:

- Capture frames directly from the network
- Display and filter captured frames immediately after capture or at a later time
- Edit captured frames and transmit them on the network (full version only)
- Capture frames from a remote computer (full version only)

You might, for example, use Network Monitor to diagnose connectivity problems when an Exchange Server 2007 server cannot communicate with other computers.

NOTE Frames and packets

A frame is a layer-2 element that encapsulates layer 3 (network layer) data. Network Monitor reads and displays encapsulations that include both data link layer elements (such as Ethernet headers and trailers) and higher-layer data from protocols such as Address Resolution Protocol (ARP), IP versions 4 and 6, Transmission Control Protocol (TCP), and DNS. A frame is distinct from a packet in that a packet encapsulates layer 3 (network layer) data.

Two versions of Network Monitor are available. The basic version ships with various Windows operating systems, for example, Windows Server 2003 and Windows Server 2008. The full version ships with Microsoft Systems Management Server (SMS). The main difference between the versions is that the full version can capture frames sent from and to remote computers, while the basic version captures frames locally.

However, this distinction holds only for networks that use hubs rather than switches to connect hosts. Most modern networks use switches, which forward frames only to the recipient computer. Switches limit the functionality of protocol analyzers such as Network Monitor by screening traffic that does not originate from or is not sent to the computer on which the protocol analyzer is running. So if your network is using switches instead of hubs (which it probably is), you will not be able to take advantage of the increased functionality of the full version of Network Monitor.

Exam Tip   The 70-236 examination objectives do not mention the full (SMS) version of Network Monitor and you are unlikely to be asked about its functionality. However, as an administrator and IT professional, you should know that this version exists, and you should be able to determine whether there is any real advantage in acquiring and using it.

Network Monitor tools comprises an administrative tool called Network Monitor and an agent called Network Monitor Driver. Both components must be installed for you to capture, display, and analyze network frames.

Using Network Monitor and Network Monitor Driver

You use Network Monitor to display the frames that a computer sends or receives. When you install Network Monitor, the Network Monitor Driver is installed automatically on the same computer. However, sometimes you need to install the Network Monitor Driver without installing the Network Monitor tool itself. For example, if you install the full version of Network Monitor and you want to capture traffic from a remote Windows computer, you need to install Network Monitor Driver but not Network Monitor on the remote computer. (This assumes that your network configuration allows you to access traffic on the remote computer.) You can install Network Monitor Driver from the Properties dialog box of the network connection where you want it to run, as shown in Figure 9-35. It installs as a network protocol.

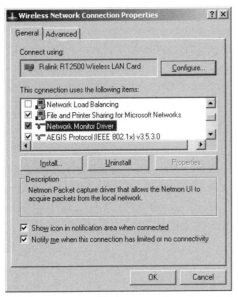

Figure 9-35 Installing Network Monitor Driver

Using Network Monitor

Network Monitor tracks the network data stream, which consists of all the information transferred over a network at any given time. This information is held in segments (known as frames), each of which contains the following information:

- The source address of the computer that sent the frame
- The destination address of the computer that received the frame
- Header information for each protocol used to send the frame
- The data (or a portion of it) being sent to the destination computer

Network Monitor can copy frames originating from or sent to the local computer to a buffer. This process is known as data capture. Typically, you need to capture only a small subset of the frames on your network. To capture a subset of frames, you can design a capture filter to isolate the information that you specify. You can filter frames on the basis of source and destination addresses, data-link-layer protocols, network-layer protocols, transport-layer protocols, protocol properties, and pattern offset.

Examining the Network Monitor Interface

When you launch Network Monitor for the first time after installation, you need to select a particular network adapter through which Network Monitor analyzes traffic.

After you select a network adapter, the Capture window appears. This window includes a graph pane, a session statistics pane, a station statistics pane, and a total statistics pane, as shown in Figure 9-36.

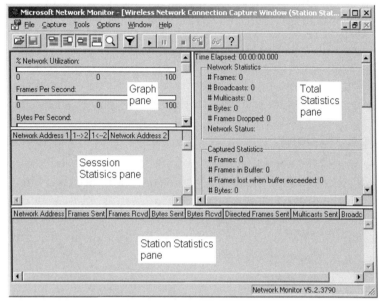

Figure 9-36   Capture window

Table 9-5 describes the type of data displayed in each of these four panes.

Table 9-5   Network Monitor Capture Window

Pane	Description
Graph	Displays the current activity as a set of bar charts
Session statistics	Displays a summary of the conversations between two hosts
Station statistics	Displays a summary of the total number of frames initiated by a host, the number of frames and bytes sent and received, and the number of broadcast and multicast frames initiated
Total statistics	Displays statistics for the traffic detected on the entire network

Capturing and Viewing Network Data

To capture data in Network Monitor you select Start in the Capture menu (or press F10 or click the Start Capture button on the toolbar). When frames are being captured, you see new data registered in the panes of the Capture window. To stop the capture, you select Stop in the Capture menu (or press F11 or click the Stop Capture button on the toolbar).

To view a capture, you select Display Captured Data from the Capture menu (or press F12 or click the Display Captured Data button on the toolbar). You can also stop and view the data in a single step by selecting Stop And View in the Capture menu.

Analyzing Captured Data

You can use Network Monitor to find out certain details about the host computer, such as the media access control address of a network interface card, the GUID of a client computer, or the port used by a protocol. However, typically you want to carry out a more detailed analysis. When you view a capture, the Frame Viewer window appears, displaying the summary pane. The summary pane displays all the captured frames in sequence, as shown in Figure 9-37.

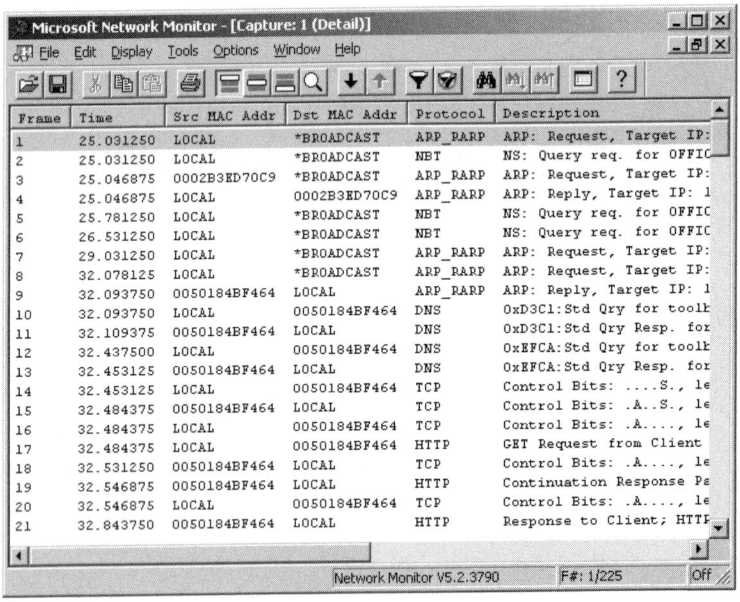

Figure 9-37   Summary pane of the Frame Viewer window

You can toggle between the original summary pane view and the three-pane view by double-clicking any frame in the summary pane. The three-pane view includes the summary pane, the details pane, and the hexadecimal (hex) pane. Figure 9-38 shows the three-pane view of the Frame Viewer window.

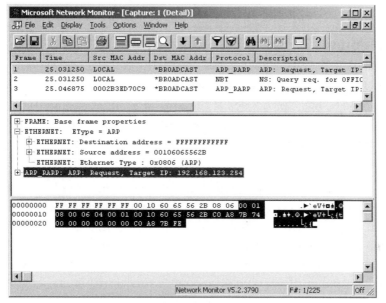

Figure 9-38   Three panes of the Frame Viewer window

Figure 9-38 shows a Network Monitor capture that records broadcast frames that use ARP and NetBIOS over TCP/IP. The summary pane lists all frames that are included in the current view of the captured data. When a frame is highlighted in the summary pane, Network Monitor displays the frame's contents in the details pane and hex pane.

The details pane displays protocol information for the frame currently highlighted in the summary pane. When a frame contains several protocol layers, the details pane displays the outermost level first. When you select a protocol in the details pane, the associated hexadecimal strings are highlighted in the hex pane.

The hex pane displays the content of the selected frame in hexadecimal format. When information is selected in the details pane, the corresponding hexadecimal data appears highlighted in the hex pane. This area can be useful, for example, to developers who need to determine precise information about a network application protocol.

You can set up a display filter that displays, for example, only frames that use the TCP protocol, or you can set up a capture filter that captures, for example, only frames from a specified source address. You can use parsers to read, analyze, and describe the contents of frames. Network Monitor includes more than 20 parsers that are responsible for parsing over 90 protocols. If this is not sufficient, you can write your own parsers. However, a detailed description of data analysis is beyond the scope of this chapter.

Network Monitor 3

Currently, Network Monitor 3 is available online, and Network Monitor 2 ships with Windows operating systems. This situation might change by the time you read this book. The basic principles of the tool have not altered in the new version—it still captures and displays frames. However, the Capture window has a pane that shows the capture filters in addition to the frame summary, frame details, and the Hex details.

Network Monitor 3 lets you can see the frames in real time while capturing data and permits simultaneous capture on multiple network adapters and multiple simultaneous capture sessions. It provides a tree view that displays frames by network conversation. A command-line version, nmcap.exe, lets you stat network captures when a specific event occurs, and the tool provides a new filtering panel with the capability to manually customize predefined filters, a new script-based protocol parser language, and script-based parsers.

The 70-236 examination is unlikely to ask questions based on this version of Network Monitor but you should be aware that it exists. Because the tool is currently in its development cycle, links to information on the Internet are at best transient, but you should be able to obtain the latest information by searching for "Network Monitor 3."

Using Exchange Troubleshooting Assistant

Exchange Troubleshooting Assistant is unlikely to be installed during an Exchange Server 2007 installation. It requires that you first install .NET Framework 1.1 (even though .NET Framework 2.0 is already installed as part of the preparation for Exchange Server 2007 installation). After you install the tool, you can access its component parts by clicking Toolbox in Exchange Management Console, selecting the tool, and clicking Open Tool in the Actions pane. Figure 9-39 shows the Exchange Troubleshooting Assistant tools.

Figure 9-39 The Exchange Troubleshooting Assistant tools

You can access the following Exchange Troubleshooting Assistant tools through Exchange Management Console:

- Database Recovery Management
- Database Troubleshooter
- Mail Flow Troubleshooter
- Message Tracking
- Performance Troubleshooter

NOTE **Database tools ship with Exchange Server 2007**

Database Recovery Management and Database Troubleshooter are Exchange Troubleshooting Assistant tools, but they also ship with Exchange Server 2007. Therefore, you do not need to install Exchange Troubleshooting Assistant to use these tools. However, if you want to use Mail Flow Troubleshooter, Message Tracking, or Performance Troubleshooter, you need to install Exchange Troubleshooting Assistant.

Best Practices Analyzer

The Best Practices Analyzer is not an Exchange Troubleshooting Assistant tool, but it has a very similar interface and mode of operation to these tools. The Best Practices Analyzer can examine a single Exchange 2007 server, a group of selected servers, or all servers in an organization. It gathers and verifies configuration information from Active Directory, WMI, the registry, and the metabase and lists any issues it discovers in order of severity with descriptions of the problem and how you can fix it.

When you open the Best Practices Analyzer, it scans for updates and gives you the option of uploading and installing any updates it detects. On the Welcome page, you can either view an existing scan or start a new scan. If you choose the latter option, you are asked to specify the Active Directory server. You then specify the type of scan to perform and give the scan a name, as shown in Figure 9-40.

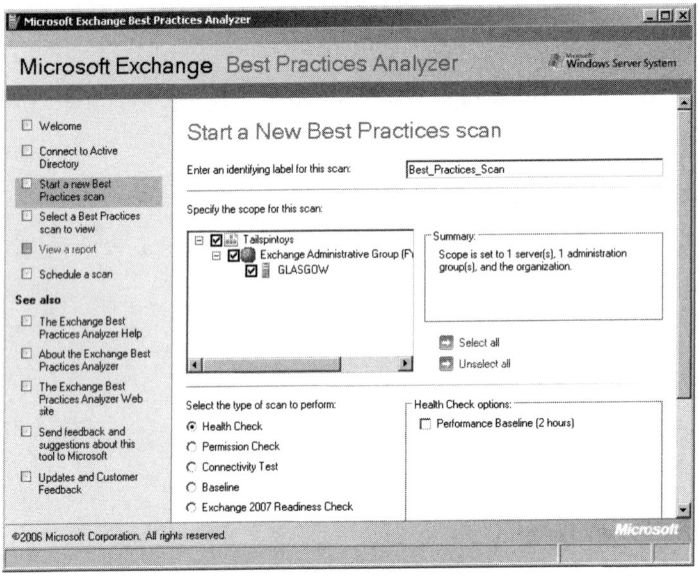

Figure 9-40   Specifying a Best Practices Analyzer scan

You can choose to start scanning immediately or schedule a scan. The tool can take a few minutes to complete a scan. When the scan completes, you can view a report.

Installing and Starting Exchange Troubleshooting Assistant

To install the Exchange Troubleshooting Assistant, you first need to download and run the .NET Framework 1.1 installation file dotnetfx.exe on the computer where you want run the tool. You then run the Exchange Troubleshooting Assistant installation file ExTRA.msi on the same computer. To find the files, access *http://www. microsoft.com/ downloads/* and search for the relevant software package. You can perform the installation on the server that the tool will be analyzing or on another computer, for example, a dedicated management station. Some functionality might be disabled if you run the tool remotely. You install Exchange Troubleshooting Assistant in the practice session later in this lesson.

Microsoft recommends that you install the Exchange Troubleshooting Assistant on a client computer or server that is running a U.S. English version of the Microsoft Windows operating system. If you want to install the tool on a computer that is outside your Exchange Server 2007 organization, you need to explicitly set the user names and passwords for logging on to the Active Directory directory service and your Exchange Server 2007 servers.

When you open the Exchange Troubleshooting Assistant for the first time (by opening any one of the tools), you are given the option of joining the Microsoft product improvement program. You are recommended to do so. The tool then searches for any updates to the Exchange Troubleshooting Assistant and gives you the option of downloading and installing any updates it detects. The Welcome screen of the chosen tool then opens.

Quick Check
- What are the four panes in the Network Monitor 2 Capture window?

Quick Check Answer
- Graph, Session Statistics, Station Statistics, and Total Statistics.

Using Performance Troubleshooter

The Performance Troubleshooter tool in Exchange Troubleshooting Assistant locates and identifies performance-related issues that could affect Exchange Server 2007 servers. It examines various settings and logs and collects data from a variety of different sources to produce recommended remedial advice. Some of the data, such as the symptom, requires user input. Other data is collected automatically. As the first step in the analysis process, you label the analysis and select a symptom, as shown in Figure 9-41.

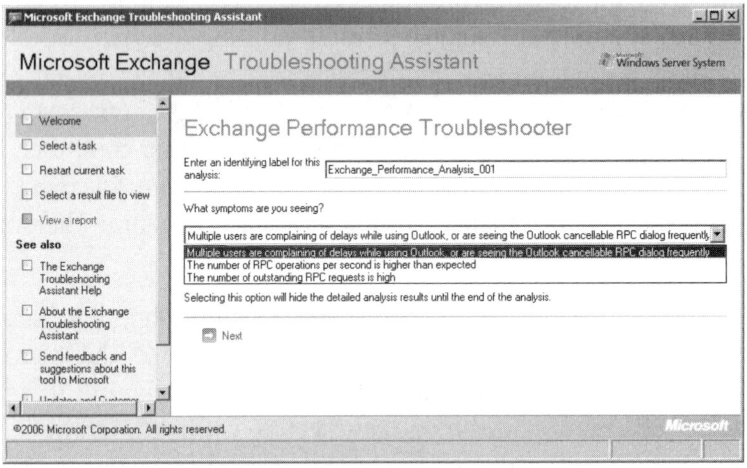

Figure 9-41   Specifying a Performance Troubleshooting symptom

The steps the tool takes depend on the symptom you specify. It can collect data from several sources, for example, the Active Directory directory service, WMI, and the registry. The tool can also capture live data to isolate the root cause of performance issues. The following data repositories are used to sample real-time data:

■ Performance Data Helper library

■ Trace data from the Microsoft Exchange Server User Monitor Tool

When the tool collects real-time data, it samples counters and logs over a period of time. This kind of collection can take several minutes (typically five minutes) to complete.

Performance Troubleshooter produces a report that displays the results of the data that the tool gathered during analysis of the server. You can select list reports, tree reports, and other reports (for example, the run-time log).

Using Mail Flow Troubleshooter

Mail Flow Troubleshooter is a diagnostic tool that asks you to input the symptoms of a mail flow problem and moves you through the correct troubleshooting path. The tool provides access to various data sources that are required to troubleshoot problems with mail flow, automatically diagnoses the retrieved data, and presents an analysis of the possible root causes of the problem. It suggests corrective actions and provides guidance to help you manually diagnose the data when automation is not possible. Figure 9-42 shows the choice of symptoms in Mail Flow Troubleshooter.

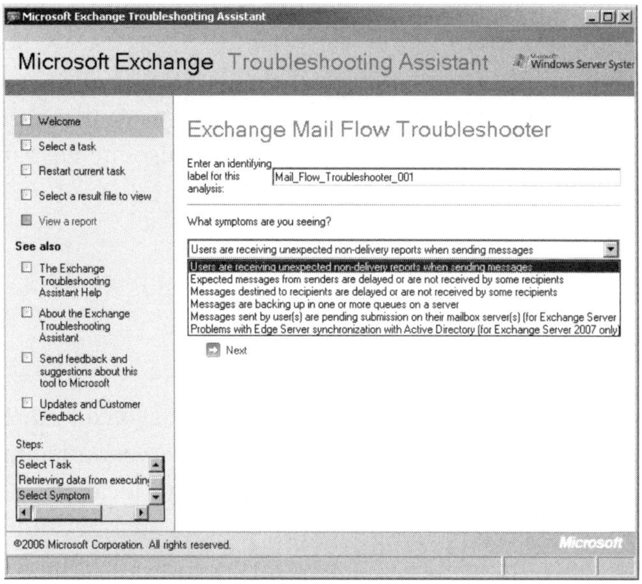

Figure 9-42 Specifying a Mail Flow Troubleshooter symptom

You need to specify the Exchange Server 2007 server and the global catalog server. The tool provides you with basic server information (for example, the Exchange Server roles that it finds). You specify a delivery status notification code (for example, 4.4.7) that you identify from NDRs your users have received. The tool scans the tracking log for the delivery status notification code and generates delivery status notification analysis results.

You can print or export the collected data. Supported export formats include XML, HTML, and CSV. Mail Flow Troubleshooter produces a report that displays the results of the data that the tool gathered during analysis of the server. You can select list reports, tree reports, and other reports. More information about reports is given in Chapter 11, "Reporting."

Using Database Recovery Management

The Database Recovery Management tool can search Exchange Server 2007 databases and available transaction log files for issues that affect database recoverability. The tool reports missing or corrupted log files and recommends steps that you can take to bring the database to a clean, mountable state. It includes a troubleshooter that detects problems with mounting databases caused by conditions that prevent successful transaction log replay and a wizard to safely move excess transaction log files and resolve "log drive full" conditions.

The tool also provides an event log filter and viewer that lets you easily view and sort events related to Exchange databases and a recovery storage group manager that can create and remove recovery storage groups. The manager can also merge mailbox contents back to original or archival mailboxes.

MORE INFO   Recovery storage groups

For more information about recovery storage groups and database recovery management, refer to Chapter 12, "Configuring Disaster Recovery."

Database Recovery Management can access the Microsoft Active Directory directory service configuration information for an Exchange Server 2007 server and automatically locate database and transaction log files in the configured path locations. When you have specified an identifying label, the server that you want to analyze, and a domain controller, the tool implements the Task Center, where you select the symptom or task that you want to address. The following functions are available in the Task Center:

- Analyze log drive space
- Repair database
- Show database-related event logs
- Verify database and transaction log files
- Create a recovery storage group
- Go to Results page

NOTE   Recovery storage group management

Exchange Management Console does not include recovery storage group management features in its primary interface. Instead, you can perform recovery storage group management from the Exchange Management Shell or from the Database Recovery Management Task Center.

Figure 9-43 shows the Task Center. Depending on the task you select, you are prompted to, for example, select a storage group and a dismounted database, or you might be asked to select a storage group into which transaction log files can be moved. When you have provided the information, the tool requires it to perform the selected task.

Figure 9-43 The Database Recovery Management Task Center

Using the Message Tracking Tool

The Message Tracking tool allows you to track e-mail messages by specifying criteria listed on the tool's Message Tracking Parameters page, shown in Figure 9-44. You use this tool in the practice session later in this lesson.

MORE INFO Using PowerShell to track messages

You can also track messages by using PowerShell commands based on the *Get-MessageTrackingLog* cmdlet. For more information, refer to Chapter 10, "Message Tracking and Mailbox Health"; search Exchange Server 2007 Help for "Get-MessageTrackingLog"; or access *http://technet.microsoft.com/en-us/library/aa997573.aspx*.

Viewing an Existing Report

You can use any of the Exchange Troubleshooting Assistant tools to view a report from a previous analysis by opening the tool and selecting the Select A Result File To View on the Welcome page. You can then select the report that you want to view from the list of locally stored reports and click View Result. You can also choose to click Export Results, Delete File, or Enter An Identifying Label. Chapter 11 discusses Exchange Troubleshooting Assistant reports in more depth.

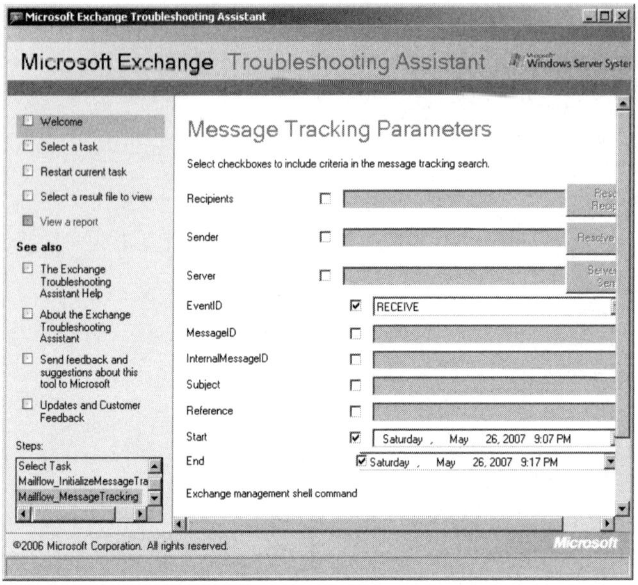

Figure 9-44 The Message Tracking Parameters page

Practice: Installing Exchange Troubleshooting Assistant and Using the Message Tracking Tool

In this practice session, you install the Exchange Troubleshooting Assistant. You then generate e-mail messages between two users and use the Message Tracking tool to track these messages. You require Internet connectivity to carry out the practices in this practice session.

In the practice session in Lesson 1, users Don Hall and Keith Harris logged on to the domain. If you do not have a client computer on your test network, then you need to put these users in the Server Operators or Account Operators security group on the domain controller to let the users log on locally at the domain controller. If you did not do this in Lesson 1, you need to do it before attempting the practices in this practice session.

▶ **Practice 1: Installing Exchange Troubleshooting Assistant**

In this practice, you install Exchange Troubleshooting Assistant on your Exchange Server 2007 server. Before you can do this, you first need to install .NET Framework 1.1. Note that if you already have Net Framework 1.1 and Exchange Troubleshooting Assistant installed on your computer you do not need to carry out this practice and will get an error message if you attempt to do so.

1. Log on to the Exchange Server 2007 server by using the Kim_Akers account.

2. Open Internet Explorer and browse to *http://www.microsoft.com/downloads.*

3. Search All Downloads for ".NET Framework 1.1."

4. Click .NET Framework Version 1.1 Redistributable Package.

5. This accesses the download page for the file dotnetfx.exe. Click Download.

6. Click Run to run the file when downloaded. If you prefer, you can click Save to save it to a convenient location and run it later.

7. Follow the steps of the Installation Wizard to install the software. You might need to make changes to Internet Information Server as specified when the software installs.

8. Browse to *http://www.microsoft.com/downloads.*

9. Search All Downloads for "Exchange Troubleshooting Assistant."

10. Click Exchange Troubleshooting Assistant.

11. This accesses the download page for the file ExTRA.MSI. Click Download.

12. Click Run to run the file when downloaded. If you prefer, you can click Save to save it to a convenient location and run it later. You need to do the latter if you have not yet installed .NET Framework 1.1.

13. Install Exchange Troubleshooting Assistant.

▶ **Practice 2: Sending and Replying to Messages**

In this practice, you send messages as Don Hall and reply to them as Keith Harris. In the next practice, you trace the messages by using the Exchange Troubleshooting Assistant Message Tracking tool. You need to have created the mailbox-enabled users Don Hall and Keith Harris before you carry out this practice. You created these users in Chapter 5, "Moving Mailboxes and Implementing Bulk Management." If you have created other mailbox-enabled user accounts, you can use them instead.

1. Log on to the domain as Don.Hall.

2. Open Microsoft Outlook and send a message to Keith Harris with the subject "Lunch tomorrow." If you prefer, you can use OWA or Outlook Express to send e-mail messages.

3. Send a message to Keith Harris with the subject "Invite Kim Akers."

4. Log on to the domain as Keith Harris.

5. Open Microsoft Outlook (or OWA or Outlook Express) and reply to both messages.

▶ **Practice 3: Tracking Messages**

In this practice, you track messages from Don Hall and Keith Harris. You need to have completed Practices 1 and 2 in this lesson before attempting Practice 3.

1. If necessary, log on to the Exchange Server 2007 server by using the Kim_Akers account.

2. Open Exchange Management Console.

3. Select Toolbox in the Console pane. In the Result pane, click Message Tracking. In the Action pane, click Open Tool.

4. If you are prompted, specify whether you want to take part in the Microsoft product improvement program. Start the tool.

5. If prompted, download and install updates to Exchange Troubleshooting Assistant. Access the Welcome screen.

6. Select the Recipients and Sender check boxes. Specify Keith Harris as the Recipient and Don Hall as the Sender.

7. Click Resolve Recipient.

8. Click Resolve Sender. Your screen should look similar to Figure 9-45. Note that the Start and End check boxes should be deselected, as shown in the figure. Deselect them if they are not.

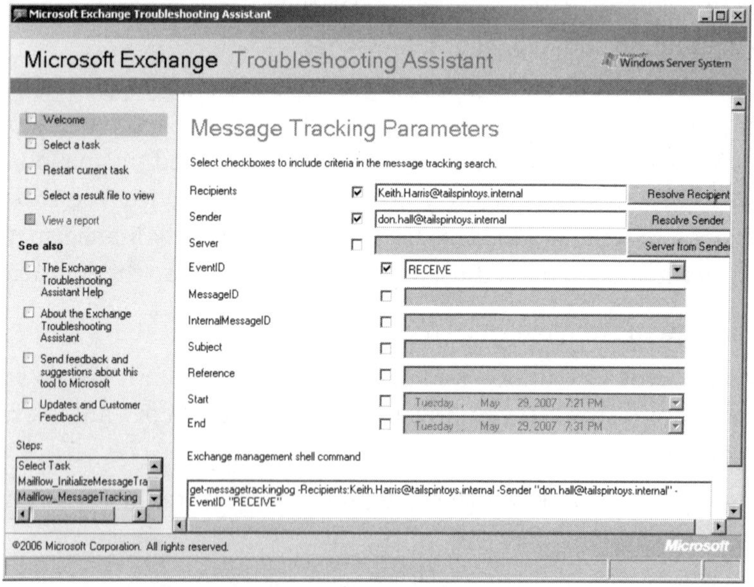

Figure 9-45   Specifying messages by sender and recipient

9. Click Next. The tool finds the messages. Your screen should look similar to Figure 9-46.

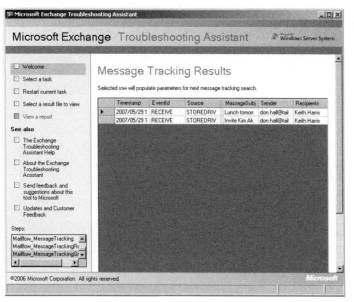

Figure 9-46   Messages from Don Hall to Keith Harris

10. Click Go Back to return to the Message Tracking Parameters page.

11. Deselect the Recipients and Sender check boxes. Select the Subject check box and specify Kim Akers, as shown in Figure 9-47.

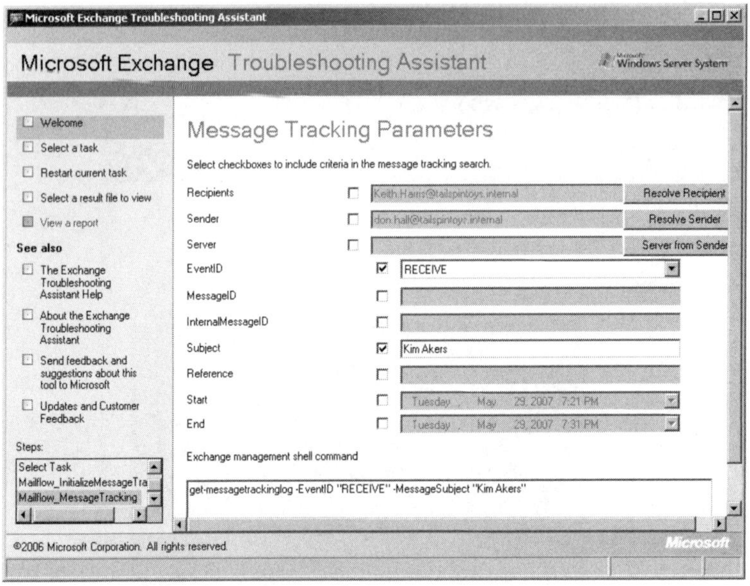

Figure 9-47   Specifying Kim Akers in the Subject box

12. Click Next. All messages with Kim Akers in the subject line are listed, as shown in Figure 9-48.

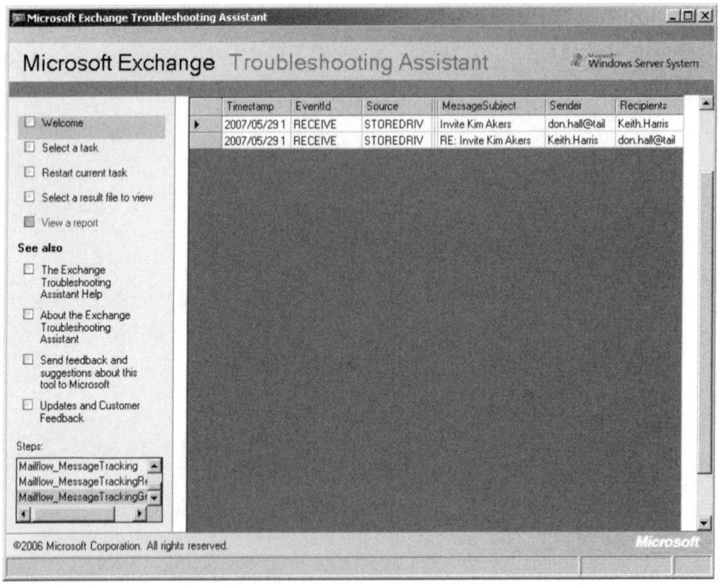

Figure 9-48   Messages with Kim Akers in the subject line

Lesson Summary

- Troubleshooting wizards are available to help diagnose hardware failure and problems with device drivers.

- You can use performance counters to measure stress on server resources and particularly to the four main subsystems: processor, memory, disk, and network. You can configure an alert to trigger when a counter value exceeds or falls below a specified threshold.

- You can use Event Viewer to monitor event logs. You can also monitor event logs by using PowerShell commands and scripts.

- You can use Network Monitor to view network traffic on your servers and HTTP-Mon to monitor OWA servers.

- Exchange Troubleshooting Assistant tools include Database Recovery Management, Database Troubleshooter, Mail Flow Troubleshooter, Message Tracking, and Performance Troubleshooter.

Lesson Review

You can use the following questions to test your knowledge of the information in Lesson 2, "Monitoring System Performance." The questions are also available on the companion CD if you prefer to review them in electronic form.

NOTE Answers

Answers to these questions and explanations of why each answer choice is correct or incorrect are located in the "Answers" section at the end of the book.

---

1. You configure an alert to trigger if the Pages/Sec counter value is 25 or greater. To which event log does the alert write an event if it is triggered?

    A. System

    B. Security

    C. Application

    D. Directory service

2. One of your colleagues has read that the value in the % Processor Time counter should not exceed 85 percent. She has therefore configured an alert to trigger when the counter reaches or exceeds that value. The alert triggers frequently. What conclusion should you draw?

    A. Your colleague has not understood processor usage.

    B. Your colleague has not set up the counter correctly.

    C. You need to install a faster processor.

    D. You need to install another processor to enable multiprocessing.

3. Which event log does not store error events?

    A. Application

    B. Directory service

    C. Security

    D. System

4. You want to analyze traffic on a specific network interface on your Exchange Server 2007 server. In particular, you want to view frames that use the RPC protocol. What tool do you use?

    A. HTTPMon

    B. Performance Logs and Alerts

    C. System Monitor

    D. Network Monitor

5. While monitoring your network, you find that the number of RPC operations per second is higher than expected. What tool can you use to analyze this problem?

    A. Mail Flow Troubleshooter

    B. Performance Troubleshooter

    C. Best Practices Analyzer

    D. Database Recovery Management

6. You want to list all events with a specified EventID in the application log. You save the following code as a PowerShell script ListEvent.ps1 in the ExScripts subdirectory. What can you enter in Exchange Management Shell to list all events with an EventID 1022?

```
Param (
[string] $ID
)
Get-Eventlog Application | where {$_.EventID -eq $ID}
```

    A. ListEvent.ps1 ID "1022"

    B. ListEvent.ps1 –ID "1022"

    C. ListEvent.ps1

    D. ListEvent.ps1–Log "System" –ID "1022"

Chapter Review

To further practice and reinforce the skills you learned in this chapter, you can perform the following tasks:

- Review the chapter summary.
- Review the list of key terms introduced in this chapter.
- Complete the case scenarios. These scenarios set up real-world situations involving the topics of this chapter and ask you to create a solution.
- Complete the suggested practices.
- Take a practice test.

Chapter Summary

- Exchange Server 2007 provides Queue Viewer and Exchange Management Shell to enable you to monitor and manage queues and the messages in these queues.
- Exchange Server Performance Monitor can determine the rates at which messages are received or sent and the lengths of queues. You can configure an alert that informs you if a counter value exceeds or falls below a specified threshold. You can also use performance counters to measure stress on server resources and particularly to the four main subsystems: processor, memory, disk, and network.
- You can use Event Viewer and PowerShell commands and scripts monitor event logs. Network Monitor monitors network traffic and HTTP Monitor monitors OWA servers.
- Exchange Troubleshooting Assistant tools let you analyze reports; track messages; and troubleshoot Exchange databases, mail flow, and performance.

Key Terms

Do you know what these key terms mean? You can check your answers by looking up the terms in the glossary at the end of the book.

- Baseline
- Categorizer
- Message queue
- Retry

- Spam
- Spam confidence level (SCL)
- Threshold

Case Scenarios

In the following case scenarios, you will apply what you have learned about monitoring. You can find answers to these questions in the "Answers" section at the end of this book.

Case Scenario 1: Checking Message Queues

You administer the Exchange Server 2007 organization at Marge's Travel. Sometimes delivery delays can occur, particularly with outgoing e-mail to other organizations. The company is also concerned with incoming malicious e-mail messages that might damage its e-mail organization and security filtering is in place. Answer the following questions:

1. Messages to the Contoso domain (@contoso.com) are taking a long time to be delivered. You want to determine whether the problem is in your organization or at Contoso. Which queue should you inspect?

2. You want to view messages that have been identified as possibly malicious. You can then delete these messages or resume delivery if you judge them to be harmless. In which queue will you find these messages?

3. You want to delete all queued messages with an SCL of 5 or greater. What command do you enter in Exchange Management Shell?

Case Scenario 2: Monitoring Exchange Server 2007 Servers

You are a senior Exchange administrator at the Adatum Corporation. Don Hall and Keith Harris report to you. Both are inexperienced in Exchange Server 2007, although Don has some Exchange Server 2003 experience. It is part of your job to advise and train them. Answer the following questions:

1. Keith wants to track messages. He opens Exchange Management Console, clicks Toolbox, selects Message Tracking in the Result pane, and clicks Open Tool in the Action pane. However, he cannot get the tool to work. What do you advise?

2. Don wants to create a recovery storage group. He opens Exchange Management Console but cannot find a recovery storage group management tool. What do you tell him?

3. The Performance Alerts tool notifies Keith that network traffic on an Exchange Server 2007 server is at an unacceptable level. He wants to find out what network frames are causing the problem and the protocols they are using. What tool should he use?

Suggested Practices

To help you successfully master the exam objectives presented in this chapter, complete the following tasks.

Monitor Mail Queues

Do Practices 1 through 3 in this section. Practice 4 is optional.

- **Practice 1: Set Up Filters**   Both Queue Viewer and Exchange Management Shell commands let you specify filters with multiple criteria. In the production environment, where you will likely have many messages in many queues, you will need powerful and versatile filtering facilities. Investigate message filtering until you are confident about setting up complex filters.

- **Practice 2: Investigate the PowerShell Cmdlets**   You enter commands in Exchange Management Shell based on the PowerShell cmdlets for managing messages and queues. Investigate the parameters that these cmdlets support and the syntax of the associated commands. Look at creating PowerShell scripts to carry out tasks that you perform frequently.

- **Practice 3: Investigate the Effects of Spam Filtering**   You were asked to disable spam filtering before attempting the practice session in Lesson 1. Enable spam filtering and attempt the practices again, noting what effect filtering has on the results.

- **Practice 4: Install and Use MOM**   The full version of MOM requires .NET Framework 1.1 and Windows SQL Server 2000 or 2005 to be installed. However, if you have an Exchange Server 2007 server with the Edge Transport role installed on your test network, you can install the client computer version of MOM without the SQL Server requirement (you still need .NET Framework 1.1). In this case, install MOM and investigate its use.

Monitor System Performance

Do all the practices in this section.

- **Practice 1: Install and Use Network Monitor**   If you have not already installed Network Monitor on your Exchange Server 2007 server, do so. Set up capture and view filters and investigate the use of this powerful tool.

- **Practice 2: Investigate the Exchange Troubleshooting Assistant Tools**   You installed Exchange Troubleshooting Assistant in the practice session in Lesson 2. Use the tools included in this software and investigate their features. Where a tool works by generating a PowerShell command, take a note of the command and search for the associated cmdlet in the Exchange Server 2007 Help files.

- **Practice 3: Use PowerShell Scripts**   PowerShell is an exceptionally powerful scripting language. Follow the For Information links in this chapter to find out more about PowerShell scripts and how they can be used to automate monitoring tasks.

Take a Practice Test

The practice tests on this book's companion CD offer many options. For example, you can test yourself on just one exam objective, or you can test yourself on all the 70-236 certification exam content. You can set up the test so that it closely simulates the experience of taking a certification exam, or you can set it up in study mode so that you can look at the correct answers and explanations after you answer each question.

MORE INFO   **Practice tests**

For details about all the practice test options available, see the "How to Use the Practice Tests" section in this book's Introduction.

Chapter 10

Message Tracking and Mailbox Health

As an Exchange administrator, you will be asked to track e-mail messages through your Exchange organization. You might be asked why a message sent by a user was not delivered or why an expected message was not received. You might be asked why a message was delayed.

Users expect to be able to connect to their mailboxes instantaneously without error messages or warnings. They expect to be able to send and receive messages without encountering problems. Typically, a user requires the e-mail system to be available 24 hours per day, seven days per week, every day of the year, and even the shortest outage or briefest delay will result in complaints.

It is your job to meet these expectations. You need to monitor the health of mailboxes by gathering and analyzing mailbox and performance statistics. You need to respond quickly to connection problems. You need to monitor by protocol and ensure that messages are being sent successfully by Simple Mail Transfer Protocol (SMTP) and are being received by Post Office Protocol version 3 (POP3) and Internet Message Access Protocol version 4 (IMAP4) revision 1 clients.

A good administrator solves problems before they occur and certainly before they become apparent to the user. An Exchange administrator needs to be good. This chapter discusses the tools you use to track messages and monitor the health of mailboxes.

Exam objectives in this chapter:
- Perform message tracking.
- Monitor client connectivity.

Lessons in this chapter:

Before You Begin

To complete the lessons in this chapter, you must have done the following:

- Installed Windows Exchange Server 2007 with the Mailbox, Client Access, Hub Transport, and Unified Messaging roles on a Windows domain controller in the Tailspintoys.internal domain. To do this, you need to have completed all the practices in Lessons 1 and 2 of Chapter 1, "Preparing for Exchange Installation," and Lesson 1 of Chapter 2, "Installing Exchange Server and Configuring Roles."

- Created mailbox-enabled users Don Hall and Keith Harris as described in Chapter 3, "Configuring Recipients, Groups, and Mailboxes." If you have not created these users but have created other mailbox-enabled users, you can use their accounts instead. However, if you use other accounts, you need to change the search criteria in the practice sessions as appropriate.

- Preferably configured a client machine running either Microsoft Outlook 2007 or Microsoft Outlook 2003–or Outlook Express or Outlook Web Access (OWA)–on your network. Failing this, you should have two users that can log on locally to your domain controller. (The practice sessions specify Don Hall and Keith Harris, but again, if you prefer, you can use other user accounts you have created.)

- Installed .NET Framework 1.1 and Exchange Troubleshooting Assistant on your Exchange Server 2007 server as described in the practice session of Lesson 2 in Chapter 9, "Monitoring."

Real World

Ian McLean

I once had a slow-delivery complaint that I solved very easily indeed. However, the follow-up was, to say the least, instructive. A senior manager had sent an e-mail to his daughter, arranging to telephone her at 7:00 PM that evening. He sent the e-mail from his office desk in the United Kingdom at 3:00 PM.

"She told me it did not arrive until she was in bed asleep," he said, "and she did not read it until the next morning." He wanted me to check the office e-mail system for excessive delays. I had only recently checked message queues and mailbox health and was confident the delay was not at my end, but I told him I would track the message. I asked him for the recipient e-mail address or, failing that, the message subject.

"I happen to have the e-mail address written down," he said. "She moved recently, and she sent it to me." I looked at the address and noticed it ended in .au. Problem solved. I reminded him about time differences. He looked a bit embarrassed and admitted that the Earth's rotation was not really the responsibility of technical support. To be fair, I think he knew about the time difference between the United Kingdom and Australia, but his daughter's family had only recently emigrated, and it had slipped his mind.

Then he paused. "You said 'subject,'" he remarked. "You can see the subjects of my e-mails?" I told him that I could track e-mail messages by a number of criteria including the subject line. "I do not want anyone seeing the subjects of my e-mails," he snapped. "Disable this immediately."

Pausing only to wonder exactly what he was putting in what was supposed to be company e-mail, I explained that written company policy stated that message subject logging should be enabled and that I could not disable it just for him. I'd need to disable it for everyone, and that required a policy change. Fortunately, I was able to identify and quote from the relevant document. The ramifications rumbled on for months, but message subject logging was not disabled.

The moral of this story is, for your own protection, know exactly what your organization's policy is for matters as sensitive as message subject logging. And know where to find the document that states that policy.

Lesson 1: Performing Message Tracking

Chapter 9 "Monitoring," introduced the Exchange Troubleshooting Assistant Message Tracking tool and the PowerShell *Get-MessageTrackingLog* cmdlet. Both the Message Tracking tool and the cmdlet access message tracking logs.

A message tracking log records message activity when messages are transferred to and from a Microsoft Exchange Server 2007 server that has the Hub Transport server role, the Mailbox server role, or the Edge Transport server role installed. You can use message tracking logs to diagnose message flow problems and generate and analyze reports about mail flow analysis.

NOTE   Client Access server role or Unified Messaging server role

Exchange servers that have the Client Access server role or Unified Messaging server role installed do not have message tracking logs unless they also have the Hub Transport server role installed.

> **After this lesson, you will be able to:**
> - Configure message tracking.
> - Read and interpret the message tracking log.
>
> **Estimated lesson time: 45 minutes**

Tracking Messages

You can track messages in the message tracking log by using the Message Tracker tool or commands based on the PowerShell *Get-MessageTrackingLog* cmdlet. You can configure a set of criteria that specify the messages you want to track. You can track messages on specific Hub Transport or Edge Transport servers where you suspect problems might be occurring or on all servers with these roles installed. You can track messages by sender or recipient on the appropriate mailbox server. You can track messages by logging on to the server you want to monitor (typically through remote desktop) or by logging on to an administrative client with the appropriate tools and specifying the Exchange Server 2007 server.

To track messages on an Exchange Server 2007 server that has the Mailbox server role or Hub Transport server role installed, you need to log on by using a domain account that is assigned to the Exchange Server Administrator role. The account must also be a member of the local Administrators group on that computer.

To track messages on an Exchange Server 2007 server that has the Edge Transport server role installed, you need to log on by using an account that is a member of the local Administrators group on that computer. You can do this by providing credentials from a client computer or by logging on directly at the server.

Tracking Messages by Using Message Tracker

As you saw in Chapter 9, you can use the Message Tracking tool to track messages. Message Tracking is an Exchange Troubleshooting Assistant tool, and you need to install .NET Framework 1.1 and Exchange Troubleshooting Assistant before you use it. You access the tool by clicking Toolbox in Exchange Management Console, selecting Message Tracking in the Result pane, and clicking Open Tool in the Action pane. Figure 10-1 shows the Message Tracking Parameters dialog box in the Message Tracking tool.

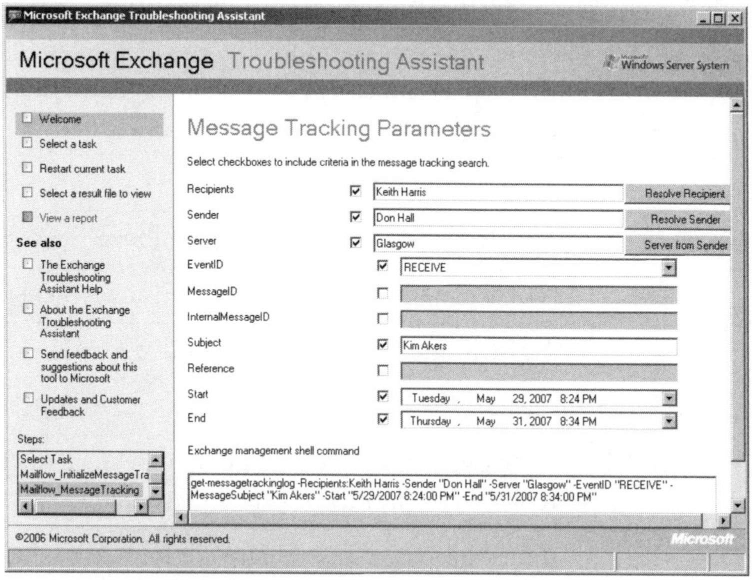

Figure 10-1   The Message Tracking Parameters dialog box

You then select the criteria for your message tracking log search. You can select any of the following search criteria by selecting the check box next to the search criterion name and entering an exact value, a partial value, or a value with embedded wildcard characters (*) in the text box next to the search criterion:

- **Recipients**   This search filter uses the recipient-address field. Multiple individual recipients that are included in a single message are logged by using a single message tracking log entry. Unexpanded distribution group recipients are logged by using the distribution group's SMTP e-mail address. Multiple recipient values can be specified by using commas as delimiters.

- **Sender**   The sender field contains the sender's e-mail address as specified in the Sender header field or in the From header field if Sender is not present.

- **Server**   The name of the Mailbox server on which the sender's mailbox resides.

- **EventID**   The event classification that is assigned to each message tracking log entry. The available values are BADMAIL, DELIVER, DEFER, DSN, EXPAND, FAIL, POISONMESSAGE, RECEIVE, REDIRECT, RESOLVE, SEND, SUBMIT, and TRANSFER. Table 10-1 describes each of these classifications.

Table 10-1   Event Classifications

Event Name	Description
BADMAIL	A message was submitted by the Pickup directory or the Replay directory that cannot be delivered or returned.
DEFER	Message delivery was delayed.
DELIVER	A message was delivered to a mailbox.
DSN	A delivery status notification (DSN) was generated.
EXPAND	A distribution group was expanded.
FAIL	Message delivery failed.
POISONMESSAGE	A message was put in the poison message queue or removed from the poison message queue.
RECEIVE	A message was received and committed to the database.
REDIRECT	A message was redirected to an alternative recipient after an Active Directory directory service lookup.
RESOLVE	A message's recipient was resolved to a different e-mail address after an Active Directory lookup.
SEND	A message was sent by SMTP to a different server.

Table 10-1 Event Classifications

Event Name	Description
SUBMIT	A message was submitted by an Exchange Server 2007 server that has the Mailbox server role installed to an Exchange Server 2007 server that has the Hub Transport or Edge Transport server role installed. Message tracking logs that are generated by the Mailbox server role contain only SUBMIT events.
TRANSFER	Recipients were moved to a forked message because of content conversion, message recipient limits, or agents.

NOTE Agent

An agent is an Exchange Transport component that extends the processing capabilities of the message transport.

■ **MessageID**   The value of the MessageID header field. If the MessageID header field does not exist or is blank, a unique value is assigned to identify the message. This value is constant for the lifetime of the message.

■ **InternalMessageID**   A message identifier integer that is assigned by the Exchange Server 2007 server that is currently processing the message.

■ **Subject**   The message's subject as specified in the Subject header field.

NOTE Message subject tracking

The tracking of message subjects is controlled by the MessageTrackingLogSubjectLoggingEnabled parameter used with the *Set-TransportServer* cmdlet on Hub Transport servers and Edge Transport servers and with the *Set-MailboxServer* cmdlet on Mailbox servers. By default, message subject logging is enabled. You can disable message subject logging by setting the value of the MessageTrackingLogSubjectLoggingEnabled parameter to $False.

■ **Reference**   Contains additional information for specific types of EventID. For EventID SEND, the Reference field contains the InternetMessageID of any DSN messages. For EventID TRANSFER, the Reference field contains the Internal MessageID of the message that is being forked. For EventID DSN, the Reference field contains the InternetMessageID of the message that caused the DSN. For all other types of EventID, the Reference field is blank.

NOTE **A forked message**

A forked message is a message copy that the categorizer creates for the original message if recipients reside in separate destinations or require different message formats.

- **Start** Uses the date-time field to look for message tracking entries that start with the specified date and time. You can use this filter by itself or with the End parameter to retrieve all message tracking log entries after the specified date-time.

- **End** Uses the date-time field to look for message tracking entries up to but not including the specified End date and time. You can use this filter by itself to retrieve all message tracking log entries before the specified date-time or with the Start parameter.

The Start date-time must be earlier than the End date-time. You can clear the check boxes next to Start or End if you do not want to filter your search by date-time. The date-time field stores information in the Coordinated Universal Time (UTC) format. However, you should enter your date-time search criteria in the regional date-time format of the computer that you are using to perform the search. The message tracking log search tools automatically convert your regional date-time query into the UTC format. The search results are automatically converted from UTC back into your regional data-time format for display.

The date-time field records the date-time of a particular message tracking event. The message origination date-time is the date-time that the message first enters the Exchange organization. The message origination date-time is stored in the message-info field for all SEND and DELIVER events.

If you select the check box next to Sender and enter a partial value in the Sender field, you can populate the rest of the sender's e-mail address by clicking Resolve Sender to resolve the names of mailbox users or mail-enabled contacts that exist in the Exchange 2007 organization. This feature works only on Hub Transport servers, but not on Edge Transport servers because Edge Transport servers do not have access to the recipient information in Active Directory.

If you select the check box next to Recipient and enter a partial value in the Recipient field, you can populate the rest of the recipient's e-mail address by clicking Resolve Recipient to resolve the names of mailbox users or mail-enabled contacts that exist in the Exchange 2007 organization. This feature works only on Hub Transport servers, but not on Edge Transport servers because Edge Transport servers do not have access to the recipient information in Active Directory.

You can automatically populate the Server field with the name of the Mailbox server on which the sender's mailbox resides by clicking Server from Sender. If you want to use that server name as a search criterion, you select the check box next to Server.

When you have specified your search criteria, you click Next to track the messages that meet these criteria.

Quick Check

- On an Exchange Server 2007 server, with which role installed can you click Resolve Recipient to populate the rest of the recipient's e-mail address after you select the check box next to Recipient and enter a partial value in the Recipient field?

Quick Check Answer

- Hub Transport role.

Tracking Messages by Using Exchange Management Shell

You can track messages by entering PowerShell commands based on the *Get-Message-TrackingLog* cmdlet in Exchange Management Shell. The following search parameters are common to both Message Tracker and Exchange Management Shell:

- Recipients
- Sender
- EventID
- MessageID
- InternalMessageID
- MessageSubject
- Reference
- Start
- End

For example, if you want to tack all messages from don.hall@tailspintoys.internal that have an EventID RECEIVE, you would enter the following command in Exchange Management Shell:

```
Get-MessageTrackingLog -EventId "RECEIVE" -Sender "don.hall@tailspintoys.internal"
```

You would typically enter the command on the Mailbox server that hosts Don Hall's mailbox. If you choose to enter the command from another computer, you can use the

Server parameter to specify the Exchange Server 2007 server on which you want the command to run. Figure 10-2 illustrates the command without the Server parameter.

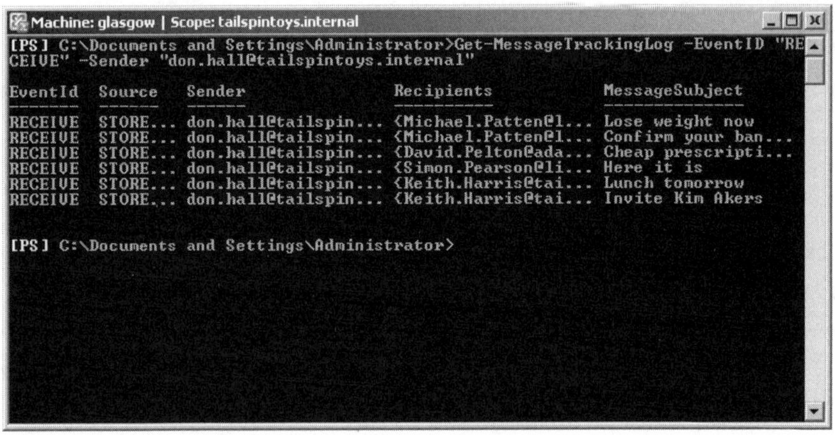

Figure 10-2   Message tracking in Exchange Management Shell

The Message Tracking tool in Exchange Management Console uses the Server search filter. This filters logged messages by comparing the entered value with the server-hostname field in the message tracking log. The *Get-MessageTrackingLog* cmdlet also has a Server parameter, but this is not used to query message tracking log entries by using the server-hostname field. Instead, the *Get-MessageTrackingLog* Server parameter specifies the Exchange 2007 server that holds the message tracking log files that you want to query. This is useful when you open Exchange Management Shell on one computer but want to query the message tracking logs on a different computer.

For example, if you are running Exchange Management Shell on the Exchange Server 2007 server Glasgow and want to track failed messages from Don Hall on the Exchange Server 2007 server Melbourne in the same domain, you can enter the following command:

```
Get-MessageTrackingLog -EventId "FAIL" -Sender
"don.hall@tailspintoys.internal" -Server "Melbourne"
```

The *Get-MessageTrackingLog* cmdlet lets you control the number of search results to display by using the ResultSize parameter. By default, a search displays up to 1,000 results, but you can change this value. Alternatively, you can display all results by using the value of Unlimited. You cannot adjust the maximum number of results displayed by the Message Tracking tool. The following command displays all messages from Don Hall that exist in the tracking logs held on the server on which it is run:

```
Get-MessageTrackingLog -ResultSize Unlimited -Sender "don.hall@tailspintoys.internal"
```

Figure 10-3 illustrates this command.

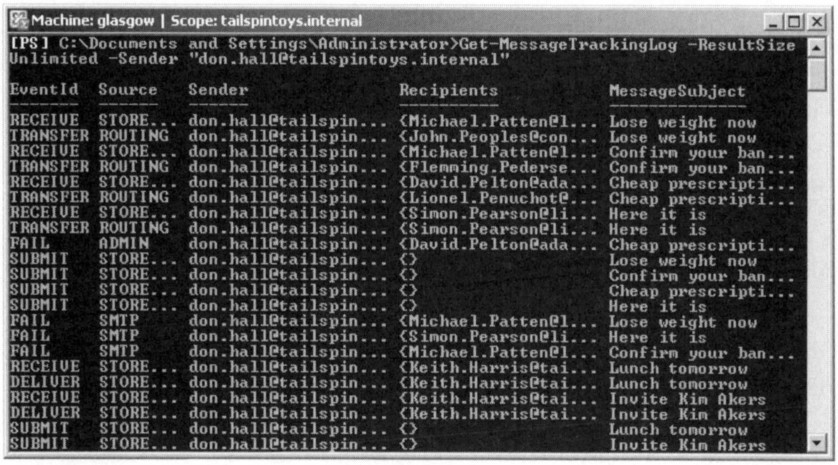

Figure 10-3   All messages from Don Hall

You can specify Start and End parameters in commands based on the *Get-Message-TrackingLog* cmdlet by using the date-time format. For example, the following command searches the message tracking log for all FAIL events from 9:00 AM on May 21, 2007, to 5:00 PM on June 3, 2007:

```
Get-MessageTrackingLog -ResultSize Unlimited -Start "5/21/2007 9:00AM" -End
"6/3/2007 5:00PM" -EventId "FAIL"
```

Figure 10-4 illustrates this command.

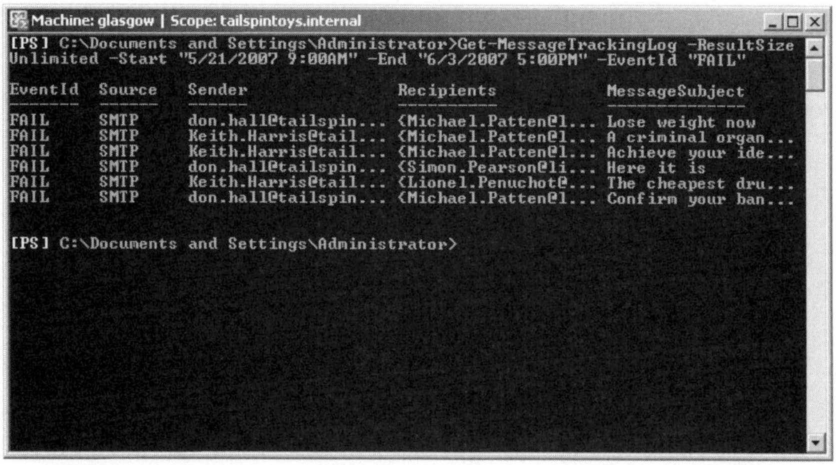

Figure 10-4   All messages between specified dates and times

> **Quick Check**
>
> - Which of the following is not a valid EventID: FAIL, RECEIVE, SEND, SUBMIT, UNDELIVERABLE, POISONMESSAGE?
>
> **Quick Check Answer**
> - UNDELIVERABLE.

Configuring Message Tracking Log Search Output

When you use a command based on the *Get-MessageTrackingLog* cmdlet to perform a message tracking log search, not all the fields are displayed for each message tracking event. By default, the following fields are displayed:

- event-id (search field EventID)
- message-source (search field Source)
- sender-address (search field Sender)
- recipient-address (search field Recipients)
- message-subject (search field MessageSubject)

You can use command output options in Exchange Management Shell to control the output of commands based on the *Get-MessageTrackingLog* cmdlet. You can display the results in a list or in a table, display or hide specific fields that are returned by the search, or send the results of the search to a file.

If the fields you want to display are long and you choose to display them in a table, the values are truncated to fit in the columns of the table. Truncation also occurs if you try to display too many different fields at the same time. The complete field values are always present if you use the list format. For example, the following command lists messages with an EventID FAIL and Sender don.hall@tailspintoys.internal in table format:

```
Get-MessageTrackingLog -EventId "FAIL" -Sender
"don.hall@tailspintoys.internal" | Format-Table
```

Figure 10-5 illustrates this command.

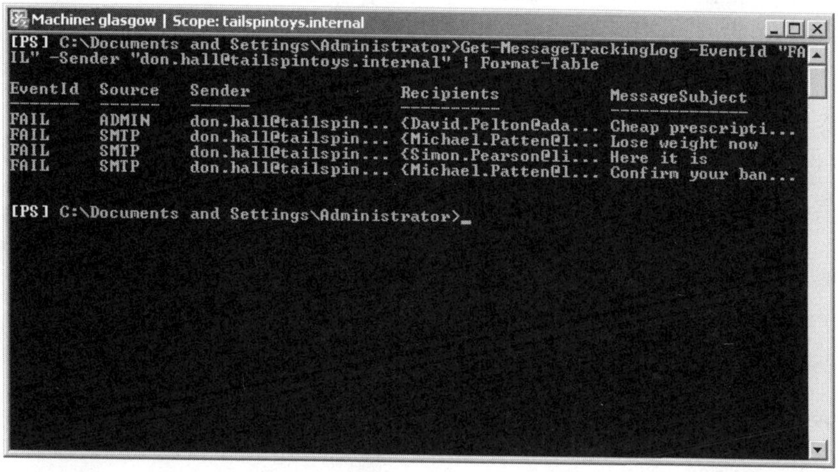

Figure 10-5   Messages in table format

You can compare this format with list format by entering the following command:

```
Get-MessageTrackingLog -EventId "FAIL" -Sender
"don.hall@tailspintoys.internal" | Format-List
```

Figure 10-6 shows a message in list format.

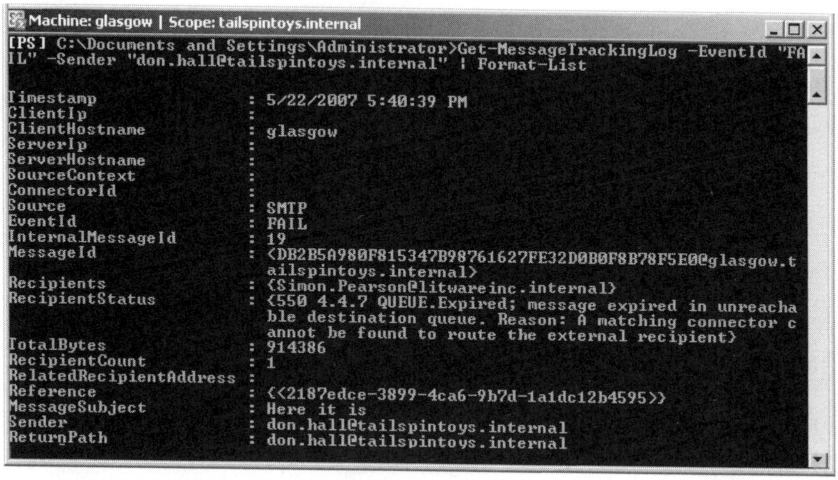

Figure 10-6   A message in list format

You can choose to display a set of field names different to those displayed as default. You specify the fields that you want to display by their search field names rather than by the field name that is used in the message tracking log (for example, Source rather than message-source). The following search field names are available for display:

- Timestamp
- ClientIp
- ClientHostname
- ServerIp
- ServerHostname
- SourceContext
- ConnectorId
- Source
- EventID
- InternalMessageID
- MessageID
- Recipients
- RecipientStatus
- TotalBytes
- RecipientCount
- RelatedRecipientAddress
- Reference
- MessageSubject
- Sender
- ReturnPath
- MessageInfo

You can use wildcards; for example, specifying Client* would display the ClientIp and ClientHostname fields. The following command displays all the events with EventID SEND in list format and shows the Sender, Recipients, RecipientCount, and RecipientStatus fields:

```
Get-MessageTrackingLog -EventId "FAIL" | Format-List Send*,Recipient*
```

Figure 10-7 shows messages with the Sender, Recipients, RecipientCount, and RecipientStatus fields displayed in list format.

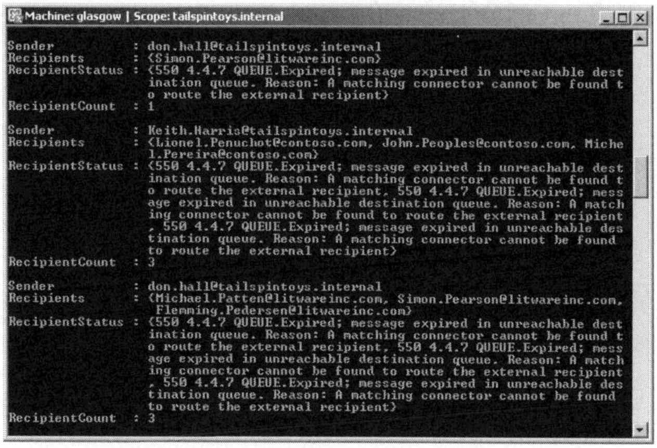

Figure 10-7 Displaying selected fields

You can modify the previous command so that it saves its output to a file C:\LogList.txt by using the following command:

```
Get-MessageTrackingLog -EventId "FAIL" | Format-List Send*,Recipient* > C:\LogList.txt
```

NOTE Creating a folder for PowerShell command output

For simplicity and clarity, the previous example creates a file in the root directory. In a production environment, you would create a folder to hold files generated by the PowerShell commands you enter in Exchange Management Shell and specify a directory path to that folder.

You can display all the events with EventID RECEIVE in table format and show the ServerIp, ServerHostname, and MessageSubject fields by using the following command:

```
Get-MessageTrackingLog -ResultSize Unlimited -EventId "RECEIVE" | Format-List
Server*,MessageSubject
```

Figure 10-8 shows selected message fields in list format.

Configuring Message Tracking

You can enter PowerShell commands in Exchange Management Shell to configure message tracking logs. You cannot carry out this task by using Exchange Management Console.

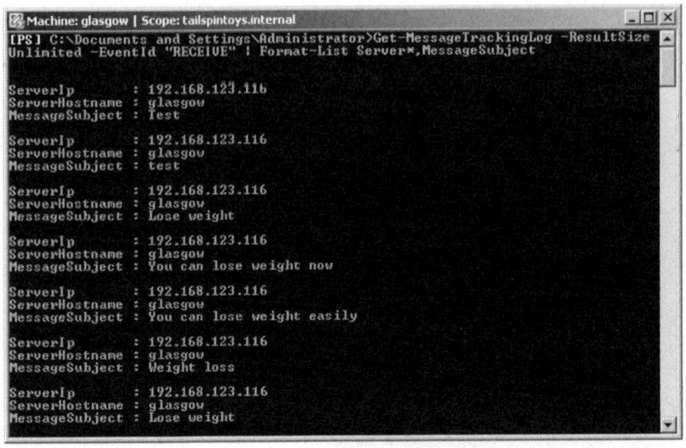

Figure 10-8   Selected message fields in list format

If you need to modify the message tracking settings on an Exchange Server 2007 server that has the Mailbox server role installed, you use commands based on the *Set-MailboxServer* cmdlet. If you need to modify the message tracking settings on an Exchange Server 2007 server that has the Hub Transport server role or Edge Transport server role installed (a transport server), you use commands based on the *Set-TransportServer* cmdlet. If a server has both the Hub Transport server role and the Mailbox server role installed, you configure settings for each role separately.

MORE INFO   *Set-MailboxServer* and *Set-TransportServer* cmdlets

For more information about the parameters and syntax used by the *Set-MailboxServer* and *Set-TransportServer* cmdlets, search Exchange Server 2007 Help for "Set-MailboxServer" and "Set-TransportServer" or access *http://technet.microsoft.com/en-us/library/aa998651.aspx* and *http://technet.microsoft.com/en-us/library/af25a915-79d7-4797-bac1-3ccd7f65129a.aspx*.

You can perform the following configuration operations by using PowerShell commands based on the *Set-MailboxServer* and *Set-TransportServer* cmdlets:

- Disable or enable message tracking
- Specify a location for the message tracking log files
- Specify a maximum size for individual message tracking log files and for the directory that contains the message tracking log files
- Specify a maximum age for message tracking log files
- Enable or disable message subject logging in message tracking logs

By default, Exchange Server 2007 deletes old message tracking log files after 30 days to limit the amount of storage that message tracking log files require. Another criteria that causes Exchange Server 2007 to delete old tracking log files is that the message tracking log directory reaches its specified maximum size.

NOTE Circular logging

The Exchange Server 2007 product documentation incorrectly refers to the process of deleting old message tracking log files as circular logging. Circular logging is a feature of the Extensible Storage Engine (ESE) to save disk space by overwriting transaction log files after the data that the log files contain has been committed to the databases. Transaction log files have nothing to do with message tracking log files. For more information about transaction logging including a section about circular logging, see "Understanding Transaction Logging" in the Exchange Server 2007 online help at http://technet.microsoft.com/en-us/library/bb331951.aspx.

Disabling and Enabling Message Tracking

Message tracking is enabled by default on all Exchange Server 2007 servers that have the Hub Transport, Mailbox, or Edge Transport server roles installed. In general, it is a good idea to track messages, but circumstances might arise, for example, if you are having temporary problems with disk storage or server performance, when you might want to disable message tracking (temporarily, it is hoped).

To disable message tracking on a transport server—a server with the Hub Transport or Edge Transport role installed—you use the MessageTrackingLogEnabled parameter. For example, to disable message tracking on the Hub Transport server Glasgow, you enter the following command:

```
Set-TransportServer Glasgow -MessageTrackingLogEnabled $False
```

If you subsequently want to enable message tracking on the same server, you would enter the following command:

```
Set-TransportServer Glasgow -MessageTrackingLogEnabled $True
```

The PowerShell commands that you would enter in Exchange Management Shell to disable or enable message tracking on a Mailbox server called Edinburgh are, respectively, the following:

```
Set-MailboxServer Edinburgh -MessageTrackingLogEnabled $False
Set-MailboxServer Edinburgh -MessageTrackingLogEnabled $True
```

Configuring the Location of Message Tracking Logs

Message tracking logs are stored by default in the C:\Program Files\Microsoft\Exchange Server\TransportRoles\Logs\MessageTracking directory. The directory must be local to the Exchange Server 2007 server on which the e-mail messages are processed. In a single-copy-cluster (SCC) environment, you should move the message tracking log directory to a physical disk resource that is located on the shared storage resource. This lets you search message tracking logs if a failover occurs. Cluster environments are discussed in Chapter 13, "Recovering Server Roles and Configuring High Availability."

If you change the location of the message tracking log directory, this does not copy any existing log files from the old directory to the new directory. Existing log files are left in the old directory. The new message tracking log directory is active almost immediately after the configuration change.

To use the Exchange Management Shell to change the location of the message tracking logs on an Exchange Server 2007 server with the Hub Transport server role or Edge Transport server role installed, you use the *Set-TransportServer* cmdlet with the MessageTrackingLogPath parameter. For example, to change the location of the message tracking log to F:\MessageTrackingLog on an Exchange Server 2007 server named Glasgow that has the Hub Transport server role installed, you would enter the following command:

```
Set-TransportServer Glasgow -MessageTrackingLogPath "F:\MessageTrackingLog"
```

To use the Exchange Management Shell to change the location of the message tracking logs on an Exchange Server 2007 server that has the Mailbox server role installed, you use the *Set-MailboxServer* cmdlet with the MessageTrackingLogPath parameter. For example, to change the location of the message tracking log to F:\MessageTrackingLog on an Exchange Server 2007 server named Edinburgh that has the Mailbox server role installed, you would enter the following command:

```
Set-MailboxServer Edinburgh -MessageTrackingLogPath "F:\MessageTrackingLog"
```

Using the MessageTrackingLogPath Parameter to Disable Message Tracking

If you set the value of the MessageTrackingLogPath parameter to $null by using a command based on the *Set-TransportServer* or *Set-MailboxServer* cmdlet, you effectively disable message tracking.

> However, if you set the value of the MessageTrackingLogPath parameter to $null when the value of the MessageTrackingLogEnabled attribute is $True, this generates error messages in the Application event log.
>
> The preferred method of disabling message tracking is therefore to use the MessageTrackingLogEnabled parameter with the *Set-TransportServer* cmdlet or the *Set-MailboxServer* cmdlet as described in the previous section of this lesson.

When you are setting up a new message tracking log directory, you need to configure the following permissions:

- Administrator: Full Control
- System: Full Control
- Network Service: Read, Write, and Delete Subfolders and Files

Figure 10-9 in shows the permissions configured for the Network Service on the folder F:\MessageTrackingLog on the Exchange Server 2007 server Glasgow.

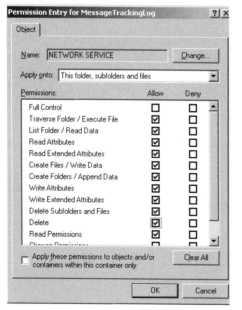

Figure 10-9   Permissions for the Network Service

By default, if the new message tracking log directory does not already exist, the Exchange Transport service uses the security credentials of the Network Service user account to create the new message tracking log directory and apply the correct permissions. Typically, the Network Service account has the rights that are required to create folders and apply permissions, and the new message tracking log directory is created with the correct permissions applied.

If, however, the new message tracking log directory already exists, the existing folder permissions are not checked. If, therefore, you move the message tracking log directory by using the MessageTrackingLogPath parameter with the *Set-TransportServer* cmdlet or the *Set-MailboxServer* cmdlet, it is a good idea to verify that the new message tracking log directory exists and has the correct permissions applied to it. If the command that changes the message tracking log directory is not successful, you can create the new message tracking log directory manually and apply the correct permissions to it before you use the appropriate Exchange Management Shell command.

Specifying a Maximum Size for Message Tracking Log Files and the Message Tracking Log Directory

The maximum size for each message tracking log file is 10 MB by default. When a message tracking log file reaches its maximum size, Exchange Server 2007 opens a new message tracking log file. This process continues until the message tracking log directory reaches its specified maximum size (by default, 250 MB) or the message tracking log file reaches its specified maximum age. After the maximum size or age limit (by default, 30 days) is reached, Exchange Server 2007 deletes the oldest message tracking log files.

Quick Check

- What parameter, used with the *Set-TransportServer* or *Set-MailboxServer* cmdlet, specifies the directory that stores tracking log files?

Quick Check Answer

- MessageTrackingLogPath.

As with the configurations described in previous sections of this lesson, you enter PowerShell commands based on the *Set-TransportServer* cmdlet to change the maximum size of individual message tracking log files on an Exchange Server 2007 server with the Hub Transport server or Edge Transport server role installed. You use commands based on the *Set-MailboxServer* cmdlet to perform the same task on an Exchange Server 2007 server with the Mailbox server role installed. In both cases, you specify the MessageTrackingLogMaxFileSize parameter.

For example, to set the maximum size of individual message tracking log files to 5 MB on an Exchange Server 2007 server named Glasgow that has the Hub Transport server role installed, you would enter the following command:

```
Set-TransportServer Glasgow -MessageTrackingLogMaxFileSize 5MB
```

To set the maximum size of individual message tracking log files to 20 MB on an Exchange Server 2007 server named Edinburgh that has the Mailbox server role installed, you would enter the following command:

```
Set-MailboxServer Edinburgh -MessageTrackingLogMaxFileSize 20MB
```

When you enter a value for the MessageTrackingLogMaxFileSize parameter, you can specify the value by using one of the following units:

- B (bytes)
- KB (kilobytes)
- MB (megabytes)
- GB (gigabytes)
- TB (terabytes)

Unqualified values are treated as bytes. The valid input range is 1 through 9,223,372,036,854,775,807 bytes. In practice, the specified size is typically in the range of 1 through 20 MB.

Exam Tip   Because Exchange administrators are accustomed to thinking of message tracking log sizes in megabytes, it is easy to forget to add the unit and specify 20 bytes when you want to specify 20 MB. Examiners are well aware of this common mistake. Look out for answers containing commands that do not specify the unit and set a message tracking log size to a very low value.

The value of the MessageTrackingLogMaxFileSize parameter must be less than or equal to the value of the MessageTrackingLogMaxDirectorySize parameter, which specifies the maximum size for the entire message tracking log directory.

By default, the maximum size for the message tracking log directory is 250 MB. As stated previously, Exchange Server 2007 deletes the oldest message tracking log files when the message tracking log directory reaches its specified maximum size.

> ### Specified and Actual Maximum Message Tracking Log Directory Size
>
> The maximum size of the message tracking log directory is calculated as the total size of all log files that have the same name prefix, for example, MSGTRK. Other files that do not follow the name prefix convention are not counted in the total directory size calculation. Renaming old log files or copying other files into the message tracking log directory could cause the directory to exceed its specified maximum size.
>
> When the Hub Transport server role and the Mailbox server role are installed on the same Exchange Server 2007 server, the actual maximum size of the message tracking log directory is larger the specified maximum size because the message tracking log files that are generated by the different server roles have different name prefixes.
>
> Message tracking log files for an Exchange Server 2007 server with the Hub Transport server role or Edge Transport server role installed begin with the name prefix MSGTRK. Message tracking log files for an Exchange Server 2007 server with the Mailbox server role installed begin with the name prefix MSGTRKM. When the Hub Transport server role and the Mailbox server role are installed on the same server and use the same message tracking log directory, the maximum size of this directory is equal to the sum of the separate size limits specified for the Hub Transport server role and the Mailbox server role.

As with previous configurations, you use the *Set-TransportServer* or *Set-MailboxServer* cmdlet to specify the maximum size of the message tracking log directory, depending on the role or roles that are installed on the Exchange Server 2007 server. You use these cmdlets with the MessageTrackingLogMaxDirectorySize parameter.

For example, to set the maximum size of the message tracking log directory to 500 MB on an Exchange Server 2007 server named Glasgow that has the Hub Transport server role installed, you would enter the following command:

```
Set-TransportServer Glasgow -MessageTrackingLogMaxDirectorySize 500MB
```

To set the maximum size of the message tracking log directory for the Mailbox server role to 150 MB on an Exchange Server 2007 server named Edinburgh that has the Mailbox server role installed, you would enter the following command:

```
Set-MailboxServer Edinburgh -MessageTrackingLogMaxDirectorySize 150MB
```

As with the maximum size for individual tracking log files, you specify the value of the MessageTrackingLogMaxDirectorySize parameter by using the units B, KB, MB, GB, and TB, and unqualified values are treated as bytes. The valid input range is 1 through 9,223,372,036,854,775,807 bytes. In practice, the specified size is typically in the range of 100 MB through 1 GB.

Quick Check

- What is the default value for the maximum size of an individual tracking log file?

Quick Check Answer

- 10 MB.

Configuring the Maximum Age for Message Tracking Logs

By default, the maximum age for a message tracking log file is 30 days. If a message tracking log file reaches its specified maximum age, Exchange Server 2007 deletes it.

To use Exchange Management Shell to change the maximum age for a message tracking log file on an Exchange Server 2007 server with the Hub Transport server or Edge Transport server role installed, you enter a command based on the *Set-TransportServer* cmdlet and the MessageTrackingLogMaxAge parameter. To perform the same task on an Exchange Server 2007 server with the Mailbox server role installed, you enter a command based on the *Set-MailboxServer* cmdlet with the same parameter.

For example, to change the maximum age of the message tracking log files for the Hub Transport server role to 45 days on an Exchange Server 2007 server named Glasgow that has the Hub Transport server role installed, you would enter the following command:

```
Set-TransportServer Glasgow -MessageTrackingLogMaxAge 45.00:00:00
```

To change the maximum age of the message tracking log files for the Mailbox server role to 20 days on an Exchange Server 2007 server named Edinburgh that has the Mailbox server role installed, you would enter the following command:

```
Set-MailboxServer Edinburgh -MessageTrackingLogMaxAge 20.00:00:00
```

You enter an age value as a time span with the format dd.hh:mm:ss, where d = days, h = hours, m = minutes, and s = seconds. The valid input range for this parameter is 00:00:00 through 24855.03:14:07. Setting the value of the MessageTrackingLog

MaxAge parameter to 00:00:00 prevents the automatic removal of message tracking log files because of their age.

Quick Check

- What PowerShell command sets the maximum size of the message tracking log directory to 400 MB on an Exchange Server 2007 server named Brisbane that has the Edge Transport server role installed?

Quick Check Answer

- *Set-TransportServer Brisbane -MessageTrackingLogMaxDirectorySize 400MB.*

Configuring Message Subject Logging in Message Tracking Logs

By default, the subject line of an SMTP e-mail message is stored in the message tracking log. However, you might want to disable message subject logging to comply with increased security or privacy requirements. Before you enable or disable message subject logging, ensure that your action conforms to organizational policy.

To enable or disable message subject logging in the message tracking logs on an Exchange Server 2007 server that has the Hub Transport server or Edge Transport server role installed, you enter a PowerShell command that uses the *Set-TransportServer* cmdlet and the MessageTrackingLogSubjectLoggingEnabled parameter. On an Exchange Server 2007 server that has the Mailbox server role installed, you use the *Set-MailboxServer* cmdlet with the same parameter.

For example, to disable message subject logging for the Hub Transport server role on an Exchange Server 2007 server named Glasgow that has the Hub Transport server role installed, you would enter the following command:

```
Set-TransportServer Glasgow -MessageTrackingLogSubjectLoggingEnabled $False
```

To enable message subject logging for the Mailbox server role (assuming it has previously been disabled) on an Exchange Server 2007 server named Edinburgh that has the Mailbox server role installed, you would enter the following command:

```
Set-MailboxServer Edinburgh - MessageTrackingLogSubjectLoggingEnabled $True
```

Table 10-2 lists the message tracking configuration parameters that you can use with the *Set-TransportServer* and *Set-MailboxServer* cmdlets.

Table 10-2   Message Tracking Configuration Parameters

Parameter	Function
MessageTrackingLogEnabled	Enables or disables message tracking
MessageTrackingLogPath	Specifies the location of message tracking log files
MessageTrackingLogMaxFileSize	Specifies a maximum size for individual message tracking log files
MessageTrackingLogMaxDirectory-Size	Specifies a maximum size for the directory that contains the message tracking log files
MessageTrackingLogMaxAge	Specifies a maximum age for message tracking log files
MessageTrackingLogSubject LoggingEnabled	Enables or disables message subject logging

Table 10-3 lists the same parameters with their default settings and value ranges.

Table 10-3   Parameter Defaults and Ranges

Parameter	Default Setting	Range
MessageTrackingLog Enabled	Enabled	Not applicable
MessageTrackingLog Path	C:\Program Files\Microsoft\Exchange Server\TransportRoles\Logs\ MessageTracking	Not applicable
MessageTrackingLog MaxFileSize	10 MB	1 through 9,223,372,036,854, 775,807 bytes

Table 10-3 Parameter Defaults and Ranges

Parameter	Default Setting	Range
MessageTrackingLog MaxDirectorySize	250 MB	1 through 9,223,372,036,854, 775,807 bytes
MessageTrackingLog MaxAge	30 days	00:00:00 through 24855.03:14:07
MessageTrackingLog SubjectLoggingEn- abled	Enabled	Not applicable

Reading and Interpreting the Message Tracking Log

By default, the message tracking log files on both Mailbox and Transport servers exist in the folder C:\Program Files\Microsoft\Exchange Server\TransportRoles\ Logs\MessageTracking. The naming convention for log files in the message tracking log directory depends on the server role that is installed. On a Hub Transport server or an Edge Transport server, the log files are named MSGTRKyyyymmdd-nnnn.log, for example, MSGTRK20070529-1.LOG. On a Mailbox server, the log files are named MSGTRKMyyyymmdd-nnnn.log, for example, MSGTRKM20070507-1.LOG. When the Hub Transport server role and Mailbox server role are installed on the same server, separate log files that use these different name prefixes are created in the message tracking log directory. Figure 10-10 shows the message tracking logs in a server that has the Hub Transport server role and Mailbox server role installed.

The placeholder yyyymmdd is the UTC date on which the log file was created, where yyyy = year, mm = month, and dd = day. The placeholder nnnn is an instance number that starts at the value of 1 each day for each message tracking log file name prefix.

Message tracking log files are text files that contain data in the comma-separated value (CSV) format. Each message tracking log file has a header that contains the following information:

- **Software** The software that created the message tracking log file. Typically, the value is Microsoft Exchange Server.

- **Version**   The version number of the software that created the message tracking log file, for example, 8.0.0.0.

- **Log-Type**   The value in this field is Message Tracking Log.

- **Date**   The UTC date-time when the log file was created. The UTC date-time is represented in the International Organization for Standardization (ISO) 8601 date-time format yyyy-mm-ddThh:mm:ss.fffZ, where yyyy = year, mm = month, dd = day, hh = hour, mm = minute, ss = second, fff = fractions of a second, and Z = Zulu, which is another way to denote UTC.

- **Fields**   The comma-delimited field names used in the message tracking log files.

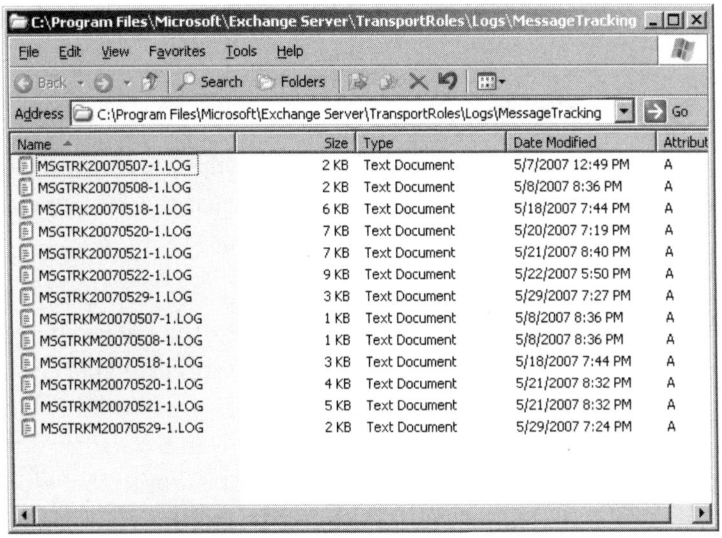

Figure 10-10   Message tracking logs

Figure 10-11 shows the contents of message tracking log files. The first file shown is a message tracking log file for the Hub Transport server role; the second is a message tracking log file for the Mailbox Transport server role. The file structures are similar, with some differences in the information they hold. Fortunately, you do not need to interpret the files manually because the PowerShell commands you enter in Exchange Management Shell and the Message Tracker tool, both of which are discussed in this lesson, do this for you.

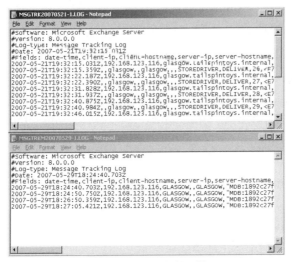

Figure 10-11   Message tracking log files

Information is written to message tracking log files until the file size reaches its maximum specified value for each log file. Then a new log file is opened that has an incremented instance number. This process is repeated throughout the day.

Typically, you track messages and access message tracking logs on a specific Exchange Server 2007 server either remotely or when logged on at the server. If you need to track messages across an organization, you might need to run the same commands or use the Message Tracker tool on several servers. Typically, you would do this from a single location. If you choose to use PowerShell commands in Exchange Management Shell, you might consider generating a PowerShell script. Chapter 5, "Moving Mailboxes and Implementing Bulk Management," discussed PowerShell scripts.

Practice: Changing the Location of the Message Tracking Log and Tracking Messages

In this practice, you change the location of the message tracking log on an Exchange Server 2007 server that has both the Hub Transport server and Message server roles installed. If you have set up your test network as specified in the "Before You Begin" section of this chapter, your Exchange Server 2007 server Glasgow will have both server roles installed.

You then send e-mail messages as the mailbox-enabled users Don Hall and Keith Harris (don.hall@tailspintoys.internal and keith.harris@tailspintoys.internal). You can use Microsoft Outlook, Outlook Express, or OWA. You sent messages logged on as these users in Chapter 9. However, if either or both users do not currently exist, you need to create them as described in Chapter 3.

You then use PowerShell commands in Exchange Management Shell to track the messages sent to and by these users.

▶ **Practice 1: Changing the Message Tracking Log Files Location**

In this practice you change the location of the message tracking log files for both the Hub Transport role and the Message Server role to C:\NewLogFiles. You do not need to create this folder before you carry out the Practice. The PowerShell commands that you enter in Exchange Management Shell create it for you.

1. Log on to the Exchange server in your domain by using the Kim_Akers account.

2. Open Exchange Management Shell.

3. Enter the following commands:

   ```
   Set-TransportServer Glasgow -MessageTrackingLogPath "C:\NewLogFiles"
   Set-MailboxServer Glasgow -MessageTrackingLogPath "C:\NewLogFiles"
   ```

   Your screen should look similar to Figure 10-12.

Figure 10-12   Commands to relocate the message tracking log files

4. Open My Computer and locate the C:\NewLogFiles folder.

5. Right-click the folder and click Properties. On the Security tab, click Advanced.

6. Ensure that the permissions on the folder are as follows:

   ❑ System: Full Control

   ❑ Network Service: Special

   ❑ Administrators: Full Control

Figure 10-13 shows the C:\NewLogFiles folder permissions.

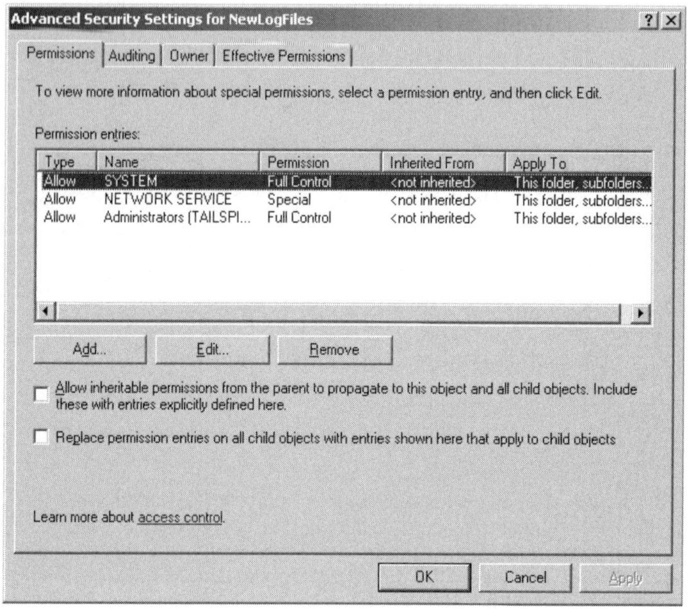

Figure 10-13   Permissions on the C:\NewLogFiles folder

7. Click Network Service. Click Edit.

8. Compare the permissions for the C:\NewLogFiles folder with those for the F:\TrackingLogs folder shown in Figure 10-9 earlier in this lesson. They should be the same (Read, Write, and Delete Subfolders and Files).

9. Open the C:\NewLogFiles folder. At this point, it should be empty because the tracking log files currently in the folder C:\Program Files\Microsoft\Exchange Server\TransportRoles\Logs\MessageTracking have not been moved to the C:\NewLogFiles folder.

▶ **Practice 2: Generating E-Mail Messages to Track**

In this practice, you log on to the domain as Don Hall and then as Keith Harris and send e-mail messages that you then track in the next practice. These messages also generate statistics that you view in the practice session in Lesson 2. If you have not created the users Don Hall and Keith Harris, you can use other user accounts, but you then need to amend the practices accordingly.

You need to be able to log on to the tailspintoys.internal domain by using the Don Hall and Keith Harris user accounts. If you do not have a client computer on your network, then you can enable the accounts to log on to your domain controller by placing them in the appropriate security group (for example, Print Operators or Backup Operators). You can use Microsoft Outlook, Outlook Express, or OWA to send the messages.

You need some large files (500 KB or larger) on the computer that you will log on to as Don and Keith to attach to messages. You can create such files by using, for example, Microsoft Paint:

1. Log on to the domain by using the Don Hall account.
2. Send the e-mail messages detailed in Table 10-4. You can include whatever text you want to (or no text at all) in the body of the e-mail. You can choose to send the messages by using Microsoft Outlook, Outlook Express, or OWA.

Table 10-4   **Don Hall's E-Mail Messages**

Recipients	Subject
Michael.Patten@litwareinc.internal Laurent.Penisson@adatum.internal John.Peoples@contoso.internal	Tuesday's meeting
Keith.Harris@tailspintoys.internal Kim_Akers@tailspintoys.internal	Meeting memos
Keith.Harris@tailspintoys.internal	Is Kim in the building?

3. Find some large files on the computer you are using. The combined size of the files you select should be at least 1 MB.
4. Send an e-mail message to Keith Harris with the subject "Suggested Graphics" and the files you selected attached.
5. Log on to the domain by using the Keith Harris account.
6. Reply to the e-mail messages you received from Don Hall.
7. Forward Don Hall's e-mail message with the large attachment to Kim Akers. If this message was not delivered because of message size restrictions, send a message to Kim Akers with the title "Suggested Graphics" and one or more large files attached.

▶ **Practice 3: Tracking Messages with Exchange Management Shell**

In this practice, you track e-mail messages by using Exchange Management Shell commands. You also check the tracking log files in their new location. You need to have successfully completed Practices 1 and 2 before attempting this practice:

1. Log on to the Exchange server in your domain by using the Kim_Akers account.

2. Open Exchange Management Shell.

3. Enter the following command to track messages from Don Hall to Keith Harris:

```
Get-MessageTrackingLog -Sender "don.hall@tailspintoys.internal" -Recipients
"keith.harris@tailspintoys.internal"
```

Your screen should look similar to Figure 10-14.

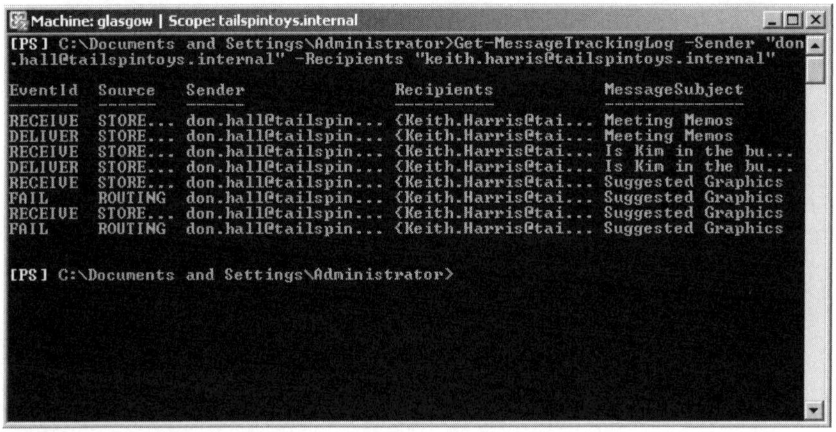

Figure 10-14 Messages from Don Hall to Keith Harris

4. Enter the following command to track failed messages from Don Hall:

```
Get-MessageTrackingLog -EventId "FAIL" -Sender "don.hall@tailspintoys.internal"
```

Your screen should look similar to Figure 10-15. There might be some differences depending on whether you have configured message size limits.

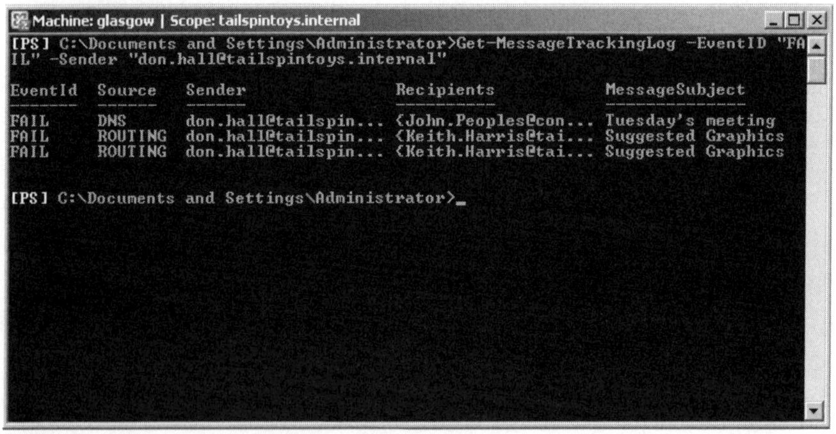

Figure 10-15 Failed messages from Don Hall

5. Enter the following command to obtain detailed information about all e-mail messages with "Kim" in the subject line:

```
Get-MessageTrackingLog –MessageSubject "Kim" | Format-List
```

Figure 10-16 shows the result of this command.

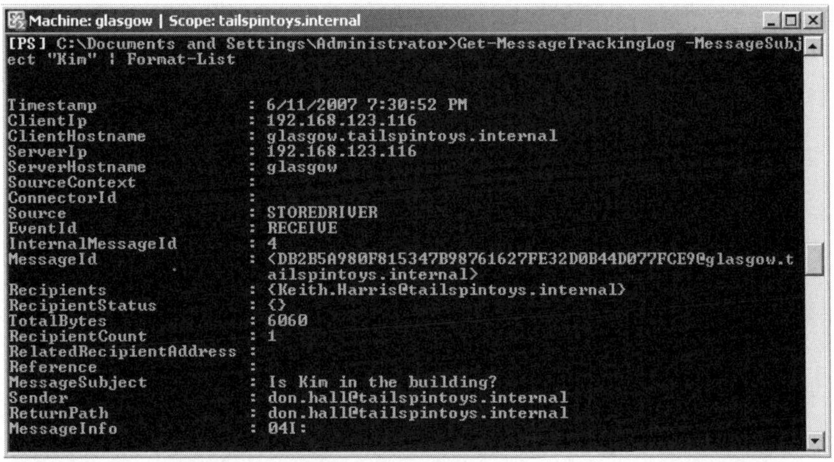

Figure 10-16 Tracing messages by subject

6. View the Sender, Recipients, and MessageSubject fields of all messages with "Kim" in the subject by entering the following command:

```
Get-MessageTrackingLog –MessageSubject "Kim" | Format-List
Sender,Recipients,MessageSubject
```

Figure 10-17 shows the result of this command.

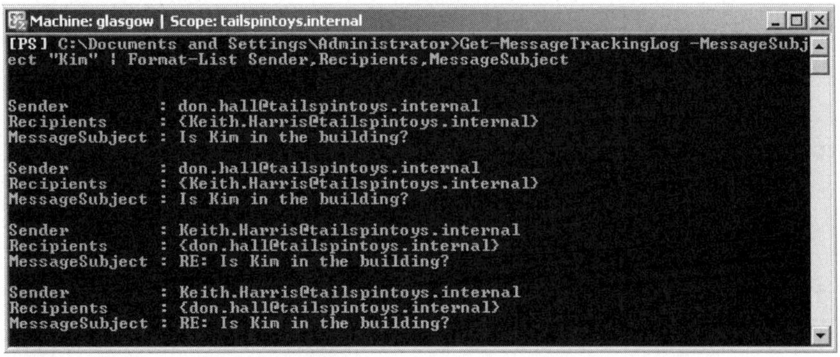

Figure 10-17 Tracing messages by subject and specifying fields

7. Access the C:\NewLogFiles folder and view a tracking log, as shown in Figure 10-18. The entries in your tracking log might differ from those shown in the figure.

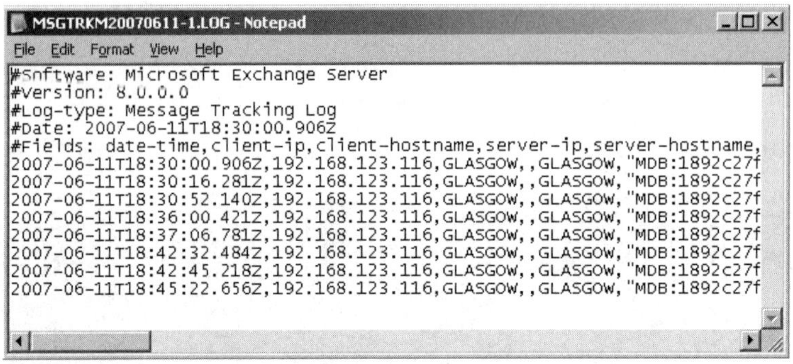

Figure 10-18   Tracking log content

Lesson Summary

- You can track messages in the message tracking log by using the Exchange Troubleshooting Assistant Message Tracker tool.

- You can use commands based on the *Get-MessageTrackingLog* cmdlet to track e-mail messages. You can display the outputs of these commands in either list or table format and view specified fields in the message tracking logs.

- You configure message tracking settings by using commands based on the *Set-MailboxServer* or *Set-TransportServer* cmdlet, depending on which server role (or roles) is installed on your Exchange Server 2007 server.

Lesson Review

You can use the following questions to test your knowledge of the information in Lesson 1, "Performing Message Tracking." The questions are also available on the companion CD if you prefer to review them in electronic form.

NOTE Answers

Answers to these questions and explanations of why each answer choice is correct or incorrect are located in the "Answers" section at the end of the book.

---

1. Which of the following is not a valid search filter for a message tracking log search?

   A. Recipients

   B. Sender

   C. Date

    D. Server

    E. EventID

    F. MessageID

    G. InternalMessageID

2. Written company policy has recently been changed and now states that the contents of the Subject line should no longer be recorded in message tracking logs. What command do you use on an Exchange Server 2007 server named Edinburgh with the Edge Transport role installed to implement this change?

    A. *Set-TransportServer Edinburgh-MessageTrackingLogSubjectLoggingEnabled $False*

    B. *Set-TransportServer Edinburgh-MessageTrackingLogSubjectLoggingEnabled $True*

    C. *Set-MailboxServer Edinburgh-MessageTrackingLogSubjectLoggingEnabled $False*

    D. *Set-MailboxServer* Edinburgh-*MessageTrackingLogSubjectLoggingEnabled $True*

3. You want to guarantee that tracking log files will never be removed by Exchange Server 2007 on a server named Chicago that has both the Hub Transport server and the Mailbox server roles installed. What commands do you enter in Exchange Management Shell? (Choose all that apply.)

    A. *Set-MailboxServer Chicago -MessageTrackingLogMaxAge 00:00:00*

    B. *Set-MailboxServer Chicago -MessageTrackingLogMaxAge $False*

    C. *Set-MailboxServer Chicago -MessageTrackingLogMaxAge 24855.03:14:07*

    D. *Set-TransportServer Chicago -MessageTrackingLogMaxAge 00:00:00*

    E. *Set-TransportServer Chicago -MessageTrackingLogMaxAge $False*

    F. *Set-TransportServer Chicago -MessageTrackingLogMaxAge 24855.03:14:07*

Lesson 2: Monitoring Client Connectivity

Mailbox health is a general term that encompasses a lot of factors. As far as your users are concerned, the system is healthy if they can connect easily and rapidly to their mailboxes and send and receive e-mail messages with no perceptible delays or problems. This in turn depends largely on connectivity between the user's client computers and your organization's Exchange Server 2007 servers. You can use the Performance console tools System Monitor and Performance Logs and Alerts to monitor connectivity, recognize potential problems, and set alerts to trigger on threshold counter values. You can use PowerShell commands and Exchange Management Console to configure protocol logging for SMTP traffic on Send and Receive connectors and monitor the results.

However, one of the first places you need to look for potential problems is in the mailbox statistics. You can obtain statistics for a single mailbox, groups of mailboxes, all the mailboxes in a database, all the mailboxes in a storage group, all the mailboxes on a server, and all the mailboxes in an Exchange organization. Obtaining mailbox statistics is straightforward; interpreting them is rather more difficult.

This lesson looks at using PowerShell commands to obtain and filter mailbox statistics and to check protocol connectivity. It also looks at how to use Perfmon counters to monitor client connectivity.

After this lesson, you will be able to:

- Monitor client connectivity by viewing mailbox statistics.
- Use Perfmon counters to monitor connectivity.
- Test protocol connectivity by using PowerShell.

Estimated lesson time: 55 minutes

Viewing Mailbox Statistics

When you need to obtain information about a mailbox, such as its size, the number of messages it contains, and the last time it was accessed, you can use Exchange Management Shell commands based on the *Get-MailboxStatistics* cmdlet. To run a command based on the *Get-MailboxStatistics* cmdlet, your account needs to be added to (at least) the Exchange View-Only Administrator role.

On an Exchange Server 2007 server with the Mailbox server role installed, you can use the *Get-MailboxStatistics* cmdlet without parameters. Figure 10-19 shows the output from this command on the server Glasgow.

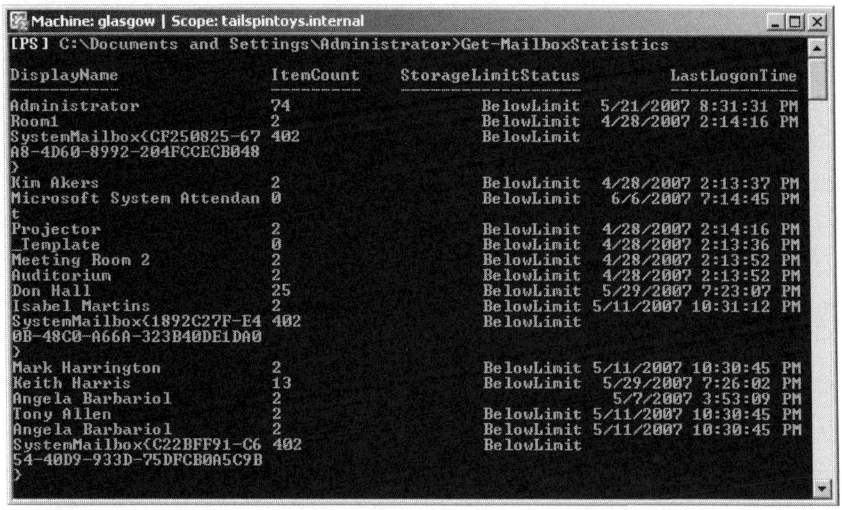

Figure 10-19   Using *Get-MailboxStatistics* without parameters

If an Exchange Server 2007 server does not have the Mailbox server role installed, you need to specify the Identity, Database, or Server parameter. You can also optionally specify the DomainController parameter.

Real World

Ian Mclean

This chapter is all about obtaining information that will tell you whether messages are being delivered and your mailboxes and Exchange organization are in a robust state of health. Many powerful tools exist for obtaining information. Information shortage is seldom a problem. But once you have all this data, what do you do with it?

Information gathering is a skill that you refine as you gain experience as an administrator. The tools are there, and you simply need to learn how to use them. Interpreting the information is an art. Responding in the best and most efficient way to the situation that your analysis has uncovered is a black art. It is not easy, but it is what they pay you for.

If, for example, one or more performance counter readings consistently return unacceptable values and you have determined that you definitely have a problem with mailbox health, then you need to find a solution. Looking at mailbox statistics might help you isolate the problem. Possibly, too, many oversized mailboxes exist, and you need to be more strict with capacity limits. You also need to test your server health and install additional memory, hard disk storage, or processing power as indicated. Possibly you need to upgrade your network or install faster network interface cards.

If you diagnose a problem in an Exchange Server 2007 server that has both the Hub Transport server and the Message server roles installed, you might need to move one of these roles to another server. If you have a server with the Hub Transport server role installed that is not coping with increased load, the answer might be to install the role in a second server for load balancing.

Finally, the blackest art of all, you need to convince those who control the budget to pay for your solution.

MORE INFO   **Load Balancing for Transport Servers**

For more information about load balancing transport servers, search the Exchange Server 2007 Help for "Load Balancing and Fault Tolerance for Transport Servers" or access *http://tech-net.microsoft.com/en-us/library/bb267003.aspx*.

Specifying the Identity Parameter

The Identity parameter specifies a single mailbox. When you provide a value for the Identity parameter, the command connects to the server where the mailbox resides and returns the statistics for the mailbox. If you want statistics for several mailboxes, you can use a command based on the *Get-Mailbox* cmdlet and pipe its output into a command based on the *Get-MailboxStatistics* cmdlet.

You can specify one of the following values for the identity parameter:

- Globally unique identifier (GUID)
- Distinguished name
- Domain\account
- User principal name
- Legacy Exchange distinguished name
- SMTPAddress
- Alias

For example, the following command returns statistics for the mailbox don.hall@tail-spintoys.internal:

```
Get-MailboxStatistics -Identity don.hall@tailspintoys.internal
```

However, if you want to see all the statistics returned by a command based on the *Get-MailboxStatistics* cmdlet, you need to pipe the output into the *Format-List* command:

```
Get-MailboxStatistics -Identity don.hall@tailspintoys.internal | Format-List
```

Figure 10-20 shows the output from this command.

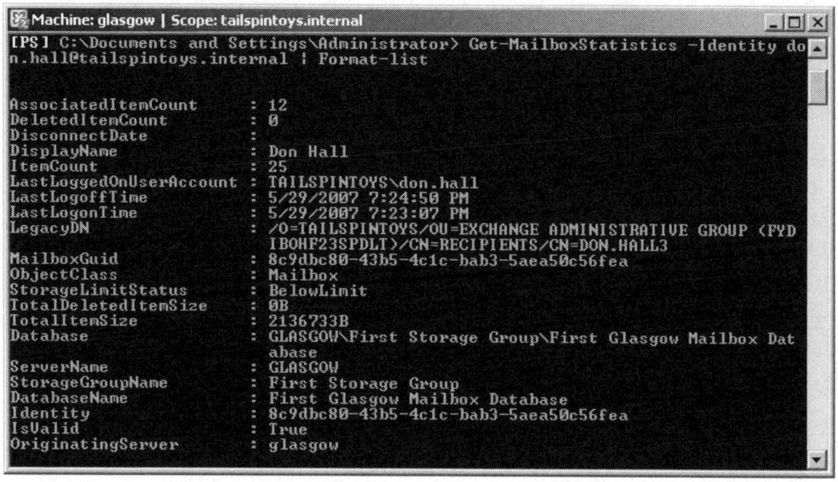

Figure 10-20   Statistics for Don Hall's mailbox

You can also pipe the output of commands based on the *Get-Mailbox* cmdlet into the *Get-MailboxStatistics* command. If, for example, you wanted statistics for the Don Hall, Keith Harris, and Kim Akers mailboxes of all users in the Accounts Department, you could use the following command:

```
Get-Mailbox -Filter { (Name -eq "Don Hall") -or (Name -eq "Keith Harris") -or (Name -eq "Kim Akers") } | Get-MailboxStatistics
```

Figure 10-21 shows the output from this command.

If you want a complete list of statistics, you can in turn pipe the output of the *Get-MailboxStatistics* command into the Format-List command:

```
Get-Mailbox -Filter { (Name -eq "Don Hall") -or (Name -eq "Keith Harris") -or (Name -eq "Kim Akers") } | Get-MailboxStatistics | Format-List
```

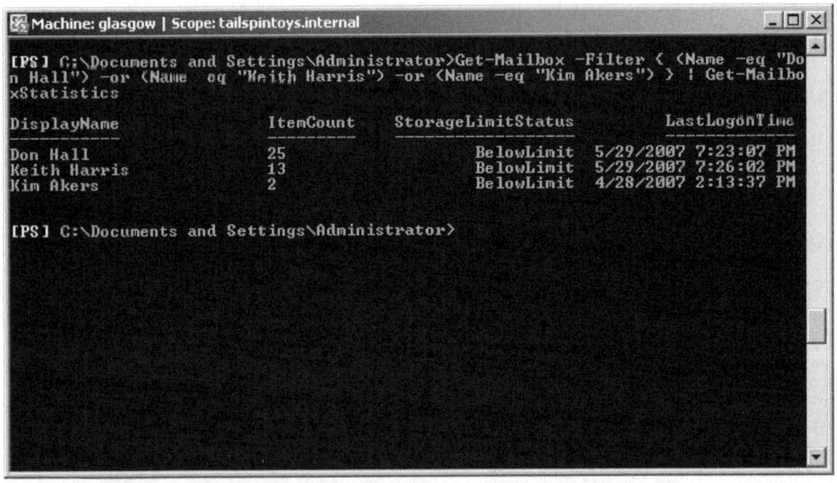

Figure 10-21 Statistics for Don Hall, Keith Harris, and Kim Akers

If you want to filter on user attributes such as Department, you can pipe the output of commands based on the *Get-User* cmdlet into the *Get-MailboxStatistics* command. For example, if you wanted statistics for all users in the Manufacturing Department, you could use the following command:

```
Get-User -Filter {Department -eq "Manufacturing"} | Get-MailboxStatistics | Format-List
```

Figure 10-22 shows the output from this command.

Figure 10-22 Statistics for all users in the Manufacturing Department

You can redirect the output of commands based on the *Get-MailboxStatistics* cmdlet into a CSV file for further analysis by software, such as Microsoft Excel, Access, or SQL Server, using the following command:

```
Get-MailboxStatistics -Identity keith.harris@tailspintoys.internal | Export-Csv
C:\KeithStats.csv
```

MORE INFO   **Export-Csv**

The *Export-Csv* command exports data to a CSV file in a format that can easily be read by other software packages. If you omitted this command and simply redirected output into a CSV file by using the > operator, the file would still be created, but the values would be in a single column, which is not a convenient format. Chapter 11, "Reporting," discusses the command in more detail. For more information about the *Export-Csv* command, access *http://www.microsoft.com/technet/ scriptcenter/topics/msh/cmdlets/export-csv.mspx*.

Using the Database Parameter

The Database parameter specifies the name of the mailbox database. When you specify this parameter, the PowerShell command returns statistics for all the mailboxes in the specified database. For example, to obtain statistics about all mailboxes in the First Glasgow Mailbox Database in the First Storage Group on the server Glasgow, you would use the following command:

```
Get-MailboxStatistics -Database "Glasgow\First Storage Group\First Glasgow Mailbox Database"
```

Figure 10-23 shows the output from this command.

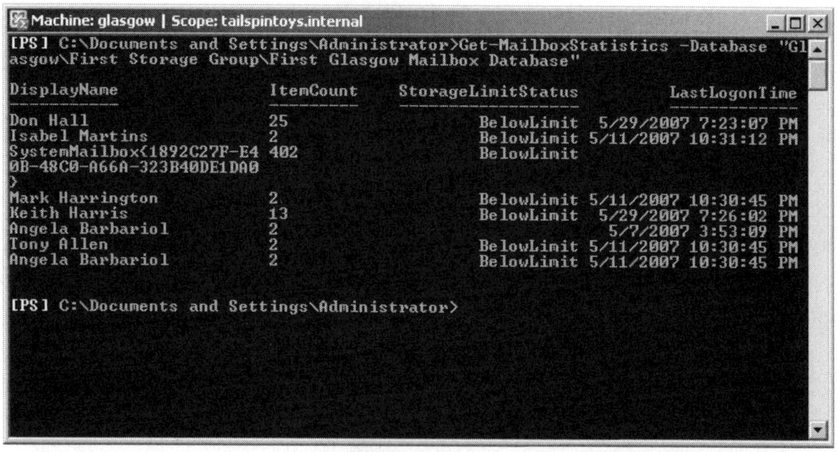

Figure 10-23   First Glasgow Mailbox Database mailbox statistics

You can use the following values to specify the Database parameter:

- Server\StorageGroup\Database
- Server\Database
- Database

However, you need to take care that if you specify only the name of a database, that name must be unique on the server where you are entering the command.

If you want to specify several databases, you can use a command based on the *Get-MailboxDatabase* cmdlet and pipe its output into a *Get-MailboxStatistics* command. For example, the following command returns statistics for all mailboxes in all databases in the storage group First Storage Group:

```
Get-MailboxDatabase -StorageGroup "First Storage Group" | Get-MailboxStatistics
```

Using the Server Parameter

The Server parameter specifies the server from which you want to obtain mailbox statistics. If you do not specify this parameter, the command returns statistics for mailboxes on the server on which Exchange Management Shell or the PowerShell console is running. You can use one of the following values:

- Fully qualified domain name (FQDN)
- Network basic input/output system (NetBIOS) name

When you specify a value for the Server parameter, the command returns statistics for all the mailboxes on all the databases, including recovery databases, on the specified server. For example, the following command obtains statistics for all the mailboxes on the Exchange Server 2007 server Glasgow:

```
Get-MailboxStatistics -Server "Glasgow"
```

If you want to specify more than one server, you can use a command based on the *Get-ExchangeServer* or *Get-MailboxServer* cmdlet and pipe its output into a *Get-MailboxStatistics* command. For example, the following command obtains detailed statistics for all mailboxes in an Exchange Server 2007 organization:

```
Get-ExchangeServer | Get-MailboxStatistics | Format-list
```

If you use a command that returns detailed statistics for all the mailboxes on a server or in an Exchange organization, you are likely to redirect the output into a CSV file because there is too much information to read from a screen display. Therefore, the previous command is likely to take the following form:

```
Get-ExchangeServer | Get-MailboxStatistics | Export-Csv C:\AllMailboxStats.csv
```

Using the DomainController Parameter

If you need to specify the FQDN of the domain controller that retrieves data from the Active Directory directory service in a command based on the *Get-MailboxStatistics* cmdlet, you can include the DomainController parameter in the command. This parameter is optional and can be used with the Server, Database, or Identity parameters, for example, using the following command:

```
Get-MailboxStatistics -Identity tailspintoys\keith.harris -DomainController
Glasgow.tailspintoys.internal | Format-List
```

You can use the DomainController parameter in concatenated commands where the output of another command is piped into a command based on the *Get-MailboxStatistics* cmdlet, although you need to be sure that you want to specify the same domain controller for every mailbox identified by these commands. You might not want to use the parameter, for example, in a command that obtains statistics for every mailbox in an Exchange organization.

Quick Check

1. The *Get-MailboxStatistics* cmdlet can take one of three required parameters. What are the required parameters?

2. The *Get-MailboxStatistics* cmdlet can take one optional parameter. What is the optional parameter?

Quick Check Answers

1. The required parameters are the following:
   - ❏ Identity
   - ❏ Database
   - ❏ Server

2. The optional parameter is DomainController.

Filtering and Analyzing Mailbox Statistics

The first step in analyzing statistics and using the results obtained to check and maintain mailbox health is to filter the output of commands based on the *Get-MailboxStatistics* cmdlet. For example, if you wanted information about the disconnected mailboxes in the database First Glasgow Mailbox Database in the storage group First Storage Group, you can use the following command:

```
Get-MailboxStatistics -Database "First Storage Group\First Glasgow Mailbox Database" | Where
{$_.DisconnectDate -ne $null}
```

MORE INFO   Comparison operators

Chapter 9 discussed the comparison operators -ne, -eq, -ge, and so on. For more information, refer to Table 9-2 in that chapter.

In a production environment, mailbox sizes are typically in the gigabyte range. However, on your test network, they are much smaller. If, therefore, you want to identify all the mailboxes on the Exchange Server 2007 server Glasgow with sizes greater than or equal to 1 MB, you can use the following command:

```
Get-MailboxStatistics -Server "Glasgow" | Where {$_.TotalItemSize -ge 1MB} | Format-List
```

Figure 10-24 shows the output from this command.

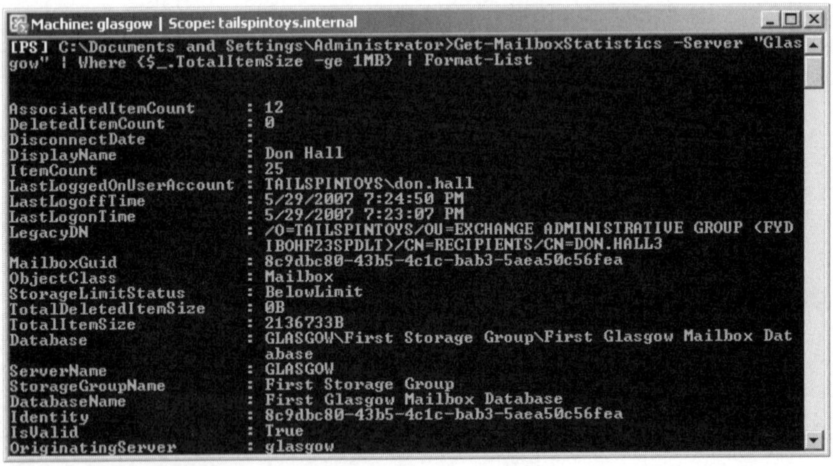

Figure 10-24   Mailbox statistics filtered by total item size

In addition, in a production environment, the number of items in a mailbox is typically in the thousands but is much lower in your test network. If, therefore, you want to identify all the mailboxes on the Exchange Server 2007 server Glasgow with an item count greater than or equal to 25, you can use the following command:

```
Get-MailboxStatistics -Server "Glasgow" | Where {$_.ItemCount -ge 25} | Format-List
```

Figure 10-25 shows the output from this command.

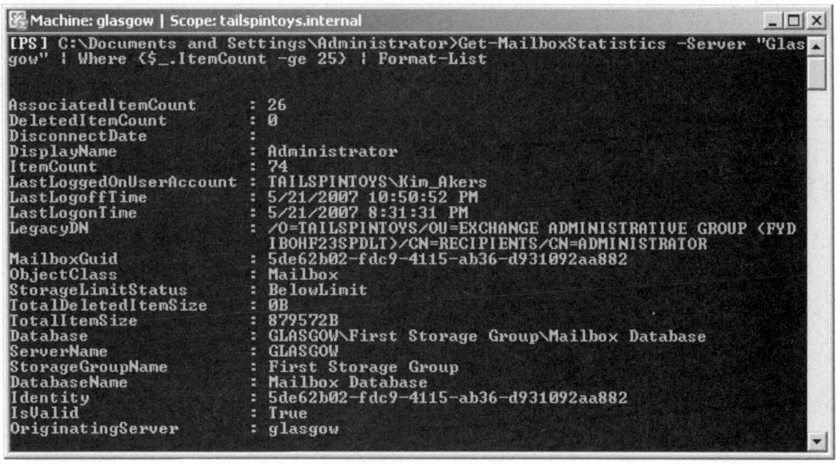

Figure 10-25   Mailbox statistics filtered by item count

You can also filter by, for example, last log-on and log-off times, storage limit status, and whether users' Active Directory accounts are valid or not valid.

You can redirect the output of commands based on the *Get-MailboxStatistics* cmdlet to CSV files and open these files with data analysis and report generation applications, for example, Microsoft Access or SQL Server. You can also use the data in applications such as Microsoft Excel that can display it in graphical form.

As always, gathering data is relatively straightforward. Analyzing the data you gather and using statistics to monitor client connectivity is more difficult, and you will learn to do this mainly through experience. If, for example, a user reports that she has not received any new e-mail messages for some time, you can look at the last log-in time statistic and make a conclusion about whether connectivity is an issue.

Quotas are frequently an issue. If a user cannot receive or send e-mail, you can look at that user's StorageLimitStatus statistic and determine whether the problem is quota related. If, on the other hand, a Mailbox server is experiencing problems, you can analyze mailbox sizes and determine whether storage limits are or could become a problem. You might then need to enforce stricter quotas, implement an archive policy, or persuade management that a hardware upgrade is required.

Quick Check

■ What PowerShell command returns detailed statistics about all mailboxes in the database First Glasgow Mailbox Database in the storage group First Storage Group that contain 1,000 or more items?

Quick Check Answer

■ *Get-MailboxStatistics -Database "First Storage Group\First Glasgow Mailbox Database" | Where {$_.ItemCount -ge 1000} | Format-List.*

Viewing Perfmon Counters

Chapter 9 introduced the Exchange Server Performance Monitor and discussed how the System Monitor component of this tool can be used to view performance counters in real time and to view counter logs that in turn enable you to generate baseline statistics that monitor general server health and issues such as mailbox health and queue thresholds.

The chapter also discussed how you can use the Performance Logs and Alerts component of the tool to add counters to logs and how you can set alerts that warn you if values in counters exceed or fall below predefined threshold levels. You used these tools and techniques to monitor queue thresholds, which are one indicator of mailbox and Exchange organization health, and to monitor the general health and resource usage of the four main server subsystems: processor, memory, disk, and network interface.

Analyzing Application Event Log Entries

By default, a triggered alert writes an event to the Application event log. You can also optionally start a performance log capture, send an administrative message, or start a program. You can use PowerShell commands based on the *Get-EventLog* cmdlet to return information in the event logs about specified events—events logged when alerts associated with mailbox counters trigger and other significant events. For example, to return detailed information about events associated with EventID 1233, you enter a command similar to the following:

```
Get-EventLog Application | Where-Object {$_.EventId -eq 1233} | Format-List
```

Figure 10-26 shows the output from this command.

You can extend this procedure to obtain information based on multiple criteria. For example, to obtain information about all warning events associated with the MSExchangeIS source, you can enter the following command:

Figure 10-26 Detailed information about events with EventID 1233

```
Get-EventLog Application | Where-Object { ($_.Source -eq "MSExchangeIS") -and ($_.EntryType
-eq "Warning") } | Format-List
```

Figure 10-27 shows the output from this command.

Figure 10-27 Searching the Application event log using multiple criteria

As with all PowerShell commands, you can redirect the output of commands based on
the *Get-EventLog* cmdlet to a CSV file for further analysis, for example, using the following command:

```
Get-EventLog Application | Where-Object { ($_.Source -eq "MSExchangeIS")  -and ($_.EntryType
-eq "Warning") } | Export-Csv C:\MSExchangeISWarning.csv
```

MORE INFO   Get-EventLog

Get-EventLog is considered a general PowerShell cmdlet and not specific to Exchange Server 2007. Therefore, it is not included in Exchange Server 2007 Help. For more information about how you can use commands based on this cmdlet, access *http://www.microsoft.com/technet/scriptcenter/topics /msh/cmdlets/get-eventlog.mspx.*

Using Information Store Mailbox Performance Counters

You can record the values in mailbox-related performance counters in log files and add counters to alerts that write events to the Application event log. Chapter 9 discussed the use of counters associated with the MSExchangeIS Mailbox performance object to monitor queues and the health of the Exchange organization. You can use the same object to monitor mailbox health and set alerts that trigger if mailbox-associated problems occur. Figure 10-28 shows this object and some of its associated counters.

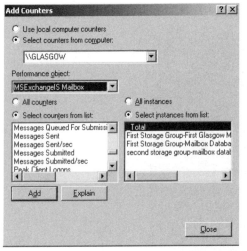

Figure 10-28   The MSExchangeIS Mailbox performance object

Table 10-5 lists and describes some of the counters associated with the MSExchangeIS Mailbox performance object. Most of these counters are directly associated with mailbox health, although some are indicators of general Exchange organization health. The queue counters were discussed in detail in Chapter 9. However, excessive queue lengths can indicate mailbox problems, server problems, or Exchange organization problems, and the related counters are therefore included in the table.

The counters that measure rates of message receipt and delivery are usually of most interest when checking mailbox health and the efficiency of message delivery.

Sometimes, however, these values need to be read in conjunction with counters that give numbers of messages processed since start-up. If the rate that messages are sent to transport is low, possibly very few messages needed to be sent to transport during this session. As with most performance counters, there are seldom absolute good and bad values. You need to judge the statistics against baseline logs to determine what threshold values you should set in alerts and whether the load on your Exchange Server 2007 servers is changing over time.

Table 10-5 Counters Associated with the MSExchangeIS Mailbox Performance Object

Counter	Function
Active Client Logons	The number of clients that performed any action within the last 10-minute time interval
Average Delivery Time	The average time between the submission of a message to the mailbox store and the delivery to all local recipients for the last 10 messages
Client Logons	The number of clients (including system processes) currently logged on
Local Deliveries	The total number of messages delivered locally
Local Delivery Rate	The rate at which messages are delivered locally
Logon Operations/Sec	The rate of log-on requests in the mailbox store
Message Opens/Sec	The rate that requests to open messages are submitted to the information store
Message Recipients Delivered	The total number of recipients that have received a message since start-up
Message Recipients Delivered/Sec	The rate that recipients receive messages.
Messages Delivered	The total number of messages delivered to all recipients since start-up
Messages Delivered/Sec	The rate that messages are delivered to all recipients
Messages Queued For Submission	The current number of submitted messages which are not yet processed by the Transport service (transport)

Table 10-5   Counters Associated with the MSExchangeIS Mailbox Performance Object

Counter	Function
Messages Sent	The total number of messages sent to transport since start-up
Messages Sent/Sec	The rate that messages are sent to transport
Messages Submitted	The total number of messages submitted by clients since service start-up
Messages Submitted/Sec	The rate that clients submit messages
Peak Client Logons	The maximum number of concurrent client log-ons since the service started
Receive Queue Size	The number of messages in the mailbox store's receive queue

The MSExchangeIS Mailbox object has other counters associated with it that test particular aspects of Exchange operation. For example, if restricted views are reused in the mailbox store, the Restricted View Cache Hit Rate and Restricted View Cache Miss Rate counters monitor this activity. The performance object provides counters that let you monitor items retained for item recovery, events related to event history, events related to virus scans, and events related to collaboration through Distributed Authoring and Versioning. However, these counters are not directly related to mailbox health.

Monitoring public stores might not be related directly to mailbox health but does relate to the health of the Exchange organization. Figure 10-29 shows counters provided by the MSExchangeIS Public performance object that assist you in monitoring public folder health and performance.

In addition to operations and counters related to the Microsoft Exchange Information Store, Exchange Server Performance Monitor provides counters related to additional performance objects that can assist you in measuring Exchange organization health and performance. For example, the MSExchangeTransport Queues object provides the Active Remote Delivery Queue Length and the Retry Remote Delivery Queue Length counters for checking remote delivery queues. For SMTP operations, the MSExchangeTransport SmtpReceive object provides a Messages Received/Sec counter, and the MSExchangeTransport SmtpSend counter provides a Messages Sent/Sec counter.

Figure 10-29   The MSExchangeIS Public performance object

Using POP3 and IMAP4 Counters

SMTP sends e-mail messages. Users typically use POP3 or IMAP4 clients, for example, Microsoft Outlook Express, to receive incoming messages. The POP3 and IMAP4 services are already installed on Exchange Server 2007 servers that have the Client Access role, but the services are disabled by default. You can enable them and set the start-up type to automatic by entering PowerShell commands in either the PowerShell console or the Exchange Management Shell. For example, to set the POP3 service start-up type to automatic and enable the service, you enter the following commands:

```
Set-Service MSExchangePop3 -StartupType automatic
Start-Service -Name MSExchangePop3
```

Figure 10-30 shows the result of these commands. Depending on how quickly the service starts, the WARNING messages might not appear.

Similarly, to set the IMAP4 service start-up type to automatic and enable the service, you enter the following commands:

```
Set-Service MSExchangeImap4 -StartupType automatic
Start-Service -Name MSExchangeImap4
```

Exchange Server Performance Monitor provides counters that let you determine the current number of POP3 and IMAP4 connections and the number of failed connections. Figure 10-31 shows the MSExchangePop3 performance object. If the service had not been enabled, the Add button would be grayed out.

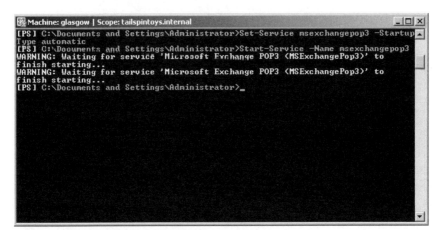

Figure 10-30   Enabling the POP3 service

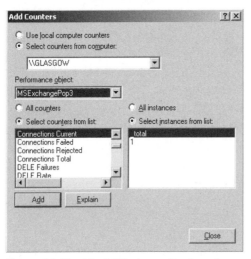

Figure 10-31   The MSExchangePop3 performance object

In addition to general counters such as Connections Current, Connections Failed, Connections Rejected, and Connections Total, the performance object provides counters related to particular POP3 commands, for example, DELE, LIST, NOOP, PASS, QUIT, RETR, RSET, STAT, STLS, TOP, UIDL, and USER. In addition, you can determine the total number of Secure Sockets Layer (SSL) connections that have been opened since the POP3 service was started. The tool therefore enables you to perform very detailed analysis of POP3 operations if you need to do so.

MORE INFO   POP3

For more information about POP3, search Windows Server Help and Support Center for "POP3" or access *http://technet2.microsoft.com/windowsserver/en/library/2843732f-4e8b-4509-9b0b-fec70e39afbc1033.mspx?mfr=true*. Note that the POP3 service is a Windows service and that this is a Windows Server 2003 link. If your computer has Windows Server 2008 installed, search the Winows Help files for "POP3."

The MSExchangeImap4 object also provides a large number of counters that enable an in-depth analysis of IMAP4 connectivity. In addition to Connections Failed, Connections Rejected, Current Connections, Active SSL Connections, Average Command Processing Time, and Total Connections counters, the performance object provides counters that let you check operations related to the APPEND, AUTHENTICATE, CAPABILITY, CHECK, CLOSE, COPY, CREATE, DELETE, EXAMINE, EXPUNGE, FETCH, IDLE, LIST, LOGIN, LOGOUT, LSUB, NAMESPACE, NOOP, RENAME, SEARCH, SELECT, STARTTLS, STATUS, STORE, SUBSCRIBE, and UNSUBSCRIBE commands.

MORE INFO   IMAP4

For more information about IMAP4, access *http://www.imap.org* and follow the links.

Managing Protocol Logging

One method of checking connectivity and mailbox health and diagnosing mail flow problems is to monitor SMTP conversations that occur between Exchange Server 2007 servers that have the Hub Transport server role or the Edge Transport server role installed. If protocol logging is enabled on Send and Receive connectors, details of these conversations are recorded in protocol logs. Protocol logs are CSV files, and you can use applications such as Microsoft Access and SQL Server to analyze the file contents and generate reports.

MORE INFO   Send and Receive connectors

For more information about Send and Receive connectors, search Exchange Server 2007 Help for "Send Connectors" and "Receive Connectors" or access *http://technet.microsoft.com/en-us/library/aa998662.aspx* and *http://technet.microsoft.com/en-us/library/aa996395.aspx*. Chapter 7, "Connectors and Connectivity," discussed creating and modifying connectors.

Protocol logging is disabled by default on all Send and Receive connectors and is enabled or disabled on a per connector basis. You also configure other protocol log options, for example, the maximum size of individual protocol logs and the maximum size of the protocol log directory, on a per connector basis for the whole server. All the Receive connectors on a Hub Transport server or an Edge Transport server share the same protocol log files and protocol log options. These protocol log files and protocol log options are configured separately from the Send connector protocol log files and protocol log options on the same server.

Quick Check

- What performance object would you select if you wanted to monitor the current number of IMAP4 connections?

Quick Check Answer

- The MSExchangeImap4 object.

You can use PowerShell commands in Exchange Management Console based on the *Set-ReceiveConnector* and *Set-SendConnector* cmdlets to enable or disable protocol logging on each Send connector or Receive connector. All other protocol log options are set by PowerShell commands based on the *Set-TransportServer* cmdlet. PowerShell commands are the main tool for configuring protocol logging and therefore form the basis of this section.

MORE INFO   Enabling protocol logging from Exchange Management Console

For more information and step-by step instructions on how to enable protocol logging from Exchange Management Console, search Exchange Server 2007 Help for "How to Configure Protocol Logging" or access *http://technet.microsoft.com/en-us/library/bb124531.aspx*.

To enable, disable, or configure protocol logging on an Exchange Server 2007 server that has the Hub Transport server role installed, your account needs to be added to the Exchange Organization Administrator role. On an Exchange Server 2007 server that has the Edge Transport server role installed, your account needs to be a member of the local Administrators group on that computer.

Enabling Protocol Logging on Send Connectors and Receive Connectors

Protocol logging is disabled by default on Send and Receive connectors. For Send connectors (other than the intra-organization Send connector, which is a special case), you enable protocol logging by entering commands based on the *Set-SendConnector* cmdlet. For Receive connectors, you enable protocol logging by entering commands based on the *Set-ReceiveConnector* cmdlet.

For example, to enable protocol logging on the Send connector "Contoso.internal Send Connector" on an Exchange Server 2007 server that has the Edge Transport server role installed, you would enter the following command:

```
Set-SendConnector "Contoso.internal Send Connector" -ProtocolLoggingLevel Verbose
```

To enable protocol logging on the Receive connector "Litwareinc.internal Receive Connector" on an Exchange Server 2007 server that has the Hub Transport server role installed, you would enter the following command:

```
Set-ReceiveConnector "Litwareinc.internal Receive Connector" -ProtocolLoggingLevel Verbose
```

To disable protocol logging on any Receive or Send connector on which you previously disabled it, you would use similar commands but set the value in the Protocol-LoggingLevel parameter to None.

MORE INFO   *Set-SendConnector* and *Set-ReceiveConnector* cmdlets

For more information about the *Set-SendConnector* and *Set-ReceiveConnector* cmdlets, search Exchange Server 2007 Help for "Set-SendConnector" and "Set-ReceiveConnector" or access *http://technet.microsoft.com/en-us/library/aa998294.aspx* and *http://technet.microsoft.com/en-us/library/bb125140.aspx*.

Enabling Protocol Logging on the Intra-organization Send Connector

The intra-organization Send connector exists on every Hub Transport server. It is implicitly created and invisible and requires no management. The intra-organization Send connector is used to relay messages to the following destinations:

- Other Hub Transport servers in the Exchange organization
- Exchange Server 2003 servers in the Exchange organization
- Edge Transport servers in the Exchange organization

By default, protocol logging is disabled for the intra-organization Send connector. If you enable protocol logging for this connector, logging occurs in the Send connector protocol logs that are configured on the Hub Transport server. You can enable or disable protocol logging for the intra-organization Send connector by using an Exchange Management Shell command based on the *Set-TransportServer* cmdlet. For example, to enable protocol logging for the intra-organization Send connector on the Exchange Server 2007 server Glasgow, you would enter the following command:

```
Set-TransportServer Glasgow -IntraOrgConnectorProtocolLoggingLevel Verbose
```

To disable protocol logging on the same connector (assuming it was enabled), you enter the following command:

```
Set-TransportServer Glasgow -IntraOrgConnectorProtocolLoggingLevel None
```

Exam Tip   The ProtocolLoggingLevel and IntraOrgConnectorProtocolLoggingLevel parameters can take one of only two values: Verbose or None. Be wary of answers to 70-236 examination questions that set these parameters to other values, for example, Off, On, True, or False.

Configuring Protocol Logs

You can use PowerShell commands based on the *Set-SendConnector* and *Set-Receive-Connector* cmdlets to configure protocol logs of all Send connectors or all Receive connectors on an Edge Transport server or a Hub Transport server. The following settings are available:

- The location of the Send connector or the Receive connector protocol log files.

- A maximum size for the Send connector or the Receive connector protocol log files.

- A maximum size for the directory that contains the Send connector or Receive connector protocol log files.

- A maximum age for the Send connector or Receive connector protocol log files.

As with message tracking logs, Exchange Server 2007 automatically purges old log files to limit the total disk space for protocol logging based on file size and file age.

IMPORTANT   Send connectors on an Edge Transport server

Do not modify the Send connectors that are located on an Exchange Server 2007 server that has the Edge Transport server role installed and is subscribed to the Exchange organization by using the Edge Subscription process. Instead, modify the Send connectors on the Hub Transport server. The change will be replicated to the Edge Transport server when synchronization next occurs.

Changing the Location of Protocol Log Files

By default, the Receive connector protocol log files on an Exchange Server 2007 server are in the local folder C:\Program Files\Microsoft\Exchange Server\TransportRoles\Logs\ProtocolLog\SmtpReceive.

To use Exchange Management Shell or the PowerShell console to configure the Receive connector protocol log directory for all Receive connectors on a Hub Transport server or an Edge Transport server, you enter a command based on the *Set-TransportServer* cmdlet. For example, to change the Receive connector protocol log files location on the Exchange Server 2007 server Glasgow to C:\ProtocolReceiveLog, you enter the following command:

```
Set-TransportServer Glasgow -ReceiveProtocolLogPath "C:\ProtocolReceiveLog"
```

By default, the Send connector protocol log files on an Exchange Server 2007 server are in the local folder C:\Program Files\Microsoft\Exchange Server\TransportRoles\Logs\ProtocolLog\SmtpSend.

To change the Send connector protocol log files location on the Exchange Server 2007 server Glasgow to C:\ProtocolSendLog, you enter the following command:

```
Set-TransportServer Glasgow -SendProtocolLogPath "C:\ProtocolSendLog"
```

Using the SendProtocolLogPath and ReceiveProtocolLogPath Parameters to Disable Protocol Logging

If you set the value of the SendProtocolLogPath parameter to $Null, this disables protocol logging for all Send connectors. Similarly, if you set the value of the ReceiveProtocolLogPath parameter to $Null, this disables protocol logging for all Receive connectors. However, setting either of these parameters to $Null when protocol logging is enabled for any Receive or Send connector, including the intra-organization Send connector, generates errors in the Application event log.

The preferred method of disabling protocol logging is to use PowerShell commands based on the *Set-SendConnector* and *SetReceiveConnector* cmdlets to set the ProtocolLoggingLevel to None on each Send connector or Receive connector. In addition, you can use the *SetTransportServer* cmdlet to set the IntraOrgConnectorProtocolLoggingLevel to None as described earlier in this lesson.

Changing the Protocol Log Size, Directory Size, and Age Parameters

Except that message tracking is enabled by default and protocol logging is disabled by default, the way that Exchange Server 2007 manages protocol log files is remarkably similar to the way it manages tracking log files. Thus, the maximum size for each protocol log file is 10 MB by default. When a protocol log file reaches its maximum size, Exchange Server 2007 opens a new protocol log file. This process continues until the directory (Send or Receive) that holds the relevant protocol log files reaches its specified maximum size (by default, 250 MB) or the protocol log file reaches its specified maximum age (by default, 30 days). After the maximum size or age limit is reached, Exchange Server 2007 deletes the oldest protocol log files.

The following commands set, respectively, the maximum size of the individual Send protocol log files on the Exchange Server 2007 server Glasgow to 5 MB, the maximum size of the individual Receive protocol log files on the same server to 20 MB, the maximum size of the Send protocol log files directory to 150 MB, and the maximum size of the Receive protocol log files directory to 400 MB:

```
Set-TransportServer Glasgow -SendProtocolLogMaxFileSize 5MB
Set-TransportServer Glasgow -ReceiveProtocolLogMaxFileSize 20MB
Set-TransportServer Glasgow -SendProtocolLogMaxDirectorySize 150MB
Set-TransportServer Glasgow -ReceiveProtocolLogMaxDirectorySize 400MB
```

As with tracking log files, sizes are in bytes unless a unit is specified, and the range is 1 through 9,223,372,036,854,775,807 bytes. The size of an individual log file cannot be greater than the size of the directory in which it resides.

To set the maximum age of Send and Receive protocol log files on the Exchange Server 2007 server Glasgow to 40 days, you would enter the following commands:

```
Set-TransportServer Glasgow -SendProtocolLogMaxAge 40.00:00:00
Set-TransportServer Glasgow -ReceiveProtocolLogMaxAge 40.00:00:00
```

As with tracking log files, you enter an age value as a time span with the format dd.hh:mm:ss, where d = days, h = hours, m = minutes, and s = seconds. The valid input range for this parameter is 00:00:00 through 24855.03:14:07. Setting the value of the SendProtocolLogMaxAge or the ReceiveProtocolLogMaxAge parameter to 00:00:00 prevents the automatic removal of the relevant protocol log files because of their age.

Quick Check

- What Send connector exists on every Hub Transport server and is implicitly created and invisible and requires no management?

> **Quick Check Answer**
> - The intra-organization Send connector.

Reading and Interpreting Protocol Logs

By default, Send connector protocol log files are located in the folder C:\Program Files\Microsoft\Exchange Server\TransportRoles\Logs\ProtocolLog\SmtpSend, and Receive connector protocol log files are located in the folder C:\Program Files\Microsoft\Exchange Server\TransportRoles\Logs\ProtocolLog\SmtpReceive.

The naming convention for log files in each protocol log directory is prefixyyyymmdd -nnnn.log. The placeholders represent the following information:

- The placeholder prefix is SEND for Send connectors or RECV for Receive connectors.

- The placeholder yyyymmdd is the UTC date on which the log file was created, where yyyy = year, mm = month, and dd = day.

- The placeholder nnnn is an instance number that starts at the value of 1 for each day.

Information is written to the log file until the file size reaches its maximum specified value and a new log file that has an incremented instance number is opened. This process is repeated throughout the day. Exchange Server 2007 deletes the oldest log files when the protocol log directory reaches its maximum specified size or when a log file reaches its maximum specified age.

Protocol log files are text files that contain data in CSV format. Each protocol log file has a header that contains the following information:

- The name of the software that created the protocol log file. Typically, the value is Microsoft Exchange Server.

- The version number of the software that created the protocol log file. Currently, the value is 8.0.0.0.

- The log type. The value of this field is either SMTP Receive Protocol Log or SMTP Send Protocol Log.

- The UTC date-time when the log file was created. The UTC date-time is represented in the ISO 8601 date-time format: yyyy-mm-ddThh:mm:ss.fffZ, where yyyy = year, mm = month, dd = day, hh = hour, mm = minute, ss = second, fff = fractions of a second, and Z = Zulu, which is another way to denote UTC.

■ The comma-delimited field names that are used in the protocol log files.

The protocol log stores each SMTP protocol event on a single line in the protocol log file. The information that is on each line is organized by fields, separated by commas. The fields that are used to classify each protocol event are listed in Table 10-6.

Table 10-6   Protocol Log Fields

Field Name	Description
date-time	The UTC date-time of the protocol event.
connector-id	The distinguished name (DN) of the connector that is associated with the SMTP event.
session-id	A GUID that is unique for each SMTP session but is the same for each event that is associated with that SMTP session.
sequence-number	A counter that starts at 0 and is incremented for each event in the same SMTP session.
local endpoint	The local endpoint of an SMTP session. This consists of an IP address and TCP/IP port number and is formatted as <IP address>:<port>.
remote endpoint	The remote endpoint of an SMTP session. This consists of an IP address and TCP/IP port number and is formatted as <IP address>:<port>.
event	A single character that represents the protocol event. The possible values for event are + (Connect), − (Disconnect), > (Send), < (Receive), and * (Information).
data	Text information that is associated with the SMTP event.
context	Additional contextual information that might be associated with the SMTP event.

You can use display, analysis, and report generation software that reads CSV files, for example, Microsoft Access, Excel, or SQL Server, to analyze protocol log files. You can also obtain information about Send and Receive connectors by entering commands based on the *Get-SendConnector* and *Get ReceiveConnector* cmdlets. For example, to get information about the Contoso.internal Send connector, you enter the following command:

```
Get-SendConnector "Contoso.internal Send Connector" | Format-List
```

Figure 10-32 shows the output from this command.

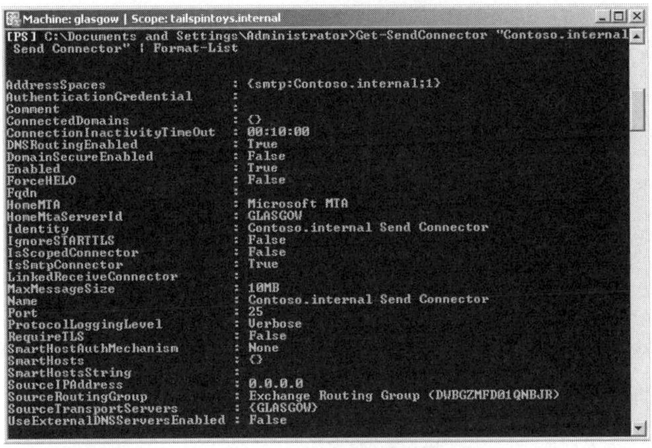

Figure 10-32   Send connector information

To get information about the Litwareinc.internal Receive connector, you enter the following command:

```
Get-ReceiveConnector "Litwareinc.internal Receive Connector" | Format-List
```

Figure 10-33 shows the output from this command.

Testing POP3 and IMAP4 Connectivity

Monitoring SMTP protocol logs lets you determine whether problems are occurring with the SMTP protocol that enables users to send e-mail messages. However, to check client connectivity, you also need to test that users can receive e-mail messages by using POP3 or IMAP4 clients. Earlier in this lesson, you saw how you could enable POP3 and IMAP4 on an Exchange Server 2007 server that has the Client Access role installed. You can check whether the services are running on a server by using the PowerShell commands *Get-Service MSExchangePop3* and *Get-Service MSExchangeImap4*. Figure 10-34 shows the output from these commands.

On the client side, you can use PowerShell commands based on the *Set-CASMailbox* cmdlet to enable or disable POP3 and IMAP4 for a specified mailbox. For example, to enable POP3 and IMAP4 for the Don Hall mailbox, you would use the following commands:

```
Set-CASMailbox -Identity "Don Hall" -PopEnabled $true
Set-CASMailbox -Identity "Don Hall" -ImapEnabled $true
```

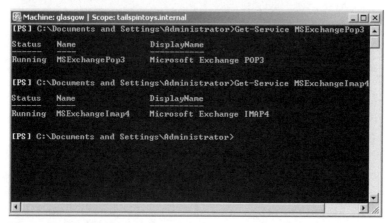

Figure 10-33   Receive connector information

Figure 10-34   Checking that services have started

The *Set-CASMailbox* cmdlet sets Client Access-related attributes for Exchange Active-Sync, OWA, POP3, and IMAP4 for a specified mailbox. The cmdlet supports the DomainController parameter, so that you cannot specify a specific domain controller for the operation.

If you want to enable POP3 or IMAP4 for more than one mailbox, you can pipe the output of a PowerShell command based on the *Get-Mailbox* cmdlet into a command based on the *Set-CASMailbox* cmdlet. For example, to enable IMAP4 for all the mailboxes in the database First Glasgow Mailbox Database in the storage group First Storage Group, you would use the following command:

```
Get-Mailbox -Database "First Storage Group\First Glasgow Mailbox Database" | Set-CASMailbox
-ImapEnabled $true
```

MORE INFO   Set-CASMailbox

For more information about PowerShell commands based on the *Set-CASMailbox* cmdlet, search Exchange Server 2007 Help for "Set-CASMailbox" or access *http://technet.microsoft.com/en-us/ library/bb125264.aspx*.

You can use PowerShell commands based on the Get-CASMailbox cmdlet to return a list of mailbox attributes that are relevant for the Client Access server role. If, for example, you wanted to check whether IMAP4 was enabled on the Don Hall mailbox, you could use the following command:

```
Get-CASMailbox -Identity "Don Hall"
```

Figure 10-35 shows the output from this command.

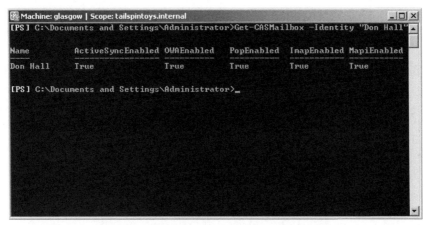

Figure 10-35   Client Access properties for the Don Hall mailbox

For more information about the properties of a mailbox you are testing for protocol connectivity, you can pipe the out of commands based on the *Get-CASMailbox* cmdlet into, for example, the Format-List PowerShell command:

```
Get-CASMailbox -Identity "Don Hall" | Format-List
```

MORE INFO   Get-CASMailbox

For more information about PowerShell commands based on the *Get-CASMailbox* cmdlet, search Exchange Server 2007 Help for "Get-CASMailbox" or access *http://technet.microsoft.com/en-us/library/bb124754.aspx*.

When the POP3 and IMAP4 services are running, you can use PowerShell commands based on the *Set-POPSettings* and *Set-IMAPSettings* cmdlets to configure the services. You can use commands based on the *Get-POPSettings* and *Get-IMAPSettings* cmdlets to check your configuration.

The *Set-POPSettings* cmdlet enables you to specify the POP3 settings for an individual or all Exchange Server 2007 Client Access servers that is running the POP3 service. By using the Server parameter, you can specify an individual Client Access server that you want to configure. You could, for example, tackle connectivity issues by increasing the value in the MaxConnectionsPerUser parameter. This parameter specifies the maximum number of connections that the Client Access server will accept from a particular user. The default value is 10. The possible values are from 1 through 1,000.

It is possible that users are connecting over POP3 but are not receiving the connection notification they expect. You can specify the message users receive on connection by setting a value in the Banner parameter, for example:

```
Set-POPSettings –Banner "You have just connected to the Tailspin Toys Exchange 2007
organization through the post office protocol (POP3). Unread e-mail messages in your inbox
are bolded."
```

PowerShell commands based on the *Get-POPSettings* cmdlet enable you to view POP3 settings on a Microsoft Exchange Server 2007 server that has the Client Access server role installed and that is running the POP3 service. The Server parameter is supported, and you can run these commands remotely. For example, the following command returns full details of the POP3 settings on the Client Access server Glasgow:

```
Get-POPSettings –Server Glasgow | Format-List
```

Figure 10-36 shows the output from this command.

PowerShell commands based on the *Set-IMAPSettings* cmdlet enable you to set specific IMAP4 settings for an Exchange Server 2007 server with the Client Access server role installed that is running the IMAP4 service. You can run this cmdlet for a single Client Access server or for all Exchange 2007 Client Access servers that have the

IMAP4 service installed. PowerShell commands based on the *Get-IMAPSettings* cmdlet return IMAP4 settings for an Exchange Server 2007 server with the Client Access server role installed that is running the IMAP4 service. The commands are similar to those used to configure POP3 settings and obtain information about these settings.

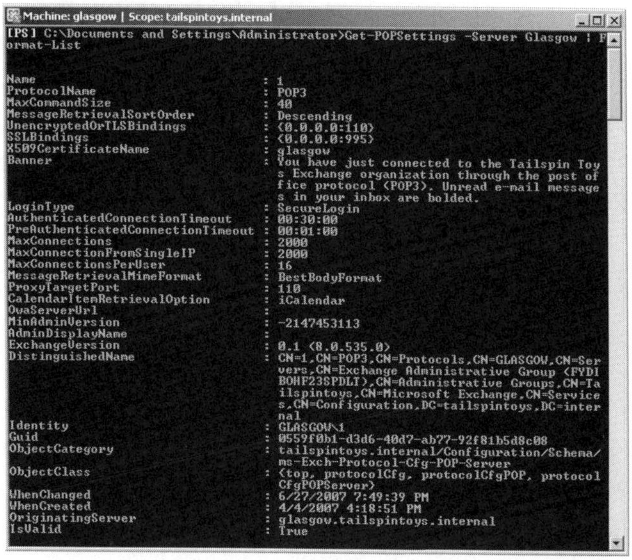

Figure 10-36 POP3 properties for the Glasgow Client Access server

---

MORE INFO *Set-POPSettings*, *Get-POPSettings*, *Set-IMAPSettings*, and *Get-IMAPSettings*

For more information about the commands associated with these cmdlets, search Exchange Server 2007 Help for the appropriate cmdlet or access *http://technet.microsoft.com/en-us/library/aa997154.aspx*, *http://technet.microsoft.com/en-us/library/aa997158.aspx*, *http://technet.microsoft.com/en-us/library/aa998252.aspx*, and *http://technet.microsoft.com/en-us/library/aa996388.aspx*, respectively.

Testing Network Connectivity

You can address client connectivity issues over POP3 or IMAP4 by determining that the required service is running on the Client Access server and the client mailbox and by ensuring that the service settings are correctly configured. You can look at the POP3 and IMAP4 performance counters to determine that connections are being established. If, however, you have a particular user logged in at a particular client computer that cannot connect and you have checked that the services are running and that the configurations are correct, the problem, by a process of elimination, is probably an unsatisfactory network connection between the client computer and the Exchange Server 2007 organization.

Most firewalls block Internet Control Message Protocol (ICMP), so pinging the appropriate Exchange Server 2007 server from the client computer or using the *tracert* command will probably not work. You can, however, use the *ipconfig* command (for example, *ipconfig /all*) to test the client's IP configuration. You can then test connectivity by using the Telnet client to connect to the appropriate port—110 for POP3, 143 for IMAP4, and 25 for SMTP—on the appropriate Exchange Server 2007 server. For example, to test POP3 connectivity to the Exchange Server 2007 Client Access server Glasgow from a client computer, you can enter the following at the client computer's Command Console (cmd.exe):

```
telnet Glasgow 110
```

If the command returns the message that the appropriate service is ready, then you know you have connectivity and the service is running. You can use the QUIT command to return to the command prompt, although if you are checking SMTP connections, it is a good idea to first enter the EHLO command to obtain more details. Figure 10-37 shows the output from an EHLO command.

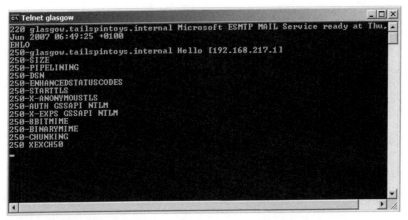

Figure 10-37   SMTP EHLO command

Practice: Reading and Filtering Mailbox Statistics

In this practice session, you read mailbox statistics by using the Identity, Database, and Server parameters. You then filter mailbox statistics to obtain information about the mailboxes that contain the largest total item size and item count. You display these statistics and capture them in a CSV file.

You will get better results from this practice session if you have generated some e-mail traffic on your test network. At the very least, you should have completed Practice 2 in Lesson 1 of this chapter. The practices assume that the mailbox-enabled users Kim Akers, Don Hall, and Keith Harris exist on your Exchange Server 2007 server.

If you have software installed that can display statistics graphically (for example, Microsoft Excel), you can expand the practice session by opening the CSV file you generate and displaying the sizes of the databases as a histogram.

▶ **Practice 1: Reading Mailbox Statistics**

In this practice, you read statistics for a single mailbox, several mailboxes, all the mailboxes in a database, all the mailboxes in a storage group, and all the mailboxes on a server. You display results in both table and list format:

1. If necessary, log on to your Exchange Server 2007 server by using the Kim_Akers account.

2. Open Exchange Management Shell.

3. To get the statistics for a single mailbox in table format, enter the following command:

    ```
    Get-MailboxStatistics -Identity keith.harris@tailspintoys.internal
    ```

    Your screen should look similar to Figure 10-38.

Figure 10-38   Statistics for Keith Harris in table format

4. To get full statistics for a single mailbox in list format, enter the following command:

```
Get-MailboxStatistics -Identity keith.harris@tailspintoys.internal | Format-List
```

Your screen should look similar to Figure 10-39.

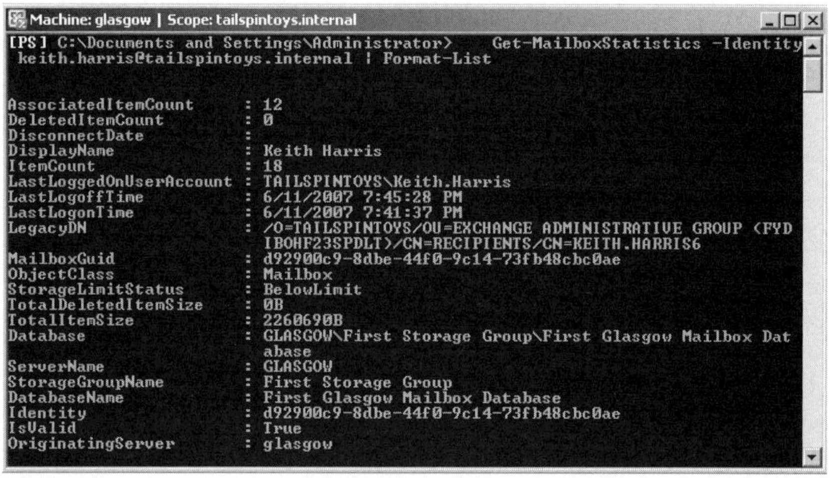

Figure 10-39   Statistics for Keith Harris in list format

5. To get the statistics for two mailboxes in table format, enter the following command:

```
Get-Mailbox -Filter { (Name -eq "Don Hall") -or (Name -eq "Keith Harris") } | Get-Mailbox
Statistics
```

Your screen should look similar to Figure 10-40.

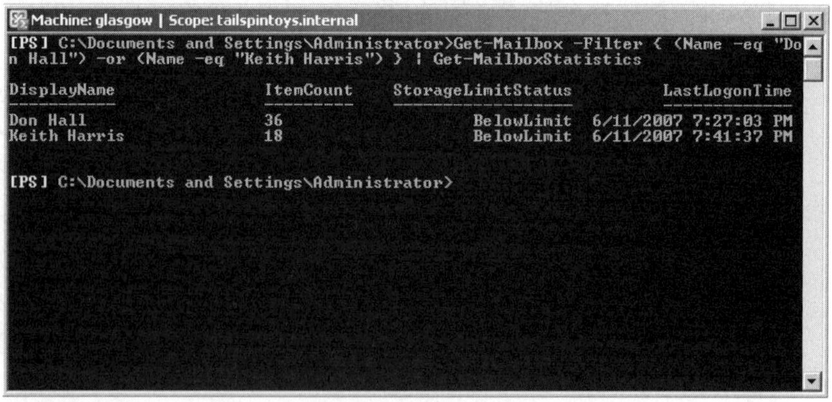

Figure 10-40   Statistics for Don Hall and Keith Harris in table format

6. To get the statistics for all mailboxes in the First Glasgow Mailbox Database in the First Storage Group in table format, enter the following command:

```
Get-MailboxStatistics -Database "First Storage Group\First Glasgow Mailbox Database"
```

Your screen should look similar to Figure 10-41.

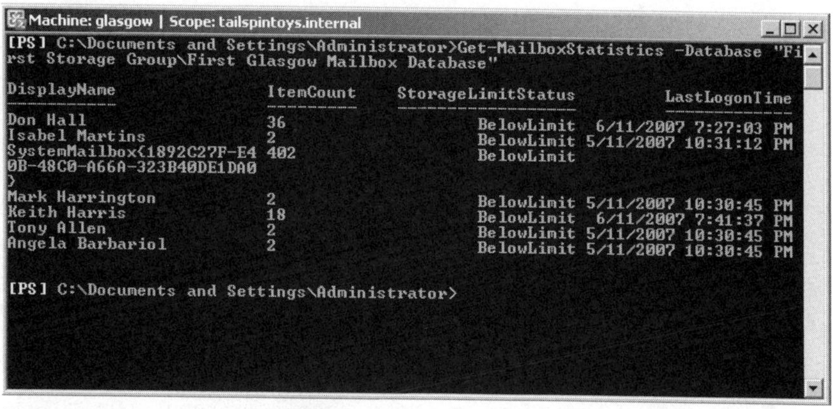

Figure 10-41 Statistics for all mailboxes in the First Glasgow Mailbox Database in table format

7. To get the statistics for all mailboxes in the First Storage Group in table format, you need to pipe a command based on the *Get-MailboxDatabase* cmdlet into the command to get mailbox statistics. Enter the following command:

```
Get-MailboxDatabase -StorageGroup "First Storage Group" | Get-MailboxStatistics
```

8. To get the statistics for all mailboxes on the Exchange Server 2007 server Glasgow, enter the following command:

```
Get-MailboxStatistics -Server "Glasgow"
```

▶ **Practice 2: Filtering Mailbox Statistics**

In this practice, you filter mailbox statistics by using the TotalItemSize and ItemCount parameters. You redirect the output of a command to a CSV file that you can display as a text file or read with reporting or statistical graphics software:

1. If necessary, log on to your Exchange Server 2007 server by using the Kim_Akers account.

2. Open Exchange Management Shell.

3. To get the statistics in table format for all mailboxes in the First Storage Group that have a total item size greater than or equal to 1 MB, enter the following command:

```
Get-MailboxDatabase -StorageGroup "First Storage Group" | Get-MailboxStatistics | Where
{$_.TotalItemSize -ge 1MB}
```

Your screen should look similar to Figure 10-42.

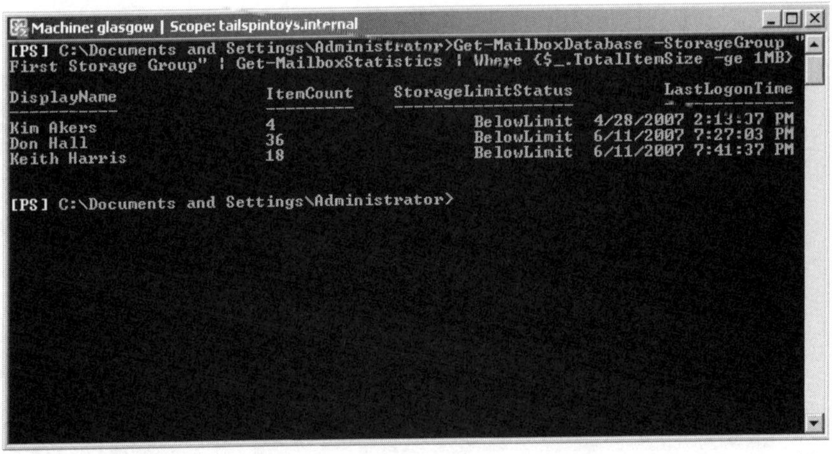

Figure 10-42 Statistics for all mailboxes in the First Storage Group with a total item size of 1 MB or more

4. To get the statistics in table format for all mailboxes on the Server Glasgow that hold 20 items or more, enter the following command:

```
Get-MailboxStatistics -Server "Glasgow" | Where {$_.ItemCount -ge 20}
```

Your screen should look similar to Figure 10-43.

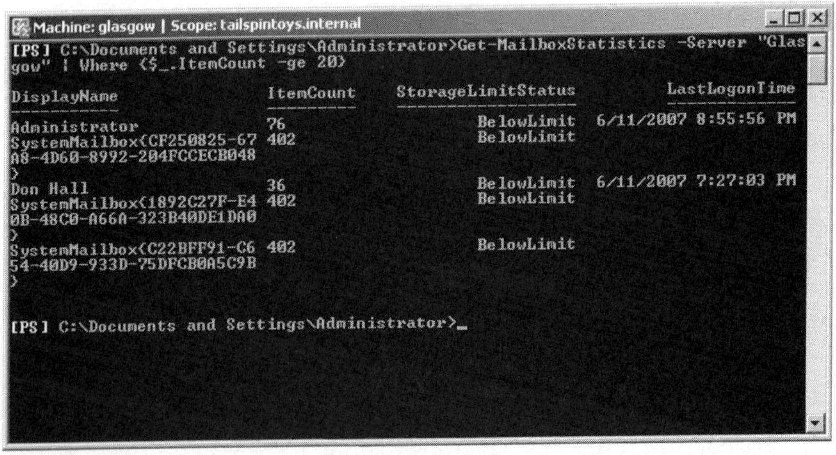

Figure 10-43 Statistics for all mailboxes on the server Glasgow with an item count of 20 or more

5. To get the statistics in list format for all mailboxes in the First Storage Group that have a total item size greater than or equal to 1 MB and redirect the output into the file C:\SizeStats.csv, enter the following command:

```
Get-MailboxDatabase –StorageGroup "First Storage Group" | Get-MailboxStatistics | Where
{$_.TotalItemSize -ge 1MB} | Export-Csv C:\SizeStats.csv
```

6. Open the file C:\SizeStats.csv with a text editor such as Microsoft Notepad. Your screen should look similar to Figure 10-44. You can open CSV files with a wide variety of software packages, for example, Microsoft Excel, Access, or SQL Server, for report generation and analysis. For example, Figure 10-45 shows the same file opened in Excel.

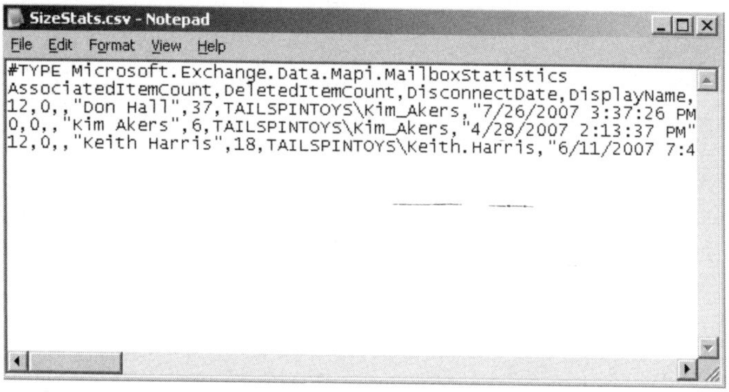

Figure 10-44   Mailbox statistics captured in a CSV file

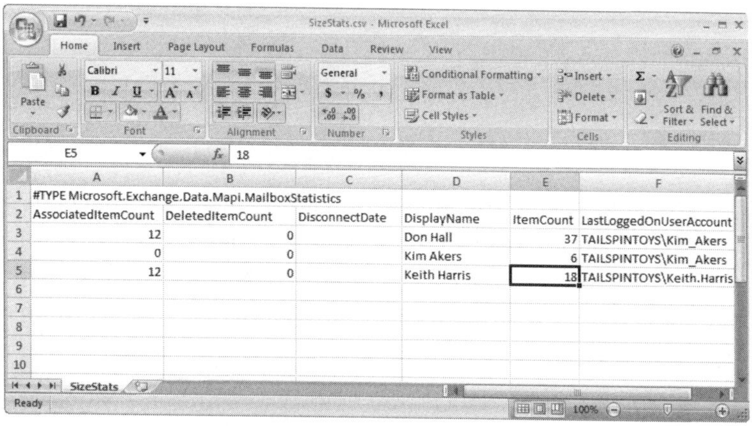

Figure 10-45   Mailbox statistics CSV file opened in Excel

Lesson Summary

- You can obtain mailbox statistics by using commands based on the *Get-Mailbox-Statistics* cmdlet.

- You can check mailbox health by looking at values in counters associated mainly with the MSExchangeIS Mailbox performance object. Alerts based on these counters write entries to the Application event log when triggered, and you can use commands based on the *Get-EventLog* cmdlet to view these entries. You can check counters associated with the MSExchangePop3 and MSExchangeImap4 objects if the POP3 and IMAP4 services are enabled.

- You configure protocol logging by using commands based on the *Set-Transport-Server*, *Set-SendConnector*, and *Set-ReceiveConnector* cmdlets. You can enable or disable protocol logging and specify the maximum size and age of protocol log files and the maximum size of the protocol log directory.

- You can use PowerShell commands to enable IMAP4 and POP3 for Client Access servers and individual mailboxes and to set and check IMAP4 and POP3 settings.

Lesson Review

You can use the following questions to test your knowledge of the information in Lesson 2, "Monitoring Client Connectivity." The questions are also available on the companion CD if you prefer to review them in electronic form.

NOTE **Answers**

Answers to these questions and explanations of why each answer choice is correct or incorrect are located in the "Answers" section at the end of the book.

---

1. You want mailbox statistics for mailboxes kim.akers@tailspintoys.internal, don.hall@tailspintoys.internal, and keith.harris@tailspintoys.internal. You want the statistics displayed in table format. What command do you enter in Exchange Management Shell on the Exchange Server 2007 server Glasgow in the tailspintoys.internal domain?

    A. *Get-MailboxStatistics −Identity "kim.akers@tailspintoys.internal, don.hall@tailspintoys.internal, keith.harrisl@tailspintoys.internal" | Format-List*

    B. *Get-MailboxStatistics −Identity "kim.akers@tailspintoys.internal, don.hall@tailspintoys.internal, keith.harrisl@tailspintoys.internal" | Format-Table*

    C. *Get-Mailbox -Filter { (Name −eq "Kim Akers") −or (Name −eq "Keith Harris") - or (Name −eq "Don Hall") } | Get-MailboxStatistics | Format-List*

    D. *Get-Mailbox -Filter { (Name −eq "Kim Akers") −or (Name −eq "Keith Harris") - or (Name −eq "Don Hall") } | Get-MailboxStatistics | Format-Table*

2. You want detailed mailbox statistics for mailboxes on the Exchange Server 2007 server Glasgow that are 1 GB or larger or that contain 5,000 items or more (or both). What command do you enter in Exchange Management Shell?

    A. *Get-MailboxStatistics -Server "Glasgow" | Where { ($_.TotalItemSize -ge 1GB) -or ($_.ItemCount -ge 5000) } | Format-List*

    B. *Get-MailboxStatistics -Server "Glasgow" | Where { ($_.TotalItemSize -eq 1GB) -or ($_.ItemCount -eq 5000) } | Format-List*

    C. *Get-MailboxStatistics -Server "Glasgow" | Where { ($_.TotalItemSize -ge 1GB) -and ($_.ItemCount -ge 5000) } | Format-List*

    D. *Get-MailboxStatistics -Server "Glasgow" | Where { ($_.TotalItemSize -eq 1GB) -and ($_.ItemCount -eq 5000) } | Format-List*

3. You want to create a performance counter log that records the total number of recipients that have received a message since start-up, the total number of messages delivered to all recipients since start-up, the rate that recipients receive messages, the rate that messages are delivered to all recipients, the total number of messages sent to transport since start-up, and the rate that messages are sent to the transport. What MSExhangeIS Mailbox counters do you add to the log? (Choose all that apply.)

    A. Local Deliveries

    B. Local Delivery Rate

    C. Message Recipients Delivered

    D. Message Recipients Delivered/Sec

    E. Messages Delivered

    F. Messages Delivered/Sec

    G. Logon Operations/Sec

    H. Messages Sent

    I. Messages Sent/Sec

4. You want to enable protocol logging on the intra-organization Send connector on the Exchange Server 2007 server Glasgow with the Hub Transport server role

installed. What command do you enter in Exchange Management Shell on that server?

   A. *Set-SendConnector "IntraOrgConnector" –ProtocolLoggingLevel Verbose*

   B. *Set-TransportServer Glasgow –IntraOrgConnectorProtocolLoggingLevel Verbose*

   C. *Set-SendConnector "IntraOrgConnector" –ProtocolLoggingLevel $True*

   D. *Set-TransportServer Glasgow –IntraOrgConnectorProtocolLoggingLevel $True*

5. You want to enable IMAP4 for the Keith Harris mailbox on the Exchange Server 2007 Client Access server Melbourne. What PowerShell command do you use?

   A. *Set-CASMailbox -Identity "Keith Harris" –ImapEnabled $true*

   B. *Set-CASMailbox -Identity "Keith Harris" –Imap4Enabled $true*

   C. *Set-CASMailbox –Server Melbourne -Identity "Keith Harris" –Imap4Enabled $$True*

   D. *Set-CASMailbox –Server Melbourne -Identity "Keith Harris" –ImapEnabled $True*

Chapter Review

To further practice and reinforce the skills you learned in this chapter, you can perform the following tasks:

- Review the chapter summary.
- Review the list of key terms introduced in this chapter.
- Complete the case scenarios. These scenarios set up real-world situations involving the topics of this chapter and ask you to create a solution.
- Complete the suggested practices.
- Take a practice test.

Chapter Summary

- You can track messages in the message tracking log by using the Exchange Troubleshooting Assistant Message Tracker tool and commands based on the *Get-MessageTrackingLog* cmdlet.

- You configure message tracking settings by using commands based on the *Set-MailboxServer* or *Set-TransportServer* cmdlet. You configure protocol logging by using commands based on the *Set-TransportServer*, *Set-SendConnector*, and *Set-ReceiveConnector* cmdlets. You can use PowerShell commands to enable the IMAP4 and POP3 services and to configure and check IMAP4 and POP3 settings.

- You can enable or disable message tracking and protocol logging and specify the maximum size and age of the associated log files and the maximum size of the directory in which they are located.

- You can obtain mailbox statistics by using commands based on the *Get-MailboxStatistics* cmdlet and check mailbox health and client connectivity by looking at values in counters associated with the MSExchangeIS Mailbox, MSExchangePop3, and MSExchangeImap4 performance objects.

Key Terms

Do you know what these key terms mean? You can check your answers by looking up the terms in the glossary at the end of the book.

- Circular logging
- Mailbox server
- Mailbox statistics
- Message subject logging
- Message tracking log
- Performance counters
- Performance object
- Protocol logging
- Transport server

Case Scenarios

In the following case scenarios, you will apply what you have learned about message tracking and mailbox health. You can find answers to these questions in the "Answers" section at the end of this book.

Case Scenario 1: Tracking Messages

You administer the Exchange 2007 organization at the Graphic Design Institute. You only recently started in the job, and you are still discovering how your predecessor set things up. Employees at the Institute have been reporting delays in the delivery of e-mail messages. You need to track specific messages by sender, recipients, and subject as part of your investigation into this problem. Answer the following questions:

1. A manager asks you to track an e-mail message sent to several recipients. She tells you that "Meeting Room 1" was in the subject line. When you try to track the message by subject, you cannot do so, and you conclude that message subject logging has been disabled on the transport server Chicago. What Exchange Management Server command do you enter to enable it?

2. The Human Resources manager Kim Akers (mailbox kim.akers@graphicde-signinstitute.com) wants you to track an e-mail message she has sent to keith.harris@Contoso.com between 9:00 AM and 5:00 PM on May 21, 2007. What command do you enter in Exchange Management Shell?

3. You find that an excessive number of tracking logs are being created on a transport server called Boston and determine that your predecessor has set the size of individual tracking log files on this server to too small a value. You want to restore this setting to 10 MB. What command do you enter in Exchange Management Shell?

Case Scenario 2: Configuring Baseline Counter Logs

You are an employed by Contoso Ltd to administer the company's Exchange 2007 organization. You want to set baselines for normal operation during quiet, typical, and busy periods. You intend using these baseline logs to track the load on your Exchange Server 2007 servers through time and to determine alert threshold levels so that you are warned about abnormal operation. Answer the following questions:

1. You want to record counter values that indicate the load on your public folders. What performance object do you select?

2. You want to monitor remote delivery queues on one of your servers. What performance object do you select, and what counters associated with that object do you add to your counter log?

3. You want to record the rate that requests to open messages are submitted to the information store, the rate that recipients receive messages, and the rate that messages are sent to the transport for one storage group on a particular server. You select the MSExchangeIS Mailbox performance object and the instance of that object that corresponds to the storage group that you want to monitor. What counters do you add to the counter log?

Suggested Practices

To help you successfully master the exam objectives presented in this chapter, complete the following tasks.

Message Tracking

Do all the practices in this section.

- **Practice 1: Read and Analyze CSV Files** Message tracking logs are CSV files that can be read by report generation and analysis software as well as the Message Tracking tool and Exchange Management Shell commands. Investigate the use of such software. If you have Microsoft Office installed on your test network, then Microsoft Access and Excel provide a good starting point for this exercise.

- **Practice 2: Investigate the Get-MessageTrackingLog Cmdlet** Search Exchange Server 2007 Help for "Get-MessageTrackingLog." Familiarize yourself with the syntax of the commands based on this cmdlet. Experiment with the various parameters that you can specify in these commands.

■ **Practice 3: Investigate the Set-TransportServer and Set-MailboxServer Cmdlets**
Search Exchange Server 2007 Help for "Set-TransportServer" and "Set-Mailbox-Server." Familiarize yourself with the syntax of the commands based on these cmdlets. Experiment with the various parameters that you can specify in these commands.

Monitoring Client Connectivity

Do all the practices in this section.

■ **Practice 1: Display and Filter Mailbox Statistics**   Pipe the output of commands based on the *Get-MailboxStatistics* cmdlet into the Format-List command and investigate the various parameters (or variables) that you can use to filter mailbox statistics. Export the output of the same commands into a CSV file by using the Export-Csv command and investigate the use of report generation and analysis software that can open CSV files.

■ **Practice 2: Investigate Performance Objects and Counters**   Exchange Server 2007 adds a large number of performance objects and associated counters to the Performance tools. Open Exchange Server Performance Monitor and use the Add Counters dialog box to identify these objects and counters. Use the Explain feature in that dialog box to find out what the various counters monitor.

■ **Practice 3: Investigate Protocol Logging**   Enable protocol logging on the connectors you configured in Chapter 7. Generate some e-mail traffic that uses these connectors and investigate the protocol logs. Look at methods of generating reports from the protocol log CSV files.

■ **Practice 4: Investigate POP3 and IMAP4 Configuration**   Search the Help files for the *Set-Service*, *Get-Service*, *Set-CASMailbox*, *Get-CASMailbox*, *Set-POPSettings*, *Get-POPSettings*, *Set-IMAPSettings*, and *Get-IMAPSettings* cmdlets and investigate the parameters associated with these cmdlets. Use the commands to enable, disable, configure, and check POP3 and IMAP4 on Client Access servers and individual mailboxes.

Take a Practice Test

The practice tests on this book's companion CD offer many options. For example, you can test yourself on just one exam objective, or you can test yourself on all the 70-236 certification exam content. You can set up the test so that it closely simulates the experience of taking a certification exam, or you can set it up in study mode so that you can look at the correct answers and explanations after you answer each question.

MORE INFO   **Practice tests**

For details about all the practice test options available, see the "How to Use the Practice Tests" section in this book's Introduction.

Chapter 11

Reporting

You can monitor the health of your servers, the operation of your Exchange organization, the size and health of your databases, and the length of your message queues and take action if any of your results indicated a present or potential problem. You can determine which users have the largest mailboxes and are sending or receiving the most messages, whether your organization is receiving more spam than usual, and whether your anti-spam measures are coping with it.

However, collecting information is only part of your job. Information is useful only if it can be correctly interpreted. Abnormal readings that warn you when a disk is near capacity or that indicate that messages are not being received are typically dealt with quickly as they happen. However, most readings do not trigger alerts. Most problems creep up on you gradually, and you will not realize they are happening unless your system performance data is displayed in a clear and meaningful manner that lets you compare against baselines and identify trends.

In addition, technical support and administration do not exist in a vacuum. You need to attend meetings and give presentations. Sometimes you need to reassure colleagues that everything is working as it should; at other times you need to warn about increased usage and justify budgeting for expansion and equipment refresh or software upgrades. Typically, management is not impressed by vague statements; it needs clearly stated and well-illustrated facts.

Collecting data is important. Analyzing that data and creating reports is arguably even more so. This chapter is about how you create reports and what reports you need to create.

Exam objectives in this chapter:
- Create server reports.
- Create usage reports.

Lessons in this chapter:

Before You Begin

To complete the lessons in this chapter, you must have done the following:

- Installed Windows Exchange Server 2007 with the Mailbox, Client Access, Hub Transport, and Unified Messaging roles on a Windows domain controller in the Tailspintoys.internal domain. To do this, you need to have completed all the Practices in Lessons 1 and 2 of Chapter 1, "Preparing for Exchange Installation," and Lesson 1 of Chapter 2, "Installing Exchange Server and Configuring Roles."

- Installed .NET Framework 1.1 and Exchange Troubleshooting Assistant (ExTRA) on your Exchange Server 2007 server as described in the practice session of Lesson 2 in Chapter 9, "Monitoring."

Real World

Ian McLean

I once knew an administrator who had grown old and wise in his job. I confess to some envy, having achieved only the former. He was very keen on reports, and those his department produced were masterpieces of clarity. Nicely labeled and annotated graphs showed trends very clearly and highlighted where future effort or investment would be advisable, histograms gave a crystal-clear illustration of the situation at a point of time, and pie charts indicated resource usage beautifully.

I was discussing other matters of mutual interest when he mentioned he was shortly attending a budget meeting chaired by a company director with a particular reputation for obduracy. This executive was immune to reasoned argument and typically took the position that if something had worked fine last year, there was no need to spend any more money on it this year. Whatever figures anyone gave her in support of a proposal she inevitably tried to use to argue against it.

My colleague asked me if I wanted to see a presentation he had prepared. I told him I had already seen and greatly admired his reports and accompanying charts. "These ones are different," he said.

His charts were now three-dimensional. Graphs loomed like sections of the Hoover dam, histograms resembled the Manhattan skyline, and pie charts looked good enough to eat. Call-outs and annotations abounded. The whole effect was like a collaboration between Picasso and Escher. It was enough to stun a whole herd of executives.

"Magnificent," I said, "but, there is only one problem. The actual data is completely obscured."

He grinned. "That is the main advantage," he said.

Lesson 1: Creating Server Reports

Several high-level tools exist that help you produce reports that indicate how well your servers are coping in a production environment. Typically, tools such as Microsoft Operations Manager (MOM) 2005 Service Pack 1 (SP1) and Microsoft System Center Operations Manager 2007 run on their own servers and work with Microsoft SQL databases to produce reports, typically by using the features of Microsoft SQL Server 2005 or 2008 Report Builder. Note that only the full version of MOM has the facilities to produce server reports; the workstation version cannot do so.

Exchange Server 2007 also provides monitoring tools that let you monitor server health performance and availability. Exchange Server Performance Monitor provides the Performance Logs and Alerts tool, which lets you display logged performance counter data in report format. The Microsoft Exchange Best Practices Analyzer (EXBPA), Exchange Performance Troubleshooter, Exchange Database Recovery Management, and Exchange Mail Flow Troubleshooter tools provide reports specific to Exchange and to the flow of e-mail traffic. Queue Viewer lets you examine queues and messages and can indicate whether an Exchange Server 2007 server is experiencing traffic surges and delays. Exchange Management Shell commands can gather information and put it in a comma-separated value (CSV) file that can be opened with report generation software. This lesson looks at these tools.

After this lesson, you will be able to:

- Create server availability reports.
- Use EXBPA to create performance and health reports.
- Create database reports.
- Create message queue reports.

Estimated lesson time: 45 minutes

Creating Server Availability Reports

You can create server availability reports that display server usage and availability reports for basic Windows Server 2003 or 2008 server and operating system operation functions and for the operation of Exchange Server 2007 running on the server. You can access information about the usage and availability of the four major server resource systems: processor, memory, disk, and network.

You can also get reports on databases and transaction logs and on queue lengths and message throughput. You can use all these reports to determine whether your servers are working as they should, where the bottlenecks are, and whether the pressure on any resource is likely to reach an unacceptable level. A report should compare current usage with baseline levels and indicate trends.

Using MOM to Create Server Availability Reports

MOM is a general tool used to monitor production servers. It can generate reports on the availability of server systems and on the operation of the various types of server that you use in a production environment, for example, file and print servers, Internet Information Server (IIS) servers, Terminal Services servers, Internet Security and Acceleration (ISA) servers, domain controllers, and so on. The full version of MOM 2005 SP1 requires that SQL 2000 Server, SQL Server 2005, or SQL Server 2008 be available in the organization and that .NET Framework 1.1 be installed on the server on which it runs.

If you want to use MOM to generate reports specific to Exchange, you need to install the Exchange Server Management Pack on the server running MOM. This pack generates reports about Exchange services, database size and whether databases are mounted, available free disk space, client connectivity, mail flow, efficiency and reliability statistics, security settings, and the current backup regime and whether circular logging is enabled.

MOM 2005 SP1 with the Exchange Server Management Pack installed also generates user reports, for example, top 100 senders or top 100 users. Lesson 2 of this chapter discusses user reports.

MORE INFO   MOM 2005 product documentation

For general information about using MOM monitoring and reporting for all servers on a production network, access *http://technet.microsoft.com/en-us/opsmgr/bb498230.aspx* and follow the links. For more information about the use of MOM 2005 SP1 with the Exchange Management Pack to generate reports specific to Exchange, access *http://www.microsoft.com/downloads/details.aspx? FamilyId=2215EEAB-41D7-423D-9F54-01F0DF4647E9&displaylang=en* and download the Exchange Server Management Pack Guide for MOM 2005.

Using System Center Operations Manager 2007

Although MOM 2005 SP1 is still widely used and provides a good method of monitoring Exchange Server 2007 servers when Exchange Management Pack is installed,

System Center Operations Manager 2007 is seen as a replacement and update, particularly for monitoring and reporting server availability.

System Center Operations Manager 2007 provides alert, state, performance, and diagram views of the network infrastructure and lets you configure new rules (similar to MOM 2005 SP1) and create groups on which rules will operate. A reporting interface is integrated into the Operations console, eliminating the need to click a hyperlink and visit a separate reporting Web site (as is required with MOM). The My Workspace facility lets you create custom views, save frequently used views and searches, and configure custom alert notification subscriptions.

The tool also provides a Health Explorer facility, which displays a hierarchical tree structure that shows the health of a server object or entity you choose to monitor. Entities are monitored on at least four parameters: availability, configuration, performance, and security.

The tool also provides the Operations Manager Command Shell, which allows administrative control from the command line. Like Exchange Management Shell, the Operations Manager Command Shell is a specially configured instance of Windows PowerShell, and you can use PowerShell commands to configure settings and obtain information; for example, the following command returns a list of open critical alerts on the server on which it runs (note that the *Get-Alert* cmdlet is available only in the Operations Manager Command Shell):

```
Get-Alert | where {$_.Severity -gt "Warning" -and $_.ResolutionState -eq 0 } | Format-List
```

The Reporting function in System Center Operations Manager 2007 is similar to that in MOM 2005 SP1 but with some important enhancements. Unlike MOM, the new tool does not use Data Transformation Services (DTS) to retrieve reporting data from the operations database. Instead, data is inserted directly into the reporting database at the same time it is inserted into the operations database.

System Center Operations Manager reports contain new smart parameter headers, providing the flexibility to define and report on specific and relative date and time ranges. The object picker in the smart parameter header provides search facilities, and the flexible date picker eliminates the need to modify report definition files to achieve a specific relative date range in recurring reports.

Figure 11-1 shows a typical System Center Operations Manager report. You can click on either the graph or the table in the report to obtain more information.

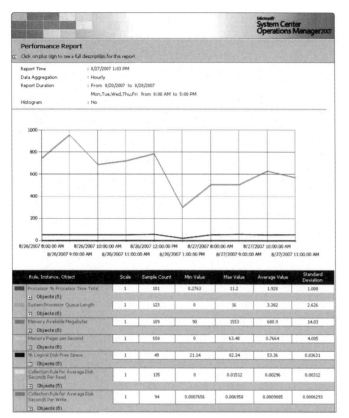

Figure 11-1   A typical System Center Operations Manager report

---

Exam Tip   As a professional Exchange administrator, you need to be aware of the tools you would use to generate reports on a busy production network. MOM 2005 SP1 and System Center Operations Manager 2007 are not mentioned specifically in the 70-236 examination objectives, and it is not practicable to install such tools on a small test network that you set up to study for the examination. You need to know that the tools exist and what they can be used for. If you have access to them on a production network, it is a good idea to have a look at them. Nevertheless, the examination is unlikely to test these tools in any depth.

Using the Reports View in Performance Logs and Alerts

The Performance Logs and Alerts tool is part of the Exchange Server Performance Monitor tool and was introduced in Chapter 9. When you create a performance log that you intend to run for a long time and that contains both historical and current data, you might typically change the capture period to, for example, 15 minutes or longer. You can set the log to run continuously and sample data periodically in Report view; you can schedule the log to run periodically, for example, at a certain time of day; or you can trigger the log to run whenever an alert triggers and then set the alert to trigger when mail flow reaches a certain level that indicates a busy period.

To create a Counter log, you open Exchange Server Performance Monitor from Toolbox in Exchange Management Console, expand Performance Logs and Alerts in the left-hand pane, right-click Counter Logs, and select New Log Settings. You need to specify a name for the log (for example, MyLog). In the Properties box for the counter log, shown in Figure 11-2, you can add entire Performance objects (this adds every counter for a selected object) or add selected counters only.

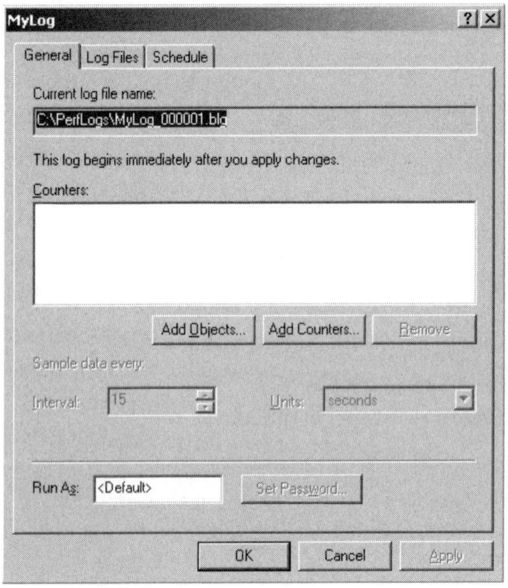

Figure 11-2   Creating a log file

Typically, you might choose to add counters that measure general server performance, for example, Processor: %Processor Time, Memory: Pages/Sec, Physical Disk: Avg. Disk Sec/Write, or Physical Disk: Avg. Disk Sec/Read. You would typically also add Exchange-specific counters associated with objects such as MSExchangeIS Mailbox or MSExchangeIS Public. Figure 11-3 shows counters being added.

When you have defined the counters you want to add, you can specify the sample interval, define the location of the log file, and schedule when the log runs. By default, the log starts as soon as it is created, and you stop it manually, but you can change these settings on the Schedule tab. You can also run the log in the context of a specified user account, in which case you need to specify a password. If you do not specify the location of the log file, it is placed in C:\Perflogs by default.

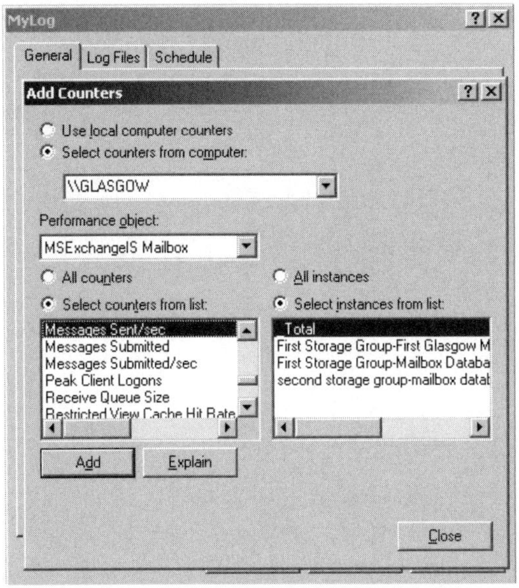

Figure 11-3   Adding counters to a Performance log

You can view a log file by opening System Monitor in Exchange Server Performance Monitor, clicking View Log Data, and selecting Log Files on the Source tab in the System Monitor Properties dialog box. You then click Add, double-click the log file you want to view, and click OK. You select Report View to view the log file. This provides a snapshot, and you need to record your snapshots over time to generate reports. In effect, this is what tools such as MOM 2005 SP1 and System Center Operations Manager do.

Figure 11-4 shows a Performance log file in Report view. Although there has been little or no Exchange activity on the server Glasgow, the memory resource of the server is under stress. In this situation, you would need to compare results with baseline logs before making a final decision, but there is a strong indication that the server needs a memory upgrade.

Creating Reports by Using EXBPA

EXBPA, introduced in Chapter 9, automatically examines an Exchange Server 2007 deployment and determines whether the configuration is set according to Microsoft best practices. The tool can examine your Active Directory and Exchange Server 2007 servers and generate a list of issues, such as suboptimal configuration settings or unsupported or not-recommended options. You can also use it to report on the general health of a system. Chapter 9 discusses the use of the tool to troubleshoot specific problems.

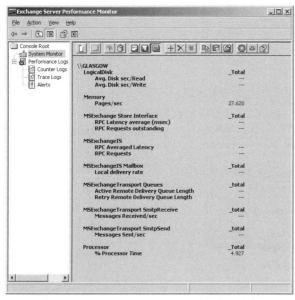

Figure 11-4   Performance log file in Report view

You can run EXBPA against an entire deployment, against a specific server, or against a set of servers. You access EXBPA by opening Exchange Management Console, clicking Toolbox, selecting the tool, and then clicking Open Tool. EXBPA first checks to find out if the tool itself needs to be updated. If you want to, you can cancel the process. On the Welcome screen, you have the choice of carrying out a new scan or accessing an existing scan.

To enable the reporting features of EXBPA, you choose to access an existing scan and then select the scan you want to view. You can then click View a report of this scan in the Best Practices Analyzer Wizard, as shown in Figure 11-5.

On the View Best Practices Report page, you can select List Reports, Tree Reports, and Other Reports. If you select List Reports, you can view Critical Issues, All Issues, Baseline, or Other Items. List Reports can be ordered by Class, Severity, or Issue. If you select Tree Reports, you can select Detailed View or Summary View. If you select Other Reports, you can access the Run Time Log. You can export reports as Hypertext Markup Language (HTML), CSV, or Extended Markup Language (XML) files. Figure 11-6 shows a List Report with All Issues selected.

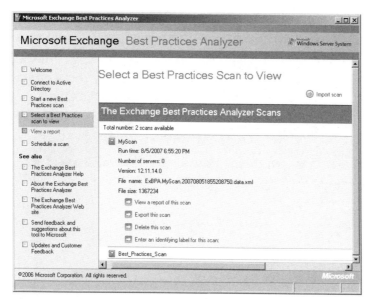

Figure 11-5   Viewing an EXBPA report

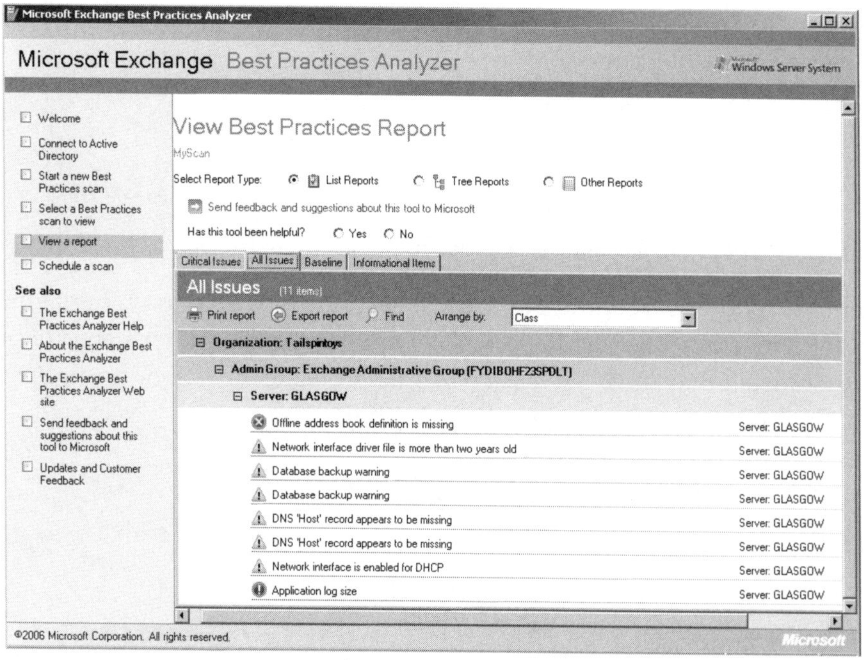

Figure 11-6   An EXBPA list report

Creating an EXBPA Performance Baseline Report

You can specify the type of scan EXBPA carries out and then create a report from that scan. If you select Health Scan, you have the option of specifying Performance Baseline. Typically, this adds two hours on to the time taken by the scan. Figure 11-7 shows this option. You can also specify the speed of your LAN or WAN.

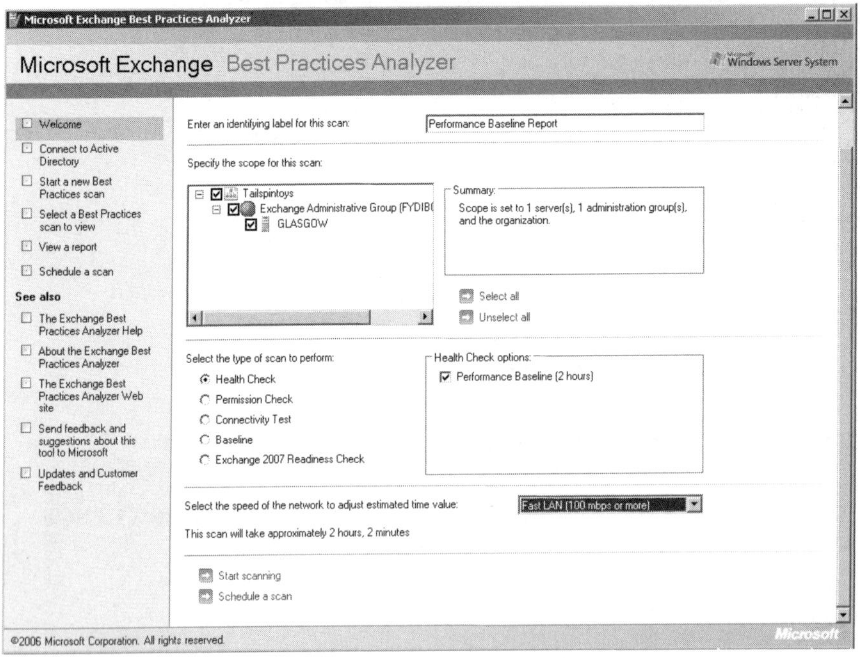

Figure 11-7   Specifying a health check with performance baseline scan

Figure 11-8 shows part of the extensive list of items on the Informational Items tab of a performance baseline List Report. You would capture a performance baseline after you first install Exchange Server 2007 or if you make any major changes to the software, Exchange organization, or network infrastructure.

Creating Health Reports by Using EXBPA

You can use EXBPA to carry out one of the following types of scan:

- Health check (with or without performance baseline)
- Permission check

- Connectivity test
- Baseline
- Exchange 2007 readiness check

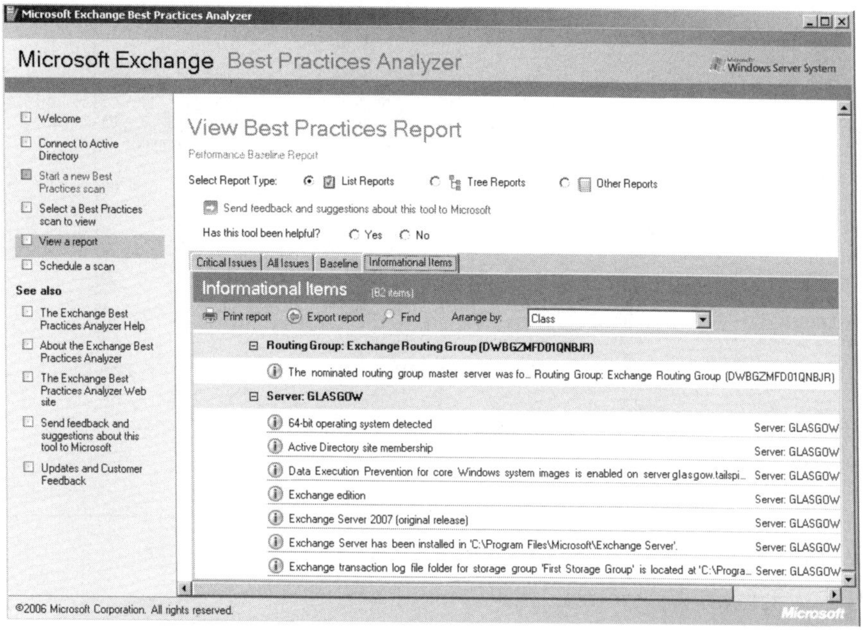

Figure 11-8 Informational items for a performance baseline report in EXBPA

If you carry out a health check without specifying performancebaseline, then the scan takes less time and returns fewer items. You should carry out such scans on a regular basis. Figure 11-9 shows the Detailed View tab of the report type Tree Reports for a health scan without the Performance Baseline option.

MORE INFO **EXBPA**

For more information about EXBPA, click The Exchange Best Practices Analyzer Help in the left-hand pane of the Microsoft Exchange Best Practices Analyzer Wizard or access *http://go.microsoft.com/ fwlink/?LinkId=33938*.

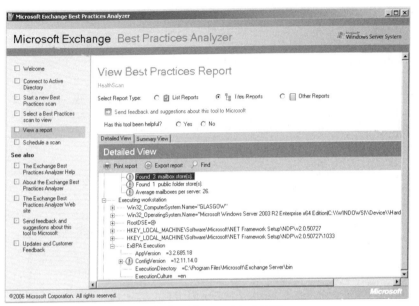

Figure 11-9   Detailed view of a health report in EXBPA

Quick Check

1.   What can you use the EXBPA tool for?

2.   What scans can EXBPA carry out?

Quick Check Answers

1.   EXBPA examines your Active Directory and Exchange Server 2007 servers and generates a list of issues, such as suboptimal configuration settings or unsupported or not-recommended options. You can also use it to report on the general health of a system.

2.   EXBPA carries out the following scans:

- ❏   Health check (with or without performance baseline).

- ❏   Permission check.

- ❏   Connectivity test.

- ❏   Baseline.

- ❏   Exchange 2007 readiness check.

Creating Database Reports

You can create database reports by using the Microsoft Exchange Troubleshooting Assistant (ExTRA) tools Exchange Performance Troubleshooter, Exchange Database Recovery Management, and Exchange Database Troubleshooter. All these tools are available from Exchange Management Console.

Using the Exchange Performance Troubleshooter

You access the Exchange Performance Troubleshooter by selecting Performance Troubleshooter in Exchange Management Console and clicking Open Tool. You can then choose to let the tool search for Exchange Troubleshooting Assistant upgrades or cancel the process. Exchange Performance Troubleshooter examines the performance of an Exchange Server messaging system and addresses issues such as slow switching between folders in Microsoft Office Outlook. It determines the most likely cause of a bottleneck and then creates step-by-step instructions to address the performance problem.

You access the reporting function in Exchange Performance Troubleshooter by clicking Select A Result File To View in the left-hand pane of the wizard and selecting from a list of troubleshooting scans. You can view or export the results. In the Tree Reports report type, you can view detailed or summary results. In the Other Reports report type, you can view the run-time log. Figure 11-10 shows the Detailed View tab for a Tree Reports report type in Exchange Performance Troubleshooter.

MORE INFO Exchange Troubleshooting Assistant

For more information about all the Exchange Troubleshooting Assistant tools, click the Exchange Troubleshooting Assistant Help in the left-hand pane of any of the wizards associated with these tools.

Using Exchange Database Recovery Management

You access Exchange Database Recovery Management by selecting Recovery Management in the Exchange Management Console and clicking Open Tool. You can choose to allow the tool to check for Exchange Troubleshooting Assistant upgrades, or you can cancel the process. You then access the Welcome page and give the job you want to perform a name.

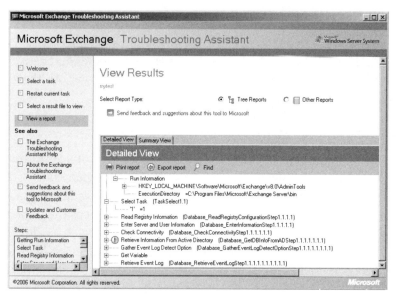

Figure 11-10 Exchange Performance Troubleshooter report

When you have named the job, you click Next to access the Select A Task page (or Task Center). A typical use for this tool is to examine an Exchange Server deployment when an Exchange Server database does not mount (the Repair Database option). Based on the problem found, the tool automatically generates step-by-step instructions to bring the database online. You can also use the tool to analyze log drive space, show database-related event logs, verify database and transaction log files, and create a recovery storage group (RSG). Chapter 12, "Disaster Recovery," discusses RSGs.

NOTE   Exchange Database Recovery Management works on dismounted databases

You can use the Repair Database and Verify Database And Transaction Log Files options in Exchange Database Recovery Management only if you have a dismounted database. If all your databases are mounted, these options return no results.

When you have completed a job by using this tool, it generates a report. Figure 11-11 shows reported Exchange transaction log statistics.

NOTE   Using Database Troubleshooter

The Exchange Database Troubleshooter lists event log entries that are relevant to databases. You start the tool in the normal way from Exchange Management Console. By default, it lists all database-related events that have occurred in the previous 120 minutes, but you can change this period.

NOTE   *Get-MailboxDatabase*

You can generate CSV files that contain data that can be used by reporting software to generate reports by using Exchange Management Shell commands based on the *Get-MailboxDatabase* cmdlet, piping the output of these commands into the *Export-Csv* cmdlet, and capturing the data in a CSV or text file. This technique is discussed later in this lesson.

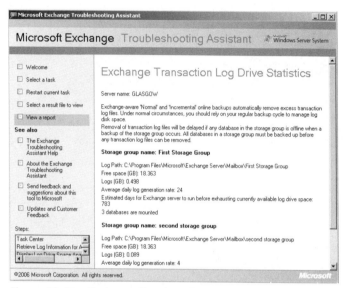

Figure 11-11   Exchange Database Recovery Management report

Creating Message Queue Reports

To determine whether e-mail is flowing smoothly through your Exchange organization, you can generate mail flow and queue reports. Exchange Management Console provides the Exchange Mail Flow Troubleshooter and Queue Viewer tools. Exchange Management Shell commands can extract information about messages and queues and redirect this into a CSV file. You can open CSV files with software that can generate reports and business graphics, for example, Microsoft Access, Excel, or SQL Server.

Using Queue Viewer

Queue Viewer can connect to all Exchange Server 2007 servers with the Hub Transport or Edge Transport server role installed. You can open the Queue Viewer tool in Exchange Management Console and create a filter to display the specific set of queues or messages that you want to monitor. You can then view the property information for these queues and messages. This can help you troubleshoot potential mail flow problems, such as messages that are queued for extended periods of time, peaks in queued messages, and spikes in queued messages. If you retain this information, you can use it to generate reports on queued messages and queue problems over an extended period of time. Figure 11-12 shows Queue Viewer filtered to display messages in the Unreachable queue on the transport server Glasgow.

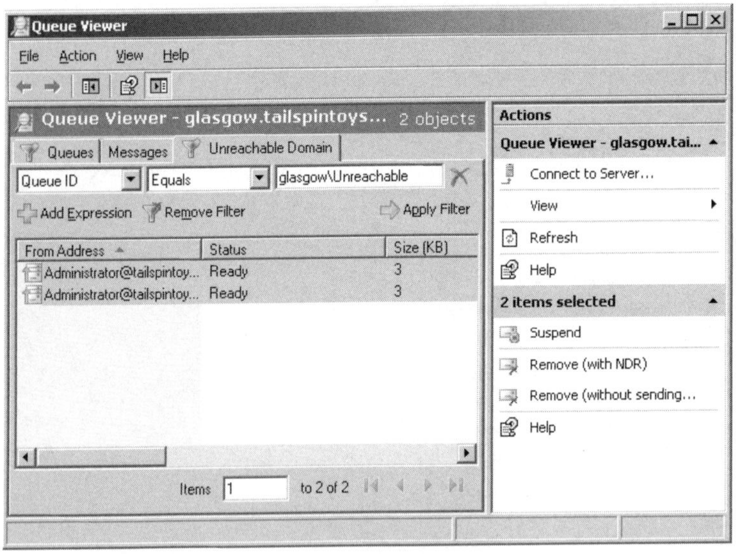

Figure 11-12 Showing messages in a queue.

Using Exchange Mail Flow Troubleshooter

The Exchange Mail Flow Troubleshooter tool provides access to the data sources you need to troubleshoot mail flow problems, such as non-delivery reports (NDRs), queue backups, and slow deliveries. The tool automatically diagnoses the retrieved data, presents an analysis of the possible root causes, and suggests corrective actions. You enter a name for the Mail Flow Troubleshooter task and specify the problem you are encountering. You can view a report for a Mail Flow Troubleshooting scan by clicking Select A Result File To View, choosing the file, and then clicking View Report. Figure 11-13 shows a report generated by specifying that messages are backing up in one or more queues.

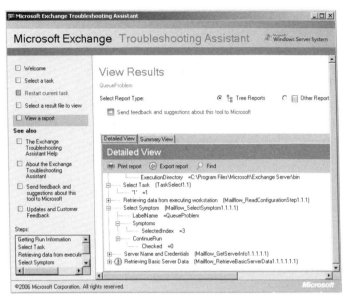

Figure 11-13 Mail Flow Troubleshooter queue.

NOTE Message Tracking tool

The Message Tracking tool, introduced in Chapter 9, examines message tracking logs. This tool is more useful for generating user reports rather than server reports and is discussed in the next lesson.

Using Exchange Management Shell Commands

Queue Viewer and Mail Flow Troubleshooter are not regarded primarily as reporting tools but rather as troubleshooting tools. An arguably superior method of generating information about queues is to use Exchange Management Shell to monitor message queues and to generate CSV files that contain the results of this monitoring. You can open CSV files with software such as Microsoft Excel, Access, or SQL Server and generate reports, graphs, histograms, and pie charts.

If you need to access queue data on a regular basis, you can create PowerShell scripts and use these in batch files that enable you to automate and schedule Exchange Management Shell operations. Chapter 5, "Moving Mailboxes and Implementing Bulk Management," describes how to use and schedule PowerShell scripts.

For example, you can enter the following command to get details of all queues on an Exchange Server 2007 transport server called Glasgow and store the results in a CSV filed called QueueDetails.csv:

```
Get-Queue -Server Glasgow | Export-Csv C:\QueueDetails.csv -Notype
```

Note that for clarity and simplicity, the CSV file is stored in the root of the C:\ drive in this example and in other examples in this chapter. If you were doing this in the real world, you would create a folder and folder path for storing your CSV files. Figure 11-14 shows the contents of the QueueDetails.csv file in a spreadsheet. In this case, Excel was used to open the file, but CSV files can be used by a wide variety of Microsoft and third-party programs.

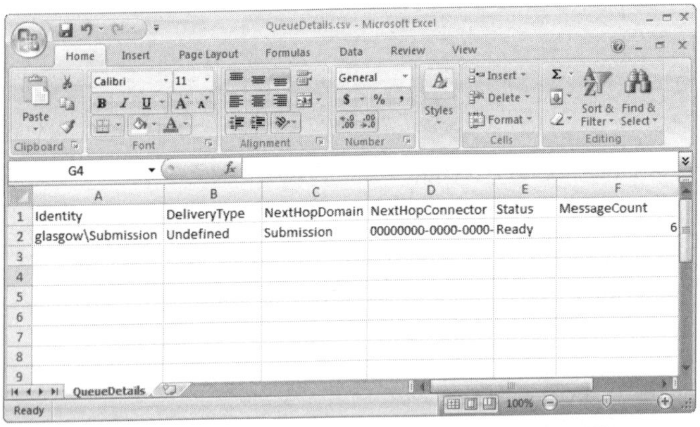

Figure 11-14   Current queues on the transport server Glasgow

---

Export-Csv

You use the *Export-Csv* cmdlet with a file path parameter in an Exchange Management Shell command. You can pipe the output of Exchange Management Shell commands that retrieve information (typically, they start with "Get") into this command and specify either a text or a CSV file to hold the data, as in the following:

```
Get-Mailbox | Export-Csv C:\MailboxDetails.csv
```

You do not need to create the target file; the command creates it for you. *Export-Csv* is very useful for capturing information that can be read and processed by report generation software.

When you use *Export-Csv* without parameters, it puts type information in the first line of the file, for example, #TYPE Microsoft.Exchange.Data.Directory.Management.Mailbox. If you do not want to capture this information you can use the Notype parameter, as in the following:

```
Get-MailboxDatabase | Export-Csv C:\MailboxDatabase.csv -Notype
```

By default, *Export-Csv* generates comma-separated ASCII values. If your report generation software requires, for example, Unicode, UTF7, or UTF8 format, you can use the Encoding parameter, as in the following:

```
Get-MessageTrackingLog -EventID Receive | Export-Csv C:\MessagesReceived.csv -Notype
-Encoding "unicode"
```

MORE INFO *Export-Csv*

For more information about *Export-Csv*, access *http://www.microsoft.com/technet/scriptcenter/topics/msh/cmdlets/export-csv.mspx.*

Practice: Using EXBPA to Generate a Health Report

In this practice session, you use EXBPA to run a best practices analyzer health scan. You view the reports that the tool generates and export a report into a CSV file.

▶ **Practice: Generating Health Scan Reports**

In this practice, you use the EXBPA tool to generate a health scan report, view the various reports, and export the detailed List Report to a CSV file.

1. Log on to your Exchange Server 2007 server by using the Kim_Akers account.

2. Open Exchange Management Console and select Toolbox.

3. Select Best Practices Analyzer and then click Open Tool.

4. On the Checking For Updates page, click Cancel This Check.

5. Click Go To Welcome Screen.

6. Click Select Options For A New Scan.

7. In the Connect To Active Directory page, ensure the Active Directory Server is GLASGOW and then click Connect To The Active Directory Server.

8. Specify ServerHealthScan as the identifying label, select Health Scan and ensure that the Performance Baseline [2 Hours] checkbox is not selected. Your screen should look similar to Figure 11-15.

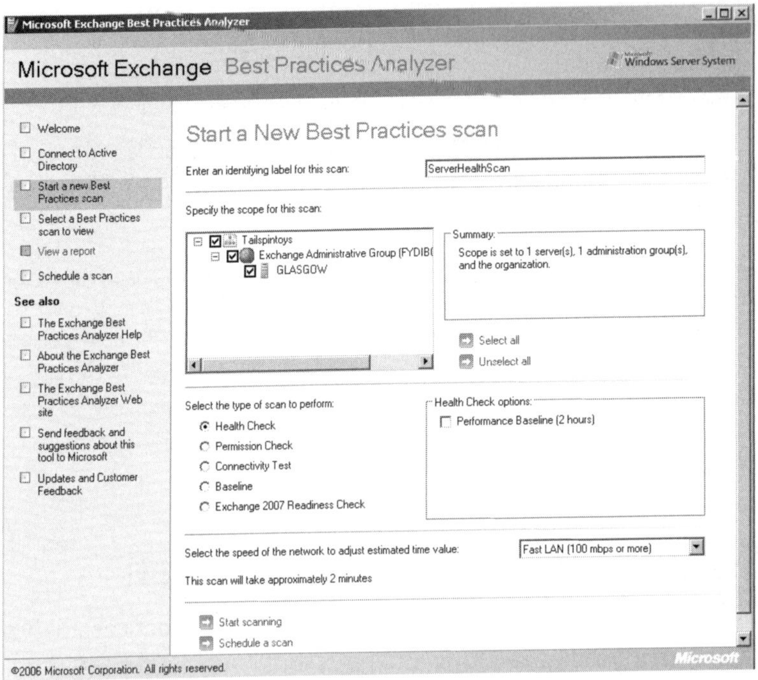

Figure 11-15 Specifying an EXBPA health scan

9. Click Start Scanning.

10. When the scan completes, click View A Report Of This Best Practices Scan.

11. On the View Best Practices Report page, select List Reports and look in turn at the Critical Issues, All Issues, Baseline, and Informational Items tabs. Figure 11-16 shows the All Issues tab. Your report might contain other items.

12. Select any issue on the All Issues report and then click Tell Me More About This Issue And How To Resolve It.

13. Read the resulting Web page and then close it.

14. On the View Best Practices Report page, select Tree Reports and look in turn at the Detailed Review and Summary Review tabs. Figure 11-17 shows the Detailed Review tab.

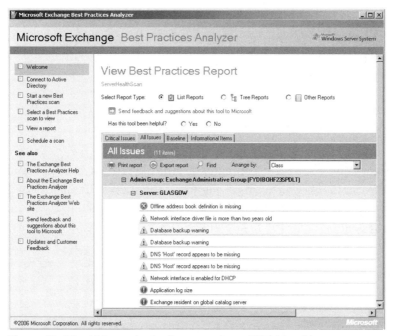

Figure 11-16   All issues in the list report in an EXBPA health scan

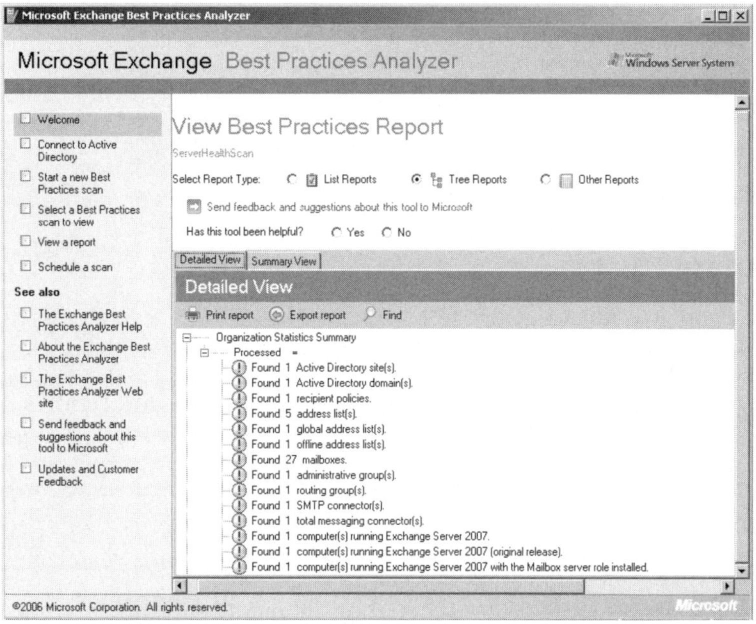

Figure 11-17   Detailed review in the tree report in an EXBPA health scan

15. Select Other Reports and view the Run-Time Log.

16. Return to the All Issues tab in List Reports that was shown previously in Figure 11-16.

17. Click Export Report.

18. Change the Save As Type specification to CSV.

19. Take a note of the path to the default (EXBPA) folder and the name of the file. Click Save.

20. Optionally, if you have a spreadsheet installed that can read CSV files, open and view the file you have saved. Figure 11-18 shows the file opened with Excel. If you do not have Excel (or another spreadsheet) installed, you can open the file with Notepad, but the result will be less informative.

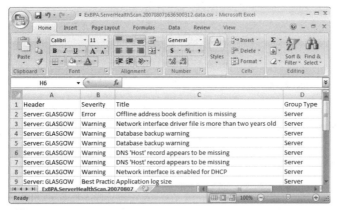

Figure 11-18 EXBPA health scan report in CSV format

Lesson Summary

- You can use MOM 2005 SP1 with the Exchange Management Pack to create server reports for Exchange Sever 2007 servers.

- System center Operations Manager 2007 monitors and reports server availability. The tool provides a Health Explorer that reports server health.

- You can use the Performance Logs and Alerts tool to record the values of counters related to the four major server subsystems and specific Exchange-related counters. You can view the results in the Reports view in System Monitor.

- EXBPA can generate reports on suboptimal configuration settings and Exchange Server 2007 server health.

- You can use Exchange Performance troubleshooter, Exchange Database Recovery Management, Queue Viewer, and Exchange Management Shell commands to generate reports on Exchange queues and databases. You can export data into CSV files that can be read by report generation software.

Lesson Review

You can use the following questions to test your knowledge of the information in Lesson 1, "Creating Server Reports." The questions are also available on the companion CD if you prefer to review them in electronic form.

NOTE Answers

Answers to these questions and explanations of why each answer choice is correct or incorrect are located in the "Answers" section at the end of the book.

---

1. Which monitoring and reporting tool provides a CLI that lets you enter Power-Shell commands?

    A. MOM 2005 SP1

    B. System Center Operations Manager 2007

    C. SQL Server 2005 Report Builder

    D. Exchange Management Pack

2. What report types are available in EXBPA? (Choose all that apply.)

    A. Other Reports

    B. Health Reports

    C. List Reports

    D. Tree Reports

3. You need to use the Performance Logs and Alerts tool to monitor e-mail messages sent per second, messages submitted per second, and receive queue size so that you can generate a report. What Performance object provides these mailbox counters?

    A. MSExchangeIS Mailbox

    B. MSExchangeIS Public

    C. MSExchange OWA

    D. MSExchange Web Nail

4. You want to pipe the output of an Exchange Management Shell command into a command based on the *Export-Csv* cmdlet to create a CSV file called MyReport.csv in the root of the C:\drive. Your report generation software requires data in Unicode format, and you do not want the CSV command to contain type information. What command should you use?

   A. *Export-Csv C:\MyReport.csv –Notype –Encoding "UTF7"*

   B. *Export-Csv C:\MyReport.csv –Encoding "unicode"*

   C. *Export-Csv C:\MyReport.csv –Notype –Encoding "Unicode"*

   D. *Export-Csv C:\MyReport.csv –Encoding "UTF7"*

5. Which of the following tasks can the Exchange Database Recovery Management tool perform? (Choose all that apply.)

   A. Analyze log drive space

   B. Determine whether Exchange Server 2007 server configuration is set according to Microsoft best practices

   C. Report on the general health of a system

   D. Show database-related event logs

   E. Generate a list of issues, such as unsupported or not-recommended options

   F. Verify database and transaction log files

Lesson 2: Creating Usage Reports

In addition to generating reports that indicate whether resources on your Exchange Server 2007 servers are or are likely to become under stress, you need reports on how these resources are being used. You need to know the number of messages in your mailboxes, which mailboxes hold the largest number of messages, and which have the largest total item size. You need to know which users are failing to clean out their mailboxes and are approaching their quota limits.

You also need to know how much spam or suspected spam is reaching your Exchange organization and whether messages that are not spam are being detected as such. If your organization is the target of virus attacks, you need to know this so that you can take the appropriate action.

Other useful information includes what types of clients and client protocols your users are using to receive messages—for example, how many user mailboxes are enabled for POP3, IMAP4, and OWA. This lesson looks at the various tools that you can use to generate usage reports.

After this lesson, you will be able to:

- Create mailbox usage and mailbox size reports.
- Create user reports.
- Create top receivers and top senders reports.
- Create number of messages reports.
- Create reports on the numbers of spam, virus, and external messages.
- Create reports on the number of users of a particular protocol.

Estimated lesson time: 45 minutes

Real World

Ian McLean

A remarkable number of users think that exceeding mailbox quota limits is a badge of honor.

They believe that having 10 GB mailboxes indicates that they work harder than anyone else and that they are good communicators. They *want* to be in the top 100 sender and receiver lists. They think of themselves as top users. When they cannot send or receive e-mail messages, this does not indicate to them that they need to clear out the junk that has been moldering in their Inboxes for years. Instead, it triggers an angry call to technical support.

Extremely hardworking people with very large mailboxes do exist, but most of the time excessive mailbox size is caused by users sending their holiday photographs to all their friends and getting more pictures sent to them in return. Audio and video files fly merrily across the ether, and nobody has ever heard of file compression.

They are the same users who take half an hour to log on in the morning because their My Documents folder is clogged with every photograph they have ever taken and all their favorite music CDs. Their desktops are so full that it is difficult to see any background.

You will not be popular, but it is your job to take a firm line. Users will not be able to use e-mail unless they clear out the garbage, and you do not believe that every message they have ever received is essential to the future of the organization or even to the future of humanity. You have reports that show that a user is consistently at or near quota limits. The user is a top receiver and sender. You need to persuade that user to moderate his or her e-mail habits.

Fortunately, company policy usually backs you up. Users should clear personal e-mails out of company Inbox and Sent Item folders. Learn what the policies are and enforce them.

As an administrator, you deal with technical problems. That is reasonably straightforward. You also need to deal with people. That is much more difficult.

Using Microsoft Operations Management to Create Mailbox Usage Reports

In a production environment, MOM 2005 SP1 with the Exchange Server Management Pack is one of the main tools for monitoring an Exchange organization and generating user reports. As stated in the previous lesson, to use the reporting function, you need the full version of MOM, which in turn requires that you have a SQL database (or data warehouse) available in your organization.

The Exchange Server Management Pack includes rules and rule groups that generate reports to view system performance and data over time and in a summarized format.

The reports are useful when comparing to a baseline standard in a centralized server environment and for an overview of the current Exchange organization.

MOM reporting queries the SQL data warehouse for the data that you want, summarizing that data and creating a formatted report. The Exchange Management Pack includes predefined reports, and you can also create custom reports. MOM uses DTS to transfer reporting data daily from the operational database to the data warehouse database.

SQL Reporting Services (specifically SQL Report Builder) generates the MOM and Exchange Management Pack reports. You can view these reports by selecting Operations in the left pane and clicking Start Reporting Console from the MOM Administrator Console or by opening the Reporting Console located in the Microsoft Operations Manager 2005 group on the Start menu. You can run reports for a specified time and select from which servers the data should be used in generating summaries and reports. You can specify chart options to display a preferred scale, chart type, and range.

An important use of MOM reporting is to identify users who have very large mailboxes and encourage them to clean out their mailbox folders. The Mailbox Size Exceptions report identifies mailboxes that have exceeded mailbox size limits configured. This report includes the following:

- Mailbox name
- Mailbox size limit
- Current mailbox size
- Number of items in the mailbox
- Location of the mailbox in the mailbox store

In addition, the Exchange Server Management Pack provides a report that reveals the top 100 users in an Exchange organization. This information is collected from the Message Tracking log on the Exchange server. This provides more detailed, informative, and easy-to-read reports than does the use of Exchange Management Shell commands based on the *Get-MessgeTrackingLog* cmdlet, although the use of Exchange Management Shell is a valid technique, especially in smaller organizations where MOM is not used. Exchange Management Shell reporting is described later in this lesson.

NOTE   **Top 100 users only**

By default, the MOM database collects only the top 100 users. The Exchange Server Management Pack has a script parameter that limits collection of the top 100 Message Tracking Log entries. Although it is possible to amend this script to collect more or all entries, Microsoft does not recommend this because it can degrade Exchange performance.

MOM 2005 SP1 and the Exchange Server Management Pack provide the following reports specific to an Exchange organization:

- Exchange Database Sizes
- Exchange Mailboxes
- Exchange Server Configuration
- Mail Delivered - Top 100 Recipient Mailboxes by Count
- Mail Delivered - Top 100 Recipient Mailboxes by Size
- Highest Growth Mailboxes
- Top 100 Mailboxes (by size)

These reports require that the Configuration Wizard is run in MOM, a Messaging Application Programming Interface (MAPI) client can log on to the system, and mail flow tests are enabled. If the Server Availability report (not an Exchange-specific report) runs without errors, this verifies that each Exchange store can be accessed by a MAPI client and implicitly verifies both Exchange and Active Directory functionality.

The Mailbox Access Account

To generate reports that use the rules that in turn rely on a MAPI logon to Exchange, you must create at least one mailbox known as the Agent Access Account on each Exchange Server 2007 mailbox server that you are monitoring. To access these mailboxes, the Exchange Server Management Pack needs to have a single domain user account known as the Mailbox Access Account that can access all the agent mailboxes on all the servers. The Mailbox Access Account must be added to the Exchange View-Only Administrator role to collect mailbox statistics information about the Exchange server for the Top 100 Mailboxes reports.

The MOM 2005 Configuration Wizard configures the Mailbox Access Account, and you should not alter this configuration; otherwise, the Exchange Server Management Pack might not be able to perform all the required tests.

Rule Groups, Rules, and Reports

The rules and rule groups that require a MAPI logon to Exchange and their associated reports are listed in Table 11-1.

Table 11-1   Rule Groups, Rule Names, and Reports

Rule Group	Rule Name	Report
Server Availability\MAPI Logon Check and Availability Reporting	Check store availability–MAPI logon	Exchange Server Availability
Server Availability\Mail Flow Verification	Send mail flow messages	Receive mail flow messages
Report Collection Rules\Mailbox Statistics Analysis	Report Collection Rules–Mailbox Statistics Analysis	Mailbox reports in Exchange Mailbox and Folder Sizes folder
Report Collection Rules\Public Folder Statistics Analysis	Report collection–public folder statistics	Public Folder reports in Exchange Mailbox and Folder Sizes folder

---

MORE INFO   Microsoft Operations Monitor

If you want to learn more about MOM, you can download extensive product documentation by accessing *http://technet.microsoft.com/en-us/opsmgr/bb498230.aspx* and following the links.

Exam Tip   As stated in the previous lesson, MOM is not specifically mentioned in the examination objectives and is unlikely to be tested in depth. Nevertheless, it is a major tool for monitoring and reporting. As an Exchange administrator you will be expected to know that it exists and that it works with the Exchange Management Pack to produce reports based on rules and rule groups. You should also learn the list of Exchange-specific reports available by default.

Quick Check

- To what Exchange Administrator role should you add the Mailbox Access Account role to collect mailbox statistics information about the Exchange server for the Top 100 Mailboxes reports?

Quick Check Answer

- The Mailbox Access Account role should be added to the Exchange View-Only Administrator role.

Creating User Reports

You can list all the messages submitted or received by a particular user by accessing the Message Tracking logs. Chapter 10, "Message Tracking and Mailbox Health," discussed these logs in detail. You can also find out what messages submitted or received by a particular user failed. MOM 2005 SP1 uses Message Tracking logs to obtain data for its user reports, and you can also access these logs through the Message Tracking tool and Exchange Management Shell commands.

Using the Message Tracking Tool

Chapter 10 discussed the Message Tracking ExTRA tool in detail. You can use this tool to specify a user as a sender or a recipient and determine the e-mail messages that the user submitted or received. Note that the SEND EventID specifies messages transferred over a send connector and does not list the messages delivered via store driver between Hub Transport servers and Mailbox servers.

You can specify all messages received or submitted within a time period, or you can uncheck the Start and End checkboxes to specify all messages that meet the other criteria. You can specify EventID, MessageID, InternalMessageID, and Reference. If subject message tracking is enabled, you can also specify a text string to search for in message subjects. Figure 11-19 lists all the messages submitted by sender Don Hall. In a production environment, you would see a lot more messages and would need to filter by other parameters to make the information usable.

Using Exchange Management Shell

You can use the Message Tracking tool if all you require is to find a message or to list messages on your screen. However, the tool is limited and does not let you extract the data it gathers in a form suitable for more detailed reports. Exchange Management Shell, however, lets you redirect output to a file and, in particular, generate CSV files that can be read by other software.

For example, the following command returns details of all messages received by Don Hall and stores the information in a CSV file:

```
Get-MessageTrackingLog -EventID RECEIVE -Recipients don.hall@tailspintoys.internal | Export-
Csv C:\DonHallReceived.csv -Notype
```

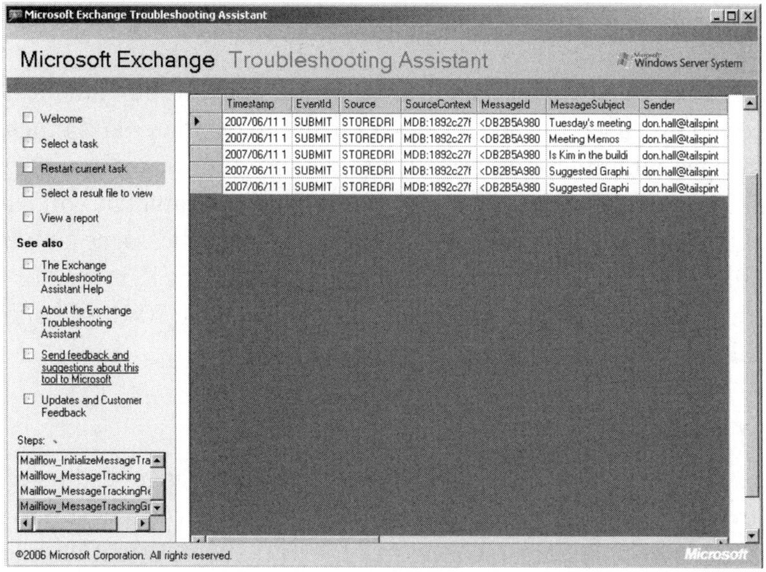

Figure 11-19   Messages submitted for sending by Don Hall

You can open CSV files with a wide variety of software programs (including Notepad). Figure 11-20 shows an extract from the DonHallReceived.csv file opened in Excel.

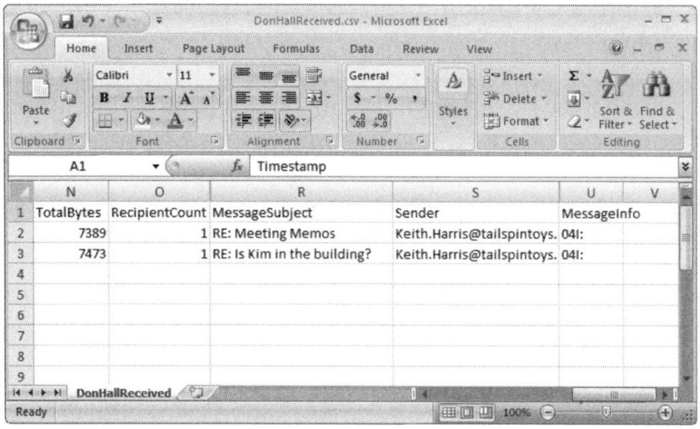

Figure 11-20   Messages received by Don Hall

You can filter your results in the Exchange Management Shell command, although it is often easier to do this in the report generation software that reads the CSV file. For example, the following command returns all messages submitted for sending by Keith

Harris that have "Kim" in the Subject line and stores this information in the file C:\KeithSubjectKim.csv:

```
Get-MessageTrackingLog -Sender keith.harris@tailspintoys.internal -EventID SUBMIT
-MessageSubject "Kim" | Export-Csv C:\KeithSubjectKim.csv -Notype
```

You can analyze the CSV file to return information about the number of messages submitted or received by a user, the messages sent between two dates and times, the total size of all messages submitted or received, and details of messages that exceed a predefined size. By using different values for the EventID parameter, you can list, for example, messages for which delivery failed or was delayed, messages for which delivery status notification was generated, messages that cannot be delivered or returned, or messages that were put in the poison message queue. Table 10-1 in Chapter 10 lists the various values that the EventID parameter can take.

Creating Mailbox Reports

MOM 2005 SP1 generates the Mailbox Size Exceptions, Exchange Mailboxes, Top 100 Mailboxes (by size), and Highest Growth Mailboxes reports. These are standard reports, and you can use the tool to configure reports that give you other information. However, if you do not have this tool in your organization or if you want more detailed and flexible reports, you can use Exchange Management Shell commands based on the *Get-MailboxStatistics* cmdlet. You can pipe the output from these commands into the *Format-List* command if you want to see them listed in detail in the Exchange Management Shell console or into a command based on the *Export-Csv* cmdlet to capture the results in a CSV file for report generation.

For example, if you wanted a report that gave details of all disconnected mailboxes on the mailbox server Glasgow, you could use the following command:

```
Get-MailboxStatistics -Server Glasgow | Where {$_.DisconnectDate -ne $null} | Export-Csv
C:\DisconnectedMailboxes.csv -Notype
```

Figure 11-21 shows part of the CSV file that this command creates. As before, this file is displayed in a spreadsheet (Excel) for clarity, but if you want to, you can open it with Notepad.

Creating Mailbox Size Reports

You can use Exchange Management Shell commands to return details of all mailboxes that have exceeded size limits and a list of the largest mailboxes in your organization.

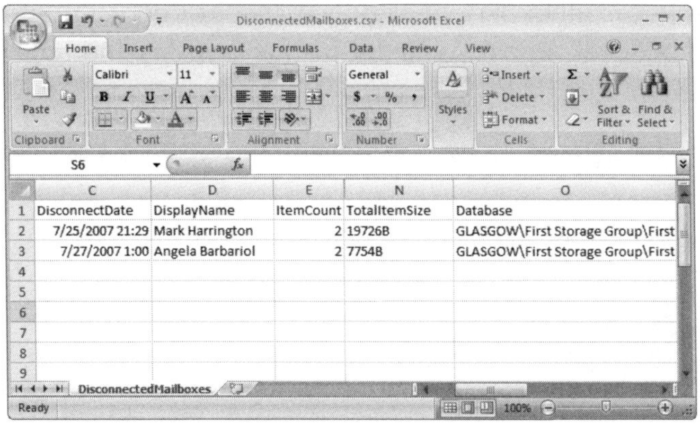

Figure 11-21   Disconnected mailboxes report

For example, to list details of mailboxes on the mailbox server Glasgow that do not have a storage limit status of "BelowLimit" and put the results in a CSV file, you would use the following command:

```
Get-MailboxStatistics –Server Glasgow | Where {$_.StorageLimitStatus -ne "BelowLimit"} |
Export-Csv C:\StorageLimit.csv -Notype
```

To list details of all mailboxes in your organization with a total item size greater than or equal to 1 GB, you would use the following command:

```
Get-MailboxStatistics | Where {$_.TotalItemSize -ge 1GB}| Export-Csv C:\BigMailbox.csv
-Notype
```

Note that if you want to try out this command on your test network, substitute MB for GB because you are most unlikely to find mailboxes in the gigabyte size range. Figure 11-22 shows an excerpt from the CSV file produced by this command, with the recommended amendment made.

Creating Number of Messages Reports

You can use Exchange Management Shell commands based on the *Get-MailboxStatistics* cmdlet to create report data for mailboxes that hold a specified number of messages or more. If you want to sort these mailboxes in order of number of messages, it is typically easier to do this by using the facilities provided by the reporting software.

To list all mailboxes on the mailbox server Glasgow that hold 1,000 or more messages and to save the mailbox details in a CSV file for further analysis and reporting, you would use the following command:

```
Get-MailboxStatistics -Server "Glasgow" | Where {$_.ItemCount -ge 1000} | Export-Csv
C:\BigItemCount.csv -Notype
```

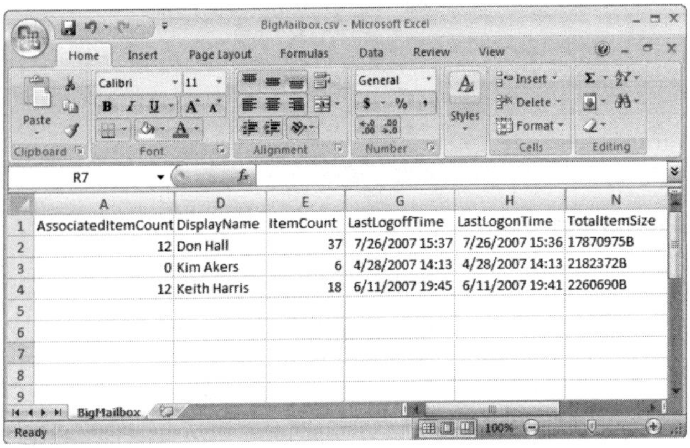

Figure 11-22   Large mailboxes report

To demonstrate this command on your small test network you would change "1000" to "10." You will probably get a report very similar to the one shown previously in Figure 11-22 because on your test network the users with the largest total item size are also the users with the largest item numbers. This is not necessarily the case in a production network.

If you want to list mailboxes in order of item numbers, it is easier to do this by loading the information into a spreadsheet or other data manipulation software program and using that program's sort facilities. The *Get-MailboxStatistics* cmdlet does not support the SortBy parameter. For example, if you chose to use Microsoft Office 2007 Excel for this purpose, you would highlight the column that holds the item count and then use the Sort & Filter function in the Editing group on the Home tab to order the data. The following command gets details about all mailboxes on the mailbox server Glasgow and saves the data in a CSV file:

```
Get-MailboxStatistics -Server "Glasgow" | Export-Csv C:\GlasgowMailboxes.csv -Notype
```

Figure 11-23 shows the relevant spreadsheet information sorted by descending order of item count.

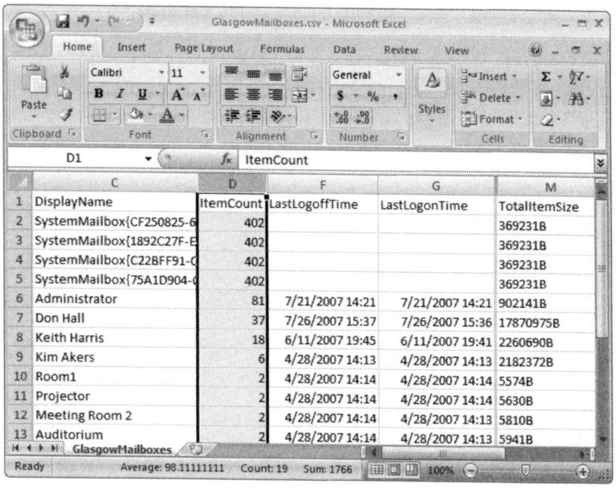

Figure 11-23 Top mailboxes by item count

You can also use the *Sort-Object* cmdlet to list items ordered by a specified property, although arguably this is less flexible than using data manipulation software. For example, to sort mailboxes in ascending order of item count and place the results in a CSV file, you could use the following command:

```
Get-MailboxStatistics | Sort-Object ItemCount | Export-Csv C:\AscendingItemCount.csv -Notype
```

Creating Top Receivers and Top Senders Reports

MOM 2005 SP1 provides the reports Mail Delivered - Top 100 Recipient Mailboxes by Count and Mail Delivered - Top 100 Recipient Mailboxes by Size. These reports are often referred to as "Top Receivers" reports.

In the previous section, you saw that you could use Exchange Management Shell commands based on the *Get-MailboxStatistics* cmdlet to obtain detailed information about mailboxes with a large total item size or a large item count. To get information specific to receivers, you can use commands based on the *Get-MessageTrackingLog* cmdlet that you used earlier in this lesson.

For example, the following command lists all receivers on the transport server Glasgow:

```
Get-MessageTrackingLog -Server Glasgow -EventID RECEIVE | Group Sender | Export-Csv
C:\GlasgowReceivers.csv -Notype
```

This command generates a very clear and simple report, shown in Figure 11-24, in which the results are displayed in order of message count. In a production environment, there would be a lot more receivers and a lot more messages.

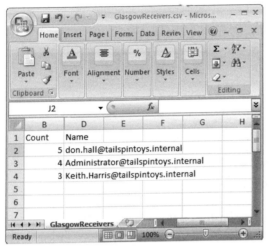

Figure 11-24   Top receivers on the Glasgow server

Similarly, the following command returns a list of senders on the same server:

```
Get-MessageTrackingLog -Server Glasgow -EventID SUBMIT | Group Sender | Export-Csv
C:\GlasgowSenders.csv -Notype
```

If you have not generated any e-mail messages on your test network for a while, you might need to send some more logged in as various users to get any result from this command. Figure 11-25 shows the CSV file. Your file is likely to contain different details.

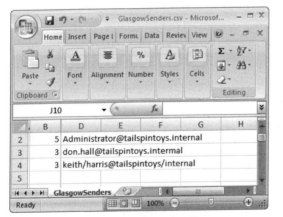

Figure 11-25   Top senders on the Glasgow server

Creating Number of Virus, Spam, and External Messages Reports

Chapter 6, "Spam, Viruses, and Compliance," discussed configuring spam detection and antivirus protection for Exchange Sever 2007. In addition to preventing viruses from damaging your servers and spam from clogging up your users' Inboxes, you need to generate reports that tell you whether the level of spam or virus attacks are increasing. If a sudden increase in e-mail messages that contain or could contain malware is detected, your organization could be under attack, and you might need to take the appropriate steps. You need to know and be able to demonstrate to others that your protection measures are working.

External messages are messages received from or sent to other e-mail organizations. You need to keep track of the numbers of such messages and ensure they are being received and transmitted without error. You also need to look out for a sudden increase in the number of external messages sent to your organization because this could indicate a Denial of Service (DoS) attack. You need to generate reports that indicate any current or possible future problems.

Virus Reporting

If you are using third-party software for virus protection, you need to refer to the manuals that accompany the software or can be downloaded from the supplier's Web site to find out how reporting is implemented. However, Microsoft recommends Microsoft Forefront Security for Exchange Server for this task, and this software therefore forms the basis of this section of the lesson.

Exam Tip   Questions about virus protection software in the 70-236 examination are likely to refer to Forefront Security for Exchange Server. It is most unlikely that you will be tested on your knowledge of third-party solutions.

Microsoft Forefront Security for Exchange Server provides reports that help you analyze the state and performance statistics of the Forefront Security for Exchange Server services through the Forefront Server Security Administrator interface. Virus-related events are written to a database file called the Virus Incident log and a text file called the Virus log.

To open the Forefront Server Security Administrator, click Start, click All Programs, click Microsoft Forefront Server Security, click Exchange Server, and then click Forefront Server Security Administrator. You can specify the Exchange Server 2007 server that you want to connect to. By default, if the tool is installed on an Exchange Server 2007 server, it suggests to connect to that server.

The Forefront Server Security Administrator user interface contains the Shuttle Navigator on the left and the work panes on the right. If you select Incidents under REPORT in Shuttle Navigator, you can view the statistics for messages and attachments, as shown in Figure 11-26.

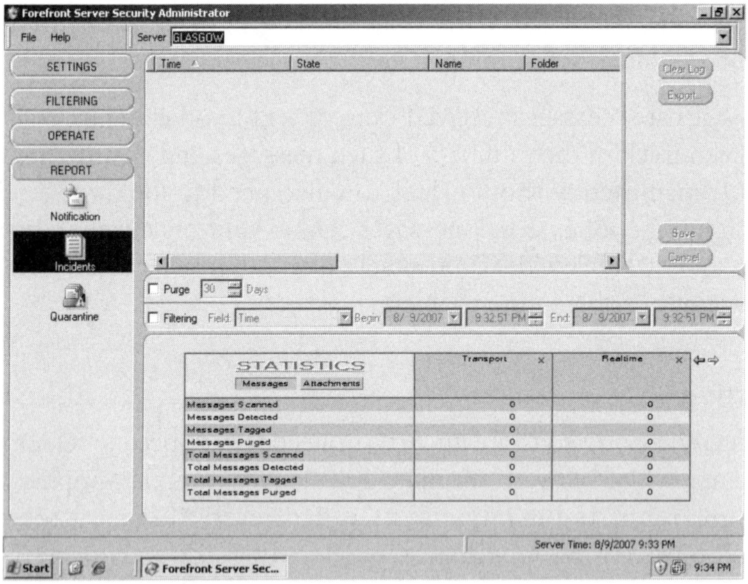

Figure 11-26   Forefront Server Security Administrator

Virus Incidents Log   The Virus Incidents log or Incidents database (Incidents.mdb) stores all virus detections or filter operations for an Exchange Server 2007 server regardless of the Forefront scan that detected the infection. Forefront Security for Exchange Server collects statistics on a per-storage-group basis for the Manual and Realtime scan jobs.

To view the Virus Incidents log, click REPORT in the left navigation shuttle. The REPORT area includes icons for accessing the work panes for Notification, Incidents, and Quarantine. Click the Incidents icon, and the Incidents work pane appears. The information that Forefront Security for Exchange Server reports for each incident (in the top section of the work pane) is listed in Table 11-2. Note that in Figure 11-26, this is blank because no viruses have been detected.

Table 11-2   Information in the Forefront Virus Incidents Log

Field	Description
Time	The date and time of the incident.
State	The action taken by Forefront Security for Exchange Server.
Name	The name of the scan job that reported the incident.
Folder	The name of the folder where the file was found. This field also reports if messages were inbound or outbound when caught by the Transport scanner.
Message	The subject line of the message or the name of the file that triggered the incident.
File	The name of the virus or name of the file that matched a file or content filter.
Incident	The type of incident that occurred. The four categories are VIRUS, FILE FILTER, SENDER FILTER, and SUBJECT FILTER. Each is followed by either the name of the virus caught or the file or content filter that triggered the event.
Sender Name	The name of the sender of the infected or filtered message.
Sender Address	The e-mail address of the sender of the infected or filtered message.
Recipient	The name of the recipient of the infected or filtered message.
Recipient Address	The e-mail address of the recipient of the infected or filtered message.
CC Name	The name or names specified in the carbon copy (CC) field.
CC Address	The e-mail addresses of recipients specified in the CC field.
Bcc Name	The name or names specified in the blank carbon copy (Bcc) field.
Bcc Address	The e-mail addresses of recipients specified in the Bcc field.

NOTE Duplicate incidents in the Virus Incidents log

Forefront Security for Exchange Server key-word filtering will scan both plain-text and HTML message body content. If it finds a match in both the HTML and the plain text, it will report two detections in the Virus Incidents log.

Virus Log By default, the Virus log (Viruslog.txt) is disabled. You can enable it from the Logging section of the General Options pane in Shuttle Navigator. To access the General Options pane, click General Options in the Shuttle Navigator Settings area. The General Options pane opens. In the Logging section, click Enable Forefront Virus Log.

When the Virus log is enabled, all virus incidents are written to the text file Virus-Log.txt under the Forefront Security for Exchange Server installation path (InstalledPath). Figure 11-27 shows a sample entry in the VirusLog.txt file.

Figure 11-27 Virus log entry

Creating Spam Messages Reports

Microsoft estimates that approximately 95 percent of attempted incoming message submissions will be eliminated by connection, sender, and recipient filtering before reaching your Exchange servers. Edge transport servers perform content filtering on the messages that do get through to assess the probability that an inbound message is spam. As described in Chapter 6, the Content Filter Agent performs various calculations by using key words and phrases, weighted words, sender reputation, and Sender ID status to arrive at a spam confidence level (SCL) rating between 0 and 9 for each message.

By default, Edge transport servers do not quarantine messages. By default, messages with an SCL of 7 or greater are deleted by the edge transport server and an NDR is generated. You can change this setting so that, for example, messages with an SCL of 9 are deleted (no NDR) while messages with an SCL of 7 or 8 are removed (NDR is sent). The remaining messages are sent to mailbox servers, where the store threshold and the recipient's safe-list information determine whether the message appears in the recipient's Inbox or the Junk E-mail folder.

You can elect to configure message quarantine. For example, you could send all messages with an SCL of 5 or 6 to a spam quarantine mailbox. You need to create this mailbox (and associated Active Directory user account), and Microsoft recommends that you first create a separate spam quarantine database in its own storage group to hold the mailbox. If use message quarantine, you need to monitor this mailbox and create regular reports on its size and the number of messages it contains. You also need to manually inspect the messages in the spam quarantine mailbox to see if it contains legitimate e-mail messages (false positives).

NOTE   Spam quarantine

For more information, search Exchange Server 2007 Help for "Configuring and Managing Spam Quarantine" or access *http://technet.microsoft.com/en-us/library/bb124897.aspx*.

> ## Anti-Spam Stamps
>
> You can inspect anti-spam stamps in message headers by using Microsoft Outlook 2007. This helps you diagnose spam-related problems and determine what actions to take on false positives and on suspected spam messages that individuals receive in their mailboxes.
>
> Anti-spam stamps contain anti-spam reports that contain information (stamps) such as the Sender ID (SID), the phishing confidence level (PCL), and the SCL of a message.
>
> For more information about anti-spam stamps, search Exchange Server 2007 Help for "Anti-Spam Stamps" or access *http://technet.microsoft.com/en-us/library/aa996878.aspx*. For information about viewing anti-spam stamps, search Exchange Server 2007 Help for "How to View Anti-Spam Stamps in Outlook 2007" or access *http://technet.microsoft.com/en-us/library/bb124595.aspx*.

Information about messages that are blocked through connection, sender, and recipient filtering will typically be held in your organization's firewall logs, and it is likely that a domain administrator rather than an Exchange administrator will read and analyze these logs.

Messages with a high SCL (typically 7 through 9) are removed or deleted by the edge transport server, and it can sometimes be difficult to get details about such messages. You can obtain details of messages that are queued on a server by using an Exchange Management Shell command based on the *Get-Message* cmdlet. For example, the following command returns details of queued messages on the edge transport server Edinburgh with an SCL of 9:

```
Get-Message -Server Edinburgh -Filter {SCL -eq 9} | Format-List
```

Note that you do not have an edge transport server in the test network recommended in this book, and if you did, it would be difficult to generate message queues of a sufficient length to get significant results from this command.

If you need the data in a CSV file that you can use to generate a report, you can replace the *Format-List* command with a command based on the *Export-CSV* cmdlet, as in the following:

```
Get-Message -Server Edinburgh -Filter {SCL -eq 9} | Export-Csv C:\VeryHighSCL.csv -Notype
```

You could also specify a range of CSVs; for example, the following command stores detailed information about messages with an SCL of 7 or greater in a CSV file:

```
Get-Message -Server Edinburgh -Filter {SCL -ge 7} | Export-Csv C:\HighSCL.csv -Notype
```

If you do not want to type this command every time you want to generate a report, you can create a PowerShell script. If you want to create a report periodically, you can embed your PowerShell script in a batch file that you can schedule to run from the Command Console (cmd.exe). Chapter 5 discusses PowerShell scripts and batch files.

One of the major advantages of configuring spam quarantine is that you can monitor and report the size of spam quarantine mailbox and the number of messages it receives as you can with any other mailbox. For example, you can save the statistics for the spam quarantine mailbox spamq@tailspintoys.internal in a CSV file by using the following command:

```
Get-MailboxStatistics -Identity spamq@tailspintoys.internal | Export-Csv
C:\SpamQuarantineStats.csv -Notype
```

As shown in Figure 11-28, you can extract the number of messages and total item size from the data saved in the CSV file. You can use the same technique to display, for example, the mailbox quota limits.

Figure 11-28   Statistics for spam quarantine mailbox

You can obtain additional details about the contents of the spam quarantine mailbox with the following command:

```
Get-MessageTrackingLog –Recipients spamq@tailspintoys.internal –EventID RECEIVE | Export-Csv
C:\SpamQuarantineData.csv –Notype
```

Figure 11-29 shows the type of information that can be extracted from the CSV file generated by this command. Note that if you try this out, you will likely get different results depending on whether you have configured spam quarantine, how you have configured spam filtering, and what messages you have sent.

External Messages and Protocol Logging

Send connectors and receive connectors handle external messages received by or sent from your Exchange Server 2007 organization. Protocol logging records the Simple Mail Transfer Protocol (SMTP) conversations that occur between e-mail servers as part of message delivery. These SMTP conversations occur on Send connectors and Receive connectors that are configured on Microsoft Exchange Server 2007 servers that have the Hub Transport server role or the Edge Transport server role installed.

If protocol logging is enabled, you can use protocol logs to generate reports on external message traffic. Protocol log files are in CSV format and can be read by report generation software. Chapter 10 discusses protocol logging in detail.

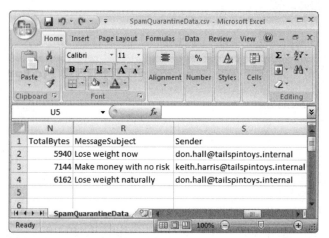

Figure 11-29 Message details in spam quarantine mailbox

Creating Reports on Number of Users of a Particular Protocol

You can determine fairly easily how many mailbox-enabled users are configured to use specific client protocols, for example, Post Office Protocol version 3 (POP3) and Internet Message Access Protocol version 4 (IMAP4), and Outlook Web Access (OWA). It is more difficult to discover how much network traffic is being generated by these protocols. This requires a network monitoring tool such as Network Monitor (Netmon.exe), which was described in Chapter 9.

NOTE OWA

OWA is regarded as a protocol in Exchange Server 2007 documentation and white papers. To be pedantic, OWA uses the Hypertext Transport Protocol (HTTP) or the Secure Hypertext Transport Protocol (HTTPS).

To list the mailbox settings relevant for client access, you would use Exchange Management Shell commands based on the *Get-CASMailbox* cmdlet. For example, to get client settings for all mailboxes in an Exchange organization, you would use the following command:

```
Get-CasMailbox
```

Figure 11-30 shows the output from this command.

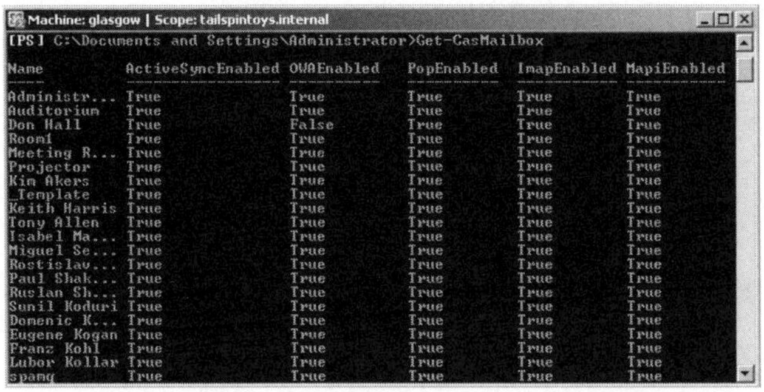

Figure 11-30   Client protocols enabled on mailboxes

You specify parameters with the *Get-CasMailbox* cmdlet to get client settings for a single mailbox or for all mailbox-enabled users in an Active Directory Organizational Unit (OU). Also, the *Get-CasMailbox* cmdlet supports the Filter parameter, but properties such as OWAenabled and PopEnabled are not filterable. Therefore, you need to capture the client settings details and process the information in the report generation software or use the *Where-Object* function. For example, the following command returns the client settings for all the mailboxes that have OWA enabled:

```
Get-CasMailbox | Where-Object { $_.OWAEnabled -eq $True }
```

MORE INFO   Filterable properties

For more information about filterable properties, search Exchange Server 2007 Help for "Filterable Properties for the -Filter Parameter" or access *http://technet.microsoft.com/en-us/library/ bb430744.aspx*.

The following command saves information about client access settings in an Exchange organization to a CSV file for further processing:

```
Get-CASMailbox | Export-Csv C:\ClientSettings.csv -NoType
```

Figure 11-31 shows only a very small subset of the data captured in the CSV file. The command returns a great deal of information, particularly about OWA settings. In a production environment, this would be a very large file and would be processed by more powerful data-manipulation software such as SQL Server.

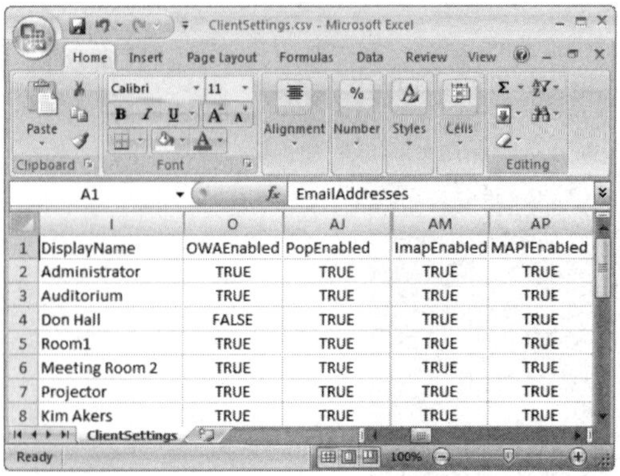

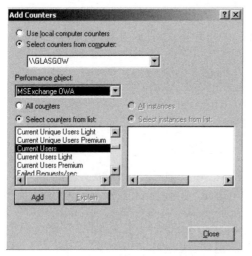

Figure 11-31 Client protocol information in a CSV file

Using Exchange Server Performance Monitor

You can use counters provided by the MSExchange OWA object in Exchange Server Performance Monitor to monitor, for example, the number of OWA users, the number of unique users, the number of proxy users, and logons per second. You can view the current values in these counters with System Monitor, or you can capture a log over an extended period with the Performance Logs and Alerts tool and compare the results with baseline logs as described in Lesson 1.

Figure 11-32 shows the MSExchange OWA performance object and some of its associated counters.

Figure 11-32 The MSExchange OWA performance object

Using the HTTP Monitoring Service

You can also generate reports specific to the OWA servers in your Exchange organization. Chapter 10 discusses the HTTP Monitoring service (HTTPMon). Although this tool has been around for some time and can be installed from the Windows 2000 Server Resource Kit, it remains a powerful tool for monitoring Web sites and applications and, in particular, OWA servers.

HTTPMon can check several Web sites, OWA servers, or applications simultaneously and export the results to a log file in CSV format or to the Windows Server event log. After you install HTTPMon, you need to run HTTPMon Configuration Manager to configure global settings for your organization and add the OWA servers you want to monitor and for which you need to generate reports. HTTPMon runs a series of tests that generate CSV files that you review and analyze to detect problems with your OWA servers. You can also review the events logged by HTTPMon in Event Viewer.

You can import the CSV file output to Excel, Access, or SQL Server for more analysis. You can also use SQL Server data and Client Monitor to track your servers and the reporting features of SQL Server to carry out additional data analysis.

HTTPMon consists of three components:

- **Real-time Sampling Service**   Monitors OWA servers (and other Web servers) in real time

- **SQL Reporting Server**   Gathers data from monitored servers and loads it into an SQL Server database

- **Client Monitor**   Displays the results from the SQL Reporting Server database as a set of Web pages

---

MORE INFO   HTTPMon

Possibly the most comprehensive site to obtain information about HTTPMon and to access downloads can be found at *http://www.httpmon.de*. This site, in spite of its Web address, is in English. Web site addresses, particularly non-Microsoft Web sites, can never be guaranteed, but this looks like a well-established site.

Practice: Creating Mailbox Reports

In this practice session, you list all the disconnected mailboxes in an Exchange organization, all the mailboxes with a total item size greater than 1 MB on a mailbox server, and all the mailboxes in a database with a total item count of 15 or more. You save your results in CSV files. In the practices, you open these files with Notepad, but if you have a spreadsheet (for example, Excel) installed on your Exchange Server 2007 server, you will find it much easier to use this for manipulating the data in the files.

▶ **Practice 1: Listing Disconnected Mailboxes**

In this practice, you list the mailboxes in your Exchange organization for which the user has been removed from Active Directory so that the mailboxes are disconnected. The practice assumes that the user mailboxes isabel.martins@tailspintoys.internal and tony.allen@tailspintoys.internal exist in your organization. If not, choose other mailboxes. The procedure also lists any other mailboxes that you might have created and disconnected while studying previous chapters.

1. If necessary, log on to your Exchange Server 2007 server by using the Kim_Akers account.

2. Open Exchange Management Shell.

3. Enter the following command:

   ```
   Remove-Mailbox -Identity isabel.martins@tailspintoys.internal
   ```

4. Confirm you want to disconnect the mailbox.

5. Enter the following command:

   ```
   Remove-Mailbox -Identity tony.allen@tailspintoys.internal
   ```

6. Confirm that you want to disconnect the mailbox.

7. Enter the following command:

   ```
   Get-MailboxStatistics | Where {$_.DisconnectDate -ne $null} | Export-Csv
   C:\PracticeDisconnect.csv -Notype
   ```

8. Open the file C:\PracticeDisconnect in Notepad.

9. Manipulate the data by inserting tab characters so that it lines up in columns. Your file should look similar to Figure 11-33.

▶ **Practice 2: Listing Mailboxes Based on Size and Item Count**

In this practice, you list details of all mailboxes on the mailbox server Glasgow with a total item size greater than or equal to 1 MB and all the mailboxes in the database Mailbox Database in the storage group First Storage Group that have a total item count of 15 or more.

1. If necessary, log on to your Exchange Server 2007 server by using the Kim_Akers account.

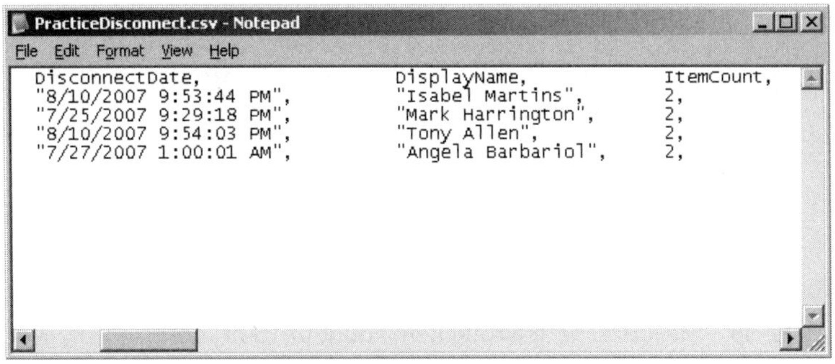

Figure 11-33 Disconnected mailboxes

2. Open Exchange Management Shell.

3. Enter the following command:

```
Get-MailboxStatistics -Server "Glasgow" | Where {$_.TotalItemSize -ge 1MB} | Select-
Object DisplayName,ItemCount,TotalItemSize | Export-Csv C:\PracticeMailboxSize.csv
-Notype
```

4. Open the file C:\PracticeMailboxSize in Notepad.

5. Manipulate the data by inserting tab characters so that it lines up in columns. This process should result in a file that looks similar to Figure 11-34.

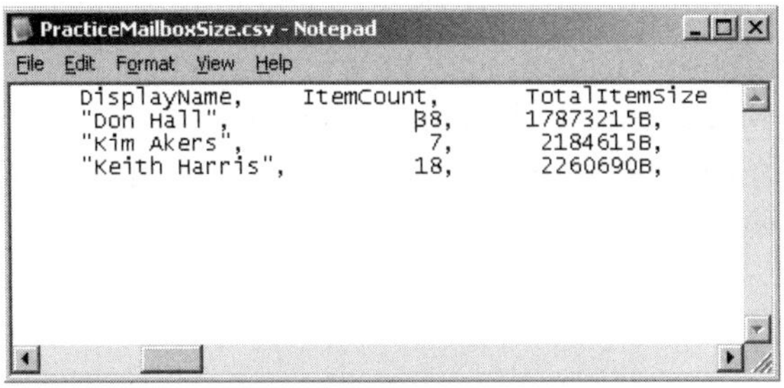

Figure 11-34 Mailboxes larger than 1 MB

6. Enter the following command:

```
Get-MailboxStatistics -Database "First Storage Group\Mailbox Database" | Where
{$_.ItemCount -ge 15} | Select-Object DisplayName,ItemCount,TotalItemSize | Export-Csv
C:\PracticeItemCount.csv -Notype
```

7. Open the file C:\PracticeItemCount in Notepad.

8. Manipulate your text file. It should look similar to Figure 11-35.

Figure 11-35   Mailboxes with a total item count of 15 or more

Lesson Summary

- MOM 2005 SP1 with the Exchange Management Pack can generate reports that include Top 100 Recipients, Top 100 Users, and Highest Growth Mailboxes.

- You can use the Message Tracking tool to generate reports on messages received or submitted by users. You can use Exchange Management Shell commands to access the message tracking logs and obtain this information in more detail.

- You can use Exchange Management Shell commands to generate data that can be used in reports that contain total mailbox sizes, number of items, and the client protocols that are enabled for individual mailboxes.

- You can create reports on virus attacks, spam, and external messages. You can also use Exchange Management Shell and Exchange Management Performance Monitor to ascertain whether mailboxes are enabled for specific client protocols and to obtain information about the number of users currently connected by using OWA.

Lesson Review

You can use the following questions to test your knowledge of the information in Lesson 2, "Creating Usage Reports." The questions are also available on the companion CD if you prefer to review them in electronic form.

NOTE   Answers

Answers to these questions and explanations of why each answer choice is correct or incorrect are located in the "Answers" section at the end of the book.

1. Which of the following Exchange organization reports do MOM 2005 SP1 and the Exchange Management Pack provide by default? (Choose all that apply.)

    A. Mail Delivered - Top 100 Recipient Mailboxes by Count

    B. Top Public Folders by Size

    C. Highest Growth Mailboxes

    D. Information Store Integrity

    E. Mail Delivered - Top 100 Recipient Mailboxes by Size

2. Which ExTRA tool obtains information about e-mail messages, senders, and receivers by accessing Message Tracking logs?

    A. Queue Viewer

    B. Message Tracking

    C. Mail Flow Troubleshooter

    D. Database Recovery Management

3. Which of the following are components of HTTPMon? (Choose all that apply.)

    A. Best Practices Analyzer

    B. Real-time Sampling Service

    C. Client Monitor

    D. System Center Operations Manager

    E. SQL Reporting Server

4. Which of the following Exchange Management Shell commands tells you whether POP3 is enabled for the don.hall@tailspintoys.internal mailbox?

    A. *Get-Mailbox –Identity don.hall@tailspintoys.internal*

    B. *Get-MailboxStatistics –Identity don.hall@tailspintoys.internal*

    C. *Get-MessageTrackingLog –Recipients don.hall@tailspintoys.internal*

    D. *Get-CASMailbox –Identity don.hall@tailspintoys.internal*

5. Which of the following Exchange Management Shell commands directly tells you the total item count in the don.hall@tailspintoys.internal mailbox?

    A. *Get-Mailbox –Identity don.hall@tailspintoys.internal*

    B. *Get-MailboxStatistics –Identity don.hall@tailspintoys.internal*

    C. *Get-MessageTrackingLog –Recipients don.hall@tailspintoys.internal*

    D. *Get-CASMailbox –Identity don.hall@tailspintoys.internal*

Chapter Review

To further practice and reinforce the skills you learned in this chapter, you can perform the following tasks:

- Review the chapter summary.
- Review the list of key terms introduced in this chapter.
- Complete the case scenarios. These scenarios set up real-world situations involving the topics of this chapter and ask you to create a solution.
- Complete the suggested practices.
- Take a practice test.

Chapter Summary

- You can use MOM 2005 SP1 with the Exchange Management Pack to create server reports for Exchange Sever 2007 servers. The same tool can generate reports that include Top 100 Recipients and Top 100 Users reports and Highest Growth Mailboxes reports. The System Center Operations Manager 2007 also monitors and reports server availability. The tool provides a Health Explorer that reports on server health and a CLI that lets you enter PowerShell commands.

- You can use the Performance Logs and Alerts tool, EXBPA, Exchange Performance Troubleshooter, Exchange Database Recovery Management, Queue Viewer, and Exchange Management Shell commands to generate reports on Exchange server health, queues, and databases.

- You can use the Message Tracking tool and Exchange Management Shell commands to access message tracking logs and report on message traffic. You can also use Exchange Management Shell commands to generate reports on mailbox sizes, number of items, and client protocols. You can access Exchange logs (for example, protocol logs) to create reports on virus attacks, spam, and external messages.

Key Terms

Do you know what these key terms mean? You can check your answers by looking up the terms in the glossary at the end of the book.

- Bottleneck
- Performance log
- Server availability
- Server health
- Top users

Case Scenarios

In the following case scenarios, you will apply what you have learned about reporting. You can find answers to these questions in the "Answers" section at the end of this book.

Case Scenario 1: Creating Server Reports

You are the Exchange administrator for Blue Sky Airlines. Answer the following questions:

1. You are using the Operations Manager Command Shell in System Center Operations Manager 2007, and you want to obtain a list of open critical alerts. What PowerShell command do you use?

2. You want to get information about all queues on a transport server BlueSky09 and store this in a CSV file C:\QueueReports\BlueSky09.csv. You do not want to capture type information. What Exchange Management Shell command do you use?

3. You want to confirm that Blue Sky's Exchange Server 2007 servers are configured according to Microsoft best practices. What tool do you use?

Case Scenario 2: Creating Usage Reports

You have recently been appointed the Exchange administrator for Coho Vineyards. Previously, a domain administrator has administered the Exchange organization, and he admits that he has had problems in this area. Answer the following questions:

1. You predecessor tried to install MOM 2005 SP1 with the Exchange Server Management Pack on a server in the Coho domain but could not do so. You check that .Net Framework 1.1 is installed on the server and find that it is. What is likely to be the problem?

2. You cannot at the moment use MOM 2005 SP1 with the Exchange Server Management Pack to generate Top 100 Users reports. You want to find out which users have mailboxes that have a total item size greater than or equal to 4 GB. You want to export the information to a CSV file C:\MailboxReports\BigMailboxes.csv. You do not want to export type information. What Exchange Management Shell command do you use?

3. Your predecessor has configured a spam quarantine mailbox, SpamQuarantine@Coho.internal. This mailbox holds all messages with an SCL from 4 through 6, but he has never generated reports for the mailbox. You want to export the statistics (but not the type information) for the spam quarantine mailbox into the file C:\SpamReports\QuarantineMailbox on that server. You open Exchange Management Shell on Coho08. What command do you enter?

Suggested Practices

To help you successfully master the exam objectives presented in this chapter, complete the following tasks.

Creating Server Reports

Do Practices 1 and 2 in this section. Practice 3 is optional.

■ **Practice 1: Learn More about the Production Tools**   Find out as much as you can about MOM 2005 SP1 with the Exchange Management Pack installed and Microsoft System Center Operations Manager 2007. If you have access to a production network that has these tools (or one of them) installed, study the reports that the tool generates.

■ **Practice 2: Revisit Exchange Server Performance Monitor**   You saw this tool before in previous chapters. Examine it again with a view to finding out which performance objects and performance counters could provide useful data if included in reports.

■ **Practice 3: Create Reports from CSV Files**   If you have access to data manipulation and report generation software such as Access or SQL Server, open CSV files that you generate by using Exchange Management Shell commands as described in this chapter and create reports. If you have access to software that can generate business graphics, such as Excel, open the CSV files in this software and generate charts to illustrate your reports.

Creating Usage Reports

Do both practices in this section.

- **Practice 1: Investigate Other Client Protocols**   Examine protocols such as Outlook Anywhere and Outlook Exchange Transport Protocol and determine whether you can generate statistics related to their use.

- **Practice 2: Investigate HTTPMon**   Find out more about HTTPMon. If you have access to a production network that has HTTPMon installed, study the reports that it generates.

Take a Practice Test

The practice tests on this book's companion CD offer many options. For example, you can test yourself on just one exam objective, or you can test yourself on all the 70-236 certification exam content. You can set up the test so that it closely simulates the experience of taking a certification exam, or you can set it up in study mode so that you can look at the correct answers and explanations after you answer each question.

MORE INFO   Practice tests

For details about all the practice test options available, see the "How to Use the Practice Tests" section in this book's Introduction.

Chapter 12

Configuring Disaster Recovery

Messaging services are typically mission critical or at least business critical. Even if e-mail is not mission critical, the loss of messaging services can create substantial disruption. Redundancy, security, and fault tolerance are important but cannot protect you from database loss, damage, or corruption. You need to back up (at least) all critical data in your Microsoft Exchange Server 2007 organization.

As an Exchange administrator, you need to know how to correctly back up Exchange 2007, how to restore Exchange 2007, and how to repair corrupt databases when no backups are available. Disaster recovery relies on decisions you make during the initial planning process. You need to carefully consider the following:

- What you might need to recover from
- Disaster recovery considerations during the deployment process
- The organization's service-level agreements (SLAs)
- The relationship between Exchange Server 2007 servers and Active Directory directory service
- How Exchange Database technology works

In this chapter, you will consider what your restore requirements are and therefore what you need to back up. A backup job backs up several files (sometimes quite a lot of files) in a single operation, and you will learn how to create and amend backup jobs and how to monitor your backups and test their validity. You will look at the use of the Volume Shadow Copy Service (VSS), which lets you quickly restore from a backup that was taken by using a hardware-based or software-based snapshot. The chapter also looks at recovering messages, recovering and reconnecting mailboxes and recovering databases, and methods of repairing a database if recovery is not possible.

Exam objectives in this chapter:
- Configure backups.
- Recover messaging data.

Lessons in this chapter:

Before You Begin

To complete the lessons in this chapter, you must have done the following:

- Installed Windows Exchange Server 2007 with the Mailbox, Client Access, Hub Transport, and Unified Messaging roles on a Windows domain controller in the Tailspintoys.internal domain. To do this, you need to have completed all the Practices in Lessons 1 and 2 of Chapter 1, "Preparing for Exchange Installation," and Lesson 1 of Chapter 2, "Installing Exchange Server and Configuring Roles."

- You need a device to hold your backup files. This can be a second internal hard disk, an external hard disk, a tape device, or a high-capacity USB pen device. In the production environment, you will likely back up to a disk or disk array, and the practices are more realistic if you use a hard disk. You cannot back up directly to optical devices.

Real World

Ian McLean

I once came across a company that had absolutely no need to back up its data, or so I was told.

It had invested in a top-of-the-range Storage Area Network (SAN) system. The disk set was striped with parity to sustain a disk failure without service interruption and then mirrored across a fibre channel network to a disk array in another building. All spindles were hot swappable. The loss of a disk or even an entire array was easily retrievable and would have no effect on system availability.

I applauded the disk setup but tried to point out that disk failure was not the only way data could be lost. Management assured me the company had the finest antivirus software money could buy. There was no way data could be wiped by an external attack. Backup, I was told, degraded performance, and restoring data took time and was therefore unacceptable, as users required 24/7 access with no downtime at all. Test restores required additional equipment and were time consuming and useless.

In other words, the company managers had spent a lot of money on what they considered a perfect solution. My function as a consultant was to tell them how clever they had been. I wrote my report and submitted my account with no real expectation it would be paid. It was not. Two months later, the company went out of business. I never did discover why, but I can guess.

Back up your data.

Lesson 1: Configuring Backups

What you need to back up is a function of what you might need to recover from. After a failure or disaster, you might need to repair or restore one or more parts of your messaging system. You need one or more strategies in place to recover from the following situations:

- Permanently deleted mail item
- Lost mailbox
- Lost database
- Lost storage group
- Lost Exchange Server 2007 server, but your databases and transaction log files are intact
- Lost Exchange Server 2007 server, and your databases and transaction log files are also lost
- Lost computer in an Exchange Server 2007 server Network Load Balancing (NLB) cluster
- Lost computer in an Exchange Server 2007 server Windows failover cluster
- Lost database or storage group in an Exchange Server 2007 Windows failover cluster
- Lost entire Exchange Server 2007 Windows failover cluster
- Lost external services (for example, Active Directory directory services, global catalog services, certificate services, Domain Name System)
- Lost site (including all Exchange Server 2007 servers and all servers that provide external services)

If, for example, your organization loses a mailbox server (including its Exchange databases and transaction log files) and has only basic backups of the Exchange databases and transaction log files, you can likely recover the Exchange Server 2007 database files and some configuration data. However, you might not be able to recover all the data and information that existed on the original server, which could include cluster configuration information, management scripts, or system management software that resided on the server. Microsoft recommends that you document all configuration settings and changes you make to a server starting immediately after setup is complete so that you can manually reconfigure your settings, if necessary.

If, on the other hand, you back up everything in your Exchange Server 2007 organization, you will likely be able to completely restore all critical data and configuration settings. However, if you back up all the data in your organization, your backup and restore processes will be more complex and more time consuming and will require more backup media space.

To determine exactly what data that you need to back up to successfully recover from a disaster, Microsoft recommends that you practice disaster recovery procedures in a test environment before you implement a backup strategy on production servers. Additionally, after you have implemented a backup and recovery strategy, you should conduct test restore operations regularly to make sure that you will be able to recover from whatever disaster might occur.

After this lesson, you will be able to:
- Create and modify backup jobs.
- Confirm backup validity.
- Monitor backups for successful completion.
- Configure shadow copy.

Estimated lesson time: 50 minutes

Selecting a Backup Type

Later in this lesson, you will look at what you need to back up for each Exchange Server 2007 server role. However, whatever else you back up, you must protect end-user data. In Exchange Server 2007, end-user data is stored in the mailbox and public folder databases on mailbox servers. Transport data in transport queue databases is transient, and there is no need to back up the queue database.

You need to protect mailbox and public folder databases by point-in-time backups. Whatever overall disaster recovery strategy you select, mailbox and public folder databases must be protected with backups because they contain user data. A backup provides a point-in-time copy of the data that can be restored to a server at a later time.

NOTE Windows Server 2008 backup

When this chapter was written, a 64-bit version of Windows Server 2008 was not available to support Exchange Server 2007. Therefore, the practices in the chapter are written for the Windows Server 2003 backup utility (NTBackup). If your test computer's operating system is Windows Server 2008, the practices will differ from those described (although not radically). In this case, it is an instructive exercise to amend the practices to use the Windows Server 2008 backup utility.

Exchange Server 2007 provides the following methods of database backup:

- **Legacy streaming backup** Legacy streaming backup (NTBackup) uses the Extensible Storage Engine (ESE) application programming interface (API). Streaming backup technology is used by Microsoft Windows Server Backup as well as many third-party products. This technology has been available in previous versions of Exchange and has a mature feature set.

- **VSS** Exchange Server 2003 introduced support for VSS and this support is extensively enhanced in Exchange Server 2007. Microsoft provides a software VSS-based backup solution for Exchange Server through Microsoft System Center Data Protection Manager (DPM) 2007, which is a separate product that provides disk-based recovery and tape-based, long-term archival storage for a complete data protection and recovery solution. NTBackup does not support VSS. DPM 2007 or third-party backup software is required to back up the Exchange database with VSS.

Backup Categories and Types

Both backup methods support complete backup and change-only backup categories. The following types are available:

- **Full backup** A complete backup that archives every selected database and all necessary log files. When a full backup completes, it deletes log files older than the checkpoint at the time the backup started. If you perform a full backup on a daily basis, you can prevent log files from consuming space on the hard disk. Microsoft recommends daily full backups unless you use continuous replication, in which case weekly full backups are adequate. Local continuous replication (LCR) and cluster continuous replication (CCR) are discussed later in this lesson. A full backup is sometimes known as a normal backup.

- **Copy backup** A complete backup that is the same as a full backup except that log files are not deleted at the completion of the backup. You can perform a copy backup if you want to save a copy of your Exchange databases at a specific point in time, for example, for archiving.

- **Incremental backup** A change-only backup that archives the transaction log files created since the last full or incremental backup. When an incremental backup completes, it deletes log files older than the checkpoint at the time the backup started.

- **Differential backup** A change-only backup that archives the transaction log files created since the last full or incremental backup and does not delete transaction log files.

Exam Tip   Incremental backups delete (or truncate) transaction log files older than the check-point at the time the backup started. Differential backups do not. I have been getting this correct in examinations for years by simply remembering "differential does not."

MORE INFO   Circular logging

Circular logging helps control the hard disk space that is used by the log files, at the expense of overwriting older data in logs. You cannot perform a differential or incremental backup when circular logging is enabled. Circular logging is a feature of the Extensible Storage Engine (ESE). ESE maintains maintains all Exchange Server mailbox databases and public folder databases. For more information about circular logging, see "Understanding Transaction Logging" in the Exchange Server 2007 online help at *http://technet.microsoft.com/en-us/library/bb331951.aspx*.

Full backup facilitates restore operations because it gives you a single backup set to restore. Backup sets are discussed later in this lesson. Copy backup does not remove the log files. This is useful if you want to obtain a point-in-time backup without disturbing the backup plan you have in place. However, you should not rely on copy backups as your main or only backup method. Log files must be removed, or the disk storage that holds them will eventually fill up. Your Exchange Server 2007 database will then be taken offline until the log files are purged.

If you use differential or incremental backups, only changes since the last full or incremental backup are saved, the size of backup files is smaller than for a complete backup, and backup takes less time. However, these backup types require multiple backup sets to perform a full restore. Especially regarding incremental backups, if any of those backup sets are missing or not restorable, recovery can be only to the point prior to the nonrecoverable backup set.

Supported Backup and Restore Methods

Exchange Server 2007 supports all four types of Exchange backups (full, copy, incremental, and differential) when you use legacy streaming backup to back up the active copy of the Exchange database. Backups can be implemented at the database level, but there can be only one backup job running against a specific storage group. Separate storage groups can be backed up at the same time by running backup jobs in parallel. You can use legacy streaming restore to restore all four types of backups to the active copy of the database or to a recovery storage group. There is no support for restoring legacy streaming backups to any other location in the same forest, although you can perform test restores in a separate forest.

If you use VSS to create a shadow copy of a storage group, you can use all four backup types to back up the shadow copy. Backups can be selected at the storage group level, and there can be only one backup job running against a specific storage group. If you back up the shadow copy of a storage group, you cannot start another backup of the same storage group until the VSS requestor signals backup success or failure to the VSS writer of Exchange Server 2007 and completes the backup process. Separate storage groups can be backed up in parallel.

VSS backups can be restored to the same storage group, to an alternate storage group on the same or a different server, or to a non-Exchange location as supported by the Exchange 2007 Store Writer.

Creating Backup Jobs

A backup job backs up a set of files in the same operation. Backup jobs create backup sets. For example, you could perform a legacy streaming full backup of a single Exchange Server 2007 database, and this backup job would create a backup set. If you then subsequently performed legacy streaming incremental backup jobs on the same database, each of these backup jobs would create a backup set. In order to restore the database up to the latest possible point in time, you would need the backup set from the last full backup job and all the backup sets from subsequent incremental backup jobs.

NOTE   Full backup set

Sometimes confusion can arise between the terms *full backup job* and *full backup set*. Full (or normal) backup is a backup type. You can perform a full backup job on a database or a storage group and create a backup set from that backup job. However, a full backup set is created when you back up everything you need to restore a full server. An Exchange full backup set includes a backup of System State data, the Exchange binaries, and most of the data on an Exchange Server 2007 server's hard disks.

Backing up the user data in mailboxes and public folders is essential and must form part of any backup strategy. However, this is by no means the only data you might want to back up and might need to restore. The backup jobs you specify and the backup sets you generate depend on the roles performed by an Exchange Server 2007 server and the procedures you intend using to implement a restore. Backup and restore strategies are closely linked and cannot be designed independently.

Backup Jobs on a Mailbox Server

An Exchange Server 2007 server with the Mailbox server role installed (a mailbox server) hosts mailbox databases containing user mailboxes and therefore stores large amounts of user data. Your major concern in a disaster recovery scenario for a mailbox server is the user data.

IMPORTANT Recovering mailbox server settings

You can recover most of the settings for a mailbox server from the Active Directory directory service by running *Setup /mode:RecoverServer* from the Command Console. However, this does not recover damaged mailboxes, and you need to back up user data.

On a mailbox server, your backup job should include Exchange database files, including both mailbox and public folder databases and Exchange transaction log files that are specific to each storage group. These files are located by default in storage group folders in the path C:\Program Files\Microsoft\Exchange Server\Mailbox\ <storage_group_folder>. Figure 12-1 shows the contents of the First Storage Group folder on the mailbox server Glasgow.

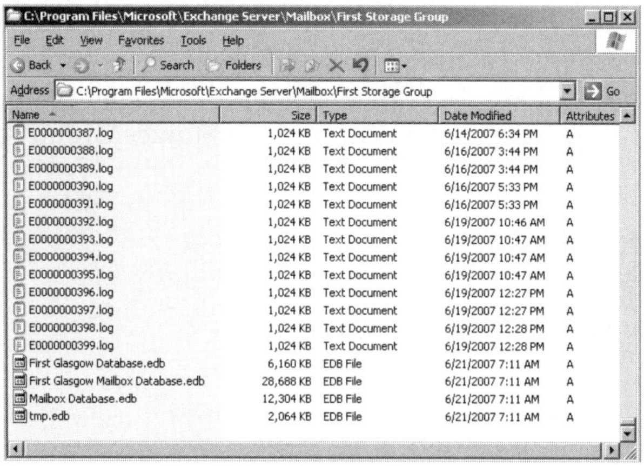

Figure 12-1 Database and transaction log files on a mailbox server

A storage group folder contains ESE (.edb) files and transaction log files. The ESE database stores all data submitted by Exchange clients. One .edb file is associated with each database. The physical size limit for .edb files is 16 TB, but only the databases of the Enterprise Edition can grow to this size. Exchange Server 2007 Standard Edition limits the individual database size to 50 GB (RTM version) and 250 GB (SP1). In practice the database size should be much smaller to satisfy SLAs for downtime—the bigger the database, the more time it takes to restore it.

MORE INFO Service-level agreements

For more information about SLAs, search for "Establishing a Service Level Agreement" in the Microsoft TechNet Library for Exchange Server or access *http://technet.microsoft.com/en-us/library/ bb124886.aspx*.

NOTE Joint Engine Technology

In previous editions of Exchange Server, the ESE database was referred to as the Joint Engine Technology (JET) database.

All changes made to the ESE database are first committed to transaction log files. Anytime a user modifies or adds to data stored in a mailbox, the change is written to a transaction log file before it is written to the database. The change is immediately committed to the database cache in RAM and then copied back to disk when the system load permits. Transaction log files are created sequentially, and this sequence is referred to as the log stream. There can be a (theoretical) maximum of 2,147,483,647 log files (0x7FFFFFFF hexadecimal) in a log stream. The transaction log files are each 1 MB in size. The number of transaction log files created depends on the client load on the server.

You should use an Exchange-aware backup application such as Microsoft Windows Server 2003 or Windows Server 2008 Backup to back up the Exchange database on a regular basis. Figure 12-2 shows the contents of the First Storage Group selected as a backup job.

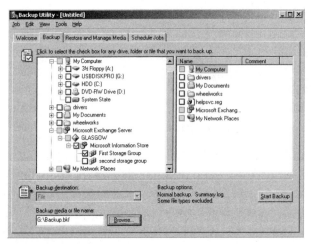

Figure 12-2 Backing up a storage group

After transaction log files are committed into the databases and backed up, they can be deleted. Exchange deletes transaction log files from the file system when a full or incremental backup occurs. If regular full or incremental backups are not performed or backups fail, transaction log files can fill all available space on your hard disk. At that point, Exchange Server 2007 dismounts your database and stops accepting data until you make more space available on the hard disk.

The Full-Text Index Catalog

The Microsoft Exchange Search Indexer service (MSExchangeSearch) enables users to perform full-text searches of documents and attachments in messages. The search index data for a specific mailbox database is stored in a catalog data directory in the same location as the database files. Figure 12-3 shows the catalog data directories associated with the First Storage Group on the mailbox server Glasgow.

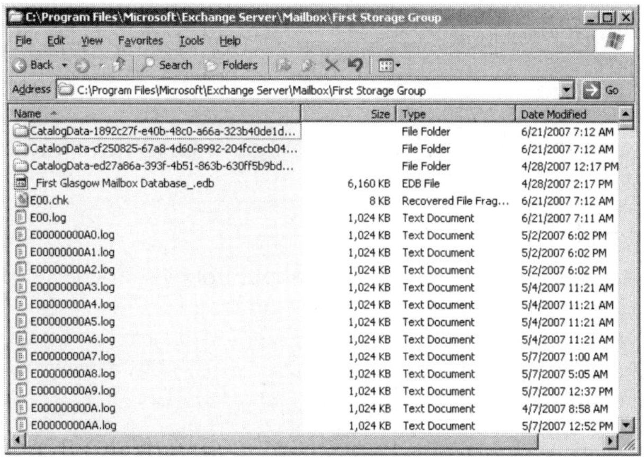

Figure 12-3   Catalog data directories

A catalog directory name follows the convention CatalogData-<guid>-<guid> where the first <guid> is the globally unique identifier (GUID) of the database, and the second <guid> represents the Instance GUID, which is used in the clustered scenario to distinguish between the nodes.

It is possible to back up the catalog directories by specifying their paths and performing a file backup. However, the search index can become unsynchronized with the database after recovery if transaction log files are played into the recovered database. Typically, you would not back up or restore catalog directories but instead rebuild the search index catalog after a restore. To do this, stop the Microsoft Exchange Search service, delete the old catalog, and then restart the service. This action forces the server to re-create the search index catalog.

For more information about how to recover your Exchange full-text search index, search Exchange Server 2007 Help for "How to Rebuild the Full-Text Index Catalog" or access *http://technet.microsoft.com/en-us/library/aa995966.aspx.*

The offline address book (OAB) is stored by default on a mailbox server in a folder in the file path C:\Program Files\Microsoft\Exchange Server\ExchangeOAB. Microsoft Outlook clients download OABs to enable clients to look up address book requests without having to connect to an Exchange server. If an Exchange organization uses public folders to store OAB information, this information is stored in the public folder database on Mailbox servers. In this case, the OAB is replicated as part of public folder replication and is backed up during public folder backup. If public folders are not used, OAB information is generated by the OABGen service on a Mailbox server, distributed by the Microsoft Exchange File Distribution service (MSExchangeFDS) on CAS servers, and downloaded by Outlook 2007 clients and mobile devices from CAS servers via the OAB virtual directory. The Autodiscover service returns the correct OAB URL to the client according to the parameters of the client connection. Chapter 4, "Public Folders," discusses the generation and storage of OAB information.

MORE INFO Public folder replication

Currently, a series of informative articles by Neil Hobson about troubleshooting public folder replication are available on the Microsoft Exchange Team Blog (You Had Me At EHLO) at *http://msexchangeteam.com/archive/2006/01/17/417611.aspx*, *http://msexchangeteam.com/archive/2006/01/19/417737.aspx*, and *http://msexchangeteam.com/archive/2006/01/23/417974.aspx*.

If you are using the Web-based distribution method via the OAB virtual directory, you need to back up the OAB files generated by OABGen on your Mailbox server. This is a file backup and is not Exchange aware, so you need to specify the path to the OAB information separately as part of your backup job, as shown in Figure 12-4.

NOTE Backing up OAB on Client Access servers

You can also back up the C:\Program Files\Microsoft\Exchange Server\OAB directory on Client Access servers that contain the local cached copy of the OAB files. This action is not essential, but doing so makes it unnecessary to replicate all the OAB files from the mailbox server when the Client Access server is brought back online after disaster recovery and saves time when recovering a Client Access server.

MORE INFO Exchange public folder database

For more information about the Exchange public folder database, search Exchange Server 2007 Help for "Managing Public Folders" or access *http://technet.microsoft.com/en-us/library/bb124411.aspx*.

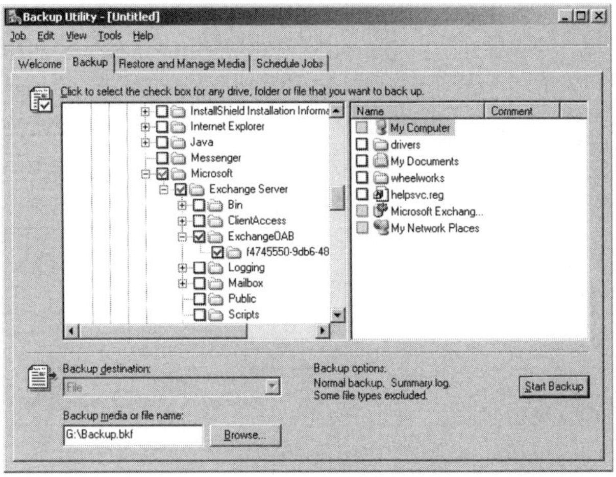

Figure 12-4   Backing up an OAB

You can also save the registry settings on a mailbox server by backing up System State data as part of your backup job or by exporting the following registry keys to files:

- HKEY_LOCAL_MACHINE\SOFTWARE\Microsoft\Exchange
- HKEY_LOCAL_MACHINE \SYSTEM\currentcontrolset\Services

Figure 12-5 shows the export of the first of these keys.

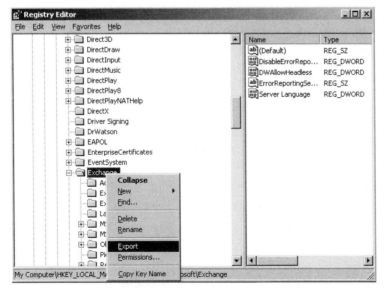

Figure 12-5   Exporting HKEY_LOCAL_MACHINE\SOFTWARE\Microsoft\Exchange

---

MORE INFO   System State data

For more information about backing up System State data, search Exchange Server 2007 Help for "How to Back Up the System State and the Exchange Program Files" or access *http:// technet.microsoft.com/en-us/library/aa997709.aspx*.

Table 12-1 summarizes the data on a mailbox server and how you back it up. You carry out an online streaming backup of Exchange database files and transaction log files in the practice session later in this lesson.

Table 12-1   Data on a Mailbox Server

Data	Location	Backup Method
Exchange database files—mailbox and public folder databases	C:\Program Files\Microsoft\ Exchange Server\Mailbox\ <storage_group_folder>	Exchange-aware backup application
Exchange transaction log files specific to a storage group	C:\Program Files\Microsoft\ Exchange Server\Mailbox\ <storage_group_folder>	Exchange-aware backup application
Exchange Search information specific to a mailbox database in a storage group	C:\Program Files\Microsoft\ Exchange Server\Mail-box\<storage_group_folder>	None—typically rebuilt after a restore
OAB	C:\Program Files\Microsoft\ Exchange Server\ ExchangeOAB	File system backup (if the Web-based distribution method is used)
OAB	Public folder (if the Exchange organization uses public folders for this purpose). Otherwise, OAB information is distributed by the Exchange File Distribution service and OAB virtual directory.	Public folder replication or backup
Windows registry	HKEY_LOCAL_MACHINE\ SOFTWARE\Microsoft\ Exchange HKLM\SYSTEM\ currentcontrolset\Services	System State backup or registry export

Backup Jobs on a Hub Transport Server

An Exchange Server 2007 server with the Hub Transport server role installed stores all its configuration data in the Active Directory directory configuration container. It also stores queues in ESE databases, message tracking and protocol logs in files, and configuration information in the registry. None of this data is essential to restoring the Hub Transport server functionality.

The queue database is used to store messages while they are being processed by agents and relayed to their final destination on the server. After the message is delivered to an internal or external host, the message is removed from the queue database. Because the data in the database is transient, this database uses circular logging, and you do not need to back it up.

The message tracking and protocol log files are used to store records of transactions that took place on the server. The message tracking logs are used as historical forensic data to view the path that a message took. The protocol logs are used to track all the conversations that take place on all the connectors on the Exchange server.

You can restore the Hub Transport server role and made it fully functional by running the *Setup/mode:RecoverServer* command. You do not need to carry out any backup jobs to restore this server role, but if you carry out a file-level backup of the message tracking and protocol log files you can restore these files to provide past information for message tracking and troubleshooting purposes. You do this in the practice session later in this lesson.

MORE INFO   *Setup/mode:RecoverServer*

For more information about the *Setup/mode:RecoverServer* command, search Exchange Server 2007 Help for "Understanding Setup/mode:RecoverServer" or access *http://technet.microsoft.com/en-us/library/aa998656.aspx*.

Backup Jobs on an Edge Transport Server

An Exchange Server 2007 server with the Edge Transport server role installed functions as a stand-alone server and does not store any end-user data in the Active Directory directory service. It stores configuration, queues, and data replicated from Active Directory in ESE databases; message tracking and protocol logs in files; and limited configuration information in the registry. The queues and logs are not essential to restoring the Edge Transport server functionality.

The queue database is used to store messages while they are being processed by agents and relayed to their final destination on the server. After a message is delivered to an internal or external host, it is removed from the queue database. Because the data in the database is transient, this database uses circular logging and is not backed up.

The message tracking and protocol log files are used to store records of transactions that took place on the server. The message tracking logs are used as historical forensic data to view the path that a message took. The protocol logs are used to track all the conversations that take place on all the connectors on the Exchange server. This data is not required to restore the server role, and you do not need to back it up. Nor do you need to back up the registry information for this server role because this information is not needed for server restore. You might decide to back up the protocol logs on an Edge Transport server for forensic or troubleshooting purposes.

Cloned Configuration

Cloned configuration backs up user-configured settings on an Edge Transport server. Most of the settings on an Edge Transport server are set by default, updated from the Web, or replicated from Active Directory. If nothing has been changed on an Edge Transport server, nothing needs to be backed up. Cloned configuration is designed to capture any administrator-modified configuration data on an Edge Transport server.

For more information about cloned configuration, search Exchange Server 2007 Help for "Edge Transport Server Data" or access *http://technet.microsoft.com/ en-us/library/aa997584.aspx*.

Backup Jobs on a Client Access Server

An Exchange Server 2007 server with the Client Access server role stores configuration data in the Active Directory directory service, the Internet Information Services (IIS) metabase, and local configuration files. Changes to IIS metabase and Active Directory data are not synchronized or duplicated. If you run the *Setup/mode:RecoverServer* command to restore your server settings, this restores your Client Access server to the default installation state and ignores all the postinstallation customization work you have carried out on the server. Virtual directories you created and customizations applied to the default virtual directories will be lost.

If the IIS metabase and Active Directory are not synchronized because of a restore or recovery operation, a client access server experiences errors. Microsoft recommends that you do not recover your IIS metabase to a Client Access server after you have run the *Setup/mode:RecoverServer* command. You should instead keep a detailed change log of customizations performed on your Client Access server. In the event that your Client Access server is recovered, you can then reference the change log and reapply the customizations.

A Client Access server stores configuration information for the OWA Web site and Web.config file, Internet Message Access Protocol (IMAP4), and Post Office Protocol (POP3) protocol settings, the Availability service, Autodiscover, Exchange ActiveSync, OWA virtual directories, and Web services configuration. It also stores some registry information, but this is not essential for restore.

Typically, a Client Access server acts as a pass-through to get to Exchange data. If multiple Client Access servers are deployed for redundancy, backup is not required. If, however, only one Client Access server exists in your organization, it might be worthwhile to back up the POP/IMAP configuration stored in\ClientAccess\PopImap. Alternatively, you could document changes to the POP and IMAP settings and redo them if you needed to rebuild the server.

MORE INFO   **Client Access server data**

For more information about Client Access server data, search Exchange Server 2007 Help for "Client Access Server Data" or access *http://technet.microsoft.com/en-us/library/aa998364.aspx*.

Backup Jobs on a Unified Messaging Server

An Exchange Server 2007 server with the Unified Messaging server role installed stores the majority of its configuration information in Active Directory, transient message queues in the file system, setup information in the registry, server-specific configuration data in XML files in the\bin folder, and custom audio files in the file system.

The C:\Program Files\Microsoft\Exchange Server\UnifiedMessaging\temp folder is used to store messages while they are being processed by the server. When the message has been submitted to a transport server for delivery, it is removed from this folder. You do not need to back up or restore the messages in this folder in order to restore server functionality. If, however, you can retrieve the e-mail message (.eml) and voice message audio (.wav) files from this directory on a failed Unified Messaging server, you can send these files to their intended recipients by copying them to the Exchange Server\TransportRoles\Pickup folder on a Hub Transport server.

Typically, the first Unified Messaging server to be associated with a dial plan becomes the prompt publishing server. On a prompt publishing server, you should back up custom audio (.wav) files for unified messaging dial plans and unified messaging auto attendants and custom audio (.wav) files for telephone user interface (TUI) or Microsoft Outlook voice access. You can do this as a file-level backup of the C:\ Program Files\Microsoft\Exchange Server\UnifiedMessaging\Prompts folder.

You do not need to back up server configuration data on a Unified Messaging server. This data is held in the Active Directory and protected by Active Directory replication or backup. You can restore the server settings by using the *Setup/mode:RecoverServer* command.

Modifying Backup Jobs

When you specify a backup job, the resulting backup set is held in the backup location in a .bkf file. You cannot modify this file directly, but you can create another backup job with the same file name and then configure the settings in Backup Job Information dialog box to choose whether the new backup overwrites or is appended to the existing backup set. Figure 12-6 shows these options.

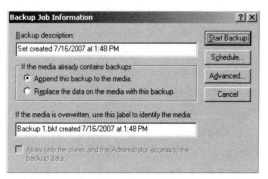

Figure 12-6 Choosing to appending to or overwrite a backup set

You would typically overwrite a backup set if you were performing scheduled daily full backups and want to retain only the latest backup set. In this situation, it is a good idea also to take regular copy backups for archiving off-site.

You would typically append a backup job to a backup set if you decide to use a file-level backup to back up additional data, for example, System State data, to an existing data set. If you create a full backup followed at intervals by incremental backups, you might want to append each incremental backup to the backup set.

If you schedule your backup job, you can specify the backup job schedule by selecting the Schedule Jobs tab of the Backup Utility, as shown in Figure 12-7.

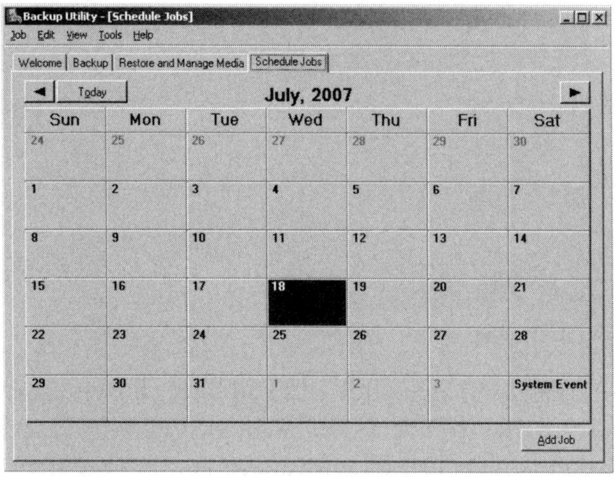

Figure 12-7   Backup Utility Schedule Jobs tab

Quick Check

■ What files should you back up on a Unified Messaging server that is also a prompt publishing server?

Quick Check Answer

■ Custom audio (.wav) files for unified messaging dial plans and unified messaging auto attendants and custom audio (.wav) files for TUI or Microsoft Outlook voice access.

Performing Restore to Confirm Backup Validity

You can choose to validate your backup by selecting the validate check box when you create the backup job, as shown in Figure 12-8. However, in order to have full confidence in your backup and restore procedures, you should restore backed-up data to a different location (a test restore) and compare the data in that location to the original data. Test restores are typically implemented on a test network in a different Active Directory forest from the production network.

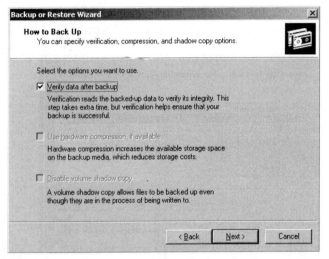

Figure 12-8   Choosing to verify backed up data

Even when your backups report as "Successful" and you have chosen to verify them, you have no absolute guarantee that the successful backup contains everything necessary to restore what you need to if data loss or software corruption occurs. Your disaster recovery plan should involve periodically testing the restore procedures to verify accuracy and test the backup media to ensure that data can actually be recovered.

In a production environment, you should perform test restores as part of your regular maintenance schedule to ensure that the backup method is correct and that disaster recovery procedures and documentation are current. Your tests also should verify that the backup media can be read from and used to restore data. Test restores have the additional advantage that they familiarize administrators with the procedures necessary for recovery so that if a real disaster occurs, recovery can be performed correctly and efficiently the first time.

IMPORTANT   Do not do a test restore to the original location

Under no circumstances should you test your restore process by restoring to the same locations that you backed up. If the restore fails and the original data is corrupted in the process, you really have a disaster and one from which you are unlikely to make a full recovery.

The ability to perform test restore is one of the main justifications for having a test network in your organization. You can then perform a restore on a different server in a different forest from the one you backed up. When test restores are performed in a nonproduction environment, users are not affected. You should vary the restore type, testing single mailbox restores, complete server restores, and full site restores.

MORE INFO **Restoring to a different server**

For more information about restoring to a different server, search Exchange Server 2007 Help for "How to Restore a Streaming Backup to a Different Server" or access *http://technet.microsoft.com/ en-us/library/aa995898.aspx*.

NOTE **Using a recovery storage group**

In Exchange Server 2007 (and Exchange Server 2003), you can use a recovery storage group (RSG) to do a test restore on the same server. However, Microsoft does not recommend this procedure in a production environment because it degrades performance on the production databases while it is being carried out. Lesson 2 of this chapter discusses RSGs.

Monitoring Backups for Successful Completion

In the production environment, a backup can take a considerable time. If, for example, you are performing a full backup of 1,000 mailboxes, each, on average, containing 4 GB of data, you are looking at transferring more than 4 TB onto a disk or tape drive that has mechanical moving parts. This does not happen instantaneously—it takes several hours.

You need to be able to monitor events that tell you whether backup is complete and whether it was successful. The NTBackup utility will generate a report indicating a successful backup and will also write to the Application log in Event Viewer. You can filter this log for events with ntbackup as the source, as shown in Figure 12-9.

Figure 12-10 shows events related to NTBackup. These events can be information, warning, or error events, depending on the success of the backup. Events with eventIDs 8000, 8001, 8002, 8003, 8018, and 8019 are of particular interest.

Event 8000, for example, indicates that the backup has started, whether the backup replaces or appends to the current backup set, and whether verify is enabled. Figure 12-11 shows this event.

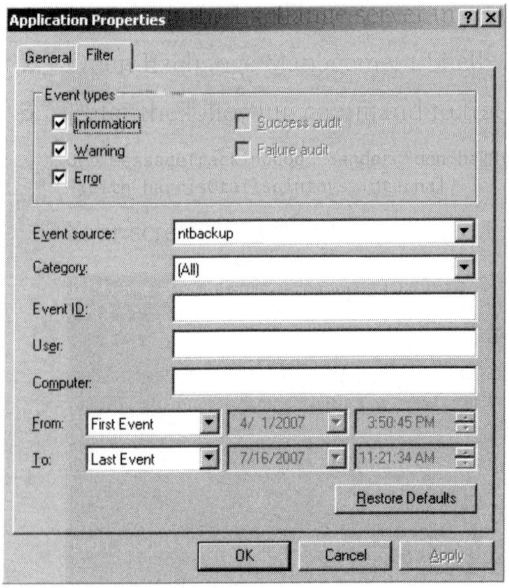

Figure 12-9 Filtering for backup events

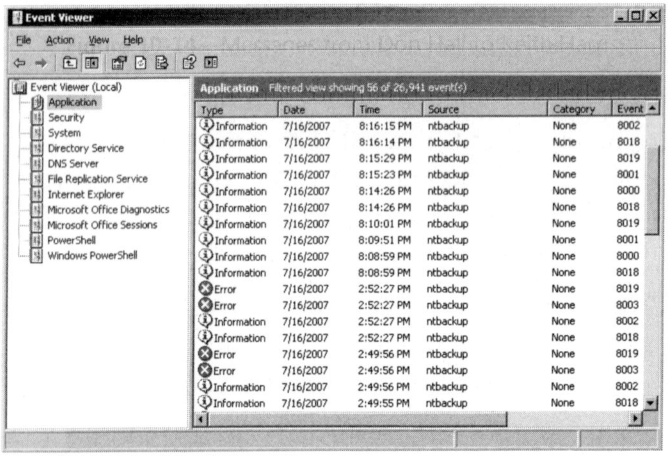

Figure 12-10 Events with source ntbackup

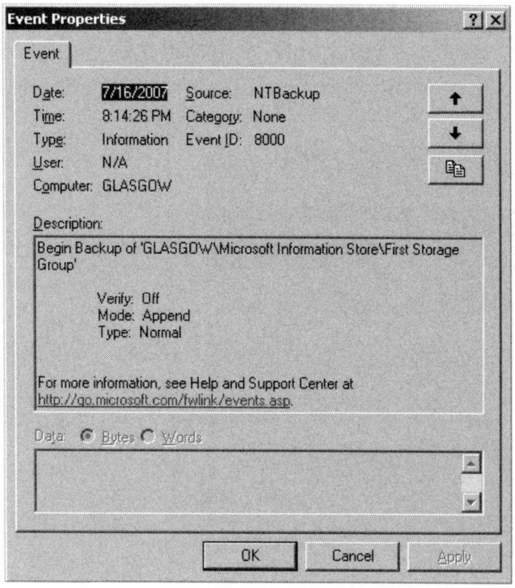

Figure 12-11   Backup start event

Event 8001 indicates that backup is complete. Figure 12-12 shows this event.

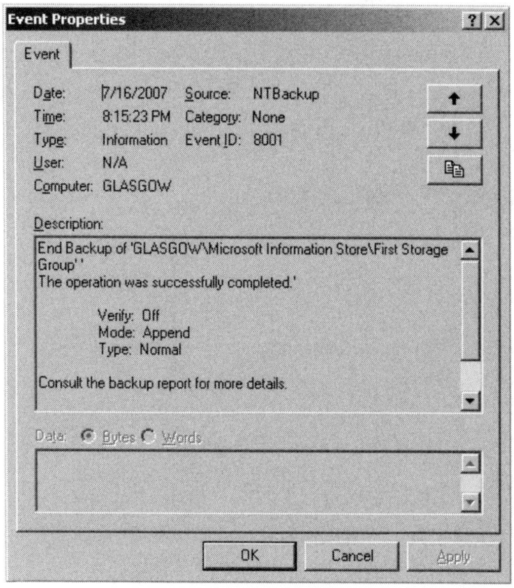

Figure 12-12   Backup complete event

Events 8002 and 8003 are restore events. Events 8018 and 8019 indicate operation completion events and can identify errors. If you click the hyperlink provided, you can get more information. Figure 12-13 shows the information provided for an 8019 event.

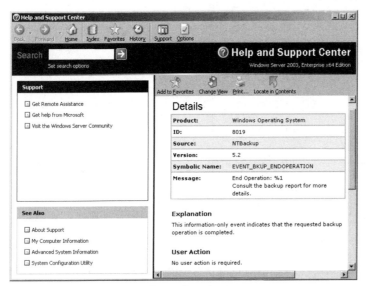

Figure 12-13   Obtaining information about an event

You can obtain information about a backup by viewing the backup log. You can do this by clicking View Backup Log when the Backup Wizard completes. Figure 12-14 shows a backup log.

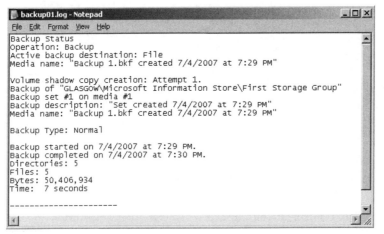

Figure 12-14   A backup log

You can use commands based on the PowerShell *Get-EventLog* cmdlet to obtain information about events in the event log. These commands can run from the PowerShell console or Exchange Management Shell. Chapter 9, "Monitoring," introduced these commands.

For example, you can list all events in the Application log with EventID 8001 by using the following command:

```
Get-EventLog Application | where {$_.EventID -eq 8001}
```

You can include commands based on the *Get-EventLog* cmdlet in PowerShell scripts and then create batch files that run the PowerShell scripts from the Command Processor (cmd.exe). The batch files can trigger executable files that could, for example, alert you if a specified event occurs. Chapter 5, "Moving Mailboxes and Implementing Bulk Management," discussed PowerShell scripts and batch files, and Chapter 9 looked at batch files that accessed event logs.

Exam Tip   You need to be aware that you can use PowerShell scripts to carry out tasks such as monitoring event logs and that you can run these scripts by using batch files. However, the 70-236 examination is most unlikely to ask you to create such scripts or batch files.

Using Shadow Copy Backup

Exchange 2007 supports VSS-based backups using the Volume Shadow Copy Service implemented in Microsoft Windows Server 2003. Typically, it takes much less time to restore a backup that was taken using a hardware-based clone than it does to restore from a streaming backup, making it easier to meet SLA time requirements that relate to the time that it takes to restore Exchange databases and thus helping you support larger database sizes.

NOTE   **Back up databases online**

When you back up an Exchange database by using the ESE streaming backup APIs or a VSS-based solution, the database must be online. Although you can back up an offline database manually, manual checksum verification is then required. In addition, taking a database offline to perform a backup results in an interruption of service to clients.

The new feature in Exchange Server 2007 when using continuous replication is the ability to run software VSS snapshot not just on the production copy but on the passive copy as well. Taking a VSS snapshot on the passive copy removes the disk load on the production logical unit number (LUN) during both the checksum integrity and the subsequent copy to tape or disk. This also frees up more time on the production LUNs to run online maintenance, messaging records management (MRM), and other tasks. Testing checksum integrity using the Eseutil tool is discussed in Lesson 2.

NOTE   Logical unit number

A LUN is a unique identifier used on a SCSI bus to distinguish between devices that share the same bus and can be used to refer to an entire physical disk or a subset of a larger physical disk or disk volume. Originally, SCSI was designed as a parallel interface that allows up to 16 devices to be connected along a single cable. Today, parallel SCSI is almost entirely replaced by more reliable serial attached SCSI (SAS) technology capable of handling several hundred devices per SAS controller. The physical disk or disk volume could be an entire single disk drive, a partition (subset) of a single disk drive, or a disk volume from a redundant array of independent disks (RAID) controller comprising multiple disk drives aggregated together for larger capacity and redundancy.

Exchange Server 2007 uses the VSS that is included in the Server operating system to take volume shadow copies of Exchange Server 2007 databases and transaction log files. If you use VSS you can restore databases more rapidly than is possible from streaming backups, and hence you can use larger databases and still meet your SLAs for restore. However, the Exchange-aware backup and restore utility (NTBackup) cannot implement VSS backups, and you need to use DPM 2007 or third-party software.

Several VSS strategies are available, and you need to test the capacity, performance, and recovery implications of each solution and ensure that any potential solution is operating within the VSS framework. VSS is a set of APIs that enables volume backups to be performed while applications on a system continue to write to the volumes. It uses requestors, writers, and providers within the VSS framework to create and restore volume shadow copies. A shadow copy of a volume duplicates all the data held on that volume at one well-defined instant in time.

As shown in Figure 12-15, VSS is stopped by default and starts on demand. If you want to use VSS you need to enable the service and set the start-up type to automatic.

VSS transparently coordinates activities of providers, writers, and requestors in the creation and use of shadow copies, furnishes the default system provider, and implements low-level driver functionality necessary for any provider to work.

During a VSS backup, the requestor initiates the backup process and instructs the Exchange Server 2007 writer to prepare a data set for backup. The writer prepares the data for backup. When the data set is ready, the writer signals the requestor to back up the data set. The provider interacts with the disk system and manages shadow copies.

When instructed by the requestor, the provider creates a shadow copy. The requestor then signals backup success or failure to the writer and completes the backup process.

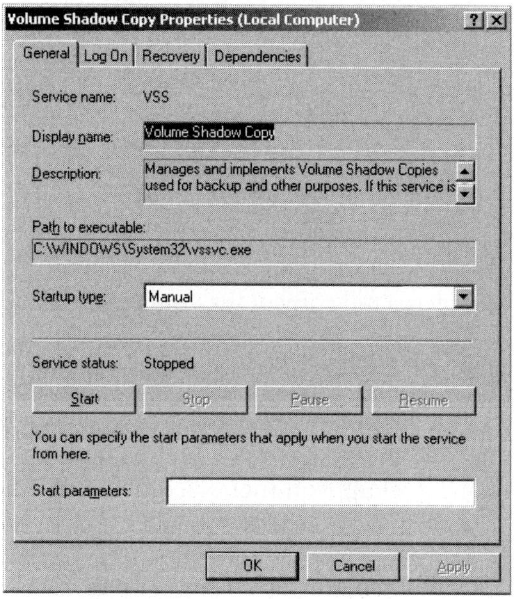

Figure 12-15   The Volume Shadow Copy Service (VSS)

MORE INFO   **Providers, requestors, and writers**

For more information about providers, requestors, and writers, access *http://msdn2.microsoft.com/en-us/library/aa384594.aspx*, *http://msdn2.microsoft.com/en-us/library/aa384596.aspx* and *http://msdn2.microsoft.com/en-us/library/aa384993.aspx*, respectively.

The Exchange writer, when instructed to do so by a requestor, prepares Exchange databases for backup. The writer does this by suspending all disk write I/O to the databases for up to 20 seconds. This is referred to as freezing the databases. The provider must be able to complete the shadow copy within this window, or the backup will be aborted. After backup finishes, the writer thaws the databases and resumes regular I/O operations.

Although no industry-standard definition or naming convention for shadow copy backup methods exists, most backup methods can be categorized as either clone shadow copies or snapshot shadow copies.

> **Quick Check**
> - During a VSS backup, what initiates the backup process and instructs the Exchange Server 2007 writer to prepare a data set for backup?
>
> **Quick Check Answer**
> - The requestor.

Clone Shadow Copies

A shadow copy set is a group of volume shadow copies that are synchronized at the same point in time. A clone shadow copy is a full copy of the volumes in a shadow copy set. A clone is independent of the original data. If all the original data is lost, the clone still persists intact. To make sure that a restorable copy is available if a failure occurs during a backup, Microsoft recommends that you use an N + 1 scheme, where N is the number of backup clones that you want to have available to restore at any time. If you decide, for example, you need only one backup, you then need two target clones that you can rotate between to prevent data loss if a failure occurs during a backup.

The third-party provider software determines how a clone is created. Some solutions prepare mirror copies in advance. These copies are then used to take a backup, providing you with a read-only copy and a live production volume. This strategy has almost no effect on the production LUNs during the backup and checksum integrity process. However, it does create significant I/O load on production LUNs before the backup.

You must make sure that you schedule time to resynchronize a clone that is no longer needed with the production LUN when you rotate through multiple clones. For restoration, the solution might resynchronize the read-only copy to the production LUN, which affects any other online storage groups that are using the same production LUN until all the data is copied. During restore, some storage arrays just change pointers to the read-only copy. This makes it writable.

Other solutions create a clone at the time of backup, where all the data in the LUN must be copied to another LUN. That data is then marked read-only. This strategy typically consumes less up-front capacity but requires all data to be copied at the time of backup. With this strategy, you must know how many gigabytes per hour a particular storage controller can support in addition to the effect on the production database LUNs during the copy. This enables you to design your LUNs correctly for maximum throughput and to plan the timing of this operation to minimize the effect on your production LUNs.

Snapshot Shadow Copies

The most important difference between a clone and a snapshot is that a snapshot is not fully independent of the original data. Snapshots are created by defining a marker at a point in time and making sure that the data can be rolled back to that marker. You can keep multiple snapshots, which typically require much less additional disk space than clones.

The most common method of creating a snapshot is copy-on-write. This method defines a snapshot at a point in time and then monitors the original data set for changes. If a change is made, the change is recorded or tracked in a separate location. Over time, therefore, the size of a snapshot will grow, especially when a snapshot is made of a quickly changing data set.

NOTE   Snapshot advantage and disadvantage

A snapshot is not an independent copy of the data. If the original data is destroyed, the snapshot data is useless because it contains only the recent changes to the data. The advantage of this backup method is that you are writing only the changes to disk instead of all the data, so the snapshot can be created very quickly. The disadvantage is that you do not have a recoverable backup if your original data is corrupted. Streaming and VSS backup technologies cannot be combined either during backups or restores. Legacy incremental backups cannot be taken after VSS full backups. You cannot combine a VSS differential backup with a legacy full backup at restore time.

Local Continuous Replication and Cluster Continuous Replication

LCR is a single-server solution that creates and maintains a copy of a storage group on a second set of disks that are connected to the same server as the production storage group. It can reduce recovery time by enabling a quick switch to a secondary copy of the data. It can also reduce the number of regular full backups that are required for data protection. VSS backup types (full, copy, incremental, and differential) can be taken from the LCR copy locations.

LCR enables the configuration, operation, verification, removal, and activation of a storage group copy. When necessary, the local copy can be made available as the production database and can be mounted. In addition, LCR does not include any special storage requirements. Any supported type of storage can be used with LCR. It also provides the ability to offload VSS backups to the passive copy of the database and logs.

You can administer LCR by using Exchange Management Console or Exchange Management Shell. For more information, access *http://technet.microsoft.com/en-us/library/bb125195.aspx*.

CCR is a high availability feature of Exchange Server 2007 that makes use of the Microsoft Windows Cluster service. CCR eliminates the Exchange information store as a single point of failure in the Mailbox server architecture, has no special hardware requirements, and has no shared storage requirements. It can reduce full backup frequency, reduce the total backed-up data volume, and help achieve the SLA for recovery time from first failure. The CCR solution can be deployed in a single data center or between two data centers.

CCR uses the database failure recovery functionality in Exchange Server 2007 to enable the continuous and asynchronous updating of a passive copy of a database with the changes that have been made to the active copy of the database. During installation of the passive node in a CCR environment, each storage group is copied from the active node to the passive node. This operation is called seeding. After the initial seeding is performed, log copying and replay are performed continuously.

In addition to new high-availability architectures for Mailbox servers, CCR facilitates scheduled maintenance and helps to keep downtime at a minimum. When you need to install updates or perform maintenance, you can move a clustered mailbox server manually to a passive node by using the *Move-ClusteredMailbox-Server* cmdlet in Exchange Management Shell. When the move operation is complete, you can then perform the required operations.

CCR supports VSS backups on the passive node. You can specify a longer backup window because the passive node does not need to maintain client connections, thereby allowing for larger databases and larger mailbox sizes.

The CCR passive copy provides the first line of defense against corruption and data loss. A double failure is required before backups will be needed. Recovery from the first failure can have a relatively short SLA specifications because no restore is required. As a result, streaming backups on the active node can be done on a weekly full cycle with a daily incremental backup strategy to keep the backup window small during work days. However, the recommended way to backup CCR-based Mailbox servers is to use a VSS-based solution on the passive node, such as DPM 2007. Backups on the passive node can be performed in

> much more frequent intervals, such as every 15 minutes an incremental backup and daily a full express backup as supported by DPM 2007. For more information, access *http://technet.microsoft.com/en-us/library/bb124521.aspx.*

Practice: Performing a Backup and Restore

The Exchange Server 2007 Server on your test network has the Mailbox, Hub Transport, and Client Access server roles installed. In this practice session, you back up the required and recommended data for each of these roles. Before you start the procedure, you need to create folders to hold the backups. If, for example, your backup medium is on the F:\ drive, create folders F:\Mailbox_backup and F:\HT_backup.

IMPORTANT In Lesson 2, you will be restoring the Don Hall mailbox

In this practice session, one of the mailboxes you will be backing up is the Don Hall mailbox that you created in Chapter 3, "Configuring Recipients, Groups, and Mailboxes." Before carrying out the practices, ensure that this mailbox contains one or more messages in its Inbox folder and is in the First Storage Group\Mailbox Database database. This does not affect the practice session in Lesson 1, but if you do not do this, the practices in Lesson 2 will not work as written.

▶ **Practice 1: Backing Up the Databases and Log Files on a Mailbox Server**

On a mailbox server, the index information, free/busy information, and the OAB can all be regenerated and typically do not need to be backed up. You therefore back up the databases and the transaction logs. This practice uses NTBackup to carry out an online streaming backup of all databases and log files in the storage group First Storage Group.

1. If necessary, log on with the Kim_Akers account.
2. Click Start. Click Run. In the Open text box, enter **ntbackup**.
3. The Backup or Restore Wizard starts. Click Next.
4. Select Back Up Files And Settings. Click Next.
5. Select Let Me Choose What To Back Up. Click Next.
6. In the left pane, expand Microsoft Exchange Server.
7. Expand Glasgow.
8. Expand Microsoft Information Store and select the First Storage Group check box, as shown in Figure 12-16, to back up all mailbox databases in this storage group and the associated log files. Note that if you want to back up all databases in all storage groups, you can select the Microsoft Information Store check box.

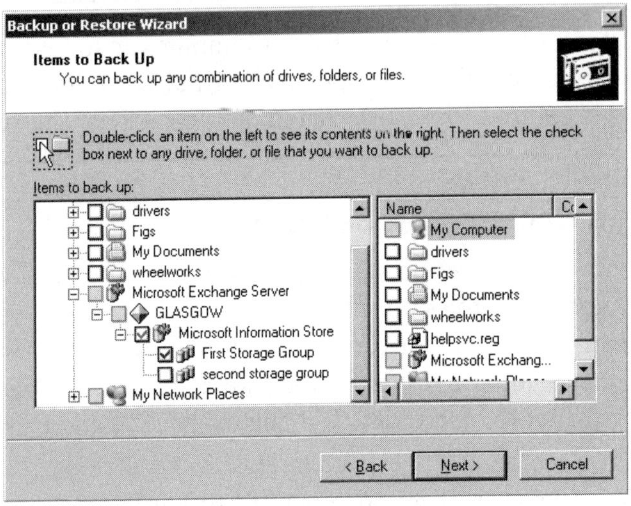

Figure 12-16 Selecting the First Storage Group for backup

9. Click Next.

10. Specify **MyMessageBackup** as the backup file name.

11. Browse to the folder you have created to hold the backup files. In Figure 12-17, this is F:\Mailbox_backup.

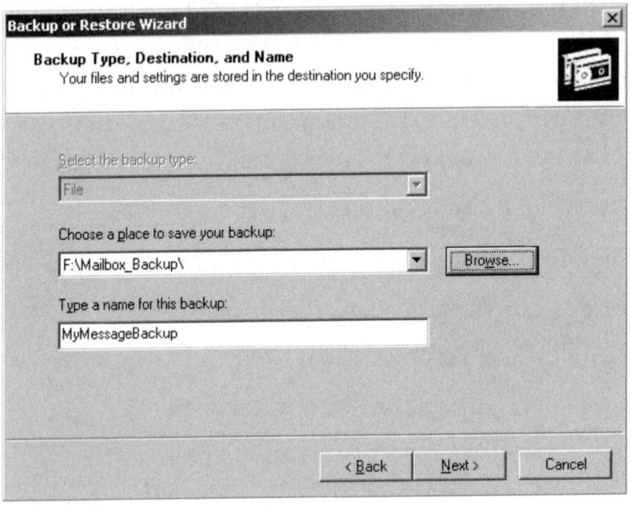

Figure 12-17 Selecting a backup location

12. Click Next. Click Advanced.

13. Specify a Normal backup as shown in Figure 12-18. A normal backup truncates the log files after the backup. Click Next.

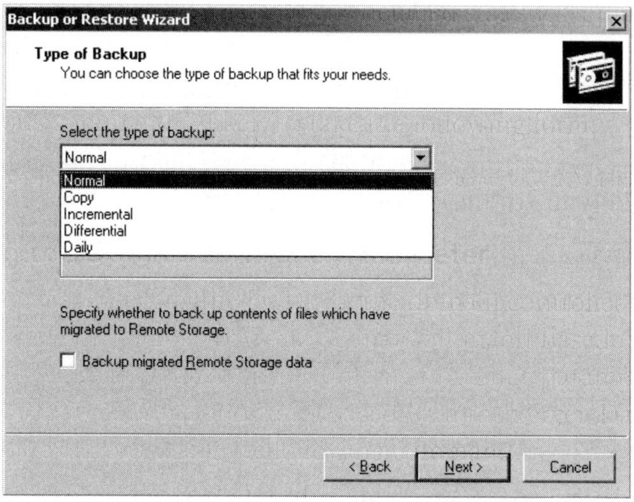

Figure 12-18   Specifying a normal (full) backup

14. Select Verify The Backup. Figure 12-8 earlier in this lesson shows this option. Note that verification takes almost as long as the backup itself. Click Next.

15. Select Replace The Existing Backups. Click Next.

16. If you wanted to run the job later, you could click Later to schedule the job for another time. However, in this instance you want backup to occur immediately, so select Now and click Next.

17. Click Finish and wait for the job to complete. Figure 12-19 indicates a successful backup. If you want to, you can click Report to see the backup log. Click Close.

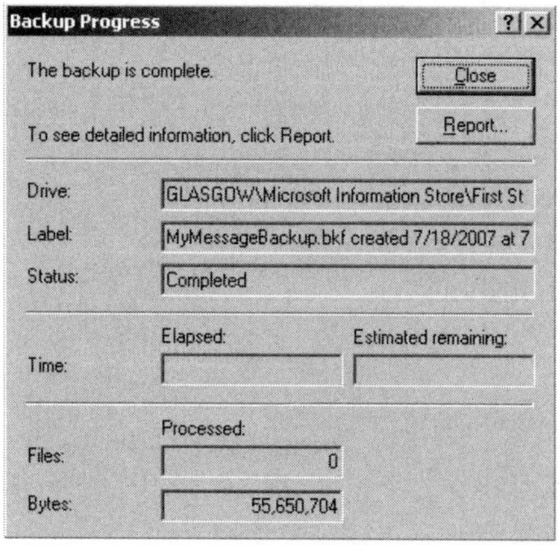

Figure 12-19   Backup completes successfully

▶ **Practice 2: Backing Up the Protocol Logs and Message Tracking Logs on a Hub Transport Server**

The log files on a Hub Transport server are not critical for a restore of an Exchange 2007 environment. However, you might choose to back up protocol logs and message tracking logs for forensic or troubleshooting purposes. This practice uses NTBackup to perform a file-level backup of these files.

1. If necessary, log on with the Kim_Akers account.

2. Click Start. Click Run. In the Open box enter **ntbackup.**

3. The Backup or Restore Wizard starts. Click Next.

4. Select Back Up Files And Settings. Click Next.

5. Select Let Me Choose What To Back Up. Click Next.

6. In the left pane, expand My Computer. Assuming that the C:\ drive contains the installation of Exchange, navigate to C:\Program Files\Microsoft\Exchange Server\TransportRoles and select the Logs check box, as shown in Figure 12-20.

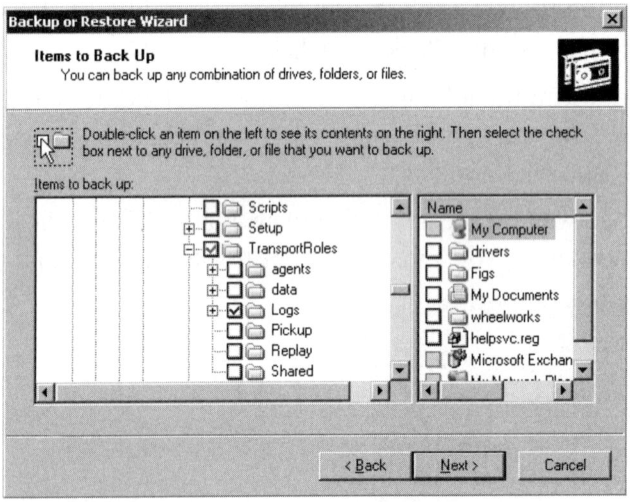

Figure 12-20   Selecting log files for backup

7. Click Next.

8. Specify **MyHubBackup** as the backup file name.

9. Browse to the folder you have created to hold the backup files. In Figure 12-21, this is F:\HT_backup.

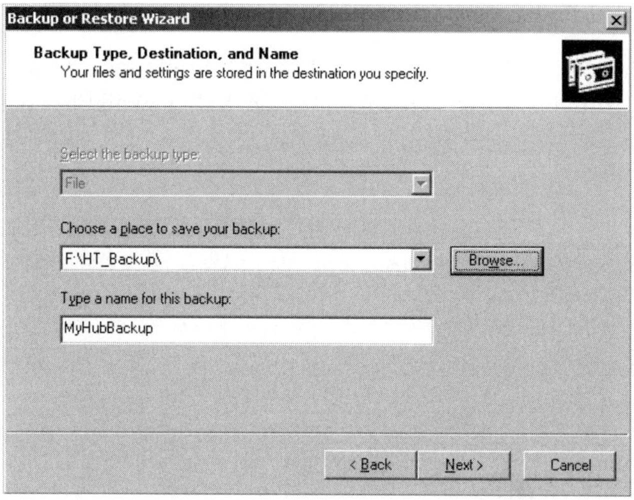

Figure 12-21   Backing up protocol and message tracking logs

10. Click Next. Click Finish and wait for the backup to complete. Click Close.

Lesson Summary

- Exchange Server 2007 provides legacy streaming backup (NTBackup) and support for the VSS. Furthermore, Microsoft provides an Exchange-aware backup solution in form of a separate product called DPM 2007 and you can also use third-party backup software to back up the Exchange database with VSS.

- Both streaming and VSS backups support the full (or normal), copy, differential, and incremental backup types.

- Mailbox servers hold user data, and this must be backed up as part of any backup plan.

- A backup job backs up a set of files in the same operation. Backup jobs create backup sets.

- You should carry out test restores to test your backup data and procedures. Although you can use an RSG for test restores, Microsoft does not recommend this procedure. To minimize user disruption, you should perform test restores on a test network in a different forest from the production network.

- You can monitor events in the Event Viewer Application log to check that a backup has completed successfully. Information is also available in the backup log.

Lesson Review

You can use the following questions to test your knowledge of the information in Lesson 1, "Configuring Backups." The questions are also available on the companion CD if you prefer to review them in electronic form.

NOTE Answers

Answers to these questions and explanations of why each answer choice is correct or incorrect are located in the "Answers" section at the end of the book.

1. On which Exchange Server 2007 server should you back up mailbox databases and transaction log files?

    A. Hub transport server

    B. Edge transport server

    C. Client access server

    D. Mailbox server

2. On which unified messaging server or servers should you consider backing up the prompts directory?

    A. All unified messaging servers in your Exchange organization

    B. The prompt publishing server

    C. Any unified messaging server that also has the Edge Transport server role installed

    D. You cannot back up the prompts directory on a unified messaging server because no Exchange-aware backup is available in NTBackup to do this

3. Which backup types are available if circular logging is enabled? (Choose all that apply.)

    A. Full

    B. Copy

    C. Differential

    D. Incremental

4. Which backup devices can you specify in the Backup Wizard? (Choose all that apply.)

   A. A second internal hard disk

   B. An external disk or disk array

   C. A tape drive

   D. A rewritable DVD drive

5. Which PowerShell command lists backup complete events?

   A. *Get-EventLog System | where {$_.EventID -eq 8000}*

   B. *Get-EventLog Application | where {$_.EventID -eq 8000}*

   C. *Get-EventLog System | where {$_.EventID -eq 8001}*

   D. *Get-EventLog Application | where {$_.EventID -eq 8001}*

Lesson 2: Recovering Messaging Data

Often when a user deletes a message or an administrator deletes a mailbox, the deleted item can be recovered without restoring backed-up data, especially if the deletion is recent. If a restore is required, then RSGs make the procedure relatively straightforward. Dial tone restores let you recover data while minimizing the disruption of service to your users. If backed-up data is not available or if a backup fails, tools are available that let you recover some if not all of the information in a damaged database.

Restores to a separate forest are still available, and this technique can, for example, be used for test restores. Fortunately, you no longer need to go through a long, complex restore process every time a user hard deletes the wrong message by mistake. The tools are there. You need to learn when and how to use them.

After this lesson, you will be able to:

- Recover messages, mailboxes, and databases.
- Repair a damaged database.

Estimated lesson time: 45 minutes

Real World

Ian McLean

Maybe I have been lucky, but it's a long time since I needed to recover an entire Exchange organization. Storage and server hardware is more reliable than it used to be, and key servers are typically clustered. Hardware is also, relatively speaking, cheaper than it used to be, and only the smallest organizations have a single domain controller, mailbox server, or other critical point of failure.

Most restore operations, in my experience, involve accidentally deleted messages or mailboxes deleted when an employee left an organization that need to be recovered for business or legal reasons. The Deleted Item Recovery feature in Outlook 2007 (which is also available in Outlook 2003 and configurable through registry settings) reduces the number of restores required. Not all users are clueless, and most realize they have hard deleted the wrong message moments after they have done so. You can save yourself a lot of grief by giving your users a little gentle training.

I am careful, however, not to grow complacent. As I said in the "Real World" section of the last lesson, hardware or media failure is not the only way to lose data, and backup is essential. I believe in a sound backup regime and regular test restores, although even they can be done in stages, testing the restore of a single storage group each time until all storage groups have been tested. I explain to management that test restores are like emergency services training. The fire service might need to deal with a major fire only occasionally but trains to do so continuously. My other analogy is the athlete who trains for months for an activity that might take only minutes.

However, I do not use the athlete analogy frequently. I am far too old and stiff for it to be credible.

Recovering Messages

Users can delete a message or other item in their own mailboxes by clicking on the item and pressing the Delete key. If a user deletes a message from the Inbox or any other server-based folder by this method, the message is actually not yet deleted but moved to the Deleted Items folder. In addition, if a user accepts or declines a meeting request, the request moves from the Inbox to the Deleted Items folder. Upon exiting, Outlook 2007 can automatically empty the Deleted Items folder according to the client configuration option "Empty the Deleted Items folder upon exiting." When Exchange Server 2007 receives the message deletion requests, it determines whether a soft or hard deletion must be performed based on criteria explained later in this section. Whenever possible, Exchange Server 2007 performs a soft deletion, also called a logical deletion to highlight the fact that the deleted items are not yet hard deleted, meaning they are not yet physically removed from the databases.

What happens if a message is soft deleted is that a flag is set on the entry for the message in the MsgFolder table to hide the message from the messaging client. Soft-deleted items are not visible in Outlook folders. The MsgFolder table is a mapping between entries in the folder table and the messages table. Message counts for the mailbox and folder are also updated. As long as an item is not soft or hard deleted, the user can easily recover it by opening the Deleted Items folder, right-clicking on the item, selecting Move To Folder, and moving the item back into the folder from which it was deleted.

During the next scheduled Exchange database maintenance process, each mailbox is examined to determine if any of the soft-deleted messages it contains have passed a configurable deleted item retention period (by default 14 days). If such a message is found, the message is hard deleted by removing the message reference from the MsgFolder table. At this point, the user can no longer recover the message in Outlook 2007 by using the

Deleted Item Recovery feature. You can configure the deleted item retention period for an individual mailbox or for a mailbox database. Individual mailbox settings override database settings for that database.

Exam Tip   The default deleted item retention period in Exchange Server 2007 is 14 days. In Exchange Server 2003, it is 7 days. Examiners often test whether candidates who have experience with a previous software version have learned about the changes in default settings in the new version.

Recovering Soft- and Hard-Deleted Items

The recoverability of a deleted message depends on the message reference in the Msg-Folder table. If a user deletes a message directly from the Inbox or another mailbox folder by using Shift+Delete or deletes an item in the Deleted Items folder and no other criteria force Exchange Server 2007 to perform a hard deletion, then the message is soft-deleted and recoverable because the message reference still exists in the MsgFolder table. On the other hand, if the user forces a hard deletion by deleting the message in the Deleted Items Recovery dialog box again, or if a system or gateway account (an account used to interface with another messaging system) performs the hard deletion, or if the message reference is removed from the MsgFolder table because the deleted item retention period has expired for the item, then the item is physically removed from the database and no longer directly recoverable in Outlook 2007. Recovering hard-deleted items requires restores from backup by using the Recovery Storage Group or a separate recovery server.

When a message is hard deleted, the message reference is immediately removed from the MsgFolder table. The message's reference count property is checked. When the message reference count drops to zero, which means that no other mailbox has a copy of the message, an entry is made in the DeletedMessages table. This indicates that the message is ready to be removed from the messages table. During the next background cleanup process, the entries in the DeletedMessages table are examined and the corresponding entries in the messages table are deleted.

By default, in Outlook 2007 a user can recover a soft-deleted message (or other item) from the dumpster by using the Deleted Message Recovery feature. On the left-hand Outlook pane, the user clicks on the folder from which the message was hard deleted. On the Tools menu, the user selects Recover Deleted Items. In the Recover Deleted Items From dialog box, the user selects the item or items to be recovered and then clicks Recover Selected Items, as shown in Figure 12-22.

In Outlook 2003, deleted items can, by default, be recovered only from the Deleted Items folder. You can change this behavior to allow the user to recover items from the dumpster by creating the registry key HKEY_LOCAL_MACHINE\SOFTWARE\

Microsoft\Exchange\Client\Options\DumpsterAlwaysOn on the user's client computer and configuring the decimal value of this key as 1. This is useful if you have a user who habitually hard deletes messages and then asks for them to be recovered.

MORE INFO   DumpsterAlwaysOn registry key

For more information about recovering hard-deleted items from the dumpster using Outlook 2003, search Exchange Server 2007 Help for "How to Recover a Deleted Item" or access *http://technet.microsoft.com/en-us/library/aa997155.aspx.*

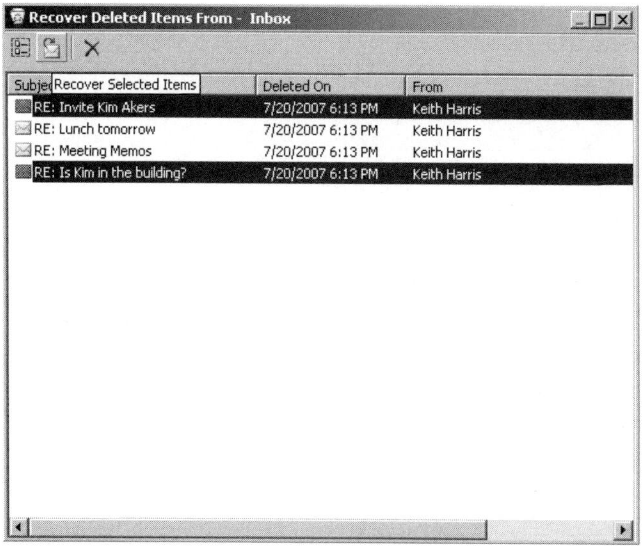

Figure 12-22   Deleted message recovery

How long messages remain in the dumpster and can be recovered by deleted item recovery depends on a number of factors. Items in the dumpster are removed during scheduled maintenance, which runs by default on a database between 1:00 AM and 5:00 AM. Figure 12-23 shows this setting on the General tab of the Properties dialog box for the mailbox database First Mailbox database. You can access this dialog box from Exchange Management Console.

Independent of scheduled maintenance, the background cleanup process runs once per hour by default. During this process, the entries in the DeletedMessages table are examined, and the corresponding entries in the messages table are deleted. You can control how often the background cleanup process runs by specifying a repetition period in milliseconds in the following registry keys:

- HKEY_LOCAL_MACHINE\SYSTEM\CurrentControlSet\Services\
  MSExchangeIS\ParametersPublic\Background Cleanup

- HKEY_LOCAL_MACHINE\SYSTEM\CurrentControlSet\Services\
MSExchangeIS\ParametersPrivate\Background Cleanup

When a message has been deleted from the dumpster, it can no longer be recovered by using deleted item recovery. If the user mailbox has been backed up when it contained the message, then the mailbox can be restored, typically into an RSG, and the recovered mailbox can be merged with the existing mailbox to restore backed-up items that were deleted subsequent to the backup. This procedure is described later in this lesson.

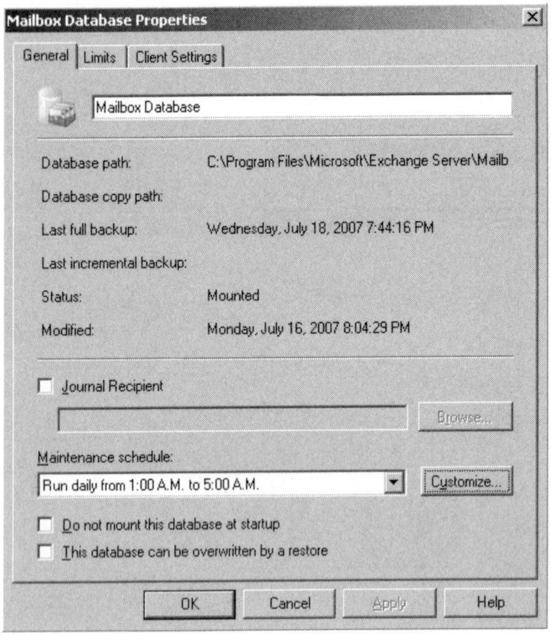

Figure 12-23   Mailbox database maintenance schedule

Configuring the Deleted Item Retention Period

You can configure the deleted item retention period for an individual user mailbox or for a mailbox database. Individual user mailbox settings override database settings. You can specify a retention time from 0 through 24,855 days. If the deleted item retention period is set to 0, Exchange Server 2007 performs an immediate hard deletion for items as soon as they are removed from the Deleted Items folder or any other mailbox folder. The longer you make the deleted item retention period, the more disk space you require for mailbox storage.

To configure the deleted item period for Don Hall's mailbox to 28 days, you would enter the following command from Exchange Management Shell:

```
Set-Mailbox "Don Hall" -RetainDeletedItemsFor 28.00:00:00
```

To configure the deleted item time for all mailboxes in the mailbox database Mailbox Database in the Storage group First Storage Group on the mailbox server Glasgow to 7 days, you would enter the following command:

```
Set-MailboxDatabase "Glasgow\First Storage Group\Mailbox Database"
-DeletedItemRetention 7.00:00:00
```

Exam Tip   Commands based on the *Set-Mailbox* cmdlet use the parameter RetainDeletedItems-For, while commands based on the *Set-MailboxDatabase* cmdlet use the parameter DeletedItemsRetention for the same purpose. Also, beta versions of Exchange Server 2007 used the parameter ItemRetention, and some technical literature still uses this in described procedures. Examiners always try to test whether you have carried out configuration for real rather than merely reading the technical literature.

You can also use Exchange Management Console to configure deleted item retention periods by accessing the Properties dialog box for the relevant mailbox or mailbox database. Figure 12-24 shows the Limits tab of a mailbox database Properties dialog box. In addition to specifying the deleted item retention period for the mailbox database, this dialog box lets you specify that items are not permanently deleted until the mailbox database is backed up. This is disabled by default. In practice, it would be a very unusual backup regime that did not back up mailbox databases at least once every 14 days.

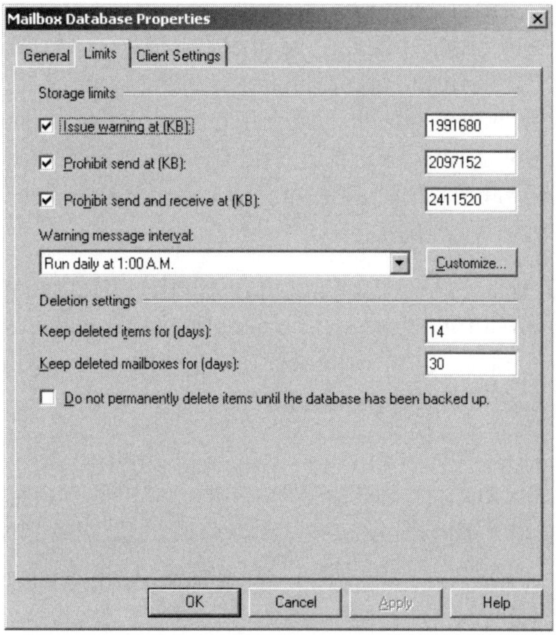

Figure 12-24   Specifying a deleted item retention period in Exchange Management Console

Recovering Mailboxes

As an administrator, you will sometimes remove mailboxes, for example, when an employee leaves an organization. Good practice guides recommend disabling mailboxes in this situation because it is not unknown for departed employees to rejoin after a short period and because the manager of a recent ex-employee might want access to that person's messages for business or legal reasons.

However, mailboxes are typically large, often several gigabytes in size. You cannot keep them forever. Also, administrators are human and make mistakes. Sometimes the wrong mailbox is removed. When you remove a mailbox, the associated Active Directory user account is deleted, and the mailbox is moved to the mailbox dumpster, where it is held for a configurable mailbox detention period (30 days by default). The mailbox is said to be disconnected.

If you want to recover the mailbox during this retention period, you need an Active Directory user account that is not mail-enabled or mailbox-enabled. You can then connect the mailbox to that account. The user account you use for this purpose will typically have the same name as the user account that was deleted. If you administer Exchange but do not have administrative rights in the domain, you need to ask a domain administrator or account operator to create the account for you.

It is important to remember that if a user account is deleted from Active Directory and an account with the same name and same permissions is created, this is not the same account. It is a new account and has a different security identifier (SID) from the account that was deleted. SIDs are unique in a domain, and the same SID cannot be used twice. Therefore, you are connecting a disconnected mailbox to a user account created for this purpose; you are connecting it to a new account. Even though the account has the same name and same permissions as the account that was deleted, it has a different SID and is not therefore the same account.

Also remember that if you remove a mailbox, for example, Keith Harris's mailbox, you cannot restore the mailbox by creating a new mailbox-enabled user called Keith Harris. This new user will have a mailbox, but it will be a new mailbox and will not contain the messages that were in the mailbox you removed.

Sometimes an Active Directory user account is deleted by mistake, but the mailbox associated with that account still exists. In this case, the effect is the same as removing the mailbox. The mailbox is held in the dumpster, and you can retrieve it by creating a new Active Directory user account (or requesting that one is created) and connecting the mailbox to that user account.

Quick Check

- Which Exchange Management Shell command would set the deleted item retention period for the mailbox database First Glasgow Mailbox Database in the storage group First Storage Group on the mailbox server Glasgow to 35 days?

Quick Check Answer

- *Set-MailboxDatabase "Glasgow\First Storage Group\First Glasgow Mailbox Database" –DeletedItemRetention 35.00:00:00.*

Recovering a Mailbox within the Deleted Mailbox Retention Period

Deleted mailbox retention enables you to recover mailboxes after they have been removed (or disconnected) without needing to restore them from backup. By default, Exchange Server 2007 retains disconnected mailboxes for 30 days after deletion, and mailbox recovery must occur during the retention period. You recover a deleted mailbox within the retention period by using either Exchange Management Shell or Exchange Management Console.

To list the deleted (or disconnected) mailboxes in the dumpster on the mailbox server Glasgow and the dates on which they were deleted, you enter the following command in Exchange Management Shell:

```
Get-MailboxStatistics -Server Glasgow | where { $_.DisconnectDate -ne $null } | select
DisplayName,DisconnectDate
```

Figure 12-25 shows the output from this command. If you do not specify the Server parameter, the command will list the disconnected mailboxes on the mailbox server on which it runs.

Connecting a Mailbox

You recover a disconnected a mailbox by connecting it to a user account. In this example, the account Mark Harrington has been created in Active Directory but does not have an associated mailbox. You can check whether this user account exists and is not disabled by entering the following command:

```
Get-User "Mark Harrington" | Format-List
```

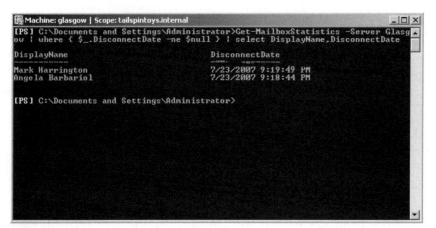

Figure 12-25   Mailboxes in the mailbox dumpster

To reconnect a disconnected mailbox in the First Glasgow Mailbox Database in the First Storage Group to user Mark Harrington when the user object exists in Active Directory directory service and has no associated mailbox, run the following command:

```
Connect-Mailbox -Database "First Glasgow Mailbox Database" -Identity "Mark Harrington"
-User "Mark Harrington"
```

If you have a number of disconnected mailboxes in a mailbox database, you can attempt to reconnect all of them with a single command, such as the following:

```
Get-MailboxStatistics -Database "Glasgow\first storage group\mailbox database" | where
{$_.disconnectdate -ne $null} | ForEach {connect-mailbox -id $_.mailboxguid -database
"Glasgow\first storage group\mailbox database"}
```

This command works for disconnected mailboxes that have equivalent Active Directory user accounts that are not associated with mailboxes.

You can also use Exchange Management Console to connect a disconnected mailbox. As with using Exchange Management Shell, a user account that does not have an associated mailbox needs to exist in Active Directory so that you can connect the mailbox to it. In Exchange Management Console, expand Recipient Configuration in the console tree and click Disconnected Mailbox. If required, click Connect To Server in the Actions pane to specify the mailbox server that holds the disconnected mailbox. Right-click the mailbox you want to connect and click Connect, as shown in Figure 12-26. Follow the steps in the Connect Mailbox Wizard.

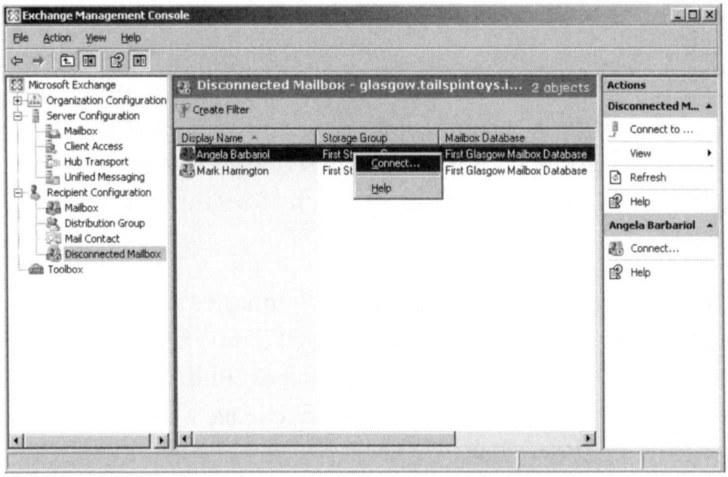

Figure 12-26 Connecting a mailbox in Exchange Management Console

Configuring the Mailbox Retention Period

You can use Exchange Management Shell or Exchange Management Console to configure the deleted mailbox retention period. If, for example, you wanted to change the mailbox retention time to 20 days for mailboxes in the database Mailbox Database in the storage group First Storage Group on the mailbox server Glasgow, you would enter the following command in Exchange Management Shell:

```
Set-MailboxDatabase "Glasgow\First Storage Group\Mailbox Database"
-MailboxRetention 20.00:00:00
```

Exam Tip Note the format for the retention period. If you see an answer in the 70-236 examination that, for example, gives a retention time of 15.00.00.00 or 30:00:00:00, that answer is wrong.

To use Exchange Management Console to configure the deleted mailbox retention period, expand Server Configuration in the console tree and select Mailbox. On the Database Management tab in the work pane, expand the storage group that contains the mailbox database that you want to configure, right-click the database, and select Properties. You can specify the mailbox retention period on the Limits tab. Figure 12-24 earlier in this lesson shows this dialog box tab.

Using Recovery Storage Groups

If a message has been deleted from a mailbox and the message retention period has expired or if a mailbox has been deleted and the mailbox retention period has expired, you need to restore from backup. If you need to recover an entire mailbox database or an entire storage group, you again need to restore from backup. Prior to Exchange Server 2003, you needed to restore to an alternative forest with the same structure, storage group names, and mailbox database names as the existing forest. Exchange Server 2003 introduced RSGs, and these have been given additional functionality in Exchange Server 2007. Other than test restores, most restores from backup now use RSGs.

An RSG is a special type of storage group that lets you mount a mailbox database, extract data from the mounted database, and copy the extracted data to a folder in an existing mailbox or merge the extracted data with an existing mailbox. In Exchange Server 2007, you can extract data by using commands based on the Exchange Management Shell *Restore-Mailbox* cmdlet or by using the Exchange Disaster Recovery Analyzer (ExDRA) tool.

You can use an RSG in the following scenarios:

- Same server dial tone recovery
- Alternate server dial tone recovery
- Mailbox recovery
- Specific item recovery

Dial tone recovery is a procedure in which you delete the files of a corrupted database or storage group so that Exchange Server can reinitialize new and empty database files, and then you restore the data from backup by using a recovery storage group. It is described later in this lesson.

An RSG differs from a normal storage group in some significant respects. Some storage group functions are disabled for RSGs. For example, all protocols except the Messaging Application Programming Interface (MAPI) are disabled. Therefore, mail cannot be sent to or from any mailboxes in a database in an RSG. Although an RSG supports MAPI, mailboxes in a database that has been mounted in an RSG cannot be accessed via Microsoft Outlook or OWA. Nor can such mailboxes be connected to Active Directory directory service accounts. These mailboxes need to be merged into existing mailboxes or copied to a folder in an existing mailbox.

System and mailbox management policies are not applied to RSGs. This prevents the system deleting items in an RSG while you are trying to salvage them. In addition, online maintenance does not run against databases in an RSG. You cannot configure databases in an RSG to mount automatically when the Exchange Information Store service is started. RSG databases mounted at the time of a cluster failover do not mount automatically after failover is completed.

If you want to change data paths after you create an RSG, you need to delete and re-create the RSG. If you want to move data files, you need to do this manually. You cannot mount public folder databases in an RSG, and you can create only a single RSG on a server. You cannot configure an RSG for replication by using LCR or CCR. Finally, you can restore to an RSG, which is its main function, but you cannot back up an RSG.

Using an RSG for Mailbox Database Recovery

You can use an RSG for mailbox database recovery where the logical information about a storage group, database, and the mailboxes in the database remains intact and unchanged in Active Directory and you need to recover a single mailbox, a single database, or a group of databases in a single storage group. You use the RSG to recover a database you have backed up or if you are repairing a database while the current copy of the database remains in production, with the eventual goal of merging the two databases.

You can also use an RSG to recover a database on a server other than the database's original server. You can then merge the recovered data back to the original server. However, probably the most common use for RSGs is to recover items that users deleted from their mailboxes and now need.

You can extract entire mailboxes from databases mounted in an RSG, including all item types, normal folders, and special folder content (such as hidden folders and notes). The format, names, and values of the content are preserved. You can also extract all message types, such as messages, calendar items, contacts, distribution lists, journal entries, tasks, notes, and documents.

NOTE RSGs on other servers

You can add a restored mailbox database to an RSG on an Exchange 2007 mailbox server other than the server where you performed the backup. However, in this case the mailbox server must belong to the same Active Directory forest as the original server.

Merging and Copying Data

When you recover a mailbox from a database mounted in an RSG, you can merge it with an active mailbox or copy it to a subfolder. If you choose the merge option, you can merge the entire recovered mailbox or a filtered subset of data from the recovered mailbox. This option adds to but does not overwrite the data in the active mailbox. So if a user has deleted a message from a mailbox and a

> backup of the mailbox contains the message, merging the restored mailbox with the current mailbox will restore the deleted message without affecting items that were added to the mailbox since the backup. Alternatively, you can copy the entire recovered mailbox or a filtered subset of data from the recovered mailbox to a subfolder in the active mailbox.

Creating a Recovery Storage Group

You can create an RSG by using Exchange Management Shell or by using the Microsoft Exchange Troubleshooting Assistant (ExTRA) Database Recovery Management tool, which was introduced in Chapter 9. The Database Management tool ships with Exchange Server 2007, and you do not need to install ExTRA in order to use it. Figure 12-27 shows the control in the Database Recovery Management tool that creates an RSG. You follow the steps in a wizard that ask you to specify the storage group associated with the RSG and the name of the RSG.

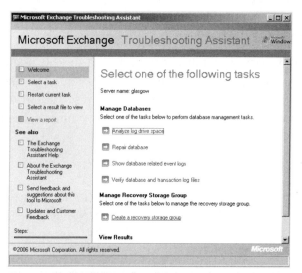

Figure 12-27   Creating an RSG in the Database Recovery Management tool

To create an RSG by using Exchange Management Shell, you use the *New-StorageGroup* cmdlet with the Recovery parameter. You can optionally specify the LogFolderPath and SystemFolderPath parameters in the command, and these determine where the RSG-related files should be located. For example, to create an RSG called Recovery Storage Group on the mailbox server Glasgow associated with the storage group First Storage Group, you would use a command similar to the following:

```
New-StorageGroup -Server Glasgow -LogFolderPath "C:\Program Files\Microsoft\Exchange
Server\Mailbox\First Storage Group\RSG" -Name "Recovery Storage Group" -SystemFolderPath
"C:\Program Files\Microsoft\Exchange Server\Mailbox\First Storage Group\RSG" -Recovery
```

Figure 12-28 shows the output of this command.

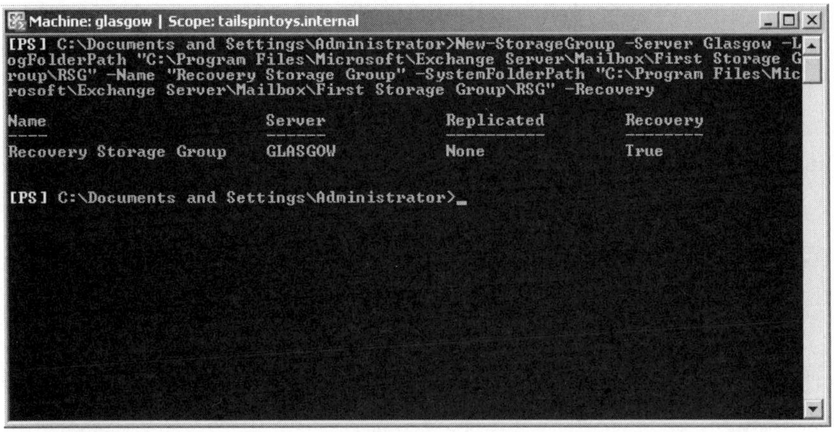

Figure 12-28   Creating an RSG with Exchange Management Shell

Next, you need to create a mailbox database within the RSG to which you can restore backed-up mailboxes. To do this, you use a command based on the *New-MailboxDatabase* cmdlet with the MailboxDatabaseToRecover parameter. For example, to add a recovery database to the RSG on a server named Glasgow with the edb file path pointing to C:\Program Files\Microsoft\Exchange Server\Mailbox\First Storage Group\RSG that you would use to recover the mailbox database First Storage Group\Mailbox Database, you would enter a command similar to the following (the EDB file path information is optional):

```
New-MailboxDatabase -MailboxDatabaseToRecover "First Storage Group\Mailbox Database"
-StorageGroup "Glasgow\Recovery Storage Group" -EDBFilePath "C:\Program
Files\Microsoft\Exchange Server\Mailbox\First Storage Group\RSG\Mailbox Database.edb"
```

If you are using a mailbox database for the recovery of backed-up data, you need to configure it to allow overwrites. You do this by running a command based on the *Set-MailboxDatabase* cmdlet with the AllowFileRestore parameter. To allow file restores for the recovery database Mailbox Database on the mailbox server Glasgow, you would use the following command:

```
Set-MailboxDatabase -Identity "Glasgow\Recovery Storage Group\Mailbox Database"
-AllowFileRestore $True
```

Typically when you add a recovery database to an RSG, restores are allowed by default. However, it is good practice to configure any database into which you intend to restore data from backup to allow file restores.

You can now restore data from backup to the recovery database you have created by using the Restore Wizard. You need to specify the path to the RSG and specify that this is the final backup set so that transaction logs for the production database are played into the restored database. You also need to specify a temporary storage path for these transaction logs. You do this in the practice session later in this lesson. When the restore operation completes, you need to mount the recovery mailbox database. In the example given, you would use the following command:

```
Mount-Database -Identity "Glasgow\Recovery Storage Group\Mailbox Database"
```

When the recovery database is mounted, you can extract data from it. For example, if Don Hall had deleted a message that needed to be recovered from backup, you could merge the Don's recovered mailbox with his production mailbox by using the following command:

```
Restore-Mailbox "Don Hall" -RSGDatabase "Glasgow\Recovery Storage Group\Mailbox Database"
```

MORE INFO   **Working with recovery storage groups**

For an informative tutorial about how to use RSGs, access *http://www.msexchange.org/tutorials/ Working-Recovery-Storage-Groups-Exchange-2007.html*.

> **Quick Check**
> - In Exchange Management Shell commands that use the *New-StorageGroup* cmdlet, what parameter specifies that you are creating an RSG?
>
> **Quick Check Answer**
> - Recovery.

Recovering Databases with Dial Tone Recovery

The Exchange Server 2007 dial tone recovery feature provides a business continuity solution for database, server, and site loss scenarios. By creating a temporary or dial tone database, you can enable users to send and receive messages while their Exchange database is being recovered or restored.

To perform a dial tone recovery on an Exchange 2007 mailbox server with a failed database, you should first move all files from the original database and transaction log folders to a temporary location in case they are required for further recovery operations. You then mount the affected database so that Exchange Server 2007 can generate and intialize new database files. The newly intialized database is an empty database, but it has the same name as the original database and all configuration settings are retained. You are warned that you are about to create an empty database.

You can use Exchange Management Shell or the Database Recovery Management tool in Exchange Management Console to configure an RSG on the original server. You then restore the database from backup into the RSG. Before you mount this database, copy log files from the failed database to the RSG so that they can be played against the restored database. Playing all the transaction logs from a failed database against a restored database is known as hard recovery and is discussed later in this lesson. Swapping the databases makes the restored database the active database that users connect to and places the dial tone database in the RSG.

You can now merge the content from the dial tone database with the active recovered database. Merging the databases gives users access to messages that were placed in the dial tone database while it was the production database. The merge process extracts messages from the dial tone database and places them in the recovered database. You can now use the Database Recovery Management tool or Exchange Management Shell to remove the RSG (you need to remove all databases it contains first). If necessary. you can manually remove the database and log files associated with the RSG.

Using Dial Tone Recovery on a Second Server

If a stand-alone server fails and needs to be rebuilt, the most efficient way to give users continuity of service is to create a dial tone database on another server and move the mailbox configuration to that server. You can then recover the failed database to the original server and move the mailbox configuration back to the original server and recovered database.

To do this, you create a mailbox database with the same name as the failed database on a second server. If there are any files that correspond to the original database, you should move them to a temporary location. They might be needed for further recovery operations. You can create the dial tone database in an existing storage group or in a new storage group. Select or create the storage group in which you will place the database, and you can then create the database by entering a command with the following syntax:

```
New-MailboxDatabase -StorageGroup <Server_Name>\<StorageGroup_Name> -Name <Database_Name>
```

You can use a command based on the *Get-MailboxStatistics* cmdlet to obtain configuration information for a specified mailbox database on the original server and pipe the output into a command based on the *Move-Mailbox* cmdlet with the Configuration-Only parameter to change the home server information in the user accounts in Active Directory and thus point all the users to their new mailboxes on that server. The syntax of the combined command is as follows:

```
Get-MailboxStatistics -Database <server1\storage group\database> | Move-Mailbox
-ConfigurationOnly -TargetDatabase <server2\storage group\database>
```

Users can now access their mailboxes on the new Exchange server. Microsoft Office Outlook 2007 clients are redirected via the Autodiscover service, OWA users are automatically redirected to the new server, and older Outlook clients (for example, Outlook 2003 clients) need to be manually configured to point to the new server.

You can now restore your original mailbox database from backup to the original mailbox server. Before you mount the recovered database in the original storage group, copy any log files from the failed database to the storage group so that they can be played against the restored database. Once the database is restored, you can use a command similar to the one you used previously to point users to their restored mailboxes on the original server, such as the following:

```
Get-MailboxStatistics -Database <server2\storage group\database> | Move-Mailbox -
ConfigurationOnly -TargetDatabase <server1\storage group\database>
```

The remaining task is to merge the databases in order to give the users access to messages that were placed in the dial tone database while it was in production. This requires you to create an RSG on the original server by using the Database Recovery Management tool and moving the dial-tone database from the second server into the RSG on the original server. After mounting the dial-tone database in the RSG on the original server, you can start the merge process to extract messages from the dial tone database and place them in the recovered database. You can then remove the RSGs on both servers.

Using Dial Tone Recovery and Keeping the Database on the Second Server

Sometimes it is not feasible to recover a failed server and recovered databases need to stay on an alternative server. You recover the failed database to the alternate server in an RSG. You then swap and merge the dial tone and restored databases and leave them on the alternate server.

To perform this procedure, you create a dial tone mailbox database on the alternative server with the same name as the failed database so that you can restore the failed database from backup to the alternative server and then merge the two databases. If any uncorrupted files exist that correspond to the original database, move them to a temporary location. They might be needed for further recovery operations.

You can create the dial tone database in an existing storage group or in a new storage group on the alternative mailbox server. You first need to select or create the storage group in which you will place the dial-tone database in and then create the database, restore the original database in the RSG from backup, and swap and merge the databases.

MORE INFO   **Demystifying dial tone recovery**

For a series of articles that demystify dial tone recovery, initially access *http://www.msexchange. org/tutorials/Exchange-Dial-tone-Restore-Method-Part1.html* and follow the links for Parts 2 and 3.

Dial Tone Portability

Exchange 2007 dial tone portability enhances the dial tone recovery scenario by allowing a dial tone recovery to take place on any Exchange 2007 mailbox server in an Exchange organization. It enhances business continuity in database, server, and site loss scenarios and enables users to send and receive e-mail messages during the recovery process. This gives you time to proceed with the recovery process and bring historical mailbox data online, without total loss of e-mail functionality.

Dial tone portability provides users with limited access to their e-mail stored in an offline folder file (.ost file) and lets you merge the dial tone and recovered databases into a single up-to-date mailbox database after the recovered database is brought back online. The feature streamlines the creation of dial tone mailboxes on alternate servers, ensures users access to the new mailbox database by automatically reconfiguring Outlook 2007 client profiles, and lets you merge the recovered data and the dial tone mailbox data by means of a wizard or a sequence of Exchange Management Shell commands.

MORE INFO   **Dial tone portability**

For more information about dial tone portability, search Exchange Server 2007 Help for "How Dial Tone Recovery Works with Dial Tone Portability" or access *http://technet.microsoft.com/en-us/library/ aa997656.aspx*.

Hard Recovery

Hard recovery is the process that changes a restored database back to a consistent state by playing transactions into the database from transaction log files. When you carry out a full backup of a database, those transaction logs that have already been written to the database (committed) are deleted (truncated). The transaction logs that have not been written to the database are backed up and are not deleted from the production database folder. The database continues in use, and committed transaction logs are not truncated until the next full or incremental backup.

Thus, if a database file is corrupted but all its transaction logs remain intact, you restore only the database and then play all the production transaction logs against it by deleting the checkpoint file so that all transaction logs play against the restored database and not just the ones that have not yet been committed to the original database. The Restore Wizard asks you to specify a temporary location to hold the production transaction logs so that they can be played against a restored database.

You specify that transaction logs are to be played against a restored database by selecting the Final Backup Set check box in the Restore Wizard. This restores all the transactions that were carried out since the last full backup so that the database is restored to the point of failure. If, however, both the database and the transaction logs are lost (for example, in a disk failure), you restore both the database and the backed-up transaction logs and play the restored transaction logs against the database. This restores the database to a consistent state, but some operations carried out after the last backup might be lost.

If hard restoration to the point of failure is a business requirement, you should store transaction log files on a different disk or disk array from your databases. This also makes for more efficient disk access. You should also not enable circular logging because this deletes transaction logs that might be needed to recover a restored database to the point of failure.

If you forget to select the Last Backup Set check box in the Restore Wizard when you restore your database, you can replay the transaction logs by using the *eseutil /CC <path name>* command and specify the path that holds the transaction log files. Note that *eseutil/C* specifies Restore mode. The second "C" is known as a mode modifier and is required. Eseutil is discussed later in this lesson.

> The hard recovery process uses a RESTORE.env file that is generated during the recovery process to determine how to restore the database files and what transaction log files must be replayed from the temporary directory that the backup was restored to.
>
> After a database is copied to its original location and the transaction log files from the temporary directory are replayed into it, hard recovery continues to replay any additional transaction log files that it finds in the transaction log file path specified for the storage group of the restored database.

NOTE Soft recovery

Soft recovery is used when a database becomes unexpectedly dismounted but does not need to be recovered from backup. In soft recovery the checkpoint file is not deleted, and only those transaction logs that are not committed are played against the database to bring it to a consistent mountable state. Like the hard recovery process, the soft recovery process also replays any additional transaction log files that it finds in the transaction log file path specified for the storage group of the restored database.

Repairing a Damaged Database

Exchange Server 2007 provides a number of tools that identify issues with mailbox databases and can repair damaged databases. Sometimes database repair involves restoring data from backup, but if this is not possible because the backup data is corrupt or does not exist, tools are provided that can recover at least some of the data from a corrupted database. The following tools are available to identify and address database problems:

- Database Recovery Management
- Database Troubleshooter
- Exchange Server Database Utilities (eseutil.exe)
- Information Store Integrity Checker (isinteg.exe)

You can access the Database Recovery Management tool and the Database Troubleshooter in the Toolbox of the Exchange Management Console. These tools provide graphical user interfaces (GUIs) for analysis and troubleshooting and provide wizards that let you, for example, recover from a database disaster, work with RSGs, recover a mailbox from a backup, and several other tasks. The monitoring and reporting functionalities of the tools are discussed in Chapter 9 and Chapter 11, "Reporting."

Using the Database Recovery Management Tool

You can use the Database Recovery Management tool to perform the following tasks:

- **Verify database and transaction log files**   Enables you to determine why databases cannot be successfully mounted and to verify restored database files to ensure that all necessary database, streaming, and transaction log files are available.

- **Analyze log drive space**   Examines dismounted databases, the checkpoint file, and log files for each storage group to identify log drive space issues.

- **Reset the log generation number**   Moves all transaction log files for a storage group to a temporary location and restarts the log generation number. This is necessary when a storage group runs out of transaction log file names.

- **Repair a database**   Repairs corrupted databases without requiring backed-up data.

IMPORTANT   Repairing corrupted databases

Using the Database Recovery Management tool to repair corrupted databases can cause permanent data loss. You should consider using this approach only if you cannot restore from backup.

- **Show database-related event logs**   Examines database-related event log entries during a specified time range. Chapter 11 discusses this functionality.

- **Create a RSG, mount or dismount the databases in the RSG, and remove the RSG** The Exchange Management Shell commands to carry out these tasks were described earlier in this lesson. You can carry out the same functions with Database Recovery Management tool.

- **Merge or copy mailbox content**   Merges or copies mailbox content from the databases in the RSG to production mailboxes. This was described earlier in this lesson.

- **Set database can be overwritten by restore option**   The Exchange Management Shell command to do this was described earlier in this lesson. You can perform the same function with the Database Recovery Management tool.

Using the Database Troubleshooter Tool

You can use the Database Troubleshooter tool to repair and analyze the following issues:

- The database will not mount.
- Log files are inconsistent.
- Log file generation has run out of numbers to name the log files.
- Drive space problems.

The Database Troubleshooter examines the Microsoft Windows Server Event Log to detect database-related issues and provides resources and possible solutions. It might, for example, refer you to Microsoft Knowledge Base articles and specific tasks in the Database Recovery Management tool.

If, for example, a database will not mount, the Database Troubleshooter executes a set of troubleshooting steps to identify the root causes of database mounting problems. The tool automatically determines the data set that is required to troubleshoot the identified symptoms and collects configuration data, performance counters, event logs, and live tracing information from Exchange Server 2007 and other sources. It then provides guidance for possible solutions with links to related database recovery management wizards.

Using Exchange Server Database Utilities (Eseutil)

Exchange Server Database Utilities (*eseutil.exe*) is a command-line tool that works with the ESE, database files, and log files that are associated with an Exchange database. You can use Eseutil to verify, modify, and repair an Exchange database file. When a database is corrupt or damaged, you can restore data from backup or repair it using Eseutil. You should always attempt a repair from backup first because an Eseutil repair can result in data loss. Eseutil is located in the Exchange default install folder, which is <SystemDrive>:\Program Files\Microsoft\Exchange Server\Bin. However, you do not need to specify this path when using Eseutil and can enter Eseutil commands directly into the Command Processor (*cmd.exe*).

You can run Eseutil against any ESE database in Exchange Server 2007. The tool can be used with ESE databases on the Exchange 2007 Hub Transport and Edge Transport server roles as well as mailbox and public folder ESE databases. In previous versions of Exchange, the tool could be used only with mailbox and public folder ESE databases.

NOTE   **Streaming files**

Exchange 2007 databases do not use streaming (.stm) files. However, the tool supports .stm files in older Exchange databases. If you are working with databases in previous versions of Exchange, use the Eseutil tool that is associated with that version of the Exchange database.

Eseutil runs from the Command Processor on one database at a time. You can use the tool to perform a range of database tasks, including repair, offline defragmentation, and integrity checks. You can use the defragmentation mode to defragment a database offline. Other Eseutil modes, such as repair, recovery, and restore, can be used to repair a corrupt or damaged database. Modes such as integrity, file dump, and checksum can be used to verify the state of a database.

Table 12-2 lists the more common Eseutil switches.

Table 12-2   Common Eseutil Switches

Eseutil Mode	Switch	Description
Defragmentation	/D	Defragments the database offline but leaves the new, defragmented database in its temporary location. This mode reduces the actual size of the database (.edb) file on the disk by discarding empty pages and by rebuilding indexes.
Repair	/P	Repairs a corrupt offline database by discarding any pages that cannot be fixed.
Restore	/C	Displays restore log file (Restore.env) and controls hard recovery after restoration from legacy online backups.
Recovery	/R	Replays transaction log files or rolls them forward to restore a database to internal consistency or to bring an older copy of a database up to date.
Integrity	/G	Verifies the page level and ESE level logical integrity of the database.
File Dump	/M	Displays headers of database files, transaction log files, and checkpoint files. Also displays database page header information and database space allocation and metadata.

Table 12-2   Common Eseutil Switches

Eseutil Mode	Switch	Description
Checksum	/K	Verifies checksums on all pages in the database, log files, and checkpoint files.
Copy File	/Y	Performs a fast copy of very large files.

NOTE   Eseutil and Isinteg

In repair mode, Eseutil fixes individual tables but does not maintain the relationships between tables. You can use the Information Store Integrity Checker (Isinteg) to check and fix links between tables if the repaired database is a mailbox or public folder database. Also in integrity mode Eseutil does not verify integrity at the application level. You can verify application-level logical integrity with Isinteg for mailbox and public folder databases. Isinteg is described later in this lesson.

MORE INFO   Eseutil modes

For more information about Eseutil defragmentation mode, search Exchange Server 2007 Help for "Eseutil /D Defragmentation Mode" or access *http://technet.microsoft.com/en-us/library/ aa997972.aspx*. For more information about Eseutil restore mode, search Exchange Server 2007 Help for "Eseutil /C Restore Mode" or access *http://technet.microsoft.com/en-us/library/ aa997899.aspx*. For more information about Eseutil recovery mode, search Exchange Server 2007 Help for "Eseutil /R Recovery Mode" or access *http://technet.microsoft.com/en-us/library/ bb123479.aspx*. For more information about Eseutil recovery mode, search Exchange Server 2007 Help for "Eseutil /G Integrity Mode" or access *http://technet.microsoft.com/en-us/library/ bb124923.aspx*. For more information about Eseutil file dump mode, search Exchange Server 2007 Help for "Eseutil /M File Dump Mode" or access *http://technet.microsoft.com/en-us/library/ bb124584.aspx*. For more information about Eseutil checksum mode, search Exchange Server 2007 Help for "Eseutil /K Checksum Mode" or access *http://technet.microsoft.com/en-us/library/ bb124276.aspx*. For more information about Eseutil copy file mode, search Exchange Server 2007 Help for "Eseutil /Y Copy File Mode" *or access http://technet.microsoft.com/en-us/library/ aa998673.aspx*.

Exam Tip   While no guarantee can be given that the examination will not ask about any of the other common Eseutil modes—and as a professional Exchange administrator you need to know about them—it is likely that the examination will concentrate on the Eseutil repair mode (*eseutil/P*).

Repairing Databases with Eseutil

Eseutil repair mode (*eseutil/P*) corrects problems in the transport server queue database, mailbox database, and public folder database. Typically, you use *eseutil/P* when you cannot restore a database from backup or when you cannot fully roll transaction logs forward.

During repair, it might be necessary to discard rows from tables or even to discard entire tables. Eseutil looks at each Exchange database page and table and ensures consistency and integrity within each table. To use Eseutil to repair a mailbox database, you need first to dismount the database (take it offline). You can do this with Exchange Management Console or an Exchange Management Shell command, such as the following:

```
Dismount-Database -Identity "Glasgow\Second Storage Group\Mailbox Database"
```

You need to confirm that you want to take the database offline. You then run *eseutil/P<file name>* to perform a database page-level and table-level repair. When you enter the command, a warning box appears, and you need to confirm you want to proceed. Figure 12-29 shows the output of the command.

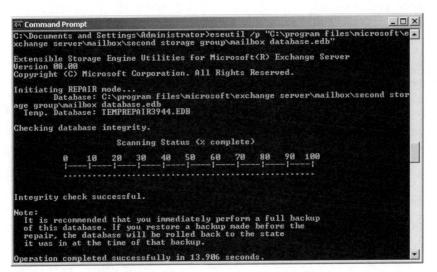

Figure 12-29   Eseutil repair mode

After you run the *eseutil/P <file name>* command, you should run *eseutil/D <file name>* to fully rebuild indexes and defragment the database. Finally, you use Isinteg to repair the database at the application level.

You need to decide whether to leave a repaired database permanently in production. Many administrators use repaired databases for data salvage only and move mailboxes as soon as possible to another database or merge the data from a repaired database into a known good database. Microsoft recommends that you not allow a repaired database to remain in production for an extended period of time.

NOTE   Repair log files

Both Eseutil and Isinteg generate detailed repair log files that list the errors found and corrected.

Using the Information Store Integrity Checker (Isinteg)

Eseutil corrects problems at the page and ESE table levels. However, Eseutil does not correct problems at the application level. Therefore, after you repair a mailbox or public folder database using Eseutil, Microsoft recommends that you run the Information Store Integrity Checker (*isinteg.exe*) to repair the database at the application level.

For example, a table in the database stores messages for all mailboxes. A separate table is used for each user's Inbox folder. Suppose that a message is lost when using Eseutil to repair the message table. Eseutil does not correlate the message with the reference to it in each Inbox folder because the tool does not have the information about the cross-table schema of the application. Isinteg is needed to compare the repaired message table with each Inbox to remove a lost message from the Inbox folder. Isinteg cannot run against Exchange Hub or Edge Transport server queue databases.

Isinteg finds and eliminates errors from the public folder and mailbox databases at the application level. The tool is not intended to be used as a part of routine information store maintenance but rather is provided to assist in disaster recovery situations. Because the Isinteg tool works at the logical schema level, it can recover data that Eseutil cannot. Isinteg repairs a mailbox or public folder database at the application level and ensures the integrity of the relationships between tables. The tool performs two main tasks:

- Patches the information store after a restore from an offline backup
- Tests and optionally fixes errors in the information store

Figure 12-30 shows the result of a set of tests (allfoldertests) run on the database Second Storage Group\Mailbox Database on the mailbox server Glasgow.

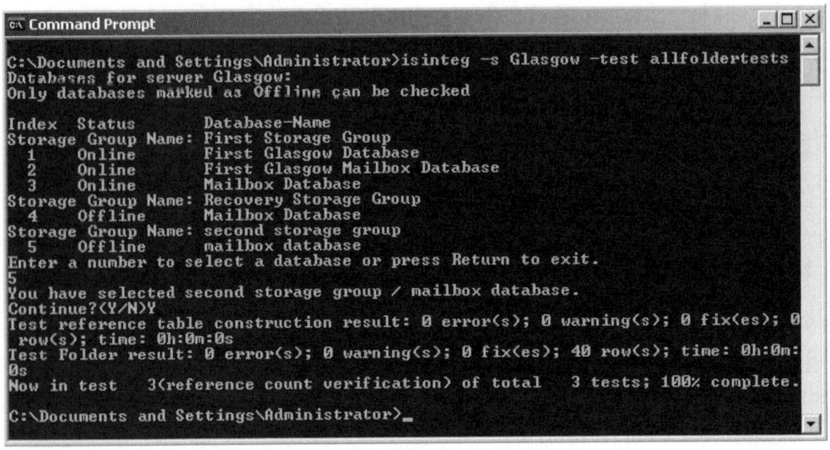

Figure 12-30 Checking integrity with Isinteg

MORE INFO Isinteg

For more information about Isinteg, open the Command Console and enter **isinteg.**

Practice: Recovering a Hard Deleted Message from Backup

In this practice session, you log on as a user and hard delete a message. You then log on as an administrator and recover the message from backup. Although in practice the user would first try to recover the message through Deleted Item Recovery, the purpose of this practice session is to familiarize you with the process of creating an RSG, recovering a mailbox from backup, and merging a recovered mailbox with an existing mailbox.

You need to have completed the practice session in Lesson 1 and backed up a storage group on your server. This practice session uses the mailbox Don Hall that you created in Chapter 3. As the practices are written, the mailbox contains one or more messages in its Inbox folder and is in the First Storage Group\Mailbox Database database. If you want to use another mailbox or if the mailbox you use is in another database, you should amend the practices accordingly.

▶ **Practice 1: Hard-Deleting Messages in the Inbox**

In this practice, you log on to the domain as Don Hall. If you have a client computer (real or virtual) in your test network, you can log on at that computer. Otherwise, you can permit Don Hall to log on at the domain controller by placing his account in the

Print Operators or Backup Operators security group. When logged on as Don Hall, you can use whatever Exchange client is available—Outlook 2007, Outlook 2003, Outlook Express, or OWA.

1. Log on to the domain as Don Hall.

2. Open your Exchange Client.

3. Access your Inbox.

4. Hard delete one or more messages by using the key combination Shift+Delete, confirming the deletion by clicking Yes in the Microsoft Outlook dialog box, and then selecting Recover Deleted Items on the Tools menu and deleting the messages in the Recover Deleted Items dialog box as well.

5. Close your Exchange client and log off.

▶ **Practice 2: Recovering Messages from Backup**

In this practice, you confirm the mailbox database that holds the Don Hall mailbox, create an RSG, recover the appropriate mailbox to the RSG from backup, and merge it with the existing mailbox.

1. Log on to the Exchange server as Kim_Akers.

2. Open Exchange Management Shell.

3. Enter the following command:

```
Get-Mailbox "Don Hall" | Format-List
```

4. Confirm that Don Hall's mailbox is in the database Mailbox Database in the storage group First Storage Group, as shown in Figure 12-31.

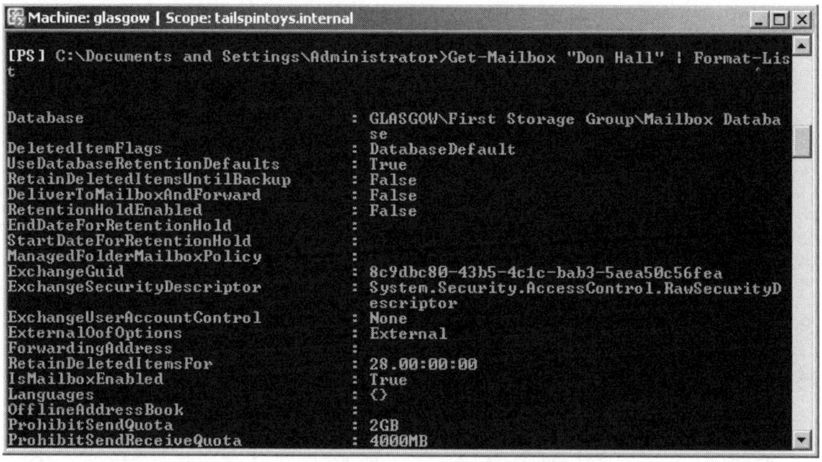

Figure 12-31 Confirming the location of Don Hall's mailbox

5. Enter the following command to create an RSG associated with the First Storage Group (note that if you created an RSG for practice while studying this chapter, you need to remove any databases in the RSG and then remove the RSG itself):

```
New-StorageGroup -Server Glasgow -Name "Recovery Storage Group" -Recovery
```

6. Enter the following command to configure a recovery database within the RSG that will recover the database that holds Don Hall's mailbox:

```
New-MailboxDatabase -MailboxDatabaseToRecover "First Storage Group\Mailbox Database"
-StorageGroup "Glasgow\Recovery Storage Group"
```

Figure 12-32 shows the result of this command.

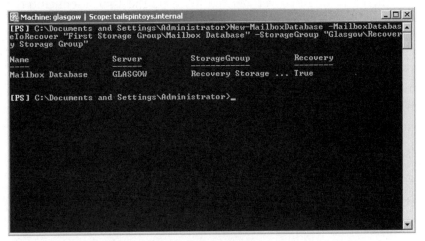

Figure 12-32 Creating a database for recovery

7. You now configure the recovery database you created to allow file restores. Enter the following command:

```
Set-MailboxDatabase -Identity "Glasgow\Recovery Storage Group\Mailbox Database"
-AllowFileRestore $True
```

NOTE Typically a new database in an RSG will allow restores

When you enter the command to allow restores, you will probably get a message that the command completed successfully but no configuration changes were made. Nevertheless, it is good practice to configure any restore database to allow restores.

---

8. Click Start, click Run, and enter **ntbackup.**

9. On the Welcome page, click Advanced Mode. On the Restore and Manage Media tab, select to restore files to an Alternate Location. Specify **C:\Program Files\Microsoft\Exchange Server\Mailbox\Recovery Storage Group.**

10. Select to restore the First Storage Group backup that you created in Lesson 1. The wizard page should look similar to Figure 12-33.

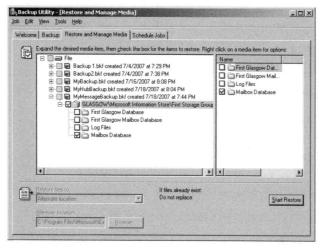

Figure 12-33 Selecting the restore path and the backup to restore

11. Click Start Restore.

12. In the Restoring Database Store dialog box, specify **C:\Program Files\ Microsoft\Exchange Server\Mailbox\First Storage Group\RSG** in the Temporary Location For Log And Patch Files box. Specify Last Restore Set so that the transaction log files will play against the restored database. Click OK.

13. When the restore completes, click Close.

14. Mount the Recovery Storage Group by entering the following command in Exchange Management Shell:

```
Mount-Database –Identity "Glasgow\Recovery Storage Group\Mailbox Database"
```

NOTE Inconsistent database

If the database does not mount, you probably forgot to check Last Restore Set in the wizard. In this case, use *eseutil/CC <file path>* to initiate a hard restore and bring the database to a consistent state.

15. Merge the recovered Don Hall mailbox with the production mailbox by entering the following command in Exchange Management Shell:

```
Restore-Mailbox "Don Hall" –RSGDatabase "Glasgow\Recovery Storage Group\Mailbox Database"
```

▶ **Practice 3: Checking Don Hall's Inbox and Deleting the RSG**

In this practice, you log on to the domain again as Don Hall and check your deleted messages have been restored. You then log on as Kim_Akers and remove the recovery database and the RSG. You need to remove all databases within an RSG (or any other storage group) before you can remove the RSG.

1. Log on to the domain as Don Hall.

2. Open your Exchange Client.

3. Access your Inbox.

4. Check that the deleted messages have been restored.

5. Log on to the Exchange server as Kim_Akers.

6. Open Exchange Management Shell.

7. Enter the following Exchange Management Shell command:

    ```
    Remove-MailboxDatabase "Recovery Storage Group\Mailbox Database"
    ```

8. Confirm that you want to remove the database. If it exists manually, remove the file C:\Program Files\Microsoft\Exchange Server\Mailbox\Recovery Storage Group\Mailbox Database.edb from your Exchange server.

9. Enter the following Exchange Management Shell command:

    ```
    Remove-StorageGroup "Recovery Storage Group"
    ```

10. Confirm that you want to remove the storage group. Manually remove any log files that exist in C:\Program Files\Microsoft\Exchange Server\Mailbox\Recovery Storage Group from your Exchange server.

Lesson Summary

■ Users can usually recover deleted items from the Deleted Items folder. In Outlook 2007, users can also recover soft-deleted items from the message dumpster, such as after emptying the Deleted Items folder, by using Deleted Item Recovery feature. Outlook 2003 can be configured to provide the same functionality.

■ You can configure the message retention and mailbox retention periods. These determine how long a soft-deleted item remains in the mailbox database and how long a deleted mailbox stays in the mailbox dumpster.

■ You can recover a deleted mailbox without needing to restore from backup provided that the deleted mailbox retention period has not expired.

- RSGs enable you to recover messages, mailboxes, databases, and storage groups without needing to recover to a recovery network in a separate forest.

- Dial tone recovery lets you recover databases with the minimum disruption to users.

- When you recover the final backup set during a recovery process, you play the existing transaction logs against the recovered databases to ensure hard recovery to the point of failure.

- You can use Eseutil or the Database Recovery Management tool to recover damaged databases where no backup is available. You can also use Eseutil to defragment a database offline. Isinteg checks database integrity at the application level.

Lesson Review

You can use the following questions to test your knowledge of the information in Lesson 2, "Recovering Messaging Data." The questions are also available on the companion CD if you prefer to review them in electronic form.

NOTE Answers

Answers to these questions and explanations of why each answer choice is correct or incorrect are located in the "Answers" section at the end of the book.

---

1. You are an Exchange recipient administrator for Contoso, Ltd. You do not have any additional administrative rights on the contoso.com domain. Mark Harrington left Contoso some time ago, and five days ago you removed his mailbox. The Legal Department at Contoso requires access to some of the messages in the mailbox, and you need to recover it. The mailbox retention period has not been changed from its default value. What is the easiest way of recovering the mailbox?

    A. Create an Active Directory account for Mark Harrington that is not associated with a mailbox. Connect the disconnected mailbox to this account.

    B. Ask a domain administrator for the contoso.com domain to create an Active Directory account for Mark Harrington that is not associated with a mailbox. Connect the disconnected mailbox to this account.

    C. Create a mailbox-enabled account for Mark Harrington.

    D. Restore Mark Harrington's mailbox from backup.

2. Which command line interface (CLI) can you use to repair a database when you cannot restore it from backup?

   A. Isinteg

   B. Database Recovery

   C. Eseutil

   D. Exchange Management Shell

3. Which Eseutil switch defragments an offline database?

   A. /D

   B. /P

   C. /R

   D. /C

4. You carry out a dial tone recovery that recovers a mailbox database from backup into the RSG you have created on the mailbox server Brisbane. You want to use the restored database as the production database on the same server. What should be your next steps?

   A. Mount the restored database. Copy log files from the failed database to the RSG and play them against the restored database. Swap the databases so that the restored database becomes the active database and the dial tone database is placed in the RSG. Merge the content from the dial tone database with the active recovered database.

   B. Copy log files from the failed database to the RSG and play them against the restored database. Mount the restored database. Swap the databases so that the restored database becomes the active database and the dial tone database is placed in the RSG. Merge the content from the dial tone database with the active recovered database.

   C. Copy log files from the failed database to the RSG and play them against the restored database. Swap the databases so that the restored database becomes the active database and the dial tone database is placed in the RSG. Mount the restored database. Merge the content from the dial tone database with the active recovered database.

   D. Merge the content from the dial tone database with the recovered database. Copy log files from the failed database to the RSG and play them against the restored database. Mount the restored database. Swap the databases so that the restored database becomes the active database and the dial tone database is placed in the RSG.

5. You need to restore Active Directory settings on a mailbox server. How should you do this? (Choose all that apply.)

    A. Restore the entire server

    B. Use the Eseutil CLI tool

    C. Carry out a System State restore

    D. Use the command *Setup/mode:RecoverServer*

6. Which Exchange Management Shell command connects Don Hall's disconnected mailbox in the mailbox database First Glasgow Mailbox Database to the Active Directory user account Don Hall?

    A. *Get-MailboxStatistics -Server Glasgow | where { $_.DisconnectDate -ne $null } | select DisplayName,DisconnectDate*

    B. *Get-User "Don Hall" | Format-List*

    C. *Connect-Mailbox -Database "Mailbox Database" -Identity "Don Hall" –User "Don Hall"*

    D. *Connect-Mailbox -Database "First Glasgow Mailbox Database" -Identity "Don Hall" –User "Don Hall"*

Chapter Review

To further practice and reinforce the skills you learned in this chapter, you can perform the following tasks:

- Review the chapter summary.
- Review the list of key terms introduced in this chapter.
- Complete the case scenarios. These scenarios set up real-world situations involving the topics of this chapter and ask you to create a solution.
- Complete the suggested practices.
- Take a practice test.

Chapter Summary

- Exchange Server 2007 provides legacy streaming and VSS backups, both of which support the full (or normal), copy, differential, and incremental backup types.
- Mailbox servers hold user data, and this must be backed up as part of any backup plan. You should carry out test restores to test your backup data and procedures. To minimize user disruption, you should perform test restores on a test network in a different forest from the production network.
- Deleted messages and deleted mailboxes can be recovered without needing to be restored from backup, provided that this is done within a configurable period.
- RSGs enable you to recover messages, mailboxes, databases, and storage groups without needing to recover to a recovery network in a separate forest. Dial tone recovery lets you recover databases with the minimum disruption to users.
- Hard recovery replays all transaction log files for the production database against a restored database. Soft recovery is carried out when a database unexpectedly goes offline but does not need to be restored from backup. Soft recovery plays uncommitted transaction log files against the database.
- You can use Eseutil, Isinteg, and the Database Recovery Management tool to recover damaged databases and check database integrity.

Key Terms

Do you know what these key terms mean? You can check your answers by looking up the terms in the glossary at the end of the book.

- Active copy
- Backup job
- Backup set
- Checkpoint file
- Consistent state
- Database
- Extensible Storage Engine (ESE)
- Hard recovery
- Inconsistent state
- Offline backup
- Online backup
- Replay
- Restore
- Soft recovery

Case Scenarios

In the following case scenarios, you will apply what you have learned about configuring disaster recovery. You can find answers to these questions in the "Answers" section at the end of this book.

Case Scenario 1: Designing a Backup Regime

You have been hired as a consultant by Coho Vineyards to design a backup regime. Currently, the company backs up all its mailbox data with a copy backup to a hard disk array every night and copies the backup files to optical storage for archive purposes once per week. The archives are held in a fireproof safe on the premises. The company considers that backups are taking too much time and that this time is getting longer. It is also concerned that the hard disks on its messaging server are getting full. Answer the following questions.

1. How would you change the backup regime?

2. One manager with a little technical knowledge suggests enabling circular logging. What advice would you give?

3. What improvements would you advise in the archive procedures?

Case Scenario 2: Restoring Data

You are the Exchange organization administrator at Blue Sky Airlines. You have no domain administrator rights. Answer the following questions.

1. One of your assistants has deleted the mailbox of an ex-employee called Keith Harris, who left the company five weeks ago. The mailbox was previously disabled. Your assistant deleted the mailbox two days ago. The mailbox retention period has not been changed from its default value. Management needs to access some messages in that mailbox. What is the first thing you need to do?

2. You need to restore an entire mailbox database on a mailbox server. The server is still operational and the hard disk is alright, but the database file is corrupted. Management wants the database restored to as near as possible to its state at the point of failure with the minimum amount of disruption to users. What do you advise?

3. You operate a test network. Management is concerned at the expense of hardware and licenses for a network that is not part of their commercial operation. How do you justify the network?

Suggested Practices

To help you successfully master the exam objectives presented in this chapter, complete the following tasks.

Performing Backups

Do all the practices in this section.

- **Practice 1: Back Up Mailbox Databases**   Back up individual mailbox databases and entire storage groups on your network. Check the backup logs and the Event Viewer Application log to ensure that the backups are successful.

- **Practice 2: Use Different Backup Types**   Carry out full, copy, incremental, and differential backups. Note the effect that each type of backup has on the transaction log files.

- **Practice 3: Back Up System State Data**   Back up and restore System State data on your Exchange server. If the Exchange server in your test network is also a domain controller, this might take longer than you anticipate.

Performing Restores

Do all the practices in this section.

- **Practice 1: Restore Mailboxes from the Mailbox Dumpster**   Delete mailboxes, create Active Directory user accounts, and reconnect the mailboxes. You should become so familiar with this procedure that you do not need to think about it.

- **Practice 2: Restore Mailboxes and Messages from Backup**   Use both Exchange Management Shell and Exchange Management Console to manage RSGs and restore mailboxes. Restore mailbox databases from backup and merge restored mailboxes with existing mailboxes.

- **Practice 3: Carry Out Dial Tone Restores**   Use dial tone restore and RSGs to carry out hard restores of mailbox databases and run the transaction logs for the original databases against the restored databases. Before you swap the dial tone database with the restored database, generate some e-mail traffic that puts messages in the dial tone database. When you merge the dial tone database with the new active database, check that these messages are copied to the new active database.

- **Practice 4: Use the Recovery Management Tool, Eseutil, and Isinteg**   Use these tools to recover databases without restoring from backup, to defragment offline databases, and to check database integrity.

Take a Practice Test

The practice tests on this book's companion CD offer many options. For example, you can test yourself on just one exam objective, or you can test yourself on all the 70-236 certification exam content. You can set up the test so that it closely simulates the experience of taking a certification exam, or you can set it up in study mode so that you can look at the correct answers and explanations after you answer each question.

MORE INFO   **Practice tests**

For details about all the practice test options available, see the "How to Use the Practice Tests" section in this book's Introduction.

Chapter 13

Recovering Server Roles and Configuring High Availability

Most Exchange administrators do not earn the big dollars because they know how to create a user mailbox or an address list. Great Exchange administrators earn their wage by being cool, calm, and confident during a crisis. For an Exchange administrator, there is no bigger crisis that you will have to resolve than recovering a mission-critical Exchange Server when some catastrophic event occurs. In the first lesson in this chapter, you will learn the procedures that allow you to recover each of the separate Exchange Server 2007 roles.

The second part of this chapter covers how you can apply different high availability strategies to each Exchange Server 2007 roles. In terms of high availability, there is no "one-size-fits-all" solution. High availability techniques that are suitable for one Exchange Server 2007 role are completely inappropriate for other roles. In the second lesson of this chapter, you will learn which high availability strategy to apply to a particular server role to best meet the needs of your organization.

Exam objectives in this chapter:
- Recover server roles.
- Configuring high availability.

Lessons in this chapter:

Before You Begin

To complete the lessons in this chapter, you must have done the following:

- Installed Exchange Server 2007 with the Mailbox, Client Access, Hub Transport, and Unified Messaging roles on a Windows domain controller in the Tailspin-toys.internal domain. To do this, you need to have completed all the practices in Lessons 1 and 2 of Chapter 1, "Preparing for Exchange Installation," and Lesson 1 of Chapter 2, "Installing Exchange Server and Configuring Roles."

No additional configuration is required for this chapter.

Real World

Orin Thomas

A long time ago, I worked as a system administrator at a company where I was responsible for managing an old Exchange server that was used to support some business-critical applications but where everyone's mailboxes were hosted on a platform other than Exchange. Having had no experience whatsoever on this alternative platform, the company employed another person to manage these mail servers specifically. A couple of months later, the mail server hosting all of senior management's mailboxes went belly up. Within about 15 minutes of this event occurring, it became painfully clear that the person employed to manage these mail servers had taken some liberties with their resumès. Not only did that person not know how to recover the mailbox server, but it turned out that the person had never actually managed any type of server before. I ended up quickly learning how to recover this type of mail server and managed to rescue senior management's mailbox data. The person who was meant to be able to do this quickly found alternate employment. Many administrators forget that disaster recovery is not just about backups but also about being able to recover from a disaster.

Lesson 1: Recovering Exchange Server Roles

In the event of a disaster, each Exchange Server role needs to be recovered in a different way. Being able to recover a server role requires knowing which aspects of the role need to be backed up. Each server role requires a separate backup strategy because each server role stores critical data in a different location. Some roles store most of their critical data within Active Directory, and others store all critical data locally.

Chapter 12, "Configuring Disaster Recovery," covered the technical details of how to back up important data. This lesson focuses more directly on the specific items that you need to ensure are backed up so that you can fully recover each server role in the event that there is a complete server failure.

After this lesson, you will be able to:

- Recover a Client Access server.
- Recover a Hub Transport server.
- Recover an Edge Transport server.
- Recover a mailbox server.

Estimated lesson time: 40 minutes

NOTE Drills are not just for making holes

If you are new to administrating servers, you may never have actually been in the position of having to recover one that has failed. That does not mean you cannot get yourself prepared. Schedule some time each month to perform recovery drills. Come up with a hypothetical failure scenario and see how quickly you are able to respond to it. Performing drills has the added benefit of allowing you to verify that you are backing up the right data. It is one thing to believe that you had backed up everything necessary in theory but quite another to prove to yourself that all the relevant information is backed up by actually using backed-up data to restore a server to full operational capacity.

Basic Recovery Procedure

Exchange Server 2007's setup routine includes a recovery option that allows for the extraction of configuration data associated with the original server from Active Directory. For certain server roles, you can achieve almost complete recovery using this technique, as almost all configuration data is stored within Active Directory and is associated with the computer account. This set of recovery steps can be used with all roles except that of the Edge Transport server, which is not joined to the domain and hence does not have configuration data associated with any computer account.

There are several common steps that you need to take prior to attempting to use *Setup* with the */m:RecoverServer* option.

- **Reset the Active Directory computer account password** If the computer account is reset, it allows you to join a replacement computer to the domain. If you delete the failed server's computer account, all Exchange configuration data stored with the computer account will be lost. If you do not reset the computer account, you will not be able to join the replacement server to the domain.

- **Install the operating system** Install Windows Server 2003 or 2008 on the replacement server using exactly the same volume and operating system configuration as the existing server. Also ensure that the replacement server has been assigned precisely the same name as the failed server.

- **Install role-specific components** Ensure that all role-specific components are installed on the server. Role-specific components were detailed in Lesson 2 of Chapter 1, "Preparing for Exchange Installation." These components must be installed prior to attempting recovery.

- **Join the replacement to the domain** Join the replacement server to the domain.

- **Run *Setup/m:RecoverServer*** The setup process will extract configuration data associated in Active Directory with the failed server's computer account and apply that as a part of the recovery process.

NOTE Remember your domain controllers

Domain controllers need to be backed up just as much as Exchange Servers do. This is especially important in small business deployments where several Exchange server roles might be installed on the only domain controller in the organization.

Some sorts of hardware failures do not require you to go through the server recovery process. For example, if your server's motherboard, processor, or power supply fails, recovery will often be a matter of replacing the failed components and booting the server. You might have to go through the Windows Product Activation process again because of the hardware changes and install new hardware device drivers, but other than that the process should be relatively painless. In general, you will need to go through the server recovery process outlined above only when you lose all the data on your storage devices or the data on your storage devices has become irretrievably corrupted.

Recover a Client Access Server

Recovering a Client Access server is a matter of rebuilding the server using the steps outlined above and then reapplying any custom configuration settings. With the exception of SSL certificates, most organizations will not apply customizations to their Client Access server. If your organization does alter a Client Access server, keep in mind the following points:

- Keep notes. Keep a log of all customizations that you make to the original Client Access server. This will assist in the recovery of the server, as not all configuration settings are associated with the computer account in Active Directory. Remember also to detail the server's volume configuration, as the recovery process requires that the recovered server's volume configuration match that of the failed server.

- Secure Sockets Layer (SSL) certificates. You can reapply for an SSL certificate from an enterprise certification authority (CA) through the Internet Information Services (IIS) console. If an SSL certificate has been obtained from a trusted third-party authority, you should keep a copy of this certificate somewhere safe. It is likely that the original certificate was transmitted through e-mail, and many organizations keep purchased certificates in a safe after they have been installed on the Client Access server.

- Custom virtual directories. If your Client Access server uses custom virtual directories, for example, to publish custom offline address books (OABs), you will need to re-create these manually once the server is recovered.

Remember to only apply customizations after you have performed the recovery process. If you apply customizations before attempting the recovery process, it is possible that these configuration changes will be overwritten by that process.

MORE INFO   **Client Access server recovery**

To find out more about recovering a Client Access server, consult the following article: *http:// technet.microsoft.com/en-us/library/aa998364.aspx*.

Recover a Hub Transport Server

Out of all the Exchange Server roles, Hub Transport servers respond most completely to being recovered using setup with the */m:RecoverServer* option. This is because Hub Transport servers store all configuration data in Active Directory. Once the server has been recovered using the process outlined earlier in this lesson, it will be able to perform its role in directing message traffic without any further intervention.

The only data that will be lost if you perform a recovery of a completely failed server using setup with the */RecoverServer* option are the message queues and the message tracking logs. In most environments, both of these components change rapidly, and any backup taken would quickly become out of date as current messages are delivered and new messages arrive. Because of their transient nature, message queue databases use circular logging and are generally not backed up.

If it is necessary to recover a particularly important message, it is possible to mount the message queue databases, located in the \Program Files\Microsoft\Exchange Server\TransportRoles\data\Queue directory on an alternate Hub Transport server. This of course assumes that it was not the loss of the storage device that caused the catastrophic failure. Generally, it is simpler to look in the Sent Items folder for a copy of a sent message or to ask the sender to retransmit it. The same applies to message tracking logs. Although they might be useful in tracking messages for later forensic analysis, the log files of other Hub Transport servers, Mailbox servers, and Edge Transport servers will also likely contain evidence of a particular message's path across your organization.

MORE INFO   **Hub Transport server recovery**

To find out more about recovering a Hub Transport server, consult the following article: *http://technet.microsoft.com/en-us/library/aa998634.aspx.*

> ## Quick Check
>   1. What must you do to the failed server's Active Directory computer account prior to attempting to use *Setup /m:RecoverServer* on the replacement server?
>   2. What will not be restored when you perform the server recovery process on a Hub Transport server after the original server fails completely?
>
> ### Quick Check Answers
>   1. Reset the failed server's Active Directory computer account.
>   2. Message queues and message tracking logs will not be restored if a Hub Transport server fails completely and must be restored using the server recovery process.

Recover an Edge Transport Server

Edge Transport servers differ from other server roles because they do not store configuration data directly in Active Directory. As you will recall from earlier lessons, Edge Transport servers are stand-alone computers located on screen subnets. Edge Transport servers are not joined to the domain. Hub Transport servers replicate the relevant Active Directory information to the Edge Transport servers by using the Microsoft Exchange EdgeSync service. On Edge Transport servers the information is stored within Active Directory Application Mode (ADAM), a local directory service.

EdgeSync Subscription

EdgeSync subscriptions are created between an individual Edge Transport server and the Hub Transport servers in the site closest to the screened subnet on which the Edge Transport server resides. For example, if an organization has two sites, one for their headquarters and one for a branch office, and the branch office site is connected to the headquarters' site by a dedicated land line and the headquarters site is connected to the Internet and uses a screened subnet, you would create an EdgeSync subscription only between the screened subnet and the headquarters site. You would not create an EdgeSync subscription between the Edge Transport server on the screened subnet and the Hub Transport servers out at the branch office site.

EdgeSync subscriptions provide a way of storing Edge Transport configurations within Active Directory. In most cases, the majority of an Edge Transport server's configuration data will be transmitted to the server using the EdgeSync process. In these cases, server recovery involves rebuilding the original server platform, installing the Edge Transport server role, and then re-creating an EdgeSync subscription.

NOTE   Network address information

As your Edge Transport server is likely to have a fully qualified domain name (FQDN) that is able to be resolved on the Internet, in many cases it will be important to ensure that the replacement server has the same Domain Name System (DNS) and IP address configuration as the failed server. If you do not replicate this aspect of the configuration, there may be problems with the delivery of inbound messages.

Cloned Configuration

Almost all settings on an Edge Transport server are set through an EdgeSync subscription, updated from the Web (anti-spam), or set by default. If you have made no custom changes to the Edge Transport server, there is little on the server that you need to back up, and recovery will consist of installing the server using the same name and IP address data and creating a new EdgeSync subscription.

Settings transferred to the Edge Transport server through EdgeSync and any custom configuration settings applied to the Edge Transport server locally are stored in ADAM. Although most of this data also exists within Active Directory and can be transferred using EdgeSync, there are some situations in which you will want to separately back up this configuration data. To back up this data, you can run a script ExportEdgeConfig.ps1, which will export the following data to an XML file:

- Log paths used by the send and receive protocols, pickup directory, and routing table
- Message tracking log path
- Transport agent status and priority configuration
- Information about Send and Receive connectors
- Accepted domain configuration
- Remote domain configuration
- IP allow and IP block list (though not block list provider configuration)
- Content filtering settings
- Attachment filters
- Recipient filtering settings
- Address rewrite settings

The script is executed using the following command from the C:\Program Files\Microsoft\Exchange Server\Scripts folder when using Exchange Management Shell:

```
./ExportEdgeConfig -cloneConfigData:"C:\EdgeData.xml"
```

This script is most often used if you wish to clone the configuration of your Edge Transport server as a part of a DNS round-robin high availability strategy. This strategy is covered in more detail in Lesson 2.

To import a cloned configuration on a new server that you wish to deploy as an Edge Transport server or on a replacement server in the event that an existing Edge Transport server has failed, perform the following steps:

1. Install Windows Server 2003 or Windows Server 2008 on the new server.

2. Install the necessary components to support the Edge Transport server role. These were detailed in Chapter 1, "Preparing for Exchange Installation."

3. Install the Edge Transport server role normally. Remember that you cannot use the */m:RecoverServer* option with this specific Exchange Server 2007 role.

4. Import the cloned configuration using the ImportEdgeConfig.ps1 script. This script is located in the same location as the ExportEdgeConfig.ps1 script and must be run from Exchange Management Shell.

5. Configure an EdgeSync subscription with the Hub Transport servers in the Active Directory site adjoining the screened subnet on which the Edge Transport server resides.

Using cloned configurations with DNS round-robin is covered in Lesson 2 of this chapter.

MORE INFO   **Edge Transport server recovery**

To find out more about recovering an Edge Transport server, consult the following article: *http://technet.microsoft.com/en-us/library/aa997584.aspx*.

Recovering a Mailbox Server

Lesson 2 of Chapter 12 explained how to recover mailbox databases and mailboxes. This section concentrates on recovering the actual mailbox server itself should you lose it, not just the mailbox databases or mailboxes themselves. Recovering clustered mailbox servers is covered in Lesson 2 later in this chapter.

To recover the mailbox server that hosts the mailboxes, you should go through the process outlined at the start of this lesson, using setup with the */m:RecoverServer* option to extract the original mailbox server's configuration data from Active Directory. Out of all the Exchange Server roles, mailbox servers are most sensitive to requiring the volume configuration of the replacement server to be exactly the same as that of the server that originally failed. Remember to document the precise configuration of the server's storage devices and volumes. If this configuration is not precisely reproduced, you are likely to encounter problems when attempting to restore mailbox and storage group data using the procedures outlined in Lesson 2 of Chapter 12.

Recovering a clustered mailbox server is a different process than recovering a mailbox server that does not use cluster continuous replication or a single copy cluster configuration. The first step to perform in recovering a clustered mailbox server is to re-create the failed cluster node and join it to the existing cluster using the Cluster Administrator tool. More detail about applying high availability solutions to Exchange

Server 2007 are covered in the second lesson of this chapter. Once the cluster has been re-created, you should ensure that all the necessary components required for a mailbox server are installed, and then you should run Exchange setup to install the passive Mailbox server role on the computer. Once the passive Mailbox server role has been successfully installed, run the following command from the command prompt:

```
Setup.com /RecoverCMS /CMSName:<name of the cluster> /CMSIPaddress:<IP Address of the Cluster>
```

This command should be run from the \Program Files\Microsoft\Exchange Server\bin directory of the reinstalled passive mailbox server. If using cluster continuous replication, you will then need to enable replication and reseed the replica database. This process is covered in more detail in Lesson 2. If you are restoring a mailbox server that uses single copy cluster, the storage groups and mailbox databases will already be present on the shared storage device. However, if the mailbox server failed because of an issue related to the shared storage hardware or firmware, you will now have to restore the data from backup, which is not necessary in case of a single storage failure in a CCR configuration.

MORE INFO   **Mailbox server recovery**

To find out more about recovering a mailbox server, consult the following article: *http://tech-net.microsoft.com/en-us/library/bb124257.aspx.*

Practice: Exchange Server 2007 Role Recovery

The practice in this section is optional and time consuming because it essentially involves installing the Hub Transport server role on a second computer twice. You should perform this practice only if you have access to the necessary hardware to host a second Exchange server. If you are using Microsoft Virtual Machine software, you will need enough RAM on the host computer to run both the existing and the new virtual machine simultaneously.

▶ **Practice 1: Installing and Recovering a Hub Transport Server**

In this practice, you will install an extra Hub Transport server into the Tailspin Toys organization. You will then create a duplicate of that server to simulate server recovery. The steps provided in this practice are of a general nature, as you will have already completed many of them in earlier practices. To complete this practice, perform the following steps:

1. Configure a Windows Server 2003 64-bit edition computer as a member of the TailspinToys.Internal domain. Name this computer RoleRecovery. Use only a single volume to host the operating system and make a note of the volume's size.

2. Ensure that Windows PowerShell and Microsoft .NET Framework version 2.0 or later are installed on the server.

3. Install the Hub Transport server role on the computer using the Exchange Server 2007 installation routine. Do not install any other Exchange Server roles on this computer.

4. Once the installation routine completes, open Exchange Management Console on the Exchange Server that you have been performing your practice exercises on. Verify that the Hub Transport server RoleRecovery is present in the list of servers when the Hub Transport node is selected under Server Configuration.

5. Shut down the server named RoleRecovery. Format the hard disk drive.

6. Reset the computer account named RoleRecovery using Active Directory Users and Computers on the TailspinToys.Internal domain controller.

7. Install Windows Server 2003 on the newly formatted computer. Assign the computer the name RoleRecovery. Install Windows PowerShell and Microsoft .NET Framework version 2.0 or later and then rejoin the server to the domain.

8. Instead of using Exchange's GUI installer, open a command prompt and change to the directory hosting the Exchange Server 2007 installation media.

9. Issue the command *Setup /m:RecoverServer* from the command prompt.

10. Once the recover routine completes, open Exchange Management Console on the Exchange Server that you have been performing your practice exercises on. Verify that the Hub Transport server RoleRecovery is present in the list of servers when the Hub Transport node is selected under Server Configuration.

Lesson Summary

- The easiest way to recover a failed server is to use *Setup /m:RecoverServer*. You can use this command successfully only if you have rebuilt a copy of the failed server that uses the same volume configuration and has the same name, you have reset the computer's Active Directory account, the server has the necessary role required components, and you have joined the replacement to the domain.

- When restoring a Client Access server, remember to reinstall any custom SSL certificates. If you are using a custom IIS virtual directory configuration, it may be necessary to manually re-create that after you have performed the role recovery process.

- All important Hub Transport data is stored in Active Directory, and this is the most straightforward Exchange server role to recover using *Setup /m:RecoverServer*.

- Edge Transport servers cannot be recovered using *Setup /m:RecoverServer*. You can back up an Edge Transport server's configuration using the Clone Configuration Scripts. To restore an Edge Transport server, install the server role on a stand-alone computer, import the cloned configuration, and then create a new EdgeSync subscription.

- When recovering a mailbox server, it is vitally important to ensure that the volume configuration on the replacement server is precisely the same as the server that it is replacing.

- Recovering a mailbox server that uses cluster continuous replication or single copy cluster requires re-creating the cluster first, installing the passive Mailbox server role, and then using the *Setup /RecoverCMS* command.

Lesson Review

You can use the following questions to test your knowledge of the information in Lesson 1, "Recovering Exchange Server Roles." The questions are also available on the companion CD if you prefer to review them in electronic form.

NOTE Answers

Answers to these questions and explanations of why each answer choice is correct or incorrect are located in the "Answers" section at the end of the book.

---

1. Which of the following Hub Transport server data is stored within Active Directory? (Choose all that apply.)

   A. EdgeSync subscription data

   B. Address lists

   C. IP address configuration

   D. Local users

   E. Local groups

2. An Edge Transport server that is configured with an EdgeSync subscription has its hard disk drives fail completely because of a power surge. After you reinstall the operating system and install the necessary components to support the Hub Transport role, which of the following should you do to return the server to full operational status? (Choose all that apply.)

   A. Reinstall the Mailbox server role

   B. Reinstall the Edge Transport role

    C. Create a new EdgeSync subscription

    D. Join the server to the domain

    E. Reinstall the Hub Transport Role

3. Which of the following Client Access server components will not be reinstalled when performing role recovery using *Setup /m:Recover*? (Choose all that apply.)

    A. SSL certificates

    B. Custom Virtual Directory configuration

    C. IMAP4 settings

    D. POP3 settings

    E. OAB publishing settings

4. You are preparing to run setup with the */m:RecoverServer* option to recover a Client Access server that was destroyed in a server room fire. You have configured the replacement server with the original server's name, installed the necessary components to support an Exchange Server 2007 Client Access server, and verified that the volume configuration of the replacement server matches that of the original. Which of the following steps must you take prior to attempting server recovery?

    A. Reset the original server's computer account

    B. Delete the original server's computer account

    C. Rename the original server's computer account

    D. Create a new computer account

5. The hard disk drives on a server assigned the Hub Transport server role fail completely. You replace the failed hard disk drive, reset the computer account in Active Directory, reinstall the operating system, join the computer to the domain, and install the necessary components to support the Hub Transport role. Which of the following steps should you perform to complete the recovery process?

    A. Use the *Setup /m:RecoverServer* command

    B. Use the *Setup /m:Install /r:ht* command

    C. Use the *Setup /m:Upgrade /r:ht* command

    D. Use the *Setup /m:Uninstall /r:ht* command

Lesson 2: Exchange Server 2007 High Availability

At its most basic, configuring Exchange Server 2007 for high availability ensures that Exchange can continue to function after the failure of critical hardware components. Each high availability strategy protects against a different type of failure, and not every high availability strategy is appropriate for a particular Exchange Server 2007 role. In this lesson, you will learn which server roles to apply particular high availability strategies to and the types of disasters a particular high availability strategy will protect against.

> **After this lesson, you will be able to:**
> - Configure local continuous replication.
> - Configure cluster continuous replication.
> - Configuring single copy clustering.
> - Configure Network Load Balancing.
>
> **Estimated lesson time: 40 minutes**

Implementing Local Continuous Replication

Local continuous replication (LCR) works on a single mailbox server by using asynchronous log shipping and log replay to create and maintain a copy of a storage group on a second set of disks. A mailbox server configured with LCR can survive the failure of a disk array, though it cannot survive the failure of the server itself.

LCR has one limitation that is worth noting. LCR restricts a storage group so that it contains exactly one database. If you attempt to use LCR on a storage group that contains more than one database, the operation will fail. LCR also cannot be used with public folder databases, though this is less of a problem as public folders can be replicated to any other public folder database in the organization and the feature is deprecated in Exchange Server 2007.

Configuring LCR

LCR can be configured using Exchange Management Console by selecting the appropriate storage group when the Server Configuration\Mailbox node is selected and then clicking Enable local continuous replication in the Actions pane. This will start the Enable Storage Group Local Continuous Replication (LCR Wizard), which involves specifying the location of the replicated data. For best results, you should locate this data on a second redundant storage array, though it is possible to configure

LCR to create a replica on an attached USB drive, if necessary. You will create an LCR replica in the practice at the end of this lesson. When you complete the wizard, you will note that the first step in configuring LCR is enabling the mailbox database within the storage group to be copied and then configuring the storage group itself.

To perform this step using Exchange Management Shell, you use the *Enable-Database-Copy* cmdlet, which has the following syntax:

```
Enable-DatabaseCopy -Identity <DatabaseID> -CopyEdbFilePath <Copy Location>
```

Once the *Enable-DatabaseCopy* operation has completed, it will not be functional until a storage group copy is enabled. Storage groups on a server using local continuous replication are managed using the following cmdlets:

- **Enable-StorageGroupCopy** This cmdlet is used to create a copy of a storage group in an LCR configuration. The mailbox database within the storage group must be copy enabled using *Enable-DatabaseCopy*. Once the *Enable-Storage-GroupCopy* cmdlet is completed, a database copy will be seeded. It is possible to stop automatic seeding by using the SeedingPostponed parameter with the *Enable-StorageGroupCopy* cmdlet.

- **Disable-StorageGroupCopy** This cmdlet is used to remove an existing copy of a storage group and the associated mailbox database. Once the command completes, the storage group and database copy configuration are removed.

- **Restore-StorageGroupCopy** When used in an LCR configuration, *Restore-StorageGroupCopy* disables LCR and makes it possible for the passive copy to be mounted.

- **Resume-StorageGroupCopy** This cmdlet is used to resume replication for a specific storage group after it has been suspended using the *Suspend-StorageGroupCopy* cmdlet.

- **Suspend-StorageGroupCopy** This cmdlet is used to block replication and replay operations for a specific storage group.

- **Update-StorageGroupCopy** This cmdlet is used to initiate or resynchronize replication. This cmdlet differs from the *Resume-StorageGroupCopy* cmdlet in that it can be used on a corrupted database or on a database that has been backed up and does not have all log files present.

- **Get-StorageGroupCopyStatus** When executed in a command, this cmdlet returns the current replication status information about an LCR copy of a storage group.

You will be utilizing these cmdlets during the practice session at the end of this lesson to create and manage local continuous replication on an Exchange Server 2007 mailbox server.

Troubleshooting LCR

LCR diagnosis is carried out using the *Get-StorageGroupCopyStatus* cmdlet. You will be using this cmdlet in the practice at the end of the lesson to check on the status of the LCR configuration that you implement. The following are a list of common errors that may arise when using LCR and how you can go about resolving them:

- *Get-StorageGroupCopyStatus* **reports database failed and not seeded**   This could be caused by a configuration problem such as the storage group on the local computer not being enabled. You should verify that the LCR copy's paths are correctly configured using *Get-StorageGroup*. When verified, use *Update-StorageGroupCopy* to seed the storage group copy.

- *Get-StorageGroupCopyStatus* **reports copy or replay queues are backed up**   A backlog of log copying could indicate that the passive copy is suspended. Resume the storage copy using the *Resume-StorageCopy* cmdlet.

- *Get-StorageGroupCopyStatus* **reports seeding is failing**   This error can arise when the active copy is being backed up. Wait for the backup process to complete. Verify that the active copy has not failed.

MORE INFO   **LCR**

To find out more about using LCR as a high availability solution, consult the following article: *http://technet.microsoft.com/en-us/library/bb125195.aspx*.

Implementing Cluster Continuous Replication

Cluster continuous replication (CCR) is the most resilient high availability strategy that you can apply to an Exchange Server 2007 mailbox server. This high availability technique uses the asynchronous log shipping and replay technology included with Exchange 2007 and the failover and management features of the Microsoft Windows Cluster service. CCR has the following features:

- No single point of failure.
- No special hardware requirements.

- Does not require the configuration of shared storage.

- Volume Shadow Copy Service backups of the passive node are supported.

CCR uses two computers that are joined in a single Microsoft Windows Cluster services failover cluster. In the event that the active node of the cluster fails, the passive node promotes itself automatically and continues to service client requests.

Configuring CCR

The first step in configuring CCR is to create the cluster. The cluster must be created using the Cluster Administrator utility included with the Enterprise editions of Windows Server 2003 and Windows Server 2008 prior to performing the installation of Exchange Server 2007. Each cluster node should also have two network adapters, one of which will be used for intracluster communication. When Exchange Server 2007 is installed, it performs a check to see if it is being installed on a computer that is configured as a part of a cluster. If it is, the cluster-aware version of Exchange Server 2007 is installed. It is not possible to convert a stand-alone mailbox server to a clustered mailbox server other than to reinstall Exchange from the beginning after the original server had been joined to a cluster.

MORE INFO **Majority node set quorum with File Share Witness**

CCR uses a new type of cluster quorum model called majority node set quorum with file share witness. To find out more about this cluster quorum model, consult the following TechNet article: *http://technet.microsoft.com/en-us/library/bb124521.aspx.*

The active node of the cluster should be installed first followed by the passive node. During the installation of the passive Mailbox server node, each existing storage group and associated mailbox databases are copied from the active node. This initial copy process is known as seeding. Once seeding is complete, log copy and replay will be performed automatically. In the event that extra storage groups or mailbox databases are added, these will automatically be copied across to the passive node.

Maintaining CCR

Once implemented, administrators should regularly monitor replication. It is vital to ensure that the passive node in the cluster is performing properly. You do not want to find out that your passive node has not been functioning properly after failover from an active node has occurred. The primary tool that you can use to monitor CCR is the

Get-StorageGroupCopyStatus Exchange Management Shell cmdlet. Running this command will inform you of the state of replication.

MORE INFO   Using *Get-StorageGroupCopyStatus* to diagnose CCR

For more information on using *Get-StorageGroupCopyStatus* to diagnose CCR, consult the following TechNet link: *http://technet.microsoft.com/en-us/library/aa996020.aspx.*

The Exchange Server 2007 Management Pack for Microsoft Operations Manager 2005 includes alerts that will notify you if the following has occurred:

- The replication service has failed on the passive node.
- The passive copy is in a failed state.
- The passive copy is lagging behind the active copy.

Service packs or updates that need to be applied to a clustered mailbox server that uses CCR should be applied to the passive node first. Once the passive node has been updated, the clustered mailbox server can be moved from the active node. This provides another benefit in that if issues arise from the application of updates, it is a simple operation to move the clustered mailbox server back to the unpatched original active node. The *Move-ClusteredMailboxServer* cmdlet is used to gracefully move the clustered mailbox server between nodes in the cluster. In the event that the active node fails, failover occurs automatically.

Quick Check

1. Which should you install and configure first when deploying CCR, the cluster or Exchange Server 2007?

2. Which cmdlet would you use in a command to resynchronize replication on an Exchange Server 2007 mailbox server configured to use LCR?

Quick Check Answers

1. When deploying CCR, it is necessary to configure the cluster first and then to deploy Exchange Server 2007. The Exchange Server 2007 setup routine will detect the clustered environment and install the cluster-aware version of Exchange.

2. *Update-StorageGroupCopy.*

Single Copy Clustering

Single copy clustering (SCC) is a high availability technique where two mailbox servers, configured as a cluster with an active and a passive node, share one storage device. The shared storage can be a directly attached disk array or a storage area network device. In the event that the server holding the active node role fails, the failover process will transfer the active node role to the passive node, and the mailbox servers will continue to service client requests. In the event that the passive node fails, the mailbox server will remain available through the active node, allowing the passive node to be repaired and brought back into the cluster.

SCCs use a shared-nothing architecture. This means that a resource being accessed by one node in the cluster cannot be accessed by other nodes at the same time. For example, a physical disk resource assigned to the first node of a two-node cluster cannot be accessed by the second node of the cluster until the first node is taken offline, the first node fails, or an administrator intervenes to move the disk resource to the second node manually. This type of move is known as a handoff. Administrators can perform a handoff using the *Move-ClusteredMailboxServer* cmdlet.

Configuring SCCs

Just as is the case with CCR, prior to installing Exchange Server 2007 in an SCC configuration, it is necessary to use the Microsoft Windows Cluster service to create a failover cluster. The Microsoft Windows Cluster service is a component of the enterprise editions of Windows Server 2003 and Windows Server 2008. The Exchange Server 2007 installation routine will detect that the server is configured to use a clustered configuration, and the cluster-aware version of Exchange Server 2007 will be installed. This will limit Exchange Server role selection to the Mailbox server role. An SCC Exchange Server 2007 clustered mailbox server requires the following elements on top of the normal components required for the Mailbox server role:

- **Shared storage** SCCs use shared storage.
- **Resource DLL** Exchange Server 2007 provides a custom resource DLL called Exres.dll to manage the Windows Cluster service.
- **Groups** In an Exchange Server 2007 SCC, a clustered mailbox server is a cluster group that contains clustered resources including an IP address, physical disk resources, the Microsoft Exchange Information Store service, and the Exchange System Attendant service.

MORE INFO   Single copy cluster installation in detail

For more information on how to install Exchange Server 2007 in an SCC configuration, consult the following TechNet article: *http://technet.microsoft.com/en-us/library/bb124899.aspx.*

Managing Disk Resources

A clustered mailbox server using SCC uses a shared storage device to host all storage group data. This shared storage must be accessible to all nodes that might host the clustered mailbox server and needs to be a part of the clustered mailbox server's resource model. Prior to performing management tasks such as managing disk volumes, all databases should be dismounted. To add new storage to an existing configuration, use the Cluster Administrator console. You should also use the Cluster Administrator, shown in Figure 13-1, to verify any configuration changes that might be made to nodes in the cluster after SCC has been configured.

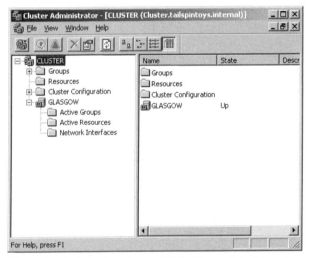

Figure 13-1   Windows Server 2003 Cluster Administrator

Managing Storage Groups and Databases

The process of creating and removing databases and storage groups on a mailbox server configured as an SCC is the same as performing these tasks on a standard mailbox server. The same applies to mounting and dismounting databases. The main difference between managing storage groups and databases on an SCC and on a standard mailbox server deployment is when you need to move the location of a storage group or database.

When moving a storage group in an SCC, use the *Move-StorageGroupPath* cmdlet from the cluster's active node. Databases will be dismounted during the move, and the new location cannot be the root directory of a volume. Databases will be remounted once the move has successfully completed. To move mailboxes on an Exchange Server 2007 server configured to use single copy cluster, use the *Move-DatabasePath* cmdlet. The *Move-DatabasePath* cmdlet automatically dismounts the mailbox database prior to removing it. The database will automatically be remounted when the move is complete. The new location of the database cannot be the root directory of a volume.

NOTE   Moving storage groups and databases

Microsoft recommends using Exchange Management Shell cmdlets to move storage groups and databases on mailbox servers configured to use SCCs rather than Exchange Management Console.

Cluster Maintenance

Prior to performing server maintenance tasks, you should ensure that the server that you are about to perform maintenance on is the passive rather than active node in the cluster. If it is necessary to perform maintenance options, such as the application of service packs or software updates, you should use the *Move-ClusteredMailboxServer* cmdlet to move the clustered mailbox server to the passive node. Always update the passive node in an SCC configuration first. That way, if problems arise when you move the clustered mailbox server prior to updating the currently active node, you can return the clustered mailbox server to the active node and roll back the updates until you are certain that they will not negatively impact your Exchange environment.

In the event that it is necessary to shut down all nodes in an SCC, for example, if there is a power outage in your building and the servers in the cluster can operate for only a short amount of time on an emergency power supply, you should first stop the clustered mailbox server prior to performing the Windows shutdown process. Use the *Stop-ClusteredMailboxServer* cmdlet on the active node and then use the *Get-Clustered-MailboxServerStatus* cmdlet to verify that the server has achieved the offline state before initiating the Windows shutdown process. Cmdlets for managing high availability configurations, including SCC configurations, are covered later in this lesson.

MORE INFO   SCC

To find out more about using SCC as a high availability solution, consult the following article: *http://technet.microsoft.com/en-us/library/bb125217.aspx.*

Implementing Network Load Balancing

Network Load Balancing (NLB) is used as a high availability strategy with Client Access servers. NLB works by distributing client requests across a group of servers. One advantage of NLB is that should the load on existing servers within the group reach an unacceptable level, it is a relatively simple procedure to add another server to the NLB group. NLB also provides fault tolerance, with the Windows NLB directing client traffic only to cluster nodes that are active. When Windows NLB detects that a member of the cluster has become inoperable, it will automatically remove it from the cluster until the member becomes operational again. Windows NLB is included in both the standard and enterprise edition of Windows Server 2003 and Windows Server 2008.

All the servers in an NLB cluster are represented by the same virtual IP address and FQDN. The actual servers within the cluster have separate IP addresses and FQDNs. Although it is possible to use a single network card for each node in a Windows NLB cluster, Microsoft recommends that each node in the cluster have two network cards so that host traffic and cluster traffic can be relegated to different network segments.

Unlike the other clustering methods covered earlier in this lesson, you can deploy NLB on a computer that will host the Client Access server role after Exchange Server 2007 has been installed. The basic process involves setting up the Client Access servers that will be members of the cluster and then joining them together in the Windows NLB cluster. You then configure clients to use the virtual FQDN of the Windows NLB cluster as the Client Access server address rather than the FQDNs of the individual Client Access servers. The Autodiscover and Availability services need to be similarly configured so that clients using it are pointed toward the virtual FQDN rather than a specific Client Access server address. Also important to remember is that the SSL certificates used by the Client Access server will need to include not only the server's original name but also the name used by the Windows NLB cluster.

MORE INFO Configuring the Availability service for NLB

To learn more about configuring the Availability service for NLB, consult the following TechNet article: *http://technet.microsoft.com/en-us/library/aa997237.aspx*.

Implementing DNS Round-Robin

DNS round-robin is a high availability strategy that is used with Edge Transport servers. DNS round-robin is relatively straightforward. Multiple DNS entries with the same host name are configured for a DNS zone. Each DNS entry is associated with a different IP address. When a client queries the DNS server for the IP address of the target host, the DNS server responds with a different IP address in a round-robin manner. Figure 13-2 displays four different entries for the host name EdgeTransport. tailspintoys.internal, which the DNS server will pass on to clients in a round-robin fashion.

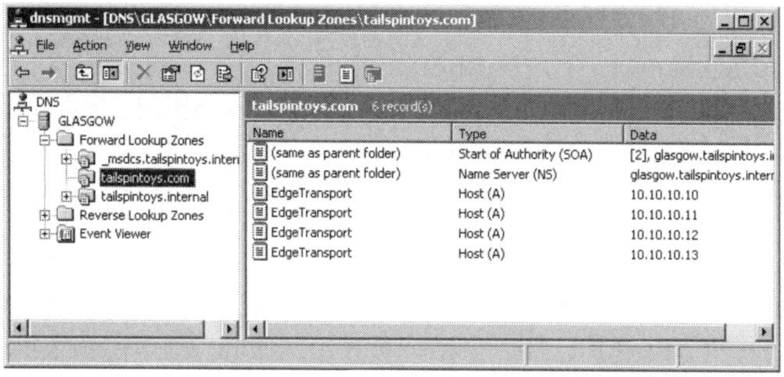

Figure 13-2   Configuring Edge Transport servers for DNS round-robin

The drawback of using DNS round-robin is that it remains unaware of server failure. For example, Contoso has two identically configured Edge Transport servers. An administrator has configured DNS round-robin for the host name mailhost.contoso.com with the IP addresses 10.10.10.10 and 10.10.10.11. The server associated with IP address 10.10.10.11 fails and becomes nonresponsive. The Contoso DNS server will remain unaware of this failure and will still provide the failed server's IP address to 50 percent of querying clients. In the event that a server using round-robin fails, it is necessary to manually delete the host record associated with that server's IP address from the DNS zone database until the server is completely restored.

MORE INFO   More on round-robin

To find out more about configuring round-robin on Windows DNS servers, consult the following TechNet article: *http://technet2.microsoft.com/windowsserver/f/?en/library/e0f49958-f290-49fc-adb4-71ed8deefd621033.mspx*.

High Availability and Exchange Management Shell

Once set up, clustered mailbox servers are managed using a set of Exchange Management Shell cmdlets. There are several interrelated cmdlet sets that will be covered over the course of the next few pages. The first set of cmdlets, listed below, are used to manage clustered mailbox servers at the server level:

- *Start-ClusteredMailboxServer* This cmdlet is used to start a Microsoft Exchange Server 2007 clustered mailbox server after it has shut down, either through the use of the *Stop-ClusteredMailboxServer* cmdlet or because of a failure. This cmdlet can be used only if the cluster exists and the data for the clustered mailbox server is available and operational.

- *Stop-ClusteredMailboxServer* This cmdlet allows an administrator to shut down clustered mailbox server operations without triggering the failover process. A restart of the server will not bring Exchange back online. The only way to activate a server after issuing this command is to use the *Start-ClusteredMailbox-Server* command.

- *Get-ClusteredMailboxServerStatus* This cmdlet is used to get basic operational information about a clustered mailbox server. This includes a list of operational computers in the cluster, a list of offline resources associated with the server, and its current state. Running this command also will return which of the six possible status states the clustered mailbox server is currently in:

    - **Online** The server is functioning normally.
    - **Partially online** One or more server resources are offline.
    - **Online pending** One or more server resources are coming offline.
    - **Offline** The server is completely offline.
    - **Offline pending** One or more server resources are in the process of going offline.
    - **Failed** The clustered mailbox server has failed.

- *Move-ClusteredMailboxServer* This cmdlet is used to gracefully transfer a Microsoft Exchange Server 2007 clustered mailbox server to an available passive node. This cmdlet is used to initiate a planned outage and is not used in the event that the active node fails. When an active node fails, automatic failover occurs. The *Move-ClusteredMailboxServer* cmdlet is covered in more detail below.

The *Move-ClusteredMailboxServer* cmdlet can be used only if a clustered mailbox server is currently not running on the target server and the target server is a member of the same cluster. If any data would be lost by running the *Move-ClusteredMailbox-Server* cmdlet, the move will be prevented, leaving the clustered mailbox server on the original node. A command based on the *Move-ClusteredMailboxServer* cmdlet takes the following form:

```
Move-ClusteredMailboxServer -Identity <HostServer> -MoveComment <String> -TargetMachine
<Destination>
```

It is necessary to include the MoveComment parameter, as the string entered here will be added to the event log. If the clustered mailbox server was offline when the command was issued, it will remain offline when transferred to the target server.

NOTE   Offline is not failed

Remember that a clustered mailbox server that is offline is in a different state than a clustered mailbox server that has failed.

Practice: Configuring and Managing Local Continuous Replication

In these practices, you will perform several exercises that will familiarize you with the configuration of LCR.

▶ **Practice 1: Configuring LCR**

In this practice, you will use Exchange Management Console to configure LCR on a new storage group and mailbox database. Rather than set LCR to replicate to a separate volume, you will configure LCR to replicate to a different folder on the same volume. This is not an ideal solution and provides no fault tolerance, but it will provide you with a demonstration of the LCR configuration process. To complete this practice, perform the following steps:

1. Log on to the Exchange Server using the Kim Akers user account.

2. Create a folder with the name and path C:\LCR-COPY.

3. Open Exchange Management Console. Navigate to the Server Configuration\Mailbox node.

4. Create a new storage group called Replicate and accept the default properties. Within the Replicate storage group, create a new mailbox database using the default settings named CloneMailbox.

5. Select the Replicate storage group and then from the Actions menu click Enable Local Continuous Replication. This will bring up the Enable Storage Group Local Continuous Replication Wizard, shown in Figure 13-3. Click Next.

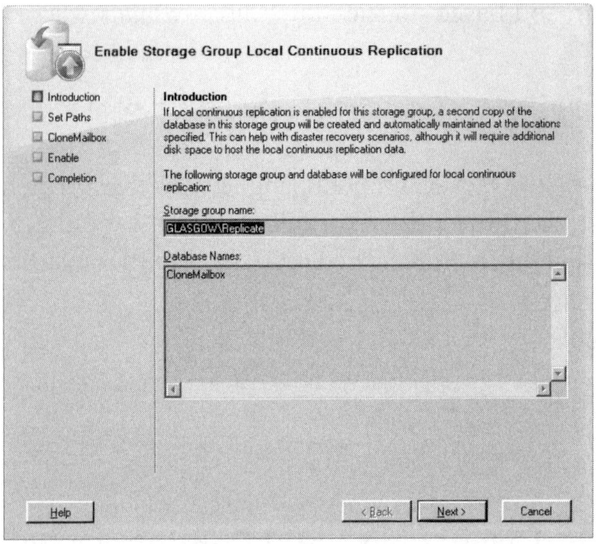

Figure 13-3   Introductory page of the LCR Wizard

6. On the Set Paths page, click Browse next to the Local continuous replication system files path textbox. Select the folder C:\LCR-COPY and click OK.

7. On the same page, click Browse next to the Local continuous replication log files path textbox. Select the folder C:\LCR-COPY and click OK. Verify that the settings on the Set Paths page match those shown in Figure 13-4 and then click Next.

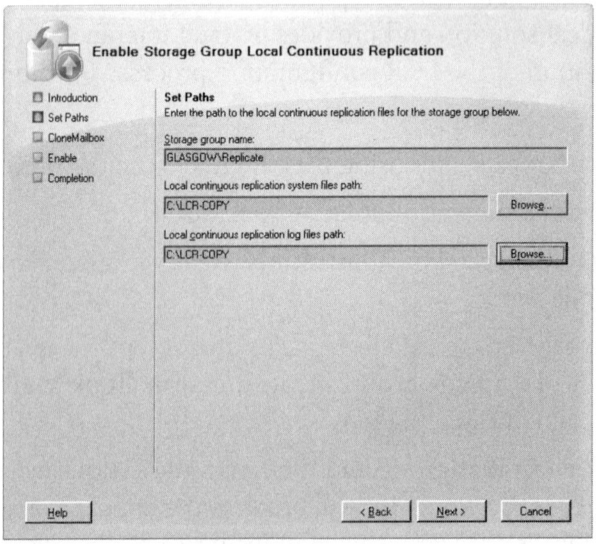

Figure 13-4   Configuring system and log file paths for the replicated storage group

8. On the page with the title CloneMailbox (this is the name of the Mailbox Database you created in step 4), click on Browse next to the Local continuous replication Exchange database file path textbox. Browse to the C:\LCR-COPY folder and click Save. Verify that the settings on the page with the title CloneMailbox match those shown in Figure 13-5 and then click Next.

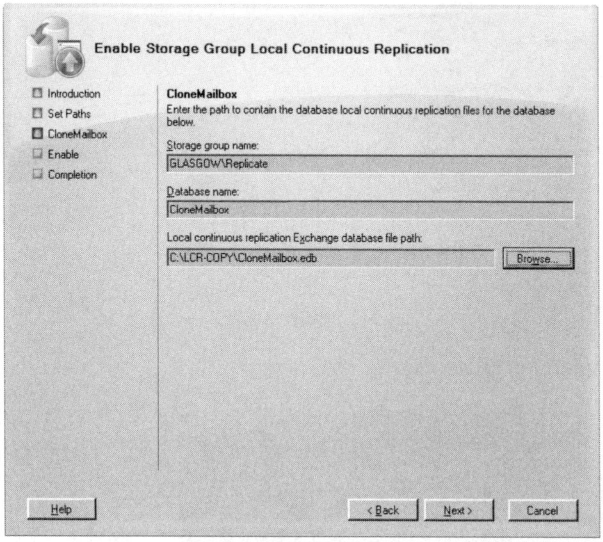

Figure 13-5   Mailbox Database LCR configuration

9. On the Enable page, click Enable. Verify that the Enable Storage Group Local Continuous Replication page matches what is shown in Figure 13-6 and then click Finish.

▶ **Practice 2: Suspending and Updating LCR**

In this practice, you will use Exchange Management Shell cmdlets to verify the mailbox server's LCR configuration. You will also suspend and resume LCR on the LCR-enabled storage group. To complete this practice, perform the following steps:

1. Log on to the Exchange Server 2007 mailbox server that you configured in Practice 1 of this lesson using the Kim Akers user account.

2. Open Exchange Management Shell.

3. In Exchange Management Shell, issue the command *Get-StorageGroupCopyStatus −Identity Replicate*. Verify that the output of this command matches that shown in Figure 13-7.

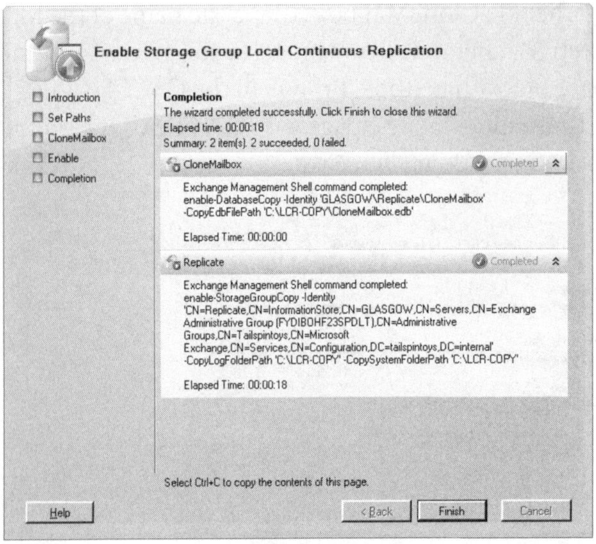

Figure 13-6 Completing LCR configuration

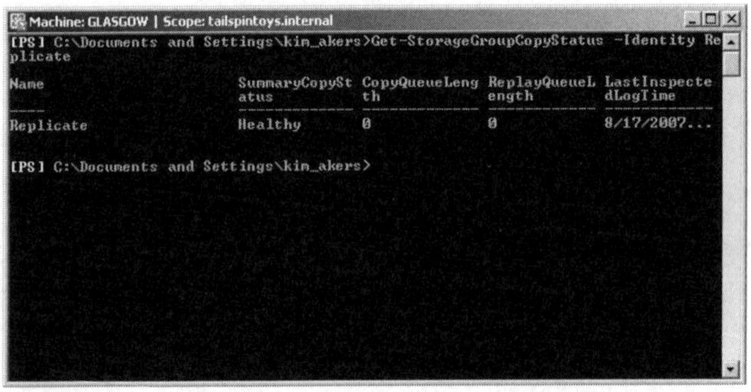

Figure 13-7 Verifying storage group copy status

4. In Exchange Management Shell, issue the command *Suspend-StorageGroupCopy –Identity Replicate*. When you are prompted to confirm this action, type **A** and press Enter.

5. Issue the command *Get-StorageGroupCopyStatus –Identity Replicate* again to verify that the Replicate storage group now has the status Suspended, as shown in Figure 13-8.

6. Issue the command *Resume-StorageGroupCopy –Identity Replicate* to resume LCR.

7. Verify that LCR has resumed by reissuing the *Get-StorageGroupCopyStatus –Identity Replicate* command.

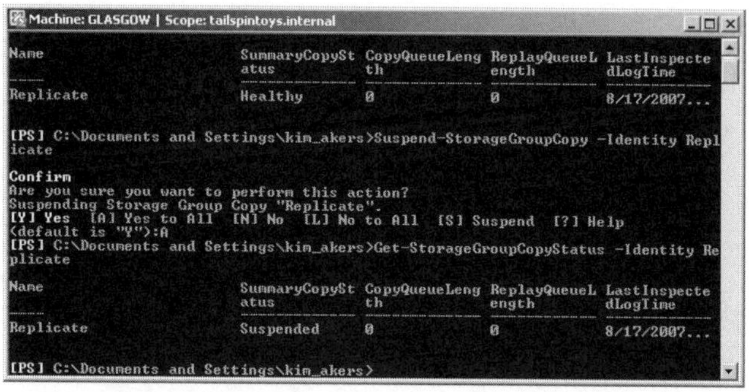

Figure 13-8 Verifying the suspension of replication

Lesson Summary

- CCR uses multiple servers and separate storage devices. When the active node in a CCR fails, the passive node takes over. A Windows Server cluster that uses separate storage devices must be configured prior to installing Exchange if you want to implement CCR.

- Single copy clusters (SCC) uses multiple servers but a shared storage device. SCC can survive the loss of a server but not the loss of the shared storage device. A Windows Server cluster that has a shared storage device must be configured prior to installing Exchange if you want to implement SCC.

- LCR uses a single server with multiple storage devices. If one storage device fails, a mailbox server configured with LCR can be configured to use the local copy of the database. LCR can be implemented on a stand-alone Exchange Server 2007 mailbox server but cannot be implemented on a server configured for CCR or SCC.

- NLB can be used with Client Access servers. A Windows NLB cluster can be configured after the Client Access server role has been installed.

- Hub Transport servers do not need to directly utilize a high availability strategy, as resiliency is built into the role. To ensure that messages are still routed between sites in the event that a Hub Transport server fails, add a second Hub Transport server to each Active Directory site.

- DNS round-robin allows the load to be spread between multiple Edge Transport servers, but the round-robin configuration must be manually changed in the event that an Edge Transport server fails.

Lesson Review

You can use the following questions to test your knowledge of the information in Lesson 2, "Exchange Server 2007 High Availability." The questions are also available on the companion CD if you prefer to review them in electronic form.

NOTE Answers

Answers to these questions and explanations of why each answer choice is correct or incorrect are located in the "Answers" section at the end of the book.

---

1. Which of the following high availability strategies support automatic failover in the event of server failure and can be applied to a mailbox server? (Choose all that apply.)

   A. NLB

   B. SCC

   C. LCR

   D. CCR

   E. DNS round-robin

2. Your organization has a single mailbox server. Which of the following solutions will allow the mailbox server to continue operating after the failure of the disk array that hosts the server's mailbox databases?

   A. LCR

   B. SCC

   C. CCR

   D. NLB

3. Which of the following high availability strategies would you implement for an Exchange Server 2007 mailbox server when you have a two-node cluster and a single shared storage device?

   A. NLB

   B. SCC

   C. LCR

   D. CCR

4. Which of the following high availability strategies would you use with the Hub Transport server role?

    A. DNS round-robin

    B. NLB

    C. CCR

    D. SCC

    E. None of the above

5. A clustered mailbox server is shut down by an administrator issuing the *Stop-ClusteredMailboxServer* command. Which of the following steps should the administrator take to restart the clustered mailbox server?

    A. Restart the server

    B. Use the *Move-ClusteredMailboxServer* cmdlet

    C. Use the *Start-ClusteredMailboxServer* cmdlet

    D. Use the *Stop-ClusteredMailboxServer* cmdlet

6. Which of the following conditions must be met to successfully initiate a *Move-ClusteredMailboxServer* operation? (Choose all that apply.)

    A. The target server must be available and must be a member of the same cluster.

    B. The target server must be available and a member of a separate cluster.

    C. A clustered mailbox server must not be running on the target server.

    D. A clustered mailbox server must be running on the target server.

    E. The server the command is run on must be in the failed state.

Chapter Review

To further practice and reinforce the skills you learned in this chapter, you can perform the following tasks:

- Review the chapter summary.
- Review the list of key terms introduced in this chapter.
- Complete the case scenarios. These scenarios set up real-world situations involving the topics of this chapter and ask you to create a solution.
- Complete the suggested practices.
- Take a practice test.

Chapter Summary

- Exchange Setup includes a recovery routine that can extract server and role information from Active Directory and apply it to a replacement server should the original fail.
- It is important to document the volume configuration of each Exchange Server computer in your organization. Also document any configuration changes that are made, such as additional virtual directories to publish OABs. These changes must be applied after the server recovery process is complete.
- SCC and CCR can be implemented only on servers that are members of clusters prior to the installation of Exchange Server 2007.
- LCR can be implemented on a stand-alone Exchange Server 2007 mailbox server.
- NLB can be used to provide high availability to Client Access servers. Hub Transport servers have resiliency built in, and Edge Transport servers should use DNS round-robin.

Key Terms

Do you know what these key terms mean? You can check your answers by looking up the terms in the glossary at the end of the book.

- Failover
- Local continuous replication

- Network load balancing
- Single Copy Cluster

Case Scenarios

In the following case scenarios, you will apply what you have learned about recovering server roles and configuring high availability. You can find answers to these questions in the "Answers" section at the end of this book.

Case Scenario 1: Recovering the Fabrikam Client Access Server

A colleague who is currently on vacation has been responsible for managing the Exchange infrastructure at a small hovercraft design business named Fabrikam. In your colleague's absence, you have been helping out at Fabrikam with the administration of their Exchange infrastructure. This morning you get a phone call informing you that because of a sprinkler malfunction, the sole Client Access server at Fabrikam has been completely lost. Replacement server hardware is available, but until the Client Access server is recovered or replaced, employees are unable to access their mailboxes.

1. What steps do you need to take prior to using *Setup* with the */m:RecoverServer* option?

2. Communication with the original Client Access server was protected by an SSL certificate issued by a trusted third-party CA. What steps need to be taken to enable secure access to the recovered server?

3. Five custom OABs were published off the default Client Access server virtual directory. What steps need to be taken to make these custom address books available to clients?

Case Scenario 2: A High Availability Solution for Coho Vineyard

You have been asked by the manager of Coho Vineyard to provide some suggestions to ensure that their business-critical Exchange infrastructure can survive certain types of failures. The company manager has e-mailed you some questions that she would like answered when you meet with her to discuss these issues. The questions are as follows:

1. What steps could be taken to ensure that mailboxes remain online in the event of a mailbox server failing completely?

2. What steps can be taken to ensure that Outlook Web Access (OWA) remains available in the event that a Client Access server fails completely?

3. What steps can be taken to ensure that messages can be transferred to and from the Internet in the event that the single Edge Transport server fails completely?

Suggested Practices

To help you successfully master the exam objectives presented in this chapter, complete the following tasks.

Recover Server Roles

Do all the practices in this section.

- **Practice 1: Hub Transport Disaster Recovery Preparation**   Prepare a list of all things that you need to back up on a Hub Transport server so that you can recover from complete server failure.

- Document the steps that you need to take to recover a Hub Transport server using setup with the recovery option, assuming that the previous server is completely unrecoverable.

- **Practice 2: Client Access Server Disaster Recovery Preparation**   Prepare a list of all things that you need to back up on a Client Access server so that you can recover from complete server failure.

- Document the steps that you need to take to recover a Client Access server using setup with the recovery option, assuming that the previous server is completely unrecoverable.

- **Practice 3: Edge Transport Disaster Recovery Preparation**   Prepare a list of all things that you need to back up on an Edge Transport server so that you can recover from complete server failure.

- Document the steps that you need to take to recover an Edge Transport server, assuming that the previous server is completely unrecoverable.

Configure High Availability

Do all the practices in this section.

- **Practice 1: Configure DNS Round-Robin**   Edit the DNS zone entries to configure DNS round-robin for a hypothetical pair of Edge Transport servers.

■ **Practice 2: Configure LCR** Create a new storage group and mailbox database. Attach a USB device to your Exchange Server and configure LCR so that the USB device holds a copy of the storage group and the mailbox database.

Take a Practice Test

The practice tests on this book's companion CD offer many options. For example, you can test yourself on just one exam objective, or you can test yourself on all the 70-236 certification exam content. You can set up the test so that it closely simulates the experience of taking a certification exam, or you can set it up in study mode so that you can look at the correct answers and explanations after you answer each question.

MORE INFO **Practice tests**

For details about all the practice test options available, see the "How to Use the Practice Tests" section in this book's Introduction.

Answers

Chapter 1: Lesson Review Answers

Lesson 1

1. **Correct Answer: D**

   A. **Incorrect:** Although it is a good idea to upgrade existing Windows 2000 server domain controllers to Windows Server 2003, Windows 2000 domain controllers can be used with Exchange Server 2007, though not as global catalog servers.

   B. **Incorrect:** There is no need to upgrade existing Exchange 2000 servers prior to the introduction of Exchange Server 2007.

   C. **Incorrect:** It is not possible to upgrade a computer running Exchange 5.5 to a computer running Exchange Server 2003.

   D. **Correct:** It is not possible to perform a direct upgrade from Exchange 5.5 to Exchange Server 2003; it is possible to migrate data only from Exchange 5.5 to Exchange Server 2003.

2. **Correct Answer: D**

   A. **Incorrect:** As Tailspintoys has a single domain forest and Exchange Server 2007 has already been deployed at another site, there is no need to prepare the schema.

   B. **Incorrect:** As Tailspintoys has a single domain forest and Exchange Server 2007 has already been deployed at another site, there is no need to prepare the domain.

   C. **Incorrect:** 32-bit domain controllers can support Exchange Server 2007 as long as they are running Windows Server 2003 SP1 or later.

   D. **Correct:** Exchange Server 2007 needs a global catalog server at each site where it is deployed. Configuring the Cootamundra domain controller as a global catalog server will meet this requirement.

   E. **Incorrect:** There is no need to promote the file server to domain controller; all that is needed is a global catalog server, and this can be achieved on the existing domain controller.

3. **Correct Answers: A and B**

   A. **Correct:** To run *Setup/PrepareSchema*, your user account needs to be a member of the Enterprise Admins and Schema Admins group.

   B. **Correct:** To run *Setup/PrepareSchema*, your user account needs to be a member of the Enterprise Admins and Schema Admins group.

   C. **Incorrect:** In a forest without an existing Exchange deployment, there will be no Exchange Organization Administrators group.

   D. **Incorrect:** To run *Setup/PrepareSchema*, your user account needs to be a member of the Enterprise Admins and Schema Admins group; it does not need to be a member of the Domain Admins group.

   E. **Incorrect:** To run *Setup/PrepareSchema*, your user account needs to be a member of the Enterprise Admins and Schema Admins group; it does not need to be a member of the Account Operators group.

4. **Correct Answer: C**

   A. **Incorrect:** If there is a preexisting Exchange Server 2003 deployment, you must run *Setup/PrepareLegacyExchangePermissions* prior to preparing the schema or domain.

   B. **Incorrect:** If there is a preexisting Exchange Server 2003 deployment, you must run *Setup/PrepareLegacyExchangePermissions* prior to preparing the schema or domain.

   C. **Correct:** If you are going to introduce Exchange Server 2007 to an environment that hosts an existing Exchange Server 2003 environment, prior to running any other commands you need to run *Setup/PrepareLegacyExchangePermissions*.

   D. **Incorrect:** It is not necessary to run *DCDIAG* prior to Exchange Server 2007 deployment, though this was a step in Exchange Server 2003 deployment.

   E. **Incorrect:** It is not necessary to run *NETDIAG* prior to Exchange Server 2007 deployment, though this was a step in Exchange Server 2003 deployment.

5. **Correct Answer: A**

   A. **Correct:** The hyphen character can be used in an Exchange Server 2007 organization name.

    B. **Incorrect:** The underscore character cannot be used in an Exchange Server 2007 organization name.

    C. **Incorrect:** The colon character cannot be used in an Exchange Server 2007 organization name.

    D. **Incorrect:** The exclamation mark character cannot be used in an Exchange Server 2007 organization name.

    E. **Incorrect:** The percent character cannot be used in an Exchange Server 2007 organization name.

6. **Correct Answer: B**

    A. **Incorrect:** It is necessary to disable link state if multiple routing groups are in use. It is not necessary to disable link state if Outlook Web Access is deployed.

    B. **Correct:** It is necessary to disable link state if multiple routing groups are in use.

    C. **Incorrect:** It is necessary to disable link state if multiple routing groups are in use. It is not necessary to disable link state if multiple administrative groups are in use.

    D. **Incorrect:** It is necessary to disable link state if multiple routing groups are in use. It is not necessary to disable link state if a front-end/back-end configuration is in use.

Lesson 2

1. **Correct Answers: B, C, and E**

    A. **Incorrect:** Server A cannot be promoted, as this was the server that failed.

    B. **Correct:** It is possible to promote a member server functioning as a file and print server to a domain controller.

    C. **Correct:** Although probably not the best server to promote from member server to domain controller because it hosts an SQL Server 2005 instance, it is possible to promote a member server running SQL Server 2005 to domain controller.

    D. **Incorrect:** Server D cannot be promoted, as it is not possible to promote a server from member server to domain controller if Exchange Server 2007 has been installed.

E. **Correct:** It is possible to promote a member server running IIS to domain controller.

2. **Correct Answers: A, B, C, and D**

A. **Correct:** The COM+ Access component needs to be installed if a computer is to be assigned the Mailbox server role.

B. **Correct:** The World Wide Web Service component needs to be installed if a computer is to be assigned the Mailbox server role.

C. **Correct:** The IIS component needs to be installed if a computer is to be assigned the Mailbox server role.

D. **Correct:** Windows PowerShell must be present to install Exchange Server 2007, so it is a necessary component of the software environment if the Mailbox server role is to be assigned.

E. **Incorrect:** ASP.NET version 2.0 is not required for the Mailbox server role.

3. **Correct Answers: C and D**

A. **Incorrect:** Microsoft Core XML Services (MSXML) 6.0 is not required for the installation of Exchange Server 2007. It is also not required for the installation of the Hub Transport server role. This component is required for the assignment of the Unified Messaging server role to an Exchange Server 2007 server.

B. **Incorrect:** RPC over HTTP Proxy is not required for the installation of Exchange Server 2007. It is also not required for the installation of the Hub Transport server role. This component is required for the assignment of the Client Access server role to an Exchange Server 2007 server.

C. **Correct:** The Microsoft .NET Framework version 2.0 is a component that must be installed prior to the installation of Exchange Server 2007.

D. **Correct:** Windows PowerShell is a component that must be installed prior to the installation of Exchange Server 2007.

E. **Incorrect:** Although MMC version 3.0 is required for Exchange Server 2007, Windows Server 2003 R2, the operating system specified in the question, already has this software installed as part of the default installation.

4. **Correct Answer: E**

A. **Incorrect:** The health check requires that Exchange already be deployed.

   B. **Incorrect:** The permissions check requires that Exchange already be deployed.

   C. **Incorrect:** The connectivity test requires that Exchange already be deployed.

   D. **Incorrect:** The baseline check works only on servers that have been deployed.

   E. **Correct:** The Exchange 2007 readiness check is the only relevant check when Exchange Server 2007 has yet to be deployed.

5. **Correct Answer: E**

   A. **Incorrect:** Ping is used to verify connectivity between two hosts.

   B. **Incorrect:** Telnet is an older protocol used for remote administration.

   C. **Incorrect:** Pathping is used to diagnose latency in network paths between two hosts.

   D. **Incorrect:** Tracert is used to display the network path between two hosts.

   E. **Correct:** The *nslookup* command can be used to query a DNS server for MX records. MX records are used to identify mail servers for a DNS zone.

Chapter 1: Case Scenario Answers

Case Scenario 1: Preparing the Active Directory Environment and Network Infrastructure at Tailspintoys for Exchange Deployment

1. If two or more routing groups exist

2. Enterprise Admins

3. At the same Active Directory site as the schema master This can include running the command on the schema master itself.

Case Scenario 2: Preparing a Windows Server 2003 Computer for Exchange Server Installation

1. No, the Core 2 Duo is a 64-bit processor.

2. Approximately 400. Exchange Server has a memory requirement of 2 GB. The server has 4 GB, and each mailbox uses approximately 5 MB of RAM.

3. Install the system volume on the first disk and configure the other two disks in RAID 1.

Chapter 2: Lesson Review Answers

Lesson 1

1. **Correct Answers: B, C, and D**

    A. **Incorrect:** Edge Transport servers are not required at sites. They are deployed on perimeter networks.

    B. **Correct:** Hub Transport, Mailbox, and Client Access servers are required at each Active Directory site in a domain where Exchange has been installed and users are accessing mail.

    C. **Correct:** Hub Transport, Mailbox, and Client Access servers are required at each Active Directory site in a domain where Exchange has been installed and users are accessing mail.

    D. **Correct:** Hub Transport, Mailbox, and Client Access servers are required at each Active Directory site in a domain where Exchange has been installed and users are accessing mail.

    E. **Incorrect:** It is not necessary to deploy the Unified Messaging server role at a site unless the functionality it provides is necessary. No mention was made of voice mail or fax storage in the question text.

2. **Correct Answer: B**

    A. **Incorrect:** You should not deploy a server that has the Edge Transport role installed in a network location directly connected to the Internet. You should place such a server on a perimeter network, which is a network that exists between two firewalls.

    B. **Correct:** Edge Transport servers should be placed on the perimeter network, which is a network that exists between two firewalls.

    C. **Incorrect:** Edge Transport servers should not be placed on an internal network. Mail routing on an internal work is handled by a Hub Transport server.

    D. **Incorrect:** Although networks can be encrypted using IPSec, it is not necessary to deploy an Edge Transport server on an encrypted network.

3. **Correct Answer: B**

   A. **Incorrect:** A code-signing certificate is used to verify the publisher of an application.

   B. **Correct:** An SSL certificate is required to secure communication between OWA and a remote client.

   C. **Incorrect:** Although IPSec is used to secure network communications locally, it is not used to secure network communication between OWA and remote clients.

   D. **Incorrect:** EFS (Encrypted File System) certificates are used to secure data on hard disk drives and cannot be used to secure network communication.

4. **Correct Answer: B**

   A. **Incorrect:** If users use primarily OWA and the processor appears to be overloaded, migrating the Client Access server to another computer will improve performance. The Hub Transport server is responsible primarily for routing mail between sites.

   B. **Correct:** If users primarily use OWA and the processor appears to be overloaded, migrating the Client Access server role to a dedicated server would reduce the performance impact on the original server.

   C. **Incorrect:** The Edge Transport server role is not deployed in this scenario, and the hints in the question point to the Client Access server role being the solution.

   D. **Incorrect:** Given that there seems to be enough disk space and no mention is made of disk queue length in the question, moving the Mailbox server role would not lead to the sort of performance increase that moving the Client Access server role would.

5. **Correct Answer: D**

   A. **Incorrect:** This command will fail. You cannot install the Edge Transport role on a computer that will host other roles.

   B. **Incorrect:** This command will fail. You cannot install the Edge Transport role on a computer that will host other roles.

   C. **Incorrect:** This command will attempt an upgrade when the question specifies an installation. The options in this answer include the Edge Transport role, which can be installed only when no other roles are present.

    D. **Correct:** Although the command *Setup/mode:Install/r:C,M,H,U* will also install the Unified Messaging server role, it will install the Client Access, Mailbox, and Hub Transport roles specified as necessary by the question.

    E. **Incorrect:** This command does not install the Hub Transport role.

6. **Correct Answers: A and B**

    A. **Correct:** The best place to install Forefront is on the Edge and Hub Transport servers. This will allow viruses and spam to be dealt with prior to their reaching user mailboxes.

    B. **Correct:** The best place to install Forefront is on the Edge and Hub Transport servers. This will allow viruses and spam to be dealt with prior to their reaching user mailboxes.

    C. **Incorrect:** You should not install Forefront on the computer hosting the Client Access server role, as this will not block viruses and spam from reaching user mailboxes.

    D. **Incorrect:** You should install Forefront on the Hub and Edge Transport server roles rather than on the computer that hosts the Mailbox server role.

    E. **Incorrect:** You should install Forefront on the Hub and Edge Transport server roles rather than on the computer that hosts the Unified Messaging server role.

Lesson 2

1. **Correct Answer: A**

    A. **Correct:** Configuring cohowinery.com as an authoritative accepted domain means that the server that hosts the Hub Transport role will accept messages sent to cohowinery.com addresses as well as cohovineyard.com addresses.

    B. **Incorrect:** There is no need to alter the settings for cohovineyard.com, as messages already arrive successfully when sent to addresses in that domain.

    C. **Incorrect:** You should not configure an internal relay domain, as there are no other Active Directory forests within the organization.

D. **Incorrect:** Remote domains are used to configure specific message format-ting policies and not to ensure that e-mail sent to a specific domain is accepted.

E. **Incorrect:** Remote domains are used to configure specific message format-ting policies and not to ensure that e-mail sent to a specific domain is accepted.

2. **Correct Answer: B**

A. **Incorrect:** Mailbox size warnings are configured through the Mailbox role. You cannot configure these warnings through the Client Access role.

B. **Correct:** Warnings about mailbox size are configured by editing the prop-erties of the relevant mailbox database. This is done by configuring the Mailbox role.

C. **Incorrect:** Although you can configure messaging format properties on Transport servers, you cannot configure mailbox warning limits.

D. **Incorrect:** Although you can configure messaging format properties on Transport servers, you cannot configure mailbox warning limits.

3. **Correct Answer: B**

A. **Incorrect:** If you add the server to the blocked server list, it will not be accessible to OWA clients.

B. **Correct:** Adding the server to the allow list will grant access to OWA cli-ents. This will change only if the server's name also appears on the block list.

C. **Incorrect:** Although the site secureshare.tailspintoys.internal should be added to the block list, the task requires you to grant access to another site. Unless you deliberately allow access, the secureshare site will still be blocked.

D. **Incorrect:** You should not add the domain suffix to the list of domains that are to be treated as internal, as this will inadvertently allow access to the secureshare site, unless the site is configured on the block list.

E. **Incorrect:** You should not allow access to the secure SharePoint site.

4. **Correct Answer: D**

A. **Incorrect:** One storage group can host a maximum of five mailbox data-bases.

B. **Incorrect:** Two storage groups can host a maximum of 10 mailbox databases.

C. **Incorrect:** Three storage groups can host a maximum of 15 mailbox databases.

D. **Correct:** The enterprise edition of Exchange Server 2007 allows for up to 50 mailbox databases and 50 storage groups; however, a single storage group can host a maximum of only five mailbox databases. Four storage groups can host a maximum of 20 mailbox databases.

E. **Incorrect:** Although five storage groups can host 16 mailbox databases, it is not the minimum number of storage groups that can be used to do so.

5. **Correct Answer: B**

A. **Incorrect:** Although the Edge Transport role has anti-spam features enabled by default, you can't install the Edge Transport role on a server that already has other roles present.

B. **Correct:** By default, the anti-spam features on Hub Transport servers are disabled. They must be enabled from the Exchange Management Shell by issuing the command *Set-TransportServer –Identity 'ServerName' –Antispam-AgentsEnabled $true*.

C. **Incorrect:** Although Forefront does provide anti-spam features for Exchange, the question asked about enabling the built-in features rather than installing an extra product.

D. **Incorrect:** Reinstalling the Hub Transport role will not enable the anti-spam features of Exchange, which are disabled by default.

6. **Correct Answer: D**

A. **Incorrect:** It is not necessary to remove the Client Access server role prior to installing the Mailbox server role.

B. **Incorrect:** It is not necessary to remove the Mailbox server role, as it has already been removed.

C. **Incorrect:** It is not necessary to remove the computer hosting Exchange from the domain and then rejoin it to the domain.

D. **Correct:** Prior to installing the Mailbox server role on a computer that has hosted that role before and since had it removed, you must remove the existing database and log files. If you do not, you will be unable to successfully install the Mailbox server role.

E. **Incorrect:** It is not necessary to reinstall the Client Access server role as this role is already present on the computer.

Chapter 2: Case Scenario Answers

Case Scenario 1: Wingtip Toys Exchange Server 2007 Deployment

1. One. Only one site has a perimeter network, as the other sites are connected to the main site using dedicated ISDN lines.

2. Three. There should be a server hosting the Hub Transport role at each site.

3. Configure the Tailspintoys.com DNS domain as an accepted authoritative domain.

Case Scenario 2: Contoso Postdeployment Role Configuration

1. Configure OWA to forbid the changing of passwords.

2. Configure the block list on the Remote File Servers tab of the OWA Web site properties to block the other two sites. If all the sites are available, it is likely that the internal Contoso domain suffix has been allowed. Alternatively, all three sites might have been added to the allow list, in which case you could remove them from the allow list, though adding them to the block list will achieve the same result.

Chapter 3: Lesson Review Answers

Lesson 1

1. **Correct Answer: C**

    A. **Incorrect:** David is not employed by Lucerne Publishing and does not require a mailbox or an Active Directory user account.

    B. **Incorrect:** There is no indication in the question that David frequently works at Lucerne Publishing's premises or that incoming e-mail needs to be forwarded to his external mailbox.

    C. **Correct:** Creating a mail contact lets Lucerne employees send e-mail to David by specifying his alias in the To line.

D. **Incorrect:** David does not need a user account or a mailbox at Lucerne Publishing, whether the mailbox is disabled or not.

2. **Correct Answer: B**

A. **Incorrect:** Terry has a mailbox at Coho Vineyard and does not require one at Coho Winery.

B. **Correct:** David needs an Active Directory user account so that he can log on to Coho Winery's domain. He is not a Coho Winery employee, and he has a mailbox at Coho Vineyards. He does not, therefore, require a mailbox at Coho Winery.

C. **Incorrect:** Creating a mail contact would not let Terry log on to the Coho Winery domain.

D. **Incorrect:** Terry does not need a mailbox at Coho Winery, whether the mailbox is disabled or not.

3. **Correct Answers: D and E**

A. **Incorrect:** The First Name field is optional. If you enter a value in this field, it is included in the default value for the Alias field.

B. **Incorrect:** The Initials field is optional. If you enter a value in this field, it is included in the default value for the Alias field.

C. **Incorrect:** The Last Name field is optional. If you enter a value in this field, it is included in the default value for the Alias field.

D. **Correct:** The Alias field is mandatory. You can accept the default or enter a new alias.

E. **Correct:** The external e-mail address field is mandatory.

4. **Correct Answer: C**

A. **Incorrect:** The *New-MailUser* cmdlet does not create a new mailbox-enabled user. The *New-Mailbox* cmdlet performs this function.

B. **Incorrect:** This answer is incorrect for the reason given in answer A.

C. **Correct:** The *New-MailUser* cmdlet creates a new mail-enabled user in this command. The ExternalEmailAddress parameter defines the external email address carol.philips@contoso.com.

D. **Incorrect:** The *New-MailUser* cmdlet creates a new mail-enabled user in this command. However, the ExternalEmailAddress parameter defines the external e-mail address carol.philips@contoso.com, not cphilips@tailspin-toys.internal.

5. **Correct Answers: A, C, D, and F**

   A. **Correct:** The Mailbox Database field is on the Mailbox Settings page of the New Mailbox Wizard. If you need to change the default mailbox database, select the mailbox database you want from the list in this field.

   B. **Incorrect:** The Organizational Unit field is on the User Information page of the New Mailbox wizard, not the Mailbox Settings page.

   C. **Correct:** The Alias field is on the Mailbox Settings page of the New Mailbox Wizard. By default, this field contains the user's first and last names, with a dot between the names. You can modify the alias in this field.

   D. **Correct:** The Server field is on the Mailbox Settings page of the New Mailbox Wizard. If you need to change the default server, select the server you want from the list in this field.

   E. **Incorrect**: The User Logon Name (User Principal Name) field is on the User Information page of the New Mailbox Wizard, not the Mailbox Settings page.

   F. **Correct:** The Storage Group field is on the Mailbox Settings page of the New Mailbox Wizard. If you need to change the default storage group, select the storage group you want from the list in this field.

Lesson 2

1. **Correct Answer: B**

   A. **Incorrect:** A security group is used to configure the rights and permissions of its members, and the question does not give this as a requirement. A security group has a fixed membership, and its membership needs to be changed manually. The question does not indicate that you are a member of the domain administration team, so you probably cannot add members to or remove them from a security group.

   B. **Correct:** The membership of a dynamic distribution group depends on filters and conditions. In this case, you could specify users with external e-mail addresses and employees of Trey Research. The group is populated from Active Directory, so consultants who no longer have accounts would not be included.

C. **Incorrect:** You could use a universal distribution group, but you would need to add or remove members manually whenever the consultant group membership changed. This requires additional administrative effort and is not the best solution.

D. **Incorrect**: A security group is not appropriate in this scenario whether it is mail-enabled or not.

2. **Correct Answer: A**

A. **Correct:** You can mail-enable an existing universal security group. However, you have no administrative rights on the domain and cannot add members to a security group.

B. **Incorrect:** You can mail-enable an existing universal security group and create a new mail-enabled security group. However, you cannot add members to a security group or set group permissions.

C. **Incorrect:** As an Exchange Organization Administrator, you can mail-enable a universal security group.

D. **Incorrect**: A universal security group can be mail-enabled. You could create a universal distribution group with the same membership of the sales group, but this would be a lot of extra work and would not be a good solution.

3. **Correct Answer: D**

A. **Incorrect:** If the group is still mail-enabled, then e-mail can still be sent to it, although nobody will receive the messages. This is not what management has asked for.

B. **Incorrect:** If you remove the group completely, you will need to create it from scratch (or perform a recovery operation) when you are asked to reinstate it.

C. **Incorrect:** You cannot change a distribution group type from universal to dynamic. Even if you could, a dynamic distribution group can still receive e-mail.

D. **Correct**: If you disable the group, e-mail cannot be sent to it, but you can mail-enable it later without needing to create the group from scratch.

4. **Correct Answer: B**

A. **Incorrect:** Exchange Management Shell cannot create or mail-enable local security groups.

B. **Correct:** The *New-DistributionGroup* cmdlet creates and mail-enables a universal security group when the Type parameter is set to Security.

C. **Incorrect:** The Type parameter is set to Security. To create a universal distribution group, the Type parameter would need to be set to Distribution.

D. **Incorrect**: The *New-DynamicDistributionGroup* cmdlet creates dynamic distribution groups.

Lesson 3

1. **Correct Answer: C**

   A. **Incorrect:** To enable scheduling, the AutomateProcessing parameter needs to be set to AutoAccept.

   B. **Incorrect:** The *Set-ResourceConfig* cmdlet is used to create custom properties.

   C. **Correct:** This command disables scheduling by setting AutomateProcessing to None.

   D. **Incorrect:** The *Set-ResourceConfig* cmdlet is used to create custom properties. In addition, a custom property for a room mailbox needs to be named in the command.

2. **Correct Answer: A**

   A. **Correct:** Network projectors are fixed resources and do not move from rooms. You should therefore create a resource room mailbox for each room, create a custom resource called NetworkProjector, and add it in each relevant room mailbox's Resource Information tab.

   B. **Incorrect:** Equipment mailboxes are used for mobile equipment that can be located in various locations. In this scenario, the static network projectors are room resources, not vice versa.

   C. **Incorrect:** This will not identify the rooms that have a network projector.

   D. **Incorrect:** Network projectors do not have rights and permissions, and the account associated with a resource mailbox is, in any case, disabled. Security groups are not appropriate in this scenario.

Chapter 3: Case Scenario Answers

Case Scenario 1: Creating Recipients

1. Mailbox-enable Kim's Active Directory user account.

2. Create a contact with the external e-mail address claus.hansen@consolidated-messenger.com.

3. Mail-enable Michelle's Active Directory user account. Specify a user logon name of m.alexander@cohowinery.com and an external address of michelle.alexander@cohovineyard.com.

Case Scenario 2: Creating Mail-Enabled Groups and Resource Mailboxes

1. You should mail-enable the Researchers universal security group and give it a user logon name of Research@baldwinmuseumofscience.com.

2. You should create a dynamic distribution group and specify that group members have external e-mail addresses and work at the university.

3. You should create room mailboxes for all rooms that staff members might want to schedule. You should create a custom resource called AudioVisual and apply it to the rooms that contain audiovisual equipment.

Chapter 4: Lesson Review Answers

1. **Correct Answer: C**

   A. **Incorrect:** This command returns information about the root public folder but not about the public folder hierarchy.

   B. **Incorrect:** This command does exactly the same as the command in answer A.

   C. **Correct:** This command returns information about the root public folder and all public folders under it.

   D. **Incorrect:** This command returns information about all the folders under the root public folder but not about the root public folder itself.

2. **Correct Answer: D**

   A. **Incorrect:** The Identity parameter needs the public folder path. Contoso is a child of the root public folder (\\), so "Contoso" should be "\\Contoso" in the command.

   B. **Incorrect:** This command returns information about Contoso and all public folders in the hierarchy under Contoso. This is not what is required.

   C. **Incorrect:** Contoso is not a system folder and is not in the \\NON_IPM_SUBTREE subtree.

   D. **Correct:** This command returns information about the Contoso public folder and 49 public folders in the hierarchy under Contoso.

3. **Correct Answer: A**

   A. **Correct:** The Path parameter specifies that Meeting Minutes is a child of Management, which in turn is a child of Contoso. New public folders are, by default, not mail-enabled.

   B. **Incorrect:** New public folders are, by default, not mail-enabled. You need to mail-enable them if you want users to be able to send e-mail messages to them.

   C. **Incorrect:** Management is a child of Contoso. It is not a top-level public folder.

   D. **Incorrect:** Meeting Minutes is a child of Management. New public folders are, by default, not mail-enabled.

4. **Correct Answer: A**

   A. **Correct:** The replication schedule specifies from Saturday 12:00 AM (normally, if inaccurately, known as Friday midnight) until Monday 12:00 AM (normally, if inaccurately, known as Sunday midnight).

   B. **Incorrect:** For replication to occur on Saturday, Sunday, and Monday, the replication schedule needs to be "Saturday.12:00 AM-Tuesday.12:00 AM."

   C. **Incorrect:** For replication to occur only on Sunday and Monday, the replication schedule needs to be "Sunday.12:00 AM-Monday.12:00 AM."

   D. **Incorrect:** The *Set-PublicFolder "\\Human Resources" -ReplicationSchedule Always* command specifies that the Human Resources public folder always uses the default replication schedule of the public folder database. Note that to use the command in the question to set custom schedules, you first need to issue the command *Set-PublicFolder "\Human Resources" –UseDatabaseReplicationSchedule $False*.

5. **Correct Answer: B**

   A. **Incorrect:** MyDatabase is a valid name for a public folder database, although it is not a very descriptive one.

   B. **Correct:** When you specify the database name, you can also select the Mount This Database check box. This mounts the database when the wizard finishes. A public folder database needs to exist and be mounted before you can create public folders.

   C. **Incorrect:** Creating a public folder database is one of the few public folder procedures for which you can use either Exchange Management Console or Exchange Management Shell.

   D. **Incorrect:** If you specify that the database is to be mounted, this happens when the wizard finishes. You do not need to restart the server.

6. **Correct Answer: B**

   A. **Incorrect:** You cannot use the Recurse parameter with the *Get-MailPublicFolder* cmdlet.

   B. **Correct:** This returns mail-related information about any public folder with the name Management or the name Management Reports, which is what is required.

   C. **Incorrect:** This returns information about the Management and Management Reports public folders but does not return mail-related information.

   D. **Incorrect:** This returns information about the Management Reports public folders but does not return mail-related information.

Chapter 4: Case Scenario Answers

Case Scenario 1: Creating and Mounting a Public Folder Database

1. By default, a pure Exchange Server 2007 organization with only Microsoft Outlook 2007 clients does not have a public folder database. You need to create and mount such a database. You also need to at least create top-level folders and possibly a folder hierarchy before users can create personal folders.

2. The system folder and public folder hierarchies are subtrees of the same public folder structure within a single public folder database. You cannot create two public folder databases on the same Exchange Server 2007 mailbox server.

3. In Trey Research's pure Exchange 2007 organization, users cannot access public folders by using OWA. You cannot enable a public folder database for OWA. Installing the latest service pack can solve this problem, but it is necessary to check whether service packs are currently supported in the production environment.

Case Scenario 2: Creating, Configuring, and Mail-Enabling Public Folders

1. *New-PublicFolder –Name "Payment Receipts" –Path \Finance\Invoices*

2. *Set-PublicFolder "\Finance\Invoices\Payment Receipts" -UseDatabaseQuota Defaults: $False*
   and
   Set-PublicFolder "\Finance\Invoices\Payment Receipts" -StorageQuota 10MB

3. *Enable-MailPublicFolder "\Finance\Invoices\Payment Receipts"*
   Set-MailPublicFolder "\Finance\Invoices\Payment Receipts" -EmailAddressPolicy-Enabled $False
   and
   Set-MailPublicFolder "\Finance\Invoices\Payment Receipts" -PrimarySmtpAddress Receipts@Contoso.com

Chapter 5: Lesson Review Answers

Lesson 1

1. **Correct Answer: D**

   A. **Incorrect:** The Move Mailbox Wizard uses the OS scheduling facilities and waits until the time selected before sending commands to Exchange Management Shell. One Exchange Management Shell command is generated for each mailbox to be moved.

   B. **Incorrect:** The Move Mailbox Wizard uses the OS scheduling facilities and waits until the time selected before sending commands to Exchange Management Shell.

C. **Incorrect:** One Exchange Management Shell command is generated for each mailbox to be moved. The mailboxes are not all moved simultaneously by a single command.

D. **Correct:** The Move Mailbox Wizard uses the OS scheduling facilities and waits until the time selected before sending commands to Exchange Management Shell. You cannot click Finish to close the console until the mailbox has been moved. A separate command is generated for each mailbox that is moved.

2. **Correct Answer: B**

A. **Incorrect:** Corrupted messages are not moved with a mailbox. If the number of corrupted messages exceeds the bad item limit, the mailbox is not moved.

B. **Correct:** If the number of corrupted messages exceeds the bad item limit, the mailbox is not moved.

C. **Incorrect:** If the number of corrupted messages exceeds the bad item limit, the mailbox is not moved. The bad item limit does not determine the number of bad items that are moved—corrupted messages are not moved with a mailbox.

D. **Incorrect:** If the number of corrupted messages exceeds the bad item limit, the mailbox is not moved. The bad item limit does not determine the number of bad items that are skipped before the remainder of bad items are moved—corrupted messages are not moved with a mailbox.

3. **Correct Answer: D**

A. **Incorrect:** Setting the SourceMailboxCleanupOptions parameter to DeleteSourceMailbox deletes the source mailbox if a mailbox is moved. However, in this case, the mailbox has corrupted messages and will not be moved because the BadItemLimit parameter is not set. In any case, corrupted messages are not moved whether a mailbox is moved or not.

B. **Incorrect:** Setting the SourceMailboxCleanupOptions parameter to DeleteSourceMailbox deletes the source mailbox if a mailbox is moved. However, a mailbox with corrupted messages will not be moved unless the BadItemLimit parameter equals or exceeds the number of corrupted messages. In this case, the BadItemLimit parameter is not set, so no mailbox move occurs. As a result, the source mailbox is not deleted. Corrupted messages are not moved whether a mailbox is moved or not.

C. **Incorrect:** A mailbox with corrupted messages will not be moved unless the BadItemLimit parameter equals or exceeds the number of corrupted messages. In this case, the BadItemLimit parameter is not set, so no mailbox move occurs. As a result, the source mailbox is not deleted.

D. **Correct:** If the number of corrupted messages exceeds the BadItemLimit setting, the mailbox is not moved. In this case, no BadItemLimit setting is specified, so the mailbox is not moved. The SourceMailboxCleanup-Options parameter setting does not affect this situation.

4. **Correct Answer: A**

A. **Correct:** The commands need to be entered at the target forest. The administrator at the target forest must provide the credentials of a user account in the source forest that has the administrative credentials required to move mailboxes.

B. **Incorrect:** Don needs to provide the credentials of a user account in the source forest that has the administrative credentials required to move mailboxes, in this case, Kim's credentials.

C. **Incorrect:** Kim cannot move mailboxes from the source forest by entering commands at this forest. Don needs to do this from the target forest.

D. **Incorrect:** This answer is incorrect for the reason given for answer C.

5. **Correct Answers: B, C, and E**

A. **Incorrect:** You can configure the IssueWarningQuota parameter for an individual mailbox by using the *Set-Mailbox* cmdlet. However, this parameter cannot be specified in the *New-Mailbox* cmdlet. The IssueWarning-Quota parameter specifies the mailbox size at which a warning message is sent to the user.

B. **Correct:** The ActiveSyncMailboxPolicy parameter can be configured when you use the *New-Mailbox* cmdlet to create a mailbox. This parameter specifies the ActiveSync mailbox policy that is enabled for the mailbox.

C. **Correct:** The ManagedFolderMailboxPolicy parameter can be configured when you use the *New-Mailbox* cmdlet to create a mailbox. This parameter specifies the managed folder mailbox policy that is enabled for the mailbox.

D. **Incorrect:** You can configure the MaxReceiveSize parameter for an individual mailbox by using the *Set-Mailbox* cmdlet. However, this parameter cannot be specified in the *New-Mailbox* cmdlet. The MaxReceiveSize parameter specifies the maximum size of messages that the mailbox can receive.

E. **Correct:** The ManagedFolderMailboxPolicyAllowed parameter can be configured when you use the *New-Mailbox* cmdlet to create a mailbox. If you specify this parameter, Exchange Server 2007 server does not warn you that messaging records management features are not supported for e-mail clients using versions of Microsoft Outlook earlier than Outlook 2007.

F. **Incorrect:** You can configure the RejectMessagesFrom parameter for an individual mailbox by using the *Set-Mailbox* cmdlet. However, this parameter cannot be specified in the *New-Mailbox* cmdlet. The RejectMessagesFrom parameter specifies the recipients from whom messages will be rejected.

Lesson 2

1. **Correct Answer: B**

   A. **Incorrect:** The target database is the database Mailbox Database in the storage group Second Storage Group, not the database Mailbox Database in the storage group First Storage Group.

   B. **Correct:** Mailboxes are selected by using the Department attribute "Accounts" and moved to the target database Mailbox Database in the storage group Second Storage Group.

   C. **Incorrect:** The target database is the database Mailbox Database in the storage group Second Storage Group, not the database Mailbox Database in the storage group First Storage Group. Also mailboxes are identified by the user's Department attribute, not by the OU in which the user accounts are stored.

   D. **Incorrect:** It is possible that all the users with a Department attribute "Accounts" are stored in the Accounts OU, but this is not stated in the question. Mailboxes are identified by the user's Department attribute, not by the OU in which the user accounts are stored.

2. **Correct Answer: D**

   A. **Incorrect:** The Name variable ($_.Name) contains the string allocated to it by the CSV file. The space character between first and second names is a part of that string.

   B. **Incorrect:** Name and Department define string variables. The values in these variables do not need to be enclosed in quotation marks.

    C. Incorrect: The commas separate the values for the variables. A CSV file treats a space directly after a comma as an end-of-line character.

    D. Correct: Probably the most common error in CSV files generated by using text editors is unwanted spaces after the comma separators. This is because we are used to putting spaces after commas when writing normal English.

3. **Correct Answer: A**

    A. Correct: The ExShell.psc1 file in the C:\Program Files\Microsoft\ Exchange Server\Bin subdirectory implements Exchange Management Shell as a PowerShell snap-in.

    B. Incorrect: The PowerShell.exe file implements the PowerShell console. It does not implement Exchange Management Shell as a PowerShell snap-in.

    C. Incorrect: PSConsoleFile is not a file. It is a PowerShell parameter that identifies the file and file path for a PowerShell snap-in.

    D. Incorrect: In beta versions of Exchange Server 2007, the ExShell.Mcf1 file implemented Exchange Management Shell as a PowerShell snap-in. However, in the production software, the ExShell.psc1 file is used for this purpose.

4. **Correct Answer: A**

    A. Correct: This lets you define the Identity parameter when you run the PowerShell script. The script then uses the $Identity variable to store the value of the Identity parameter. It moves the identified mailbox and deletes the source mailbox.

    B. Incorrect: You need to define parameters before you use them, not afterward.

    C. Incorrect: This does not permit you to define the Identity parameter. The script would fail because there would be a null value in the $Identity variable.

    D. Incorrect: This lets you define the Identity parameter and moves the appropriate mailbox. However, it does not delete the source mailbox.

5. **Correct Answer: D**

    A. Incorrect: If you select more than one mailbox in Exchange Management Console, the Properties function is no longer available. You cannot schedule changes to mailbox properties in exchange Management Console; you can schedule only mailbox moves. There is no Set Properties Wizard.

B. **Incorrect:** You cannot schedule Exchange Management Shell commands.

C. **Incorrect:** You cannot schedule PowerShell scripts directly in Exchange Management Shell. You need to run Exchange Management Shell from the Command Console and use the Scheduled Tasks applet in Control Panel to schedule this operation.

D. **Correct:** You can schedule tasks that run in the Command Console. Typically, you specify the task in a batch file and schedule when the batch file runs.

Chapter 5: Case Scenario Answers

Case Scenario 1: Configuring and Moving Mailboxes

1. *Get-Mailbox -Database "First Storage Group\Mailbox Database" | Move-Mailbox -TargetDatabase "Second Storage Group\Adatum Employees Mailbox Database" -SourceMailboxCleanupOptions DeleteSourceMailbox*

2. *Set-MailboxDatabase "Second Storage Group\Adatum Employees Mailbox Database" –IssueWarningQuota 4GB*

3. *Move-Mailbox "Kim Akers" -TargetDatabase "Second Storage Group\Adatum Employees Mailbox Database" -SourceMailboxCleanupOptions DeleteSourceMailbox -IgnorePolicyMatch*

Case Scenario 2: Implementing Bulk Management

1. Save the spreadsheet file as a CSV file.

2. You create a CSV file from the text file (similar to the IdentifyUsers.csv file shown in Figure 5-15 earlier in this chapter). You could call the file, for example, UsersTo-Move.csv. Your PowerShell script should then contain the following code:

```
Import-CSV "C:\UsersToMove.csv" | ForEach-Object –Process {Get-Mailbox –Identity
$_.Identity} | Move-Mailbox -TargetDatabase "First Storage Group\Second Contoso Mailbox
Database" -SourceMailboxCleanupOptions DeleteSourceMailbox
```

3. The batch file should contain the following code:

```
PowerShell.exe -PSConsoleFile "C:\Program Files\Microsoft\Exchange
Server\Bin\ExShell.psc1" -Command ". 'C:\Program Files\Microsoft\Exchange
Server\Scripts\ ConfigureQuotas.ps1'"
```

Chapter 6: Lesson Review Answers

Lesson 1

1. **Correct Answer: C**

   A. **Incorrect:** Although the recipient will be informed when an attachment is stripped, the sender will not be.

   B. **Incorrect:** The sender and the recipient are not informed when attachment filtering is set to silent delete.

   C. **Correct:** Setting the attachment filtering behavior action to reject will ensure that the sender is informed that the message containing the attachment has been rejected.

   D. **Incorrect:** Connector exceptions are used to allow specific connectors to be exempt from attachment filtering.

2. **Correct Answer: A**

   A. **Correct:** It is possible to configure a block list entry to expire after a set amount of time.

   B. **Incorrect:** IP block lists override IP allow list. If an item is on both the block list and the allow list, removing it from the allow list will not make a difference to message acceptance.

   C. **Incorrect:** Adding the server's SMTP address to the allow list will not block messages from that address.

   D. **Incorrect:** As messages are being received from the SMTP server's IP address, that address must not be on the block list; hence, it will be impossible to remove.

3. **Correct Answer: C**

   A. **Incorrect:** Attachment filtering is used to remove attachments; it is not used to filter e-mail on the basis of the properties of its sender's address.

   B. **Incorrect:** In this instance, if you blocked the sender's SMTP server's IP address, you would also block incoming e-mail from other clients of your organization.

   C. **Correct:** When using sender filtering, you are able to filter by a specific sender's e-mail address or a sender's e-mail address domain. In this case, you would block the sender's e-mail address domain.

D. **Incorrect:** Recipient filtering works on the basis of who is receiving the message rather than who is sending the message. In this question, you want to configure a filter on the basis of where the message is coming from.

4. **Correct Answer: C**

A. **Incorrect:** Enabling or disabling the Optimize For Performance By Not Rescanning Messages Already Virus Scanned–Transport option will not ensure that messages stored on mailbox servers are rescanned when antivirus definitions are updated.

B. **Incorrect:** Enabling or disabling the Perform Reverse DNS Lookup option will not ensure that messages stored on mailbox servers are rescanned when antivirus definitions are updated.

C. **Correct:** Configuring the Scan On Scanner Update setting forces Forefront Security for Exchange Server to rescan messages stored on a mailbox server for viruses after antivirus definitions have been updated.

D. **Incorrect:** Configuring the Quarantine Messages settings will not ensure that messages stored on mailbox servers are rescanned after antivirus definitions are updated.

5. **Correct Answer: C**

A. **Incorrect:** The Disable All option disables Forefront scans.

B. **Incorrect:** Configuring the Enable Store Scanning option means that only messages located on servers assigned the Mailbox servers role will be scanned and that messages transmitted to hub transport servers will not be scanned.

C. **Correct:** In this situation, you would enable transport scanning. This will ensure that messages are scanned as they are transmitted through hub transport servers but not when they are stored on mailbox servers.

D. **Incorrect:** Although this setting will ensure that messages are scanned as they are transmitted through hub transport servers, it will also ensure that messages are scanned when they are stored on mailbox servers.

6. **Correct Answer: B**

A. **Incorrect:** Stopping anti-spam updates will not allow messages containing the word "Hovercraft" to always pass through the content filter.

B. **Correct:** You should configure the word "Hovercraft" as a nonblocked word on the Custom Words tab of Content Filtering properties. This will ensure that messages containing the word "Hovercraft" are not dropped by your edge transport server.

C. **Incorrect:** If you enter the word "Hovercraft" as a blocked word, messages containing the word will automatically be blocked.

D. **Incorrect:** Exempting the address hovercraft@tailspintoys.com will not ensure that messages containing the word "Hovercraft" will always pass through the content filter.

Lesson 2

1. **Correct Answer: A**

A. **Correct:** Managed content settings allow you to specify the retention period for messages in a managed folder. It is also possible to specify what is to be done with messages when the retention period expires. It is possible to configure messages to be moved to another managed folder where they could be reviewed before being permanently deleted.

B. **Incorrect:** Transport rules apply only to messages being passed through hub or edge transport servers. They do not apply to messages that have been stored for some time in mailboxes.

C. **Incorrect:** Retention hold is a method by which records management can be temporarily disabled.

D. **Incorrect:** A managed folder mailbox policy is used to collect managed folders into logical groupings; it is not used to specify retention policies.

2. **Correct Answers: B and D**

A. **Incorrect:** It is not necessary to install IIS on hub transport server to implement Windows Rights Management Services.

B. **Correct:** It is necessary to install the Windows Rights Management Services Client with SP2 and enable the Active Directory Rights Management Services Prelicensing Agent on each hub transport server to ensure that message classifications restricting access work.

C. **Incorrect:** It is necessary to install only one Windows Rights Management Services server in an organization. It is not necessary to install the server on each hub transport server.

D. **Correct:** It is necessary to install the Windows Rights Management Services Client with SP2 and enable the Active Directory Rights Management

Services Prelicensing Agent on each hub transport server to ensure that message classifications restricting access work.

    E. **Incorrect:** It is not necessary to install IPSec on each hub transport server to get Windows Rights Management Services to work.

3. **Correct Answer: B**

    A. **Incorrect:** Messages marked A/C privilege have a banner that informs readers that the message contains privileged information. This will not stop the message being read by users in the way that a message marked company confidential would be.

    B. **Correct:** Messages classified as company confidential can be opened only by individuals assigned the correct permissions through Windows Rights Management Services.

    C. **Incorrect:** Messages marked as company internal cannot be sent to external addresses but can be opened by anyone from within the organization.

    D. **Incorrect:** Messages marked with no restriction can be opened by anyone within the company and can be transmitted to people outside the organization.

4. **Correct Answer: C**

    A. **Incorrect:** If a new rule is created, the existing rule will still be in effect.

    B. **Incorrect:** If the existing rule is edited so that Sam Abolrous's account is a condition, the rule will apply only to messages from Sam Abolrous.

    C. **Correct:** If you want to have a transport rule apply to everyone except a small number of people, configure those people's user accounts as exceptions to the rule.

    D. **Incorrect:** If a new rule is created, the existing rule will still be in effect and will still apply.

5. **Correct Answer: A**

    A. **Correct:** If the message is blind carbon copied, the CEO will receive the message without the senior manager being aware that his communication is being monitored.

    B. **Incorrect:** If a recipient is added, both the senior manager and the person to whom the message is being sent will be aware that the message is being forwarded to the CEO.

C. **Incorrect:** If all the senior manager's e-mails are redirected, it will become clear this his communication is being monitored, as none of it will reach its destination.

D. **Incorrect:** If all the senior manager's e-mails are dropped, the CEO won't know their contents, and the senior manager may suspect he is under surveillance because none of his e-mails are getting through.

6. **Correct Answer: D**

A. **Incorrect:** Legal disclaimers cannot be added by configuring accepted domain settings; they are added by configuring transport rules.

B. **Incorrect:** Legal disclaimers cannot be added by configuring e-mail address policies; they are added by configuring transport rules.

C. **Incorrect:** Legal disclaimers cannot be added by configuring filtering rules; they are added by configuring transport rules.

D. **Correct:** Legal disclaimers can be added to messages by configuring transport rules on hub transport servers.

Chapter 6: Case Scenario Answers

Case Scenario 1: Exchange Server 2007 as an Anti-Spam Solution for Coho Vineyard

1. Sender reputation can be automatically configured to block the IP address of SMTP servers that repeatedly send spam to the organization.

2. Add the IP address of the customer's SMTP servers to the IP allow list.

3. Add the explicit words to the blocked list on the Custom Words tab of Content Filtering Properties.

Case Scenario 2: Configuring Message and Transport Compliance for a Law Firm

1. Message classification. An attorney–client message classification, which is one of three classifications built into Exchange Server 2007, provides a banner that explains that the message contains privileged information.

2. Configure a transport rule that redirects messages that contain text involving the celebrity's name to the directors of the law firm.

3. Configure a transport rule that inserts the appropriate text on outgoing messages.

Chapter 7: Lesson Review Answers

Lesson 1

1. **Correct Answer: D**

   A. **Incorrect:** By default, Send and Receive connectors are created when you install the Edge Transport server role.

   B. **Incorrect:** By default Send and Receive connectors are created when you install the Edge Transport server role.

   C. **Incorrect:** It is not necessary to re-create the Edge subscription for an existing Edge Transport server if another Edge Transport server is added. It is necessary to re-create the subscription if you add an additional Hub Transport server.

   D. **Correct:** By default, the necessary connectors are created when you install an Edge Transport server. Even though this is the case, messages cannot flow until the server undergoes the Edge subscription process.

2. **Correct Answer: B**

   A. **Incorrect:** The Client usage type allows clients such as Outlook to communicate with Hub Transport servers.

   B. **Correct:** The Internal usage type uses Exchange Server authentication as its default authentication mechanism. This authentication type is used to allow Exchange servers within the organization to communicate with each other.

   C. **Incorrect:** The Internet usage type does not use authentication.

   D. **Incorrect:** The Partner usage type uses mutual TLS authentication.

3. **Correct Answer: C**

   A. **Incorrect:** You would use the Internal rather than Internet usage type in this situation.

   B. **Incorrect:** The Client usage type is used to allow clients to send messages.

   C. **Correct:** The Internal usage type is used to allow legacy Exchange bridgehead servers to communicate with Hub Transport servers.

   D. **Incorrect:** The Partner usage type is used to allow external partners to transmit messages directly to an organization. You would not implement this usage type to allow a legacy Exchange bridgehead server to connect to a Hub Transport server.

4. **Correct Answer: A**

   A. **Correct:** Send connectors are created at the organizational level. This means that you need to create them only once.

   B. **Incorrect:** Unlike Receive connectors, Send connectors need to be created only once, as their configuration data is stored within Active Directory.

   C. **Incorrect:** Unlike Receive connectors, Send connectors need to be created only once, as their configuration data is stored within Active Directory.

   D. **Incorrect:** Unlike Receive connectors, Send connectors need to be created only once, as their configuration data is stored within Active Directory.

   E. **Incorrect:** Unlike Receive connectors, Send connectors need to be created only once, as their configuration data is stored within Active Directory.

5. **Correct Answer: C**

   A. **Incorrect:** An Internal Send connector is used to forward message data to mail servers within the organization.

   B. **Incorrect:** An Internal Receive connector is used to receive message from servers within the organization.

   C. **Correct:** An Internet Send connector can be used to forward mail to a smart host that will in turn forward the messages to a specific external organization.

   D. **Incorrect:** Internet Receive connectors are used to receive message traffic from sources outside the organizational network.

6. **Correct Answer: C**

   A. **Incorrect:** The correct syntax is *open mail.server.hostname 25*. Mail.contoso.com is the host name of the mail server, and port 25 is the SMTP server port. This answer is incorrect because the mail server name is incorrect.

   B. **Incorrect:** The correct syntax is *open mail.server.hostname 25*. Mail.contoso.com is the host name of the mail server, and port 25 is the SMTP server port. This answer is incorrect because port 23 is specified instead of port 25.

   C. **Correct:** The correct syntax is *open mail.server.hostname 25*. Mail.contoso.com is the host name of the mail server, and port 25 is the SMTP server port.

D. **Incorrect:** The correct syntax is *open mail.server.hostname 25.* Mail.con-toso.com is the host name of the mail server, and port 25 is the SMTP server port. This answer is incorrect because SMTP is used instead of OPEN.

E. **Incorrect:** The correct syntax is *open mail.server.hostname 25.* Mail.con-toso.com is the host name of the mail server, and port 25 is the SMTP server port. This answer is incorrect because SMTP is used instead of OPEN.

Lesson 2

1. **Correct Answer: E**

    A. **Incorrect:** The time without user input setting defines the amount of time that a device is not used before it is necessary for a password to be reentered.

    B. **Incorrect:** Password Expiration defines the maximum age of a password before it needs to be changed.

    C. **Incorrect:** Enable Password Recovery allows a password to be recovered in the event that it is forgotten.

    D. **Incorrect:** The Require Encryption setting is used to ensure that all data stored on the device is encrypted.

    E. **Correct:** The Number Of Failed Attempts Allowed setting allows you to configure a device to delete all user data and reset itself to its default con-figuration if a specified number of incorrect passwords are entered in succession.

2. **Correct Answer: C**

    A. **Incorrect:** User account passwords are independent of device passwords.

    B. **Incorrect:** Disabling ActiveSync will not recover David's password.

    C. **Correct:** You can learn the recovery password for David's device using the Exchange Management Shell command *Get-ActiveSyncDeviceStatistics -Mailbox:"alias" -ShowRecoveryPassword:$true.*

    D. **Incorrect:** Performing a remote wipe will remove all of David's data, which is what he is trying to avoid.

3. **Correct Answer: B**

    A. **Incorrect:** IPSec certificates do not use subject alternative names.

    B. **Correct:** For the Autodiscover service to work for Outlook 2007 clients that are remotely connecting using Outlook Anywhere, you must ensure that the SSL certificate is configured with a subject alternative name that matches autodiscover.domain.name, where domain.name is the organization's DNS suffix.

   C. **Incorrect:** EFS certificates do not use subject alternative names and are not used by Outlook Anywhere or the Autodiscover service.

   D. **Incorrect:** Outlook Anywhere with Autodiscover does not use client certificates, which are generally used for authentication.

4. **Correct Answer: C**

   A. **Incorrect:** Outlook Anywhere is the new name for RPC over HTTP and allows clients on the Internet to connect to Exchange without using a VPN.

   B. **Incorrect:** Although IMAP4 is a client access protocol, it will not automatically update free/busy calendar data.

   C. **Correct:** The Availability service allows Outlook 2007 clients to receive automatic updates when there are changes to free/busy data.

   D. **Incorrect:** Although POP3 is a client access protocol, it will not automatically update free/busy calendar data.

5. **Correct Answer: D**

   A. **Incorrect:** The appropriate command syntax is *CASMailbox -Identity kim_akers@tailspintoys.internal −IMAP4Enabled $false*.

   B. **Incorrect:** The appropriate command syntax is *CASMailbox -Identity kim_akers@tailspintoys.internal −IMAP4Enabled $false*.

   C. **Incorrect:** The appropriate command syntax is *CASMailbox -Identity kim_akers@tailspintoys.internal −IMAP4Enabled $false*.

   D. **Correct:** This command will disable IMAP4 for Kim Akers's user account.

Chapter 7: Case Scenario Answers

Case Scenario 1: Contoso Connector Configuration

1. Partner Receive connector.

2. Internet Send connector.

3. Specify the connector to accept only traffic from IP addresses associated with Fabrikam servers.

Case Scenario 2: Coho Vineyard Mobile Devices

1. The phones should be running Windows Mobile 6.0 or later. In the event that they are running Windows Mobile 5, it will be necessary to install the Messaging and Security Feature Pack.

2. The Autodiscover feature can be used to provision mobile devices in the same way that it can be used to provision Outlook 2007 clients.

3. Force the data to be encrypted, require the device to use a password, and configure the device to be remotely wiped if the incorrect password is entered multiple times in succession.

Chapter 8: Lesson Review Answers

Lesson 1

1. **Correct Answers: B, C, and E**

   A. **Incorrect:** Although being a member of the Exchange Organization Administrators role will allow use of the *Test-ExchangeSearch* cmdlet, the role confers more privileges than are necessary.

   B. **Correct:** To use the *Test-ExchangeSearch* cmdlet, a user account must be a member of the Exchange Recipient Administrator role and the Exchange Server Administrator role on each mailbox server and be a member of the Local Administrators group on each mailbox server.

   C. **Correct:** To use the *Test-ExchangeSearch cmdlet*, a user account must be a member of the Exchange Recipient Administrator role and the Exchange Server Administrator role on each mailbox server and be a member of the Local Administrators group on each mailbox server.

   D. **Incorrect:** Members of the Exchange View-Only Administrator role do not have enough privileges to utilize the *Test-ExchangeSearch* cmdlet.

   E. **Correct:** To use the *Test-ExchangeSearch* cmdlet, a user account must be a member of the Exchange Recipient Administrator role and the Exchange Server Administrator role on each mailbox server and be a member of the Local Administrators group on each mailbox server.

2. **Correct Answer: B**

   A. **Incorrect:** The command *Set-Mailbox "Kim Akers" –ExternalOofOptions External* will allow out-of-office messages to be sent by Kim to recipients outside the organization.

  B. **Correct:** The command *Set-Mailbox "Kim Akers" –ExternalOofOptions InternalOnly* will configure Kim's mailbox so that out-of-office messages cannot be sent to recipients external to the organization.

  C. **Incorrect:** Just as it is possible to configure out-of-office settings on a per-mailbox basis, it is also possible to set them for all users on a per-remote-domain basis. Configuring these settings on a per-remote-domain basis will not configure them specifically for Kim Akers's user account.

  D. **Incorrect:** Just as it is possible to configure out-of-office settings on a per-mailbox basis, it is also possible to set them for all users on a per-remote-domain basis. Configuring these settings on a per-remote-domain basis will not configure them specifically for Kim Akers's user account.

3. **Correct Answer: B**

  A. **Incorrect:** The command will not update the contents of the default OAB but will change the default OAB to the one named NewOAB.

  B. **Correct:** The Exchange Management Shell command *Set-OfflineAddressBook –Identity NewOAB –IsDefault %true* will set the default OAB to NewOAB.

  C. **Incorrect:** The command will not move the default OAB but will change the default OAB to the one named NewOAB.

  D. **Incorrect:** The command will not reindex the default OAB but will change the default OAB to the one named NewOAB.

4. **Correct Answer: D**

  A. **Incorrect:** The use of %s%1g in the command means that the entire surname and the first letter of the given name will be used in the SMTP address. This answer would require the string %g.%s@cohovineyard.com.

  B. **Incorrect:** The use of %s%1g in the command means that the entire surname and the first letter of the given name will be used in the SMTP address. This answer would require the string %g1.%s@cohovineyard.com.

  C. **Incorrect:** The use of %s%1g in the command means that the entire surname and the first letter of the given name will be used in the SMTP address. This answer would require the string %s.%g@cohovineyard.com.

  D. **Correct:** The use of %s%1g in the command means that the entire surname and the first letter of the given name will be used in the SMTP address.

5. **Correct Answer: A**

    A. **Correct:** To configure the appropriate access, the UNCAccessEnabled parameter needs to be set to $false, and the WSSAccessEnabled parameter needs to be set to $true.

    B. **Incorrect:** This answer is incorrect because access is granted to the Windows File Shares.

    C. **Incorrect:** This answer is incorrect because access is granted to the Windows File Shares and access blocked to SharePoint sites.

    D. **Incorrect:** This answer is incorrect because access is blocked to SharePoint sites.

6. **Correct Answer: A**

    A. **Correct:** If a mixture of Windows Mobile devices is being used, it is possible that some of these devices are running versions of the Windows Mobile operating system that are not fully compliant with Exchange ActiveSync mailbox policies. If the policy is set so that nonprovisionable devices are unable to sync, these devices will be unable to successfully complete the ActiveSync process.

    B. **Incorrect:** The blocking of nonprovisionable devices is the cause of the problem in this question, not its solution.

    C. **Incorrect:** This problem is related to the blocking of nonprovisionable devices and is not related to passwords.

    D. **Incorrect:** This problem is related to the blocking of nonprovisionable devices and is not related to passwords.

Lesson 2

1. **Correct Answer: A**

    A. **Correct:** The *Set-MailPublicFolder* cmdlet is used to configure mail-related public folder settings.

    B. **Incorrect:** *Enable-MailPublicFolder* enables messages to be sent using e-mail on the public folder. This cmdlet is not used to configure mail-related settings.

    C. **Incorrect:** *Add-PublicFolderClientPermission* is used to add permissions to the public folder. This cmdlet is not used to configure mail-related settings.

D. **Incorrect:** The *Set-PublicFolderDatabase* cmdlet is used to configure the attributes of public folders. Mail-related settings are configured at the public folder level rather than at the public folder database level.

2. **Correct Answer: D**

   A. **Incorrect:** This command will configure a public folder to accept only messages from a specific distribution list. It is not used to forward public folder messages to another address.

   B. **Incorrect:** This command is not distribution list related.

   C. **Incorrect:** This command is not distribution list related.

   D. **Correct:** This command will configure a public folder to accept only messages from a specific distribution list.

3. **Correct Answer: C**

   A. **Incorrect:** Although the *Set-PublicFolderDatabase* cmdlet can be used to configure settings such as replication period and schedule, it cannot be used to configure the specific public folders that will be replicated.

   B. **Incorrect:** The *Set-MailPublicFolder* cmdlet is used to configure mail settings. It cannot be used to configure replication settings.

   C. **Correct:** The *Set-PublicFolder* cmdlet can be used to create replicas of the public folder on appropriately configured mailbox servers.

   D. **Incorrect:** The *Update-PublicFolder* cmdlet is used to start content synchronization; it cannot be used to configure the specific public folders that will be replicated.

4. **Correct Answers: A and C**

   A. **Correct:** The replication schedule of a public folder can be set on both the public folder and the public folder database level. To set it on the public folder database level, use with the *Set-PublicFolderDatabase* cmdlet.

   B. **Incorrect:** The *Update-PublicFolder* cmdlet is used to initiate synchronization but cannot be used to set an actual schedule.

   C. **Correct:** The replication schedule of a public folder can be set on both the public folder and the public folder database level. To set it on the public folder level, use with the *Set-PublicFolder* cmdlet.

   D. **Incorrect:** The *Set-MailPublicFolder* cmdlet is used to configure mail-related properties and cannot be used to configure the replication schedule of a public folder.

   E. **Incorrect:** Although *New-PublicFolder* can be used to set a folder's initial replication schedule, it cannot be used to modify the schedule of an existing public folder.

5. **Correct Answer: C**

   A. **Incorrect:** You cannot use the *Add-PublicFolderAdministrativePermission* cmdlet to view administrator permissions assigned to a public folder.

   B. **Incorrect:** The *Get-PublicFolderClientPermission* cmdlet will display client permissions to a public folder but will not display administrator permissions for the folder.

   C. **Correct:** The *Get-PublicFolderAdministrativePermission* cmdlet will allow you to view the administrator permissions assigned to a particular public folder.

   D. **Incorrect:** You cannot use the *Add-PublicFolderClientPermission* cmdlet to view administrator permissions assigned to a public folder.

Chapter 8: Case Scenario Answers

Case Scenario 1: Address Lists at Coho Vineyard

1. Create an address list tailored to the Barossa Valley region.

2. You could configure an address list that uses the Recipient is in a Department option and set that option to Distributor.

3. No steps need to be taken. All Rooms is one of the default address lists.

Case Scenario 2: Public Folder Management at Fabrikam

1. Configure public folder client permissions.

2. Configure public folder administrator permissions.

3. Configure the public folder database replication settings. Configure the public folder database replication settings rather than the replication settings of each public folder.

Chapter 9: Lesson Review Answers

Lesson 1

1. **Correct Answers: A and D**

    A. **Correct:** Servers with the Hub Transport role installed implement internal routing of all messages. Servers with this role are transport servers, and Queue Viewer can connect to them.

    B. **Incorrect:** Servers with the Client Access role installed proxy Internet client traffic to the correct mailbox server (similar to the front-end server in earlier versions of Exchange). Queue Viewer cannot connect to such servers unless the Hub Transport role is also installed.

    C. **Incorrect:** Servers with the Mailbox role installed host user mailboxes. Queue Viewer cannot connect to such servers unless the Hub Transport role is also installed.

    D. **Correct:** Servers with the Edge Transport role installed are located outside an organization's internal network and provide on-premise e-mail security, antivirus, and anti-spam services for Exchange. Servers with this role are transport servers, and Queue Viewer can connect to them.

    E. **Incorrect:** Servers with the Unified Messaging role implement private branch exchange integration, which enables voice mail and fax messages to be delivered to Exchange mailboxes and provides voice dial-in capabilities to Exchange Server. Queue Viewer cannot connect to such servers unless the Hub Transport role is also installed.

2. **Correct Answer: D**

    A. **Incorrect:** The unreachable queue contains messages that cannot be routed to their destinations. It does not hold all messages that are received by a transport server before processing.

    B. **Incorrect:** A remote delivery queue holds messages that are being delivered to a remote server by using SMTP. It does not hold all messages that are received by a transport server before processing.

    C. **Incorrect:** A mailbox delivery queue holds messages that are delivered to a mailbox server by using encrypted Exchange RPC. It does not hold all messages that are received by a transport server before processing.

D. **Correct:** All messages that are received by a transport server are held in the Submission queue before processing. The categorizer uses the submission queue to store messages that need to be resolved, routed, and processed by transport agents.

3. **Correct Answer: B**

A. **Incorrect:** The *Remove-Message* cmdlet removes a message. It does not suspend it. Messages cannot be exported to queues, only to folders.

B. **Correct:** By default, the WithNDR parameter is set to &True, and NDRs are sent when a message is removed. If you did not want to send an NDR, you would need to add *-WithNDR $False* to the command.

C. **Incorrect:** The *Remove-Message* cmdlet removes the specified message. By default, the WithNDR parameter is set to &True, and NDRs are sent when a message is removed.

D. **Incorrect:** The *Remove-Message* cmdlet removes the specified message. There is no Exchange Management Shell cmdlet that transfers messages between queues.

4. **Correct Answer: C**

A. **Incorrect:** The *-ge* operator specifies "greater than or equal to." All messages with an SCL of 6 or greater are listed. Therefore, all messages with an SCL of 6 will be in the list.

B. **Incorrect:** The *-ge* operator specifies "greater than or equal to." All messages with an SCL of 6 or greater are listed.

C. **Correct:** The *-ge* operator specifies "greater than or equal to." All messages with an SCL of 6 or greater are listed. Therefore, all messages with an SCL less than 6 will not be in the list.

D. **Incorrect:** The *-ge* operator specifies "greater than or equal to." All messages with an SCL of 6 or greater are listed. Therefore, all messages with an SCL greater than 6 will be in the list.

5. **Correct Answer: D**

A. **Incorrect:** The MSExchangeIS performance object does not provide a Messages Queued For Submission counter.

B. **Incorrect:** The MSExchangeIS performance object does not provide a Receive Queue Size counter.

C. **Incorrect:** The MSExchangeIS Mailbox:Messages Queued For Submission counter returns the current number of submitted messages that are not yet processed by transport.

D. **Correct:** The MSExchangeIS Mailbox:Receive Queue Size counter returns the number of messages in the mailbox store's receive queue.

Lesson 2

1. **Correct Answer: C**

    A. **Incorrect:** The system log stores system events that are logged by Windows Server and Windows Server system services. Triggered alerts write events to the application log, not the system log.

    B. **Incorrect:** The security log stores security-related audit events. Triggered alerts write events to the application log, not the security log.

    C. **Correct:** Triggered alerts write events to the application log.

    D. **Incorrect:** The directory services log, found only on domain controllers, stores events related to the Active Directory directory service. Triggered alerts write events to the application log, not the directory services log.

2. **Correct Answer: A**

    A. **Correct:** The average value in the % Processor Time counter should not exceed 85 percent. However, the value in this counter frequently exceeds this value and typically reaches 100 percent whenever a program starts. The alert your colleague has configured triggers frequently during normal processor operation.

    B. **Incorrect:** An alert on a value in the % Processor Time greater than 85 percent triggers frequently during normal processor operation. There is no indication that the alert has been incorrectly configured.

    C. **Incorrect:** An alert on a value in the % Processor Time greater than 85 percent triggers frequently during normal processor operation. There is no indication that the processor resource is under stress.

    D. **Incorrect:** It is probably a good idea to have more than one processor. However, it is not essential, and the lack of a second processor is not the reason that the alert is triggering.

3. **Correct Answer: C**

   A. **Incorrect:** The application log stores error, warning, and information events.

   B. **Incorrect:** The directory service log stores error, warning, and information events.

   C. **Correct:** The security log stores audit success and audit failure events. It does not store error events.

   D. **Incorrect:** The system log stores error, warning, and information events.

4. **Correct Answer: D**

   A. **Incorrect:** HTTPMon monitors Web servers. It is used in an Exchange Server 2007 organization to monitor OWA servers. It does not capture or display network traffic.

   B. **Incorrect:** Performance Logs and Alerts allows you to create logs that capture performance counter values and configure alerts that trigger when a counter value exceeds or goes below a specified threshold limit. It does not capture or display network traffic.

   C. **Incorrect:** System Monitor displays performance counter values in real time or values captured in performance logs. It does not capture or display network traffic.

   D. **Correct:** Network Monitor captures and displays network traffic on a specified interface. You can set a capture filter so that it captures RPC traffic.

5. **Correct Answer: B**

   A. **Incorrect:** Mail Flow Troubleshooter asks you to input the symptoms of a mail flow problem and moves you through the correct troubleshooting path. It does not analyze the symptom that the number of RPC operations per second is higher than expected.

   B. **Correct:** In Performance Troubleshooter, one of the symptoms you can select is that the number of RPC operations per second is higher than expected. The tool will analyze this problem and suggest possible solutions.

   C. **Incorrect:** Best Practices Analyzer gathers and verifies configuration information. It does not analyze the symptom that the number of RPC operations per second is higher than expected.

   D. **Incorrect:** Database Recovery Management searches Exchange Server 2007 databases and available transaction log files for issues that affect database recoverability. It does not analyze the symptom that the number of RPC operations per second is higher than expected.

6. **Correct Answer: B**

   A. **Incorrect:** ID is a patameter and needs to be preceded by the "-" character.

   B. **Correct:** This lists all events in the application log with EventID 1022.

   C. **Incorrect:** No default is set for the ID parameter, so you need to specify it in the command line.

   D. **Incorrect:** There is no Log parameter, and you cannot specify a log other than application.

Chapter 9: Case Scenario Answers

Case Scenario 1: Checking Message Queues

1. The remote delivery queue for contoso.com

2. The poison message queue

3. *Remove-Message −Filter {SCL −ge 5} -WithNDR $False*

Case Scenario 2: Monitoring Exchange Server 2007 Servers

1. Message Tracking is part of Exchange Troubleshooting Assistant, and Keith needs to install this software. However, he first needs to install .NET Framework. Alternatively, you could advise Keith to check out the *Get-MessageTrackingLog* PowerShell cmdlet.

2. Don should click Toolbox Exchange Management Console and open the Database Recovery Management tool. He can create a recovery storage group from the Task Center in this tool.

3. Network Monitor.

Chapter 10: Lesson Review Answers

Lesson 1

1. **Correct Answer: C**

   A. **Incorrect:** The Recipients search filter uses the recipient-address field. Multiple recipient values can be specified by using commas as delimiters.

B. **Incorrect:** The Sender search filter uses the sender's e-mail address as specified in the Sender header field or in the From header field if Sender is not present.

C. **Correct:** The Start and End search filters specify a start date and time and an end date and time. However Date is not itself a search filter.

D. **Incorrect:** The Server search filter contains the name of the Mailbox server on which the sender's mailbox resides.

E. **Incorrect:** The EventId search filter uses the event classification that is assigned to each message tracking log entry. Available values are BADMAIL, DELIVER, DEFER, DSN, EXPAND, FAIL, POISONMESSAGE, RECEIVE, REDIRECT, RESOLVE, SEND, SUBMIT, and TRANSFER.

F. **Incorrect:** The MessageID search filter uses the value in the Message-ID header field. If the Message-ID header field does not exist or is blank, an arbitrary value is assigned.

G. **Incorrect:** The InternalMessageID uses the value of a message identifier integer that is assigned by the Exchange Server 2007 server that is currently processing the message.

2. **Correct Answer: A**

A. **Correct:** This command disables message subject logging on the transport server Edinburgh.

B. **Incorrect:** This command enables message subject logging on the transport server Edinburgh if it is currently disabled. You want to disable message subject logging, not enable it.

C. **Incorrect:** The Exchange Server 2007 server has the Edge Transport server role installed. Therefore, it is a transport server. It cannot have the Message server role installed because no additional server roles can be installed on a server that has the Edge Transport server role installed. You cannot use commands based on the *Get-MessageServer* cmdlet on this server.

D. **Incorrect:** This answer is incorrect for the reason given for answer C. Also, the MessageTrackingLogSubjectLoggingEnabled parameter needs to be set to $False, not $True.

3. **Correct Answers: A and D**

A. **Correct:** This command ensures that mailbox log tracking files will never be removed by circular logging because they have reached their maximum age.

B. **Incorrect:** The MessageTrackingLogMaxAge cannot take the value $False. You need to set it to be infinite by using the value 00:00:00.

C. **Incorrect:** This command ensures that mailbox log tracking files will be very old indeed before they are removed by circular logging because they have reached their maximum age. However, the question stipulates that you need to guarantee they will never be removed because they have reached their maximum age.

D. **Correct:** This command ensures that transport log tracking files will never be removed by circular logging because they have reached their maximum age.

E. **Incorrect:** This answer is incorrect for the reason given for answer B.

F. **Incorrect:** This answer is incorrect for the reason given for answer C.

Lesson 2

1. **Correct Answer: D**

    A. **Incorrect:** The Identity parameter in commands based on the *Get-Mailbox-Statistics* cmdlet can take the value of only a single mailbox.

    B. **Incorrect:** This answer is incorrect for the reason given for answer A.

    C. **Incorrect:** This command gets statistics for the three mailboxes but displays them in list format, not table format.

    D. **Correct.** This displays the statistics in the required format. The pipe to Format-Table is optional because this is the default.

2. **Correct Answer: A**

    A. **Correct:** This command returns statistics for mailboxes with a total item size greater than or equal to 1 GB or with a total item count greater than or equal to 5,000 (or both).

    B. **Incorrect:** This command returns statistics for mailboxes with a total item size exactly equal to 1 GB or with a total item count exactly equal to 5,000 (or both).

    C. **Incorrect:** This command returns statistics for mailboxes that have a total item size greater than or equal to 1 GB and also have a total item count greater than or equal to 5,000.

    D. **Incorrect.** This command returns statistics for mailboxes that have a total item size exactly equal to 1 GB and also have total item count exactly equal to 5,000.

3. **Correct Answers: C, D, E, F, H, and I**

    A. **Incorrect.** The Local Deliveries counter returns the total number of messages delivered locally. The question does not ask for this information.

    B. **Incorrect:** The Local Delivery Rate counter returns the rate at which messages are delivered locally. The question does not ask for this information.

    C. **Correct:** The Message Recipients Delivered counter returns the total number of recipients that have received a message since startup. The question asks for this information.

    D. **Correct:** The Message Recipients Delivered/sec counter returns the rate that recipients receive messages. The question asks for this information.

    E. **Correct:** The Messages Delivered counter returns the total number of messages delivered to all recipients since startup. The question asks for this information.

    F. **Correct:** The Messages Delivered/sec counter returns the rate that messages are delivered to all recipients. The question asks for this information.

    G. **Incorrect:** The Logon Operations/sec counter returns the rate of logon requests in the mailbox store. The question does not ask for this information.

    H. **Correct:** The Messages Sent counter returns the total number of messages sent to transport since startup. The question asks for this information.

    I. **Correct:** The Messages Sent/sec counter returns the rate that messages are sent to the transport. The question asks for this information.

4. **Correct Answer: B**

    A. **Incorrect:** You use the *Set-TransportServer* cmdlet, not the *Set-SendConnector* cmdlet, to enable or disable protocol logging on the intra-organization Send connector.

    B. **Correct:** This command enables protocol logging on the intra-organization Send connector of the specified server.

C. **Incorrect:** This answer is incorrect for the reason given for answer A. In addition, to enable protocol logging, you specify the parameter value Verbose, not $True.

D. **Incorrect.** To enable protocol logging, you specify the parameter value Verbose, not $True.

5. **Correct Answer: A**

A. **Correct:** This command enables IMAP4 on the Keith Harris mailbox.

B. **Incorrect:** The parameter that lets you enable or disable the IMAP4 service is ImapEnabled, not Imap4Enabled.

C. **Incorrect:** The *Set-CASMailbox* cmdlet does not support the Server parameter. You need to enter the command on the Client Access server that holds the mailbox.

D. **Incorrect.** The *Set-CASMailbox* cmdlet does not support the Server parameter. In addition, the parameter that lets you enable or disable the IMAP4 service is ImapEnabled, not Imap4Enabled.

Chapter 10: Case Scenario Answers

Case Scenario 1: Tracking Messages

1. *Set-TransportServer Chicago -MessageTrackingLogSubjectLoggingEnabled $True*

2. *Get-MessageTrackingLog −Sender "kim.akers@graphicdesigninstitute.com" −Recipients "keith.harris@Contoso.com" -Start "5/21/2007 9:00AM" -End "5/21/2007 5:00PM"*

3. *Set-TransportServer Boston -MessageTrackingLogMaxFileSize 10MB*

Case Scenario 2: Configuring Baseline Counter Logs

1. The MSExchangeIS Public performance object.

2. You select the MSExchangeTransport Queues object and monitor the Active Remote Delivery Queue Length and the Retry Remote Delivery Queue Length counters.

3. The Message Opens/sec, Message Recipients Delivered/sec, and Messages Sent/sec counters.

Chapter 11: Lesson Review Answers

Lesson 1

1. **Correct Answer: B**

    A. Incorrect: MOM 2005 SP1 is a monitoring and reporting tool, but it does not provide a CLI that lets you enter PowerShell commands.

    B. Correct: System Center Operations Manager 2007 provides the Operations Manager Command Shell CLI, which is a specially configured instance of Windows PowerShell that lets you use PowerShell commands to configure settings and obtain information.

    C. Incorrect: Tools such as MOM 2005 SP1 and System Center Operations Manager 2007 use SQL Report Builder to generate reports from the data they have gathered during the monitoring process. Report Builder is not a monitoring tool and does not provide provide a CLI that lets you enter PowerShell commands.

    D. Incorrect: The Exchange Management Pack works with MOM 2005 SP1 to provide monitoring and reporting facilities specific to Exchange. It does not provide a CLI that lets you enter PowerShell commands.

2. **Correct Answers: A, C, and D**

    A. Correct: Other Reports is a report type available in EXBPA.

    B. Incorrect: You can carry out a health scan in EXBPA and generate reports from that scan. However, Health Reports is not a report type.

    C. Correct: List Reports is a report type available in EXBPA.

    D. Correct: Tree Reports is a report type available in EXBPA.

3. **Correct Answer: A**

    A. Correct: The MSExchangeIS Mailbox Performance object provides the Messages Sent/sec, Messages Received/sec, and Receive Queue Size counters.

    B. Incorrect: The MSExchangeIS Public Performance object provides counters related to public folders. It provides Messages Sent/sec, Messages Received/sec, and Receive Queue Size counters, but these are for public folders, not mailboxes.

C. **Incorrect:** The MSExchange OWA Performance object provides counters related to OWA users. It does not provide the Messages Sent/sec, Messages Received/sec, and Receive Queue Size counters.

D. **Incorrect:** The MSExchange Web Mail Performance object provides counters related to Web mail facilities, such as appointments, forms, and attachments. It does not provide the Messages Sent/sec, Messages Received/sec, and Receive Queue Size counters.

4. **Correct Answer: C**

A. **Incorrect:** This command exports data to the file in UTF7-encoded format. You require Unicode.

B. **Incorrect:** This command will include type information in the exported data. You need to specify the Notype parameter.

C. **Correct:** This command specifies Unicode encoding and does not export type information.

D. **Incorrect:** This command exports type information and specifies UTF7 encoding.

5. **Correct Answers: A, D, and F**

A. **Correct:** You can use the Exchange Database Recovery Management tool to analyze log drive space.

B. **Incorrect:** You use EXBPA, not the Exchange Database Recovery Management tool, to determine whether Exchange Server 2007 server configuration is set according to Microsoft best practices.

C. **Incorrect:** You use EXBPA, not the Exchange Database Recovery Management tool, to report on the general health of a system.

D. **Correct:** You can use the Exchange Database Recovery Management tool to show database-related event logs.

E. **Incorrect:** You use EXBPA, not the Exchange Database Recovery Management tool, to generate a list of issues, such as unsupported or not-recommended options.

F. **Correct:** You can use the Exchange Database Recovery Management tool to verify database and transaction log files.

Lesson 2

1. **Correct Answers: A, C, and E**

   A. **Correct:** MOM 2005 SP1 and the Exchange Management Pack provide the Mail Delivered - Top 100 Recipient Mailboxes by Count report by default.

   B. **Incorrect:** MOM 2005 SP1 and the Exchange Management Pack do not provide the Top Public Folders by Size report by default.

   C. **Correct:** MOM 2005 SP1 and the Exchange Management Pack provide the Highest Growth Mailboxes report by default.

   D. **Incorrect:** MOM 2005 SP1 and the Exchange Management Pack do not provide the Information Store Integrity report by default. You can use the Isinteg CLI tool to check information store integrity. Chapter 12 discusses Isinteg.

   E. **Correct:** MOM 2005 SP1 and the Exchange Management Pack provide the Mail Delivered - Top 100 Recipient Mailboxes by Size report by default.

2. **Correct Answer: B**

   A. **Incorrect:** Queue Viewer lets you list queues and messages and can indicate whether an Exchange Server 2007 server is experiencing traffic surges and delays. It does not obtain information about e-mail messages, senders, and receivers by accessing Message Tracking logs.

   B. **Correct:** The Message Tracking tool obtains information about e-mail messages, senders, and receivers by accessing Message Tracking logs.

   C. **Incorrect:** The Mail Flow Troubleshooter tool provides access to the data sources you need to troubleshoot mail flow problems, such as NDRs, queue backups, and slow deliveries. It does not obtain information about e-mail messages, senders, and receivers by accessing Message Tracking logs.

   D. **Incorrect:** You can use the Database Recovery Management tool to examine an Exchange Server deployment when an Exchange Server database does not mount (the Repair Database option). Based on the problem found, the tool automatically generates step-by-step instructions to bring the database online. You can also use the tool to analyze log drive space, show database-related event logs, verify database and transaction log files, and create an RSG. The tool does not obtain information about e-mail messages, senders, and receivers by accessing Message Tracking logs.

3. **Correct Answers: B, C, and E**

    A. **Incorrect:** EXBPA is an Exchange Server 2007 tool that automatically examines an Exchange Server2007 deployment and determines whether the configuration is set according to Microsoft best practices. It is not a component of HTTPMon.

    B. **Correct:** The Real-time Sampling Service is a component of HTTPMon. It monitors OWA servers (and other Web servers) in real time.

    C. **Correct:** Client Monitor is a component of HTTPMon. It displays the results from the SQL Reporting Server database as a set of Web pages.

    D. **Incorrect:** System Center Operations Manager provides alert, state, performance, and diagram views of the network infrastructure and lets you configure new rules and create groups on which rules will operate. It is not a component of HTTPMon.

    E. **Correct:** SQL Reporting Server is a component of HTTPMon. It gathers data from monitored servers and loads it into an SQL Server database.

4. **Correct Answer: D**

    A. **Incorrect:** Commands based on the *Get-Mailbox* cmdlet tell you whether the mailbox exists and return information such as the display name, alias, server name, and quota settings. They do not tell you whether POP3 is enabled.

    B. **Incorrect:** Commands based on the *Get-MailboxStatistics* cmdlet return statistics such as the total item count and last logon time. They do not tell you whether POP3 is enabled.

    C. **Incorrect:** Commands based on the *Get-MessageTrackingLog* cmdlet list messages received or submitted by the specified mailbox or mailboxes. They do not tell you whether POP3 is enabled.

    D. **Correct:** Commands based on the *Get-CASMailbox cmdlet* return the value of the PopEnabled parameter for the specified mailbox or mailboxes. This tells you whether POP3 is enabled for a mailbox.

5. **Correct Answer: B**

    A. **Incorrect:** Commands based on the *Get-Mailbox* cmdlet tell you whether the mailbox exists and return information such as the display name, alias, server name, and quota settings. They do not tell you the total item count.

    B. **Correct:** Commands based on the *Get-MailboxStatistics* cmdlet return statistics such as the total item count and last logon time.

    C. **Incorrect:** Commands based on the *Get-MessageTrackingLog* cmdlet list messages received or submitted by the specified mailbox or mailboxes. It is possible to configure such a command to list all the messages in a mailbox but then you would need to count them manually. Commands based on this cmdlet do not directly tell you the total item count.

    D. **Incorrect:** Commands based on the *Get-CASMailbox* cmdlet tell you whether client protocols such as IMAP4, POP3, or OWA are enabled for the mailbox. They do not tell you the total item count.

Chapter 11: Case Scenario Answers

Case Scenario 1: Creating Server Reports

1. *Get-Alert | where {$_.Severity -gt "Warning" -and $_.ResolutionState -eq 0 } | Format-List*

2. *Get-Queue −Server BlueSky09 | Export-Csv C:\QueueReports\BlueSky09.csv -Notype*

3. EXBPA

Case Scenario 2: Creating Usage Reports

1. Coho does not use SQL Server, or your server cannot connect to an SQL database.

2. *Get-MailboxStatistics | Where {$_.TotalItemSize -ge 4GB} | Export-Csv C:\MailboxReports\BigMailboxes.csv −Notype*

3. *Get-MailboxStatistics −Identity SpamQuarantine@Coho.internal | Export-Csv C:\ SpamReports\QuarantineMailbox −Notype*

Chapter 12: Lesson Review Answers

Lesson 1

1. **Correct Answer: D**

    A. **Incorrect:** A hub transport server holds message queues that are transient and do not need to be backed up. You might decide to back up protocol logs and message tracking logs.

B. **Incorrect:** An edge transport server does not hold mailbox databases or transaction log files. You might decide to back up protocol logs.

C. **Incorrect:** A client access server does not hold mailbox databases or transaction log files unless the server also has the Mailbox server role installed. If only one client access server exists in your organization, you might consider backing up the POP/IMAP settings.

D. **Correct:** Mailbox databases and transaction logs reside on a mailbox server and should always form part of a backup strategy.

2. **Correct Answer: B**

A. **Incorrect:** You can back up custom audio prompts on the prompt publishing server. You do not need to back up prompts on any other unified messaging server.

B. **Correct:** You should consider backing up custom audio prompts on a unified messaging server that is also the prompt publishing server.

C. **Incorrect:** An edge transport server cannot have any additional server roles installed. You cannot therefore have the Edge Transport and Unified Messaging roles installed on the same server.

D. **Incorrect:** Although it is true that you cannot use NTBackup to carry out an Exchange-aware backup of the prompts directory on a unified messaging server, you can still use the tool to perform a file-level backup.

3. **Correct Answers: A and B**

A. **Correct:** Full or normal backup is available whether circular logging is enabled or not.

B. **Correct:** Copy backup is available whether circular logging is enabled or not.

C. **Incorrect:** Partial backups, incremental or differential, are not available if circular logging is enabled.

D. **Incorrect:** This answer is incorrect for the reason given for answer C.

4. **Correct Answers: A, B, and C**

A. **Correct:** You can back up to a folder in a second hard disk on the same server.

B. **Correct:** You can back up to a folder on an external hard disk, disk array, or other disk-based storage solution.

C. **Correct:** Tape drives are not as common as they used to be and reliability issues exist. Nevertheless, you can specify a tape drive as a backup destination.

D. **Incorrect:** You cannot back up directly to optical storage. For archive purposes, you can back up to a disk and then copy the backed-up files to optical storage media.

5. **Correct Answer: D**

A. **Incorrect:** NTBackup writes to the Application log, not the System log. Also, events with an EventID 8000 are backup start events.

B. **Incorrect:** Events with an EventID 8000 are backup start events.

C. **Incorrect:** NTBackup writes to the Application log, not the System log.

D. **Correct:** This command lists backup complete events (EventID 8001) stored in the Application log.

Lesson 2

1. **Correct Answer: B**

A. **Incorrect:** You have no administrative rights to the contoso.com domain. You cannot create an Active Directory account that is not associated with a mailbox.

B. **Correct:** This is the recommended method for recovering a disconnected mailbox from the mailbox dumpster.

C. **Incorrect:** This creates a new user and a new mailbox. It does not recover the disconnected mailbox in the dumpster.

D. **Incorrect:** You can restore from backup, but the deleted mailbox retention period has not expired, and it is easier to reconnect the mailbox.

2. **Correct Answer: C**

A. **Incorrect:** The Isinteg CLI checks database integrity. This can be part of the recovery process, but you use Eseutil to carry out the actual recovery.

B. **Incorrect:** The Database Recovery Management tool can recover a damaged database. However, it is a graphical user interface (GUI), not a CLI.

C. **Correct:** You use Eseutil in repair mode (*eseutil/P*) to repair a damaged database.

D. **Incorrect:** No Exchange Management Shell commands exist that repair a damaged database when no backup is available.

3. **Correct Answer: A**

A. **Correct:** The *Eseutil/D* command defragments an offline database.

B. **Incorrect:** The *Eseutil/P* command repairs an offline database.

C. **Incorrect:** The *Eseutil/R* command replays transaction log files or rolls them forward to restore a database to internal consistency.

D. **Incorrect:** The *Eseutil/C* command displays the restore log file and controls hard recovery.

4. **Correct Answer: B**

A. **Incorrect:** You need to play the log files from the failed database against the restored database before you mount this database.

B. **Correct:** This is the correct procedure.

C. **Incorrect:** The restored database cannot become the active database unless you have first mounted it.

D. **Incorrect:** Merging the dial tone and restored databases writes any database operations that occurred while restore was taking place into the active restored database. It is the final operation after the restore process, not the initial one.

5. **Correct Answers: C and D**

A. **Incorrect:** Restoring the entire server will restore Active Directory settings provided that you have backed up System State data as part of your backup set. However, you do not need to restore the entire server to restore System State data.

B. **Incorrect:** You cannot use *Eseutil* to restore System State data.

C. **Correct:** If you have backed up System State data, the best way to restore Active Directory settings is to carry out a System State restore.

D. **Correct:** If you have not backed up System State data, you can use the *Setup/mode:RecoverServer* command to restore default Active Directory settings. However, you will also need to manually reinstate any changes you made to the default settings.

6. **Correct Answer: D**

    A. **Incorrect:** This command lists all the disconnected mailboxes on the mailbox server Glasgow.

    B. **Incorrect:** This command checks that the user Don Hall exists in Active Directory and returns details about the user account (for example, whether it is associated with a mailbox).

    C. **Incorrect:** This connects a disconnected mailbox in the database Mailbox Database.

    D. **Correct:** this connects the disconnected mailbox to the correct user account.

Chapter 12: Case Scenario Answers

Case Scenario 1: Designing a Backup Regime

1. Copy backups do not truncate committed transaction log files. These files are filling the hard disk space on the mailbox servers and resulting in larger backups that take more time. The scenario does not state that clustering (LCR or CCR) is used, so a full backup every night and a copy backup once per week for archiving purposes would be a reasonable regime. Alternatively, if time or storage space is limited, consider a regular (weekly) full backup with nightly incremental or differential backups.

2. Circular logging will delete transaction log files and solve the disk storage problems. However, if circular logging is enabled, data cannot be recovered to the point of failure, and differential and incremental backups are not possible. Replacing copy backups with full backups is a better solution.

3. Coho should consider off-site as well as on-site archive storage. Even if the safe is fireproof, its contents might not survive flood or earthquake damage. An organization can survive the loss of its premises. It cannot survive the loss of its data.

Case Scenario 2: Restoring Data

1. You need to ask a domain administrator or account operator to create an Active Directory account for Keith Harris that is not associated with a mailbox.

2. You can carry out a dial tone recovery so that users can send and receive e-mail while recovery is taking place. Because the mailbox server has not experienced a

hardware failure, you can recover to that server. Because disk storage is alright, the transaction log files should be available to be played against the restored database and ensure recovery to the point of failure. You can then merge the dial tone database with the recovered database so that any messages users sent or received while recovery was taking place are not lost.

3. A test network has many purposes. You can test software updates and service packs before applying them to the production network. You can test third-party software. However, the main advantage of a test network in a separate forest is that you can perform test restores to ensure the disaster recovery processes you have in place are carried out quickly and efficiently.

Chapter 13: Lesson Review Answers

Lesson 1

1. **Correct Answers: A and B**

    A. **Correct:** EdgeSync subscription data is stored within Active Directory.

    B. **Correct:** Address lists are stored within Active Directory.

    C. **Incorrect:** An individual server's IP address configuration is not stored within Active Directory.

    D. **Incorrect:** An individual server's local user configuration is not stored within Active Directory.

    E. **Incorrect:** An individual server's local group configuration is not stored within Active Directory.

2. **Correct Answers: A and B**

    A. **Correct:** EdgeSync subscription data is stored within Active Directory.

    B. **Correct:** Address lists are stored within Active Directory.

    C. **Incorrect:** An individual server's IP address configuration is not stored within Active Directory.

    D. **Incorrect:** An individual server's local user configuration is not stored within Active Directory.

    E. **Incorrect:** An individual server's local group configuration is not stored within Active Directory.

3. **Correct Answers: A and B**

    A. **Correct:** A Client Access server's SSL certificates are not stored within Active Directory and will need to be reobtained either from backup or from the issuing CA.

    B. **Correct:** Custom Virtual Directory configuration is not stored within Active Directory and will need to be manually applied after the Client Access server is recovered.

    C. **Incorrect:** Client Access server IMAP4 settings are stored within Active Directory and will be recovered during role recovery.

    D. **Incorrect:** Client Access Server POP3 settings are stored within Active Directory and will be recovered during role recovery.

    E. **Incorrect:** OAB publishing settings are stored within Active Directory and will be recovered during role recovery.

4. **Correct Answer: A**

    A. **Correct:** Prior to performing recovery, you need to reset the original server's Active Directory account.

    B. **Incorrect:** If you delete the original computer's account, all the original computer's Client Access server configuration information will be lost.

    C. **Incorrect:** There is no need to rename the original server's computer account, as you have given the replacement computer the same name as the original server.

    D. **Incorrect:** If you create a new account, it will need a separate name. A new account will not retain the original Client Access server data of the original account.

5. **Correct Answer: A**

    A. **Correct:** In this situation, you would use the */m:RecoverServer* option, which will take existing data within Active Directory and use it to recover the server role.

    B. **Incorrect:** If you use the command *Setup/m:Install/r:ht*, you will perform a clean install, and no data about the original server will be recovered from Active Directory.

    C. **Incorrect:** You cannot use setup with the upgrade option if Exchange is not already installed on the computer.

    D. **Incorrect:** You would not use the */Uninstall* option when Exchange is not already installed.

6. **Correct Answers: B and D**

    A. **Incorrect:** NLB cannot be applied to mailbox servers.

    B. **Correct:** SCC supports automatic failover.

    C. **Incorrect:** LCR does not support automatic failover in the case of server failure.

    D. **Correct:** CCR supports automatic failover.

    E. **Incorrect:** DNS round-robin cannot be applied to mailbox servers.

7. **Correct Answer: A**

    A. **Correct:** LCR uses multiple disk arrays connected to the same mailbox server. In the event that one disk array fails, the mailbox server can fail over to the second disk array.

    B. **Incorrect:** An SCC strategy does not protect against the failure of a disk array, as only one copy of the mailbox databases exists in this configuration.

    C. **Incorrect:** CCR relies on there being more than one mailbox server.

    D. **Incorrect:** NLB cannot be used as a high availability strategy for mailbox servers.

8. **Correct Answer: B**

    A. **Incorrect:** NLB cannot be implemented as a high availability strategy for Exchange Server 2007 mailbox servers.

    B. **Correct:** The SCC high availability strategy is used when you have two-cluster nodes that use a shared storage device.

    C. **Incorrect:** The LCR strategy is used when you have two separate storage arrays connected to a single Exchange Server 2007 mailbox server.

    D. **Incorrect:** CCR is used when you have a two-node cluster that use separate storage devices.

9. **Correct Answer: E**

    A. **Incorrect:** DNS round-robin should not be used with Hub Transport servers. High availability can be achieved with Hub Transport servers by adding a second server with this role to a site.

B. **Incorrect:** NLB should not be used with Hub Transport servers. High availability can be achieved with Hub Transport servers by adding a second server with this role to a site.

C. **Incorrect:** CCR should be used only with Mailbox servers, not Hub Transport servers.

D. **Incorrect:** SCCs should be used only with Mailbox servers, not Hub Transport servers.

E. **Correct:** Resiliency has been designed into the Hub Transport server role. Adding a second Hub Transport server to a site will provide a high availability solution without having to use DNS round-robin, NLB, CCR, or SCC.

10. **Correct Answer: C**

A. **Incorrect:** Restarting the server will not restart the clustered mailbox server.

B. **Incorrect:** Although the *Move-ClusteredMailboxServer* cmdlet can be used to activate a passive node, it cannot be used to restart a clustered mailbox server that has been stopped with the *Stop-ClusteredMailboxServer* cmdlet.

C. **Correct:** The *Start-ClusteredMailboxServer* cmdlet is the only way to restart a clustered mailbox server that has been stopped through the *Stop-Clustered-MailboxServer* cmdlet.

D. **Incorrect:** The *Stop-ClusteredMailboxServer* cmdlet is used to stop a clustered mailbox server; it cannot be used to start a clustered mailbox server.

11. **Correct Answers: A and C**

A. **Correct:** For a *Move-ClusteredMailboxServer* operation to work, the target server must be available and must be a member of the same cluster.

B. **Incorrect:** You cannot move a clustered mailbox server to a server that is not a member of the same cluster.

C. **Correct:** You can move a clustered mailbox server only to a server that is not currently running a clustered mailbox server.

D. **Incorrect:** You cannot move a clustered mailbox server to a server that is currently running a clustered mailbox server.

E. **Incorrect:** The server that the command is run on must be working normally and cannot be in a failed state.

Chapter 13: Case Scenario Answers

Case Scenario 1: Recovering the Fabrikam Client Access Server

1. Reset the computer account in Active Directory, rebuild the server using the same name and volume configuration, install the necessary components to support the Client Access server, and join the computer to the domain.

2. Obtain and install a new certificate from the original issuing authority unless the originally issued certificate can be recovered.

3. Rebuild the custom OABs; this will republish them to their original location.

Case Scenario 2: A High Availability Solution for Coho Vineyard

1. Set up a mailbox cluster that uses CCR.

2. Add a second Client Access server and configure a Windows NLB cluster with the existing Client Access server.

3. Configure a second Edge Transport server using the cloned configuration process and an EdgeSync subscription. Use DNS round-robin to balance traffic between servers. Reconfigure the DNS settings if a Edge Transport server fails.

Glossary

Active copy   The master, mountable copy for the storage group.

ActiveSync   This service allows the transfer of messaging and calendaring data to a mobile device from an Exchange Server 2007 mailbox.

Address list   A collection of recipient addresses that can be accessed when a client is connected to Exchange.

Attack surface   The port, services, and applications that can respond to requests from the network. Shutting down ports, services, and applications reduces attack surface.

Autodiscover   This service allows Outlook 2007 and Windows mobile clients to be automatically configured given an e-mail address and password.

Availability service   This service provides up-to-date calendaring information.

Backup job   The act of backing up a set of files at the same time.

Backup set   The set of files created by a backup job.

Baseline   A set of readings (typically performance counter values) that define the normal operating parameters of a system. You take baselines for quiet, normal, and busy periods, whenever there is a significant system change, and regularly to determine if the load on your resources is increasing over time.

Block list   A block lists is a list of items that you do not want to allow. This list can consist of senders, recipients, or domains.

Bottleneck   The resource that is under most stress. You can never eliminate bottlenecks. If you allocate more resources to a bottleneck, the next most stressed resource becomes the bottleneck.

Bulk management   Performing the same operation on more than one Exchange entity at the same time—for example, configuring or moving several mailboxes.

Categorizer   An Exchange transport component that processes all inbound messages and determines what to do with them on the basis of information about their intended recipients.

Checkpoint file   A file that tracks the progress of transaction logging. The checkpoint file has a pointer to the oldest log file that contains data that has not yet been written to the database.

Circular logging   Helps control the hard disk space that is used to store log files by overwriting older data in logs.

Cluster continuous replication (CCR)   A high availability feature of Microsoft Exchange Server 2007 that combines the asynchronous log shipping and replay technology built into Exchange 2007 with the failover and management features provided by the Microsoft Windows Cluster service. The CCR process achieves high availability by using separate servers with separate storage devices to replicate storage group and mailbox data.

Comma-separated value (CSV) file   An implementation of a delimited text file that uses commas to separate values. CSV files can be read by most report-generating software packages.

Compliance   A set of legal requirements or policies that must be implemented through Exchange Server configuration.

Consistent state   If the database is in a consistent state, the database can be remounted without any kind of transaction log replay. Changing a database from an inconsistent state to a consistent state generally involves two processes: restoring the database from a backup that was completed while the database was online and replaying the transaction log files into the restored database.

Contact   An entity in Active Directory that is not a user account. Contacts cannot log on to the domain. A contact is typically mail-enabled, and its purpose is to allow users to send e-mail (typically to an external e-mail address) by specifying the contact's name in the To or Cc lines.

Custom attribute   An attribute that describes an object in Active Directory other than standard attributes, such as Location or Employer. You can use custom attributes, for example, to define membership of a dynamic distribution group.

Database   In the context of disaster recovery, database is a generic term that refers to either a mailbox store or a public folder store.

Dynamic distribution group   A mail-enabled group that does not have a fixed membership and whose members are identified dynamically using filters and conditions each time e-mail is sent to the group.

E-mail address policy   A policy that determines the format of an e-mail address.

Equipment mailbox   A resource mailbox used to identify items of equipment that typically do not have a fixed location and can be used anywhere in an organization's premises.

Extensible storage engine (ESE)   The database engine that Exchange uses.

Failover   The process by which the passive component becomes active when the existing active component fails.

Hard recovery   The process that changes a restored database back to a consistent state by playing transactions into the database from transaction log files.

Inconsistent state   If the database is in an inconsistent state, it cannot be remounted, and transaction log replay needs to be performed.

Link state   Routing protocol used by previous versions of Exchange.

Local continuous replication   A process by which high availability is achieved using separate storage devices attached to the same mailbox server.

Exchange ActiveSync mailbox policy   A policy, applied to users, that is used to manage a Windows Mobile device.

MX record   A special type of record that defines the hosts in a DNS zone that can accept mail.

Mail-enabled user   A user that has a user account in Active Directory but does not have a corresponding mailbox. E-mail sent to this user is forwarded to the user's mailbox in another organization. Mail-enabled users have external e-mail addresses.

Mailbox database   A database for storing mailboxes. The mailbox database manages the data in mailboxes, tracks deleted messages and mailbox sizes, and assists in message transfers. A mailbox database is stored as an Exchange database (.edb) file.

Mailbox-enabled user   A user that has both a user account and a mailbox in an Active Directory domain.

Mailbox server   An Exchange Server 2007 server that has the Mailbox server role installed.

Mailbox statistics   Values for parameters associated with a mailbox, such as item count, last logon time, last logoff time, total item size, and whether a valid account exists in Active Directory.

Message queue   A temporary location that holds e-mail messages that are waiting to enter the next stage of processing. Message queues exist on Exchange Server 2007 servers that have the Edge Transport or Hub Transport role.

Message subject logging   Storing the subject line of an SMTP e-mail message in the message tracking log. Message subject logging is enabled by default, but you can disable it if required.

Message tracking log   Records message activity when messages are transferred to and from a Microsoft Exchange Server 2007 server that has the Hub Transport server role, the Mailbox server role, or the Edge Transport server role installed.

Mounting a database   The process of preparing a database for use. A public folder database needs to be mounted before public folders can be stored in it.

Network load balancing   A process by which client load is shared between identically configured servers using a virtual address.

Offline address book   A point-in-time collection of recipient addresses based on an existing address list.

Offline backup   A backup made while the Exchange services are stopped. When you perform an offline backup, users do not have access to their mailboxes.

Online backup   A backup made while the Exchange services are running.

Out-of-office message   An automatic message that informs senders that the recipient is currently unavailable. These messages are almost always configured by recipients prior to their going on leave.

Outlook anywhere   This service replaces RPC over HTTP and allows external Outlook 2007 clients to access a protected Exchange Server 2007 infrastructure without requiring a VPN.

Performance counters   Counters related to a performance object that monitor aspects of performance associated with that object. For example, the Messages Delivered/sec counter in the MSExchangeIS performance object monitors the rate that messages are delivered to all recipients.

Performance log   A file that records (logs) counter values that indicate resource usage.

Performance object   An entity that describes an aspect of server performance and provides performance-related counters. For example, the MSExchangeIS Mailbox object provides counters that monitor the performance of mailboxes in the information store.

Perimeter network   A network location between the Internet and your organization's network. This network location is bounded by two firewalls.

Protocol logging   Can be enabled on Send and Receive connectors to monitor SMTP conversations that occur between Exchange Server 2007 servers that have the Hub Transport server role or the Edge Transport server role installed.

Public folder   A folder that users can access directly with client applications such as Microsoft Outlook. Users can place files in public folders so that other users can access them.

Public folder database   A dedicated database in a storage group used to store public folders. There can be only one public folder database on an Exchange Server 2007 server.

Public folder hierarchy   Sometimes known as the public folder tree or the IPM_Subtree. A structured list of the public folders in a public folder database showing parent/child relationships.

Public folder replication   The process by which public folder databases replicate public folder information to Exchange servers that hold content replicas of the folder. Information about the public folder hierarchy and public folder permissions can be replicated in addition to public folder content.

Receive connector   This type of connector handles incoming SMTP traffic.

Recipient template   A recipient object (e.g., a mailbox) that is used as a template or pattern for creating similar objects. Using this technique allows you, for example, to configure the mailbox template with nondefault settings (e.g., you could alter the storage quota or the maximum message size from the database defaults).

Replay   A process in which Exchange examines the transaction log files for a storage group to identify transactions that have been logged but have not been incorporated into the databases of that storage group. The replay process then uses the information in the transaction logs to bring the database to a consistent state.

Resource forest   A forest that contains mailboxes but not their associated user accounts. Typically, you create a resource forest when an organization wants to outsource the administration of e-mail and retain the administration of Windows user accounts.

Resource mailbox   A mailbox that enables users to identify and schedule a resource within an organization, for example, a room or a piece of equipment, by including the resource mailbox in a meeting request.

Restore   To return the original files that were previously preserved in a backup to their location on a server.

Retention   The period of time that data is kept before it is irrevocably deleted.

Retry   The status of a delivery queue when Exchange Server 2007 attempts to resend the queued messages at regular intervals. You can force a retry so that an attempted resend occurs immediately.

Send connector   A connector that handles outgoing SMTP traffic.

Server availability   A level of service provided by applications, services, or systems on a server.

Server health   An indication of the stress that is placed on server resources and on major applications that run on a server, such as Exchange Server 2007.

Single copy cluster   A process by which high availability is achieved using two Mailbox severs that share the same storage device.

Soft recovery   An automatic transaction log file replay process that occurs when a database is remounted after an unexpected stop. Soft recovery uses the checkpoint file to determine which transaction log file to start with when it sequentially replays transactions into databases. In hard recovery, the checkpoint file is deleted, and all available transaction files are played against a recovered database.

Spam   Unsolicited advertising and other unwanted e-mail messages.

Spam confidence level (SCL)   Indicates the likelihood of a message being spam. The higher the SCL, the higher the likelihood of spam. The SCL value is an integer from 0 through 9.

Storage group   An Exchange feature that allows you to group databases into a common container that shares a single transaction log set.

Room mailbox   A resource mailbox that enables users to identify a room and schedule its use (if scheduling is enabled). Custom attributes associated with a room mailbox can identify equipment and facilities permanently located in the room.

Root public folder   The folder at the top of the public folder subtree, also known as the IPM_Subtree. The root public folder is denoted by a backslash (\). Top-level public folders are children of the root public folder.

Spam confidence level   A score assigned to an incoming message that indicates the likelihood that the message contains spam rather than legitimate communication.

SSL (Secure Sockets Layer)   A method of establishing identity and of encrypting communication using a digital certificate.

Schema   A set of definitions for all object classes that can exist within an Active Directory forest.

Security group   A group in Active Directory that can be used to grant or deny permissions to its members. A universal security group can be mail-enabled, although many are not.

Sender reputation level   A score assigned to a sender's address based on analysis of the message traffic.

Site   A collection of IP subnets defined within Active Directory.

Spam   Unsolicited e-mail of a commercial nature.

Storage quota   A size limit for a public folder (or a mailbox). Several quota levels can be specified, for example, Warning and Prohibit Post.

System folder   A folder that users cannot access directly with client applications such as Microsoft Outlook. Client applications such as Outlook use system folders to store information such as free/busy data, offline address lists, and organizational forms. Other system folders hold configuration information that is used by custom applications or by Exchange itself.

Threshold   A value for an operational parameter above or below which you need to be notified so that you can take appropriate action.

Top-level public folder   A public folder that is a child of the root public folder. Users cannot create top-level public folders by using Microsoft Outlook.

Top users   Users who have the most number of messages or the largest total message size in their mailboxes.

Transport server   An Exchange Server 2007 server that has the Hub Transport or Edge Transport server role installed.

Universal distribution group   A group with a fixed membership used to facilitate sending e-mail to its members. A single e-mail sent to the group mailbox goes to every member of the group.

Virus   Executable content that can infect a computer after being executed by a user.

Index

Additional Windows (R2) Resources for Administrators

Published and Forthcoming Titles from Microsoft Press

Microsoft® Windows Server™ 2003 Administrator's Pocket Consultant, Second Edition

William R. Stanek ● ISBN 0-7356-2245-0

Here's the practical, pocket-sized reference for IT professionals supporting Microsoft Windows Server 2003—fully updated for Service Pack 1 and Release 2. Designed for quick referencing, this portable guide covers all the essentials for performing everyday system administration tasks. Topics include managing workstations and servers, using Active Directory® directory service, creating and administering user and group accounts, managing files and directories, performing data security and auditing tasks, handling data back-up and recovery, and administering networks using TCP/IP, WINS, and DNS, and more.

MCSE Self-Paced Training Kit (Exams 70-290, 70-291, 70-293, 70-294): Microsoft Windows Server 2003 Core Requirements, Second Edition

Holme, Thomas, Mackin, McLean, Zacker, Spealman, Hudson, and Craft ● ISBN 0-7356-2290-6

The Microsoft Certified Systems Engineer (MCSE) credential is the premier certification for professionals who analyze the business requirements and design and implement the infrastructure for business solutions based on the Microsoft Windows Server 2003 platform and Microsoft Windows Server System—now updated for Windows Server 2003 Service Pack 1 and R2. This all-in-one set provides in-depth preparation for the four required networking system exams. Work at your own pace through the lessons, hands-on exercises, troubleshooting labs, and review questions. You get expert exam tips plus a full review section covering all objectives and sub-objectives in each study guide. Then use the Microsoft Practice Tests on the CD to challenge yourself with more than 1500 questions for self-assessment and practice!

Microsoft Windows® Small Business Server 2003 R2 Administrator's Companion

Charlie Russel, Sharon Crawford, and Jason Gerend ● ISBN 0-7356-2280-9

Get your small-business network, messaging, and collaboration systems up and running quickly with the essential guide to administering Windows Small Business Server 2003 R2. This reference details the features, capabilities, and technologies for both the standard and premium editions—including Microsoft Windows Server 2003 R2, Exchange Server 2003 with Service Pack 1, Windows SharePoint® Services, SQL Server™ 2005 Workgroup Edition, and Internet Information Services. Discover how to install, upgrade, or migrate to Windows Small Business Server 2003 R2; plan and implement your network, Internet access, and security services; customize Microsoft Exchange Server for your e-mail needs; and administer user rights, shares, permissions, and Group Policy.

Microsoft Windows Small Business Server 2003 R2 Administrator's Companion

Charlie Russel, Sharon Crawford, and Jason Gerend ● ISBN 0-7356-2280-9

Here's the ideal one-volume guide for the IT professional administering Windows Server 2003. Now fully updated for Windows Server 2003 Service Pack 1 and R2, this *Administrator's Companion* offers up-to-date information on core system administration topics for Microsoft Windows, including Active Directory services, security, scripting, disaster planning and recovery, and interoperability with UNIX. It also includes all-new sections on Service Pack 1 security updates and new features for R2. Featuring easy-to-use procedures and handy work-arounds, this book provides ready answers for on-the-job results.

MCSA/MCSE Self-Paced Training Kit (Exam 70-290): Managing and Maintaining a Microsoft Windows Server 2003 Environment, Second Edition

Dan Holme and Orin Thomas ● ISBN 0-7356-2289-2

MCSA/MCSE Self-Paced Training Kit (Exam 70-291): Implementing, Managing, and Maintaining a Microsoft Windows Server 2003 Network Infrastructure, Second Edition

J.C. Mackin and Ian McLean ● ISBN 0-7356-2288-4

MCSE Self-Paced Training Kit (Exam 70-293): Planning and Maintaining a Microsoft Windows Server 2003 Network Infrastructure, Second Edition

Craig Zacker ● ISBN 0-7356-2287-6

MCSE Self-Paced Training Kit (Exam 70-294): Planning, Implementing, and Maintaining a Microsoft Windows Server 2003 Active Directory® Infrastructure, Second Ed.

Jill Spealman, Kurt Hudson, and Melissa Craft ● ISBN 0-7356-2286-8

For more information about Microsoft Press® books and other learning products,
visit: **www.microsoft.com/mspress** *and* **www.microsoft.com/learning**

Additional SQL Server Resources for Administrators

Published and Forthcoming Titles from Microsoft Press

Microsoft® SQL Server™ 2005 Reporting Services *Step by Step*
Hitachi Consulting Services ● ISBN 0-7356-2250-7

SQL Server Reporting Services (SRS) is Microsoft's customizable reporting solution for business data analysis. It is one of the key value features of SQL Server 2005: functionality more advanced and much less expensive than its competition. SRS is powerful, so an understanding of how to architect a report, as well as how to install and program SRS, is key to harnessing the full functionality of SQL Server. This procedural tutorial shows how to use the Report Project Wizard, how to think about and access data, and how to build queries. It also walks the reader through the creation of charts and visual layouts to enable maximum visual understanding of the data analysis. Interactivity (enhanced in SQL Server 2005) and security are also covered in detail.

Microsoft SQL Server 2005 Administrator's Pocket Consultant
William R. Stanek ● ISBN 0-7356-2107-1

Here's the utterly practical, pocket-sized reference for IT professionals who need to administer, optimize, and maintain SQL Server 2005 in their organizations. This unique guide provides essential details for using SQL Server 2005 to help protect and manage your company's data—whether automating tasks; creating indexes and views; performing backups and recovery; replicating transactions; tuning performance; managing server activity; importing and exporting data; or performing other key tasks. Featuring quick-reference tables, lists, and step-by-step instructions, this handy, one-stop guide provides fast, accurate answers on the spot, whether you're at your desk or in the field!

Microsoft SQL Server 2005 Administrator's Companion
Marci Frohock Garcia, Edward Whalen, and Mitchell Schroeter ● ISBN 0-7356-2198-5

Microsoft SQL Server 2005 Administrator's Companion is the comprehensive, in-depth guide that saves time by providing all the technical information you need to deploy, administer, optimize, and support SQL Server 2005. Using a hands-on, example-rich approach, this authoritative, one-volume reference book provides expert advice, product information, detailed solutions, procedures, and real-world troubleshooting tips from experienced SQL Server 2005 professionals. This expert guide shows you how to design high-availability database systems, prepare for installation, install and configure SQL Server 2005, administer services and features, and maintain and troubleshoot your database system. It covers how to configure your system for your I/O system and model and optimize system capacity. The expert authors provide details on how to create and use defaults, constraints, rules, indexes, views, functions, stored procedures, and triggers. This guide shows you how to administer reporting services, analysis services, notification services, and integration services. It also provides a wealth of information on replication and the specifics of snapshot, transactional, and merge replication. Finally, there is expansive coverage of how to manage and tune your SQL Server system, including automating tasks, backup and restoration of databases, and management of users and security.

Microsoft SQL Server 2005 Analysis Services *Step by Step*
Hitachi Consulting Services ● ISBN 0-7356-2199-3

One of the key features of SQL Server 2005 is SQL Server Analysis Services—Microsoft's customizable analysis solution for business data modeling and interpretation. Just compare SQL Server Analysis Services to its competition to understand/grasp the great value of its enhanced features. One of the keys to harnessing the full functionality of SQL Server will be leveraging Analysis Services for the powerful tool that it is—including creating a cube, and deploying, customizing, and extending the basic calculations. This step-by-step tutorial discusses how to get started, how to build scalable analytical applications, and how to use and administer advanced features. Interactivity (which is enhanced in SQL Server 2005), data translation, and security are also covered in detail.

Microsoft SQL Server 2005 Express Edition
Step by Step
Jackie Goldstein ● ISBN 0-7356-2184-5

Inside Microsoft SQL Server 2005:
The Storage Engine
Kalen Delaney ● ISBN 0-7356-2105-5

Inside Microsoft SQL Server 2005:
T-SQL Programming
Itzik Ben-Gan ● ISBN 0-7356-2197-7

Inside Microsoft SQL Server 2005:
Query Processing and Optimization
Kalen Delaney ● ISBN 0-7356-2196-9

For more information about Microsoft Press® books and other learning products, visit: **www.microsoft.com/mspress** *and* **www.microsoft.com/learning**

System Requirements

We recommend that you use an isolated network that is not part of your production network to do the practice exercises in this book. The computer that you use to perform practices requires Internet connectivity. It is possible to perform all the practices in this training kit if you decide to use a single computer that is configured as a domain controller and has Exchange Server 2007 installed. Both the Windows Server and Exchange Server software need to be 64-bit editions.

Hardware Requirements

Your computer or computers should meet (at a minimum) the following hardware specification:

- Personal computer with a 1-GHz or faster 64-bit processor.
- 1.5 GB of RAM (2 GB if you plan to use virtual machine software).
- 60 GB of available hard disk space (100 GB if you plan to use virtual machine software).
- DVD-ROM drive.
- Keyboard and Microsoft mouse or compatible pointing device.
- The practices in Chapter 12, "Disaster Recovery," require a second hard disk, either internal or external. You can carry out the practices by using a high-capacity USB flash memory device (4 GB or greater), but the practices are closer to real life if you use a hard disk.
- Note that while the current edition of Microsoft Virtual PC and Virtual Server do not support 64-bit guest operating systems, third-party virtual machine host software such as VMware Server does. You must ensure that your processor's virtualization extensions are enabled when attempting to run 64-bit guest operating systems.

Software Requirements

The following software is required to complete the practice exercises:

- An evaluation or full edition Windows Server 2003, Windows Server 2003 R2, or Windows Server 2008 64-bit Enterprise Edition.
- An evaluation or full edition of Windows Exchange Server 2007.

What do you think of this book?

We want to hear from you!

Your feedback will help us continually improve our books and learning resources for you. To participate in a brief online survey, please visit:

microsoft.com/learning/booksurvey

...and enter this book's ISBN-10 or ISBN-13 number (appears above barcode on back cover). As a thank-you to survey participants in the U.S. and Canada, each month we'll randomly select five respondents to win one of five $100 gift certificates from a leading online merchant. At the conclusion of the survey, you can enter the drawing by providing your e-mail address, which will be used for prize notification only.*

Thank you in advance for your input!

Where to find the ISBN on back cover

Example only. Each book has unique ISBN.

Stay in touch!

To subscribe to the *Microsoft Press® Book Connection Newsletter*—for news on upcoming books, events, and special offers—please visit:

microsoft.com/learning/books/newsletter

Save 15%

on your Microsoft® Certification exam fee

Present this discount voucher to any participating test center worldwide, or use the discount code to register online or via telephone at participating Microsoft Certified Exam Delivery Providers. See microsoft.com/mcp/exams for locations.

Microsoft | Learning

Good for 15% off one exam fee in the Microsoft Certified Professional Program

Offer expires 12/31/2012

Your voucher discount code

Redeemable at Microsoft Certified Exam Delivery Providers worldwide.
For locations, visit: **www.microsoft.com/mcp/exams**

Promotion Terms and Conditions

- Offer good for 15% off one exam fee in the Microsoft Certified Professional Program.
- Voucher code can be redeemed online or at Microsoft Certified Exam Delivery Providers worldwide.
- Exam purchased using this voucher code must be taken on or before December 31, 2012.
- Inform your Microsoft Certified Exam Delivery Provider that you want to use the voucher discount code at the time you register for the exam.

Voucher Terms and Conditions

- Expired vouchers will not be replaced.
- Each voucher code may only be used for one exam and must be presented at time of registration.
- This voucher may not be combined with other vouchers or discounts.
- This voucher is nontransferable and is void if altered or revised in any way.
- This voucher may not be sold or redeemed for cash, credit, or refund.

X13-92079